SOFTWARE COMMUNICATION SKILLS

Other books by Robert L. Glass available from Prentice-Hall:

Modern Programming Practices
Real-Time Software
Software Maintenance Guidebook

SOFTWARE COMMUNICATION SKILLS

Robert L. Glass

Software Engineering Program
Seattle University

Prentice-Hall, Inc., Englewood Cliffs, New Jersey 07632

Library of Congress Cataloging-in-Publication Data

GLASS, ROBERT L. (date)
Software communication skills.

Bibliography: p.
Includes index.
1. Computer software. 2. Electronic data processing documentation. I. Title.
QA76.754.G53 1988 005.1 87-2461
ISBN 0-13-821679-7

Editorial/production supervision and interior design: Kathryn Gollin Marshak
Cover design: Edsal Enterprises
Manufacturing buyer: S. Gordon Osbourne

Printed in the United States of America

10 9 8 7 6 5 4 3 2 1

ISBN 0-13-821679-7 025

PRENTICE-HALL INTERNATIONAL (UK) LIMITED, *London*
PRENTICE-HALL OF AUSTRALIA PTY. LIMITED, *Sydney*
PRENTICE-HALL CANADA INC., *Toronto*
PRENTICE-HALL HISPANOAMERICANA, S.A., *Mexico*
PRENTICE-HALL OF INDIA PRIVATE LIMITED, *New Delhi*
PRENTICE-HALL OF JAPAN, INC., *Tokyo*
PRENTICE-HALL OF SOUTHEAST ASIA PTE. LTD., *Singapore*
EDITORA PRENTICE-HALL DO BRASIL, LTDA., *Rio de Janeiro*

Contents

Preface

Writing a book about software communication skills is not unlike strolling through a minefield—there are so many serious problems to avoid. For instance, one area of mines surrounds the title of the book itself. *Communication,* in the software world, is a pretty loaded word. A book with *that* word in its title sounds as if it might be about networks and distributed processing.

Well, this one is not about that. This one is about the writing and talking that software people must do to get their job done. And that brings us to another area of mines. Why write a book about communication when all of us, from first grade on, have been learning about it all our lives? Is there really anything left to say?

The truthful answer to that one is no, there's not. But there's a problem here. For all that we software folk have learned about communicating over the years, we still don't do it very well. People out there beyond our profession, in fact, think we are pretty awful at it. Perhaps it's time to revisit all those things we already know, by taking a refresher course in communication but focusing on the unique problems that software people face. That's what this book is all about.

There's another minefield here. Given the subject area we've just defined, does the world really need another book? There must be a dozen or more competitors talking about communication or documentation for software people, with more appearing all the time.

In response to that, let me tell you a story. I teach a course in technical communication in the graduate school's software engineering program at Seattle University. Our master's degree students must have had at least two years of experience building software before they can get into our program. To my way of thinking, that makes them a pretty sophisticated bunch of people, in a software sense, who know too much to be talked to like inexperienced undergraduates. When I went to choose a textbook for the class, I found that almost everything on the subject was written by technical writers who had lots of good things to say about how to write but nothing to say about the relationship between the software and the writing. They were the wrong books for my audience. Faced with that problem, I decided to try to write the right book. This is the result of that process.

I found another problem with the other books available in this subject area. None of them incorporated into their discussion the existing national and international standards for software documentation available to us. Whether you decide to use these standards or not, it is important to know of their existence. That minefield has also been avoided in this book—the standards are presented as appendices, and the value of their content is discussed in the main part of the book.

The audience that I see for this book, then, is the audience I deal with at Seattle U—software professionals who already know something about software and want to be better at communicating about it. Perhaps they are already software managers; perhaps they aspire to be software managers; or perhaps they want to do their technical job better—but they all see communication skills as an important part of their professional growth process.

I enjoy that audience. I was a software professional myself for nearly 30 years before turning to the academic world. I, too, have built significant pieces of software. In addition to the textbook material in this book, I'll share with you some personal anecdotes about my own experiences as a professional who has encountered lots of communication problems over the years! Some will help you learn, and some are simply fun stories to share. A few are personally embarrassing—but communication, after all, is an area where we expose ourselves to some public audience, and the result of that exposure is often either euphoria or embarrassment, much more so than in most other areas of our professional lives.

There are some people who have helped me in the process of producing this book. Marvin Herard, a Seattle University professor from the Fine Arts department, has done some fine chapter illustrations and contributed an artistic tone that my limited art skills could never have provided. Ed Presson, who has done the art for many of my previous books, has taught me the value of introducing art into the communication process. Several guest speakers I have invited into my classroom, especially Beryl Gorbman, have helped me see this minefield better from the technical writer's point of view. And my students, who have helped me shape and focus this material and whose merciless critiques have steered this book away from a few additional minefields onto some better ground, deserve the most thanks of all.

There are personal minefields around a professional career in the software field. The most obvious of them are those that involve communication. Join with me in learning a little more about our communication choices. I hope you'll enjoy the trip!

Robert L. Glass

SOFTWARE COMMUNICATION SKILLS

Communication involves people, it involves messages, and it involves media. Aimed into the air from a source, the messages may be heard by the intended audience, or they may hang in the air for anyone to receive. Television, radio, and other signals swirl about us, waiting to be listened to or watched.

CHAPTER 1

Fundamentals of Communication

The reporter and the photographer walked along the top of the levee. Water lapped only inches below their feet as the river threatened to burst its banks. Sweaty workers strained in clusters, pouring sand into sandbags and stacking the sandbags along the top of the levee, trying desperately to hold back the awesome force of the water.

The Army Corps of Engineers and community volunteers had been working for hours in a life-and-death battle against potential flooding. If the water were to wash over the levee, its momentum would eventually tear out a section, and the water would then be free to rush rapidly into the fields and homes formerly protected by the levee. The situation was desperate.

The reporter paused periodically and asked questions of the workers. Some were happy to stop their work and answer. Others, their emotions deadened by the fatigue in their bodies, angrily asked the reporter to go away. Unobtrusively, the photographer snapped pictures of both reactions.

When the reporter came to the Army Corps of Engineers officer, she paused for a longer period. "How is the fight going?" she asked. "Are you winning or losing? What is the flood-stage level? When will the peak be reached? What level will that be? Can you contain that level of water?" The tired officer responded as best he could, using as a basis the computer-printed reports he received from headquarters and his years of experience doing battle with the mighty river. It felt like they were winning, but only time would tell.

That afternoon, on the newsstands the headline announced RIVER CRESTS TONIGHT. LEVEES HOLDING, and below it there were pictures of grimy and tired volunteers, their expressions clearly showing the exhaustion they felt. The battle was hard, said the pictures, but they were winning it, said the text.

Communication is more a part of our daily lives than we often realize. We talk, we write, we read, we observe, we gesture, we sketch, we touch, and we process all that data that we have sent and received in such diverse ways. Communication is fundamental to the functioning of humanity.

The riverbank story brings the importance of communication alive. We see communicators doing their job—talking, listening, taking notes, taking pictures and re-forming those notes and pictures into a more useful final product. The final product, the finished newspaper, is useful in the sense that it brings to its readers an accurate representation of the facts and emotions of an event—in this case a critical event.

We rely on communication for many things. Let us look a little further into how that communication happens and see what we can learn about doing it better.

In the story there were several forms of communication: oral, as the reporter talked to various people; graphic, as the photographer snapped pictures; and written, as the reporter took notes and translated them into a publishable report. We will discuss all those forms of communication, but before we do, let us see what characteristics they all have in common.

In each type of communication someone defines a message, selects a medium for that message, deals with some human considerations in putting that message onto that medium, and finally creates the final product. We will consider each of those facets in the next few sections.

Each form of communication also has completeness guidelines that are (happily) straightforward and simple; they are sometimes called the journalistic *W*'s. If a communication answers the following questions, it is probably doing the basic job it is supposed to do.

1. *Who* is the communication about?
2. *What* is the communication about?
3. *When* did the event being communicated happen?
4. *Where* did the event being communicated happen?
5. *Why* is this communication worthwhile?
6. (sometimes) *How* did the event being communicated happen?

1.1 WRITTEN COMMUNICATION

The statement, "It must be true if it's written down," inaccurate as it is, says a lot about the importance of written communication. There is a lasting quality to the written word that tends to give it more credibility than the spoken word. Consequently, those who choose to communicate in writing should feel a sense of special responsibility:—both popular belief and force of law demand that what is written be accurate.

Successful writing involves several fundamental steps: preparing the right message, selecting the right media, overcoming inertia, and producing the right product. Each of these topics is elaborated in the following sections.

1.1.1 The Right Message

Communication need not be goal-oriented. Written communication, however, usually is. The writing may be intended to entertain, or to inform, or to stir to action; it is important to create a message that supports the chosen goal.

There are several fundamental rules that you as a writer should keep in mind when presenting your message.

Know Your Subject. Do not write until you are ready to write. If you are going to write an informative description of the COBOL programming language, be sure you understand COBOL before you attempt to do so.

Know What You Want to Present. Focus what you write. If you are discussing the report generation facilities of the COBOL programming language, concentrate your effort and energy on just that topic. Do not discuss the MOVE CORRESPONDING verb unless it has some bearing on report generation.

Know What You Want to Accomplish. Whatever you write, do it in a way that supports the goal of the writing.

Know Your Audience. People will read what you write. You need to know who they are, and to write for them. If your audience is composed of COBOL novices, don't use any terms you haven't previously defined. If your audience is composed of COBOL experts, don't bore them with unnecessary definitions; move quickly to the technical meat of the matter. Keep the reader clearly in mind as you write. Read the completed material from the point of view of the intended audience as a form of checkout.

Outline Your Material. You don't program, in general, without a design. Analogously, you shouldn't write without an outline. Think about, plan, and build a framework for what you want to write.

Allocate Length Constraints Against the Outline. Sometimes you are given limited space in which to say what you want to say. Sometimes common sense dictates placing limits on what you say (people may be less likely to read 100 pages than 2 pages). Either way, that space constraint should be budgeted against your outline. It is likely that the introduction deserves considerably less space than the technical content. Decide how much each deserves, and stick to it.

Consider Styles and Choose One. Style is an elusive but vital quality of writing. A dictionary definition, ''characteristic mode of writing, as determined by period, literary form, personality, etc.,'' is not very satisfying. But neither is the [STRUNK79] definition, ''an increment in writing,'' ''the sound the author's words make on paper.'' Let us just say that style is to writing as

Melinda Jones loved to write, and for the most part, she was good at it. She spun a good story, capturing the reader's attention with a good pacing of excitement and mood.

But there was one thing Melinda lacked—that elusive thing called style. Melinda's prose was interesting, but the words just didn't paint pictures or set up cadences or do any of the other things that the words themselves can do to supplement their context.

I discovered this about Melinda when she and I exchanged our writings, critiquing one another for the pleasure of the act and the value of the feedback. Somehow, although I felt free to critique all the other aspects of Melinda's writing, I could never bring myself to critique her style. ''You either have it or you don't,'' I reasoned, ''and why critique her for something she can't fix?''

Time passed, and our relationship drifted a bit. It was a couple of years before Melinda and I exchanged writings again. Much to my surprise, I found in Melinda's new writings all the positive essence of the old but with the beauty of a refreshing and new style, all her own!

''What have you been doing recently?'' I asked, out of curiosity as much as personal interest.

''Taking a writing class,'' she answered. ''It's a writing circle, where we all receive assignments and then read the results to each other, critiquing what we hear.''

So, I had been wrong. From Melinda I learned some important good news. Even that elusive thing called style can be taught. Melinda learned her lesson well. She went on from there to make a career out of writing.

personality is to the human being: It is the personal, distinctive imprint placed upon the whole. Do you intend to be formal in your presentation or informal? Are you taking a high-level or a detailed approach? Will you be journalistic (conclusions first, least important material last) or professional (summary first, technology in the middle, and conclusions last)? Is there an existing model that is generally accepted for the kind of work you are doing? If so, follow that model (unless you have good reason for doing otherwise). To evaluate the stylistic quality of your work, read what you write—aloud. Listen for the sound *your* words make on paper.

Flesh Out the Outline. Your "design" work is now complete; it is time to "code" the finished product. Working from the outline, put words to the framework. Only now should you concern yourself with specific choices of words and phrases.

Seek and Use Competent Reviewers. We know from bitter experience that completed code is rarely correct. Find one or more people who understand your subject area as well as you and solicit their critique. Then shed your ego defenses and respond to those critiques by modifying your writing. This is the checkout phase of writing.

Seek and Use Editorial Helpers. The skills of software proficiency, writing talent, and grammatical correctness sometimes seem almost mutually exclusive. Get someone with one or both of the latter skills to review your work. Grammar and spelling checker software can also help. Poor English detracts from an otherwise fine writing effort.

1.1.2 The Right Media

"The right message," in the previous section, dealt with the issue of content. "The right media," in this section, deals with the issue of form.

Content should usually take precedence over form. Sometimes content must be tailored to form, or decisions about the two should interact. Only rarely should form dictate content.

What is meant by form, or media?

"Now" Versus Lasting Material. Is the message a transient one, to be delivered, acted on, and forgotten? Or is it more permanent, to be referred to more than once? Select carefully how the message is to be presented, based on your answers to these questions. Memos, for example, tend to be transient—good for now material but usually discarded or filed in such a way as to inhibit later reference. Manuals, on the other hand, are usually permanent works with tables of contents and/or indexes to allow for ease of reference. A message about how best to use a COBOL language feature of your compiler, for example, should be distributed as an insert to a manual about COBOL pro-

gramming; but the announcement of the availability of a new version of a computer product could well be a memo.

Paper Quality. Every year, automobile manufacturers announce their new products via slick-paper brochures that feel and smell almost as good as the new cars themselves. On the other hand, the telephone book is printed on paper as thin and cheap as possible. Think about the implication of each. Which is appropriate for your message? There are social protocols that assist in answering this question. Internal product manuals meant for technical people are usually readable but austere. Marketing material is usually supported by high-quality, image-building media. User manuals for customers fall somewhere in between. More care is usually taken with communication to upper management than to peers or subordinates.

Type Quality. Hand in hand with the issue of paper quality is the issue of type quality. Should your material be typeset? Typewritten? Letter-quality printed? Dot-matrix printed? Done in calligraphy? Or even handwritten? The same social protocols that apply to paper quality apply here.

Illustrations. Just as the photographer's pictures captured a viewpoint in the flood story that no amount of text could have accomplished, so too, illustrations can be an important element in a written presentation. Sometimes illustrations can stand alone, as in cartooning (see Figure 1-1). At other times they may be used to supplement text. Either way, one picture is worth a thou-

Figure 1-1 Creativity and standardization.

sand words. But before you use an illustration, be sure that you really want those thousand words!

Figures and Tables. Text is not always the clearest form of presentation. Facts that need emphasis or contrast are sometimes lost in paragraphs of text. Figures and tables may be used to emphasize information, especially data, that may otherwise be glossed over by your reader. Figures may be illustrations or charts, whereas tables are usually matrices of numbers and headings. Careful use of tables and figures can transform murky text into clear supportive description.

Example Table: Readability Factor of Text Versus Tables

	Comprehension Quotient	Fog Factor	Speed of Grasping	Retention Factor
Text	0.4	0.8	4 seconds	1 minute
Table	0.6	0.2	1 second	30 minutes

(This is an example table only; the data are nonsense!)

1.1.3 Overcoming Inertia

Let's face it—many software professionals hate to write. Let's face it again—most software professionals have to do it anyway! The result of this unpleasant pair of facts is that software professionals often have a serious problem overcoming the inertia that inhibits the starting and continuing and completion of a writing project. (This is different from *writer's block,* which occurs when people want to write but can't think of anything to say).

There are ways of attacking, and perhaps overcoming, this inertia problem that involve finding ways to increase the enjoyment of the act of writing. One way is to automate the task as much as possible. Use a word processor with a good text editor to reduce the fatigue of creating and the inhibition to rewrite. Use a thought organizer such as ThinkTank [ANDER85] if you find it helps you with your prewriting organization. Use a spelling checker to facilitate the production of correct material.

Another way to overcome inertia is to write for your audience first but to write for yourself as well. Within reason, use a writing style that gives you pleasure. Use humor if you're good at it. Use art and graphics if they help make your point. If you are interested in what you write, your reader is more likely to be interested in it, too.

Organization also helps overcome the inertia problem. An outline, as we discussed previously, puts the material in focus, as does having a clear understanding of your goals. And once the planning is complete, chop the writing into accomplishable subtasks. *War and Peace* wasn't written in one sitting.

Write a comfortable portion of the text at a time. Reward yourself for completing it.

It is probably true that if others enjoy reading what you have written, you will come to enjoy writing it more. Get help in learning to create a better product. To improve your style, join a writing class or group. If you don't know of one, ask at the English department of a convenient college or university. To improve your grammar, read [STRUNK79]. Then practice your skills, getting regular feedback from someone whose opinions are accurate and nonthreatening. In writing as in sports, winning isn't everything, but it's sure a lot better than losing.

Another stimulus to writing well is reading good writing. Try best-selling fiction (it's better than best-rated television!), good humor, the classics, even national advertising. E. B. White is a marvelous writer; Edwin Newman playfully dissects the English language. Good writing style can be both acquired and absorbed. Try to do both.

1.1.4 The Right Product

Like a software product, written communication that has been correctly planned (designed) and written (implemented) should be correct. And like a software product, inevitably it will not be. For all the care put into its creation, it will contain requirements errors (attacking the wrong goals), design errors (faulty focus), coding errors (poorly chosen words and phrases), data-entry errors (typographical errors), and more. The written product, like a software product, will need checkout. There is a proper order to follow in this checkout process, based on a hierarchy of concerns, as follows:

1. *Ideas.* Examine the ideas first. If they aren't right, no amount of word twiddling will fix them.
2. *Organization.* Make sure the organization of your ideas presents them in a consistent and logical order. If it doesn't, fix it before proceeding.
3. *Style.* Check the writing style to see whether it is (a) appropriate to the reader, (b) appropriate to the writer, and (c) consistent. Especially if there is more than one writer, ensure that the style is consistent throughout the work.
4. *Words and phrases.* Now, and only now, begin working on word and phrase choices. If a word jars or misleads the reader, replace it. If another word is more interesting or colorful without detracting from the meaning, use it. There are two common mistakes at this level: changing wording too soon and spending too long on wording changes. Remember, there is no best program; some are just better than others.
5. *Grammar.* Correct all grammatical errors. Poor grammar may cause the reader to believe that the writer is ignorant.

Getting my first book published was a coup, a monumental achievement, an unexpected and fantastic highlight of my life. How was I to know that it would also lead to one of my most embarrassing moments?

You may have heard of the book. It is called *The Universal Elixir and Other Computing Projects Which Failed,* and it's still being sold, a few copies a month. It's a humorous, anecdotal book about the computing world for computing people to read, and there's not a lot of competition for it in that domain, even now, nearly a decade later.

So how could an apparent success like that be the cause for an embarrassing moment? Well, if you're asking that question, your knowledge of grammar is about at my level—passable, but by no means perfect.

Get out your [STRUNK79] and look up the difference between *which* and *that.* You'll see that the title of my book used the wrong word, not just tucked away obscurely inside somewhere—but out on the cover, for everyone to see!

6. *Spelling.* Be sure the spelling is correct. Use a spelling checker if one is available. Spelling is important because misspelling detracts from your ideas and your credibility.

Within this hierarchy of concerns there are some important subissues. During checkout is a good time to ensure that your writing is focused and lean. Remove ambiguity. Justify or eliminate redundancy. Simplify complexity. Tighten elaborate explanations. Make generalities specific. Use a positive emotional tone. Make writing forms consistent and perhaps even rhythmic. Emphasize nouns and verbs. Strive for clarity above all else.

Checkout is an iterative process. As you work on the "right product," you must evaluate your writing critically and repeatedly. Polishing and editing require rereading the material more times than you may wish to. To do less may result in an inferior product.

1.2 SPOKEN COMMUNICATION: FORMAL

We have already noted that written communication has some unique attributes, particularly in the area of requirements for accuracy.

There are unique aspects to formal spoken communication, as well. By formal communication, we mean a situation where the speaker is appearing before an audience. The speaker in this situation is putting himself or herself on the line with every word that is uttered. Unlike the reader of written communication, the listener can challenge the speaker immediately and demand an instant response. For an entirely different reason, then, the speaking communicator has a special need for accuracy.

A good way and a bad way exist to respond to that need. Some politicians have mastered the art of the bad way—they ensure that their spoken communication is so bland as to be not worth challenging. The good way is to be knowledgeable and therefore confident enough in your subject area to minimize the chances of being wrong.

The creation of spoken communication involves several fundamental steps (in many ways analogous to the steps already discussed for written communication): preparing the right message, selecting the right media, overcoming fear, and producing the right performance. Each of these topics is elaborated in the following sections.

1.2.1 The Right Message

The most important aspects of assuring that your spoken communication contains the right message are very similar to those already presented for written communication:

1. Know your subject.
2. Know what you want to present.
3. Know what you want to accomplish.
4. Know your audience.
5. Outline your material.
6. Allocate time (not length) constraints against the outline.
7. Consider styles, and choose one.
8. Flesh out the outline.

Within those aspects, however, there are some differences. Stylistically, the speaker has a choice that the writer does not: Will the presentation involve talking *to* the audience, as in the traditional lecturer-listener situation, or talking *with* the audience, as in the traditional seminar style? The answer may be dependent on the perceived level of sophistication of the audience and thus may even change during the presentation. Dynamic change is difficult; consider the possibility of such a transition beforehand.

Audience interaction is another aspect of the dynamic nature of spoken communication. You should decide in advance how to encourage or discourage it, how to control it when it happens, and whether to allow interspersed questions or to save them until the end.

In addition, audiences sometimes consist of groups that may respond quite differently to some parts of your presentation. Some advance thought should be given to such groups and how to handle them.

Spoken communication is, as we have said, far more transient than written communication. A word once spoken is gone and cannot be referred back to in order to clarify a more current point. Therefore, the speaking communicator has more of a need to "keep score," to remind the listener periodically of what has gone before and what is to come. This requirement can be expressed by the adage

Tell 'em what you're gonna tell 'em	(Present the audience with an outline of where you're going.)
Tell 'em	(Present the material itself.)
Tell 'em what you told 'em	(Present the audience with a summary.)

1.2.2 The Right Media

Media choices for the speaker are far different from those for the writer. In fact, although spoken communication is far more dynamic than written communication, some media forms (such as audio or video tape) actually separate the speaker from the listener, eliminating the opportunity for interaction.

At the highest decision-making level, the media choices for a speaker are exciting. There are mass communication approaches, such as television and radio; within that choice, presentations range from highly dynamic live, through semidynamic live-audience taped, down to fully taped, nondynamic. There are recorded communication approaches such as audio and video tape that allow the listeners to schedule the communication at their convenience. And there is face-to-face, fully dynamic communication.

Often media choices are made for the speaker by the organizer of the event; but if the speaker is also the organizer (e.g., an entrepreneur preparing an introductory sales presentation), then these choices belong to the speaker.

Where the communication occurs is also important. If the listening group is small, the facility used should be small (a few people in a large room feel isolated and out of place). If the presentation is meant to be impressive, then the facility should be impressive. If the presentation is meant to be interactive, the facility should facilitate interaction (a conference table, or chairs drawn in a circle, encourage face-to-face communication). If the presentation is to be lengthy, the facility should be comfortable. The facility should provide enough space (so that the audience will not feel cramped), adequate temperature control, and enough air flow to inhibit the sleepiness that results from reused air. Offices and conference rooms are usually good for small, interactive, and impressive presentations. Auditoriums are good for large, comfortable presentations. Classrooms and banquet halls are good for medium audiences but lack comfort for long presentations.

Audio-visual (AV) support is usually desirable to help the speaker enliven the presentation and perhaps to provide supplementary information (a listener can read a lot faster than a speaker can speak, and written supplements allow the speaker to bypass the content constraints imposed by time). Some common visual assists are listed.

1. Viewfoils on overhead projectors provide for the rapid presentation of written or drawn support material in a somewhat flexible way (new viewfoils can be created on the spot, if desired). They are inadequate for audiences over 100 or so in size unless the equipment is better than average.
2. Slides in a slide projector provide for the rapid presentation of written, drawn, or photographed support material in a polished but relatively inflexible way (on-the-spot changes are not possible) to audiences of any size.
3. Flip charts provide for the personal presentation of informal material in an intimate audience setting.
4. Chalkboards provide a slow but highly flexible capability for presenting words and sketches.

Audio enhancement of the spoken presentation can be provided by either of the following:

1. Fixed microphones, which require the speaker to remain within proximity of the mike.
2. Mobile microphones, which allow the speaker to move about but require paying attention to the cord.

Computing systems can also be used for AV assistance to enhance both the speech and its textual support. A demonstration displayed on a computer's

> The speaker critiques had come in from the audience, telling me what they had liked and not liked about my presentation. Nearly universal among the "not liked" were my viewfoils. They were too busy, not very neat, and difficult to read.
>
> I pleaded guilty, to myself, on all counts. After all, I had prepared the viewfoils as memory props for myself, not as works of art for the audience. It was a trick I had learned, to transfer my memory from my mind to some kind of hard copy, in order to avoid worrying about forgetting what I was going to say. But what I was learning now was another dimension of that lesson. If my memory props were visible to the audience, they must match their needs as well as mine.
>
> The members of the audience were right, of course. They usually are.

screen can be dramatic. Multiple-screen and enlargement systems are beginning to be available for displaying such screens to larger audiences.

These approaches should be supplemented by handout packets containing the presentation material if the material is worthy of such a lasting and costly treatment.

There is one other category of AV support that should not be overlooked—the speaker's own memory props. As we will see in the next section, speaker self-confidence is a vital part of a quality oral presentation. Anything that allows the speaker to relax, such as the knowledge that there is no chance of forgetting the presentation material, is useful. That is the role of the memory prop. The first consideration in memory prop material should be the AV support. Properly chosen AV material will not only enliven the presentation but will also provide the speaker with memory cues. If necessary, these can be supplemented by a set of notes carried by the speaker on unobtrusive note cards (e.g., 3 by 5 cards).

1.2.3 Speaker Confidence

People fear public speaking more than any other calamity that might befall them. Surveys have shown that this fear is worse than the fear of nuclear war or of getting hit by a truck. Overcoming this fear—and building speaker confidence—is thus a critical part of any presentation.

The confidence I felt when I agreed to teach the COBOL course was beginning to vanish. The students asked questions I wasn't prepared to answer—enough of them that I was beginning to get embarrassed by the number of times my answer was "I don't know."

The problem was predictable, but I was too early in my career to realize it. My only training for teaching the course had been the COBOL class I had taken from our local IBM representative and one small program I had written. I was certainly not a COBOL expert—I barely qualified as a novice.

The class dragged on through the days of its schedule, and with increasing pain I began formalizing the lesson I was learning: Never teach a course unless you're really prepared to teach it. And preparation means more than just having taken the course yourself. It means going over the material, trying it out with variants and nuances, until you understand not only the material to be presented but also the questions that will inevitably be triggered by it.

There is no substitute for knowledge in the world of the speaker. And knowledge can best be obtained from experience.

The process for building confidence, fortunately, is relatively straightforward. There are two keys to that process: knowing your material when you speak and having successful speaking experiences as frequently as possible.

If you lack confidence in your knowledge of your material, there is no way you can have confidence in yourself. Prepare for your presentation by reviewing the fundamentals underlying the material, if necessary, and by reviewing the specifics to be presented. Consider questions that might arise and what your response should be. Assure yourself that when you stand up to speak, the presentation material is not going to be a problem for you. If you don't have that assurance, then don't speak.

Speaking frequently is the key to overcoming self-doubt. It is important that such presentations be in a supportive setting, where feedback is helpful and criticism, if any, is constructive. There are many ways to practice, such as speaking to friends and peers, joining the Toastmasters organization, or speaking into an audio or video tape recorder and critically listening to and/or watching the playback. Once you have spoken relatively successfully a few times, the fear starts to go away.

The fear, however, rarely vanishes completely. People who perform frequently, such as actors, come to see the remaining fear as a friend. Understanding their fear, they prepare a little harder for their performance. On stage, their fear sets their adrenalin flowing, getting them "up" for the performance. From this point of view, a lack of fear of speaking is more dangerous than the presence of the fear.

It is important to note the origin of this fear, namely, focusing on yourself and your own flaws instead of on your audience and your own strengths. As you move the focus of attention outside yourself, the fear diminishes to manageable proportions.

> The speakers who were scheduled to take the podium during the afternoon returned from their lunches and took their places on the platform. I was to be the first speaker, and my hands trembled with the fear I always feel before appearing.
>
> Out of curiosity, I turned and looked down the row of eminent speakers aligned with me. The futurist next to me also had a hand that trembled. So did the head of data processing for a leading oil company. And so did the professor from a noted university.
>
> I had heard before that everyone has a fear of speaking, but somehow I'd never really internalized it. Now I could see it for myself.
>
> The person who isn't afraid of speaking must be rare, indeed. None of them were there that afternoon, at any rate!

Words were coming out of the speaker's mouth, one after the other, in fine cadence. But the content of the words was vacuous. It was like listening to a discussion about the weather.

Except it wasn't supposed to be a discussion about the weather. It was supposed to be a session on software reliability at a major computing conference. And the speaker was wasting our time. How, I wondered, could anyone stand up before an audience with so little to say?

Later, after the conference ended, I got the answer. Someone who knew the speaker had seen him just before the vacuous presentation and asked him how he felt. "Just fine, considering that I didn't have time to prepare anything," the speaker had said.

Here was the other side of the lesson. I had already learned nervousness is nearly universal among speakers; however, the lack of it may be an even greater problem than the presence of it. The speaker who went ahead and spoke without anything to say might have had the gift of steel nerves, but we all suffered for it.

1.2.4. The Right Performance

There is a performance quality to any spoken presentation. Even if your presentation is a formal description of a new technical concept, the manner in which you present your material helps determine your effectiveness in getting your ideas across. To that extent, then, when you are giving a talk you are "on stage," and it is worth considering the analogy that your presentation is a theatrical performance.

For example, there arises the question of rehearsal. Theatrical performances, in general, require rehearsals, but many times presentations do not. If it is vital that the presentation be letter-perfect, then rehearsal may be in order. Otherwise, except for timing verification, rehearsal is relatively uncommon. Many believe that rehearsal of a presentation reduces its spontaneity and thus its effectiveness. And of course, to the extent that audience interaction is desired, rehearsal is not possible.

What about the theater itself? It is always wise for the speaker to check the performance environment. Where is the best place for the speaker to be? How will AV support be placed and handled? Is the necessary equipment present and working? Can the audience see and hear well? For a long presentation, is a pitcher of water available for the inevitable parched throat? A wise speaker checks the theater and thinks about these issues prior to the performance.

I fidgeted a little, knowing that when dinner was over it would be time for me to stand up and make the evening's presentation. Still, professional society groups in general are made up of friendly folks, and I'd appeared in this kind of setting more than a dozen times before. It was just my natural fear of speaking, I reasoned.

There was one thing that bothered me, however. Our dinner was being served in a restaurant, and there was no place that I could see set aside for my talk. I asked my host where I would be speaking. He looked uneasy, and suddenly I felt uneasy as well. "There is a problem," he said. "The restaurant forgot to get the meeting room ready, and we aren't sure where you'll speak."

He hailed the restaurant owner, and both of us got up from the table to go look at the meeting room. It was hopeless! Lettuce and carrots from the salad preparation littered the floor and tables. Spills darkened the carpet. An odor prevailed. There was no way the room could be readied for my presentation.

We returned to the table, eyes downcast. What could we do? The only place in the restaurant that could accommodate us was the main dining room, and there were other diners present.

When you have to, you're capable of doing things you'd never dream of doing otherwise. We rearranged the tables in one corner of the dining room, grouping the audience into the corner, and I stood in the middle of that restaurant, in the presence of all the other disinterested diners, and spoke to my host professional society group. The other diners might have thought it peculiar, but not one said a word!

Checking the speaking room well before a performance may seem both superfluous and the mark of a worrywart, but failing to check it can prove even more embarrassing.

During the performance, there are some key speaker concerns. These may be peripheral to the message and the medium, but they still make a big difference in how well the presentation is accepted.

Have a Strong Opening. Get the audience's attention at the outset. Be challenging, or be controversial, or be funny, but get the audience conditioned to want to listen to what you have to say.

Take Control. This is *your* audience for the duration of your talk, and what goes on in your theater is under your control. It is up to you to ensure that the audience behavior is appropriate. Inhibit side discussions and other audience self-distraction. No one else will do it for you.

> The agony of anticipation had been worse than anything I'd ever imagined. Being the presiding officer at the college journalism conference was an honor, but it wasn't an honor I had sought. It had come to me by lot.
>
> And now the day itself had come. For the first time, I was in charge of a meeting. And this was no small meeting. College journalists from all over the state were there.
>
> It started out well enough. There are only so many ways to start a meeting, and the one I had chosen had worked. We were off to an acceptable start, my meeting and I.
>
> But then came trouble. A controversial issue arose, and the meeting fragmented. It wasn't the diversity or even the ferocity of the opinions that was the trouble. It was that the meeting disintegrated into small meetings, all over the room, as people argued the issue with their neighbors. And, in the front row, one of the participants even started a side discussion with me.
>
> In the years since that meeting, I have learned the lesson. But I didn't know it that day. The fragmented meeting limped on and eventually the group came back together of its own accord. But a lot of important time and energy had been lost.
>
> What was the lesson I didn't know that day? The leader of a meeting—or the speaker at a meeting—has a responsibility beyond the obvious one of presenting material. It is his or her job to control the meeting. As an old supervisor of mine once shouted into a buzzing session, ''Let's have *one* meeting here.'' A unified approach is what the audience really wants. And it's the job of the speaker to ensure it.

Get the Audience on Your Side. It is important to challenge an audience and to avoid shying away from controversy. But it is also important to be tactful in doing so. Don't insult the audience's intelligence with too much overview or its interest level with peripheral detail. Don't challenge cherished beliefs, if possible, but if you must, do it with tact and the approach that we're all basically on the same (human) side here.

Handle Interaction. If there's too little, stimulate it (ask questions, even rhetorical ones). If there's too much, inhibit it (explain that you can accept only one more comment, in the interest of time). This is just another facet of taking control.

Use Anecdotes. A fact-filled presentation is a wonderful thing to behold, but it soon fatigues the mind. There are a couple of reasons for spinning

The speaker had done it again. He had presented a perfectly legitimate bias, but he had done it in such a way as to alienate that part of the audience that disagreed with him.

I personally don't care much for the Basic programming language. It lacks some important capabilities that I think even a minimal language must have. But I wouldn't tell an audience that in such a way as to make the Basic devotees feel like nerds, for two reasons: First, because I just don't like to do that to people, and second, because I don't want to start creating enemies in an audience. They'll rear up and bite back when you least expect it.

Sure enough, at a key emotional moment later in the presentation, the speaker was challenged, hostilely and uncomfortably. The biased seeds sown earlier had borne ugly fruit.

tales that illustrate the point you're trying to make—it's a change of pace for the audience, a chance to relax the mind for a little while; and the visual image of an anecdote may more effectively set the point into the mind and enhance it with an emotional framework.

Read the Audience. Speaking is, as we have seen, usually a dynamic environment. A good speaker reads and then plays the audience. Does the audience seem to come alive during certain parts of the talk? Figure out what those parts are, and do more of that. Is the audience yawning? Check the temperature and airflow, and correct them if necessary and possible. Throw in an extra anecdote if you have a good one, seek audience interaction, or enliven the talk in some other way.

Getting to know your audience is a dynamic thing. As your presentation progresses, you may get feedback that your original assessment of the audience capability and interest was wrong. If so, adjust your material to the newly perceived level.

Monitor Timing. There is almost always a proper ending time for a talk. Meet it. If you must go overtime, apologize and then show that you mean it by closing as soon as possible. Audiences are extremely intolerant of overtime speakers, and rightfully so.

Watch the Little Things. Don't hide behind the podium. Use a microphone only if you need it. Don't put your hands in your pockets (if you feel them getting away from you, clasp them behind your back). Enunciate clearly, speak slowly, and vary your tone and inflection. Don't chew gum.

As the performance comes to a conclusion, there are several things that you should do in addition to speaking:

There are some special problems in speaking before an audience of 325. I knew some of them. I was about to learn some others.

The problem I was prepared for was the problem of interaction. Not many people, except those with peculiar axes to grind, are willing to speak out in an audience of that size. And yet my speaking style is at its best with audience interaction.

Thinking about the problem in advance, I had armed myself with some tools to stimulate the audience. I asked them at the beginning to identify themselves by job task, and by kind of application orientation, and by several other categories that demanded that they get used to at least raising their hand in the group. Then I prepared some rhetorical questions, hoping that would stimulate some response. And finally I decided to present some of my more outrageous technical biases to stimulate some agreement or disagreement.

It worked. The problem was, it worked too well. One hour into the talk, it was Speaker 20 minutes, Audience 40. Things were clearly out of hand.

As I continued to speak and work the solution out in the back of my mind simultaneously, an old friend in the back of the room came to my rescue. "I came here to hear the speaker, not the audience," said my friend, "and I'm getting damn tired of not getting what I came for."

A startled hush fell over the audience. It had been scolded, but the scolding was really for me, I knew. It was, after all, my job not only to stimulate the interaction but to inhibit it as well. With the help of my friend, I now did what I should have done. "I welcome your interaction," I said into the silence, "but it's my job to limit it. I'll take one more comment on this issue, and then we must move on."

And so it went, nicely controlled but with good interaction, for the remainder of the session.

1. Monitor the time (that pretty well has to happen as a parallel, real-time process).
2. Emphasize the objectives of the presentation (these should have been built into the outline).
3. Measure what you perceive to be the results of the presentation (this will be a combination of planned presentation and ad-lib based on the results (if any) of the audience interaction).
4. Identify action items (again, these should have been a part of the outline).

It was the other problem in speaking before an audience of 325 that nearly threw me. I am used to using viewfoils on an overhead projector as my memory props. They had served me well over the years. But not this day. With over 325 people in an audience, you are taxing the technology of some overhead projectors and screens. People in the back just aren't going to be able to see the material. And that's what happened, in the middle of the audience interaction problem we just talked about, on this day.

When the audience began complaining about not being able to see, the seminar producers and I tried to work the problem in real time. We moved the projector, and the table it sat on, back and forth, and at the same time I tried to present the technical material.

It was a disaster! Nothing would help, and the audience was becoming restless. At last, we admitted defeat. It was simply not possible to find any position for the projector that would solve the problem.

What's the lesson here? For a large audience and mediocre projector or screen technology, use 35-millimeter slides. The precision is better, and the projection can meet the needs of almost any large audience.

The audience should leave the performance with the feeling that something *was* accomplished or is about to be.

1.3 SPOKEN COMMUNICATION: INFORMAL

Informal spoken communication is simply one-on-one or one-on-few communication. The techniques are totally different from those for formal communication, but the results are just as important—and perhaps more so.

By its nature informal communication has not usually been planned by the speaker. This is not entirely true, of course—we have all "rehearsed" what we planned to say to someone. But the elaborate planning of message, media, and performance that characterize formal spoken communication are not at work here.

Thus informal spoken communication is largely improvisational. You would think that there was not much to be said about this kind of communication. But that is not true. Look at Figure 1-2. Here we see a model of the typical informal communication process. There is a speaker and one (or more) listeners. There is a message passing from one to the other(s). There are filters that inhibit the successful flow of the message. And there is, potentially, feedback by means of which the listener completes the communication circuit and attempts to certify the message.

It was a couple of days before my scheduled user-group keynote address that I realized there was a problem. The problem wasn't my speech. I felt good about that. I had done some research on the topic and supplemented it with my own experience, and I had a talk the audience would enjoy and I would feel good about presenting.

No, the problem was more subtle. How would I check the timing of my hour-and-a-half talk? My speech was immediately followed on the schedule by lunch. A hungry audience, I realized, can easily become a hostile audience.

My normal technique for a timing check is to make a silent presentation of the material. But in this case, I just didn't have an extra hour and a half to devote to that level of preparation. After some thought, I came up with another way.

For each memory prop in my presentation, I allocated a certain amount of time cumulatively so that if I stuck to my allocation I would finish on time. Then on each memory prop I wrote the start time and stop time for that material. Now I wouldn't have an overall timing test of my material, but at least I had some milestones to check against along the way.

On the day of the speech, it worked amazingly well. For most of the memory props, my guess had been right on. For those where it wasn't, I shrank or expanded my material to fit the preallocated time. And when lunchtime came, the talk came to an end—right on schedule, and with no audience hostility!

What kinds of filters do we put up to inhibit informal communication? There are many: your emotional mood (if you feel depressed, you probably don't absorb as much information as you do at other times); your physical comfort (if you've been sitting in a too-firm chair for two hours, your attention is divided between your communication and your something else); your mindset (if certain words trigger your mind, you may pursue your own thoughts

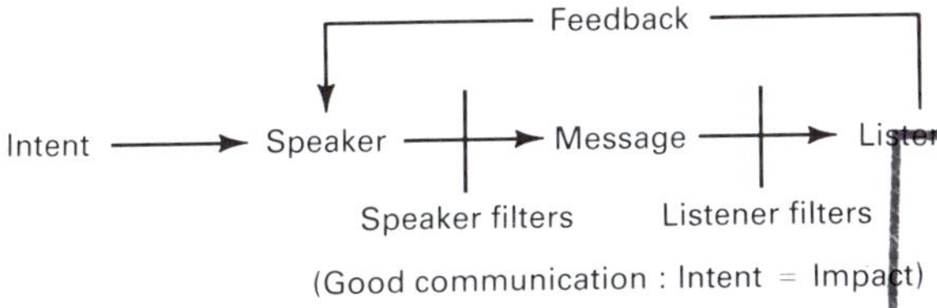

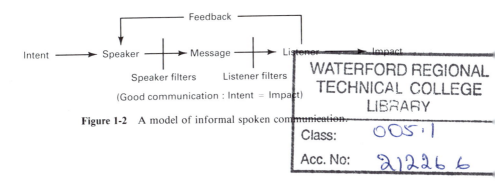

Figure 1-2 A model of informal spoken communication.

Have you ever thought about how a beat reporter gathers information? (A beat reporter is someone who makes the rounds of an assigned set of news sources, gathering information worthy of being made into news stories.)

You might have thought that the reporter stops at each place on the beat, asks, "What's new?," writes it down, and moves on. If you thought that, you'd be wrong. When I was a young cub reporter (before I turned to a life in computing), I tagged along with several full-fledged reporters making their rounds and found out what happens.

The reporter stops in at the news source—say, the police station—and strikes up a conversation with the clerk on duty (and later with the police chief). Perhaps 10 minutes into the conversation the question, "What's new?" comes out, but in a subtle, conversational way. This is a friend making the rounds of his or her contacts, not a reporter brusquely soliciting news.

I thought about that. "What a waste of time," was my first thought. And then I thought again. People's lives aren't necessarily prioritized around "What's new?" The answer to that question is buried somewhere in the conscious (or even subconscious) and needs a chance to work its way out naturally. It was an important lesson in how people—all of us—really communicate.

rather than the communication at hand); distractions (if there is noise nearby, your concentration will be divided).

What should be done to minimize the effect of filters?

Identify the Filters. If the speaker or the listener is aware of a filter at work, it may be important to stop the communication, identify the filter, and seek to remove it before going on.

Provide Feedback. To keep the speaker and the listener focused, the listener needs to present back to the speaker his or her interpretation of what has just been communicated. This must, of course, be more than just "You said X"; it must be more like "What I hear you saying, if I may change the words a little, is Y". The speaker can then confirm or revise the interpretation.

Communicate at More Than One Level. Often it is enough to communicate at a logical level, involving only the mind. But just as often, logic is only a part of the communication process. The emotions are the other part. If a communication involves motivating change, for example, then the emotional mindset of the listener must be reached by the speaker before the communication can be successful.

There are additional filter-removal techniques that can be assigned to the speaker and to the listener. Among the speaker tasks are the following:

Avoid Unsupported Generalizations. If you say "everybody says . . . ," your listeners may spend as much time figuring out who "everybody" is as they do listening.

Avoid Dogmatic Statements. If you say "XYZ is always true," your listeners may spend their energy looking for exceptions.

Avoid "You" Statements. If you say "you should LMN . . . ," your listeners may spend their time figuring out how not to.

Avoid Inappropriate Questions. If you ask Why questions your listeners may focus on defensive Because answers.

Avoid Inappropriate Direction. If you ask the audience if they want to do something you want them to do, they may choose not to.

Among the listener tasks are the following:

Be Committed to Listening. Focus your attitude, your time, and your attention on the speaker and the subject.

Listen Actively. Try to identify the speaker's key points. Ask clarifying questions. Make reinforcing responses. Paraphrase the speaker's words in your feedback.

With these basic techniques, the speaker and the listener can work cooperatively to improve the chances of making intent equal impact.

1.3.1 Assertiveness

Participants in a communication process have certain rights. They have the right to

- Be treated with respect.
- Have their own feelings and opinions, and express them.
- Ask questions, even "dumb" ones.
- Prioritize the expectations of others with their own (as long as they are aware of and respect organizational hierarchies).
- Make mistakes and be responsible for them.

Dealing with those rights involves many factors, one of which is shown in Figure 1-3. Here we see a continuum of attitudes toward those rights: non-assertiveness, where people do not recognize they have rights; assertiveness, where people deal with their rights; and aggressiveness, where people assume too many rights.

The proper communications role—in fact, the proper human relations

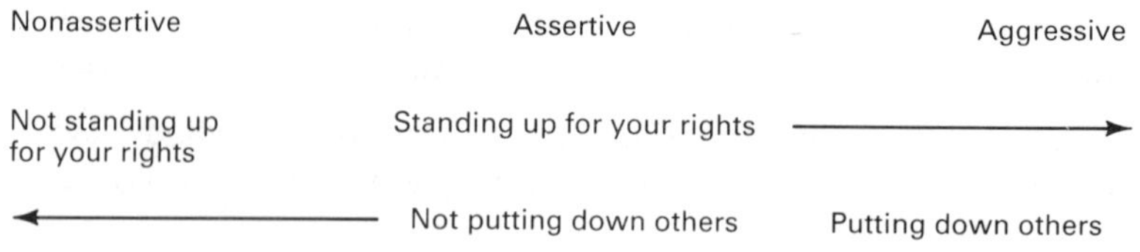

Figure 1-3 Assertiveness and its continuum.

role—is the middle, assertive road. The extremes lead to unhealthy communication and perhaps even to unhealthy actions.

However, being assertive is not a natural state for all people. Women and minorities, for example, who over the years have found themselves put down by a biased society, sometimes need to be trained to reclaim the capability. Thus assertiveness training is a frequently offered course in women's centers.

1.3.2 Conflict

Conflict is inevitable in life situations. Conflict is inherently neither bad nor good; only the methods of handling conflict may be bad or good.

Most of us hate conflict. We feel threatened by it. We know that it generates anger and other unpleasant emotions, and our natural tendency is to avoid it. Avoiding conflict can be a severe mistake. Generally there is an issue at stake in conflict. The nature of the issue, and not the tendency to avoid conflict, should determine the reaction.

It is important to evolve the belief that conflict is manageable. This belief can come only from experience. Thus opportunities to try conflict management and conflict resolution should be sought rather than avoided.

This advice is, of course, more easily given than taken. It is like telling a speaker "relax—your tension is not helping you." The following set of guidelines may be helpful in determining when to deal with conflict and when to avoid it. Dealing with conflict is sometimes called *confrontation*. The chart contrasts confrontation and avoidance.

Confront if . . .	Avoid if . . .
A small problem will grow.	The issue is trivial.
A relationship is threatened.	You don't care about the relationship.
A decision is required.	Time delay will help.
The alternative is a "bad" de facto decision.	A "cooling down" is needed.
Morality, morale, or productivity are threatened.	The cost of confrontation exceeds the benefit.
	Others can resolve better.

Confrontation is probably the most difficult form of communication. The speaker and the listener are usually at some measure of risk—personalities are often drawn into conflict along with issues, and the confronter may have to deal with personal attacks as well as intellectual ones.

But as with any other risky situation, the opportunities present in confrontation may also be significant. The person who handles conflict and confrontation well may be much more successful in life's experiences, whether they are professional or personal.

Technical communication is like basic communication except that the messages focus on specific kinds of content. They may be about circuitry, or graphical illustrations of phenomena, or mathematical expressions, or anatomical studies, or even illustrations of the evolution of Asian characters from their original pictorial form.

CHAPTER 2

Fundamentals of Technical Communication

The engineer was frustrated. For the third time in three months the problem had been presented to the mathematical support group. For the third time, their answer wouldn't work. It was a tough problem, to be sure. The wing geometry of a naval airplane, twisted to allow super-slow carrier landings, was not easy to visualize, let alone to convert into a mathematical model.

Still, the problem had been carefully and thoroughly presented. There was the blueprint for the wing and its leading-edge component, which had been the basis for the discussion. There were the face-to-face meetings with the mathematicians, poring over the blueprint and discussing its implications. There were the supplementary sketches, drawn where the blueprint's two-dimensional limitations were too severe for a three-dimensional problem. There was the feedback discussion, as the mathematicians played back to the engineer their understanding of the problem. Why was a solution so elusive?

The engineer reported the inability of the group to solve the problem to upper management. Upper management reacted by forming an audit team to investigate the situation. The audit team interviewed the engineer and the mathematicians, analyzed the source material they had shared in working the problem, and reported its decision: The failure to solve the problem was a failure of communication. It was not, as it might have been, a failure of technical capability, or of lack of knowledge, or of maliciousness, or of personality conflict. For all their attempts, the engineer and the mathematicians had never communicated quite well enough to be working on the same problem. With this finding, the engineer and the mathematicians went on to explore the problem even more thoroughly (using a more formal feedback system), and eventually they communicated well enough to create a solution to the problem.

Let us look at the implications of this story. The first and most important point this story makes is that communication is a truly vital part of technical problem solving. Proper communication leads to solved problems; improper communication leads to unsolved ones. There are dollars, schedules, products, and perhaps even lives at stake in our technical communications.

The second point this story makes is that communication comes in many forms. Recall all the kinds of communication in the story:

- Face-to-face discussion
- The blueprint
- Sketches
- Feedback discussion
- Reporting to management
- Audit investigation
- Interviews
- The written report

In other words, communication was verbal, it was written, and it was graphic. It is not uncommon for technical communication to take all these forms.

Given that technical communication is vital and takes many forms, what portion of the technologist's work involves communication? A study* has shown time expenditures by white-collar workers (including technical people as a subset) to be as follows:

46%	Meetings and telephone calls
25%	Administration
16%	Analysis/other
13%	Document creation

If we presume that these data are correct for the technical specialist—and their correctness will of course differ in different settings—then the white-collar technologist is spending 59% of his or her time in communication, only a small fraction (16%) in more technically oriented work, and the remaining significant chunk of time (25%) in administrative support, some of which no doubt also involves communication.

*Data from a Booz, Allen & Hamilton 15-company study published in 1984 in *Business Computer Systems*.

We have seen from both an anecdotal and a statistical point of view that communication is fundamental to the technical process. It is important to learn more about it.

In many ways, the problems of technical communication are not so different from those of basic communication. All the concerns of the previous chapter—preparing the right message, presenting it via the right media, overcoming inertia, and presenting the right product—are the fundamental problems of the technical communicator, as well. There are, however, some additional concerns for the technical communicator. It is those concerns that form the substance of this chapter.

Because technical communication is much more often product- and *goal-oriented* than is basic communication, it is important to pay special attention to those goals. In addition, the complexity of technology often leads to more *diverse layers of content*—technical knowledge can be absorbed at many levels. That diversity requires special preparation. It demands special languages; sometimes it demands *informal languages* and sometimes, *formal ones.* The skilled technical communicator must understand all the levels of diversity, the languages that go with each, and when it is appropriate to use a formal or informal language. This is no small mix of tasks!

There is also the problem of *creation.* The technologist must overcome inertia and even personal resistance to prepare material. If the technologist is not comfortable with or good at communicating, then he or she must seek help.

The technical person also has special *terminology* to consider. The complex and ever-expanding nature of technology brings with it a specialized vocabulary; sometimes that vocabulary helps communication, and sometimes it hinders it. The effective technical communicator must know when to use such vocabulary and when not to.

In addition, there is the issue of *communication facilitation.* Communication is so vital to technology that thought must be put into ways of making it happen and helping it happen. For example, the *environment* in which communication is conducted may be vital to the success of the communication. Should communication be conducted in meetings, or as one-on-one contacts, or by phone or mail, or by some other method?

Finally, there is the issue of *information storage and retrieval.* It is not enough to communicate information. That information must also be saved, and retrieved, and used again. Let us explore each of these areas in more depth.

2.1 THE IMPORTANCE OF GOALS

In the technical world, communication is almost always designed to achieve some result. Your first focus should be on that result. What is the goal of this communication? What is the audience for this communication? In what way can I cause this audience to seek, or join me in seeking, this goal? It is vital that you state the goals at the beginning of the communication, that you address them periodically during the communication, and that you make them a part of the summary and conclusion of the communication.

If processes are being described or defined, make sure those processes support the goals. If actions are being sought, select the best actions for achieving the desired goals. If there are expectations implicit in processes and actions, make them explicit. Within the constraints of the sophistication level of your audience, go the extra mile in leaving no doubt as to your intentions.

There are hidden agendas in some technical (and nontechnical) communications. You may, for example, be negotiating a compromise solution to an issue, and your planning may have armed you with a set of fallback levels, or giveaways, or bargaining chips with which you can respond to offers from the other side. In this case, of course, the openness of the previous paragraph is inappropriate. Even so, in this context there are always higher-level goals, above the level of the negotiation details, that can be made explicit and around which both communicators can build the remainder of their compromises. The problem in communication is rarely one of giving away too much information—it is much more often a lack of openness and clarity. In the event that you do find yourself communicating in a hidden-agendas environment, it is still important to keep the hidden agenda clearly in mind during the communication, to express and deal with the visible goals that buttress or form the invisible ones, and to plan the transition from the visible goals to the hidden ones. This kind of communication, with one "hand" behind the back, is far more complicated than the more normal, cards-on-the-table way of doing business.

Some communicators focus on goals by means of a *goals analysis tree* (see Figure 2-1). If your communication goal is to obtain management ap-

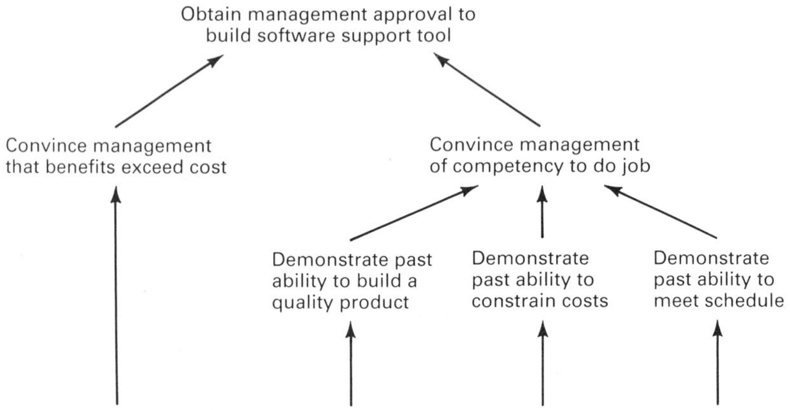

Figure 2-1 Example goals analysis tree.

proval to build a new software support tool, such as a powerful debugger to support the programmers in your company, then that overall goal may be broken down into supportive but subordinate goals. One support goal would be to convince your listener that debugging time using current methodologies was taking too long and costing too much. Another support goal would be to convince your listener that you are competent enough to build the product in question to a reasonable quality level, with reasonable cost, and on a schedule that meshes with your organization's other activities. Each of those support goals could then be broken down into its own set of support goals. The competency goal could be supported, for example, via three goals: demonstrating past ability to build a complex quality product, demonstrating past ability to constrain costs to a reasonable level, and demonstrating past ability to meet reasonable schedule constraints. The resulting set of goals is a hierarchical tree, in the same sense that a requirements specification may flesh out into a top-down, hierarchical tree-structure design.

Checklists are handy devices for ensuring that planned effort meets original goals. In validating your planned communication from this point of view, consider these questions:

1. Is it clear to your listener why you are communicating?
2. Is it clear who is to take action and what that action is to be?
3. Are your goals stated early in the presentation?
4. Do you avoid confusing the issue with irrelevant side goals?
5. Are you prepared for objections and questions?
6. Does your summary leave the listener prepared to act?

Working with a checklist such as this requires practice. To help with that practice, the book *Writing at Work—the Russell and Associates Papers* [RUSS85] can be particularly useful. It contains examples of technical communication, some good and some bad, and asks the reader to critique them, then provides its own critique. Some of the examples are extremely relevant to the software person; some others are so badly done that they are funny.

The enemy of communication is miscommunication. Focusing on and working with goals is one way of defeating that enemy.

2.2 DIVERSITY OF LEVELS OF CONTENT

The technology of computing can be approached by reading your daily newspaper, by reading *Scientific American,* by reading *Datamation* or *Byte,* or by reading the *Journal of the ACM.* Each of these approaches is legitimate, but each is dramatically different in the level of technology it represents.

The technical communicator must choose the level of technology to be presented. Nearly always, this choice will be determined by the nature of the audience. (It is almost a fundamental law of communication that the audience should define the presentation.)

Is Your Audience Technology-naive? Then be prepared to present only a simplified overview of what you know. This audience will get lost quickly in detail and may be lost in too much overview as well. Intimate technical terminology will confuse and even alienate them. The naive audience is probably the most difficult for the technical communicator to address, since it demands so much attention and habit change.

Is Your Audience Technically Knowledgeable on a Broad Level? This is the typical management audience. Here again, an overview, high-level approach is most appropriate. Details will bore this audience. (And erroneous details may not be discovered. This audience is subject to victimization!) The overview presented should either fit the world view held by the audience or explain why it does not. What this audience misses at the detail level, it will not usually miss at the high level. In many ways this is the easiest audience to address, since it understands most of the technical terminology and yet is not able to dispute the communicator on technical inaccuracies at the detail (most vulnerable) level.

Is Your Audience One of Technical Peers? Then your presentation must begin with sufficient overview to brief the audience on the larger picture but move swiftly into the technical details of interest. Here, too much overview will bore the audience, and too much simplification will insult it. This is also, potentially, a difficult audience to address, because of the likelihood that it will find flaws in the presentation. (Often, however, that is the purpose of this kind of communication—flaw detection has enormous value, even though it may be embarrassing.)

The diversity of audiences affects not only the technical content of the presentation but other matters as well. Should the presentation include exhibits? Charts or graphs? It is often true that words are an inefficient way of presenting information, and an object or illustration can be used to accelerate the communication process.

An exhibit might take the form, for example, of holding up a floppy disk to explain microcomputer storage media to a mainframe audience. This is a situation where no amount of words could ever replace the image of the object itself in the audience's mind. There are some important issues to deal with in considering the use of exhibits, however. Does the exhibit help clarify a point that needs to be made? Does it reinforce that point, and not distract? An ill-chosen exhibit is like a poorly told joke—it leaves the audience wondering what it missed (or what you missed).

Charts and graphs take many forms: pie charts, bar charts, line graphs, dot charts, and more. The type of chart chosen should support the point to be made or the information to be presented. For example, pie charts are good for showing parts of a whole; bar charts, for ranking or comparing several items; line graphs, for showing change in one or several items; and dot charts, for comparing change in several items.

Again, the critical factor in deciding the level of detail is understanding who makes up the audience and targeting to them. That understanding comes from a variety of information—the educational level, the motivation, the organizational level, the experience level, and the style preferences. A lawyer preparing a case for trial, for example, will go out of his or her way to understand the character of the judge assigned to try the case. Dossiers on judges are sometimes maintained in legal offices for this purpose. The presentation approach that might sway one judge might alienate another.

If your audience does not have a specific name—let's say you're writing a user manual—then perhaps you will want to invent one. Danny Debugger is easier to visualize as the reader of your debugger user manual, for example, than a faceless programmer with undefinable skills. As you write, write for Danny Debugger. And when you're through writing, review what you wrote as if you were Danny Debugger. "Walking a mile in the other person's moccasins" is one of the best ways of evaluating the worth of what you have done.

Software, being one of the fastest-changing technologies around, is more vulnerable than most to the problems of diversity of levels of content. Not only the level of content but also the date of it may confuse the audience. A presentation effective for a 1980 audience is unlikely to work in 1990. The terminology may be obsolete, the concerns may be obsolete, and the technical content may be obsolete. There is no alternative for the software presenter but to be up-to-date. Software audiences are notoriously intolerant of outdated material!

For a number of reasons, then, the technical presenter must be aware of many aspects of the technology being presented. Failing to do so may lead to a totally inadequate presentation. Acknowledging and planning for the problem can form the foundation for an effective piece of communication.

2.3 THE PROBLEMS OF CREATION

Creation of technical material has many facets. The material must be conceived, organized, prepared, enabled, and refined. Each of these actions implies a unique set of problems.

The first problem sometimes encountered is called *writer's block*—the creator simply can't think of anything to say, as if the mind had suffered "brain clamp." The best solution to freeing the mind is *brainstorming*. (Brainstorming is a technique in which the mind is allowed to spawn and develop ideas uncritically; it is especially useful, in addition to overcoming brain clamp, when nontraditional ideas are needed.) Brainstorming may be facilitated by utilizing a stream-of-consciousness technique (jotting down whatever is occurring in the mind) until the material begins to focus on the problem at hand. Brainstorming may be focused by forcing the reluctant mind to prepare an outline for the material even though the material itself hasn't come to mind yet.

Once writer's block is overcome and the brain clamp is released, there are some organizational techniques for keeping the mind moving in the proper direction. The creator may choose to focus on the most familiar problem in order to make the most confidence-building progress. Or an already-confident creator may choose to focus on the most difficult problem in order to make the most real progress.

The *storyboard* is a way of laying out information in modules, moving them around to find the best information flow and layout. Some creators use the walls of a large room to serve as a storyboard, taping paragraphs and sections in various places as the content evolves. (It is essential, even using a storyboard approach, to work with a well-defined outline—excellent modules placed in an unplanned sequence read as badly as poor modules.)

If the technologist is truly not comfortable with or good at communication, things get more difficult. There are only three choices: (1) have the technologist do the communicating even if he or she is ineffective at it; (2) shift the communication responsibility to another technical person or to a team of such people; or (3) shift the responsibility to a skilled communicator.

The first choice has limited appeal. If the technical person is truly ineffective at communication, then the use of that person in communicating may be counterproductive to reaching the desired goal. A long-term fallback plan involving special training in communication for such a person is advisable; technical people simply cannot remain ineffective communicators and be effective at their technology.

The second, or team choice, is relatively common, particularly in a team-technology setting, where the knowledge of the technical subject is spread among several people. The best communicator from the team can then be used for the necessary presentations. Only in the event that the presentation is so specialized that only one person can prepare it does the problem persist.

The third, or skilled-communicator, choice is becoming increasingly common. Technical writers are frequently used to prepare user manuals for new software products, for example, not only because they have the requisite writing skills, but also because they may better be able to wear the moccasins of the often computer-naive reader than the technologist who built the product. In fact, because of the frequent failure of technologists to do an adequate job of preparing user manuals for microcomputer products, there has sprung into existence a new industry of how-to computer books for the naive audience that are really only user manuals being sold in bookstores. Some publishing companies have made contractual arrangements with software companies to write, publish, and sell the "official" user manual, delivering a contractually defined number of manuals to the vendor before selling the rest through bookstores. And one well-known software company, Microsoft, has actually formed a publication subsidiary to perform this role.

One task that cannot be effectively delegated by technologists to nontechnologists is minute-taking at technical meetings. When technologists are speaking to each other, they have free rein to use their technology-intimate vocabulary, and in fact they should not be restrained from doing so, since communication would be considerably slowed. But clerical note-takers who do not understand this vocabulary have been known to produce very bizarre minutes from what appeared to be fairly straightforward meetings by trying to interpret or even spell terms they did not understand. There is no substitute for the use of technical specialists for minute-taking at technical meetings.

There are some common communication ground rules that should be fairly universally observed by technologists and their helpers:

1. If you take a position, support that position with reference material whenever possible.
2. Offer your audience the option of pursuing your topic further through a bibliography of relevant material.
3. Give thanks to those whose information you have used, and name the people whenever possible.
4. If you present unsupported personal opinions, identify them as such.

These ground rules may be seen as constraints on creativity, but they also serve to produce a far more credible product.

2.4 THE COMPLICATION OF TERMINOLOGY

Have you ever heard someone speak on your favorite technical subject in a foreign language? Whether the speech occurred in a formal setting or was among a small group of people, you probably experienced frustration as you tried to understand what was being said. Some people even feel anger in that kind of circumstance. Few of us are very good about listening to sounds whose meaning we don't understand.

Computing people speak a foreign language—foreign, at least, to noncomputing people. We use words like *byte* and *throughput* that came into existence along with our technology. We use words like *IMS* and *CPU* that are abbreviations, in fact, for other words that came into existence along with our technology. Worst of all, from the point of view of communicating with computer-naive people, we are so comfortable with these new, foreign words that we don't even realize that we are using them. The result is an enormous communication gap between computing and noncomputing people.

The person we were interviewing was impressive, all right. He seemed to know the technology, was on top of the latest buzzwords, and dropped just the right mix of computing-relevant names to impress us without being showy.

Still, there was this nagging feeling. Something just didn't seem right. He was a leading candidate for the managerial position we had open, and all the things that tapped our logic said this was the person to choose; but still, there was that nagging feeling . . .

His formal presentation progressed, still as impressive and smooth as ever. And then it happened. We could hardly believe it.

One of the leading computers of the day, in small installations at least, was the IBM 1401. This computer was customarily referred to as the "fourteen oh one," and although no one had ever told us how that got started, we all knew that pronunciation to be correct.

But the speaker had said "fourteen hundred and one." We listened carefully, disbelieving. He said it again. The terminology was right, but the pronunciation was all wrong. For all his credentials and smoothness and buzzwords and name-dropping, the speaker was a fraud. He'd never worked around a computing installation, or he'd have gotten it right.

The interview ended fairly quickly after that. We asked a few more pointed, less polite questions, and the facade crumbled. He had faked the résumé, faked the credentials, and studied just enough computerese to get by—almost.

The problem is even more complicated than that. We have invented subvocabularies in our technical world that only people in our computing subculture can understand. For example, IBM mainframe users have a whole alphabet soup of abbreviations that no one with a non-IBM background can understand. (It is even rumored that some of this specialized vocabulary was invented by IBM to help keep its customers captive!) The result is that there are communications barriers between people within the computing world.

There is also a communication barrier between computer practitioners and computer academics. In many cases one concept is described by different words in the two worlds, and occasionally the same word is used to mean two different things. Students fresh out of a university may hear professionals talking about something foreign sounding and not realize (until they ask what the term means) that it is a concept they already understand. For example, in most of the computing practitioner world and in the academic world as well, the word *file* refers to a collection of data. But in some parts of the computing world, the term *data set* is used for that same purpose.

Part of me wondered what I was doing there. But the other part felt strangely at home.

My talk to the Munich audience wasn't scheduled until that afternoon, but I had dropped in early to check the room and see how things were going. My speech would be supported by translators converting my English into German, but the current speakers were using German. I understood only about one word in one hundred, not enough to pick up any meaning at all. I wondered if it was worth staying; I wondered how rude it would be to leave in the middle of the talk.

As I was feeling uneasy about sitting through a talk I couldn't understand, I also had a sensation of déjà vu—this was an experience I'd had before. But where?

And then I remembered. It was just like the computer science colloquia at the university back home. The talks there were in English, of course, but the terminology was so specialized to the subject that I gleaned no more meaning from it than if the speaker had been using German! They were Ph.D. candidate talks aimed only at other Ph.D. candidates.

I settled back and listened as the German speaker went on. It was an experience I'd had before.

Words themselves in the computing field sometimes evolve their meanings. The word *specification* is a case in point. For many people it means a statement of the requirements that define a problem to be solved. But as researchers have tried to use the specification as the text from which code is automatically generated, the meaning of specification has recently changed; sometimes it means high-level design and sometimes even low-level design. It is vital when reading the literature to verify that a term is being used in the way that you understand it or to adjust your thinking to the new definition.

Some computing words are ambiguous even in their normal usage. *System,* for example, tends to mean whatever its user wants it to mean. *Verification* and *validation* refer to processes for establishing product reliability. Verification means ensuring that the evolving product meets the specification for this life-cycle stage, and validation means ensuring that the evolving product meets the overall requirements; however, in some cases the words are used with their meanings exactly reversed.

Old words are also given new meanings by computing people. A *bug,* for example, is more than an insect. *Impact* is not just the crater left by a meteoroid.

And finally, there is the computing acronym. *COBOL* has been with us so long that we all know what it means (COmmon Business-Oriented Lan-

> I know that I don't use perfect English. Language is a tool, I believe, and just as I occasionally use a screwdriver as a prying device, I'll use a word or a phrase in an unusual way.
>
> Still, it was a surprise when the letter came. I'd written an article for a professional journal, having fun with my subject as I usually try to do, using colorful English when it spiced things up a bit. Some of it had survived the editor's knife, some had not. The letter talked about some of my questionable words that survived.
>
> The letter came from one of those rules-oriented language people—you know the kind, infinitives are never to be split and prepositions are never to end a sentence. What made this letter memorable, however, was the graphic art that accompanied it to help make the point.
>
> The picture was of a giant hole in the ground. "This is an impact," said the accompanying text. "Do not say 'the technology had an impact on something.' That is not an impact." The letter writer was right, of course. I had misused the word *impact.* But the use of the picture to reinforce the judgment call has had more of a lasting impact on me (ouch!) than anything else in the letter.

guage), but what about JOVIAL (Jules's Own Version of the International Algorithmic Language)? All of us have worked on projects, I am sure, with our own specialized abbreviations and acronyms. One project's *MSU* might be another project's *LCU. LSI* begat *VLSI.* Is a *VM* system more powerful than a 512K one? Perhaps we are worse than bureaucrats; we have invented a language—or a set of languages—all our own, and we are in general happy about it.

There are some commonsense rules for the use of these acronyms. If your audience is likely to be familiar with an acronym, define it at the first reference or in a glossary and then use it as much as you wish. If the audience is not likely to understand it, either don't use the acronym at all or define it periodically throughout the text. Since repeated definitions are annoying, it is probably better not to use the acronym at all unless it is a critical part of the material being presented.

Most acronyms are presented in all capital letters (oddly, Fortran (FORmula TRANslation) often is not). Sometimes periods are put after each letter, but if the acronym is treated as a word (e.g., COBOL) no periods are included.

In spite of this confusion, our subculture languages serve us well. They allow us to converse quickly and effectively on specialized topics without the slowdown factor of using phrases where a short word would do. These specialized words are the symbols of our profession, and usually they facilitate communication in a very effective way.

The problem arises, however, when we begin using these specialized words with people who don't understand them. Then—as in the first paragraph of this section—frustration and perhaps even anger set in among our listeners. It is important to realize that the problem is not theirs to solve—it is ours. We have invented the new and specialized vocabulary, and it is up to us to use it when it is appropriate, and either avoid using it or explain it when it is not. In many ways this is the worst communication problem of the computing professional—the language has become so natural to us that we often fail to realize that we are using it. The result is that computing people have a reputation for obfuscatory communication. We mask the message without even realizing that we are doing it.

The solution, as with so many of the problems of communication, is to bear our audience in mind when we communicate and to listen to and evaluate ourselves as we communicate. It is an example, again, of walking in the other person's moccasins.

One other communication problem that can affect technical communication is deliberate miscommunication. Some people intentionally miscommunicate, either to impress others with their knowledge or to cover up the fact that they aren't sure what they're talking about. (It is ironic that the pompously knowledgeable and the nonknowledgeable both use this technique, and it is difficult to distinguish between them.) Correcting for deliberate miscommunication is a challenge. Faced with this problem, the frustrated communicator should either try to strip away the obfuscation and get to the meat or avoid the person and the problem entirely.

2.5 FACILITATION OF COMMUNICATION

Communication is at the same time a natural and a nonnatural phenomenon. That is, most of us communicate at several levels without even thinking about it; some psychologists even believe that some forms of communication are vital to life itself.

But communication blockage is also a common problem. O. Henry's wonderful story "The Gift of the Magi" tells us what happens when two people are better at loving each other than they are at communicating with each other (the woman cuts off and sells her long hair to buy a watch fob for the man, and the man sells his watch to buy tortoise shell combs for the woman).

Communication may just happen if we don't do anything to facilitate it, but then again it may not—with disastrous results. Mechanisms to facilitate communication are vital to the functioning of most societies.

What are some examples of the facilitation of communication? The counselor, working with a couple to get them to listen to, express, and understand the important feeling they may not have been sharing; the retreat, at which a group of people leave their normal place of interaction and go to a special place for the specific purpose of communication; the facilitator, who works with a group of people to get them to share ideas, problems, or feelings. And finally, there is the institutional organization.

The organization? What does it have to do with communication? The answer is, a lot. An *organization* is a system used to define people relationships in an institutional setting. It is usually represented by an organization chart. There is usually some sort of hierarchy of leadership (Figure 2-2), stretching from the top officer of the institution to the lowest-ranked employee. This chart not only reflects the organization of power and function, it also steers the flow of communication.

There are many sayings in our society having to do with communication and the organization. The *open-door policy* means that any subordinates may visit and communicate with their supervisor at any time they need to. *Going over your boss's head* means communicating at a level frowned on by the organization. IBM has a policy called "Speak Up," by means of which employees at all levels can bypass the organization and send a message to the company's leaders. The organization shapes institutional communication in profound ways; furthermore, it was designed to do just that.

How well *does* the organization work as a shaper of communication? How well *should* it work? These are two important questions that must be dealt with in an institutional setting. One answer to the first question is best supplied by an anecdote.

When the researchers at Xerox's successful research facility, the Palo Alto Research Center (often called Xerox PARC), were initially exploring the subject of office automation, they decided that the first order of business was to find out what really happened in a functioning office work place. To that end, they had a series of meetings with the office staff of another part of the Xerox Corporation to find out the tasks being performed and the communication lines being used there. At the conclusion of the series of meetings, as the researchers prepared to go back to PARC to think about and model what

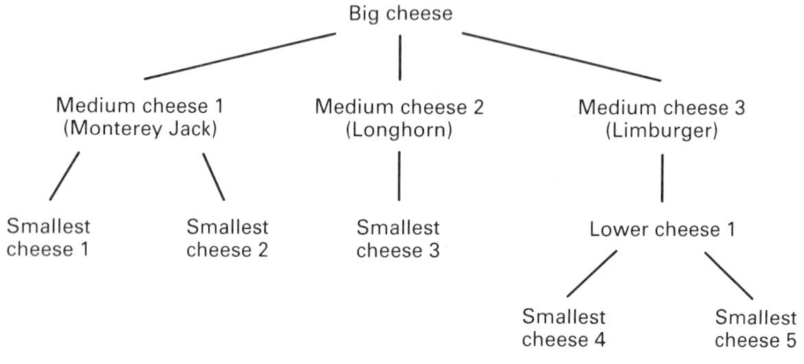

Figure 2-2 Example organization chart.

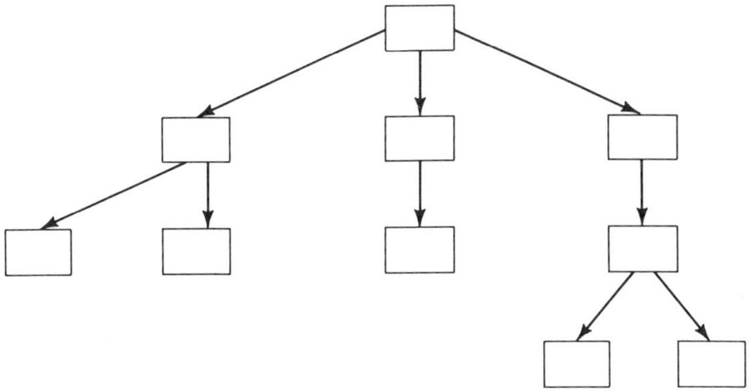

Figure 2-3 Example communication flow as management may think it happens.

they had learned, a clerical person took one of the researchers aside and said "I wish the managers hadn't been present at these meetings. Then we could have told you what *really* happens in the office!"

The organization, then, may be a funnel through which communication flows, or the lines of communication may simply exist on paper. The important question is, What *should* happen?

Figures 2-3 and 2-4 show two kinds of communication flow in an organization: the first as the manager may think it flows and the second as it actually happens. What kinds of communication are there, and how important are they?

Through Management Channels. This is the kind of communication management had in mind when it constructed the organization chart. Direc-

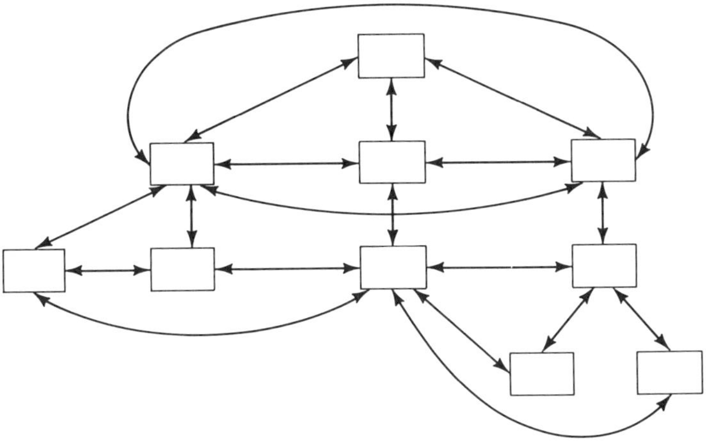

Figure 2-4 Example communication flow as it actually happens.

tion flows downward; feedback flows upward. It sounds crisp and efficient, and it may in fact be. But it may also be counterproductive. The feedback mechanism may atrophy as the channels get choked with downward flow only. Important peer communication may get inhibited, forcing technical "reinvention of the wheel."

Through Technical Channels. Groups must communicate on group problems and solutions. Individuals must communicate to know their individual tasks. Communication avenues must be opened between technologists and technical key people, in a twentieth-century master/apprentice relationship. New groups should be formed when they share common knowledge whose spread could benefit the institution (this is the purpose of the Special-Interest Group subfunction of the Association for Computing Machinery, for example). Perhaps staff positions should even be established to help disseminate or to coordinate the creation of information of common value.

Through Special Information Channels. A library is an organizational entity set up purely to facilitate communication, as is a document or information center [IW86].

Through the Grapevine. All institutions have an unofficial flow of information, whether they want one or not. The grapevine is amorphous and subject to gross distortion of its contents; but it may be useful, at times, for planned information release to test reactions. Politicians, for example, are well known for "leaking" trial decisions in order to observe the public response before deciding whether the decision is a wise one.

By Accident. All too often, the actual flow of communication in an organization is by happenstance. Whoever carpools together, or sits next to each other, or has a friend in common may actually be the conduit through which information spreads. The information that flows in these ways may or may not be desirable information. This is the mechanism, for example, by means of which false rumors are most often propagated.

It is important for an institution to plan its communication mechanisms and to ensure that they are working in order to inhibit the less desirable forms of communication flow. What *kinds* of information should flow through these various channels? Anything that will help the institution function more effectively.

1. Management information: direction, advice, feedback, procedures and policies, support, motivation, criticism, and an organizational overview (the "big picture").
2. Technical communication: advice, feedback, support, motivation, criticism, guidelines, specific direction, consultation.
3. Special information: written management communication, written technical communication, audio-visual support, reference information.

It is not so surprising, when we view the options for information flow and content, that communication is a problem in the institutional setting. It is vital—and as institution size grows, ever more vital—to plan for and facilitate communication flow.

2.6 ENVIRONMENT FOR COMMUNICATION

There are many ways of facilitating communication, as we discussed in the last section. One of the more important ways is to create an environment that fosters it.

Surprisingly little work has been done in this area in support of software people. Even the recent focus on workstations has not yet caused much change; facilities vary widely—some may work in one-person offices, others in several-person cubicles, and still others in a so-called bullpen, where row upon row of desks extend side by side in an open, warehouse-type area. Interestingly enough, although in most professions the individuality of the workplace is a measure of the prestige of the worker, this may not be true in computing. The internationally known computer scientist has been known to work in a bullpen, and the novice in a private office.

Cost, of course, is a factor in office space decisions. Large companies often try to reduce direct costs by reducing the square footage provided for each employee. Unfortunately, there are few studies that provide data on the indirect costs of reduced productivity incurred by such decisions.

There is one significant exploration of office environments available to us. IBM decided, in the mid-1970s, to build an optimum facility for use by software people. The architectural exercise to design such a facility and the resulting product are described in [MCCU78] and illustrated in Figure 2-5. (A similar facility built by Honeywell for its software developers is described in [SD82]. The latter reference is more recent—it places heavier emphasis on automated workstation tools for the software developer, for example—but it is less complete in its discussion. An interesting discussion of the workstation environment from the microcomputer *user* point of view is found in [PC85].)

The IBM study selected the private office as the appropriate workplace, with a great deal of communication-facilitating trappings: the blackboard for transient work either by the individual or with a group; bulletin board space for more lasting messages; reference storage and transient storage for the various artifacts a software person must use; plenty of work surface to allow spreading out the documents that support these efforts; and a guest chair, to accommodate two-person conferences.

A great deal of thought went into this proposal. I would like to suggest, however, an alternative model for the software specialist. To develop one, let's first take a look at the requirements for this person.

First, there is the need for private, analytical work, where the person

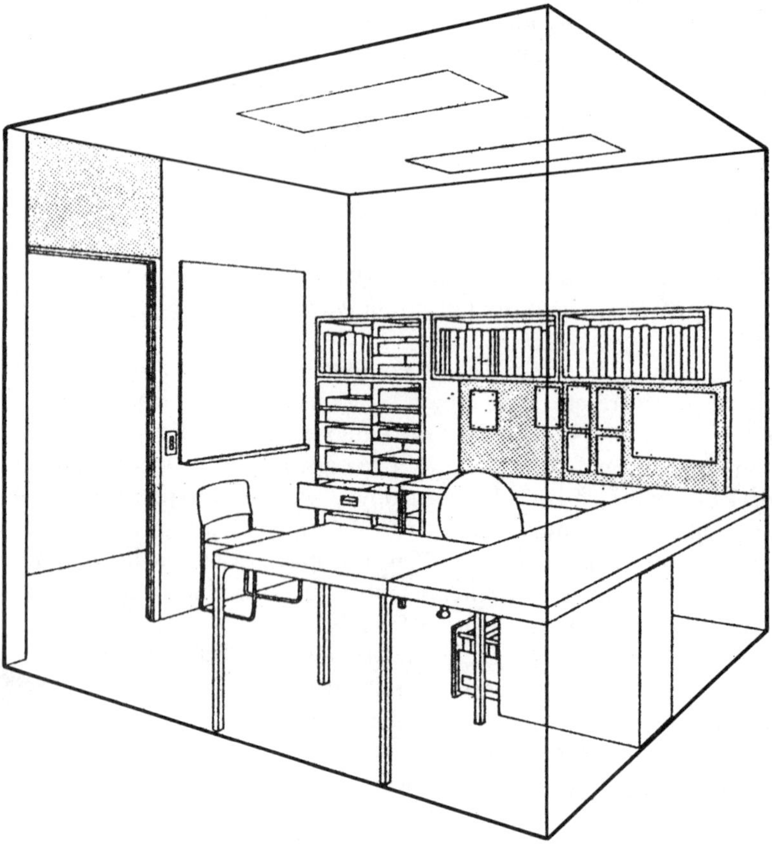

Figure 2-5 IBM Santa Teresa Laboratory programmer office space. Gerald M. McCue, "IBM's Santa Teresa Laboratory—Architectural design for program development," *IBM Systems Journal*, 17, no. 1(1978): 17. Copyright © 1978 International Business Machines Corporation. Reprinted with permission.

thinks through a design, or assimilates requirements information, or evolves a difficult code. In this setting, the software developer has a need for uninterrupted silence.

Second, there is a need in most software environments for team communication. Although the software developer may work alone at times, that work typically evolves from an assignment created in a team setting. It is vital to have a workplace where the team can communicate on a spontaneous basis. Communication that can't happen spontaneously often doesn't happen at all, and software errors result.

Third, there needs to be a place where a group of people can meet for the sole purpose of a group discussion.

It is difficult to satisfy these diverse needs in one setting. The analytical need demands silence, while the group-meeting need demands verbal communication. The team environment stresses interruptability, but there are times when interruptions are harmful. Because of these conflicting needs, it is my belief that the environment best able to facilitate communication ought to have three separate elements: the work carrel, the team cubicle, and the conference room.

The Work Carrel. This is where the software developer retreats, complete with the materials needed to support deep thinking, when a problem arises that can't be solved in the hubbub of the other environments. The carrel is much like a library carrel, available to whoever needs it. Silence is demanded in the carrel area. Shelves for written materials are plentiful. A terminal or computer is available to access needed files of information. The emphasis here is on facilitating thought.

The Team Cubicle. This is the normal workplace of the software developer, the location of his or her desk, terminal or computer, and storage facilities. The number of people in the cubicle should be the number in the team who have need for close communication. Often this may be as small as two or as large as seven. Here silence is the norm, but it is expected that software people are free, with discretion, to interrupt each other and ask questions or share ideas. Here, too, the social rapport essential to team functioning may be developed.

The Conference Room. This is the group-meeting area, probably a conference table surrounded by a dozen or so chairs, and perhaps expandable for

> The need for the work carrel is not new. Neither are innovative attempts to simulate the carrel.
>
> Emory Earplug (a name contrived to hide his true identity) was a pioneer in the area. Needing deep silence in the middle of a taxing software design exercise, he went out to the flight line of his aerospace company, the place where they tested the jet engines, and returned to his office with a pair of flight-line earmuffs. When Emory had on his muffs, the whole world was his work carrel.
>
> Wanda Walkman has a more recent solution to the same problem. She wraps a radio around her ears when she needs to tune the world out, and turns on the music.
>
> John McJohn is a little less subtle. When John is deep in the mire of trying to understand a thicket of requirements just dropped on him by a new customer, he retires to the men's room—the third stall from the left. Here, in what he calls "Flushing Meadows," he is seldom interrupted by anything more intrusive than running water!

larger-attendance training meetings. (There may, however, be a need for training facilities in addition to conference facilities.) Here the planning sessions, reviews, customer interfacing, and perhaps even sales presentations can be held.

These ideas are not necessarily popular. Most people, including software developers, would prefer a private office as their home base, much like the one presented in the IBM work. Few institutions provide this totality of facilities to their software developers. Cubicles are common, conference rooms are common, but carrels are not.

Obviously, software can be successfully developed in a variety of environments, and no one has established a best setting. The issue is, however, important. Studies have shown [GLASS80] that the most persistent of software errors, those that escape detection in the early stages of software development and are not found until maintenance, are errors where the software to solve a problem is too simple for the complex problem being solved. It is as if the human mind is trying to retain more details than it is capable of holding. Communication is one way of boosting the retention power of the human mind. Isolated, uninterrupted work time is another. The proper environment can help in both of these areas.

2.7 MEETINGS

In the previous section we mentioned the need for a conference room for the software developer. This opens the door to a vital yet mundane topic—meetings.

A *meeting* is a communication session involving two or more people. Nearly always, meetings are held to facilitate goals. Careful attention is needed to steer the meeting toward achieving those goals.

Consider the goals as paramount in the process; achieving the goals may involve *not* having a meeting, for example. Before a meeting is held, not only should the goals be well defined and understood by all, but the way in which a meeting will assist in achieving the goals should also be defined. The goal of a meeting may be to share information, to change attendee beliefs, or to strengthen attendee beliefs, for example. Which goal you are trying to accomplish will make a big difference in how the meeting is conducted.

As part of this goals-oriented process, determine the attendees consistent with the goals. Inviting peripheral people wastes their time and yours. Failing to invite critical people may waste the entire meeting.

Consider the method of conducting the meeting most likely to achieve the goals. Is it important to control and focus the meeting on a specific set of information to be presented? Or is it important to give the attendees a chance to air their opinions and emotions? The answers to these two questions may steer the meeting in two very different directions.

The following sets of questions form a checklist for making decisions about meetings.

> The two teenagers squirmed uncomfortably in their chairs. They had told two conflicting stories about what had happened the night before. The patient father of the boy, with a wisdom that surprised me, had immediately called for a face-to-face meeting. It was working.
>
> Seeing that both their stories could not be true, they began correcting their previous stories, a little at a time, until what we had was the truth. Without the meeting, we might never have known what had happened.
>
> I was struck by the importance of the communication process. It was not only important to be able to communicate, I now realized; it was important to know some techniques and when to use them, as well.

Meeting Planner. Is the meeting worth calling? Is the goal one that could be achieved by moving information rather than people? Is the meeting well planned? Are the facilities appropriate to the goal? Are the meeting time and place known and acceptable to all?

Meetings are generally most useful when divergent opinions need to be assimilated into one, or when there is a lot of information to be presented and questions are expected, or when circumstances dictate a face-to-face confrontation rather than the less personal alternatives of telephoning or letter writing. Meetings are expensive—the cost is the average salary of the attendees multiplied by their number, and it escalates rapidly.

Is the meeting well focused? Has the goal of the meeting been made known in advance to the attendees? Are the attendees the right ones? Has an agenda been prepared that focuses the meeting on these goals? Have preparations been made for recording discussions (where necessary), decisions, and action items? Is the person in charge good at keeping a meeting focused?

Meeting Conductor. Is the meeting well conducted? Are the speakers introduced and the agenda presented at the outset? Is necessary background information provided? Are all viewpoints expressed, so that everyone feels involved and represented? Are the multiplicity of viewpoints narrowed toward action items and decisions? Are side meetings inhibited? Are individual viewpoints of little interest to most attendees channeled into side meetings after the main one? Is the meeting wrapped up at the end, with action items and decisions highlighted? If the subject has emotional overtones, does the meeting touch the emotions as well as the logic of the situation?

Meeting Participant. Do you understand the purpose of the meeting? Do you understand the result of the meeting? Is your understanding the same as that of the other attendees? Have you asked questions to clarify any confusion? Have you coordinated any surprises you need to present? Are you judicious in your use of meeting time, leaving some for others? Do your comments stick to the meeting subject? Do you help move the meeting toward an appropriate conclusion?

Meetings may be conducted in a variety of ways. They may occur in a classroom, a conference room, an office, or a hallway. They may be scheduled—most of the points just discussed apply to scheduled meetings—or they may be unscheduled (important goals are sometimes achieved in unplanned, perhaps even serendipitous, ways). They may occur in person, by telephone, or by electronic mail. They may occur on demand, such as via an open-door management policy, or via an authoritative management policy.

We mentioned previously that some meetings may be held just to allow the attendees to ventilate their thoughts and feelings. That kind of meeting needs a little more discussion, since at first it seems to be much less goal-oriented than the other kinds of meetings we have been talking about. However, there is still a clear-cut goal; it is just a more subtle one.

The goal of such a meeting may often be to make people feel involved in a decision-making process. For example, an institution is about to install a new productivity system to assist clerical workers in performing their jobs more efficiently. If the new system is thrust on the workers without preparing them for it, they may well resist the change and destroy its effectiveness. It is good people policy and good communication policy to hold exploratory meetings before the final decision is made and the new system installed to allow the

The minority history class I was teaching in my church's adult-education program seemed to be going well. I had covered a lot of material, all of which showed the cultural history and contributions of America's minorities in ways that history books had for suspicious reasons failed to teach us.

It was important to me not just to present material but to effect change. What I was presenting, it seemed to me, showed clearly that the threads of racist self-interest had denied the beauties of American freedom to a significant number of American people. It was a perversion of the American way; it was un-American! It was time for those of us who cared to do something about it.

But when the class ended and I got the attendee feedback, I learned an important lesson. The material I had presented had indeed been received, but it had not taken root. And the reason was clear.

I had touched my audience logically, but I had not touched them emotionally. And it was deep in the emotions that the roots of racism were anchored. I had presented too much material; I had spent too little time asking the audience for their reactions to what I was presenting.

It was an important failure, but it was an important lesson, as well. There are many ways to reach an audience. It is important to reach them in the ways that count.

clerical workers to participate in some of the decision making. If the decision is perceived to have had their support, the workers are much more likely to cooperate in making it a success.

This motivational, ventilating kind of meeting must be handled with exceptional care. The decisions being made must be legitimate, not simply rubber-stamping decisions already made. The venting of emotional reactions must be allowed, but decisions must also be pursued and achieved. Such meetings tend to feel disorganized, so it is important that the meeting leader understand the dynamics in order to make them successful.

Meetings, then, may be held for a variety of reasons. But no matter what the reason, the tasks of planning and organizing the meeting remain very similar. The goals of the meeting must be clearly in mind and explicitly stated. The organization of the meeting must facilitate the achievement of the goals. The results of the meeting must be recorded and distributed.

2.8 INFORMATION STORAGE AND RETRIEVAL

Communication is nearly always based on information. The information may serve as the raw material of the communication, or it may be the product of the communication; therefore, it is important to develop ways of filing, retrieving, and disseminating information.

Communication concepts that fail to plan for storing and retrieving information are as ineffective as buying new carpeting but failing to buy a vacuum cleaner. Information that is saved in an ill-conceived, inaccessible system will be impossible to use when it is needed later on.

The human mind has an infinite capacity for storage, but not an omnipotent power of retrieval. It may, in fact, be that ill-conceived, inaccessible system discussed in the last paragraph! Therefore it is necessary to hone the storage and retrieval powers of the human mind and to supplement these powers with some sort of organized, physical filing system.

How should information be organized for retrieval? Commonly, topics are developed and organized alphabetically by topic name. Then information pertaining to a particular topic is placed in that topic's area.

Sometimes alphabetizing of topics is too time consuming. In that case or in a case where some information is used much more frequently than others, the topics may be arranged in order of most recent access. The likelihood is that the topic needed at a particular point in time will be near the front of the file because it was probably used recently.

Information may also be stored chronologically, in a sort of push-down stack. Many people record information in a journal, for example, and to retrieve it they remember approximately when it would have been entered into the journal and then go there to look for it.

An information storage and retrieval system is highly personal and reflects the way in which the organizer's mind works; therefore, if anyone else is ever going to need to use a system, its operation has to be documented briefly at the beginning of the file.

Another facet of the information problem is its dissemination. Suppose you have some information to distribute about a software product you have created. How should you do it?

An important first question to ask is, How will the recipient use it? Is this information transient—to be read and discarded—or is it reference material, to be filed and retrieved?

If the information is transient, then a simple memo or note is an effective way to spread it. But if the information is permanent, a more organized system is desirable. If the information is part of a whole, such as a write-up for a new software tool that supplements some tool write-ups already distributed, then it is important for the sender to plan the storage and retrieval on behalf of the recipient. A planned and organized document, with preassigned section numbers encompassing present and future information, should be sent out prior to the release of any information or coincident with the release of the first information.

If information being disseminated is worth keeping, it is the responsibility of the sender, not the receiver, to plan the method of keeping it. If the sender does not make a plan, some recipients will make effective use of the information but others will not.

2.9 LANGUAGE FORMALITY

Technical communication of computing information has some additional interesting choices beyond those present in many other technical disciplines. We have invented a lot of new languages for the communication of information. Programming languages, as an example, are vehicles for communicating control information from a person (the programmer) to a machine (the computer).

The question then arises, What level of language is appropriate for communicating information? Programming languages are very formal languages, with lots of rules for how things must be done. In fact, the computer will not obey the language information until it has had all rule deviations removed from it (by syntax checking and semantic testing). Natural language, to the contrary, has a minimal number of rules, and most of those may be violated without preventing the communication from achieving its result. Natural language is rich and flexible; programming languages are terse and potentially powerful.

Your first answer to the question, What level of language is appropriate for communicating information? is probably "the language the audience is most likely to understand." If you are talking to a person, you use a natural language—one that they know already. If you are talking to a computer, you use a programming language—one that it knows already (via a compiler).

The importance of the question begins to arise when we talk about languages for representing the intermediate byproducts of the programming process. What language should we use for stating a requirements specification, for example? Or, what language should we use for stating a design representation?

Here, our intuition at first appears to be helpful. Since the audience for a design is either a designer or a programmer, the language chosen should be understandable with minimal effort by that kind of person. In recent years, the *program design language,* or *pseudocode,* has evolved as an appropriate choice.

Controversy arises, however, when we begin to think about a language for specifying requirements. Who is the audience for this document? First, the systems analyst who develops the requirements must read it. Second, the designer who translates requirements into design must be able to read it. And finally, but not less importantly, the user who originally presented the requirements must be able to read it.

This is a diverse audience. The designer, for example, is likely to be a technical specialist, comfortable with working in somewhat formal languages. The systems analyst, by tradition, may be more people- and application-oriented and less computing-oriented. And the user is unlikely to be computing-oriented and therefore unlikely to be comfortable with other than natural language.

Out of this spectrum of choices, then, it is necessary to define an appropriate language level for requirements communication. Computer scientists, who perceive formalism as concise and unambiguous, vote for formal languages. Computer practitioners, who deal with customers and feel that user communication is a vital first level of defense against solving the wrong problem through misunderstanding the requirements, vote for informal languages.

This is no small controversy. The literature of the computing field is full of papers on new formal languages and examples of their use. Claims are made for the future benefits of these formal languages, even extending to statements such as "we will automatically be able to generate code from requirements specifications" and "formal methods for demonstrating the consistency of a specification with the program derived from it will eliminate the need for software testing."

It is important for you at least to be aware of this controversy. If you are a systems analyst, not only do you need to be aware, but you need to make your own decision as to which methodology to use. Some references are given at the end of the book to help you learn more ([AVIZ84], [IEEE85], [MEYER85]). One of them, [AVIZ84], involves an experiment in which three different levels of specification language were used, ranging from informal to formal. The results were mixed, but they tended to show formal languages to be weaker than one might have expected in areas where they were thought to be strong. Interestingly enough, English was in many respects the best form used.

A life cycle is an evolution of form. From the upper right-hand corner, reading downward and then moving serpentinely, we see a step-by-step series of transitions.

CHAPTER 3

Communication in the Software Life Cycle

The software developer was surprised, perhaps even amazed. She had worked on several software projects before, but always smaller ones. This new assignment, however, put her on a team of 100 programmers developing a complex, many-faceted software system.

It wasn't the numbers of programmers that amazed her, however. In the briefing for new team members she'd just attended, she had been surprised by the formality on the project: formal documentation requirements—even a specification tree, spelling out the documentation in an elaborate hierarchy; review requirements, spelling out who was to say what to whom periodically throughout the project; audit requirements, calling for a specialist team to examine project progress if special problems arose; reporting requirements, detailing what should be in activity reports, to whom they were to be distributed, and how often they should be produced; identified project specialists, who could be counted on to provide answers to difficult questions in their areas of specialty.

The software developer thought about this giant overhead system of formality. What is all this for? she thought to herself. And then the answer came—it was to facilitate communication. The documentation described to interested readers something they needed to know about the project. The reviews gave the developers a chance to get feedback in case they were steering an erroneous course. The audits provided the same mechanism but as a response to problems. The reporting let management know what was happening. The project specialists could give quick answers to questions that might otherwise take hours to get answered. All this elaborate formalism was there to assist communication. The software developer was amazed at the amount of extra work necessary to maintain and enhance communication on a large project.

"But why haven't I run into this level of formality before," the software developer wondered. "Why didn't we do all those things on that four-person project I just finished last month?" She thought some more, and then she realized that all those communication functions had happened on the smaller project, too; the degree of effort put into communication had just been considerably smaller.

Documents were smaller, and some kinds were omitted. Reviews were simpler and often informal. One audit had been necessary, but it just sort of happened, its results were assimilated, and it was forgotten. Reports to management, who sat in the same office area, were usually verbal. And each programmer was his or her own technical specialist—no one was assigned to be responsible for any particular area of expertise, except by default when one of them got ahead of the others in a particular area.

Communication, the software developer began to see, is the glue that holds the team together, no matter what its size. The degree of communication, translated into the degree of formalism, was the only difference between the small project and the big project.

The software developer had learned an important lesson, one that still eludes some software practitioners and theorists. The principles of software engineering—that comprehensive set of concepts found in any book on the subject—are not a cure-all to be applied to any project, no matter what its nature. They are, instead, a menu of ideas, all tested and found worthwhile, from which the software developer must make selections appropriate to the project at hand. Is the project large? Choose from the formal side of the menu. Is the project critical? Choose from the rigorous side of the menu. Is the project quick and dirty? Choose from the low-budget side of the menu. Is the project tightly scheduled? Choose (but carefully!) from the time-minimizing side of the menu. The skilled software engineer, then, is not just one who knows the principles of software engineering. He or she is one who has also developed the ability to know when to apply them.

Since many of the principles of software engineering are communication facilitators, this same pick-from-the-menu idea is at the heart of what we discuss next. In this section we talk about all the kinds of communication that may be applied to a software project. Read this material at two levels: Absorb it, but at the same time develop a set of criteria by means of which you will be able to decide how and when to apply it.

On the largest of software projects, the communication methods, as we have seen, may be very formal and even cumbersome appearing. If the software is part of a larger system, there may be a tree structure of system components, with the software coming at one or more places in the tree (see Figure 3-1).

Corresponding to the system tree there may be a specification tree, showing all the kinds of documentation to be produced for the system. Figure 3-2 shows what a portion of such a tree might look like. The entire tree would have the structure of Figure 3-1, showing the full documentation set for each system and subsystem element.

Again, this level of formality is the lifeblood of the large project, but the small project simply doesn't possess or need such elaborate tree structures. Because of this diversity of approaches, it is important to put any further discussions into some sort of project-independent framework.

The framework for this discussion is a concept commonly called the software *life cycle.* Students of software engineering have defined this life cycle in different ways, but all definitions retain a common core of concepts. Since the life cycle serves only as a framework for the material being presented, we stick as closely to the core definition as we can.

The life cycle is the set of steps that occur in the process of solving a problem via software. The first step is that of problem definition: What is the problem to be solved? In some communities this is known as *requirements definition,* and in others, *systems analysis.* We will use the former term.

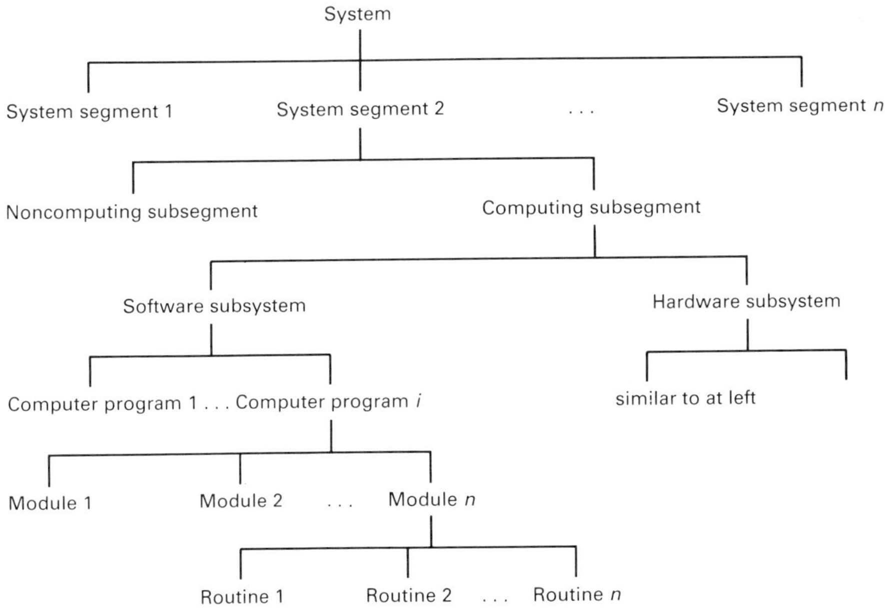

Figure 3-1 Tree structure of a large system involving software.

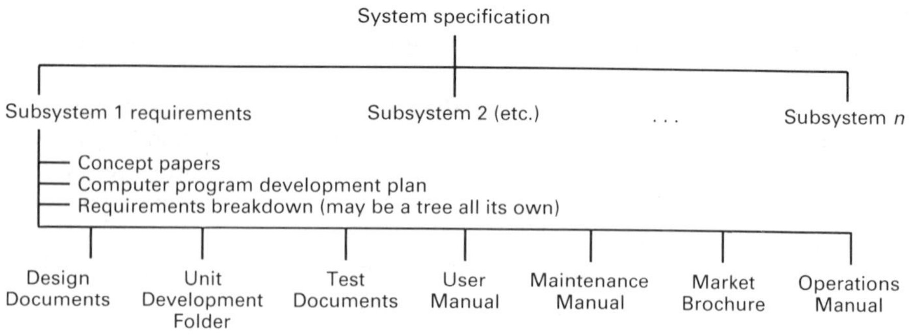

Figure 3-2 Specification tree for a large system involving software.

Once the problem is understood, the next step in the software life cycle is deciding how to solve the problem. This conceptual step is commonly known as *design*. Some software specialists break design down into components, such as preliminary design and critical design, or functional design and detailed design, but we need not go that far here.

Once the design is conceptualized well enough to code the problem solution for a computer, the *implementation* phase begins. Here the ideas of the design are translated into a form that a computer can process. Some software specialists include as part of implementation the first stages of testing, often known as *unit testing*.

The coded solution, no matter how well prepared, will not work without testing. The checkout phase is the time for this error-removal activity. Checkout begins with small program components and progresses to the integrated software whole. Checkout may be both static (performed without executing the program on the computer, such as *desk checking* or *formal verification*), or dynamic (performed by executing the program and examining the results) [GLASS79]. The progression of subphases within checkout generally includes *unit testing* (unless it was counted as being part of the implementation phase), *integration testing* (where the units are put together into a software whole), and (in more elaborate projects) *system testing,* where the software is wed to the other components of a total system and tested in that environment.

An interesting view of the life cycle and its relationships to software communication is presented in Figures 3-3 and 3-4. These figures are taken from [BRUCE82] and reflect a large-system, DoD-oriented (Department of Defense), real-time-application view of communication and the life cycle. Figure 3-3 shows the life cycle as it relates to the production of various software documents, and Figure 3-4 shows the relationship between those documents and the reviews that examine them.

As we mentioned before, there are different types of life cycles. Some specialists advocate a form of development that eliminates unit testing in favor of continual, evolving integration testing (known as *top-down implementa-*

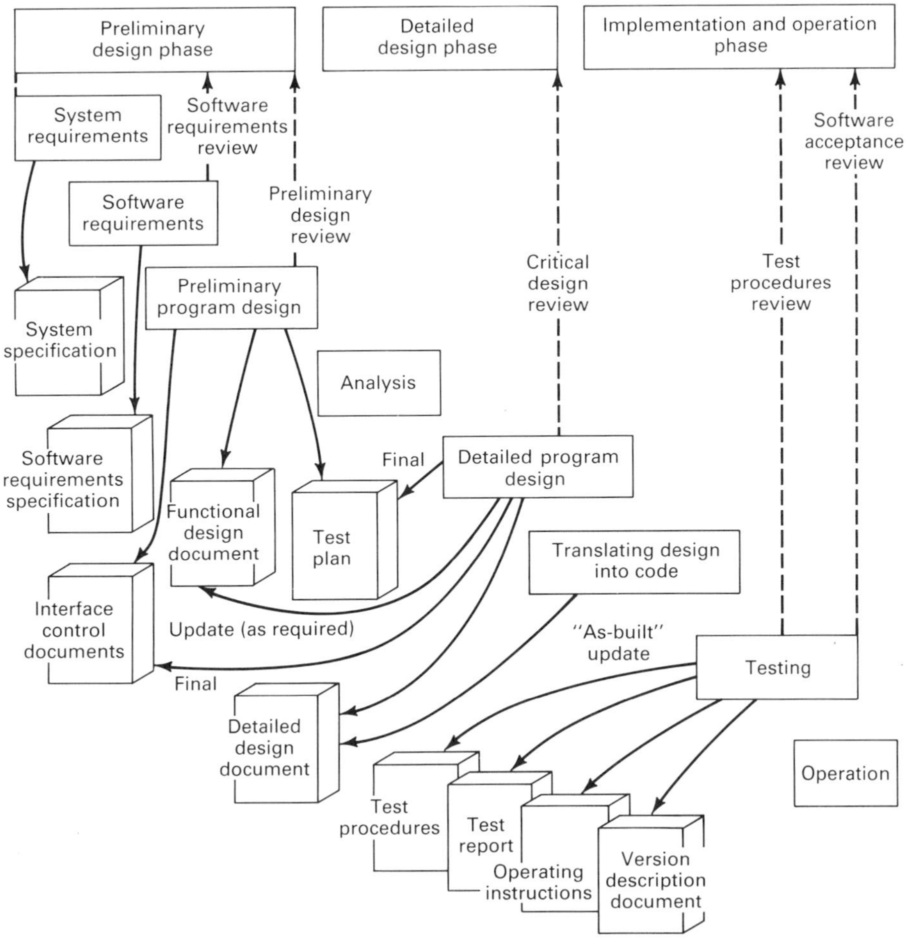

Figure 3-3 The software life cycle and software documents. Bruce and Pederson, *The Software Development Project.* (New York: Wiley-Interscience, 1982), p. 10. Copyright © 1982 by John Wiley & Sons. Reprinted by permission.

tion). Some specialists advocate the use of *prototyping,* in which a pilot software product is built to explore difficult requirements or design issues. Some specialists are bothered by the apparently hard lines between the phases of the life cycle, believing that the actual development process is iterative and on occasion, may move backward from (say) implementation to (say) design before moving forward again.

There is value to the life cycle, and there is value to the varying viewpoints we have discussed. It is the core of the life-cycle concept that is useful here; the nuances can be left to the preferences of the reader.

In this book we add two more phases to the software life cycle. One we

Name	Purpose	Materials Reviewed
SRR (software requirements review)	Verify software requirements	Software requirements specification
PDR (preliminary design review)	Verify design approach and interfaces	Functional design document Interface control documents (requirements and preliminary design sections) Test plan (preliminary)
CDR (critical design review)	Verify detailed design and test plan	Detailed design document Interface control documents (final) Test plan
TPR (test procedures review)	Verify test procedures	Test plan Test procedures
SAR (software acceptance review)	Verify test results and completed product (code and documentation)	Test procedures Test report Operating instructions Version description document "As-built" updates Functional design document Detailed design document

Figure 3-4 Software reviews and documents. Bruce & Pederson, *Software Development Project*, p. 12.

call *project startup,* the process by which the very existence of a problem is explored, and permission is sought to find a solution. The other we call *project windup,* the process in which the problem solution is tidied and in some sense laid to rest. Startup is discussed in Section 3.1, the life cycle is discussed in Section 3.2, and windup is discussed in Section 3.3.

3.1 PROJECT START-UP

The initiation of a technical project is a curious blend of technology and communication. As we will see, communication plays a much more important role than you may imagine in the success or failure of this activity.

The process of project start-up is highly dependent on the political environment in which it occurs, but there are some common elements that are independent of environment. Only in the one-person company, where the roles of manager, technical specialist, and producer are blended into one, do we find a situation where there is little communication required in the start-up process. Elsewhere there is an identifiable core process that is used and can be applied in most decision-making situations.

3.1.1 Start-up Communication Process

Seeing a problem and realizing that there may be a solution is, of course, a technical issue. On the other hand, selling someone on the notion that there is a problem and that it should be solved is a political, social, and—especially from our point of view—a communication issue. Let us explore for the moment the process by which a new idea might be translated into a project.

Suppose you have come to realize, through either serendipity or clever and careful analysis, that the production of widgets at your company can be substantially improved. Suppose further that you have decided to pursue this issue in the name of corporate efficiency as well as personal fame and glory. The steps you take toward achieving this goal might come from the following list:

1. *Establish needs.* Once you perceive the problem, you need to understand precisely what it is. This is a technical step.
2. *Obtain management approval.* With the problem well defined, you are ready to plan for a solution. You need management to allocate the necessary resources. This is a communication step.
3. *Form a study team and prepare a study plan.* If you need help in planning the approach, this step—primarily a communication step—follows.
4. *Obtain management approval of the plan.* Return to management again for another communication step.
5. *Prepare the study team.* Train the participants in the study so that they are prepared to start at your level. This, too, is a communication step.
6. *Gather the study information.* What do you need to know to present an appropriate study conclusion? If the information to be gathered is to be extracted from people, this is yet another communication step.
7. *Validate the study information.* Does the information gathered make sense? This is largely a technical step, but it may involve some communication.
8. *Prepare the study report.* Weave the findings of the study team into a document that describes the process, presents the findings, and proposes direction—a communication step.
9. *Present the study report* (to management and to study participants). Tell all the interested parties what you have learned, both those from whom you want action and those who deserve to know—more communication.
10. *Press for permission to proceed.* If your study report demonstrated what you expected it to, request resources for providing a problem solution—once again, communication.

The project start-up process, as we have seen, is deeply communication-oriented, which may come as a surprise to you. We tend to think of an inventor as a technical genius who hibernates in a laboratory until he or she dashes forth to dazzle the world with some new finding. For the most part that simply is not the case. The invention of the clever 3M Post-it Note Pad (the little sheets of (usually yellow) paper with adhesive on one end) is said to have taken 10 years from idea to production. You can believe that very little of that time was spent on technical issues. The bulk of it was on communication—convincing management that the idea was worthwhile. In fact, it may be said that the prime difference between someone who succeeds in a corporate structure and someone who stagnates is the ability to communicate successfully. Certainly the ability to conceive and enable an idea is fundamental to success in most corporate environments.

At the beginning of the chapter we discussed the formality of the large-project environment. In that formal environment, there is a recognized set of steps that follow the new-idea process just described. You should follow these steps in seeking and obtaining permission to begin a technical project. The steps are (1) the concept presentation, often accompanied by a concept paper; (2) the request for proposal and the proposal; and (3) the contract and contract negotiations.

We discuss these three items as if this level of formality were required in every setting. In fact, for the smaller or less critical project, these same steps and processes will probably be present but in a much less visible way. The concept presentation may be written on the back of an envelope in a spur-of-the-moment meeting with management. The request for proposal and the proposal may be skipped entirely, particularly in a noncompetitive environment; and the contract may be notes on a piece of paper, or (probably all too often) it may be verbal. Once again, the decision on formality must be specific to the project. Bear in mind, however, that the "easy" decision to be informal may have tragic implications if it later turns out that a formal trail of processes is necessary for technical, legal, or political reasons.

3.1.2 Start-up Written Communication

In the most formal of settings, the written communication that occurs in project start-up is almost like a dance between the group of people we might call *doers* (the people who want to do the job) and the group of people we might call *funders* (the people who are expected to provide the resources to do the job). There is a predefined set of steps that each group takes in response to an action of the other.

The first dance step is the presentation of the concept, either in verbal or written form or both. The concept is often presented by the doers, but it may also be presented by the funders if there is a job they would like to do but are unable to do themselves. Once the concept paper has been approved and permission to go ahead has been obtained, the funders begin to seek qualified doers. Sometimes this search takes the form of a *sources sought* announcement, in which the funder describes the problem in general terms and asks for responses from doers who have the appropriate capabilities. Government agencies use a publication called the *Commerce Business Daily* to present a sources sought; less formal approaches might include phone calls or letters to possible doers known to the funders. The response to a sources sought is a *qualification letter,* in which the doers concisely describe why they are capable of doing the desired work.

Those doers whose qualification letters are acceptable are then sent a *request for proposal,* or RFP, which spells out in technical, legal, and contractual detail the task to be performed. The RFP step is generally used if the contractual process is to be competitive and proposals from a variety of doers are to be solicited and evaluated. If the process is to be noncompetitive—often referred to as a *Sole Source procurement*—then the RFP step can be skipped.

The response to an RFP is a *proposal.* (If the process is noncompetitive, then the proposal may be sent independent of the existence of an RFP. If the proposal is initiated by the doer, it is called an *Unsolicited proposal.*) The proposal is an elaborate statement of the capability of the doer to perform the task in question.

Next the funder engages in a proposal evaluation process. During this process, the funder sometimes conducts contract negotiations with one or more proposed doers, generally those considered to be finalists in the competition, in order to get the best possible and most realistic proposal both technically and costwise. Following the negotiations, a *contract* is awarded, and the doer, appropriately monitored by the funder, begins work.

The steps in the dance we have just described are illustrated in Figure 3-5.

3.1.2.1 Concept Paper. The concept paper is the first step toward project start-up. Its purpose is to define a problem to be solved, motivate

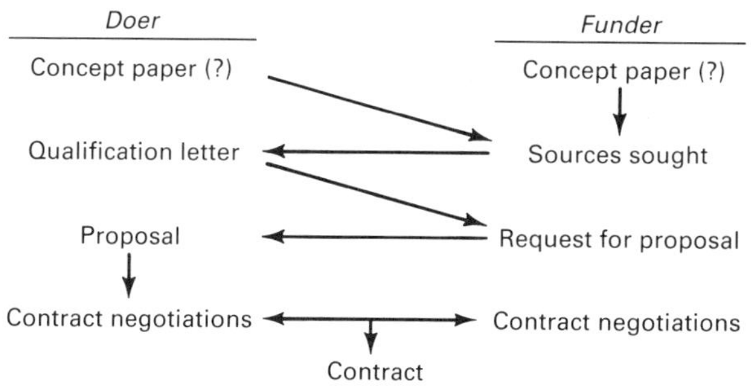

Figure 3-5 Project start-up formal dance.

support for the solution of the problem, and obtain permission and resources to begin that solution.

The content of the concept paper should contain the following:

- An explanation of the problem
- An analysis of initial solution ideas
- A first approximation of costs for a solution (dollars, schedule, people)
- A first approximation of benefits of a solution
- Any other motivation to approve solving the problem
- Qualifications of the doers to provide a solution

Since a concept paper is usually addressed to upper-level management, it should be concise. Bulky technical support materials should take the form of supplementary documents or appendices or in some other way be separated from the mainstream of the concept paper itself.

There is no standard form for a concept paper. One possible outline is the following:

1.0 Problem statement
2.0 Objectives
3.0 Approach to the problem (overall)
4.0 Approach to the problem (detailed)
5.0 Cost/benefit analysis (initial)
6.0 Qualifications

3.1.2.2 Request for Proposal and Proposal. After approval to proceed with a problem solution has been given, the next move is up to the funder. The goal is to obtain one or more proposals from qualified doers that may be used to pick the final doer.

If a list of appropriate doers is not readily available, the funder must seek such a list. As we mentioned previously, one means of doing so is a published advertisement known as a sources sought, which looks like a classified advertisement in a newspaper and states tersely what talents and capabilities are being sought. Interested bidders respond to the sources sought with a qualification letter, which explains why the bidder can perform the job, based on past experience, capability, and interest. A qualification letter is often written according to a simple outline like the following:

1.0 Cover letter to introduce the qualification letter
2.0 Cover page for qualification letter
3.0 Capabilities and facilities
4.0 Related experience
5.0 Resumés of appropriate people

The next significant step in this process is the issuance of the request for proposal, or RFP. An RFP in practice is a considerably more elaborate document than might be expected. Most government agencies, for example, encumber the RFP with a number of preprepared paragraphs or pages that are necessary for legal or managerial reasons but are often technically unimportant. These preprepared paragraphs are often referred to as *boiler plate,* a term left over from journalistic days gone by when such material was kept in metal form, ready to print, so that it did not need to be rekeyed for each presentation.

Among the boiler plate, and not always in obvious places, is found the critical content of the RFP:

- The restrictions on the bidders (if yours is a large company and bidders are restricted to small businesses, don't waste your time going further)
- The requirements definition (what is to be done)
- The statement of work (tasks necessary to do it)
- Constraints on the bidders (budget and schedule limitations for the proposal or the job itself or both)
- Deliverables (what is to be delivered with the proposal; what is to be delivered when the job is complete)
- The type of contract (fixed-price, cost-plus-fee, etc.)
- The proposal evaluation criteria (how the funder will decide who wins)

As an example of how difficult it sometimes is to separate this material from the boiler plate, the contract deliverables are often included as an appendix entitled "Contract Deliverables Requirements List" (CDRL), and the CDRL may contain boiler plate as well as important technical material.

Upon receipt of the RFP, it is necessary to decide whether to bid on the job. This is no small decision, since the writing of a proposal involves spending resources that will not be reimbursed. The complexities of the bid decision are discussed further in Section 3.1.3.2.

If the decision to bid is made, then a proposal must be written. The purposes of a proposal seem relatively straightforward, yet in fact they are inextricably complex: to win a contract, to ensure making enough money on the contract, and to permit the doer to do a respectable, quality job. A contract can be won either by making a low bid or by proposing a top-quality project—opposite approaches. Making enough money means bidding an amount high enough to permit making a profit, while not being so high as to preclude winning the contract. Doing a quality job means bidding higher than any competitor proposing a shoddy job, thus once again risking losing the contract. Even at the goals level, a proposal is a tricky piece of business.

The content of a proposal is little easier. First, it must blend technical credibility and salesmanship—no small task. It must demonstrate an understanding of the problem to be solved. It must be convincing as to the doer's proposed method of solution. It must show both corporate and individual relevant experience. It must demonstrate corporate stability and commitment. It must present a coherent management strategy and organizational approach. It must emphasize the evaluation criteria. It must propose and substantiate costs and schedules. And it must do all those things in a positive, convincing way.

The form a proposal takes is sometimes, though not always, dictated by the RFP. If it is, obviously that form should be followed. (Antagonizing the funder is no way to win a contract!) If it is not, then there are a variety of forms that may be employed. Roughly following the RFP outline may be one way, since it will be easier for the funder to evaluate. The following form has been used frequently and encompasses the content material described earlier in this section.

1.0 Executive summary (summarize the proposal for the busy reader)
2.0 Introduction
3.0 Problem statement
4.0 Objectives
5.0 Approach to solution
    5.1 Scope of work
    5.2 Statement of work
    5.3 Deliverables
6.0 Relevant experience
7.0 Management plan
    7.1 Organization
    7.2 Schedule
    7.3 Personnel (including résumés)
8.0 Quality assurance
9.0 Facilities
10.0 Appendices

Note that this outline makes no provision for cost figures. Often the cost proposal is prepared separately from the material we have just described (the technical proposal) to facilitate the funder's evaluation process, which may involve evaluating cost and technology separately.

There are several other important factors to consider in writing a proposal. For schedule and consistency reasons, it is often necessary to reuse information from previous proposals (or other sources). If this is done, the material must be refocused to the current proposal. If you propose person A to do Task X, person A's résumé should emphasize an ability to do X, and the relevant-experience section should show lots of X, for example.

> The proposal had been thrown together pretty hurriedly. Proposals always are, it seems. But why had the contractor rejected it? We asked for a debriefing.
>
> Some of the results of the debriefing surprised us. We had had some technical deficiencies, and once they were pointed out, we could see what we had done wrong.
>
> But there was a problem with our résumé section, as well. "Our résumés?" we thought to ourselves, surprised. We looked back at our proposal. Of all the sections thrown together hurriedly, these (we now saw) had been thrown together with the least care. Most were broad based and unfocused on the proposal tasks.
>
> But one was far worse than the rest. It was directed toward a particular job application the person had made a few weeks back, and it was totally inappropriate for the task at hand. In our haste, we had thrown it in without noticing. It was the last time we'd make that particular mistake!

Prior to writing the proposal, it is vital to develop

- Complete information about the RFP
- A pricing strategy
- A technical strategy
- Any teaming strategy

The technology-price tradeoff may play a critical role in whether the proposal will be a winner or not. If the quality is too low or the bid is too high, you may be disqualified by the funder, for example. If you have areas of technical weakness in either writing the proposal or doing the job, you may want to seek teaming support, a long-lead process that should be well underway before the writing of the proposal.

During the writing of the proposal, it is important to emphasize your areas of strength and uniqueness. Confront and present solutions to your areas of weakness, and avoid slipping from substantive discussions into pure sales pitch. It is surprising how often technical people avoid saying good things about themselves, and it is equally surprising how often managers put in glowing phrases with no technical content behind them.

Upon completion of the first draft of the proposal, there are still several things that you must do:

1. Solicit and act on a knowledgeable review and critique.
2. Make sure that the evaluation criteria are adequately dealt with.

> Writing a winning proposal is a complicated matter and is a bit like shooting into the darkness. No matter how well you know the territory, you're not sure whether you have a hit or a miss. This proposal was more complicated than most. There were three parts to it, for the three different software tools described in the RFP.
>
> Our position was a little unusual. We had already built one of the tools, and we could pull it off the shelf to bid it. Why not make it a price leader and price the other two tools a little high to take advantage of the price advantage we had on the first tool and to buffer the risk we would be undertaking on the others? We congratulated ourselves on a clever strategy and wrote the proposal.
>
> When the awards were announced, however, our self-congratulation faded. We had won, all right—but only on the first tool. The contractor had split the award into three parts, and all we won was our price leader—cleverly priced too low to make any profit!

3. Provide the funder with a cross-reference, linking proposal paragraphs with RFP tasks.

In any technical writing, it is important for the writer to place himself or herself in the place of the reader. The same situation, with some special implications, is true here. The easier it is for the funder to review your proposal, the more favorably it will be looked upon.

3.1.2.3 Contract. The contract—goal of all the previous steps in the dance—is a vitally important anticlimax to what has preceded it. Often the meat of the contract is a blend of phrases from the RFP and the winning proposal.

A properly drawn contract is the agreement between the funder and the doer as to what is to be done, how it is to be done, and the terms and conditions constraining the doing. It will be referred to frequently in the contract performance period to follow, sometimes with acrimony; ("I don't have to do that task—it's not within the scope of the contract!") therefore, this baseline document must be prepared with special care. Not only technical people and their managers must examine it, but contracts specialists and legal professionals should also be called upon to give it their blessing.

Ambiguity and omission are the worst sins of the contract writer. If it isn't stated, it won't be done. If it isn't stated clearly, it probably won't be done either. The wording of the contract must be succinct and concise. These are also the goals of most of the preceding documents, but here they take on special importance.

It was the preliminary design review for our subcontractor, and it was obvious that the subcontractor hadn't done a good job of getting ready for it.

All the documents that our contract called for had been written, but the design was shaky. I was becoming upset. The subcontractor was building a compiler, and I knew quite a bit about compilers. I had built several in industry, and I'd even published a paper on the subject in *ACM Surveys,* volume 1, number 1. I felt that I was the ranking technical expert on our team, and I felt it my responsibility to get the subcontractor onto firmer ground.

But the subcontractor was resistant. Again and again, I would ask for agreement on some additional technical detail, and again and again the subcontractor would refuse. My upset feelings were turning to anger. Finally, I broke under the strain. I accused the subcontractor of unethical performance in blistering words that I would not repeat here, and I demanded that my ideas be incorporated. And once again, the subcontractor refused. "Your demands are out of scope," said the contractual lead.

In the heat of the moment, I was too angry to realize what that phrase meant. It was months before I finally understood all that it meant.

Fundamentally, what it meant was that I was wrong. For all the technical correctness of my position, I was asking for things that weren't spelled out in the contract. They were "out of the scope of the contract." And since they weren't in the contract, we weren't going to get them—no matter how much profanity I shouted.

Some of the lessons we learn about communication are subtle and painless. That one wasn't, though. I will remember that painful lesson every time someone mentions the subject of contracts!

Contracts cannot always say precisely what is to be done. For example, in advanced technology it is often not known how to do something or what should be done until early project phases have explored alternatives. In this situation, the contract cannot define a goal task explicitly, but it can define the task that will lead to the explicit definition of the goal task and the process by which the goal task will then be determined. For example, if the contract is for a large-matrix spreadsheet program but the final definition of *large* will be determined by later analysis, specify a date upon which the evaluation is to be complete, constraints between which *large* must fall, the decision criteria for the final definition of *large,* and the voting process for making the decision. Without this kind of specification, expensive contractual disputes are often the result. No one would logically define *large* to be 65, but a doer in trouble in some other area of the contract might!

Contracts must also specify such details as the following:

- Period and place of contract performance
- Contractual deliverables, both products and reports
- Ownership of contractual deliverables, especially source code
- Costs, fees, payment schedules
- Key personnel (by-name specification of particular doers)

Terms and conditions common to contracts are best read about elsewhere. In passing, we note that software contracts are usually either fixed price (the cost is determined in advance, independent of subsequent events) or cost plus (the cost is determined by legitimate ongoing expenses). Both types of contracts may also provide incentives for cost, schedule, or quality performance better than that called for in the contract. Funders usually prefer fixed-price contracts to reduce dollar risk; doers usually like cost-plus contracts for the same reason.

3.1.3 Start-up Spoken Communication

We saw earlier that the new-idea start-up process involves lots of communication, some of it written and some of it verbal. The written communication, we have just seen, is a sort of ''dance'' between the doer and the funder to reach agreement on beginning the project.

That dance may be as formal as the steps that we enumerated in the last section, or, like other forms of communication, it may be less formal, the formality level being determined by the nature of the project. If the project is more informal in nature, much of the communication discussed in the last section will be all or in part spoken. We consider the nature of this spoken communication in this section.

3.1.3.1 Concept Presentation. Whether the project is formal or informal, the final go-ahead to begin a project will probably result from a meeting. Thus, even if a concept paper is prepared, there will almost always need to be a concept presentation.

Attendees at the meeting will be representatives of the doers, representatives of the funders, interested parties, and supporting decision makers. The presentation will usually be made by the doers.

The content of the concept presentation will be largely that of the concept paper, discussed earlier in Section 3.1.2.1, modified to fit the mode of a spoken rather than a written presentation. Since like any spoken presentation, the concept presentation will be done in real time, the emphasis should be on decisions and action. If all goes well, the decision to go ahead may be made at or immediately after the meeting.

If a concept paper has been prepared, the concept presentation will be more effective if the attendees have read it beforehand, and the presentation focuses on attendee reaction to the written word. In this case, the presenters should give a brief overview, make sure that the attendees have indeed read the concept paper, and move on to the key points and the decision making.

If no concept paper has been prepared or read beforehand, then the concept presentation must start from scratch and cover all the ground that the paper would have covered. At the conclusion of the presentation, it is essential that the presenters summarize their case and request action.

3.1.3.2 Bid Decision. As the project start-up dance continues, the point is eventually reached where a final decision must be made by the doers that they really want to bid on doing the job. If the project was initiated by the doers, the yes answer to this question is probably a foregone conclusion; but if the doer is one of several candidate doers, given the cost of preparing a proposal, he or she needs to make sure that the bid preparation money will be well spent, with some likelihood of a profitable, winning proposal for a quality product.

For some very large projects, the preparation for the project and the bid decision may begin well in advance of the actual events. In these situations, many companies engage in corporate intelligence operations, gathering information about the funder and the project to fortify what will eventually be presented in the RFP. This is often accomplished through site visits by doer representatives to the funder location. Sometimes the visitors are doers themselves, and sometimes they are hired intelligence gatherers who represent one or more companies at one or more funder locations. In either case, there is much oral communication, of a very specialized form at that.

The information so gathered may be fundamental to the bid decision process. What follows is a checklist prepared by one company for determining [illegible] to bid on projects. (Note the number of times that intelligence information plays a role in the decision making.) If the answer to more than a few of the questions on the checklist is no, the company should not bid.

1. Is the program real?
2. Will an RFP really be issued?
3. Do we have a genuine and known capability in this problem area?
4. Do we know the funder?
5. Have we influenced the RFP?*

*Life is not always fair, especially in the world of industrial competition. Some RFPs are perfunctory, with the winner already decided in advance. This practice, is, of course, unethical and probably illegal.

6. Is our technical/proposal homework on schedule?
7. Does the funder consider us to be a front-runner?
8. Are appropriate resources (money, people, facilities) available to do the proposal? To do the job?
9. Can we make a profit from either this or following contracts?
10. Do we have credible, strategic advantages?

3.1.3.3 Contract Negotiation. Contract decisions by funders are often elaborate processes. If the decision is competitive, precautions must be taken to ensure a fair and accurate decision. Quite often two teams of proposal evaluators are defined, one to evaluate the technical proposal and one to evaluate the cost proposal. In some situations, these two teams are not allowed to talk to each other.

Proposal material is generally considered proprietary to the company that prepared it, and steps must be taken to safeguard it. Often a special, lockable room is set aside for each proposal evaluation team. Proposal evaluators are expected to minimize or eliminate contact with bidders and to ensure that any clarifications passed on to or from one bidder are passed on to the others, when appropriate.

As the decision process approaches a conclusion, two things often happen: One or more bidders are eliminated from the competition for nonconforming or inadequate proposals, and one or more of the finalists are contacted for final preaward negotiations. These final negotiations are exercises in careful communication. Details of one bidder's proposal must not be shared with another bidder, and yet the goal of the negotiations may be to supplement one proposal's promises with the best of another's. Bid negotiations are also conducted to pin down ambiguous technical and cost-proposal sections or to modify the task list by knowledge that has come to the funders since the RFP was issued.

Like any other negotiations, bid negotiations are conducted less openly than other forms of communication. Both teams of negotiators usually have *hidden agendas*—lists of issues on which concession is possible or impossible—that they will disclose to the other team only if the others expose some of their own. [CART82] contains a fascinating description of the open and hidden agendas of the negotiators in the Israel-Egypt peace talks conducted by President Carter in 1978. The successful negotiator will be a communicator who deals well with both open and hidden agendas and who knows how to plan strategies of transition from open to hidden information. Teams of specialists are often used because of their expertise in such areas.

The result of a contract negotiation is essentially a modified proposal—the original proposal as modified by the minutes of the negotiation meeting. Following the set of contract negotiations with the bidding finalists, the funder resumes evaluation, using the modified proposals, and works toward a final award decision.

It is not unusual for written and verbal communication to be used together to solve problems. Contract negotiation is a particularly striking example of the need for both forms of communication, with an interesting variety in the forms of verbal communication that occur.

3.2 PROJECT IMPLEMENTATION

The software salesperson and the programmer were on safari in Africa, and they had come to the cabin where they would spend the night. After the two of them had unloaded their gear, the programmer decided to clean up the cabin, and the salesperson opted to scout around a bit.

Before long, the salesperson came bounding back out of the bush, with a lion in hot pursuit. Near the cabin, the salesperson suddenly stepped aside and threw open the cabin door, and the lion darted into the cabin with the programmer. "You skin this one," shouted the salesperson, "and I'll go find another!"

That story has more than one element of truth to it. It is often the lot of the programmer to solve a problem dumped precipitously on him or her. For the purposes of this section, however, the point of the story is that once the *project start-up* phase is over, the *project implementation* task is only just beginning—and the implementation phase is often considerably more complicated, certainly technically deeper (and perhaps even more dangerous), than what has preceded it.

It is tempting to come to the conclusion that, after the communication-intensive project start-up phase, the communication needs of the implementation phase are minimal. For anyone who has been through a software development experience on a project of any significance, that is a naive position to take. Certainly the kinds of communication change dramatically from project start-up to project implementation, but the need for communication remains vital.

3.2.1 Implementation Communication Process

As the implementation phase begins, there is a heavy need for planning—a communication-intensive process. As the planning draws to a conclusion, project-specific and general standards are often defined and documented. As the project itself takes form, there are certain categories of both written and spoken communication that accompany that process. Whole books have been devoted to just this part of the software project communication process.

The written form of communication for this phase is generally called *software documentation* and is a vital part of software implementation communication. Seminars on software documentation, for example, are among the most popular ongoing technical presentations in the software field.

The spoken form of communication for this phase has no generic name, but it encompasses such important concepts as audits, reviews and walk-throughs.

Recently an organizational adjunct called the *information center* has been defined whose purpose is to focus this implementation communication. Typically, the information center is a service organization, helping the software developers via general-purpose tools, training, consultation, and access to data. Tool selection, training definition, and database administration may thus fall within the information center's jurisdiction.

Regardless of who the communicators are, however, there are certain fundamental parts to the software implementation communication process. These processes will be covered in more depth in the sections that follow.

3.2.2 Implementation Written Communication

In the early stages of the development of a software project, the product being developed is an idea supported by written and oral communication; since the idea may be nebulous or at least transient, the communication media often *become* the product: What is the concept? Read the concept paper.

But as software development proceeds, a split begins to form between the product and its communication support. This is especially true of its written communication, called *documentation;* the software product begins to evolve into two parts: the software itself, such as the code and its listings, and the documentation describing the code. The creation of both of these is a significant and important problem. All too often, emphasis is placed on the software itself—without which there is no product—to the exclusion of the documentation. Although obviously if there are not sufficient resources, it is the documentation that must suffer—too often there is not enough budget or time to complete both the software and its documentation—this is usually a short-term decision that loses cost-effectiveness in the long term. Software without a useful user manual or maintenance manual cannot be used to its full potential.

Some authors have found a semantic solution to this problem by defining software to be the code *and* its documentation; the implication is that without documentation there is no product. This solution has a lot of appeal, but it has the disadvantage that nontechnically oriented managers of software development begin to emphasize the documents (which they can read and understand) instead of the code (which they cannot). In this book we make the choice that software is the code and that documentation supports but is not part of software. The remainder of this section deals with software documentation. First we look at several *kinds* of documentation.

3.2.2.1 Transient Documentation Versus Permanent Documentation. Some documentation is produced to support an event in the software life cycle and then is filed away or discarded. For example, a computer program development plan is written to tell what is going to be done during the software construction process, but once the construction is well underway or complete, it is of historical significance only. This documentation is *transient.*

Other documentation is produced to support the full life of the software product. For example, a user manual will be essential to product function until the product itself is no longer useful. This documentation is *permanent.*

This distinction is seldom made in software documentation, but it is an important one. Clearly, permanent documents should be treated with at least as much care as transient ones. But the opposite is often true. A plan written to support a review milestone may receive far more attention than a maintenance manual written to support a maintenance programmer. Yet most plans are transient, ignored after the review, and all maintenance manuals (to the extent that they are written at all!) are permanent.

A key decision that must be made when a document is defined is whether it is to be a transient or permanent document. Projected use of the document, and installation philosophy about documents, will determine that decision. Once it is made, its ramifications should be considered. Should the transient document be given the editorial polish and the production pizazz of a permanent one? Should the transient document be kept up-to-date after its baseline event has passed? The answer to these questions should frequently be no, but there are cases (e.g., a formal review of a product with a customer may call for an image-enhancing plan document) where a no would be incorrect.

There is some controversy attached to the transient-permanent dichotomy. We will see in a subsequent section that in this book much software documentation (requirements spec, development plan, design document, coding document, testing document) is considered to be transient. This reflects the fact that it is common software practice not to retrofit corrections into these documents once the event they support has passed. For example, once coding starts, the design document gradually becomes obsolete as the coder reworks some design choices to enhance codability.

However, there is a strong belief in some circles that the maintenance of software—that is, the implementation of changes to a software product—must be conducted by reviewing and changing each of the defining software documents prior to reworking the code itself. For example, revising a product to allow it to process 12 input parameters rather than 6 would require revising the requirements spec and the design document prior to revising the code. Clearly in this situation, most documents become permanent. The requirements spec must be, and will always be, accurate and up-to-date. Because this approach is rarely used in practice, however, this book treats such documents as transient.

A more detailed discussion of transient and permanent documents follows, in Sections 3.2.2.5 and 3.2.2.6.

3.2.2.2 Tutorial Documentation Versus Reference Documentation. Some documentation is produced to assist in *learning* about a software product; other documentation is produced to aid an experienced user in *remem-*

bering about a software product. Learning documentation is commonly called *tutorial* documentation, while remembering documentation is commonly called *reference* documentation. There is an enormous difference between the two.

Tutorial documents should be readable, paced by, and organized to the expected reader's knowledge level. For example, consider the user manual for a word processing system. It is typically written for a clerical person, so it must explain all its nonclerical terms as they are first used; it must pace the material so that it does not overload its nontechnical reader; it must make frequent use of illustrations and art; and it may be written in a folksy or colloquial way. Because of these requirements, it will probably be a thick document, with lots of words and pictures, but easy and fast to read. In effect, a tutorial document is a do-it-yourself manual for a software product.

Reference documents are nearly the opposite of tutorial documents. They should facilitate the finding of material, so their organization rather than their readability is the key to their success. The reader should be able to turn immediately to the information needed rather than to have to read all the preceding material to get it. From a computing point of view, a tutorial document is accessed like a sequential file, whereas a reference document is accessed like a random or indexed file.

Take the reference card for a typical computing system. On the card are several sets of key information, easily distinguished from one another and therefore easily found. Each set of information is also compacted and ordered for ease of search. The character set, for instance, is probably defined in character order rather than numeric order, and the instruction set is in order by mnemonics. You wouldn't be able to *read* the reference card to learn something—it is too terse. But you could certainly find a piece of information you needed, once you knew what set of information it was in and how to find it within that set.

Although we have used a clerical user manual as an example of a tutorial document and a programmer reference card as an example of a reference document, do not succumb to the temptation to see tutorials as material for the nontechnical person and reference as material for the technical person. A clerical word processor user, for example, might want a reference manual to summarize the commands tersely, and a programmer might want a principle-of-operation tutorial manual as a first readable introduction to the computer. In short, tutorial documents are written to be read, whereas reference documents are written to be referenced.

One problem in the current state of software development is that there is rarely sufficient budget available to prepare both tutorial and reference documentation, and usually what *is* prepared is a compromise between the two. Note that the two documents are dramatically different, and a suitable compromise is touchy business. All too often, in fact, such compromises are failures. A tutorial-reference document is frequently not very good at either function.

If such a compromise is required of you, the best solution is probably a tutorially written document with a comprehensive indexing system. Even better is a tutorial document supplemented by a terse reference card. Less desirable, but most commonly used, is a mediocre tutorial document organized in a structure that can be referenced.

The key to tutorial-reference documentation, compromise or not, is writing with the reader in mind. It is the need of the reader that establishes the difference between tutorial and reference documentation, and that need should underlie every decision made in preparing the documents.

There is a trend emerging in software documentation that is clearly related to this tutorial-reference distinction. As computers and software reach further into the everyday world of the general public, it is becoming increasingly obvious that traditional kinds of documentation are totally inappropriate. *Tutorial material should be built into the functioning of the program.* At every software-user interaction the software should make perfectly clear what the user should do next, for example, in tutorial-like presentations given to the user as the program executes. Often the user choices are presented in menu form, where the user knows exactly what his or her choices are, and explicit and directive feedback is given when an improper choice is made. Frequently, complicated procedures are presented as menus that lead to other menus (a *hierarchy* of menus), so the user is led step by step through the interaction process. In today's state of the art, this is probably tutorial documentation at its finest.

Analogously, reference documentation may be available through the program itself. Often, the user is presented with one additional choice as a program interacts—a *help* choice. Help is merely access to on-line documentation. Those "documents" may be presented as either tutorial or reference material. Tutorial help documents are readable and understandable; reference help doc-

> The whole idea of user-friendly software had been pretty much an abstraction to me. I mean, of course we ought to build software that's easy to use. Haven't we always?
>
> That's the way I felt until I bought a computer for my son's graduation present. While it sat in my house waiting for the big event, I thought to myself "Why don't I just use this for a few days?"
>
> That was easier said than done. The manuals accompanying the machine were in three volumes, and each was an inch thick. No way, I decided, was I going to spend the time to read that much material for only a few days' benefit; I wanted a machine I could turn on and have it teach me how to use it. And then I realized *that's* what user-friendly software is really all about.

uments are terse and easily referenced. In either case, the user is able to peruse the desired material as the program functions and without needing to go and find the appropriate document.

But the distinction between tutorial on-line documentation and reference on-line documentation involves more than menus and help functions. To an experienced user, for instance, a hierarchy of menus leading the user through an interactive interface is an aggravating nuisance. This kind of user would prefer, perhaps, a terse command structure that relies on the fact that the user has already learned the menu choices and no longer needs to have them presented—a simple command word, or string of command words, saying "do this, this, and then this." The help function can now be used to aid the occasional lapse of memory of this experienced user.

Thus the very structure of the software may have a tutorial interface portion and a reference interface portion. As with the budget problem of preparing both tutorial and reference documents, this solution is more often discussed than implemented. Still, the trend toward self-help programs is clear, and the question here is really simply, How helpful need we be?

This kind of on-line documentation, of course, can be used only on a computer whose software works with a user in interactive mode. But time-sharing and personal computing are commonplace now and becoming even more so. And this kind of documentation is most relevant to user documents; it is less clear that other kinds of documents, such as maintenance manuals or marketing manuals, would benefit from this approach.

Still, the trend is clear. Certain kinds of documents should often not be documents at all, but program functions. Tutorial user documents are frequently handled in this way. Reference user documents, to a lesser extent, are also handled in this way. For an average computer program, this new trend may result in up to half of the development resources' being expended on the user interface. The knowledgeable software manager or developer must consider this possibility and plan for it, and he or she must see this method as a new medium to be exploited. The result, if it is properly managed, will be optimally useful software and documentation.

3.2.2.3 Prose Versus Graphic Documentation. The word *documentation* tends to imply words strung together in proper syntactic and semantic sentences and paragraphs. This emphasis, however, ignores the maxim that one picture is worth one thousand words. Dealing with this issue requires dealing with an important side issue, the computer processing of documentation. What are the relative roles of the prose and graphic approaches to documentation?

In the 1960s, before the advent of good text editors and word processors, documentation was handled in a traditional manner using typewriters and hard-copy originals. At that time, nonprose supplements to text such as graphs and charts could be cut and pasted into textual layouts, and that manual process was little more difficult than the preparation and revision of the text itself. As a result, nonprose documentation such as flow charts was nearly universally accepted.

Times changed. Serious questions were raised about the value of flow charts [SHNEID77], but even more importantly, the preparation of prose text was gradually automated. In the 1970s it began to be the norm for documents to be created and revised on the computer and for document preparation to be initiated from the computer's document data base. At this point, graphic approaches became a nuisance. Incorporating such nonprose material into a computer-prepared document became a manual interruption of an otherwise automated process. For these and other reasons, the flow chart lost favor, and the semiprose program design language became the most commonly used design representation. (Specifics and examples of these approaches are presented in the part of Section 3.2.2.5 entitled "Design Documentation.")

Another decade has passed, and the automation of graphics technology is rapidly catching up with the automation of textual technology. The advent of high-resolution graphics terminals, good graphics software packages, and laser printers now makes it possible to integrate graphics and text automatically. However, the word *possible* in the previous sentence is a key word. What can be done and what is in fact done are two different things. It is still the state of the practitioner's art to prepare text and graphics separately. The result is predictable—graphic approaches are still avoided in many documents.

Two exceptions are notable. Marketing documents, those slick-paper, multicolor works of art that tout a product's virtues, make heavy use of graphics. So do true tutorial documents. It is as if there is a budgetary boundary between text and graphics, and the boundary may be surmounted only when the reasons for doing so are compelling.

Putting aside the side issue of the computer processing of documentation, we are still left with the question, Which is more *effective,* prose or graphic documentation?

That issue is largely case-specific. For example, understanding a component in the context of its whole is probably best accomplished with graphics. The pie chart transmits the information much more succinctly than a paragraph of words. The memory map of a program is another example—some sort of rectangular diagram is simply a natural way to both send and receive that information.

Capers Jones highlights this issue exceptionally well in [JONES79]. Discussing design language approaches, he says, "There is no real doubt that graphics-based languages excel over character-string languages in both speed of information transfer and overall clarity. . . . Indeed, recent and surprising findings in the domain of perceptual psychology lead to the conclusion that the image-processing portion of the human sensory apparatus is separate and distinct from the character-string interpretation portion, and works considerably more rapidly. . . . "

To further illustrate the notion that the choice of text versus graphics may be case-specific, consider the problem of representing program logic and data logic in a document. Program logic can rather comfortably be presented in text form, in semitext form (such as a program design language), or in graphic form (such as a flow chart). But data logic is nearly impossible to visualize without graphics. Both data structure and data flow are almost always presented in graphical form. [JONES79] says, "The set of graphics languages seems more supportive of data analysis than character-string languages. A few authors even go so far as to observe that really understanding data relationships *requires* some form of graphics for the human mind to visualize what is going on." Some books (e.g., [MARTIN75]) are devoted to elaborating upon this idea.

One might suspect that the use of graphics is not only case-specific but individual-specific. Some people function much better from pictures and others, from words. It is important once again to remember the fundamental principle of communication: It is the nature of the reader, and not the writer, that should determine the form and content of the material being presented. In this case, the meaning is clear. *Helpful graphic material should be included in documents even when it is a nuisance to the writer to do so.*

There are some situations where graphics are simply better than text, no matter what the case or who the individual. In *The Visual Display of Quantitative Information,* [TUFTE83] discusses how graphics may be used to enhance the presentation of numeric data. He includes several guidelines for such graphic displays. They should do the following:

- Show the data.
- Induce the viewer to think about the substance rather than about methodology, graphic design, the technology of graphic production, or something else.
- Avoid distorting what the data have to say.
- Present many numbers in a small space.
- Make large data sets coherent.
- Encourage the eye to compare different pieces of data.
- Reveal the data at several levels of detail, from a broad overview to the fine structure.
- Serve a reasonably clear purpose: description, exploration, tabulation, or decoration.
- Be closely integrated with the statistical and verbal descriptions of a data set.

As a case in point, the author presents what he calls "the best statistical graphic ever drawn," a map/graph showing the terrible fate of Napoleon's army in invading Russia in 1861. The graph (Figure 3-6) shows as few other

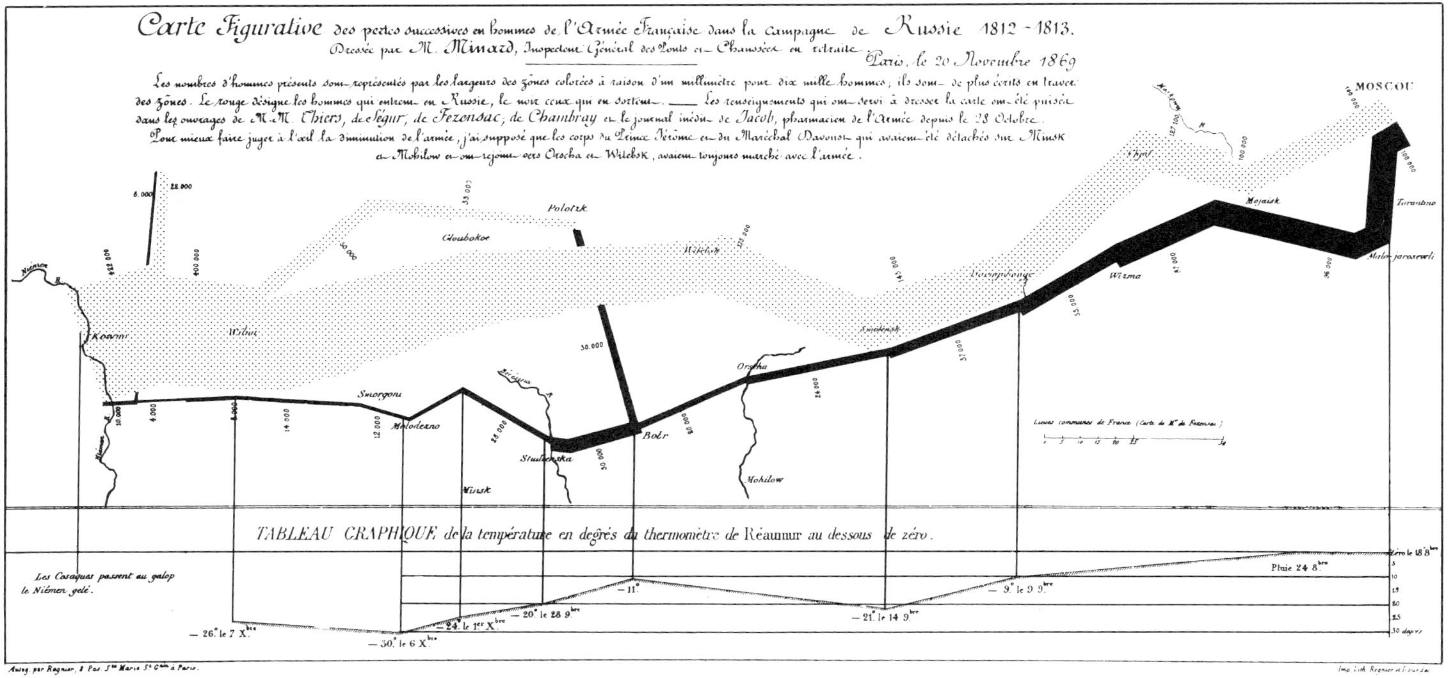

Figure 3-6 Napoleon's army in Russia, 1812. Charles Joseph Minard, *Tableaux Graphiques et Cartes Figuratives de M. Minard*, in Edward R. Tufte, *The Visual Display of Quantitative Information,* (Cheshire, CT: Graphics Press, 1983), p. 41. Six variables are plotted: the size of the army, its location on a two-dimensional surface, direction of the army's movement, and temperature on various dates during the retreat. (Notes courtesy of [TUFTE83].)

approaches could how severe were the losses that Napoleon suffered. The reader is encouraged to compare the effect of this figure with the guidelines for graphics just listed.

This classic graph done by Charles Joseph Minard (1781–1870), a French engineer, shows the terrible fate of Napoleon's army in Russia. Beginning at the left on the Polish-Russian border, the thick band shows the size of the army (422,000 men) as it invaded Russia in June 1812. The width of the band indicates the size of the army at each place on the map.

In September the army reached Moscow, which was by then sacked and deserted, with 100,000 men. The path of Napoleon's retreat from Moscow is depicted by the darker, lower band, which is linked to a temperature scale and dates at the bottom of the chart. As the graph shows, the crossing of the Berezina River was a disaster, and the army finally struggled back into Poland with only 10,000 men remaining.

In another example of the unique advantages of nontextual material, [TUFTE83] presents a very early use of graphics to show geographical data for medical purposes. Figure 3-7 displays an area in central London in 1854 where deaths from cholera were epidemic. Dr. John Snow, investigating the deaths, plotted their location and the location of the water pumps in the area. Nearly all the deaths centered on one water pump, that on Broad Street. Dr. Snow had the handle of that pump removed, and the epidemic, which had taken 500 lives, was ended.

Of course, geography is not the only area where graphics excels. Figure 3-8, again from [TUFTE83], shows 2200 pieces of weather data for the city of New York in 1980, plotted and summarized in a meaningful way. Temperature and relative humidity are plotted over time. Contrasts with norms are shown. Precipitation data is also presented.

Figure 3-9, from *Time* magazine, shows the price fluctuation in the stock of Apple computer (with emotional overtones!). The price drop in Apple computer stock is seen as a worm emerging from an apple.

Finally, graphics and text can be combined for a particularly interesting effect. Figure 3-10, again from [TUFTE83], shows a self-explanatory example of the use of this effect, prepared by the statistician W. J. Youden. Figures 3-11 through 3-15 are other examples. In each case, the graphics is the text and the text is the graphics.

These examples show graphics as a medium for the communication of information among all kinds of people. We have also previously discussed in this section of use of graphics for programming, particularly in the design phase.

The belief is growing in some software circles that the entire art or science of programming will eventually use a graphic approach. For a survey of papers that take this point of view, see [IEEE85b]. For the most part, this is an area of discontinuity between software theory and software practice. Few if any instances of completely graphic programming are known in practice.

Many people who are comfortable with preparing text do not feel ca-

Figure 3-7 Investigation of a cholera epidemic, 1854. E. W. Gilbert, "Pioneer Maps of Health and Disease in England," *Geographic Journal*, 124 (1958), 172–83. On this street map, deaths from cholera are represented by dots, and the location of pumps is indicated by crosses. The Broad Street pump is located at the center of the map, just to the right of the D in Broad Street.

pable with graphics. If you believe your graphics skills are lacking, try a motivational book like [HANKS77] or a few sessions on a graphics support system like Macintosh MacPaint. Automation has made even graphics skills somewhat easier to come by! In fact, art may be created completely by the use of a computer (see [PRUEITT84]).

3.2.2.4 Documentation Standards. We have already seen that there are many kinds of software documentation, and many choices of how to prepare it. Is there any order in this potential chaos?

Well, there is good news and bad news on this issue. The good news is that there exist software standards that provide outlines for program docu-

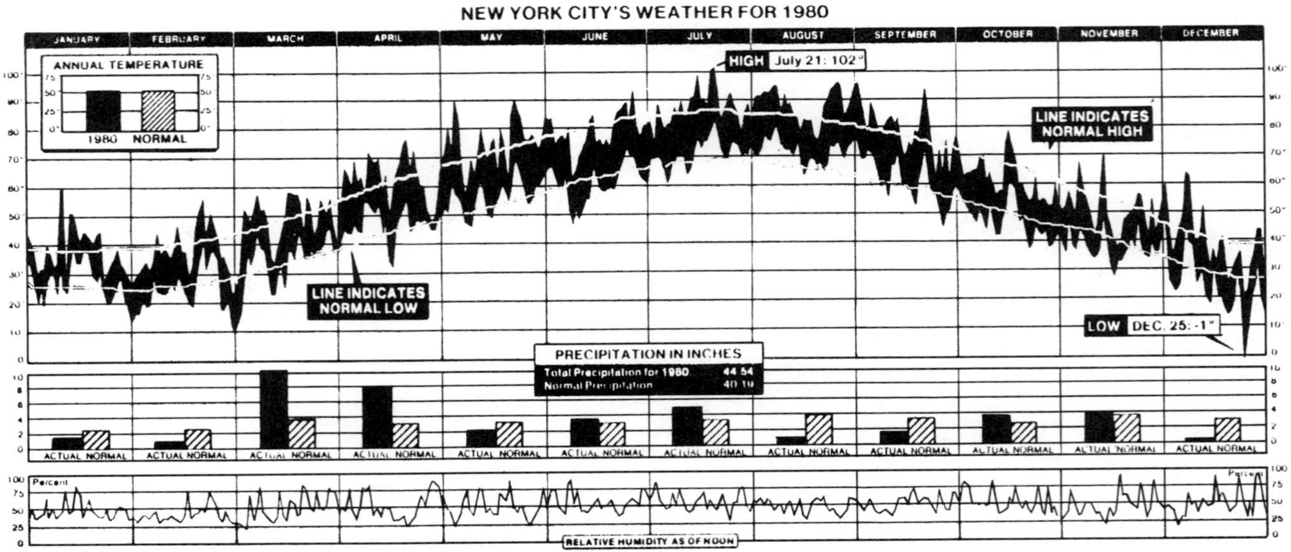

Figure 3-8 New York City's weather, 1980. "New York City's Weather for 1980," *The New York Times*, Jan. 11, 1981, p. 32. Copyright © 1981 by The New York Times Company. Reprinted by permission.

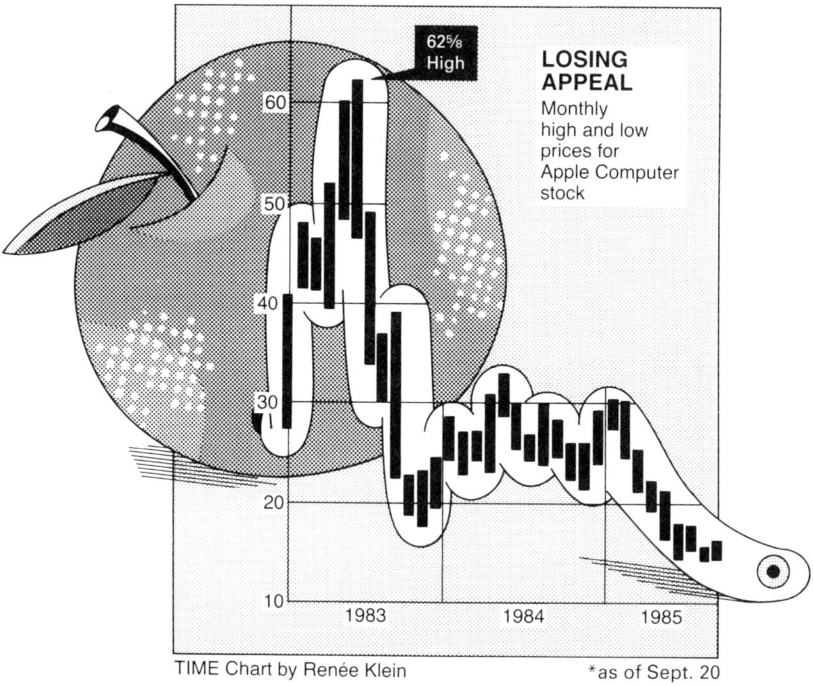

Figure 3-9 Apple stock prices, 1983–1985. Copyright © 1985 Time Inc. All rights reserved. Reprinted by permission from *Time*.

THE
NORMAL
LAW OF ERROR
STANDS OUT IN THE
EXPERIENCE OF MANKIND
AS ONE OF THE BROADEST
GENERALIZATIONS OF NATURAL
PHILOSOPHY ◆ IT SERVES AS THE
GUIDING INSTRUMENT IN RESEARCHES
IN THE PHYSICAL AND SOCIAL SCIENCES AND
IN MEDICINE AGRICULTURE AND ENGINEERING ◆
IT IS AN INDISPENSABLE TOOL FOR THE ANALYSIS AND THE
INTERPRETATION OF THE BASIC DATA OBTAINED BY OBSERVATION AND EXPERIMENT

Figure 3-10 A mixture of graphics and text. Tufte, *Visual Display*, p. 143.

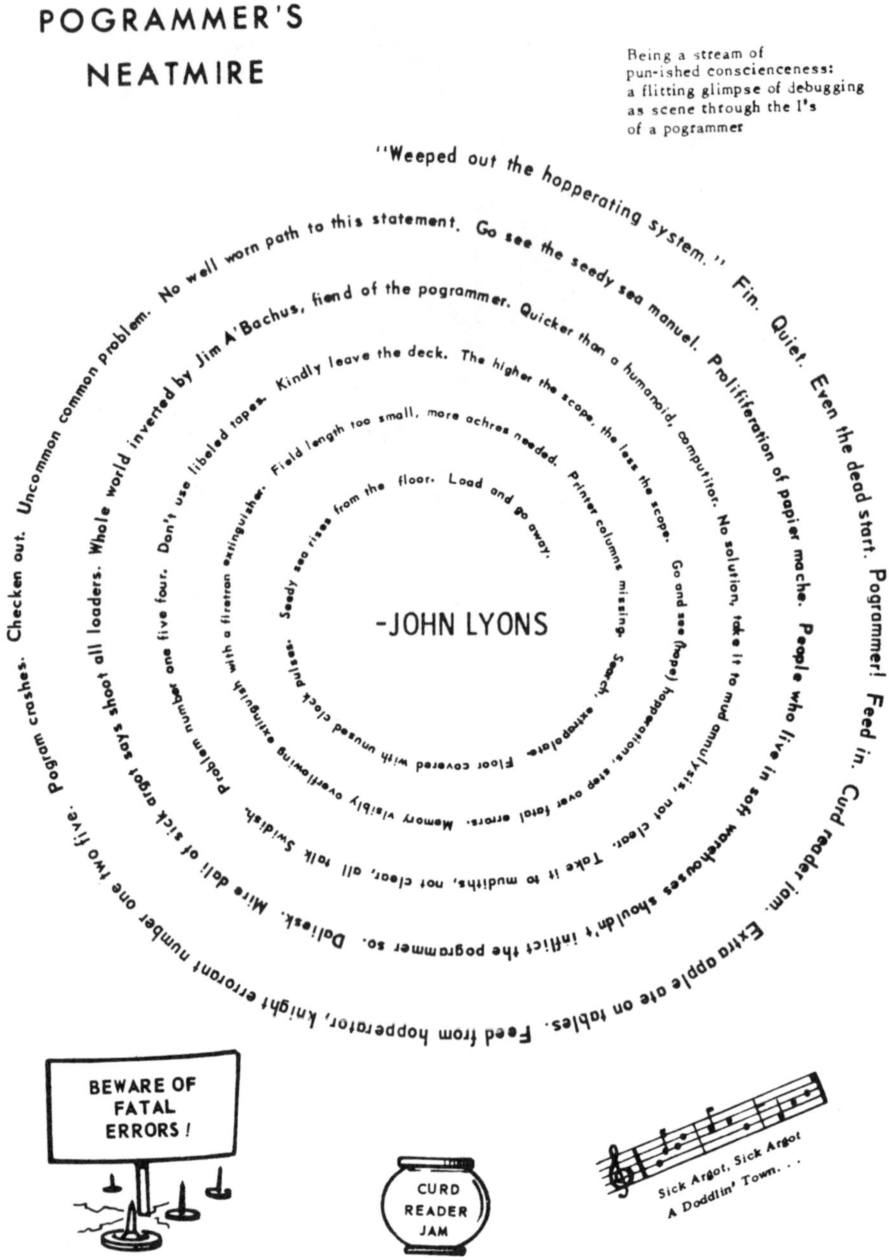
POGRAMMER'S
NEATMIRE
Being a stream of
pun-ished conscienceness:
a flitting glimpse of debugging
as scene through the I's
of a pogrammer
"Weeped out the hopperating system." Fin. Quiet. Even the dead start. Pogrammer! Feed in. Curd reader jam. Extra apple ate on tables. Feed from hopperator, knight errorant number one two five. Pogram crashes. Checken out. Uncommon common problem. No well worn path to this statement. Go see the seedy sea manuel. Prolififeration of papier mache. People who live in soft warehouses shouldn't inflict the pogrammer so. Daliesk. Mire dali of sick argot says shoot all loaders. Whole world inverted by Jim A'Bachus, fiend of the pogrammer. Quicker than a humanoid, computitor. No solution, take it to mud annulysis, not clear. Take it to mudiths, not clear, all talk Swidish. Problem number one five four. Don't use libeled tapes. Kindly leave the deck. The higher the scope, the less the scope. Go and see (hope) hopperations, stop over fatal errors. Memory visibly overflowing extinguish with a firetran extinguisher. Field length too small, more achres needed. Printer columns missing. Search, extrapolate. Floor covered with unused clock pulses. Seedy sea rises from the floor. Load and go away.
-JOHN LYONS
BEWARE OF FATAL ERRORS!
CURD READER JAM
Sick Argot, Sick Argot
A Doddlin' Town. . .

Figure 3-11 Text as graphic. *PGR Quarterly Newsletter*, Fall 1968, p. 2.

Figure 3-12 Tish Murphy, "Maze," p. 11. Reproduced, with permission, from *Words*, ed. Mark Soppeland. Copyright © 1980 by William Kaufmann, Inc., Los Altos, CA 94022. All rights reserved.

Figure 3-13 Mark Soppeland, "Wrench," in Soppeland, *Words*, p. 72.

mentation and define the content of each section of the outline. The bad news is that there is more than one such standard!

First, let's discuss the value of software documentation standards. In any software shop at any point in time, a large number of computer programs are in various states of usability. Many will be in production and several will be in development. Accompanying each of these will be some family of documentation. Given the multiplicity of programs in a shop, it is desirable that the support documentation for each program (1) consist of essentially the same set of documents, (2) have each comparable document written to the same outline, and (3) have roughly the same kind of content in each comparable section of the outline. In other words, documentation within a shop should be—and generally is—standardized as to structure, form, and content. In many cases, there is a manual for the software shop that describes what the standards are and how to prepare documentation in accordance with them.

The preceding describes *local* standardization of software documentation. It is local in the sense that the standard applies only to that shop. The question then arises, Are there *global* standards? The answer is yes, although few people are yet aware of them. First and probably of broadest interest is the global standard prepared by the National Bureau of Standards (NBS) in

Figure 3-14 Jonathan Peterson, "Build," in Soppeland, *Words*, p. 121.

1976—*Federal Information Processing Standard Publication* 38 (FIPS PUB 38). FIPS PUB 38 is essentially, at the national level, the standards manual we discussed earlier. It tells what documents should be written, what their organization should be, and what their content should be. In general, it is written for business data processing application software, but that only marginally limits its broader usefulness. FIPS PUB 38 is available to the public from the NBS or through the federal superintendent of public documents. Appropriate sections are included as Appendix A.1 of this book.

Figure 3-15 Tish Murphy, "Ego," in Soppeland, *Words,* p. 132.

The second most commonly used software documentation standard is the U.S. DoD *Military Standard Specification Practices* 490 (MIL-SPEC-490). Prepared originally in 1968, it was updated in 1985 with the creation of DOD-STD-2167, *Military Standard Defense System Software Development.* In general, this DoD standard emphasizes the documentation needs of real-time, *embedded* computer systems—those where a computer and its software are a part of some larger system. Appropriate sections are included as Appendix A.2 of this book.

The Department of Defense, in fact, has yet another documentation standard, this one for data-processing as opposed to real-time systems: DOD-7935.1-STD, *Automated Data Systems (ADS) Documentation Standard.* It is largely included in Appendix A.3 of this book.

In addition to the NBS and DoD standards is an emerging set defined by the IEEE (Institute of Electrical and Electronics Engineers). The IEEE has a very active standards body, with standards being planned and defined on an ongoing basis. The current software standards are defined in [IEEE84].

In the future, as a more comprehensive set of standards is developed by IEEE, it will be vital for the software practitioner to be aware of it as well as the others. To keep abreast of IEEE standards, write to IEEE Standards Board, 345 E. 47th St., New York, NY 10017.

The unfortunate part of all this standardization activity is that there is no standardization! That is, although there is some agreement on the structure, form, and content of software documentation among the standards, there is also substantial disagreement. It is possible to follow one standard or another slavishly or to pick and choose among them. It is not, however, possible to follow the "national standard" for software documentation, because there is none. FIPS PUB 38 probably comes closest to becoming such a national standard because it addresses a more common application area.

The approach that we take to these standards in this book is to bring up a documentation topic (e.g., the requirements spec), discuss what some of the standards have to say on the subject, and then contrast and critique them. You are thus left to choose a documentation solution, if you wish, from among the available standards. In general, the closer you adhere to some established standard, the more likely the resulting documentation is to be broadly useful.

Because of the magnitude of the software documentation problem and the cost of its solutions, automated software *documentation packages* that assist the programmer with its preparation are beginning to become available. The broad use of such a package in a computing shop will also tend to impose standards on the shop's documentation. [SNYD83] is a summary of such packages available in 1983; however, you are encouraged to pursue a more recent report, since packaged software is a relatively volatile product.

An examination of these documentation packages shows that they tend to address important fringe problems of the software documentation problem rather than to provide a solution to the total problem. This is not to belittle such packages; rather, it further illustrates how complex the documentation problem really is. Here is a partial list of the specific services performed by such products:

Data dictionary.	Keeps track of all names of program variables, and their meanings.
Cross-reference.	Keeps track of all the places in a program where an entity is used, most commonly variables or files.
Library usage.	Keeps track of modular, reusable code usage.
Operations usage.	Helps the programmer prepare an operator's manual.
System flow.	Shows an overview of logic flow in a system.
System structure.	Shows an overview of static structure of a system.
Writer's guide.	Helps the programmer know what documentation to prepare.

[SNYD83] lists some 29 packages that have these and other capabilities. Once a documentation standard is established, such packages may be useful in lowering the cost or increasing the timeliness and thus the quality of some aspects of the documentation.

The overall point of this discussion is that all computing shops need to have a well-defined set of software documentation standards that are prepared with adequate awareness of the national standards and of the automated services available to help support them.

3.2.2.5 Transient Documentation. We saw earlier that transient documentation is produced to support a specific event and then is no longer kept up to date. Eventually it is filed as a historical record or discarded.

The most obvious example of transient documentation is the concept paper, discussed earlier in Section 3.1.2.1. The concept paper is prepared to promote the acceptance of a concept; once that acceptance is achieved and the concept is developed into an actual product, the concept paper rapidly becomes obsolete. No one would suggest going back and rewriting the concept paper to match the as-built product; there would be no point to it, since the goal of the preparation of the concept paper had long since passed. In addition, the rewrite would destroy a historical record of the evolution of the product. Instead, the concept paper is typically filed away in the archives. If the history is of sufficient interest, someday it may become part of a paper or book on the product. If not, it will eventually be discarded.

In practice, implementation documentation is also generally treated as being transient. As mentioned earlier, this custom is controversial. Before discussing the format and content of the documents themselves, let us deal with that controversy.

The *requirements specification* is generally thought of as the first document in the implementation documentation process. It is the *what* of the software product: It defines the problem to be solved by the product to be built.

Usually the requirements specification is used to support a requirements review (the goal of which is to achieve mutual user-producer agreement on the requirements) and the beginnings of the design process. Once the design is well underway, the requirements specification generally is increasingly ignored and perhaps overridden by subsequent revisions agreed upon by the user and producer. Thus it is transient.

There is another approach to software development in which the requirements specification plays a more vital role. Here, the requirements are seen as a vital product baseline to be kept up-to-date until product completion. Perhaps if the technology becomes feasible, they can even serve as a basis for formal verification or proof of correctness ([HANT76], [DEMILL77]). Even here, however, the requirements specification is transient—its time of usefulness is simply extended to the point of product usage.

A third approach to software development (discussed earlier) sees the requirements specification as a baseline for software maintenance as well as development. In this approach, all software changes must begin with the necessary changes to the requirements specification. With this view, the requirements specification is not transient, since it is kept valid for the life of the product; however, this view is rarely used in practice. Because this is intended to be a practical book, it will present the viewpoint that the requirements specification is transient.

The *software development plan* is a description of the process to be used in creating the software. If it is prepared in written form at all (often it is not), it is generally used to support an early product review, perhaps a preliminary design review, and to give guidance to the team of software developers. Clearly, this is a transient document.

Design documentation is the *how* of the software product: It defines how the requirements specification (which is the *what* of the product) is to be implemented. Usually design documentation is used to support one or more design reviews and to give guidance to the coding process. Once coding is complete, the design document is rarely referred to. In fact, the coding process often overrides detail definitions. Thus the design documentation is transient.

There are two circumstances in which the design document may not be transient. In one, sometimes used in practice, the design documentation evolves into a software maintenance document. As coding progresses and is completed, the design document is modified to match the as-built product. The final document is then renamed the maintenance document and clearly becomes permanent product documentation.

The other circumstance was discussed earlier under the requirements specification. In this view, maintenance of software must involve revising not just the code but its requirements and design document as well. If this revision is done, the design document becomes permanent. However, as mentioned previously, it is rarely done.

The *interface control document* is used on large software projects to define the junctions between product components. It is a design-type document in that its purpose is to describe how interfaces will be implemented. Its importance is that it helps ensure that the people responsible for constructing the product components will build them in a plug-compatible manner. The previous discussions of design documentation also hold here; under most circumstances, the interface control document is a transient document.

Coding documentation is a mixed bag. Often it consists of informal notes written to guide the implementation team, sometimes aggregated into a *unit development folder.* This is clearly transient documentation, since it has little or no value once the product is complete.

On the other hand, the coding documentation may be an in-depth evolution of the design document, intended to further evolve into a maintenance document. In this case, code documentation is nontransient. Note how different these approaches to coding documentation are. An up-front decision must be made as to which approach is to be employed and thus whether coding documentation is to be transient or not.

Testing documentation is the collection of documents that are used to define the software testing process. They often consist of a test plan/procedure describing what is to be done and how, and a test report, describing how it all came out. Here we have another example of largely transient documents; once the testing is finished, the documents have historical value only. However, since maintenance of software involves retesting, the test plan/procedure (but not the report) may have more lasting value.

You may wonder if the distinction between transient and permanent documentation is an important one, since you may not have run into it before. Given the distinction, the temptation is to say that transient documentation is less important than permanent documentation. This is a mistake. Transient documentation is often prepared to support higher-level management in decision making: Is this concept worthwhile? Are these requirements the ones the customer meant? Does this design satisfy the requirements? As such aids, transient documents are often prepared with more care and expense than permanent ones.

There are two reasons that the distinction is important. One is that, if you use the distinction as you plan a software development, you are forced to make some early decisions about the documentation approach. The most important questions to ask are, Where will the (permanent) software maintenance document come from? Will there be one at all? Will it evolve from a transient document or documents?

The second reason is that, in today's software state of the art, permanent documentation is frequently given short shrift. User manuals are often inadequate. Maintenance manuals are commonly not produced at all. Marketing material is usually interspersed among the material in the user manual. The result is that enormous attention is being paid to transient documents and little to permanent ones. The reason is that transient documents tend to be read by managers, and permanent documentation only by workers. This is a dangerous trend, and the use of the words *permanent* and *transient* may help put it in better perspective. Permanent documentation is not necessarily more important than transient documentation, but it is *as* important.

Requirements Specification. *What* is the problem the software product is to solve? That question is the one the requirements specification is written to answer.

Like any other broad-scale question, this one can be broken down into a more specific set of questions:

1. What are the functions to be performed?
2. What algorithms must be used to perform the functions? (This question is a little dangerous, because it begins to lead the spec writer into the realm of "*how* are we to do this?" which usually should be avoided in a requirements spec. Sometimes, however, it is necessary to talk about

how in order to define the *what* completely (e.g., "Poobah's Method will be used on this problem because of its accuracy"). Only where there are clearly preferable algorithms should a requirements spec tell how to do something.)

3. What are the interfaces between the software product and its outside world?
4. What performance is to be achieved by the software system? (size, speed, capacity, etc.)
5. What programming methodologies *must* be used in order to achieve the desired result? (modular programming, structured programming, etc.) Again, only "must" methodologies should be requirements.
6. What growth capability should the software product possess?
7. What requirements exist for the data to be input, to be output, and to be kept in a data base?
8. What must be done to verify that the final software product is acceptable?

Where do the answers to these questions come from? In most situations, someone from the software organization (often known as a systems analyst) talks to one or more people from the customer organization in order to define precisely what problem is to be solved. In some situations, especially where the software is part of some larger system (for example, the software in a computer in a navigation airplane), the software requirements may alternatively be extracted from a requirements document already prepared for the total system (the system specification).

In either case, the problem of requirements gathering is one of

- Reading or listening carefully
- Knowing which things written or said pertain to software and which may be ignored
- Organizing these relevant extracted requirements
- Subjecting this first pass at the requirements to a consistency analysis to spot areas of customer confusion
- Challenging information sources to ensure a continuing accurate, consistent picture
- Preparing a first draft of these requirements in some customer-readable form
- Subjecting this draft requirements specification to customer review and critique
- Polishing the first draft into a final draft via this critique

Notice from this description that the preparation of a requirements specification involves intensive interaction with a customer. This is perhaps the most human-factors-oriented phase of the software development process; and

Gathering the requirements for a system, even a large system, probably sounds like a relatively easy task. It's not. Let me describe for you one situation where the job of gathering requirements was not only hard, it was actually impossible!

The system requirements for the F-222 (a fictitious name) aircraft occupy documents whose binders would fill a whole shelf in a library. In those documents are *all* the requirements for the entire system. Let's assume that your job is to go through those binders and extract those requirements that have software relevance.

That was the job of some friends of mine on the project. They pored through those binders for weeks on end, trying desperately to cull the requirements that would drive the software system they were to create. As a completeness check, they had several people do the job in parallel and compare notes. The problem was that no pair of people agreed on the set of requirements they had extracted.

At that point, the people went back through the binders looking for requirements they had missed. And as they did so, each of them found requirements that not only had they not found before, but no one else had found either!

They repeated that process several times over a several-week period before the awful truth began to hit them—they were not going to be able to reach closure on the iterative process of gathering requirements! At that point, they made a very practical decision. They froze the requirements to be the set they were currently working with and moved on to design the solution. If they could miss a requirement after that much work had been put into finding them, they reasoned, the customer would never miss them either. To the best of my knowledge, they were right!

because it is, it is not uncommon to find this phase handled by someone other than a designer, programmer, or tester, someone with more people-oriented skills than the computer-oriented programmer normally has.

Notice also that in the definition of the requirements specification, a baseline is being laid for the product to follow. Any mistake at this stage is critical to the final product; no amount of clever design or programming can overcome the obstacle of faulty requirements. Because of this, the systems analyst is often more highly skilled, and paid, than a programmer.

It is particularly important to define requirements in such a way that it is both logically and legally possible to determine if they have been achieved in the final software product. A vague requirement will be treated as if it were not there at all.

Picture yourself as a software specialist trying to convince a judge or jury that the software you have written meets a performance requirement of processing 10 cases a minute. That one is easy, of course; you produce some computer-printed timing data that show that 10 cases were processed in 52 seconds. Now picture yourself in the same circumstance trying to show that your software meets the requirement that it be "modular." You know when software is modular, but a judge or jury does not, and it is extremely difficult to think of a way of convincing them that it is.

It is tempting to say that quantized requirements, such as "10 cases a minute," are better than qualitative ones, such as "modular." And in general, they are. The problem here is that it is not always meaningful to quantize. For example, it is common practice now to quantize modularity by requiring that there be no more than 50 (75? 100? 150?) lines of code per module, but in fact this is diverting modular programming from a functional concept to a numerical one, and the purpose of modularity begins to be lost.

What *can* be said here is that requirements must be both *meaningful* and *testable*. Achieving those sometimes-conflicting goals requires wisdom, thought, and a thorough understanding of software development. Thus the systems analyst must be skilled in both human-factors considerations *and* in the technology of software (as well as, of course, the technology of the customer).

One of the most critical problems of software development is that of unstable requirements. Either the systems analyst does an inadequate job, or the customer cannot fully grasp the problem to be solved during such a conceptual stage. In either case, as the software product evolves, some new requirements creep into the picture, or some old ones change. A catastrophe may be in the making, since for all the "softness" of software, it is still not flexible enough to absorb flexing requirements. Thus it is important in writing the requirements specification to define not only what is to be built but also what is to be done about changes to what is to be built. In this way, when and if the changes are encountered, there will be a well-defined process for handling them.

From all this discussion, a picture of the process of preparing a requirements specification emerges, as shown in Figure 3-16.

The preceding sections have discussed the kinds of questions a requirements specification must answer and the process of preparing one. But what might the form and content of such a document be?

There are many possible answers to that question, and several national standards deal with it. What follows will be a discussion of two of those standards.

NBS's FIPS PUB 38 breaks down requirements documentation into two documents—one containing *functional* requirements, and one containing *data* requirements. DOD-STD-2167, on the other hand, defines a requirements specification similar to the NBS functional one, but it offers an additional

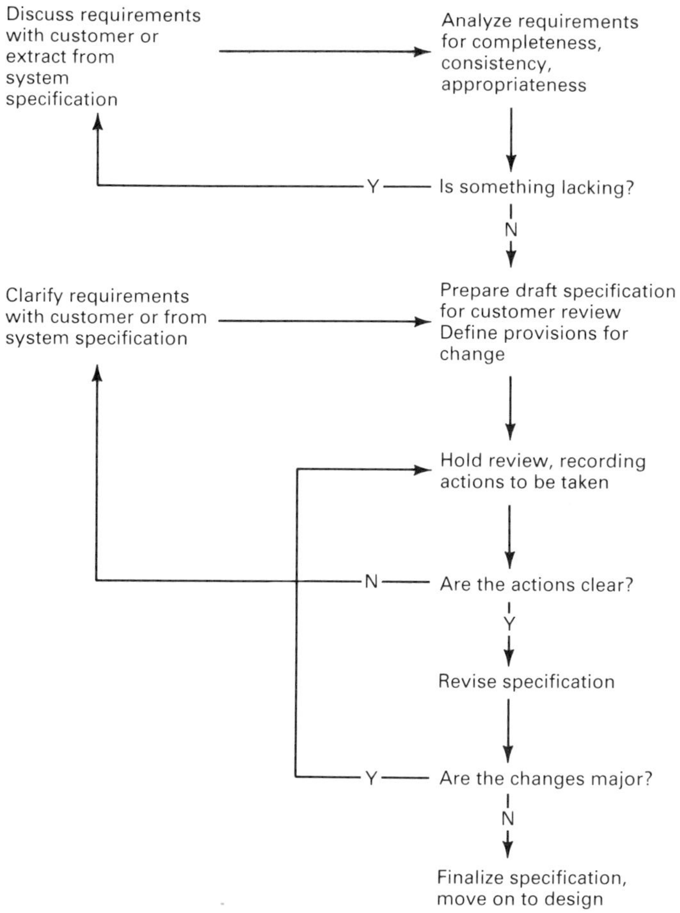

Figure 3-16 Systems analysis.

interface requirement document instead of a data one. The following sections will compare and contrast the NBS and DoD requirements documents.

Both outlines begin with some introductory outline material.

NBS Functional Requirements Document	*DoD Software Requirement Specification*
1. General information	1. Scope
1.1 Summary	1.1 Identification
1.2 Environment	1.2 Purpose
1.3 References	1.3 Introduction
	2. Applicable documents

The purpose of this introduction is to make sure that the reader has a proper overview of the software product before reading further—what it is to do, where it is to be used, and what other written material describes it. Thus although the outline topic words appear different, the opening content is pretty much the same. (Note that the full definition of the content of each document section is found in Appendix A of this book.)

Next, however, the NBS outline expands significantly on the problem to be solved. There is nothing comparable in the DoD documentation.

NBS

2. Overview
    - 2.1 Overview
    - 2.2 Objectives
    - 2.3 Existing methods and procedures
    - 2.4 Proposed methods and procedures
    - 2.5 Summary of improvements
    - 2.6 Summary of impacts
        - 2.6.1 Equipment impacts
        - 2.6.2 Software impacts
        - 2.6.3 Organizational impacts
        - 2.6.4 Operational impacts
        - 2.6.5 Development impacts
    - 2.7 Cost considerations
    - 2.8 Alternative proposals

The NBS approach heavily emphasizes that the software system is a revision of some prior solution (manual or automated), and the new system is expected to have a number of impacts on the present method of operation. Often DoD software is implementing a new concept (e.g., the software that controls the navigational computer in a smart missile), and there may be no "existing methods and procedures" to discuss.

Meanwhile, the emphasis of the DoD spec in its next section is on methodologies and interfaces.

DoD

3.0 Requirements
    - 3.1 Programming requirements
        - 3.1.1 Programming language(s)
        - 3.1.2 Compiler/assembler
        - 3.1.3 Programming standards
    - 3.2 Design requirements
        - 3.2.1 Sizing and timing constraints
        - 3.2.2 Design standards
        - 3.2.3 Design constraints

3.3 Interface requirements
- 3.3.1 Interface relationships
- 3.3.2 Interface identification and documentation
- 3.3.3 Detailed interface requirements

Here again, the two standards differ. In the real-time world, there is a necessary heavy emphasis on interface between the software and its environment.

It is in the next section that both outlines get down to the true point of the document, the requirements.

NBS	*DoD*
3. Requirements	3.4 Detailed functional and performance requirements
3.1 Functions	3.4.X (Name X) function
3.2 Performance	3.4.X.1 Inputs
3.2.1 Accuracy	3.4.X.2 Processing
3.2.2 Validation	3.4.X.3 Outputs
3.2.3 Timing	
3.2.4 Flexibility	
3.3 Inputs-outputs	
3.4 Data characteristics	
3.5 Failure contingencies	
4. Operating environment	3.5 Adaptation
4.1 Equipment	3.5.1 System environment
4.2 Support software	3.5.2 System parameters
4.3 Interfaces	3.5.2 System capacities
4.4 Security and privacy	
4.5 Controls	

The two outlines have some strong common threads. They both stress the definition of functions and their input and output, and the definition of the environment in which the software product will be used. The NBS approach stresses performance considerations, and the DoD, capacities, both of which are important and are omitted from the other outline. (Do we care how fast the program is, how big it is, or how much data it will hold?) NBS touches on validation, which we will see is the subject of a whole section of the DoD document. Clearly there is, to this point, similarity but not unanimity on how to write the fundamental portion of a standard requirements document!

If this difference is disturbing, the concluding section is even more so.

NBS	*DoD*
5. Development plan	3.6 Quality factors
	3.6.1 Correctness requirements
	3.6.2 Reliability requirements

DoD

3.6.3 Efficiency requirements
3.6.4 Integrity requirements
3.6.5 Usability requirements
3.6.6 Maintainability requirements
3.6.7 Testability requirements
3.6.8 Flexibility requirements
3.6.9 Portability requirements
3.6.10 Reusability requirements
3.6.11 Interoperability requirements
3.6.12 Additional quality requirements
3.7 Software support
3.8 Traceability
4.0 Qualification requirements
4.1 General qualification requirements
4.2 Special qualification requirements
5.0 Preparation for delivery
6.0 Notes
10.0 Appendices

The NBS document veers off in the direction of how the software is to be developed, whereas the DoD places heavy emphasis on the quality of the product (touched on in NBS Section 3.2.2).

Recall that the NBS data requirements are treated in a separate document.

NBS Data Requirements Document

1. General information
   1.1 Summary
   1.2 Environment
   1.3 References
   1.4 Modification of data requirements
2. Data description
   2.1 Static data
   2.2 Dynamic input data
   2.3 Dynamic output data
   2.4 Internally generated data
   2.5 Data constraints
3. Data collection
   3.1 Requirements and scope
   3.2 Input responsibilities
   3.3 Procedures
   3.4 Impacts

The NBS document places far more emphasis on data considerations than the DoD approach (note paragraphs 3.4.X.1 and 3.4.X.3 of the DoD outline). You can see that the NBS had a different, data-oriented set of applications in mind.

Meanwhile, recall that the DoD has a separate interface requirements document.

DoD Interface Requirements Document

1. Scope
    - 1.1 Identification
    - 1.2 Purpose
    - 1.3 Introduction
2. Applicable documents
3. Requirements
    - 3.1 Interface relationships
    - 3.2 Interface identification and documentation
    - 3.3 Detailed interface requirements
        - 3.3.1 Software/software
            - 3.3.1.X (Name X interface)
        - 3.3.2 Software/hardware or critical item
            - 3.3.2.Y (Name Y interface)
4. Qualification requirements
6. Notes
10. Appendices

The side-by-side presentation of these two standards might be quite depressing if you were hoping for a universal cookbook outline for the writing of requirements specifications. Obviously, if one of the standards is adopted, then the unique good features of the other are not provided for. However, a better viewpoint is the following: You are encouraged to choose whichever outline seems preferable, and then make sure that either within that outline, or in special added sections, the unique and worthwhile aspects of the other are included. In that way, the resulting requirements specification will have the benefit of the best thinking of both the NBS and DoD.

How do you choose which outline is preferable? Well, the NBS outline is best suited for the data-oriented, commercial data processing kind of application, whereas the DoD outline is oriented more toward the real-time or scientific application. Thus the nature of the application may well dictate the form of the requirements specification that will be written.

Development Plan. The requirements specification, which describes what product is to be built, is an essential part of the software development process. The development plan, however, is less commonly prepared.

The purpose of a development plan is to describe the *processes* that will be used to create the software. It does not attempt to describe the software itself but rather the tasks, methods and philosophies that will occur as the development proceeds.

For very large software projects involving a large number of people, a development plan, prepared in some formal manner, is probably essential. For tiny software projects, the development plan typically resides in someone's head, and that is probably as it should be. And for the vast gray area between very large and tiny, some sort of written plan ranging from complete but informal to a series of memos to the troops on "how we'll do business" is advisable.

The question, What processes will be used? can be broken down into a more specific set of questions:

1. Technical questions
   a. What development philosophy will be used?
   b. What are the specific elements of that philosophy?
   c. What methods will be used?
   d. What tasks will be performed?
   e. What products (deliverable, nondeliverable) will be created (programs, documents)?
   f. How will product maintenance occur?
2. Management questions
   a. What management philosophy will be used?
   b. What organization will be employed?
   c. What facilities will be utilized?
   d. What procedures and controls will be imposed?
   e. How will changes be handled?

Where do the answers to these questions come from? Generally they are drawn from the past experience of the technical and management project participants, with that experience being extrapolated to cover the present problem. "We did it this way before" or "We can improve on what we did before by doing this" greatly influence what goes into a development plan.

The NBS document series does not place heavy emphasis on the development plan, although we have seen provision for it in Section 5 of the Functional Requirements Specification. But the DoD offers a specific and elaborate outline for this kind of document.

Software Development Plan

1. Scope
   1.1 Identification
   1.2 Purpose
   1.3 Introduction

2. Referenced documents
3. Resources and organization
   - 3.1 Project resources
     - 3.1.1 Contractor facilities
     - 3.1.2 Government-furnished equipment, software, and services
     - 3.1.3 Personnel
   - 3.2 Software development
     - 3.2.1 Organizational structure
     - 3.2.2 Personnel
     - 3.2.3 Resources
   - 3.3 Software configuration management
     - 3.3.1 Organizational structure
     - 3.3.2 Personnel
     - 3.3.3 Resources
   - 3.4 Software quality evaluation
     - 3.4.1 Organizational structure
     - 3.4.2 Personnel
     - 3.4.3 Resources
   - 3.X Other software development functions
4. Development schedule and milestones
   - 4.1 Activities
   - 4.2 Activity network
   - 4.3 Procedures for risk management
   - 4.4 Identification of high-risk areas
5. Software development procedures
   - 5.1 Software standards and procedures
     - 5.1.1 Software development tools, techniques, methodologies
     - 5.1.2 Critical-component selection criteria
     - 5.1.3 Software development library
     - 5.1.4 Software development files
     - 5.1.5 Documentation formats for informal tests
     - 5.1.6 Design and coding standards
     - 5.1.7 Formal reviews
   - 5.2 Software configuration management
     - 5.2.1 Configuration identification
     - 5.2.2 Configuration control
     - 5.2.3 Configuration status accounting
     - 5.2.4 Configuration audits
     - 5.2.5 Preparation for configuration authentication
     - 5.2.6 Configuration management major milestones
   - 5.3 Software quality evaluation
     - 5.3.1 Procedures, methods, tools and facilities
     - 5.3.2 Activities
   - 5.4 Additional software development procedures

Software Development Plan

5.5 Commercially available, reusable, and government-furnished software
5.6 Data rights and documentation for software
5.7 Nondeliverable software, firmware, and hardware controls
5.8 Software developed for hardware deliverables
5.9 Installation and checkout
5.10 Interface management
6. Notes
10. Appendices

This outline is perhaps more detailed than many projects will warrant. Most of the outline speaks for itself—the organizational distinction between the product (Section 5) and management of the product (Sections 3 and 4) is crisp—but you may be confused by the terms *deliverable* and *nondeliverable* products. Deliverable products are those named in the requirements—specific computer programs or documents in specific form (e.g., program XYZ's object code), which are required to be delivered to the customer or user. Nondeliverable products are those built, perhaps unexpectedly, as part of the pro-

> You might expect that the software development plan would be written *before* the software itself is written. Well, that certainly is the normal way of doing business. But on the XYZ project, things got done in funny ways sometimes.
>
> The customer forgot, for example, to schedule the delivery of the software development plan on the system master schedule. One day, an alert programmer noticed that although the plan was required, it had never been written or delivered because there was no milestone to call for it and thus trigger its creation. The customer had two choices at this point: to skip the plan, because it made no sense to write one telling how you were going to do something you'd already done, or to insist that it be written because the contract called for it.
>
> Customers are not always as logical as we would like them to be. In this case, the XYZ customer insisted that he wanted a plan. And so we wrote him one. It didn't describe what we actually did, of course, because it would have taken too long to poll all the doers to find out how they did what they did. So it described how we thought they might have done it, or should have done it, or how the literature advised us to do it.
>
> When we handed it to the customer, he was happy. Another deliverable had been delivered!

cess of building deliverables—test cases, or debugging tools, are the most common examples. They enter into this discussion only because provision is made for both kinds of products in the development plan.

The development plan is a blueprint for how to do business. Whether it is followed to the letter of the law, or in spirit, is up to the leadership of the software project.

Design Documentation. *How* is the problem that the software product is to address going to be solved? That question is the one to be answered by the design and its documentation.

However, this answer is not quite so simple as those of the preceding documents. The process of creating a software design is an iterative process, one in which the designer conceives of a solution at ever-deepening levels of detail, some of which negate previous design "solutions" and cause them to be redone. The initial written communication of a design, at a fairly high level, may be a series of pictures such as HIPO diagrams (hierarchical diagrams that show Input, Process, and Output for each mode in a hierarchy) to enable the designer to record and replay the first cut at the design. As the design progresses, it is expressed in whatever mechanism is most convenient to facilitating the designer's mental processes—organized (or perhaps even disorganized!) notes, sketches, text. These design notes, as the design begins to gel, get formalized into some sort of design "language" or representation—program design language (PDL), flow charts, Nassi-Shneiderman charts, data flow diagrams, decision tables, or whatever medium (or combination of media) the designer finds helpful (see Figure 3-17).

At some point in time there will probably be a formal or informal design review. When that happens, the design notes and design language must be organized into a somewhat more formal design document. At this intermediate level, the result is a functional design document in which the broad functional requirements are allocated to software components. And later, at a relatively fine-grain level, there will be a detail design in which sufficient design solutions are presented to enable the design to be coded.

Generally these four levels of design (design overview, working design, functional design, detail design) are simply a continuum of steps in producing a design document. That is, the overview material of the original design becomes a high-level part of the functional design document, and the functional design document is elaborated to become the detail design document. Seen in this way, the documentation of the complex design process remains relatively simple.

Into what questions can the *how* problem of design be decomposed?

1. What algorithms are needed to solve the problem stated in the requirements?
2. What program structure can best support those algorithms?

Program Design Language

```
Open Book;
While Page Not Back Cover;
    Read Page;
    Turn Page If Odd-Numbered;
End While;
Close Book;
```

Nassi-Shneiderman Chart

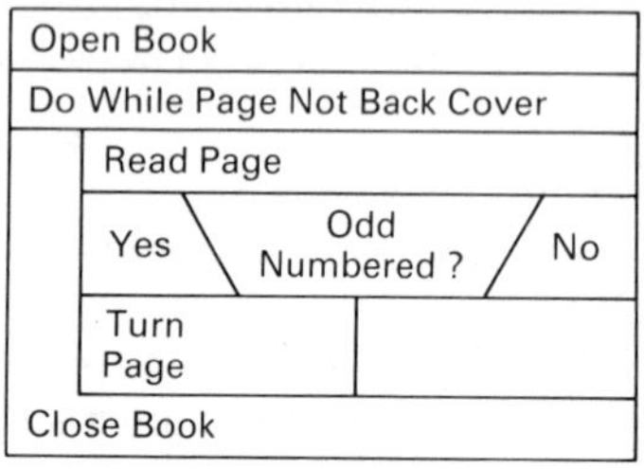

Flow Chart

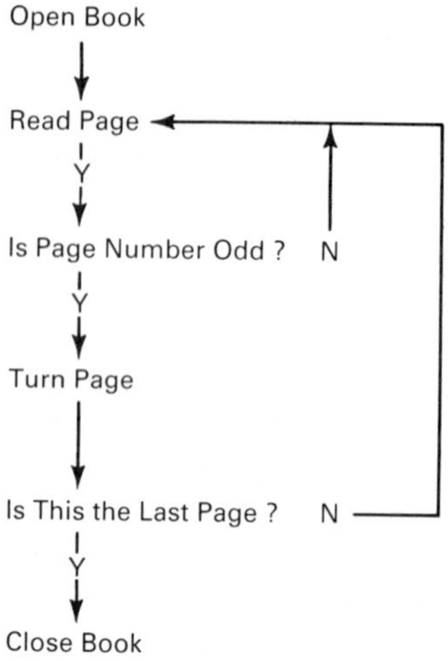

Data Flow Diagram

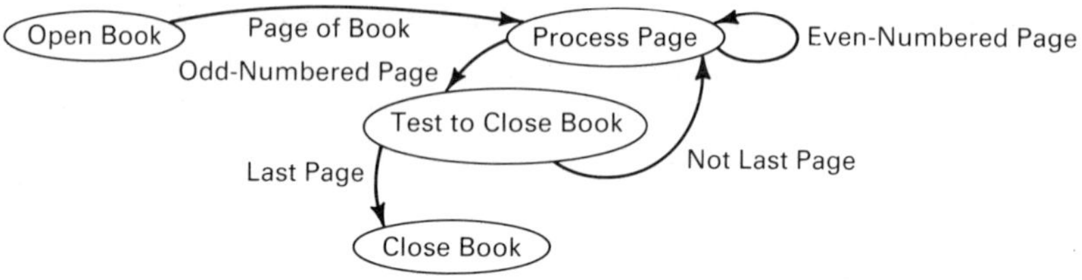

Decision Table

Conditions				
Page = First	Y	N	N	N
First < Page < Last and Even	N	Y	N	N
First < Page < Last and Odd	N	N	Y	N
Page = Last	N	N	N	Y
Actions				
Open Book	X			
Read Page	X	X	X	X
Turn Page	X		X	
Close Book				X

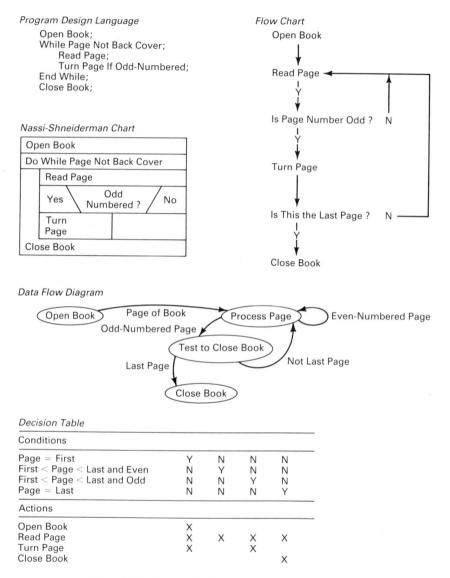

Figure 3-17 Some design languages and representations.

3. What data structure and data flow can best support those algorithms? (For heavily data-oriented programs, the selection of data flow/structure may precede the selection of algorithms.)
4. Are the chosen solutions compatible with the performance requirements? (If not, the design must be redone.)
5. What methodologies best support the chosen algorithms and structures?

6. What internal as well as external interfaces will exist in these structures?
7. How will the requirements be traceable into the design?
8. How will user errors and operational errors be handled?

Where do answers to these questions come from? Unlike the answer to that question in the section on requirements specification, the process of answering these questions is decidedly analytical rather than social. These answers pour out of the mind of the designer as the designer's training and experience wrestle with the problem as stated in the requirements. *Pour* in the preceding sentence is somewhat of a misnomer; if the problem is simple and/or the designer is bright, a design may indeed pour out quickly. But if the problem is complex and/or the designer is not quite so bright, a design may require months or occasionally years of work before it is ready to be coded.

In truth, because so much of the design process occurs within the mind, we in software understand the design process a lot less well than we'd like to. Fortunately, however (from the point of view of this book), we understand the final product of a design—namely, the design documentation—a lot better than we understand the process.

Even so, there is some controversy surrounding the issue of how detailed a detailed design should be. Some say it should be complete, sufficient in detail that the coding process can be almost mechanical. Others say it need go only far enough to allow the intended programmer, at whatever skill level that programmer has, to write the code. This could result in dramatically different thicknesses of design documentation, since a design for a "mechanical" coder must be considerably more detailed than the design for a professional programmer, for example. This controversy remains unresolved at present. Fortunately, choosing a side in the controversy is a matter of level of detail in the

> The programmer grumbled, stared at the design document, and grumbled again.
>
> The designer had produced an impeccable-looking, carefully thought out, extremely detailed design. The programmer had a problem, though. For all the detail it contained, the design didn't quite solve the whole problem.
>
> How could the programmer bend the design to fit the problem to be solved? To do so would mean thinking like the original designer.
>
> The programmer couldn't do it. Scrapping the carefully prepared design, the programmer prepared her own. It may have wasted the previous designer's efforts, but it was the only way to get the problem solved.
>
> Has this ever happened to you?

document and not of fundamental organization of the document, so what follows is appropriate to either side of the controversy. Let us, then, look at the NBS and DoD approaches to standard design documentation.

The NBS uses three design documents: at the system level (assuming that the software product will consist of several programs), a system or subsystem specification; at the program level, a program specification; and for the system or program data, a data base specification.

The DoD acknowledges the difference between system and program entities—there is a system segment specification, which contains system requirements, for example—but then uses four design documents to record the design of the software itself: the "Software Top Level Design Document," the "Software Detail Design Document," the "Data Base Design Document," and the "Interface Design Document."

Looking at the system specification, we find the following outlines, which begin in a similar way, but then the DoD outline becomes much more demanding.

NBS System/Subsystem Specification

1. General information
    - 1.1 Summary
    - 1.2 Environment
    - 1.3 References
2. Requirements
    - 2.1 Description
    - 2.2 Functions
    - 2.3 Performance
        - 2.3.1 Accuracy
        - 2.3.2 Validation
        - 2.3.3 Timing
        - 2.3.4 Flexibility
3. Operating environment
    - 3.1 Equipment
    - 3.2 Support software
    - 3.3 Interfaces
    - 3.4 Security and privacy
    - 3.5 Controls
4. Design characteristics
    - 4.1 Operations
    - 4.2 System/subsystem logic
5. Program specifications
    - 5.1 Program i specification

DoD System/Segment Specification

1. Scope
2. Applicable documents
3. Requirements
    - 3.1 System definition
        - 3.1.1 Missions
        - 3.1.2 Threat
        - 3.1.3 System modes and states
        - 3.1.4 System functions
            - 3.1.4.X Function X
        - 3.1.5 System function relationships
        - 3.1.6 Configuration allocation
        - 3.1.7 Interface requirements
        - 3.1.8 Government furnished property
    - 3.2 System characteristics
        - 3.2.1 Physical requirements
    - 3.3 Processing resources
    - 3.4 Quality factors

- 3.5 Logistics
- 3.6 Precedence (prioritized requirements)

4. Qualification requirements
   - 4.1 General
   - 4.2 Formal tests
   - 4.3 Formal test constraints
   - 4.4 Qualification cross-reference
5. Preparation for delivery
6. Notes
10. Appendices

At the program level, we again contrast the NBS and DoD approaches:

NBS Program Specification

1. General information
   - 1.1 Summary
   - 1.2 Environment
   - 1.3 References
2. Requirements
   - 2.1 Program description
   - 2.2 Functions
   - 2.3 Performance
     - 2.3.1 Accuracy
     - 2.3.2 Validation
     - 2.3.3 Timing
     - 2.3.4 Flexibility
3. Operating Environment
   - 3.1 Equipment
   - 3.2 Support software
   - 3.3 Interfaces
   - 3.4 Storage
   - 3.5 Security and privacy
   - 3.6 Controls
4. Design characteristics
   - 4.1 Operating procedures
   - 4.2 Inputs
   - 4.3 Program logic

DoD Software Top Level Design Document

1. Scope
2. Referenced documents
3. Requirements
   - 3.1 Architecture
   - 3.2 Functional allocation
   - 3.3 Memory and processing time allocation
   - 3.4 Functional control and data flow
   - 3.5 Global data
   - 3.6 Top-level design
     - 3.6.X Design element X (inputs, local data, interrupts, timing and sequencing, processing, outputs, adaptation data)

DoD Software Detailed Design Document

1. Scope
2. Referenced documents

NBS Program Specification	*DoD Software Detailed Design Document*

4.4 Outputs
4.5 Data base
    4.5.1 Logical characteristics
    4.5.2 Physical characteristics
	3. Requirements
	    3.1 Interface design
	        3.1.X Interface X
	    3.2 Global data
	    3.3 Detailed design
	        3.3.W Element W (inputs, local data, process control, processing, utilization of other elements, limitations, outputs)

Here again we see the wide disparity in existing documentation standards. The NBS program specification replays many of the topics covered in the requirements specification, but in a program-specific manner. The DoD section titled "Requirements" is in reality the place where the evolving design is documented, and the expectation is that this documentation will be prepared at a high level, just as the NBS section "Design characteristics" is expected to contain material at the program level but not necessarily below that.

That disparity is not major, but still it causes some measure of despair. It is apparent that, even after the more than 30 years that design documentation has been produced, we are a long way from agreement on what it ought to contain.

The DoD methodology, by including a "Software Detail Design Document" as well as the top-level one, provides for the inevitable elaboration of the design as it approaches the point at which coding may begin. Note that the DoD top-level and lower-level design documents have a sufficiently different outline that it is apparent that the latter can evolve from the former only by some rework. Thus it is obviously the DoD intention that the detail design not supersede the top-level one. Let us explore why this is so.

To discuss this issue, we must back up a little and cover a new topic. The eventual result of all the design effort, of course, is a software product. Part of that product will be the listing of the code that constitutes the product. Part of that listing will be commentary describing the function of the code in order to make the code more understandable. Most software experts now agree that, to the extent that it is feasible, the design representation should become much of that commentary. That is, if the design representation is computer-readable text (note that PDL satisfies this requirement, and that most other design representations do not), then the design can be inserted into the program along with its code.

Now we return to the issue. If the design—and its representation—are elaborated from a functional design to a detailed design, and especially if this detailed design is the kind that allows near-mechanical translation, then is not the design as complex as the code and, in fact, redundant?

There appear to be two common solutions to this problem. One is to acknowledge the redundancy but include the complete design representation as commentary anyway, probably in the form of a set of PDL followed by the set of code that implements it (rather than PDL line by code line). The other solution is to preserve the functional (top) level of design representation and let it, rather than the detail level, become the code commentary. This solution is closer to the traditional expectation for commentary, since it tends to result in a line of fairly high-level PDL followed by the code that implements it.

There is another issue related to this one. How far need the detail design process go before it can be terminated in favor of coding? Here I am going to express a personal bias. I prefer a design to go only as far as needed by the subsequent professional coder rather than down to the mechanical translation level, and I then prefer that that somewhat high level of design become the program commentary. I prefer this approach because (1) it minimizes the cost of overlap between design and code, since the designer is not doing work the coder could do; and (2) it enhances the readability of the listing, since the design complements and is not redundant to the code.

I must acknowledge, however, that there is strong disagreement with my preference. In particular, the DoD detail design documents frequently descend to the completeness of a code-to recipe.

Moving further along the path of design documentation, we come to the NBS data base specification and its DoD equivalent.

NBS Data Base Specification

1. General information
   1.1 Summary
   1.2 Environment
   1.3 References
2. Description
   2.1 Identification
   2.2 Using software
   2.3 Conventions
   2.4 Special instructions
   2.5 Support software
3. Logical characteristics
4. Physical characteristics
   4.1 Storage
   4.2 Access
   4.3 Design considerations

DoD Data Base Design Document

1. Scope
2. Referenced documents
3. Requirements
   3.1 Data base management systems overview
   3.2 Data base structure (description, file, interrelationships by file)
   3.3 Data base file design (file record, field, item definitions, references)

4,5. No content

6. Notes

10. Appendices

Bearing in mind that a data base may serve a collection of computer programs, breaking this document out into a separate one makes a great deal of sense. Now the data base design, both its logical and physical aspects, can be expressed independently of any of the (several?) programs that may utilize it.

But again there are severe differences between the form and content of the NBS and DoD documents. DoD makes provision for discussing the data base management system, then moves to a very hierarchical description of the structure of the data "files." NBS approaches the problem with a more overview-oriented outline. However, there is sufficient latitude in both outlines that their content *could* end up being similar.

There is one final possible level of design documentation, one that is probably unnecessary for small software projects but absolutely essential for huge ones. This is the *interface design document,* or IDD. If an IDD is prepared, it will be written very early in the design process (in order to document all the interfaces of the software system before design of the components that must satisfy those interfaces gets underway).

DoD Interface Design Document

1. Scope
2. Referenced documents
3. Requirements
   - 3.X (Name X) Interface
     - 3.X.1 Summary
     - 3.X.2 Item summary
     - 3.X.3 Item formats

4,5. No content

6. Notes

10. Appendices

It must be remembered here that the essential role of the IDD is to define and control all interfaces at the outset of design so that all subsequent design can proceed from a common baseline. The interfaces may include not just software-software component interfaces but software-hardware and software-human interfaces as well. Looked at in that light, the IDD becomes quite an important document, not just because it controls interfaces, but because it gives them visibility and accessibility as well.

Here, then, we see that design documentation is an umbrella covering a variety of concepts:

- Design overview information
- Design assists
- Functional design documents

- Detail design documents
- Design embedded in code as commentary
- Data base design documents
- Interface control document

The final document describing a design may consist of only one or two volumes, but the process of getting there—like the design process itself—may be quite complex.

Coding Documentation. As the construction of a software product evolves from systems analysis into design and then into coding, the nature of the task evolves as well. Systems (requirements) analysis is based on human communication and problem technology; design, on thought and solution technology; and the coding phase, on language and the computer.

Because of these different orientations, the documentation product of the coding phase is significantly different from the documentation products of the earlier phases. First and foremost, the documentation product of the coding phase is the listing of the as-coded program product. The listing must describe not only a *working* program product but a *readable* and *understandable* program product as well.

Readability and understandability are goals undertaken on behalf of the eventual software maintainer rather than the software developer. As a result, there is a great temptation on the part of the developer to place considerably higher priority on getting the program working rather than making it understandable. As with many other maintenance-oriented decisions, this is a short-term decision that fails to be cost-effective in the long term.

What constitutes a readable and understandable program listing?

Most important is a well-modularized program, with separable functions produced as callable modules so that the reader of the program can read that function once and understand its role every place it is called. Next most important is a well-structured program, one whose logic flows smoothly and largely in a forward direction, its readability assisted by indentations keyed to program logic.

Data and logic names must be carefully chosen so that the meaning is inherent in the name—DO VALIDITY TEST has a clear meaning, but DOVT does not; ERROR FLAG explains its own role, but ERFL does not. With this goal in mind, it is often useful to let subroutines and procedures be named as verbs, since they produce action, and to let data items be nouns, since actions are performed on them. (Some companies require names to be chosen based on the structure, rather than the meaning, of an entity (e.g., all names in program XYZ must be of the form XYZ.ABC). This approach helps the reader of a program to follow its structure, but helps very little in understanding its function.)

Finally, the readable and understandable program product should contain clarifying commentary. If the modules and structure and program-naming conventions are still not enough to make the program self-documenting, then carefully chosen comments must be added. One solution to a large part of the commentary problem is to embed the computer-readable, high-level design in the code, as we discussed in the preceding section. This still may not be enough, however. Commentary must be sufficient to fill the following needs:

1. To define the role of each program module—its function, its inputs and outputs, its assumptions, limitations and restrictions, its error processes, and historical information—the developer's name, the date of development and the date, purpose, and implementor of each change.
2. To define the role of each program subfunction (straight sequence of code, loop, begin-end block, etc.).
3. To define each interface, both as to requirements for satisfying the interface and the nature of the interface users.
4. To define each data variable, both aggregate and simple items, as to its role and meaning.
5. To explain all complex or anomalous sections of code.

It should also be noted that too much commentary and erroneous commentary are worse than none at all.

The rudiments of readable and understandable code are well understood by most programmers. The problem lies in the doing of it, not in failing to know what to do. The solution to the problem is one of motivation. Programmers should be asked, at or near the end of program checkout, to make one last pass over the program from the point of view of readability and to add the elements we have discussed above that were not added during development. Clearly it is preferable to solve this problem during the initial writing of the code, since modularity and structure (for example) are hard to add on after the fact. But since that approach is usually not enough, the extra pass is often necessary. This pass may be part of the peer review process, an oral communication approach, which we wil discuss later in Section 3.2.3.3.

Contemporary technology does not always support the creation of readable and understandable programs. The Basic programming language inhibits modularity, for example, and Fortran inhibits readable naming conventions. There are two ways to deal with this problem: Avoid technologies mired in the old ways, or use the technology as well as you can. It is important to ensure that the inadequacies of a technology are not used as an excuse for giving up on the achievement of readability and understandability.

In addition to the role of the program listing as coding documentation, there is one other kind of coding documentation that is sometimes used, especially on large software projects. It is called the *unit development folder*

(UDF) (see TRW's description of their UDF in [GLASS82]), and it is rather different from the kind of documentation we have discussed up until now.

The UDF is a folder, a repository for a loose collection of related information, rather than a document. Into the UDF is put anything relevant to a particular program unit (a unit may be considered to be some isolatable fraction of a total program product, usually a compilable program or subprogram). The UDF contains at least the following: a description of the unit; the activities and schedule for the creation of the unit; other documentation for the unit (requirements, design, test plan, etc.); the current (and perhaps historical) listing(s) of the unit; information describing how the unit is used and how it is configuration managed; a log of error reports, corrections, and status; and any other design and implementation notes. Several companies use UDFs, but the idea has been best explained in the literature by TRW. Their outline of a UDF follows:

TRW Unit Development Folder

0. Cover sheet and schedule
1. Requirements information
2. Current working-design information
3. A list of the testable functional capabilities of the unit
4. Source code listing
5. Test plan
6. Results of review of the test plan
7. Test case results
8. Problem reports
9. Notes

The advantage of the UDF approach is that it provides a place to keep things that might otherwise not be kept at all, such as test case results; it also ensures that all information relevant to a unit will be kept together and thus will be able to be referenced.

The primary activity of the coding phase is coding, so we have seen a change during this phase in the nature of the documentation for communication. The program listing, which is the natural focus of the coding phase, gets a lot of attention as a documentation product as well; and the loose collection of documentation pertinent to the coding process is collected and organized into a unit development folder. Note that the listing is really not a transient program document, since it will last the length of the product. The UDF probably is transient, unless it is kept up to date during maintenance of the unit.

Testing Documentation. Does the software product do what it is supposed to do? That is the question that is explored in the test phase of software development. For a straightforward software product, testing is usually straightforward also. But for a complex software product, testing complexity escalates rapidly. Some excellent descriptions of how to test are found in [GLASS79], [MYER76], and [MYER79].

As testing complexity escalates, the need for testing documentation emerges. Testing activity must be designed to answer such questions as those that follow, and a document called the *test plan* is written to provide those answers. Sometimes the test plan is broken into two documents: The first, the test plan, tells *what* testing will be conducted; and the second, the *test procedure,* tells *how* those tests will be conducted. In either case, there is also a *test report,* which documents the results of the tests.

A test plan answers the following kinds of questions:

1. What test philosophy or combination of test philosophies is to be used? Requirements-driven ("black box") or structure-driven ("white box")? Analysis (such as proof of correctness) or testing? Top-down or bottom-up?
2. How thorough is the testing to be? All requirements? All structure? All inputs? All combinations of requirements or structure or inputs? All error conditions?
3. How will the degree of thoroughness be measured?
4. What *are* the tests? Inputs? Expected outputs? Tolerances on expected outputs?
5. How do the tests correlate with the testing philosophy: Which tests test which requirements? Which structure? Which inputs? Which combinations?
6. What facilities and resources are needed for the testing? Where? When?
7. What procedures and approvals are needed for the testing?
8. What people, in what roles, are needed for the testing?

Where do the answers to these questions come from? First, they come from a thorough analysis of the requirements of the software product, keeping testability in mind; then from a thorough analysis of the structure of the software product, focusing on how to build a test case that exercises a given structural element; and then, correlating those findings, from the engineering of a set of test cases that optimally exercise as many requirements (preferably, all) and as much structure (preferably, at least 80%) as possible.

What form might such documents take? The NBS approach uses two documents, a Test Plan and a Test Analysis Report. DOD-STD-2167 contains descriptions of four documents, the Test Plan, Test Description, Test Procedures, and Test Report. Those outlines follow.

NBS Test Plan

1. General information
   - 1.1 Summary
   - 1.2 Environment and pretest background
   - 1.3 References
2. Plan
   - 2.1 Software description
   - 2.2 Milestones
   - 2.3 Testing (one section per location)
     - 2.3.1 Schedule
     - 2.3.2 Requirements
     - 2.3.3 Testing materials
     - 2.3.4 Test training
3. Specifications and evaluation
   - 3.1 Specifications
     - 3.1.1 Requirements
     - 3.1.2 Software functions
     - 3.1.3 Test/function relationships
     - 3.1.4 Test progression
   - 3.2 Methods and constraints
     - 3.2.1 Methodology
     - 3.2.2 Conditions
     - 3.2.3 Extent
     - 3.2.4 Data recording
     - 3.2.5 Constraints
   - 3.3 Evaluation
     - 3.3.1 Criteria
     - 3.3.2 Data reduction
4. Test description (one per test)
   - 4.i Test
     - 4.i.1 Control
     - 4.i.2 Inputs
     - 4.i.3 Outputs
     - 4.i.4 Procedures

DoD Software Test Plan

1. Scope
2. Referenced documents
3. Plans for informal testing
   - 3.1 Unit testing (requirements, responsibilities, schedule)
   - 3.2 Integration and test planning (requirements, responsibilities, test classes, schedules)
   - 3.3 Resources required for informal testing
4. Plans for formal testing
   - 4.1 Formal test requirements
   - 4.2 Formal test responsibilities
   - 4.3 Formal test classes
   - 4.4 Formal tests
   - 4.5 Formal test levels
   - 4.6 Formal test summary
   - 4.7 Formal test schedule
   - 4.8 Data recording, reduction, and analysis
   - 4.9 Formal test reports
   - 4.10 Resources required for formal testing
5. Test planning assumptions and constraints
6. Notes

10\. Appendices

DoD Software Test Description

1. Scope
2. Referenced documents
3. Formal test descriptions
   - 3.X Formal test X
     - 3.X.Y Test case Y (initialization, input, intermediate

DoD Software Test Description

test results, output, evaluation criteria)

4. Assumptions and constraints
5. No content
6. Notes
10. Appendices

DoD Software Test Procedure

1. Scope
2. Referenced documents
3. Test schedule and procedures
   3.1 Schedule
   3.2 Pretest procedures
   3.3 Test procedures
   3.4 Data reduction and data analysis procedures
4. Assumptions and constraints
5. No content
6. Notes
10. Appendices

The DoD is more thorough here, with separate documents for planning the test, defining specific tests, and discussing how they will be carried out. The NBS approach of using one document is more concise.

As for test result documentation, the prime goal is to provide a written record of how the testing went. Was it a success? A conditional success? What conditions? A failure? What workarounds were employed? What happens next? Are we unconditionally through? Conditionally through, with reruns? Do we start over from scratch? What recommendations are made? What retest schedule or estimates are there? The Test Results document should answer all these questions.

NBS Test Analysis Report

1. General information
   1.1 Summary
   1.2 Environment
   1.3 References

DoD Software Test Report

1. Scope
2. Referenced documents
3. Test report
   3.1 Summary of tests

2. Test results and findings
   2.i Test (one per test)
      2.i.1 Dynamic data performance
      2.i.2 Static data performance
3. Software function findings
   3.i Function (one per function)
      3.i.1 Performance
      3.i.2 Limits
4. Analysis summary
   4.1 Capabilities
   4.2 Deficiencies
   4.3 Recommendations and estimates

   3.2 Test history
   3.3 Test results
      3.3.X Formal test X
   3.4 Test evaluation and recommendations
4. Deviations
5. No content
6. Notes
10. Appendices

There is an interesting philosophical problem with these outlines. Both are thorough, covering each test in detail. Preferable, however, would be an exception report, focusing on problems and solutions and relegating test detail to an appendix or to references to the test plan.

Test documentation is probably the least read of all software documentation. Whereas in the preceding life-cycle phases the documentation at the end of one phase served as a baseline for the next, in testing, the documents—especially the test results document—serve as more of a historical record. As with all transient documentation, this fact of temporal usage does not negate the value of the document, it helps only to keep that value in perspective.

Other Documentation. The possibilities for the creation of other software documentation by the harried software professional are enormous. The DoD standards, for example, define these additional possibilities:

- Software configuration management plan
- Software quality evaluation plan
- Software standards and procedures manual
- Computer support diagnostic manual
- Computer resources integration support document

The IEEE is working on, or has defined, some of these:

- A standard for system design description language
- A standard for information model description language

- A standard for software verification and validation plans
- A standard for software development plans
- A standard for user documentation
- A standard for quality assurance plans
- A standard for software test documentation
- A standard for software configuration management plans

As the complexity of a software project increases, the need for these documents becomes increasingly apparent. The configuration management plan, some sort of quality plan, and a standards and procedures manual are part of even medium-sized software projects, for example.

In this book, however, we have chosen to include only the "mainline" software documents. The reader who wants to learn more about the DoD documents should see Appendix A.2; about the IEEE work, [IEEE84] or the reference in Section 3.2.2.4.

3.2.2.6 Permanent Documentation. Documentation that is permanent is intended to last the life of the software product. It may be delivered at a certain event, such as a user manual at a design review, but once delivered and reviewed, its usefulness has just begun.

The most obvious example of permanent documentation is the user manual. We have all seen user manuals, probably for some software support tool such as an operating system, a compiler, or a library of software parts. Our first exposure to a user manual is typically tutorial—we need to read the manual, usually from beginning to end, to find out how to use the software product. After that, the exposures are more commonly reference ones—we need to look up in the manual a fact that has slipped our mind, such as the exact syntax for a piece of command language or programming language. As we continue to use the product, those exposures become less and less frequent.

This declining usage curve of a permanent document does not detract from its permanence, however. If we interrupt our usage of product A for a period of time to use a different operating system or programming language, when we return to use product A again we may well need to repeat the learning cycle and therefore start over again on the documentation usage curve. Thus the potential for both tutorial and reference usage of a permanent document by one or many readers remains present during the life of the software product.

The documentation that follows is the implementation documentation that in practice is treated as permanent.

The *user manual* is written from the point of view of the user and tells everything that needs to be known about how to use the product. The rationale for its being a permanent document has already been presented.

The *operations manual* is written from the point of view of a computer operator and tells everything that an operator needs to know to facilitate proper execution of the product. It is a permanent document for the same kinds of reasons that a user manual is permanent.

The *maintenance manual* is written from the point of view of the maintainer and tells how the product functions internally. It serves as a basis for all maintenance activities, both repair and enhancement. It is usually true for software products that active maintenance parallels usage. That is, as users discover product errors (presumably as time goes on, they are fewer and more obscure), there must be maintenance to repair them. And as users discover areas where product functionality can be improved, there must be maintenance to make those improvements (this kind of maintenance may decline or increase over time). Since the maintenance activity itself is ongoing, the maintenance manual is almost always a permanent piece of documentation.

The fourth category of permanent documentation is the *marketing material*. This is the tool for convincing potential users that the software product is worth using. It may be as simple as an in-house memo announcing the availability and value of the product or as complex as a polished and expensive brochure that argues to the world at large that the product is worth using (and buying). Although the form of the marketing manual may differ dramatically, the nature and usage of it does not. It is the first piece of documentation to which any potential new user is exposed, and this process continues as long as there are new users.

User Manual. What does the user need to know in order to make the software product useful? That is the question the user manual must answer.

The question can be broken into several more detailed questions:

1. What capabilities does the product offer?
2. How and where can the product be accessed?
3. What input must be prepared to use the product?
4. What output will be produced by a product run, and how is the output interpreted?
5. What limitations and restrictions does the product have?
6. What resources does the product use (time, main memory, external storage)?
7. What error diagnostics are there, and how should the user respond to them?

The answers to these questions come from an intimate knowledge of the requirements for the software product and from the product itself. For example, capabilities and inputs are probably specified in the requirements spec, whereas limitations and resource utilization may be known only by the implementors of the product.

The user manual is probably the best example of the reference-tutorial document dichotomy mentioned earlier, in Section 3.2.2.2. There are learning costs associated with the initial use of a software product; the tutorial manual addresses that problem. Continued use of a software product requires fast access to detail-level information; the reference manual addresses that problem. All the ramifications of on-line training, help functions, and self-teaching programs come into play here. The world of the user manual is currently dynamic, perhaps even unstable.

There are good reasons (or bad, depending upon your viewpoint) for this instability. Over the years, in spite of the importance of the user manual, some very bad user manuals have been written. It is almost as if software people have found it impossible to think enough like a user to write the kind of manuals users need. Various solutions to this problem have been tried, the most common being the use of technical writers to prepare user documents. This practice tends to produce a very readable manual but creates two new problems. For one, the technical writer can easily find the answers to the key user manual questions when they are answered in another spec (e.g., the requirements spec); but those questions that can be answered only by understanding the software product itself are beyond the direct reach of the technical writer. This obstacle gives rise to the second new problem, that the technical writer must have some of the implementation team's time in order to get that class of questions answered. This is not a bad situation, but it does mean that at least some portion of the implementor's time must be devoted to user-manual preparation even if a technical writer has responsibility for the document.

What constitutes a bad user manual? There are the obvious things, like poor organization or poor writing. But more commonly, the problem is more subtle. The usual problem with a bad user manual is that it is trying to do too many things. Many bad user manuals contain information that the implementor cares about, but the user does not (for example, what programming language or data base system was used to create the program). Other bad user manuals contain marketing puffery intended to impress rather than assist the user (for example, saying that the program is "fast" or "simple"). It is vital to keep in mind at all times who the user manual is being written for—the user.

There is another, more surprising, reason why so many bad user manuals have been written. Little emphasis has been placed, in some circles, on the value of a good user manual. Until recently, the DoD documentation standards treated the user manual almost as an afterthought. That is one of the reasons why this book makes such a distinction between permanent and transient documents. The old DoD approach tended to treat the transient documents that support project development milestones as being more important than the permanent documents that are simply product deliverables.

Let us take a look at the NBS and DoD user-manual outlines.

NBS User Manual

1. General information
   - 1.1 Summary
   - 1.2 Environment
   - 1.3 References
2. Application
   - 2.1 Description
   - 2.2 Operation
   - 2.3 Equipment
   - 2.4 Structure
   - 2.5 Performance
   - 2.6 Data base
   - 2.7 Inputs, processing, outputs
3. Procedures and requirements
   - 3.1 Initiation
   - 3.2 Input
     - 3.2.1 Input formats
     - 3.2.2 Sample inputs
   - 3.3 Output
     - 3.3.1 Output formats
     - 3.3.2 Sample outputs
   - 3.4 Error and recovery
   - 3.5 File query

DoD User's Manual

1. Scope
2. Referenced documents
3. Instructions for use
   - 3.X Capability X
     - 3.X.Y Function Y (initialization, execution options, user inputs, system inputs, execution, termination, restart, outputs, interrelationships)
4. Errors
   - 4.X Error message X
5. Diagnostic features
6. Notes
10. Appendices

Both outlines start out in a semantically similar way, if you are willing to see "application" and "capabilities" as topic headings addressing the same ground. Both go on to deal with the vital usage details under "procedures and requirements" or "instructions for use." But NBS tempts the writer toward irrelevancies, with sections titled "structure" and "data base," which might result in descriptions of internal program organization of no interest to the user. The dilemma here is that all the outline-specified information is important, but not all of it is important in a user manual.

There is another, more subtle, dilemma. Both outlines presented here could be useful for structuring user information, but they tend to be stodgy and dull. It might be better, for example, to use this structure as a list of topics to be covered, but to cover them in a way that also supports the following:

- Tutorial learning and/or reference use
- Early user overviews of the product
- Interesting, perhaps graphics-supported usage descriptions
- A lively writing style

The student was angry. The user manual he had handed in was just the kind he was used to writing at work; it even fulfilled the government contractual requirements for his project there.

But it was all wrong for this assignment. Now his product was a commercial piece of microcomputer software, destined for a marketplace (if all went well) of tens of thousands of people. And people in that marketplace are used to friendly, reasonably pretty, easy-to-use documents that lead them carefully and thoroughly by the hand through the steps necessary to make the product work. The user manual he had turned in was stodgy, poorly focused, and encumbered by lots of introductory paragraphs that delayed the user in getting to the meat of the subject. In short, it was a by-the-numbers document designed for a small component in a big system, with readers who couldn't expect and wouldn't get friendly documents.

The student wouldn't, or couldn't, understand. How could something that passed all the government tests at work get a failing grade here in the classroom?

The advent of the personal computer era may mark the onset of a solution to the user manual problem. Mass computer products for the computer-naive customer must solve the problem of bad or dull user manuals or face economic failure. The result is that some bad user documents are still being produced, but some brilliantly innovative approaches are being tried as well. Here especially, the traditional mainframe documentor may have a lot to learn from his or her (youthful) microcomputer brethren.

Operations Manual. What does a computer operator need to know in order to make the software product work? That is the question the operations manual must answer.

There are some historical implications to this question. To those computer people who are accustomed to timesharing or personal computing, for example, the question may not make sense. In those circumstances, the user of the software product is its operator, and so "operations" documentation properly belongs in the user manual. It is in the realm of batch-oriented software or software with complex resource or scheduling requirements that a separate operations manual begins to make sense. Then the task of the operations manual is to inform the operations personnel of those complexities in such a way that the correct procedures for running the software will be followed.

Subordinate questions that must be answered by an operations manual include the following:

1. How is the software product initiated?
2. What are its unique operational requirements—data, devices, other resources?
3. How is the execution of the software product facilitated and monitored?
4. How is unsuccessful execution detected, and what should be done about it?
5. How is successful execution detected, and how is a run terminated?
6. What security precautions must be taken?
7. Is the job initiated by a user (on demand) or by operations (on schedule)? If by operations:
    a. What is the schedule?
    b. What interrelationships does this job have with others?
    c. What input data are required, and where do they come from?
    d. How is the output data separated and distributed?
    e. What kinds of data control must be imposed?
    f. How does the operator-user obtain the necessary user manual information?

It is important to point out once again that in many circumstances an operations manual is unnecessary. Where it *is* necessary, it is permanent documentation, since it is useful for the life of the product.

Where do the answers to all these questions come from? They come from the same sources as the user manual information—the product requirements and from the product itself. It is entirely possible and appropriate for the person who prepares the user manual to prepare the operations manual as well. While gathering material for inclusion in either manual, that person must keep in mind the nature of the intended reader or user of the manual. In general, a user and an operator need to be told rather different kinds of things and in rather different ways. An operator, for instance, may need a "cookbook" approach that leads him or her rapidly, simply, and with no ambiguity through the series of steps necessary to operate the software.

The form that an operations manual might take is presented below.

NBS Operations Manual

1. General information
    1.1 Summary
    1.2 Environment
    1.3 References
2. Overview
    2.1 Software organization
    2.2 Program inventory
    2.3 File inventory

DoD Computer System Operator's Manual

1. Scope
2. Referenced documents
3. Computer system operations
    3.1 Preparation and setup
    3.2 Operating procedures
    3.3 Input and output
    3.4 Monitoring procedures
    3.5 Off-line routines

NBS Operations Manual

3. Description of runs
   3.1 Run inventory
   3.2 Run progression
   3.3 Run description I
      3.3.1 Control inputs
      3.3.2 Operating information
      3.3.3 Input-output files
      3.3.4 Output reports
      3.3.5 Reproduced output reports
      3.3.6 Restart/recovery procedures
4. Non-routine procedures
5. Remote operations

DoD Computer System Operator's Manual

   3.6 Recovery procedures
   3.7 Special procedures
4. Diagnostic features
5. No content
6. Notes
10. Appendices

The basic content of the two manuals may be the same, but NBS dabbles in extraneous matters. Should the NBS operator understand the "software organization" (that is, how the software is structured)? In some circumstances, the answer to this question might be yes, but to make it organizationally required content in all operations manuals is presumptuous and perhaps even dangerous.

Thus once again the "standard" outlines for document organization are useful but must be taken with a fairly heavy dose of understanding, knowledge, and common sense.

Maintenance Manual. What does the maintainer need to know in order to keep the software product useful to the user? This is the question the maintenance manual must answer.

There are some interesting implications to this question. First, notice that the maintenance manual is written for the maintainer. This means that, unlike many of the preceding software documents, it is written by and for people who understand software and speak at least some "computerese." No elaborate explanations of common computer terms and concepts need be provided; on the other hand, the technical meat of the document must be presented in depth and correctly.

Second, notice that the maintainer is providing a service to the user. The goal of software maintenance—and, therefore, of the maintenance manual—is to keep the user satisfied with the function and performance of the software product. This means that the maintenance manual must provide sufficient information not only to allow the maintainer to understand the product but also to allow him or her to modify it to correct errors, to add capability, or to improve performance. This is no small task. Simply detailing the function of a software product is an enormous and often onerous task. Doing that task in such a way that the maintainer is provided with a crystal ball that potentially allows revision of the product to meet future goals makes the task considerably more complicated.

Because of all these requirements, the maintenance manual has become a controversial piece of documentation. Based on surveys taken at software maintenance seminars I have presented, I would estimate that less than 10% of software products are supported by any maintenance manual at all. At the same time, DoD requirements often result in maintenance manuals that contain elaborate levels of detail and increase the cost of the product by at least half again. The practitioner's state of the art, then, is one of extremes—no manual at all, or one of enormous cost and content. Tangled in this controversy is the question of what is actually being maintained, which was discussed earlier in the book. For those who espouse the belief that maintenance should involve not just changes to the program, but changes to all the documents and analysis that led to the program, all those prior documents become part of the maintenance documentation. In that case, maintenance documentation takes on a whole new dimension.

There is yet another view of maintenance documentation, and it is the one I believe in. In this view, the maintenance manual should provide an overview of the software product sufficient to allow reading the listing to obtain the remaining levels of detail. This view reflects an important reality: No matter how well motivated the preparation of the maintenance document is, as time goes by and a software product is modified, the actual program and its maintenance documentation begin to diverge. Either someone forgets to update the manual at all, or the written description of the software change does not actually reflect the change itself. For this reason, software maintainers typically go straight to the product listing to begin a maintenance task, ignoring the (possibly) inaccurate manual altogether.

If the maintenance manual and the listing complement one another, however, then there is little or no redundancy and there is considerably reduced opportunity for digressions or errors. According to this viewpoint, the purpose of the manual itself should be to provide a top- and midlevel definition of the software (see Figure 3-18 for a hierarchical picture of these ideas):

1. *Overall structure description.* Words and pictures showing how the entire system hangs together. A functional block diagram, showing components, should be included. Better yet, this diagram would show (a) overlay structure, if any; (b) execution order; and (c) data flow. It may take several diagrams to achieve this.
2. *Overall data base summary.* Words and pictures showing the role of the

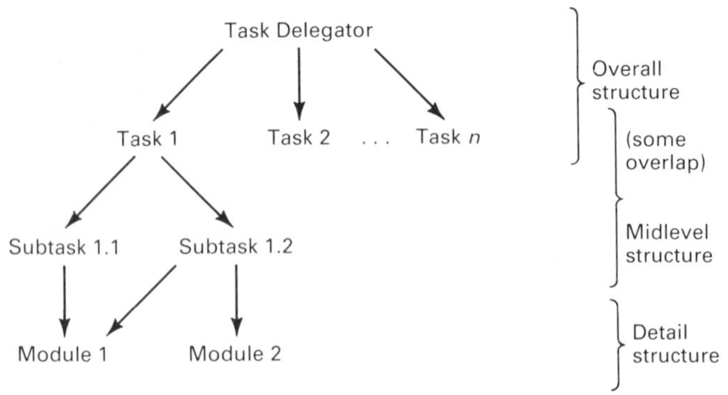

Figure 3-18 Typical software system, viewed as levels.

data base in the total systems: files and structures, and their content, layout, and usage.

3. *Design decision data.* Historical notes showing what design alternatives were entertained and how and why design decisions were made. (Often readable handwritten material, photocopied into the manual, is preferable to a retyped version, since retyping may decrease both the style and accuracy of the original.)
4. *Underlying philosophy.* Words explaining the beliefs of the designers and implementors that were the basis of the product creation process.
5. *Midlevel structure.* Words and pictures that bridge the gap between the summary of the overall structure, (1), and the detail level of the listing. This is a vital component of maintenance documentation, and it is the most commonly omitted. It is omitted because it is essentially an open-ended concept (for simple software, there may not be a midlevel structure; for complex software, there may be several middle levels), and it is sometimes easier to ignore open-ended problems than to solve them. We will return to this issue.
6. *Midlevel data base.* Words and pictures that show the data base(s) necessary to support the structure of (5).
7. *Pointers to detail-level information.* Links that tell the maintenance manual reader where to go in the listing to obtain the final levels of detail. Here we have the bridge that connects the manual and the listing.

This approach to the maintenance manual places a requirement on the software developer to create a readable product listing that can easily be referenced. The listing, to complement the manual properly, must contain (as discussed previously) the following:

1. *Good modularity.* Separate product functions must be satisfied by separate program components.

2. *Good structure.* Control logic must be distinguishable by crisp separation and clear indentation.
3. *Readable names.* The names chosen for data and logic items must support the reading of the code by being self-explanatory.
4. *Commentary.* The areas where readability is still lacking after (1), (2), and (3) must be supplemented by commentary.

It is important to pursue the notion of midlevel documentation a bit further. Recall that this material represents an open-ended problem and is rarely provided for in maintenance manuals. Fortunately, there is a model in another discipline for how to attack this problem.

For a complex engineering product like an airplane, the product is supported and defined by a series of blueprints. The problem of blueprint technology has a lot in common with the problem of maintenance documentation. At the top level, there is a single blueprint that depicts the total system. Within that total system, there are many components. Each of those components is elaborated in its own top-level blueprint, which points to the total system blueprint as its predecessor and is pointed to on the total system blueprint as one of many successors.

This process of levels of blueprint with interlinked connections continues. The total system blueprint, as we have seen, will point to a number of subordinate but still relatively high-level successor blueprints, each of which will point back to its predecessor and to its more detailed successors.

This, too, is an open-ended process. The nesting depth of the interlinked structure is defined by the complexity of the product. In Figure 3-19 there are

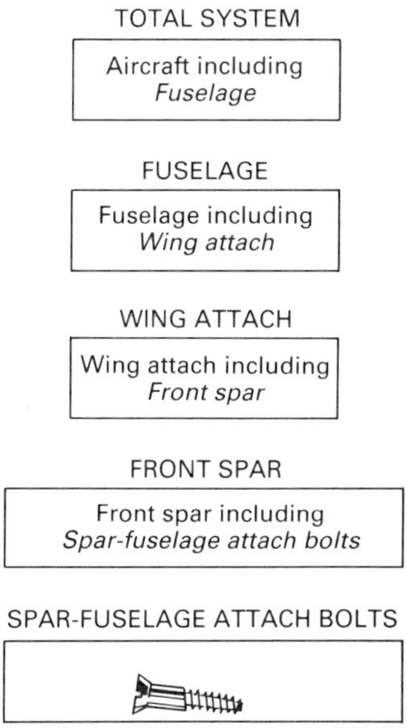

Figure 3-19 Blueprint hierarchy.

five levels from top to bottom. The true number of such levels would actually be whatever was necessary to define the product well enough to allow it to be manufactured.

Thus the software maintenance manual may need to be a complex series of interlinked "blueprints" (note that this is a top-down product representation), each of which defines a component of the software product sufficiently to allow it to be understood *at that level.* For all the complexity of this description, however, it is likely that the resulting document will still be simpler, as well as more useful, than the DoD "document in minutiae" approach, and it is unlikely that the resulting document will be more than two or three levels deep in most cases. Recall that the final level of detail, the "bolt itself," is deferred to the listing. In software, this level still contains a great deal of complexity (which is why readable listings are so important). (For a more complete discussion of maintenance documentation, see [GLASS80].)

The approach described here differs dramatically from what practitioners currently do and from the existing standards. Here, for contrast, are the standards:

NBS Program Maintenance Manual

1. General information
   - 1.1 Summary
   - 1.2 Environment
   - 1.3 References
2. Program descriptions
   - 2.i Program i description
     - 2.i.1 Problem and solution method
     - 2.i.2 Input
     - 2.i.3 Processing
     - 2.i.4 Output
     - 2.i.5 Interfaces
     - 2.i.6 Tables
     - 2.i.7 Run description
3. Operating environment
   - 3.1 Hardware
   - 3.2 Support software
     - 3.2.1 Operating system
     - 3.2.2 Compiler assembler
     - 3.2.3 Other software
   - 3.3 Data base

DoD Software Product Specification

1. Scope
2. Applicable documents
3. Requirements
   - 3.1 Top-level design*
   - 3.2 Detailed design*
   - 3.3 Listings
   - 3.4 Data base design*
   - 3.5 Data base listing
   - 3.6 Interface design*

4,5. No content

6. Notes

10. Appendices

*Reference to another document is allowed.

4. Maintenance procedures
   4.1 Programming conventions
   4.2 Verification procedures
   4.3 Error-correction procedures
   4.4 Special maintenance procedures
   4.5 Listings and flowcharts
   Data limitations

The change didn't work. I was devastated. It wasn't just that it didn't work. The program blew up even before it got a chance to work, in a section of code that I hadn't touched.

I was maintaining a huge compiler, and for weeks I had been carefully fashioning a modification to the code generator to allow it to generate code for a different target computer. I had written the code, gotten it reviewed, and been through it myself a dozen times, and I was sure it would work. When it didn't, I tried all the obvious things and got no new clues at all. In desperation, I started backing out pieces of the change, one by one.

Time passed, and the compiler still wouldn't budge past the place where it was blowing up. Finally, I took out the last piece of added code. It still didn't work! But it had to—I had restored it to the status it was in before I started modifying it. And it had worked then.

Suddenly, I remembered. In addition to changing the code, I had changed the link map around a little, too. That had to be the problem.

I studied the linkage procedure, and slowly I began to realize that one of the main data structures—the compiler's symbol table, in fact (for you compiler buffs out there!)—overlaid an area where some executable procedures also resided. The order of linkage was vital, and my tinkering had destroyed that. The way I had set it up, the symbol table was clobbering some needed procedural code.

I restored the old link procedure, started over again with my new code, and—voila! It did indeed work the first time, now. But I sure wished that someone had spent a little more time in the maintenance manual warning about the perils of changing the link map.

The standards differ dramatically. DoD essentially calls for a skeleton document to house the documents already produced during the design phase. The implication, of course, is that those early documents must be updated if necessary to match the as-built product.

Both standards provide for a description of multiple program components (NBS in Section 2.i, DoD in the referenced documents), but neither provides any mechanism for bridging the gap between that level of detail and the top level. Note, however, the important NBS emphasis on *how* maintenance is to be performed (Sections 3 and 4). By reusing the documents from early in the life cycle, the DoD fails to provide for this important part of the software maintenance manual.

Here then, we see controversy and turmoil—maintenance manuals rarely written or badly written or too-elaborately written or allowed to grow obsolete, and in fact important disagreements on what is being maintained and how much of the total product documentation should support maintenance. The one position upon which all would agree is that, whatever maintenance documentation is, it certainly belongs in the category "permanent."

Marketing Material. What will convince a prospective purchaser or user of a software product that obtaining it would be a wise choice? is the question the marketing material must answer.

> It was an important clue.
>
> The pages of the maintenance manual were yellowed and wrinkly, as if they had been around for awhile. But they weren't worn or pencil marked; it looked as though they hadn't been used very much.
>
> The maintenance programmer scanned the table of contents to find the section she needed and turned to the page describing the section of code she believed she needed to modify. The description was reasonably clear—it was a pleasant surprise, since in her experience most maintenance manuals were written hurriedly by people who believed (or whose management believed) that they had something better to do.
>
> With the maintenance manual open in front of her, she searched the listing until she found the code in question and began to read it. A frown crossed her face. The code didn't match the document.
>
> Her suspicions were confirmed. The maintenance manual, written in haste in the first place, had not been kept up to date. She checked the change log in the listing—sure enough, her section of code had been modified about 6 months after the manual came out. And no one had thought to change the maintenance manual.

The phrase *purchaser or user* in the previous paragraph is a clue that the target audience of marketing material is diverse and product-dependent. If the software product is built for sale, for example, the target audience is the entire software-user world (or at least that segment of that world that would find the product useful); then the marketing material may have all the cost and pizazz of a Madison Avenue blitz. But if the software product is built by an institution's software department for in-house use only, that does not mean there will not be or should not be marketing material—it means only that such material will take a more conservative form. Seen in this light, the announcement memo, which says "this product is now available to our users," is one form of marketing material.

It is important to realize that marketing material not only channels promotional material into a receptacle designed for that purpose, but it also channels promotional material out of inappropriate receptacles. It is common, for example, to find promotional phrases in user manuals, such as "this is the best XYZ around," "it is fast and reliable," "it will solve all your LMN problems." Those kinds of blatant statements are appropriate in marketing material (assuming they are supported by the necessary facts); in a user manual, they are offensive (if they are indeed factual, the user manual can make those same points by detailing functionality and presenting performance speeds and error rates).

Because marketing material is so product-dependent (and in fact environment-dependent), it is difficult to discuss in general terms. A glance at the marketing material for some other product type (e.g., cars or stereos) will quickly show that there is no form or even content standard for this kind of document; however, there are some categories of information that tend to be found in marketing materials:

- The strengths of the product
- The effectiveness of the product
- The user-friendliness of the product
- The uniqueness of the product
- The advanced state of the product
- The quality of the product
- The cost-effectiveness of the product
- The competitive benefits of use of the product
- The experience, knowledge, and stability of the product creators
- The support for the product—documentation, maintenance, and consultation

Notice that these categories are appropriate whether the resulting information is placed in a slick-paper brochure or an announcement memo; whether

The advertisement was beautiful. It was a multiple full-page spread with lots of colors, a good mix of words and space and graphics, and the text showed careful preparation. But it was all wrong.

It was an advertisement for microcomputer software, a brand new data base product. But the ad was placed in *Datamation* magazine. Microcomputer readers do not regularly read *Datamation.* To reach its intended audience, the ad should have been in *Byte* or *PC* or one of the other seemingly dozens of magazines oriented toward that marketplace.

The entrepreneur with more venture capital money than marketing knowledge had come out of the mainframe software world. He advertised in the journal he knew best. But it was the wrong one.

This is a story with a happy ending, however. The entrepreneur, poorer but wiser, refocused his next advertisements onto the right target. And his product rose to be the number two data base system in the marketplace.

it is accompanied by creative graphics or typed on standard typing paper; and whether the information is couched in emotion-inflaming phrases or itemized in a factual list.

The sky is no limit for the kinds of approaches to marketing materials. Because of this, especially if the material is part of an elaborate marketing campaign, it may be well to use marketing professionals in the preparation of marketing materials—market research professionals to target the appropriate audience; public relations or advertising professionals to create the appropriate approach; and typesetters and printers to translate the material into a quality product. These are skills not commonly found in software professionals.

All this effort may sound terribly expensive. It is, of course, far too expensive for that in-house product announcement memo. But in the modern world of software products—where the market is vast, the sales potential is enormous, and the competition is vigorous—entrepreneurs say that it takes more than a quarter of a million dollars to launch a software-product marketing campaign. This statement, of course, is true primarily for software in the broad microcomputer marketplace; in the mainframe and mini world, the sales volumes are considerably smaller and the marketing approach is more targeted. However, in all those worlds the quality of the marketing material is still perceived as being a clue to the quality of the software product. That means that the cost of the material itself must be balanced against the cost of failing to sell the product!

In this section, we have primarily discussed marketing material. That material is only part of a marketing campaign. For the in-house product, that campaign may also include an announcement meeting, product demonstrations, and selection of advance users who will help spread the word. For the product for sale, that campaign may also include magazine and television advertisements, presentations at computer shows and symposia, and direct mail distribution of the marketing materials. In short, a marketing campaign can and should utilize all the written *and* oral communication skills discussed in this book.

3.2.3 Implementation Spoken Communication

There is a lot of written documentation that accompanies the development and use of a software product. But there is a lot of spoken communication inherent in the process, as well.

As the project evolves, the written documentation is never complete enough to convey the information it is supposed to. Inevitably, a detail or an ambiguity can be understood only by talking to the information source.

As the testing proceeds, a mysterious bug may occur that the developer, despite the full application of a potent analytical mind, cannot fathom. Explaining that bug to a colleague is often the next step in the debugging process; the fresh viewpoint necessary to make an explanation of the problem, or the fresh viewpoint of the colleague, often makes the problem become clear. At predefined milestones, formal reviews are held to expose project progress to peers, managers, or customers. In times of trouble, audits are conducted to solve problems. As team harmony develops, informal reviews and walkthroughs are used.

In short, the spoken communication processes are probably as prevalent and as vital as the written ones.

3.2.3.1 Formal Reviews. The developers of a software product need to pause periodically in the development process and evaluate how they are doing. Formal reviews are a way of making sure that happens, and they ensure that an outside look supplements the developers' biased inside one.

Formal reviews are usually scheduled into the development process from the beginning. The number of reviews held varies from environment to environment and project to project—for critical or large software, there may be four or more; for smaller or noncritical software, there may be two or fewer.

The reviews are generally held at milestones in the product development.

- A *requirements review* may be held when the final requirements definition is ready to be baselined.
- A *preliminary design review* may be held after the high-level design has been completed, to make sure it is on track with the requirements.
- A *critical design review* may be held before the design is translated into code, to make sure that good code is not written to a bad design.

- A *test review* may be held after unit testing is complete and before more elaborate testing, to make sure that the testing is necessary and sufficient.
- An *acceptance test review* may be held to make a final inspection of the product and its results.

Such reviews generally have several characteristics in common: They are scheduled in advance, they are run by a predefined agenda, they are attended by a predefined attendance list; and the action taken is either approval to proceed, approval to proceed with changes, or a stop-work decision (the latter rarely occurs).

Attendees at formal reviews generally run the full spectrum from technical peers, to developmental and quality assurance management, to customers and/or their representatives. Early in the life cycle the emphasis is heavy on customer participation; as the development proceeds, the implementation details tend to be of less interest to customers, and the attendance focuses more on peers.

The level of the review and its accomplishments may well be determined by who is invited. If there is a heavy concentration of peer invitees, then technical details will likely be attentively covered but the overview may not. If managers and customers predominate, the overview will be well analyzed but the details probably will not. Thus it is important to choose an attendee mix that matches the goals of the review or to hold more than one review at some milestones to cover more than one level of information.

There are two rather different approaches to the conduct of a formal review. The more traditional review is a stand-up lecture process, where the presenter—usually the knwoledgeable technical person—makes a presentation, and the attendees respond with questions, comments, and criticism.

At the other extreme is the review where the review material is distributed to the attendees in advance, they read it and present written questions, comments, and critiques, and the review meeting itself covers the responses to the written critiques. The traditional method obviously is a lower-budget approach, since the attendee time expenditure is confined to the meeting itself. The written-material approach tends to move more swiftly into problem areas and cover more ground. Thus the choice is effectively between a low-cost and a high-benefit approach.

An elaborate description of what the Department of Defense expects in software formal reviews and audits may be found in [DOD1521].

3.2.3.2 Audits. Periodic pauses for review in the software development process may not be enough. Problems may arise that require immediate attention and that cannot wait for a scheduled review. The *problem audit* is one response to this situation.

Since problem audits are often called in response to an emergency situation, it is difficult to define in general terms what should or will happen. Such an audit usually begins with an information-gathering phase, where the audit team gets a clear definition of the problem and what is necessary to solve it. This process involves talking to people at all levels of the project and reading whatever documentation exists. Often it involves comparing the technical plan for the project, if there is one, with the actual progress of the project, looking especially for deviations. For a project of some complexity, it may not be possible to process all the information that is available. In this case, sampling methods may be used to gain a broad picture at minimal expense.

The problem audit is not the only kind of audit. Some software methodologies call for scheduled audits—the *functional configuration audit* and the *physical configuration audit*—to occur at the time of product delivery. The functional audit is designed to review product performance by looking at test results, and the physical audit looks at the product itself by review of listings and documentation. Other such "general" audits may be scheduled to supplement the review process.

Audits may be conducted for specialized purposes, such as to determine the adequacy of the assigned technical or management personnel, or their training. The feasibility study is a kind of audit performed early in the project to determine if the situation warrants proceeding with the project. Thus audits are called for an enormous variety of reasons and may therefore take many forms.

If the audit is not a scheduled one, then someone must take responsibility for calling it. Generally this is a manager sufficiently far up the hierarchy to have the authority to do so or a *quality assurance* organization whose ongoing work gives them reason to believe an audit may be necessary. Participants in an audit must be top-level technologists and nimble managers who are capable and who have the confidence of the project key people, to create a high likelihood that their findings will be worthwhile and accepted.

The result of an audit is an audit report, perhaps presented in writing or verbally or both. An outline for such a report, from [BRYAN82], is presented in Table 3-1. The report must cover at least these areas: a statement of the problem, a description of the audit process, the audit findings, and recommendations. Specific categories of findings are suggested in the figure; they may or may not apply to a specific audit situation.

The distribution of the audit report should be limited to those with a need to know. It should be presented to the manager who called the audit, and usually as well to at least the management level of the subject of the audit. However, in some cases it may be wise to present only the recommendations to the audit-subject management, since the other content may be personal or even inflammatory.

Audits are a difficult form of communication, not because of what they are but because of the circumstances surrounding them. In a problem audit especially, the audit may need to be confrontational if some members of the

TABLE 3-1 Software Audit Report Outline

1. Introduction
   1.1 Purpose (of report)
   1.2 Identification (of software audited)
   1.3 Project references
   1.4 Overview (of report)
2. References
3. Procedure (for audit)
4. Findings
   4.1 Conformance with standards
   4.2 Configuration identification
   4.3 Results of requirements evaluation
   4.4 Traceability matrix (requirements to product)
   4.5 Results of verification
   4.6 Results of validation
   4.7 Configuration status accounting (list of components changed as a result of the audit)
5. Conclusions
6. Recommendations

Note: This outline is taken from an article on software quality [BRYAN82]; it takes a configuration management approach to the audit.

project team attempt to inhibit the information-gathering process. Generally, however, the audit team will choose a friendly mode of operation and defer confrontation to those who must act on its findings.

3.2.3.3 Informal Reviews and Walkthroughs. The formal review process is an effective method for steering a project in the direction of its correct goals. Informal reviews are another important process that can be used to supplement the formal review.

There are various names for such informal reviews, including *walkthroughs* and *peer reviews.* The underlying reason for informal reviews, like the underlying reason for the formal review, is that several minds are more likely to see the project clearly.

Amazing success has been claimed for informal reviews. "Walkthroughs are one of the most effective ways known to improve the quality of a computer program," says [YOURDON77]. In fact, "programming groups using walkthroughs report . . . reductions in the number of errors . . . by as much as a factor of 10." "The payoff is tremendous. If I had it to do over, I would insist on independent code inspection as a mandatory part of the verification process for the entire program," says [SPECTOR84].

The walkthrough process is simple. Technological peers, often in teams of two to four, take a line-by-line look at the review material, considering it in as much technical depth as they are able. The technical material may be, in turn, the requirements specification, the design, the code, or the test cases.

I was in trouble. My integrity and my on-the-job wisdom were in conflict.

The audit team I had joined had completed its audit. There was a communication problem at the upper management level, we had concluded, between our software subcontractor and our company. We had even made a presentation of our findings to the subcontractor before we ended the audit and came home.

But our upper manager—the one who had been faulted, the one who had appointed the audit team—wouldn't accept the audit finding; in fact, the manager was directing us to change the audit conclusions. The number-one person on the audit team, not noted for integrity, was going to do it.

I felt like a fool. The conclusions we had so carefully wrought were going to be overturned by someone who hadn't even talked to any of the principals. And we were going to come back to our subcontractor with a revised report that clearly contradicted our verbal presentation.

My on-the-job wisdom told me to lie low, say nothing, let the managers make fools of themselves in the name of business. But my integrity said that my professional reputation was at stake.

I called my friends at the subcontractor, told them what was happening, told them I disapproved, and apologized. It was a dumb political move, but it felt like the right move in spite of that.

I seemed to get a little more respect from the subcontractors after that. And, as far as I could tell, my manager never found out.

The purpose of the walkthrough is to detect problems, not to correct them; correction is a subsequent and probably nonteam process.

In spite of its simplicity, there are some pitfalls in the walkthrough process. The self-discipline demanded of the participants as they focus on an in-depth understanding of the material being reviewed is extremely taxing. Most reviewers find they are able to continue for only an hour at a time. In that hour, only about 100 lines of material are likely to be covered, according to those with experience in the process. Thus the communication involved in walkthroughs is exceedingly demanding, and progress is both slow and expensive. Some peer reviews are carried out by individuals who review the material in a nonteam setting before getting together for a team discussion. This system may alleviate some of the fatigue problems, but it is not clear whether it improves the error-detection process or not.

> Peer code reviews, the in-depth kind we were doing, generally took an hour for about 100 lines of code—we had read that in the literature. And, we knew, an hour was about all the time a review session should last.
>
> But we didn't know why. We were a group of friends, working together to code review a joint product before shipping it, and we had decided to do the job right. We met in my recreation room and fortified ourselves with chips and dips and liquid refreshments; the nearby refrigerator was on an open-door policy.
>
> Then we settled back with listings and documents to do the deed. An hour later our camaraderie was a shambles. The intensity of reading, understanding, and ferreting out problems in the code had left our emotions badly frayed, our defense mechanisms up, and our commitment to tact ebbing. Raw nerve ends shot sparks into the air.
>
> It was time to quit. We had covered exactly 112 lines of high-level language code. The literature had been right. And now we knew why!

The roles played by walkthrough participants may be loosely defined, or they may be carefully defined. It is vital, of course, that the walkthrough have a presenter (the person responsible for the material under review) and a scribe (the person who notes action items). Other participants may play the roles of the maintainer (ensuring that the software is maintainable), the standards-enforcer (ensuring that the software conforms to standards), and the user (ensuring that the software is responsive to the needs of those who originally presented the problem).

At the conclusion of the walkthrough, the scribe should have a list of action items. The walkthrough participants then decide on a course of action: acceptance of the material as is, acceptance with revisions as noted in the action items, or rejection to be followed by rework and a new walkthrough. This material constitutes the *walkthrough report.* Since the review is informal, the form of the report is not as important as the actions it defines to be carried out.

The walkthrough, then, is a high-leverage activity—lauded for its benefits, demanding in its costs—that also has several fringe benefits. First, software developers who know that their work will be reviewed may be more conscientious in its creation. Second, developers examining one another's work are likely to pick up stylistic and technical knowledge from each other, improving the skill level of all participants. Third, participants in walkthroughs are one step along the process toward serving as backup technologists in the event that something happens to the developer in charge.

3.3 PROJECT WIND-UP

The completion of a software project often comes a long time after its inception. The struggle to implement, test, and release a useful and acceptable product to the user is such a difficult job that common sense says there ought to be an opportunity to breathe and ruminate at the end.

Unfortunately, this is far from the true situation. As a project nears completion, the ending is often an anticlimax, with most programmers gone elsewhere when the end finally comes. Under these circumstances, project endings are usually untidy. Pieces of needed documentation are often left dangling, and the product is sometimes rushed into usage with some of its rough edges still unsmoothed. The programmer who developed the software, if not moved on to another project, is probably busy improving the user readiness of the product and in general completing the transition from developer to maintainer.

Because of these unpleasant facts, the discussion that follows must be treated as an ideal rather than as a description of software practice. Project wind-up all too often simply doesn't happen at all. If it did, this section describes what that process might be.

3.3.1 Wind-up Communication Process

The most famous project wind-up communicator was Fred Brooks, whose masterpiece *The Mythical Man-Month* [BROOKS74] is a book about what he learned from the pioneering and sometimes difficult experience of managing the creation of the first behemoth operating system, OS/360, for IBM mainframe computers. Brooks' lessons are a classic in making the most of the project wind-up phase; Brooks left IBM to join the faculty of the University of North Carolina and from that vantage point had the time and hindsight to be able to think about what went right and what went wrong.

Few if any of us have a similar opportunity. Project wind-up tends to be a high-stress time for correcting all the problems that there wasn't time to correct during development.

Foremost in the project wind-up process is the packaging and delivering of the software product. Whether the customer is 10,000 microcomputer users at locations scattered across the globe or one key organization in the same building of the same company, the software product must be tidied and documented in such a way that the user(s) will have no trouble getting it to do what they want.

Only after that process is well under way can the opportunity arise to commemorate the project. If the project or the developmental approach is unique, perhaps a professional paper or conference presentation is in order. If the project is of major scope, perhaps it can be a basis for a book. The software developer who gets the opportunity to evolve development work into a publishable paper or book is rare, but the need is always there—there is a desperate shortage of "lessons from the practitioner" in the computing literature.

3.3.2 Wind-up Written Communciation

The writing that occurs at the end of a project is usually pretty feverishly done. Although most software experts believe the maintenance manual should be produced before the project ending, what maintenance documentation is produced is often produced in those waning moments as the project winds down. Maintenance documentation was discussed earlier.

There are still some other pieces of documentation business at the end, however. The completed product must be documented and packaged for distribution or shipping. Installation instructions must be prepared for the eventual users.

3.3.2.1 Delivery and Installation Information. When a software product is ready for delivery, the developer has been testing it for so long that there is a tendency to believe that the whole world must by now know how to operate it. That, of course, is not true. The developer must at this point put on the hat of the user and prepare the information that will allow the user to reach a comfort level in being able to use the product.

When the product is physically moved to its new location, there must be an accompanying description of what is being moved. This delivery information may take the form of an invoice, a listing of the items being packaged and shipped. If there are floppy disks or tapes, how are they labeled? What is on them? In what order? In what format? What is different about this version of the product? Why? This packaging information need not be wordy, but it must be accurate and readable or the users will not have any idea what they have received.

The DoD defines a document, the *version description document,* to serve this purpose. Its outline follows:

DoD Version Description Document

1. Scope
2. Referenced documents
3. Version description
    - 3.1 Inventory of materials released
    - 3.2 Inventory of packing contents
    - 3.3, 3.4 Description of changes
    - 3.5 Adaptation data

3.6 Interface compatibility
3.7 Bibliography of reference documents
3.8 Operational description
3.9 Installation instructions
3.10 Possible problems and known errors
4,5. No content
6. Notes
10. Appendices

As with the standards discussions of an earlier section, this outline at least furnishes a check list for document content if not a blueprint for producing it.

This packaging and delivery information merely tells what has been shipped. The user also needs to know what to do with it. There must be some form of *installation guide* that describes how the physical media are to be made into a usable product. Typically, the installation guide consists of step-by-step directions for handling the physical media and how to introduce it into its environment. If backup of the product is important, the user should be presented with some suggestions for backup methodologies as well.

Only when the product has been received and installed will the user need the ultimate user documents, the *user manual* and (sometimes) the *operator's manual.* These two documents were discussed previously. It is important to note that all these user-oriented documents must be written with the user clearly in mind. If the software developer is not able to do so, then in this area especially a technical writer may play an important role. In either case, it is important for a real or simulated user to evaluate the delivery, installation, user, and operator documents before they are released to actual users. How many of us have had the experience of trying to decipher complex delivery instructions, only to be frustrated or to fail? "Put tab A into slot B" may have seemed easy to the product developer, but to the user the meaning is often elusive at best.

3.3.2.2 Conferences, Papers, and Books. The world of computing is hungry for information. The computing professional who is able to commemorate his or her project activity in a presentation or a paper has many choices. Conferences on an enormous variety of topics are held each year, and the list of computing publications—newspapers, magazines, and journals—is rich and varied.

If you find yourself in the happy but unusual position of having the time and resources to prepare a presentation on some facet of your work, you must answer some immediate questions.

Should you present? Is what you know and want to share sufficiently new and interesting that others will want to know about it? Are you aware

> "This paper contains nothing new or interesting."
>
> It was like a shotgun blast in the gut. I couldn't believe I was reading it. But the reviewer who had read my paper didn't like it much and had said so, in what seemed to me to be the cruelest possible way.
>
> Where did that cruelty come from? Usually in our society we protect one another with hedging words or small lies to avoid hurting one another's feelings. But reviewers for technical journals are anonymous. And this one had taken advantage of that anonymity. I will never know who it was who thought I had nothing new or interesting to say, but I will always remember that he or she said it!
>
> (How did I react? Once I got past the pain, I was angry. I sent that paper off to another technical journal, and then another, until it was indeed finally accepted and published. So what we have here is a success story. But what I remember most is the pain that preceded the success.)

enough of the work of others in your field that you can put your accomplishment into perspective? Can you write and/or speak well, or are you teamed with someone who can? Only after the answer to all these questions is yes should you contemplate the next question in this series.

Where should you present? Is what you want to share deeply technical and narrowly focused? Then one of the professional conferences or journals should probably be your target. Is your information more broadly focused? One of the commercial conferences or periodicals may be a better choice. Is your information timely and, therefore, newsworthy? Then one of the news-format publications makes sense.

Why should you present? Do you want acknowledgment, perhaps even fame? The professional journals can provide that. Conferences can, too, and probably more intensely (at the moment of presentation) but fleetingly (conference presentations in the form of proceedings are often not as readily referred to as periodicals). Do you want payment for the presentation you will do? The commercial periodicals usually provide that. Oddly, in fact, the journals that pay provide only moderate fame, and the journals that provide fame do not pay! In general, there are no payments available to conference speakers.

Should you speak or write? Conference presentations have fringe benefits. You become known and seen in your field. You meet others, some of whom you may have heard about before. You listen to the presentation of others, and you learn in the halls and in the hallways. You travel. But writing for a periodical has fringe benefits, too. You become known, perhaps more

> The anonymous reviewer had really gotten into the draft of my book. But not in a negative way. He (I found out later that it was a "he") had not only read the material in depth and liked it but, with his own creative juices flowing, had also written some additional words that really added to what I had said in a stylistic and technically meaningful way.
>
> The words were good, really good. In fact they were so good that I decided that I wanted to use them in the book. I wrote to the publisher, asking if I could get the reviewer's permission to use the words and if the reviewer was willing to be named. The publisher responded that he was, on both counts.
>
> Not all my experiences with anonymous reviewers have been good ones. But for every bad experience, it seems there is at least one that makes it all worthwhile. In this case, I had met a reviewer who cared—and contributed.

lastingly, in your field. You do not have to spend the time and resources necessary to travel. You do not have to speak. You may get paid.

Table 3-2 lists some of the current computing conferences that publish proceedings. Table 3-3 lists some of the computing periodicals and their areas of specialty. Table 3-4 lists some publishers of computing-oriented books. The field of computing is in great flux. Although these tables are up to date at the time of publication of this book and describe journals or publishers that have been successful over the years, you should double-check the accuracy of these lists before acting on their contents.

What is the process of preparing a presentation? Often it is more cal-

TABLE 3-2 Computing Conferences that Publish Proceedings

ACM Computer Science Conference
ACM National Conference
ACM Principles of Programming Languages
ACM SIGGRAPH (graphics)
ACM SIGOPS (operating systems)
COMPCON (IEEE)
COMPSAC (IEEE)
Computers in Aerospace (AIAA)
International Conference on Software Engineering
International Conference on System Science (Hawaii)
National Computer Conference/Fall Joint/Spring Joint
SoftFair

Note: This is only a sampling of computer conferences. Refer to the activities calendar of such periodicals as *Communications of the ACM* to obtain a full listing at any specific time.

TABLE 3-3 Computing Periodicals

Periodical	Material Published
ACM Software Engineering Notes	CSci, Prof.
ACM Computing Surveys	Tutorial
ACM Transactions on Database Systems	CSci
ACM Transactions on Programming Languages and Systems	CSci
ACM Journal	CSci, Research
Advances in Computers	Prof.
Bell Systems Technical Journal	Prof., Research
Business Computer Systems	EDP, Prof.
Byte	Popular, Micro
Communications of the ACM	CSci, Prof.
Computer Journal	CSci
Computerworld	News
Computing Reviews	Reviews
Data Management	EDP, Prof.
Datamation	Prof.
Dr. Dobb's Journal	Micro
IEEE Computer	CSci, Prof.
IEEE Software	CSci, Prof.
IEEE Spectrum	CSci, Prof.
IEEE Transactions on Communications	CSci
IEEE Transactions on Computers	CSci
IEEE Transactions on Software Engineering	CSci
IEEE Transactions on Systems, Man, and Cybernetics	CSci
Information Week	News
Infosystems	Popular
Info World	News
Journal of Systems Management	Prof.
Journal of Systems and Software	CSci, Prof.
Mathematics of Computation	CSci
Microcomputing	Micro
PC	Micro
Perspectives in Computing/IBM	Prof.
Software: Practice and Experience	CSci, Prof.

Note: This is only a sampling of computing periodicals. Due to the high mortality rate of some new publications, it is not possible to produce a complete list.

Legend:

All: All categories of readers listed here
CSci: Computer science
EDP: Commercial data processing
Micro: Microcomputer
News: News material
Popular: General (nontechnical)
Proceedings: Conference proceedings
Prof.: Computing professionals
Ref.: Reference material
Research: In-depth material on highly technical subject
Reviews: Review material
Tutorial: Elementary approach to highly technical subject

TABLE 3-4 Publishers of Computer-Oriented Books

Publisher	Material Published
Academic Press, Inc., P. O. Box 733 Old Chelsea Station, New York, NY 10113	CSci
Association for Computing Machinery, 11 W. 42nd St., New York, NY 10036	Proceedings
Addison-Wesley Publishing Co., Reading, MA 01867	All
AFIPS Press, 1815 N. Lynn St. Suite 800, Arlington, VA 22209	Proceedings
Auerbach, 6560 N. Park Dr., Pennsauken, NJ 08109	EDP, Prof., Ref.
CBS College Pub. (Holt, Rinehart and Winston), 383 Madison Ave., New York, NY 10017	All
Computer Science Press, 11 Taft Ct., Rockville, MD 20850	CSci
Computing Trends, P. O. Box 22012, Seattle, WA 98122	Prof., Humor
Creative Computing Press, 39 E. Hanover St., Morris Plains, NJ 07950	Popular
Datapro Research Corp., 1805 Underwood Blvd., Delran, NJ 08075	EDP, Prof., Ref.
Digital Press, Digital Equipment Corp., 12-A Esquire Rd., Billerica, MA 01862	Prof.
Elsevier/North-Holland, P. O. Box 1663 Grand Central Station, New York, NY 10163	All
IEEE Computer Society, 1109 Spring St. Suite 300, Silver Spring, MD 20910	Proceedings, Tutorials for CSci
ITT Bobbs-Merrill, 4300 W. 62nd St., P. O. Box 7080, Indianapolis, IN 46206	Popular, Micro
Krieger Publishing Co., P. O. Box 9542, Melbourne, FL 32902	EDP, CSci
Little, Brown and Co., 200 West St., Waltham, MA 02154	All
McGraw Hill, 1221 Avenue of the Americas, New York, NY 10020	All
Microsoft Press, 10700 Northrup Way, Bellevue, WA 98004	Popular, Micro
MIT Press, 28 Carleton St., Cambridge, MA 02142	CSci, Research
Prentice-Hall, Inc., Englewood Cliffs, NJ 07632	All
QED Information Sciences, QED Plaza, P. O. Box 181, Wellesley, MA 02181	EDP, Prof.
Science Research Associates, Inc., 155 N. Wacker Dr., Chicago, IL 60606	CSci, Prof.
Springer-Verlag, 175 Fifth Ave., New York, NY 10010	CSci
Sybex, Inc., 2344 Sixth St., Berkeley, CA 94710	Popular, Micro
Yourdon Press, 1133 Avenue of the Americas, New York, NY 10036	EDP, Prof.

Legend:

All: All categories of readers listed here
CSci: Computer science textbooks
EDP: Commercial data processing
Micro: Microcomputer
News: News material
Popular: General (nontechnical)
Proceedings: Conference proceedings
Prof.: Computing professionals
Ref.: Reference material
Research: In-depth material on highly technical subject
Reviews: Review material
Tutorial: Elementary approach to highly technical subject

endar-consuming than you might ever imagine. First, of course, is the preparation of the material. For a conference the material may be an abstract or a full paper, whichever the conference organizers require to make a judgment about which topics to include or exclude from the conference. For a periodical the material is generally the full paper. For a book the material is most likely a table of contents, a couple of important sample chapters, and a "prospectus" or description of the content of the book and the reasons the publisher should consider publishing it.

Next comes the judgment process. The submitted material is reviewed for appropriateness. This process, if it involves formal reviewers of a periodical with a significant backlog, may take months. Following the judgment process comes the judgment, usually "accept" or "accept if you revise it" or "reject." The judgment is normally accompanied by the findings that resulted in the judgment.

Once material is accepted, then it gets in line for the presentation process. If the presentation is at a conference, of course the date is known and can be planned for. If the presentation is in a periodical, an approximate publication date is usually provided. If the presentation is a book, a contract is signed and the material must be expanded into a full book and resubmitted for additional reviews.

Thus the calendar time for a presentation varies enormously with the type of presentation. For a conference, it is the time until the conference is held. For a periodical, it is largely the time until the paper is accepted, which is usually measured in months. (Some periodicals publish material unreviewed, thus shortening these timing considerations considerably. These publications, ironically, can publish fresher material but with less prestige than the refereed journals.) For a book, the calendar time until publication is likely to be 3 to 4 years. (If your book is especially timely or has enormous sales potential, that time can be shortened.)

The form of a presentation depends on the place it is presented. Conference proceedings often require the material to be submitted in camera-ready form, typed on special paper; formal periodicals use a style that is process oriented, with conclusions last and a heavy emphasis on references, bibliographies, and acknowledgments; informal periodicals generally want the most important information presented first and the details last, and with no references or bibliographies. Obviously, it is important to know the target for your presentation before you prepare it.

The preparation and presentation of material on a project, then, is a serious and time-consuming undertaking. On the one hand, it should be begun only if the time and resources are clearly available to finish it. On the other, it may be the most important and memorable achievement of the presenter's career!

3.3.3 Wind-up Spoken Communication

Project wind-up is in some ways a misnomer. What is a wind-up for the software developers is actually the beginning for the software maintainers. In this section we see a mixture of the spoken communication that the developers may do in finalizing the project and the spoken communication that commonly occurs in maintenance.

In the previous section we discussed the possibility of presenting a paper at a conference. Although that involves oral communication, we included it there because it has so much in common with the presentation of technical papers. In this section we will briefly discuss two kinds of wind-up communication: presentations and debriefings. Then we will talk about the maintenance role of user support.

3.3.3.1 Marketing Presentations. Once the project is complete or nearly complete, it is time to tell the world about it. In general, this world should be fairly limited, however! Users, potential users, and management are the audiences for this form of communication.

These meetings may be termed *marketing presentations.* The reason for the meeting is to promote the product (and perhaps yourself). Your goal is generally to inform—management, about what you have done, and users, about what you have done for them—but with some (tactful) bragging. It is your chance to tell those people who care about your accomplishment what your project is and what is especially worthwhile about it. Refer to the subsection of Section 3.2.2.6 entitled "Marketing Material" for further discussions of the content and form of the written equivalent of this kind of presentation.

Oral marketing presentations have their own set of ground rules. IBM, master of the marketing presentation, advocates an outline something like the following:

- *Introduction, jokes, "what I've done since we last met."* Establish a comfort zone between you and your audience.
- *Initial benefit statement.* Explain why you're worth listening to.
- *Agenda.* Tell 'em what you're going to tell 'em.
- *Problem.* Define the problem for which you're offering a solution.
- *Solution overview.* Provide a general explanation of your solution.
- *Features/benefits.* Explain the specifics of your solution, in benefit terms.
- *Summary.* Tell 'em what you told 'em.
- *Close the business.* Ask for their support.

> Establishing a comfort zone with the audience is an important part of the oral presentation, whether the speaker is doing marketing or not. And anecdotes can be a big help in bringing a group together; however, anecdotes can be overdone. It was on a call to a particularly good customer that I found myself telling a story. Suddenly I felt uneasy. Had I told this group this story before? Choosing my words carefully, I asked them.
>
> A tactful customer gave a classic response. "We love your stories every time you tell them," he said. And then he blushed. He hadn't realized that his answer confirmed that not only had I told the story before, but probably several times. Then it was my turn to blush.

As the presentation proceeds through an outline like this, questions and comments will likely arise. If they do, each interaction should be treated as important, perhaps even as an opportunity.

- Make sure you understand the point being made. Restate it, and ask for concurrence.
- Empathize with the questioner if appropriate.
- Respond to the comment.
- Ask the questioner if your response was satisfactory. If not, try again using a different approach.
- If appropriate, reclose the business.

3.3.3.2 Debriefings. A presentation is made by a doer to some interested party or parties. A *debriefing,* on the other hand, is usually an evaluation of that presentation by its audience.

An example is in order. Suppose you and your teammates have worked for 6 weeks on a proposal for a software project, and you have just received word that the funders who evaluated it have rejected it. Perhaps the rejection was in the form of announcing a winner other than you in a competitive award, or perhaps the rejection was specific to you. In either case, one logical reaction on your part (after the more obvious emotional ones) is to wonder what you did wrong.

The debriefing is a response to that wondering. The decision makers, in a debriefing, explain what was found wanting in the presentation. A debriefing usually consists of these elements:

The lead sentence of the story in *Computerworld* read "XXX (a person's name) has marketing in his blood." That intrigued me. I wanted to find out what XXX had done that impressed a reporter that much. I read on.

XXX, it turned out, was a vice-president of a leading computer company that had just suffered the worst year in its history. And the presentation the reporter had covered was made by XXX to a group of shrewd high-level managers, the kind who might become future customers of his.

First, XXX confronted the problems. "We *have* had a bad year," he admitted, and gained a hundred points of listener confidence in doing it. His audience knew his company's status, and he knew they knew it. There was nothing to be gained by hiding and everything to lose. "But here's what we're doing to fix our problems," he went on. And he enumerated a half-dozen managerial and technical steps the company had taken to improve its profit and product picture.

Marketers aren't always known for their openness and honesty. But here was a refreshing case where marketing honesty was not only the right way to go ethically, it was also the right way to go in a marketing sense. That's what had impressed the reporter—and me, as well.

- An overview of the context of the rejection
- A general discussion about the rejected presentation
- An explanation of what is good about the presentation
- An explanation of what is bad about the presentation
  - Overall negative impressions
  - Detailed negative impressions
- Conclusions

A debriefing, taken with the appropriate emotional attitude, can be an extremely important event. A good debriefing can turn this time's failure into next time's victory. The emphasis should be on looking to the future, not on looking at the past.

3.3.3.3 User Support. *User support* is a multifaceted term. Taken at face value, it covers all the things the doer of a software project does to help the user use the product. We have already discussed such user support as user manuals, installation manuals, and delivery instructions. Here we will discuss a new topic, the spoken communication that occurs between a user and a user-support person in response to a user problem.

No matter how well (or how badly) the other user-support material is done, there will be occasions when the user simply doesn't "get it." Not getting it may mean that the user is unable to understand an appropriate explanation, or a failure of an explanation to be clear, or a product problem that no amount of written explanation could have anticipated.

In these circumstances many institutions have an identified person or persons whose job is to help the user. At colleges and universities, and sometimes in industry, these people are referred to as *consultants;* others call them *troubleshooters*. Their task is to push aside a user obstacle in order to allow the user to proceed. Sometimes the communication between the user and the consultant is in person. Other times, there is a hot-line telephone link between them. Especially in the world of large user populations, such as in microcomputer software, many of the calls are long distance, often over a toll-free line.

The consultant needs both skill and information in playing this role. The skill is personal knowledge and experience in the product the user is using. The information is the record of existing and past user reports, often kept as a data base and sometimes accessed by the consultant on line via a terminal.

If a user has a problem with a specific product feature, the consultant needs to analyze that problem from several points of view. Does the user really understand what he or she is doing? Is he or she doing it properly? If the answer is yes, is the explanation faulty? If not, is the product faulty? If either is faulty, is this a previously reported problem? If so, is there a workaround while the problem is being fixed? When will a fix be available? If the problem has not been reported previously, the consultant must also search for a workaround for the user while preparing a report. The world of the consultant is complex.

It is made more complex by the existence of multiple versions of a program product. If there is indeed a problem with the product or its explanation, what machine is the user running on? What operating system? What version of the product? If the version is an old one, has this problem been fixed in a later version? If the context for the answer is wrong, the answer will be worthless, or worse.

The world of the consultant is also harried. Users with problems are often not in good moods. Whether the problem is theirs or the product's, they may greet an explanation with a mixture of relief and anger. The consultant's communication role, then, involves both knowledge and tact. Because of the interpersonal nature of the consultant's work, users sometimes seek out and stay with a particular consultant for repeat problems because of their psychological compatibility with that person.

One of the depressing things about the job of consultant is that it deals primarily with problems, not successes. But there are rewards. Some consultants have reported that after helping a user with a problem, they have been sent roses or chocolates as a thank you for their efforts!

The bar charts of technology are superimposed over the grizzled face of someone born before the computing revolution. How can the technologist communicate with the computer naive?

CHAPTER 4

Technical Communication with a Nontechnical Audience

In several preceding sections this book has addressed the topic of communication by a technologist with a nontechnical audience. (*Nontechnical* in this case is meant to cover people who use computers but do not work as computing professionals.)

In Section 2.4 we discussed the complication of the special terminology that technologists use and how it is sometimes a barrier between the technologists and nontechnologists. In Section 3.2.2 we discussed several documents that are prepared for nontechnical readers: the user manual, the operations manual, and marketing material. In Section 3.3.2, in a similar vein, we discussed delivery and installation information. And in Section 3.3.3 we discussed user support.

We return to that subject area here because it is particularly troublesome. For all the logic and knowledge of skilled software specialists, we have a very poor track record in being able to communicate outside our field. This section focuses again on that problem.

Complaints pop up repeatedly in the computing press—computing people just don't know how to talk to the general public, or at least they don't know how to write for them. In one column of one publication [BUSCS84], retail dealers of computers were asked the question, What complaints—or praise—do you hear most regarding software documentation? The answers,

> The two politicians were livid. They had gone to great lengths to arrange for presentations by high-technology companies in their area to potential international customers. And the technologists had "blown it."
>
> "These guys know their product, know their technology," said one of the politicians, "but they can't present information worth beans." "At least, if they're poor communicators, they could get some good communication help," said the other politician. "But no—they have to do it themselves and botch the job."
>
> There was no saving the situation. The potential customers, muttering to themselves about the presentation they had heard but not understood, filed out of the room. There were no sales today. And, perhaps, not ever.

from five software dealers scattered from California to New York, contained these thoughts:

- " . . . we have to make up for the sins of the manufacturers by bridging the gap with a set of instructions . . . an idiot sheet."
- "Documentation should be written in more concise terms in a language the user can understand. It seems to be addressing the wrong crowd . . . [it is] aimed at the go-between, not at the user himself."
- "The documentation is not complete. The bulk of it has been written by a person . . . who has to learn how to speak English."

These are strong words. If there is one most serious problem in the world of software communication, this is it. The concerned software communicator must confront this in order to be successful.

There are some steps that can be taken toward solving the problem. They are presented below. As you take those steps, you encounter a choice. Do you want communication with nontechnical users to be presented by technologists or by technical communication specialists (often called *technical,* or *tech writers*)?

The technologist, by virtue of knowing the technical material, has a better starting place for preparing it. But the technical writer, by virtue of knowing how to handle the technical material, has a better "finishing place." In theory, the technologist may take less time to prepare the material; but the technical writer probably draws a lower salary, and thus may cost less. The key to the decision is whether the technologist has the skills to produce an effective presentation. Many do not, and the decision in that case is clearly in favor of the technical writer. For those who do have the skills, the decision can go either way.

Suppose you have decided to have your technologist prepare the material. It is vital to do it with the reader/listener clearly in mind. These steps, suggested by technical communication specialist Beryl Gorbman, can help in that process:

1. Define the reader, in terms of educational level, motivation to read your product, position in the organization, style preferences, customary reading materials, and present knowledge.
2. Draw up a composite of the reader (give them a name or identity if it helps). Do a psychological profile. Is your product geared to an upwardly mobile corporate professional who will concentrate or to a disenchanted ditch digger with an unpleasant hangover?
3. Write to that person. Close your eyes and try to pretend that you are that person. Imagine that person reading your material.
4. Tell the person what they need to know, no more, no less.
5. Accept the general truth that technical documents are often, by nature, quite boring. Do your best to liven them up. Remember that the readers are the customers. It's your job to keep them interested.
6. Define the tone of your language and keep it consistent. Never, never use passive voice unless you are deliberately shielding information (i.e., "It was decided . . . " By whom?).
7. Avoid huge monoliths of text. Break up the text with drawings, screens, or photos. Use a lot of white space.
8. Use expert help. An editor will make sure that language and form are consistent, that you aren't explaining too much or too little, and that your work is grammatically correct. A graphics designer will make your document attractive and readable.

If you decide to use a technical communication specialist, the question arises, Where can you find one? Perhaps your company already has an organization of them; if not, this is a skill that may be advertised for in your general newspaper classified section or obtained via a recruiting firm. Various professional societies exist for technical communication specialists—the Society for Technical Communication, the Association for Computing Machinery Special Interest Group for Documentation (SIGDOC), and the IEEE Communication Society are some examples. Contacting one of them in your area may be a good avenue to pursue.

Many people today are choosing to specialize in this area. It should be possible to find individuals or specialty firms fairly easily. When engaging someone, it is important to look at samples of his or her past work to be sure that what he or she can do is similar to what you want done.

Let us look at another facet of the communication gulf between technologists and nontechnologists. It works both ways. We software folk may not be very good at writing for the nontechnical audience, but that audience is pretty bad about evaluating our technical material, as well.

I've seen a lot of bad user manuals in my time. They come with software products, or they're created by people I work with, or they're turned in as assignments by my students.

Do you want to see an example of what a bad one looks like? Here's one contributed by Beryl Gorbman that can't be traced to anyone in particular—there's no point in causing embarrassment—but it illustrates some of the kinds of things that can be done wrong.

"Report Space is the verb name for this interactive, fast, and friendly word processor whose user manual you are now reading. It has three main modes of operation—edit mode, input mode, and ruler mode. Edit mode is the normal mode of operation, wherein the user can page through a document or invoke a special word processing feature, which includes entering input or ruler modes.

"Ruler mode enables the user to change or create a new ruler. A ruler defines the current left margin, right margin, and tab settings for the following body of text. Whenever the format of the printed page must be changed, or the user wants to go from inputting FILL text to NOFILL text, a new or different ruler must be used.

"Input mode enables the user to put new text into a document from the CRT keyboard. When Report Space is invoked on a new item, a default ruler is set up and ruler mode is entered. Once ruler mode has been exited, at which time the user enters edit mode, from which ruler or input modes can be easily reached."

The manual went on, but I will include no more. After all, the sensitive documentor can stand only so much computerese, so much passive language, so much fuzzy thinking!

Jerry Weinberg, author of several software-oriented books, summed up his frustrations in an article entitled "Publishers Know Zero About Computing."* Weinberg expressed his frustration that editors simply couldn't see a market for *The Psychology of Computer Programming,* and its publication was delayed for a year while he got letters saying " . . . it just is not worthwhile pushing this project any further . . . it may be wise to forget the book concept entirely." The book, once published, went on to sell over 60,000 copies!

"I believe the problem stems from the rapidly changing nature of the business," Weinberg says. "By the time an editor has learned anything about what the market will bear, the market has turned. . . . "

*Published in a now-defunct journal called *Computer Career News.*

That comment pretty well sums up the relationship between our technology and the public in general. For those of us inside the field, keeping up with the technology is a bit like trying to stay on a bucking bronco. Imagine the difficulty for those outside the field. Although there is an amazing and increasing amount of knowledge out there in the world beyond our profession, the public will not be able to keep up with what we inside the field know.

And that, of course, is the problem. It is our job to bridge that gap. We can do it ourselves, or we can hire appropriate help. Either way, the gap must be bridged.

All technologies evolve. Information flow has moved well beyond the pony express, and air travel beyond the Wright Brothers.

CHAPTER 5

Automation of Technical Communication

Reader, beware! Here we enter into exciting but shaky ground. In this section we will discuss the same general topics we covered earlier but from a new point of view. We ask the question, What can we automate in this process?

Some of this ground is fairly firm. This book, for example, was created by interaction between the author and a word processor. The production of the finished material was assisted by computers in the publication process. Some of the source material was sent to the author via electronic mail. All these processes are, to varying degrees, common examples of the automation we are talking about.

But there is much more to come—so much more that it is difficult to predict in which direction this new technology is moving and will move. In this chapter we will discuss what is known and predictable in the automated office as we near the end of the twentieth century.

The term most commonly accepted for our topic here is *office automation*. Even though what we are talking about goes beyond the clerical implications of that familiar term, it is a convenient one. Let us discuss what office automation is.

5.1 WHAT IS OFFICE AUTOMATION?

Office automation is the collection of technologies that support white-collar workers. What white-collar workers? Clerical, technical, managerial persons—anyone whose job involves working with paper and ideas instead of hardware is included in this category. By this broad definition, lots of technologies are part of office automation. The typewriter, for example. The telephone. The stapler.

It is the new and dramatically changing technologies, however, that make office automation a force to be reckoned with. The copy machine revolutionized distribution and backup in the office. The word processor revolutionized the preparation of text material. The graphics system is just beginning to revolutionize the preparation of nontext material. Many more revolutions are coming. The big question is *when* more than it is *what*.

Currently the term office automation defines a relatively well-defined collection of technologies.

- *Reproduction* is any technology that assists the copying of material.
- *Word processing* is any technology that assists in the creation and formatting of textual material.
- *Graphics* is any technology that assists in the creation and formatting of nontextual material.
- *Distribution* is any technology that assists in the dissemination of textual and nontextual material.
- *Communication* is any technology that assists humans in communication.
- *Records management* is any technology that assists in saving and accessing information.
- *Administration* is any technology that assists in performing other administrative tasks.

Of these terms, several are by now so commonplace that no further discussion is needed. The copying machine is so ubiquitous that it not only supports the reproduction needs of the average office, but it may well have replaced the drinking fountain as the mecca for social gatherings! The word processor, often including a spelling checker and perhaps a grammar checker and outline processor, is the personal tool of many who create, or perform clerical tasks on, text. Graphics software, fast evolving but still primitive in the average office, is at least known in most environments. But what do we mean by distribution, or communication, or records management, or administration?

By distribution we mean mail systems—technology such as electronic or voice mail that complements the traditional telephone and postal systems for sending and receiving information. Some contemporary companies have elaborate electronic mail systems and swear by them. Many others have none.

By communication we mean technologies that assist human beings in direct communication. Defining this technology is a somewhat more elusive process than it was for the previous ones. Mail systems, of course, help their users communicate. But so, too, do teleconferencing systems, bulletin boards, telephone "gab lines," and a host of thought-of and unthought-of technologies that will help humans break down the barriers to communication.

By records management we mean information filing and retrieval systems. The data base management system is a common example.

By administration we mean a miscellaneous collection of capabilities not provided above. The electronic calendar, by means of which the user keeps track of what he or she is to do when, is one example. The spreadsheet program, by means of which the user manipulates matrices of data and text, is another.

Gluing many of these technologies together is another technology of its own—the network. Local area networks (LANs) and wide area networks (WANs) are mechanisms for integrating all the technologies just described and data processing technology, as well. Although network technology is a vital consideration in the future of data processing and office automation, it is peripheral to our discussion here. You may want to look at [WEITZ80] for more information on networks.

An interesting summary of the marketplace in advanced communication technology is given in [GLOSS83]. The book discusses such commercially available communication media as accessible public data bases, bulletin board systems, computer conferencing, typesetting, and remote shopping and bank-

> I was looking forward to what my guest speaker on office automation had to say. Whereas I had a peering-in-from-the-outside knowledge of what the subject was all about, he had been out in the trenches, working as a consultant. Besides that, he was a former computer science professor, and I counted on that to add perspective to his experiences.
>
> But I was wrong. For the consultant in office automation, the subject area is largely one of educating the small businessperson about the rudiments of the subject. My speaker knew that subject very well, with lots of good war stories to share. But my audience, the group that he was addressing, was pretty knowledgeable. They already knew the rudiments of office automation. They wanted something more sophisticated.
>
> They were disappointed. And so was I. The state of the art of office automation, I had learned once again, was deeply subjective.

ing. The good news is that the book is complete and timely; the bad news is that it may grow out-of-date rapidly.

5.2 WHAT IS THE STATUS OF OFFICE AUTOMATION?

The current status of office automation is pretty much dependent on whose facility you wish to examine. To some, it is a roaring success, well defined, and full of excitement. To others, it is vendor hype, paper promises and products, and, according to one editorial writer in the office automation world, "a mess." Where you stand on that spectrum is pretty much a function of how successful you have been with however much of office automation you have tried. The picture is, to be brief, mixed.

Because of the explosive growth of office automation in this quarter-century, there is a temptation to think it is a new field. To examine that belief further, it is worthwhile to step back a little and look at the history of the office before we discuss today and all its tomorrows.

5.2.1 History of Office Automation

There are some surprises in the history of office automation. First, it is indeed a short history, dating back not much farther than 100 years. Second, some technologies we might have expected to have been around forever are not only recent but have followed more exciting concepts that we would presume to be newer. The discussion that follows relies heavily on an article entitled "Historical Lessons for the Automated Office."*

Prior to the turn of the century, most written communication in industry was conducted outside the company, not inside. Inside the company people talked to each other, they did not write to each other. Because of this, the demands placed on communication devices were not severe, and the stimulus for more advanced communication devices was not present.

When the stimulus did appear, things began to change rapidly. Look at the following time line to see how much and how fast:

- 1870 The mimeograph machine is invented.
- 1870s The typewriter is mass-produced.
- 1876 Operator-assisted phone is invented and quickly put into mass usage.
- 1893 Vertical file is introduced at Chicago World's Fair.

*Marcus, M. L., and J. Yates, "Historical Lessons for the Automated Office." Reprinted from *Computer Decisions,* June, 1982, pp. 116–119, 260. Copyright © 1982, Hayden Publishing Company.

- 1899 Direct-dial telephone becomes available.
- 1900+ Carbon paper is invented.
- 1914 New York School of Filing begins training clerks in filing methods.
- 1965 Photocopying becomes commonly available.
- 1965 Typewriters with text storage become available.
- 1975+ Word processing becomes commonly available.

It is almost as if the approach of a new century has been a trigger to speed the advance of office automation. A spate of products was introduced in the last quarter of the nineteenth century, including the vertical file cabinet (isn't it incredible that that idea hasn't been around "forever"?). Another spate of products has been introduced in the last quarter of this century. In both centuries, the rate of change has been phenomenal. Word processing is an excellent example. In 1978, word processing was an $830 million business internationally, and the cost of a product was around $20,000. Two years later the business had grown to $2 billion, and the product price had fallen to $5000. Will the future of office automation continue to move at its recent pace? We will look at that subject in the next section. But before we do, let's look a bit at the process by which new technology is absorbed into society.

At the outset, society often drives technology. Some kind of "necessity is the mother of invention" force causes technology to explore, create, try out, and produce a new product. Then after the new product is available, society takes a while to absorb it. There is rethinking and replanning and retraining to be done. Finally, the full force of the new technology bursts upon society and a societal "breakthrough" (many years in the making) occurs. Now this new technology, having caused a revision in how society functions, has created a new set of "necessities." Invention is mothered again, and the cycle repeats itself.

Look back at the office automation time line. It was 20 years after the mimeograph machine and the typewriter before the vertical file cabinet was invented. (You can almost see the stacks of typed and mimeographed paper teetering as the need for better filing techniques grew ever stronger.) Out comes the file cabinet, but 20 years elapses again before courses are taught in how to use it.

Looking at the future is often a matter of extrapolating from the past. In the context of the necessity-invention-breakthrough cycle, consider some of today's technologies: microfiche, computer storage of text and video data (could the vertical file cabinet become obsolete?), video teleconferencing, and more. We may not be able to predict which technologies will become societal breakthroughs or when, but we can predict some things about the process by which they will come about.

5.2.2 Future of Office Automation

It is easy, although surprising, to look at the past of office automation. It is not so easy to look at the future. We have already seen that, in the futures business, technology tends to move faster than we predict, but society tends to move slower. A safe prediction about the future of office automation, then, is that the technology will move forward faster than society will absorb it.

But what does that really mean? Let's look at electronic mail as one example.

In 1982 there were 125,000 computer-based mailboxes in this country, transmitting around 70,000,000 messages per year. (By 1985 the number of boxes was closer to 300,000; by 1990, 1,700,000.) Those electronic systems are concentrated in a few companies—Digital Equipment Corporation has built a successful corporate culture around its electronic mail system, for example, and Texas Instruments had over 12,000 mailboxes in 1985. But many other companies, as we mentioned previously, had not chosen to pay the start-up costs involved in this new technology. With a technology like this, we can expect to see fill-in expansion—more companies beginning to use the existing technology—rather than dramatic increases in technical capability.

What sort of capability is present in an electronic mail system? First of all, the ability to send and receive written mail via a computer network and its associated terminals. Messages may be created, edited, and dispatched to one or several locations. Recipients may be notified when mail arrives, or they may choose to scan their mailboxes at a convenient time. Mail may be prioritized; for example, if it is marked "urgent," it will be put at the top of the recipient's queue. It may be *registered,* in which case the recipient or his or her computer system must acknowledge its receipt. It may be linked onto other networks, even that of the U.S. Postal Service.

Why would someone want electronic mail instead of the more traditional forms of communication? First, it's nearly instant and thus has timing advantages over both corporate and U.S. mail systems. Second, it's a noninterrupt system, so the recipient scans his or her mail at a convenient time, and not on demand, as with the telephone. Third, material sent may easily be kept by the user and/or sent to others; the process of copying a message is simpler than that with traditional mail, and of course much better than with traditional telephones, where no copy of a conversation may legally be kept at all.

Corporate users of electronic mail at Digital Equipment find their system to be the focal point of corporate communication. They broadcast informational notices and exchange personal messages using the system, and they have found that the use of traditional mechanisms like the telephone and the conventional grapevine has diminished.

Of course, there are disadvantages to electronic mail, as well. The instant interaction of a telephone is sometimes vital for problem solving, and the ability to traditionally mail preprinted material is vital for information dissemination. The communication of emotions as well as facts is difficult without direct contact. The lack of the massive networks of traditional systems also hurts, and the cost of disk storage (perhaps $500 per user) is another negative factor, but these latter two factors will probably be corrected as time passes and the prevalence of electronic systems increases.

How would you justify the cost of electronic mail? That's a difficult question because statistics about people's work habits and how they are helped or hindered by communication are hard to determine. But the difficulty is not new. Think about how, at the turn of the last century, you would have gone about justifying the cost of a telephone system in your company.

Written electronic mail is not the only form of mail being explored. Voice systems are available, as well. With this kind of system, voice messages instead of textual ones are stored and forwarded. For the most part, such systems are in other ways analogous to electronic mail, although messages may be initiated and received over standard push-button telephones; thus the instruments and the network are already in place.

Interestingly, there are some social advantages to such mail systems, as well as technical ones. If the goal of a contact is to pass information rather than to be social, then chitchat can be eliminated. "Telephone tag," in which two or more people leave telephone messages for return calls but never actually make contact, can be circumvented. Even the time-zone problem, where the recipient may not be at work when you want to send a message, can now be overcome. And of course, for the handicapped, electronic mail or voice mail may be the only effective communication medium available.

These simple facts do not begin to cover the interest in, and the controversy surrounding, this or any other new technology. A scan of the publications that deal with office automation shows such headlines as "Office Automation is Your Headache," or "Electronic Mail—a Mixed Blessing?" or "Electronic Mail—A Smart Way to do Business?" or even "Electronic Mail: A New Medium for the Message." Clearly, even among professionals in the field, there is a mixed set of messages about this new technology. To the extent that there is research and experimentation, however, these findings seem to hold true:

- Overcoming the initial inertia of people will cost 10 times as much as you think it will.
- Once people make the transition to the new technology, they hold onto it with a "death grip."

For a fairly recent analysis of the options for both in-company and outside-company electronic mail, see [PC85]. In any fast-moving technology such as this, however, beware—information that is more than a couple of years old may not be worth looking at.

Electronic mail is not, of course, the only fast-changing element of office automation. Computer voice systems are another area of rapid change. Current capabilities including systems that talk to you (even your car may be telling you to close its door, or your soft drink machine to insert your money), and systems to which you can talk (Pfizer drug has a sales order system into which a sales rep can speak an order using a limited vocabulary). Voice communication is exciting, but there is even more excitement ahead. How about a conference call situation in which the participants have terminals, not telephones, and the information shipped may be text or graphics? Experiments in the use of such systems for group decision making were made in the early 1980s.

Take that idea, and add video screens. Some companies, such as Boeing, began using video teleconferencing in the same time period (Boeing claims to have saved 1.5 million miles of staff travel between Seattle-area plants alone during a 4-year time period). Over 100 U.S. companies currently use such systems, and growth of their use is predicted to be well over 100% in the next 5 years. But, as with other aspects of the office automation technology, a warning note was sounded in [CULLEN86]: The technology to date is pretty cumbersome and pretty expensive.

How about accessing a library of information on your own home TV? Such systems are commonly available in Europe—the British Post Office provides such a service, and France has made this capability part of its national communication planning and implementation.

There are significant barriers to the achievement of these new technological advances, of course. One of the most significant is the lack of standards across computer company lines. Each company invents and adheres to its own way of doing business, even if it hinders the spread of technology because users cannot interact across computer company lines. What if a de facto standard had not emerged in VCR equipment, for example? The spread of VCR technology, and its mass availability, would never have happened. Or to be even more mundane, what if the size of the base of a light bulb had never been standardized? The very existence of commonly available, cheap electrical service would have been threatened.

Yet we have computing companies each with its own data file format, and only clumsy interface file definitions, such as the DIF technology,* to bridge the gap. Clearly the enemy of the advance of office automation lies primarily in the resistance of those who must adjust to new technology, but

*A file format developed to allow microcomputer data files created by one program (e.g., Visicalc) to be used by another (e.g., Wordstar).

there are enemies inside our own field, as well. We will return to this topic in Section 5.2.3, "Research in Office Automation."

The automation of technical communication, then, is an area of enormous excitement, some fear, and a lot of resistance. That blend should be a volatile and interesting one to watch in the years ahead.

5.2.3 Research in Office Automation

Volatile as the practical uses of office automation may be, research into the area continues at an increasing pace. The answer to the question, How can these new techniques be used in innovative new ways? is the major thrust of the researcher.

For example, "should textual material be limited to its traditional printed form?" is one question being explored [YANK85]. Table 5-1 shows the advantages of printed (traditional) material over electronic display of textual material. Notice that electronic display gives an increase in flexibility in the way information is presented (e.g., constant update of rapidly changing subject areas is possible) but at a cost in integrity (e.g., what is a "book" if its content is constantly changing?).

TABLE 5-1 Traditional versus Electronic Print Media

Characteristic	Traditional Advantages	Disadvantages
Information integrity	A version never changes Never inaccessible due to hardware problems	Inflexible Reader cannot change, annotate Can't modify layout to reader preference
Physical entities	Portable Easy to browse, explore Allows underlining, marking	2-D information only Text and graphics must be static Costly to keep up to date Hard to locate specific information No sound, motion Difficult to have multiple indices
Advanced technology	Well-defined, accepted standards Support disciplines in place: typography, graphic design, photo reproduction Easy to read	Joint authorship difficult Rekeying is error prone

Pursuing the benefits of this flexibility, researchers are looking toward the following areas for the true benefits of electronic text:

- *Connectivity.* The reader may scan referenced or related text simply by calling it up in a window adjacent to the original material.
- *Audiovisualization.* Graphics and sound may supplement text (a discussion of a tiger is much more credible if the reader sees a videotaped tiger move and hears it growl).
- *Creation or revision support.* Text that must be written to a predefined outline (e.g., FIPS PUB 38 requirements) can be created more easily if a text-processing system can impose the appropriate outline on the writer.

New concepts to support workers in teams are also being explored. Asynchronous systems, in which the users send and receive information at a time of their choosing, were discussed in the previous section. But simultaneous systems, more advanced than the now-ubiquitous telephone, are also being explored. The U.S. Department of Defense is particularly interested in these real-time conference systems, for such tasks as

- Crisis handling
- Design and development by team
- Debugging by team
- Time-critical consensus determination

A good discussion of progress in these areas is contained in [SARIN85].

One barrier to progress, which lies on the borderline between practice and research, is standards. Even something as conceptually simple as text interchange between computers is fraught with problems. Not only have we invented vendor-dependent character sets and numeric representation conventions, but we use completely unstandardized control codes within the text to define its function (e.g., a paragraph indicator in word processing text).

Considerable effort is being put into the standards area by a variety of national, regional, international, and societal organizations. Progress is being made [HORAK85], [BONO85], but it is slow and fraught with the complication of conflicting vendor business goals (e.g., IBM invented the EBCDIC character set in spite of the existence of the international standard ASCII). It may be that progress will not be made in the critical standards areas until the international organizations (International Telephone/Telegraph Consultative Committee (CCITT), International Organization for Standardization (ISO), and European Computer Manufacturers Association (ECMA)) are joined by user groups with clout born of anger from the frustration of using too many incompatible systems.

Thus research into automation of communication is as exciting as text with audio and visual components and as mundane as standardization of the underlying technology. In an era evolving as rapidly as this one, such variance and perhaps even instability are to be expected. Out of it will come the communication methodologies that 21st-century humankind will take for granted.

Looking ahead is looking at the meeting point of the parallel lines that frame our lives. Tatting up is examining the artifacts that lie among those converging lines.

CHAPTER 6

Summary

Communication is something we all do but with varying degrees of success. Technical communication in the software field is something we all do, with lesser degrees of success. Simply stated, software people, for whatever reason, have the reputation of being some of the world's worst communicators.

The solution to that problem is no simpler than the solution to any other serious problem. It is a matter of learning what to do, exercising the new-found skills, seeking sympathetic but useful criticism, and refining the exercised skills until the product they produce does the job it is supposed to do. It's a simple, predictable solution, but one much harder to put into practice than to talk about.

But there is an overriding factor that, properly applied, can accelerate the process of useful software communication: The communicator *must* think like the target of the communication. The level of communication, the manner of presentation, even the words chosen must be chosen because they communicate to the chosen listener. It is a classic case of not being able to succeed until you have walked a mile in the other person's moccasins.

One of the most necessary pieces of software communication is the documentation that inevitably accompanies a software product. Even if the software developer rarely communicates in any other way—and that, in this decade, would be a rare situation indeed—there is the necessity for producing requirements specs, and design representations, and user manuals, and marketing support materials, and more.

Fortunately there are some standards that have been and are being defined to help steer the software developer into appropriate ways of doing these kinds of documentation. But unfortunately the standards that do exist tend to differ from one another, so the software developer is still left at loose ends for guidance on how best to do the job.

As with any other facet of software productivity, the successful software communicator must possess a blend of knowledge and experience. That knowledge must include the fundamentals of *all* communication, specific knowledge of software communication, awareness of the methodologies available, and the judgment to create a proper blend out of this knowledge. Experience, added to knowledge, hones the knowledge into a usable form. It has been the intention of this book to present the necessary knowledge, stimulate and shape the necessary judgment, and make that mix more palatable with a collection of fairly personal anecdotes. It is now your turn to decide how well the book has accomplished its intentions.

6.1 BIBLIOGRAPHY

ALAVI84 Alavi, M., "An Assessment of the Prototyping Approach to Information Systems Development," *Communications of the ACM,* June 1984.

ANDER85 Anderson, C., "The Organized Writer," *PC Magazine,* May 14, 1985.

AVIZ84 Avizienis, A., and J. P. J. Kelly, "Fault Tolerance by Design Diversity: Concepts and Experiments," *IEEE Computer,* August 1984.

BOEHM84 Boehm, B. W., T. E. Gray, and T. Seewaldt, "Prototyping vs. Specifying: A Multiproject Experiment," *IEEE Transactions on Software Engineering,* May 1984.

BONO85 Bono, P. R., "A Survey of Graphics Standards and Their Role In Information Interchange," *IEEE Computer,* October 1985.

BRUCE82 Bruce, P., and S. M. Pederson, *The Software Development Project: Planning and Management.* New York: Wiley-Interscience, 1982.

BROOKS75 Brooks, F. P., Jr., *The Mythical Man-Month.* Reading, MA: Addison-Wesley, 1975.

BRYAN82 Bryan, W. L., S. G. Siegel, and G. L. Whiteleather, "Auditing Throughout the Software Life Cycle: A Primer," *IEEE Computer,* March 1982.

BUSCS84 "Business Computer Products—Dealer Field Report," *Business Computer Systems,* October 1984.

CART82 Carter, J., *Keeping Faith.* New York: Bantam Books, 1982. Contains a detailed account of former President Carter's mideastern peace negotiations.

CULLEN86 Cullen, G., "Videoconferencing: A Long Way From Fulfilling Its Promise," *InformationWEEK,* April 21, 1986.

DEMILL077 DeMillo, R. A., R. J. Lipton, and A. J. Perlis, "Social Processes and Proofs of Theorems and Programs," *Proceedings of the Fourth Symposium on Principles of Programming Languages,* 1977.

DOD1521 Military Standard for Technical Reviews and Audits for Systems, Equipment, and Computer Software, MIL-STD-1521B. Washington, DC: U.S. Government Printing Office, June 4, 1985.

DOD7935.1-STD Department of Defense Automated Data Systems Documentation Standards. Washington, DC: U.S. Government Printing Office, April 24, 1984.

FIPS PUB 38 Federal Information Processing Standards Publication 38, "Guidelines for Documentation of Computer Programs and Automated Data Systems." National Technical Information Service: Springfield, VA, Feb. 15, 1976.

GLASS79 Glass, R. L., *Software Reliability Guidebook.* Englewood Cliffs, NJ: Prentice-Hall, 1979.

GLASS81 Glass, R. L., "Persistent Software Errors," *IEEE Transactions on Software Engineering,* March 1981.

GLASS81a Glass, R. L., *Software Maintenance Guidebook.* Englewood Cliffs, NJ: Prentice-Hall, 1981.

GLASS82 Glass, R. L., *Modern Programming Practices.* Englewood Cliffs, NJ: Prentice-Hall, 1982.

GLOSS83 Glossbrenner, *The Complete Handbook of Personal Computer Communication: Everything you Need to Know to Go On-Line with the World.* New York: St. Martin's Press, 1983.

HANKS77 Hanks, K., and L. Belliston, *Draw! A Visual Approach to Thinking, Learning, and Communicating.* Los Altos, CA: William Kauffman, 1977.

HANT76 Hantler, S. L., and J. C. King, "An Introduction to Proving the Correctness of Programs," *ACM Computing Surveys,* September 1976.

HECKEL83 Heckel, P., "Designing Translator Software," in R. L. Glass, *Real-Time Software.* Englewood Cliffs, NJ: Prentice-Hall, 1983.

HORAK85 Horak, W., "Office Document Architecture and Office Document Interchange Formats: Current Status of International Standardization," *IEEE Computer,* October 1985.

IEEE84 *Software Engineering Standards.* New York: IEEE and Wiley-Interscience, 1984.

IEEE85 "Requirements Engineering Environments," special issue of *IEEE Computer,* April 1985.

IEEE85b "Visual Programming," special issue of *IEEE Computer,* August 1985.

IW86 "Info Centers a Hive of Activity," special issue of *InformationWEEK,* April 14, 1986.

JONES79 Jones, C., "A Survey of Programming Design and Specification Techniques," *Proceedings of "Specifications on Reliable Software",* April 1979.

MARTIN85 Martin, J., and C. McClure, *Diagramming Techniques for Analysts and Programmers.* Englewood Cliffs, NJ: Prentice-Hall, 1985.

MARC82 Marcus, M. L., and J. Yates, "Historical Lessons for the Automated Office," *Computer Decisions,* June 1982, pp. 116–119, 260.

MCCR82 McCracken, D. D., and M. A. Jackson, "Life-Cycle Concept Considered Harmful," *ACM Software Engineering Notes,* April 1982.

MCCU78 McCue, G. M., "IBM's Santa Teresa Laboratory—Architectural Design for Program Development," *IBM Systems Journal,* 17, no. 1 (1978).

MEYER85 Meyer, B., "On Formalism in Specifications," *IEEE Software,* January 1985.

MIL-STD-483A Military Standard Configuration Management Practices for Systems, Equipment, Munitions, and Computer Programs. Washington, DC: U.S. Government Printing Office, June 4, 1985.

MIL-STD-490 Military Standard Specification Practices. Washington, DC: U.S. Government Printing Office, October 30, 1968.

MYER76 Myers, G. J., *Software Reliability Principles and Practices.* New York: Wiley-Interscience, 1976.

MYER79 Myers, G. J., *The Art of Software Testing.* New York: Wiley-Interscience, 1979.

PC85 Special reports on "Corporate Communications," especially related to electronic mail systems, and "Designing Computer Workspace," on computer user environments; *PC Magazine,* Sept. 3, 1985.

PETERS77 Peters, L., and L. Tripp, "Comparing Software Design Methodologies," *Datamation,* November 1977.

PRUEITT84 Prueitt, M. L., *Art and the Computer.* New York: McGraw-Hill, 1984.

RUSS85 Russell, J. S., *Writing at Work—the Russell and Associates Papers.* New York: Holt, Rinehart and Winston, 1985.

SARIN85 Sarin, S., and I. Greif, "Computer-Based Real-Time Conferencing Systems," *IEEE Computer,* October 1985.

SCHUTTE83 Schutte, W. M., and E. R. Steinberg, *Communication in Business and Industry.* New York: Holt, Rinehart and Winston, 1983.

SD82 "Honeywell Designs for Software Productivity," *Systems Development,* March 1982.

SHNEID77 Shneiderman, B., R. Mayer, D. McKay, and P. Heller, "Experimental Investigation of the Utility of Detailed Flowcharts in Programming," *Communications of the ACM,* June 1977.

SNYD83 Snyders, J., "Documentation Packages Write Up Front," *Computer Decisions,* June 1983.

SPECTOR84 Spector, A., and D. Gifford, "Case Study: the Space Shuttle Primary Computer System," *Communications of the ACM,* September 1984.

STRUNK79 Strunk, W., Jr., and E. B. White, *The Elements of Style.* New York: Macmillan, 1979.

TUFTE83 Tufte, E. R., *The Visual Display of Quantitative Information.* Cheshire, CT: Graphics Press, 1983.

WEITZ80 Weitzman, C., *Distributed Micro/Minicomputer Systems.* Englewood Cliffs, NJ: Prentice-Hall, 1980.

YANK85 Yankelovich, N., N. Meyrowitz, and A. van Dam, "Reading and Writing the Electronic Book," *IEEE Computer,* October 1985.

YOURDON80 Yourdon, E., *Structured Walkthroughs* (2nd ed). Englewood Cliffs, NJ: Prentice-Hall, Inc., 1980.

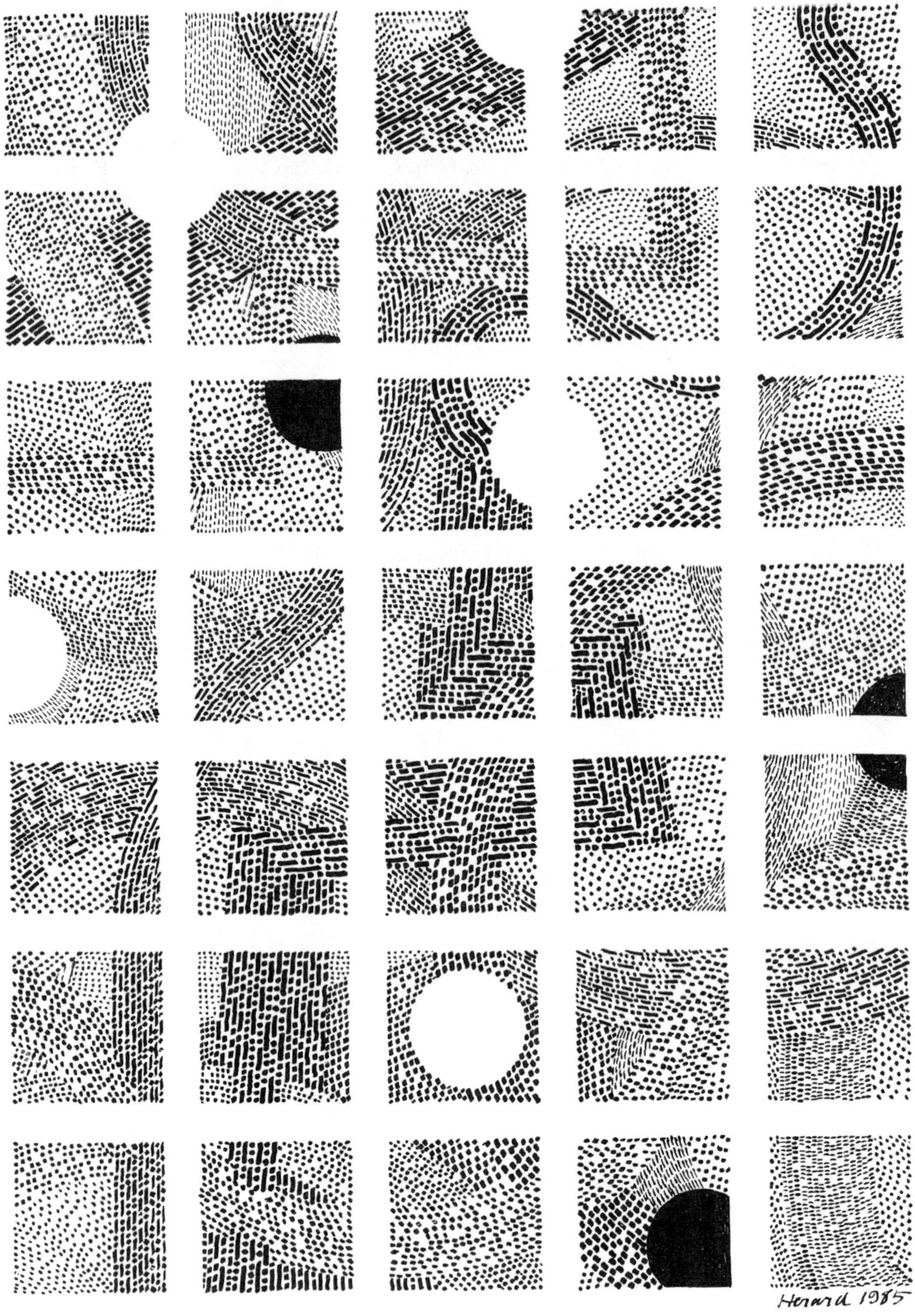

Even in a field as soft and swirly as software, it is possible to utilize standards. They become a grid of regularity and predictability superimposed over the intangible software product.

APPENDIX A

Documentation Standards for Software

This appendix contains a fuller description of the currently defined documentation standards for software. These descriptions are compared and contrasted in material earlier in this book. They are included here for reference and for more complete content only. Because these standards may evolve over time, the reader who intends to use these standards is advised to obtain the latest version from the source of the standard.

A.1 FIPS PUB 38

The material that follows is pages 3 through 55 of Federal Information Processing Standards Publication 38, "Guidelines for Documentation of Computer Programs and Automated Data Systems," Feb. 15, 1976.

GUIDELINES FOR DOCUMENTATION OF COMPUTER PROGRAMS AND AUTOMATED DATA SYSTEMS

Contents

Figures

Introduction

The planning, design, development, and implementation of computer programs and automated data systems[1] represent a considerable investment of human and automated resources. To maximize the return on this investment, and to provide for cost-effective operation, revision, and maintenance, sufficient documentation is needed at each stage of the software development life cycle. This publication has been prepared in response to that need.

Documentation provides information to support the effective management of ADP resources and to facilitate the interchange of information. It serves to:

—Provide managers with technical documents to review at the significant development milestones, to determine that requirements have been met and that resources should continue to be expended.

—Record technical information to allow coordination of later development and use/modification of the software.

—Facilitate understanding among managers, developers, programmers, operators, and users by providing information about maintenance, training, changes, and operation of the software.

—Inform other potential users of the functions and capabilities of the software, so that they can determine whether it will serve their needs.

The quality and consistency of software documentation depend on management commitment and the technical environment. The criteria for evaluating the adequacy of documentation will vary directly with the perceived need for documentation. The utility, quality, and acceptability of the documents prepared will provide a measure of the management judgment exercised in implementing the documentation guidelines.

This publication provides guidelines for the content of software documentation and examples of how management might determine when and how to utilize the ten document types described. Part 1 states the purpose of each document type and its relationship to the software life cycle. Part 2 discusses considerations in using these documentation guidelines including examples of agency or organization level guidance criteria that can be applied to determine the extent of documentation required. Part 3 presents the content guidelines for the ten document types.[2]

[1] Throughout this FIPS PUB 38 "software" is used in lieu of "computer program and/or automated data system."

[2] Note that the Software Summary for Describing Computer Programs and Automated Data Systems (FIPS PUB 30) is considered a component of documentation, in this context.

PART 1. DOCUMENTATION WITHIN THE SOFTWARE LIFE CYCLE

1.1. Scope. Computer programs and automated data systems evolve in phases from the time that an idea to create the software occurs through the time that that software produces the required output. It is recognized that there are in current usage many different terminologies to identify these phases and the stages within these phases. Three phases applicable to the software life cycle are: initiation, development, and operation. The development phase is further subdivided into four stages.

This publication provides content guidelines for ten document types generally prepared during the development phase. Figure 1 relates the preparation of the ten document types to the stages in the development phase. The amount of documentation produced is flexible, and this flexibility is discussed in Part 2. Content guidelines for the ten document types is provided in Part 3. Each of these document types can stand alone or be combined with others to meet specific documentation requirements.

FIGURE 1. *Documentation within the software life cycle*

<table>
<tr><th>INITIATION PHASE</th><th colspan="4">DEVELOPMENT PHASE</th><th>OPERATION PHASE</th></tr>
<tr><td></td><td>Definition Stage</td><td>Design Stage</td><td>Programming Stage</td><td>Test Stage</td><td></td></tr>
<tr><td></td><td>Functional Requirements Document</td><td>System/ Subsystem Specification</td><td>Users Manual</td><td></td><td></td></tr>
<tr><td></td><td></td><td>Program Specification</td><td>Operations Manual</td><td></td><td></td></tr>
<tr><td></td><td>Data Requirements Document</td><td>Data Base Specification</td><td>Program Maintenance Manual</td><td></td><td></td></tr>
<tr><td></td><td></td><td colspan="2">Test Plan</td><td>Test Analysis Report</td><td></td></tr>
</table>

1.2. Phases. While the terminology used to describe the phases is arbitrary, it provides a convenient framework within which the development of software may be discussed.

1.2.1. Initiation. During the Initiation Phase, the objectives and general definition of the requirements for the software are established. Feasibility studies, cost-benefit analyses, and the documentation prepared within this phase are determined by agency procedures and practices.

1.2.2. Development. During the Development Phase, the requirements for the software are determined and the software is then defined, specified, programmed, and tested. Documentation is prepared within this phase to provide an adequate record of the technical information developed.

1.2.3. Operation. During the Operation Phase, the software is maintained, evaluated, and changed as additional requirements are identified.

1.3. Stages. While the terminology used to describe the stages is arbitrary, it provides a convenient framework within which the development of the ten document types may be discussed. It is recognized that not all of the document types are required to document software in every case and that in some cases the various document types may need to be combined. The flexible nature of these guidelines is discussed in Part 2.

1.3.1. Definition. During the definition stage, the requirements for the software and documentation are determined. The Functional Requirements Document and the Data Requirements Document may be prepared.

1.3.2. Design. During the design stage, the design alternatives, specific requirements, and functions to be performed are analyzed and a design is specified. Documents which may be prepared include the System/Subsystem Specification, Program Specification, Data Base Specification, and Test Plan.

1.3.3. Programming. During the programming stage, the software is coded and debugged. Documents which may be prepared during this stage include the Users Manual, Operations Manual, Program Maintenance Manual, and Test Plan.

1.3.4. Test. During the test stage, the software is tested and related documentation reviewed. The software and documentation are evaluated in terms of readiness for implementation. The Test Analysis Report may be prepared.

1.4 Document Types. The purpose of each of the ten document types, described in further detail in part 3, is defined in the following paragraphs.

1.4.1. Functional Requirements Document. The purpose of the Functional Requirements Document is to provide a basis for the mutual understanding between users and designers of the initial definition of the software, including the requirements, operating environment, and development plan.

1.4.2. Data Requirements Document. The purpose of the Data Requirements Document is to provide, during the definition stage of software development, a data description and technical information about data collection requirements.

1.4.3. System/Subsystem Specification. The purpose of the System/Subsystem Specification is to specify for analysts and programmers the requirements, operating environment, design characteristics, and program specifications (if desired) for a system or subsystem.

1.4.4. Program Specification. The purpose of the Program Specification is to specify for programmers the requirements, operating environment, and design characteristics of a computer program.

1.4.5. Data Base Specification. The purpose of the Data Base Specification is to specify the identification, logical characteristics, and physical characteristics of a particular data base.

1.4.6. Users Manual. The purpose of the Users Manual is to sufficiently describe the functions performed by the software in non-ADP terminology, such that the user organization can determine its applicability and when and how to use it. It should serve as a reference document for preparation of input data and parameters and for interpretation of results.

1.4.7. Operations Manual. The purpose of the Operations Manual is to provide computer operation personnel with a description of the software and of the operational environment so that the software can be run.

1.4.8. Program Maintenance Manual. The purpose of the Program Maintenance Manual is to provide the maintenance programmer with the information necessary to understand the programs, their operating environment, and their maintenance procedures.

1.4.9. Test Plan. The purpose of the Test Plan is to provide a plan for the testing of software; detailed specifications, descriptions, and procedures for all tests; and test data reduction and evaluation criteria.

1.4.10. Test Analysis Report. The purpose of the Test Analysis Report is to document the test analysis results and findings, present the demonstrated capabilities and deficiencies for review, and provide a basis for preparing a statement of software readiness for implementation.

PART 2. DOCUMENTATION CONSIDERATIONS

Documentation preparation should be treated as a continuing effort, evolving from preliminary drafts, through changes and reviews, to the documentation and software delivered. The extent of documentation to be prepared is a function of agency management practices and the size, complexity and risk of the project.

2.1. Responsibilities. Separable responsibilities which are inherent in the flexible nature of these guidelines are:

a. Definition of agency guidance to project managers as to what documentation should be prepared under various conditions and, perhaps, to what levels of extent, detail, and formality. See Examples A and B in paragraph 2.5.

b. Determination by a project manager of the documentation plan for a specific project, including:

(1) What document types apply and should be prepared.
(2) The formality, extent, and detail of the documentation.
(3) Responsibilities and a schedule of preparation for the documentation.
(4) Procedures and schedule of review, approval, and distribution and the distribution list.
(5) Responsibilities for documentation maintenance and change control through the development phase.

The formality, extent, and level of detail, and other determinations by the project manager in specific cases will be more consistent if agency guidance and criteria are established. In general, as the size, complexity, and risk of a project increase, so does the need for formality, extent, and level of detail of the documentation. The Users, Operations, and Program Maintenance Manuals should be formal since they support the use of the software, particularly if the software will be used outside of the developing organization or if extensive changes are expected during the life of the software.

2.2 Document Audiences. Each document type is written for a particular "audience." The audience may be an individual or a group of individuals who are expected to use the document contents to perform a function, e.g., operation, maintenance, design, programming. The information should be presented using the terminology and level of detail appropriate to the audience.

2.3. Redundancy. The ten document types in this guideline have some apparent redundancy. This apparent redundancy is of two types. Introductory material has been included in each document type to provide the reader with a frame of reference. This information has been included to provide the "stand alone" approach, and understanding of the document with a minimum need for cross-referencing to parts of other documents that may have been produced. A second type of apparent redundancy is that most document types specify, for example, descriptions of inputs, outputs, and equipment to be included. The information that should be included in each of the document types, differs in context and, perhaps, in terminology and level of detail, since the information is intended to be read by different audiences and at different points in the software life cycle.

2.4. Flexibility. Flexibility in the use of the document content guidelines is provided by the basic organization of contents. An attempt has been made to provide an internally consistent organization scheme. The following paragraphs describe various options which should be considered.

2.4.1. "Sizing" of Document Types. Each document type outline may be used to prepare documents that range from a few to several hundred pages in length. The size depends on the size and complexity of the project and the judgment of the project manager as to the level of detail necessary for the environment in which the software will be developed or run.

2.4.2. Combining and Expanding Document Types. It is occasionally necessary to combine several document types under one cover or to produce several volumes of the same document type. Document types that can be combined into one are, for example, the Users, Operations, and Program Maintenance Manuals. When this is done, the substance of the contents covered by each document type should be presented using the outline of that document type, for example, Part I–Users, Part II–Operations, and Part III–Program Maintenance.

When a system is extremely large or is to be documented in a modular fashion, a document may be prepared for each module. In some cases, the size of a document may necessitate that it be issued in multiple volumes to allow ease of user reference. In such cases, the document should be separated at a section division. The contents of the Test Plan document type, for example, may be separated between the sections of plan, specifications and evaluation, and specific test descriptions.

2.4.3. Format. The content guidelines in Part 3 have been prepared using a generally consistent format. Use of this particular format is encouraged but is not essential. It is a tested and accepted format.

2.4.4. Sequencing of Contents. In general, the order of the sections and paragraphs in a particular document type should be the same as shown in the content guidelines in Part 3. The order may be changed if it significantly enhances the presentation.

2.4.5. Documenting Multiple Programs or Multiple Files. Many of the document type content outlines anticipate and are adaptable to documenting a system and its subsystems, multiple programs, or multiple files. All of these outlines can, of course, be used for a single system, subsystem, program, data base, or file.

2.4.6. Section/Paragraph Titles. In general, the titles of sections and paragraphs should be the same as shown in the content guidelines. The titles may be modified to reflect terminology unique to the software being documented if the change significantly enhances the presentation. Sections or paragraphs may be added or deleted as local requirements dictate.

2.4.7. Expansion of Paragraphs. Many of the document types have paragraphs with a general title and a list of factors that might be discussed within that paragraph. The intent of the content guidelines is not to prescribe a discussion of each of these items, but to suggest that these items be considered in writing that paragraph. These and all other paragraphs may be expanded and further subdivided to enhance the presentation.

2.4.8. Flowcharts/Decision Tables. The graphic representations of some problem solutions are treated best in the form of flowcharts, others in the form of decision tables. Either may be included in or appended to the documents produced.

2.4.9. Forms. The use of specific forms is dependent on practices in an agency. Some of the information specified in a paragraph in the content guidelines may be recorded on such forms. If so, the form can be referenced from the appropriate paragraph. The use of standard forms is encouraged.

2.5. Examples of Documentation Guidance and Criteria. The formality, extent, and level of detail of documentation to be prepared is a function of agency ADP management practices and the size, complexity, and risk of a project. The following examples were taken from two Federal agency directives, but are amended to conform to the naming of document types in this publication. The examples illustrate how criteria could be established to aid project managers in determining the extent and level of detail of documentation required.

Example A presents a scheme using development cost and document audience as two criteria to establish thresholds for documentation requirements. See the following pages and Figure 2.

Example B presents a scheme using twelve criteria with weighting factors and a scale of the total weighted criteria to establish formal documentation requirements. Figure 3 illustrates the application of the weighted criteria shown in Figure 4. The procedure to use these tables is:

1. Weight the software by each of the twelve criteria in Figure 4.
2. Sum the weights assigned. (Total weighted criteria.)
3. Find the row in Figure 3 that lists the document types to be prepared.

FIGURE 2. EXAMPLE A. *Cost and/or usage threshold criteria for extent and formality*

Level	If PROJECT COST:	Or USAGE	Then DOCUMENTATION ELEMENTS	And EXTENT OF EFFORT
1	Less than $1000 Or One Man-month	One Shot (Single Use)	Software Summary plus any incidentally produced documentation.	No special effort, normal good practice.
2	$1000 to $5000	Special or Limited Purpose or Application	Level 1 plus Users Manual and Operations Manual.	Minimal documentation effort, spent on informal documentation. No formal documentation effort.
3	Over $5000	Multipurposed, or Multiuser	Level 2 plus Functional Requirements Document, Program Specification, Program Maintenance Manual, Test Plan, Test Analysis Report, and System/Subsystem Specification.	All basic elements of documentation should be typewritten, but need not be prepared in finished format for publication or require external edit or review.
4	Over $5000	Publicly Announced, or Critical to Operations	Level 3 produced in a form suitable for publication.	At a minimum, all basic elements prepared for formal publication, including external review and edit.

EXAMPLE A. LEVELS OF DOCUMENTATION

DEFINITIONS OF LEVELS

To protect against both over and under documentation, computer program documentation has been divided into four levels. From lowest to highest these levels of documentation are: (1) minimal level, (2) internal level, (3) working document[3] level, and (4) formal publication level. The criteria determining these levels of documentation are described in the following paragraphs, and summarized in Figure 2. Additional criteria peculiar to an installation and/or judgment relative to program sharing potential, life expectancy, and usage frequency are also appropriate factors to be considered in the determination of documentation levels.

MINIMAL LEVEL (LEVEL 1)

Level 1 documentation guidelines are applicable to single use programs, or one-shot jobs, of minimal complexity. Although no significant documentation cost should be added, there exists the requirement to show what type of work is being produced and what a given program really does. Hence, it is desirable to keep on file for a minimum period of time the documentation which results from the development of the programs, i.e., program abstract, compile listing, test cases, etc. The criteria for categorizing a program as Level 1 can be its expected usage or the resource expended in its generation, in man-hours or dollars, and may be modified for the peculiar requirements of the installations. Suggested resource expenditure criteria are programs requiring less than one man-month effort or less than $1,000 (these are not assumed to be equal).

INTERNAL LEVEL (LEVEL 2)

Level 2 documentation applies to special purpose programs which, after careful consideration of the possible interest of others, appear to have no sharing potential and to be designed for use only by the requesting scientist or manager in an environment over which he has cognizance. Large programs which have a short life expectancy also fall into this level. The documentation required (other than Level 1) is that necessary for deck setup and modifications. This requirement can be satisfied by the inclusion of detail input/output formats, setup instructions, and the liberal use of comment cards in the source deck to provide clarification in the compile listing. In summary, the effort spent toward formal documentation for Level 2 programs should be minimal.

[3] The term "working document" or "working paper" as used in this guideline refer to typewritten documents, not necessarily prepared in finished format suitable for publication nor subject to external editorial review.

WORKING DOCUMENT LEVEL (LEVEL 3)

This level applies to programs which are expected to be used by a number of people in the same installation or which may be transmitted on request to other installations or to contractors or grantees. The format of the documentation at this level should include, as a minimum, all elements of documentation. All basic elements of documentation should be prepared in typewritten form, but not necessarily in a finished format suitable for publication. Normally, it will not be formally reviewed or edited above the review required for a working paper. However, if there are certain programs important to the activities of the installations, but not considered appropriate for publication, then local more stringent documentation review standards should be applied.

FORMAL PUBLICATION LEVEL (LEVEL 4)

This level applies to programs which are of sufficient general interest and value to be anounced outside the originating installation. This level of documentation is also desirable if the program is to be referenced by a scientific publication or paper. The format of the documentation at this level should comply with the guidelines on elements of documentation suitable for inclusion in one of the scientific and technical publication series with the attendant review and editing procedures.

Also considered to be within this level are those programs which are critical to the activities of the installation. These programs should be documented in a formal, rigorous manner, with in-depth review and special configuration control procedures enforced. Recurring management applications, such as payroll, should be considered for inclusion in this category so as to maintain an accurate history of conformation to changing laws, rules, and regulations.

FIGURE 3. EXAMPLE B. *Total weighted documentation criteria vs required document types*

(See Figure 4 to determine total weighted criteria.)

TOTAL WEIGHTED CRITERIA	Software Summary	Users Manual	Operations Manual	Program Maintenance Manual	Test Plan	Functional Requirements Document	System/Subsystem Specification	Test Analysis Report	Program Specification	Data Requirements Document	Data Base Specification
0-12*	X										
12-15*	X	X									
12-26	X	X	X	X	X			**		***	***
24-38	X	X	X	X	X	X		**		***	***
36-50	X	X	X	X	X	X	X	X		***	***
48-60	X	X	X	X	X	X	X	X	X	***	***

NOTES: * Additional document types may be required at lower weighted criteria totals to satisfy local requirements.

** The Test Analysis Report logically should be prepared, but may be informal.

*** Preparation of the Data Requirements Document and Data Base Specification is situationally dependent.

FIGURE 4. EXAMPLE B. *An example of weighting for twelve documentation criteria (See Figure 3 for application of total weighted criteria to determination of required documentation types.)*

	WEIGHTS				
Criteria	1	2	3	4	5
1. Originality required	None—reprogram on different equipment	Minimum—more stringent requirements	Limited—new interfaces	Considerable—apply existing state of art to environment	Extensive—requires advance in state of the art
2. Degree of generality	Highly restricted. Single purpose	Restricted—parameterized for a range of capacities	Limited flexibility. Allows some change in format	Multi-purpose. Flexible format. Range of subjects	Very flexible—able to handle a broad range of subject matter on different equipment
3. Span of operation	Local or utility	Component command	Single command	Multi-command	Defense Department. World wide.
4. Change in scope and objective	None	Infrequent	Occasional	Frequent	Continuous.
5. Equipment complexity	Single machine. Routine processing	Single machine. Routine processing. Extended peripheral system	Multi-computer. Standard peripheral system	Multi-computer. Advanced programming. Complex peripheral system	Master control system. Multi-computer auto input/output and display equipment.
6. Personnel assigned	1–2	3–5	5–10	10–18	18 and over
7. Developmental cost	1–10k	10–50k	50–200k	200–500k	Over 500k
8. Criticality	Data processing	Routine operations	Personnel safety	Unit survival	National defense
9. Average response time to program change	2 or more weeks	1–2 weeks	3–7 days	1–3 days	1–24 hours
10. Average response time to data inputs	2 or more weeks	1–2 weeks	1–7 days	1–24 hours	0–60 minutes
11. Programming languages	High level language	High level and limited assembly language	High level and extensive assembly language	Assembly language	Machine language
12. Concurrent software development	None	Limited	Moderate	Extensive	Exhaustive

PART 3. CONTENT GUIDELINES FOR DOCUMENT TYPES

Part 3 provides content guidelines for the following ten document types discussed in Parts 1 and 2.

The document types are presented in the order of development within the software life cycle. Included for each document type are a table of contents and a description of the contents of that document type. The page numbers given in the table of contents for each document type are those within the boxes.

3.1 Functional Requirements Document

The purpose of the Functional Requirements Document is to provide a basis for the mutual understanding between users and designers of the initial definition of the software, including the requirements, operating environment, and development plan.

Contents

Functional Requirements Document

1. GENERAL INFORMATION

1.1. **Summary.** Summarize the general nature of the software to be developed.

1.2. **Environment.** Identify the project sponsor, developer, user, and computer center or network where the software is to be implemented.

1.3. **References.** List applicable references, such as:

a. Project request (authorizations).
b. Previously published documents on the project.
c. Documentation concerning related projects.
d. FIPS publications and other reference documents.

2. OVERVIEW

2.1. **Background.** Present the purpose and scope of the software, and any background information that would orient the reader. Explain relationships with other software.

2.2. **Objectives.** State the major performance objectives of the software, including examples. Identify anticipated operational changes that will affect the software and its use.

2.3. **Existing Methods and Procedures.** Describe the current methods and procedures that satisfy the existing objectives. Include information on:

a. Organizational and personnel responsibilities.
b. Equipment available and required.
c. Volume and frequency of inputs and outputs.
d. Deficiencies and limitations.
e. Pertinent cost considerations.

Illustrate the existing data flow from data acquisition through its processing and eventual output. Explain the sequence in which operational functions are performed by the user.

2.4. **Proposed Methods and Procedures.** Describe the proposed software and its capabilities. Identify techniques and procedures from other software that will be used or that will become part of the proposed software. Identify the requirements that will be satisfied by the proposed software. Include information on:

a. Organizational and personnel responsibilities.
b. Equipment available and required.
c. Volume and frequency of inputs and outputs.
d. Deficiencies and limitations.
e. Pertinent cost considerations (developmental as well as operational).

Illustrate the proposed data flow to present an overall view of the planned capabilities. Describe any capabilities in the existing software that may be changed by the proposed software. State the reasons for these changes. Explain the sequence in which operational functions are to be performed by the user.

Functional Requirements Document

2.5. **Summary of Improvements.** Itemize improvements to be obtained from the proposed software, such as:

a. New capabilities.
b. Upgraded existing capabilities.
c. Elimination of existing deficiencies.
d. Improved timeliness, e.g., decreased response time or processing time.
e. Elimination or reduction of existing capabilities that are no longer needed.

2.6. **Summary of Impacts.** Summarize the anticipated impacts of the proposed software on the present system, in the following categories:

2.6.1. Equipment Impacts. Summarize changes to currently available equipment, as well as new equipment requirements and building modifications.

2.6.2. Software Impacts. Summarize any additions or modifications needed to existing applications and support software in order to adapt them to the proposed software.

2.6.3. Organizational Impacts. Summarize organizational impacts, such as:

a. Functional reorganization.
b. Increase/decrease in staff level.
c. Upgrade/downgrade of staff skills.

2.6.4. Operational Impacts. Summarize operational impacts, such as modifications to:

a. Staff and operational procedures.
b. Relationships between the operating center and the users.
c. Procedures of the operating center.
d. Data (sources, volume, medium, timeliness).
e. Data retention and retrieval procedures.
f. Reporting methods.
g. System failure consequences and recovery procedures.
h. Data input procedures.
i. Computer processing time requirements.

2.6.5. Developmental Impacts. Summarize developmental impacts, such as:

a. Specific activities to be performed by the user in support of development of the proposed software.
b. Resources required to develop the data base.
c. Computer processing resources required to develop and test the new software.

2.7. **Cost Considerations.** Describe resource and cost factors that may influence the development, design, and continued operation of the proposed software. Discuss other factors which may determine requirements, such as interfaces with other automated systems and telecommunication facilities.

2.8. **Alternative Proposals.** If alternative software has been proposed to satisfy the requirements, describe each alternative. Compare and contrast the alternatives. Explain the selection reasoning.

Functional Requirements Document

3. REQUIREMENTS

3.1. Functions. State the functions required of the software in quantitative and qualitative terms, and how these functions will satisfy the performance objectives.

3.2. Performance. Specify the performance requirements.

3.2.1. Accuracy. Describe the data accuracy requirements imposed on the software, such as:

a. Mathematical.
b. Logical.
c. Legal.
d. Transmission.

3.2.2. Validation. Describe the data validation requirements imposed on the software.

3.2.3. Timing. Describe the timing requirements imposed on the software, such as, under varying conditions:

a. Response time.
b. Update processing time.
c. Data transfer and transmission time.
d. Throughput time.

3.2.4. Flexibility. Describe the capability for adapting to changes in requirements, such as:

a. Changes in modes of operation.
b. Operating environment.
c. Interfaces with other software.
d. Accuracy and validation timing.
e. Planned changes or improvements.

Identify the software components which are specifically designed to provide this flexibility.

3.3. Inputs-Outputs. Explain and show examples of the various data inputs. Specify the medium (disk, cards, magnetic tape), format, range of values, accuracy, etc. Provide examples and explanation of the data outputs required of the software, and any quality control outputs that have been identified. Include descriptions or examples of hard copy reports (routine, situational and exception) as well as graphic or display reports.

3.4. Data Characteristics. Describe individual and composite data elements by name, their related coded representations, as well as relevant dictionaries, tables, and reference files. Estimate total storage requirements for the data and related components based on expected growth.

3.5. Failure Contingencies. Specify the possible failures of the hardware or software, the consequences (in terms of performance), and the alternative courses of action that may be taken to satisfy the information requirements. Include:

Functional Requirements Document

a. Back-up. Specify back-up techniques, i.e., the redundancy available in the event the primary system element goes down. For example, a back-up technique for a disk medium would be to record periodically the contents of the disk to a tape.
b. Fallback. Explain the fallback techniques, i.e., the use of another system or other means to accomplish some portion of requirements. For example, the fallback technique for an automated system might be manual manipulation and recording of data.
c. Recovery and Restart. Discuss the recovery and restart techniques, i.e., the capability to resume execution of software from a point in the software subsequent to which a hardware or software problem occurred, or the re-running of the software from the beginning.

4. OPERATING ENVIRONMENT

4.1. Equipment. Identify the equipment required for the operation of the software. Identify any new equipment required and relate it to specific functions and requirements to be supported. Include information such as:

a. Processor and size of internal storage.
b. Storage, online and offline, media, form, and devices.
c. Input/output devices, online and offline.
d. Data transmission devices.

4.2. Support Software. Identify the support software and describe any test software. If the operation of the software depends on changes to support software, identify the nature and planned date of these changes.

4.3. Interfaces. Describe the interfaces with other software.

4.4. Security and Privacy. Describe the overall security and privacy requirements imposed on the software. If no specific requirements are imposed, state this fact.

4.5. Controls. Describe the operational controls imposed on the software. Identify the sources of these controls.

5. DEVELOPMENT PLAN

Discuss in this section the overall management approach to the development and implementation of the proposed software. Include a list of the documentation to be produced, time frames and milestones for the development of the software, and necessary participation by other organizations to assure successful development.

3.2 Data Requirements Document

The purpose of the Data Requirements Document is to provide, during the definition stage of software development, a data description and technical information about data collection requirements.

Contents

Data Requirements Document

1. GENERAL INFORMATION

1.1. Summary. Summarize the general nature of the software for which these data requirements are being defined.

1.2. Environment. Identify the project sponsor, developer, user organization, and computer center where the software is to be installed. Show the relationships of these data requirements and those of other software.

1.3. References. List applicable references, such as:

a. Project request (authorization).
b. Previously published documents on the project.
c. Documentation concerning related projects.
d. FIPS publications and other reference documents.

1.4. Modification of Data Requirements. Describe or reference procedures for implementing and documenting changes to these data requirements.

2. DATA DESCRIPTION

Separate the data description into two categories, static data and dynamic data. Static data is defined as that data which is used mainly for reference during operation and is usually generated or updated in widely separated time frames independent of normal runs. Dynamic data includes all data which is intended to be updated and which is input during a normal run or is output. Arrange the data elements in each category in logical groupings, such as functions, subjects, or other groupings which are most relevant to their use.

2.1. Static Data. List the static data elements used for either control or reference purposes.

2.2. Dynamic Input Data. List the dynamic input data elements which constitute the data intended to be changed by a normal run or during online operation.

2.3. Dynamic Output Data. List the dynamic output data elements which constitute the data intended to be changed by a normal run or during online operation.

2.4. Internally Generated Data. List the internally generated data of informational value to the user or developer.

2.5. Data Contraints. State the constraints on the data requirements. Indicate the limits of the data requirements with regard to further expansion or utilization, such as the maximum size and number of files, records, and data elements. Emphasize the constraints that could prove critical during design and development.

Data Requirements Document

3. **DATA COLLECTION**

3.1. **Requirements and Scope.** Describe the type of information required to document the characteristics of each data element. Specify information to be collected by the user and that to be collected by the developer. It should be logically grouped and presented. Include:

a. Source of Input. Identify the source from which the data will be entered, e.g., an operator, station, organizational unit, or its component group.
b. Input Medium and Device. Identify the medium and hardware device intended for entering the data into the system. In those cases where only certain special stations are to be legitimate entry points, they should be specified.
c. Recipients. Identify the intended recipients of the output data.
d. Output Medium and Device. Identify the medium and hardware device intended for presenting output data to the recipient. Specify whether the recipient is to receive the data as part of a hard copy printout, a symbol in a CRT display, a line on a drawing, a colored light, an alarm bell, etc. If the output is to be passed to some other automated system, the medium should be described, such as magnetic tape, punched cards, or an electronic signal to a solenoid switch.
e. Critical Value. One value from a range of values of data may have particular significance to a recipient.
f. Scales of Measurement. Specify for numeric scales, units of measurement, increments, scale zero-point, and range of values. For non-numeric scales, any relationships indicated by the legal values should be stated.
g. Conversion Factors. Specify the conversion factors of measured quantities that must go through analog or digital conversion processes.
h. Frequency of Update and Processing. Specify the expected frequency of data change and the expected frequency of processing input data. If the input arrives in a random or in an "as occurred" manner, both the average frequency and some measure of the variance must be specified.

3.2. **Input Responsibilities.** Provide recommendations as to responsibilities for preparing specific data inputs. Include any recommendations regarding the establishment of a data input group. Specify by source those data inputs dependent on interfacing software or unrelated organizations.

3.3. **Procedures.** Provide specific instructions for data collection procedures. Include detailed formats where applicable, and identify expected data communications media and timing of inputs.

3.4. **Impacts.** Describe the impacts of these data requirements on equipment, software and the user and developer organizations.

3

3.3 System/Subsystem Specification

The purpose of the System/Subsystem Specification is to specify for Analysts and Programmers the requirements, operating environment, design characteristics, and program specifications (if desired) for a system or subsystem.

Contents

System/Subsystem Specification

1. **GENERAL INFORMATION**

   1.1. **Summary.** Summarize the specifications and functions of the system/subsystem to be developed.

   1.2. **Environment.** Identify the project sponsor, developer, user, and computer center or network on which the system is to be implemented.

   1.3. **References.** List applicable references, such as:

   a. Project request (authorizations).
   b. Previously published documents on the subject.
   c. Documentation concerning related projects.
   d. FIPS publications and other reference documents.

2. **REQUIREMENTS**

   2.1. **Description.** Provide a general description of the system/subsystem to establish a frame of reference for the remainder of the document. Include a summary of functional requirements to be satisfied by this system/subsystem. Show the general interrelationship of the system/subsystem components.

   2.2. **Functions.** Specify the system/subsystem functions in quantitative and qualitative terms and how the functions will satisfy the functional requirements.

   2.3. **Performance.** Specify the performance requirements.

   2.3.1. Accuracy. Describe the data accuracy requirements imposed on the system or subsystem, such as:

   a. Mathematical.
   b. Logical.
   c. Legal.
   d. Transmission.

   2.3.2. Validation. Describe the data validation requirements imposed on the system/subsystem.

   2.3.3. Timing. Describe the timing requirements imposed on the software, such as, under varying conditions:

   a. Response time.
   b. Update processing time.
   c. Data transfer and transmission time.
   d. Throughput time.

   2.3.4. Flexibility. Describe the capability for adapting the program to changes in requirements, such as:

The organization of the contents of Sections 2, 3, 4, and 5 may vary according to the purpose of the documentation. See Example following this content guideline, page 28.

System/Subsystem Specification

a. Changes in modes of operation.
b. Operating environment.
c. Interfaces with other software.
d. Accuracy and validation and timing.
e. Planned changes or improvements.

Identify the system/subsystem components which are specifically designed to provide this flexibility.

3. OPERATING ENVIRONMENT

3.1. Equipment. Identify the equipment required for the operation of the system/subsystem. Identify any new equipment required and relate it to specific functional requirements to be supported. Include information, such as:

a. Processor and size of internal storage.
b. Storage, online and offline, media, form, and devices.
c. Input/output devices, online and offline.
d. Data transmission devices.

3.2. Support Software. Identify the support software and describe any test software. If the operation of the system/subsystems depends on changes to support software, identify the nature and planned date of these changes.

3.3. Interfaces. Describe the interfaces with other software.

3.4. Security and Privacy. Describe the overall security and privacy requirements imposed on the system/subsystem. If no specific requirements are imposed, state this fact.

3.5. Controls. Describe the operational controls imposed on the system/subsystem. Identify the sources of these controls.

4. DESIGN CHARACTERISTICS

4.1. Operations. Describe the operating characteristics of the user and computer centers where the software will be operational.

4.2. System/Subsystem Logic. Describe the logic flow of the entire system/subsystem in the form of a flowchart. The flow should provide an integrated presentation of the system/subsystem dynamics, of entrances and exits, computer programs, support software, controls, and data flow.

5. PROGRAM SPECIFICATIONS

5.1. Program (Identify) Specification. Specify the system/subsystem functions to be satisfied by the computer program.

a. Describe the program requirements.
b. Describe the operating environment.
c. Describe the design characteristics of the program including inputs, program logic, outputs, and data base.

5.N. Program (Identify) Specification. Describe the remaining computer programs in a manner similar to the paragraph above.

System/Subsystem Specification

EXAMPLES OF ALTERNATIVE SECTION OUTLINES

Sections 2, 3, and 4 of this specification may follow one of several alternative outlines depending on the purpose to which the documentation is directed. Examples of alternative purposes and the corresponding outline are shown below.

Example A: When this document is directed to the documentation of a given system and is not to specifically include the documentation of any subsystem, the appropriate title would be "System Specification." The outline for the specification would be:

REQUIREMENTS
- Description
- Functions
- Performance

OPERATING ENVIRONMENT
- Equipment
- Support Software
- Interfaces
- Security and Privacy
- Controls

DESIGN CHARACTERISTICS
- Operations
- Logic

Example B: When this documents is directed to the documentation of a given subsystem, the appropriate title would be "Subsystem Specification." The outline for the specification would be the same as Example A above.

Example C: When this document is directed to the documentation of a system and its subsystems, the appropriate title would be "System and Subsystem Specifications." The outline, in brief, for the specification would be:

System REQUIREMENTS
System OPERATING ENVIRONMENT
System DESIGN CHARACTERISTICS
Subsystem 1 (Identify)
- REQUIREMENTS
- OPERATING ENVIRONMENT
- DESIGN CHARACTERISTICS
- PROGRAM SPECIFICATIONS

Subsystem 'n' (Identify)

Example D: In any of the above examples, the program specifications may be documented within as a separate section; as subsections to each subsystem section; or may be documented in a separate document, "Program Specification."

3.4 Program Specification

The purpose of the Program Specification is to specify for programmers the requirements, operating environment, and design characteristics of a computer program.

Contents

Program Specification

1. **GENERAL INFORMATION**

1.1. **Summary.** Summarize the specifications and functions of the computer program to be developed.

1.2. **Environment.** Identify the project sponsor, developer, user, and computer center where the computer .program is to be run.

1.3. **References.** List applicable references, such as:

a. Project request (authorization).
b. Previously published documents on the subject.
c. Documentation concerning related projects.
d. FIPS publications and other reference documents.

2. **REQUIREMENTS**

2.1. **Program Description.** Provide a general description of the program to establish a frame of reference for the remainder of the document. Include a summary description of the system/subsystem functions to be satisfied by this program.

2.2. **Functions.** Specify the functions of the program to be developed. If the program in itself does not fully satisfy a system/subsystem function, show the relationship to other programs which in aggregate satisfy that function.

2.3. **Performance.** Specify the performance requirements.

2.3.1. Accuracy. Describe data accuracy requirements imposed on the program, such as:

a. Mathematical.
b. Logical.
c. Legal.
d. Transmission.

2.3.2. Validation. Describe the data validation requirements imposed on the program.

2.3.3. Timing. Describe the timing requirements imposed on the program, such as, under varying conditions:

a. Response time.
b. Update processing time.
c. Data transfer and transmission time.
d. Throughput and internal processing time.

2.3.4. Flexibility. Describe the capability for adapting the program to changes in requirements, such as:

Program Specification

a. Modes of operation.
b. Operating environment.
c. Interfaces with other programs.
d. Accuracy, validation, and timing.
e. Planned changes or improvements.

Identify the components of the program which are designed to provide this flexibility.

3. OPERATING ENVIRONMENT

3.1. Equipment. Identify the equipment required for the operation of the program. Include information on equipment required, such as:

a. Processor and size of internal storage.
b. Storage, online and offline, media, form, and devices.
c. Input/Output devices, online and offline, and capacities.
d. Data transmission devices.

3.2. Support Software. Identify the support software and describe any test programs. If the operation of the program depends on changes to support software, identify the nature and planned date of these changes.

3.3. Interfaces. Describe all interactions with the operator. Describe all interactions with other software, including sequence or procedure relationships and data interfaces.

3.4. Storage. Specify the storage requirements and any constraints and conditions.

a. Internal. Describe and illustrate the use of internal storage areas, including indexing and working areas. Briefly state the equipment constraints and design considerations that affect the use of internal storage.
b. Device. List by device type all peripheral storage required. Briefly state any constraints imposed on storage requirements by each storage device. State requirements for permanent and temporary storage, including overlays.
c. Offline. Describe the form, media and storage requirements of all offline storage.

3.5. Security and Privacy. Describe the security and privacy requirements imposed on the program, the inputs, the outputs, and the data bases. If no specific requirements are imposed, state this fact.

3.6. Controls. Describe the program controls such as record counts, accumulated counts, and batch controls. Identify the sources of these controls.

4. DESIGN CHARACTERISTICS

4.1. Operating Procedures. Describe the operating procedures and any special program functions or requirements necessary for its implementation. Describe the load, start, stop, recovery, and restart procedures. Describe all other interactions of the program with the operator.

Program Specification

4.2. Inputs. Provide information about the characteristics of each input to the program, such as:

a. Title and tag.
b. Format and type of data, such as a record layout.
c. Validation criteria.
d. Volume and frequency.
e. Means of entry.
f. Source document and its disposition, or specific interface source.
g. Security and privacy conditions.

4.3. Program Logic. Describe the program logic. The logical flow should be presented in graphic form (flowcharts, decision logic tables) supplemented by narrative explanations.

4.4. Outputs. Provide information about the characteristics of each output from the program, such as:

a. Title and tag.
b. Format specifications, such as a report format.
c. Selection criteria for display, output, or transfer.
d. Volume and frequency.
e. Output media.
f. Description of graphic displays and symbols.
g. Security and privacy conditions.
h. Disposition of products.
i. Description of sequence of displays, display contents, fixed and variable formats, and display of error conditions.

4.5. Data Base. Describe the logical and physical characteristics of any data base used by the program.

4.5.1. Logical Characteristics. Describe for each unique set, file, record, element, or item of data, its identification, definition, and relationships.

4.5.2. Physical Characteristics. Describe in terms of this data base, the storage requirements for program data, specific access method, and physical relationships of access (index, device, area), design considerations, and access security mechanisms.

3.5 Data Base Specification

The purpose of the Data Base Specification is to specify the identification, logical characteristics, and physical characteristics of a particular data base.

Contents

Data Base Specification

1. GENERAL INFORMATION

1.1. **Summary.** Summarize the purpose of the data base and general functions of the using software.

1.2. **Environment.** Identify the project sponsor, developer, user organization, and computer center where the software and data base are to be installed.

1.3. **References.** List applicable references, such as:

a. Project request (authorization).
b. Previously published documents on the project.
c. Documentation concerning related projects.
d. FIPS publications and other reference documents.

2. DESCRIPTION

2.1. **Identification.** Specify the code name, tag, or label by which the data base is to be identified. If the data base is to be experimental, test, or temporary, specify this characteristic and effective dates or period. Any additional identification information should also be given.

2.2. **Using Software.** Identify all software intended to use or access this data base. Identify for each: the software name, code name, and any release or version number.

2.3. **Conventions.** Describe all labeling or tagging conventions essential for a programmer or analyst to use this data base specification.

2.4. **Special Instructions.** Provide any special instructions to personnel who will contribute to the generation of the data base, or who may use it for testing or operational purposes. Such instructions include criteria, procedures, and formats for:

a. Submitting data for entry into the data base and identification of a data control organization.
b. Entering data into the data base.

Where these instructions are extensive, reference appropriate sections of other documents.

2.5. **Support Software.** Describe briefly all support software directly related to the data base. Descriptions should include name, function, major operating characteristics, and machine run instructions for using the support software. Cite the support software documentation by title, number, and appropriate sections.

Examples of support software are:

a. Data base management systems.
b. Storage allocation software.
c. Data base loading software programs.
d. File processing programs.
e. Other generating, modifying, or updating software.

Data Base Specification

3. LOGICAL CHARACTERISTICS

A data base is a logical arrangement of data. Sets (aggregates), files, records, elements, and items of data may vary in their logical arrangement and relationships. The organization of the content of this section should provide a meaningful presentation of the logical organization of the data base.

Define each unique set (aggregate), file, record, element, or item of data providing information, such as:

a. **Identification.** Name and tag, or label.
b. **Definition.** Standard or unique; purpose in data base; using software; media; form; format and size; update criteria and conditions; security and privacy restrictions, limitations, or conditions (update or access); integrity and validity characteristics; controlling data elements or items; and graphic representation.
c. **Relationships.** Superior and inferior relationships; update and access relationships.

4. PHYSICAL CHARACTERISTICS

4.1. **Storage.** Specify the storage requirements for the data base and any constraints and conditions.

a. Internal. Describe and illustrate the use of internal storage areas set aside for data including indexing and working areas. Briefly state the equipment constraints and design considerations that affect the use of internal storage.
b. Device. List by device type all peripheral storage required for the data base. Briefly state any contraints imposed on storage requirements by each storage device. State requirements for permanent data storage and temporarary data storage, including overlays.
c. Offline. Describe the form, media and storage requirements of all offline data storage.

4.2. **Access.** Describe the access method and specify the physical relationships of access (index, device, area). Describe all physical access security mechanisms.

4.3. **Design Considerations.** State the design considerations for the handling of this data base, such as blocking factors. Emphasize those physical relationships important to the efficient utilization of the data base.

See Examples of Content Organization for Section 3 on page 36.

Data Base Specification

EXAMPLES OF CONTENT ORGANIZATION FOR SECTION 3

Example A: Simple structure in which the data base is composed only of data elements:

Element 1 (Identification, Definition, Relationships)
Element 2 (Identification, Definition, Relationships)
Element N (Identification, Definition, Relationships)

Example B: Simple hierarchial structure in which the data base is composed of files, records, and data elements:

File 1 (Identification, Definition, Relationships)
    Record 1 (Identification, Definition, Relationships)
        Element 1 (Identification, Definition, Relationships)
        Element N (Identification, Definition, Relationships)
    Record N (Identification, Definition, Relationships)
File N (Identification, Definition, Relationships)

Example C: A structure in which a data base is composed of data elements and sets of data with an organization based on multiple or specific relationships between elements and sets:

Element 1 (Identification, Definition, Relationships)
Element N (Identification, Definition, Relationships)

Set 1 (Identification, Definition, Relationships)
Set N (Identification, Definition, Relationships)

Example D: Any of the above structures, but with a substantial number of sets, files, records, elements, or items of data. Outline in graph or chart form the structure, levels, and relationships with each chart element denoting the Identification of the set, etc., portrayed. Supplement the graph or chart with a suitably organized listing of all sets, etc., with the appropriate Definition and Relationships information.

3.6 Users Manual

The purpose of the Users Manual is to sufficiently describe the functions performed by the software in non-ADP terminology, such that the user organization can determine its applicability and when and how to use it. It should serve as a reference document for preparation of input data and parameter, and interpretation of results.

Contents

Users Manual

1. **GENERAL INFORMATION**

   1.1. **Summary.** Summarize the application and general functions of the software.

   1.2. **Environment.** Identify the user organization and computer center where the software is installed.

   1.3. **References.** List applicable references, such as:

   a. Project request (authorization).
   b. Previously published documents on the project.
   c. Documentation concerning related projects and software.
   d. FIPS publications and other reference documents.

2. **APPLICATION**

   2.1. **Description.** Describe when and how the software is used and the unique support provided to the user organization. The description should include:

   a. Purpose of the software.
   b. Capabilities and operating improvements provided.
   c. Functions performed.

   2.2. **Operation.** Show the operating relationships of the functions performed to the organization that provides input to and receives output from the software. Describe security and privacy considerations. Include general charts and a description of the inputs and outputs shown on the charts.

   2.3. **Equipment.** Describe the equipment on which the software can be run.

   2.4. **Structure.** Show the structure of the software and describe the role of each component in the operation of the software.

   2.5. **Performance.** Describe the performance capabilities of the software including where appropriate:

   a. Quantitative information on inputs, outputs, response time, processing times, and error rates.
   b. Qualitative information about flexibility and reliability.

   2.6. **Data Base.** Describe all data files in the data base that are referenced, supported, or kept current by the software. The description should include the purpose for which each data file is maintained.

   2.7. **Inputs, Processing, and Outputs.** Describe the inputs, the flow of data through the processing cycle, and the resultant outputs. Include any applicable relationships among inputs or outputs.

Users Manual

3. PROCEDURES AND REQUIREMENTS

This section should provide information about initiation procedures, and preparation of data and parameter inputs for the software. The scope, quality, and logical arrangement of the information should enable the user to prepare required inputs and should explain in detail the characteristics and meaning of the outputs. It should also describe error, recovery, and file query procedures and requirements.

3.1. Initiation. Describe step-by-step procedures required to initiate processing.

3.2. Input. Define the requirements of preparing input data and parameters. Typical considerations are:

a. Conditions—e.g., personnel transfer, out of stock.
b. Frequency—e.g., periodically, randomly, as a function of an operational situation.
c. Origin—e.g., Personnel Section, Inventory Control.
d. Medium—e.g., keyboard, punched card, magnetic or paper tape.
e. Restrictions—e.g., priority and security handling, limitations on what files may be accessed by this type of transaction.
f. Quality control—e.g., instructions for checking reasonableness of input data, action to be taken when data appears to be in error, documentation of errors.
g. Disposition—e.g., instructions necessary for retention or release of all data files received, other recipients of the inputs.

3.2.1. Input Formats. Provide the layout forms used in the initial preparation program data and parameter inputs. Explain each entry, and reference it to the sample form. Include a description of the grammatical rules and conventions used to prepare input, such as:

a. Length—e.g., characters/line, characters/item.
b. Format—e.g., left justified.
c. Labels—e.g., tags or identifiers.
d. Sequence—e.g., the order and placement of items in the input.
e. Punctuation—e.g., spacing and use of symbols (virgule, asterisk, character combinations, etc.) to denote start and end of input, of lines, of data groups, etc.
f. Combination—e.g., rules forbidding use of groups of particular characters, or combinations of parameters in an input.
g. Vocabulary—e.g., an appendix which lists the allowable character combinations or codes that must be used to identify or compose input items.
h. Omissions and Repeats—e.g., indicate those elements of input that that are optional or may be repeated.
i. Controls—e.g., header or trailer control data.

3.2.2. Sample Inputs. Provide specimens of each complete input form. Include:

a. Control or header—e.g., entries that denote the input class or type, date/time, origin, and instruction codes to the software.
b. Text—e.g., subsections of the input representing data for operational files, request parameters for an information retrieval program.

Users Manual

c. Trailer—e.g., control data denoting the end of input and any additional control data.
d. Omissions—e.g., indicate those classes or types of input that may be omitted or are optional.
e. Repeats—e.g., indicate those positions of the input that may be repeated.

3.3. **Output.** Describe the requirements relevant to each output. Typical considerations are:

a. Use—e.g., by whom and for what.
b. Frequency—e.g., weekly, periodically, or on demand.
c. Variations—e.g., modifications that are available to the basic output.
d. Destination—e.g., computer area, remote terminal.
e. Medium—e.g., printout, CRT, tape, cards.
f. Quality control—e.g., instructions for identification, reasonableness checks, editing and error correction.
g. Disposition—e.g., instructions necessary for retention or release, distribution, transmission, priority, and security handling.

3.3.1. Output Formats. Provide a layout of each output. Explanations should be keyed to particular parts of the format illustrated. Include:

a. Header—e.g., title, identification, date, number of output parts.
b. Body—e.g., information that appears in the body or text of the output, columnar headings in tabular displays, and record layouts in machine readable ouputs. Note which items may be omitted or repeated.
c. Trailer—e.g., summary totals, trailer labels.

3.3.2. Sample Outputs. Provide a sample of each type of output. For each item on a sample, include:

a. Definition—e.g., the meaning and use of each information variable.
b. Source—e.g., the item extracted from a specific input, from a data base file, or calculated by software.
c. Characteristics—e.g., the presence or absence of the item under certain conditions of the output generation, range of values, unit of measure.

3.4. **Error and Recovery.** List error codes or conditions generated by the software and corrective action to be taken by the user. Indicate procedures to be followed by the user to ensure that any restart and recovery capability can be used.

3.5. **File Query.** Prepare this paragraph for software with a file query retrieval capability. Include detailed instructions necessary for initiation, preparation, and processing of a query applicable to the data base. Describe the query capabilities, forms, commands used, and control instructions required.

If the software is queried through a terminal, provide instructions for terminal operators. Describe terminal setup or connect procedures, data or parameter input procedures, and control instructions. Reference related materials describing query capabilities, languages, installation conventions and procedures, program aids, etc.

3.7 Operations Manual

The purpose of the Operations Manual is to provide computer operations personnel with a description of the software and of the operational environment so that the software can be run.

Contents

Operations Manual

1. GENERAL INFORMATION

1.1. **Summary.** Summarize the general functions of the software.

1.2. **Environments.** Identify the software sponsor, developer, user organization, and the computer center where the software is to be installed.

1.3. **References.** List applicable references, such as:

a. Project request (authorization).
b. Previously published documents on the project.
c. Documentation concerning related projects.
d. FIPS publications and other reference documents.

2. OVERVIEW

2.1. **Software Organization.** Provide a diagram showing the inputs, outputs, data files, and sequence of operations of the software. Runs may be grouped by periods of time cycles, by organizational level where they will be performed, or by other groupings.

2.2. **Program Inventory.** Identify each program by title, number, and mnemonic reference.

2.3. **File Inventory.** Identify each permanent file that is referenced, created, or updated by the system. Include the title, mnemonic reference, storage medium, and required storage.

3. DESCRIPTION OF RUNS

3.1. **Run Inventory.** List the various runs possible and summarize the purpose each run. Show the programs that are executed during each run.

3.2. **Run Progression.** Describe the manner in which progression advances from one run to another so that the entire run cycle is completed.

3.3. **Run Description (Identify).** Organize the information on each run into the most useful presentation for the operating center and operations personnel involved.

3.3.1. Control Inputs. List the run stream control statements needed for the run.

3.3.2. Operating Information. Provide information for the operating center personnel and management, such as:

a. Run identification.
b. Operating requirements.
c. Initiation method, such as on request, at predetermined time, etc.
d. Estimated run time and turnaround time.
e. Operator commands and messages.
f. Contacts for problems with the run.

Operations Manual

3.3.3. Input-Output Files. Provide information for files created or updated by the run, such as:

a. File name or label.
b. Recording medium.
c. Retention schedule.
d. Disposition of file.

3.3.4. Output Reports. For each output report or type of report, provide information such as:

a. Report identification.
b. Medium.
c. Volume of report.
d. Number of copies.
e. Distribution.

3.3.5. Reproduced Output Reports. For those reports that are computer- generated and then reproduced by other means, provide information such as:

a. Report identification.
b. Reproduction technique.
c. Dimensions of paper or other medium.
d. Binding method.
e. Distribution.

3.3.6. Restart/Recovery Procedures. Describe procedures to restart the run or recover from a failure.

3.4 **Run Description (Identify).** Present information about the subsequent runs in a manner similar to that used in paragraph 3.3.

4. NON-ROUTINE PROCEDURES

Provide any information necessary concerning emergency or non-routine operations, such as:

a. Switchover to a back-up system.
b. Procedures for turnover to maintenance programmers.

5. REMOTE OPERATIONS

Describe the procedures for running the programs through remote terminals.

3.8 Program Maintenance Manual

The purpose of the Program Maintenance Manual is to provide the maintenance programmer with the information necessary to understand the programs, their operating environment, and their maintenance procedures.

Contents

1

Program Maintenance Manual

1. **GENERAL INFORMATION**

1.1. **Summary.** Summarize the general nature of the software to be maintained.

1.2. **Environment.** Identify the project sponsor, developer, user and computer center or network where the software is implemented.

1.3. **References.** List applicable references, such as:

a. Project request (authorizations).
b. Previously published documents on the project.
c. Documentation concerning related projects.
d. FIPS publications and other reference documents.

2. **PROGRAM DESCRIPTIONS**

Describe the program and programs in the system/subsystem for the maintenance programmer. If a complex system is being described, provide a general description of that system identifying each program and its functions.

2.1. **Program (Identify) Description.** Identify the program by title, tag or label, and programming language.

2.1.1. Problem and Solution Method. Describe the problem to be solved or the program function and the solution method used.

2.1.2. Input. Describe the input to the program and provide a layout. Identify the medium used. Include information, such as codes, units of measurement, format, range of values, or reference a data element directory.

2.1.3. Processing. Describe processing features and purposes important to the maintenance programmer, such as:

a. Processing logic.
b. Linkages.
c. Variables and constants.
d. Formulas.
e. Error handling provisions.
f. Restrictions and limitations.
g. Locations, settings, internal switches and flags.
h. Shared storage.

2.1.4. Output. Describe the output of the program and provide a layout. Identify the medium used.

2.1.5. Interfaces. Describe the interfaces with other software, such as data formats, messages, parameters, conversion requirements, interface procedures, and media.

2.1.6. Tables. Identify each table and its items. Describe the location, structure, and purpose of each.

Program Maintenance Manual

2.1.7. Run Description. Describe or reference the operating procedures to run the program, including loading, operating, terminating, and error handling.

2.2. **Program (Identify) Description.** Describe the second through nth computer program in a manner similar to that used in paragraph 2.1.

3. **OPERATING ENVIRONMENT**

3.1. **Hardware.** Identify the equipment required for the operation of the system. Describe any unusual features used. Relate the hardware to each program. Include information such as:

a. Processor and size of internal storage.
b. Storage online or offline, media, form, and devices.
c. Input/output devices, online and offline.
d. Data transmission devices.

3.2. **Support Software.** Identify the support software needed for each computer program.

3.2.1. Operating System. Identify and describe the operating system including the version or release number and any unusual features used.

3.2.2. Compiler/Assembler. Identify and describe the compiler or assembler including the version or release number and any special features used.

3.2.3. Other Software. Identify and describe any other software used including data management systems, report generators, etc.

3.3. **Data Base.** Describe or reference documentation on the data base used. Include information such as codes, units of measurement, format, range of values, or reference a data element directory.

4. **MAINTENANCE PROCEDURES**

4.1. **Programming Conventions.** Identify and describe the programming conventions used.

4.2. **Verification Procedures.** Describe the verification procedures to check the performance of the programs, either general or following modifications. Include a reference to test data and testing procedures.

4.3. **Error Correction Procedures.** Describe all error conditions, their sources, and procedures for their correction.

4.4. **Special Maintenance Procedures.** Describe any special procedures required for the maintenance of the programs. Include information such as periodic purges of the data base, temporary modifications needed for leap years or century changes, etc.

4.5. **Listings and Flowcharts.** Reference, append, or describe the method for obtaining copies of listings of the programs and flowcharts.

3.9 Test Plan

The purpose of the Test Plan is to provide a plan for the testing of software; detailed specifications, descriptions, and procedures for all tests; and test data reduction and evaluation criteria.

Contents

Test Plan

1. GENERAL INFORMATION

1.1. Summary. Summarize the functions of the software and the tests to be performed.

1.2. Environment and Pretest Background. Summarize the history of the project. Identify the user organization and computer center where the testing will be performed. Describe any prior testing and note results that may affect this testing.

1.3. References. List applicable references, such as:

a. Project request (authorization).
b. Previously published documents on the project.
c. Documentation concerning related projects.
d. FIPS publications and other reference documents.

2. PLAN

2.1. Software Description. Provide a chart and briefly describe the inputs, outputs, and functions of the software being tested as a frame of reference for the test descriptions.

2.2. Milestones. List the locations, milestones events, and dates for the testing.

2.3. Testing (Identify Location). Identify the participating organizations and the location where the software will be tested.

2.3.1. Schedule. Show the detailed schedule of dates and events for the testing at this location. Such events may include familiarization, training, data, as well as the volume and frequency of the input.

2.3.2. Requirements. State the resource requirements, including:

a. Equipment. Show the expected period of use, types, and quantities of the equipment needed.
b. Software. List other software that will be needed to support the testing that is not part of the software to be tested.
c. Personnel. List the numbers and skill types of personnel that are expected to be available during the test from both the user and development groups. Include any special requirements such as multishift operation or key personnel.

2.3.3. Testing Materials. List the materials needed for the test, such as:

a. Documentation.
b. Software to be tested and its medium.
c. Test inputs and sample outputs.
d. Test control software and worksheets.

2.3.4. Test Training. Describe or reference the plan for providing training in the use of the software being tested. Specify the types of training, personnel to be trained, and the training staff.

Test Plan

2.4. Testing (Identify Location). Describe the plan for the second and subsequent locations where the software will be tested in a manner similar to paragraph 2.3.

3. SPECIFICATIONS AND EVALUATION

3.1. Specifications.

3.1.1. Requirements. List the functional requirements established by earlier documentation.

3.1.2. Software Functions. List the detailed software functions to be exercised during the overall test.

3.1.3. Test/Function Relationships. List the tests to be performed on the software and relate them to the functions in paragraph 3.1.2.

3.1.4. Test Progression. Describe the manner in which progression is made from one test to another so that the entire test cycle is completed.

3.2. Methods and Constraints.

3.2.1. Methodology. Describe the general method or strategy of the testing.

3.2.2. Conditions. Specify the type of input to be used, such as live or test data, as well as the volume and frequency of the input.

3.2.3. Extent. Indicate the extent of the testing, such as total or partial. Include any rationale for partial testing.

3.2.4. Data Recording. Discuss the method to be used for recording the test results and other information about the testing.

3.2.5. Constraints. Indicate anticipated limitations on the test due to test conditions, such as interfaces, equipment, personnel, data bases.

3.3. Evaluation.

3.3.1. Criteria. Describe the rules to be used to evaluate test results, such as range of data values used, combinations of input types used, maximum number of allowable interrupts or halts.

3.3.2. Data Reduction. Describe the techniques to be used for manipulating the test data into a form suitable for evaluation, such as manual or automated methods, to allow comparison of the results that should be produced to those that are produced.

4. TEST DESCRIPTIONS

4.1. Test (Identify). Describe the test to be performed.

4.1.1. Control. Describe the test control, such as manual, semi-automatic, or automatic insertion of inputs, sequencing of operations, and recording of results.

Test Plan

4.1.2. Inputs. Describe the input data and input commands used during the test.

4.1.3. Outputs. Describe the output data expected as a result of the test and any intermediate messages that may be produced.

4.1.4. Procedures. Specify the step-by-step procedures to accomplish the test. Include test setup, initialization, steps, and termination.

4.2. Test (Identify). Describe the second and subsequent tests in a manner similar to that used in paragraph 4.1.

3.10 Test Analysis Report

The purpose of the Test Analysis Report is to document the test analysis results and findings; present the demonstrated capabilities and deficiencies for review; and provide a basis for preparing a statement of software readiness for implementation.

Contents

Test Analysis Report

1. GENERAL INFORMATION

1.1. Summary. Summarize both the general functions of the software tested and the test analysis performed.

1.2. Environment. Identify the software sponsor, developer, user organization, and the computer center where the software is to be installed. Assess the manner in which the test environment may be different from the operational environment and the effects of this difference on the tests.

1.3. References. List applicable references, such as:

a. Project request (authorization).
b. Previously published documents on the project.
c. Documentation concerning related projects.
d. FIPS publications and other reference documents.

2. TEST RESULTS AND FINDINGS

Identify and present the results and findings of each test separately in paragraphs 2.1 through 2.N.

2.1. Test (Identify).

2.1.1. Dynamic Data Performance. Compare the dynamic data input and output results, including the output of internally generated data, of this test with the dynamic data input and output requirements. State the findings.

2.1.2. Static Data Performance. Compare the static data input and output results, including the output of internally generated data, of this test with the static data input and output requirements. State the findings.

2.N. Test (Identify). Present the results and findings of the second and succeeding tests in a manner similar to that of paragraph 2.1.

3. SOFTWARE FUNCTION FINDINGS

Identify and describe the findings on each function separately in paragraphs 3.1 through 3.N.

3.1. Function (Identify).

3.1.1. Performance. Describe briefly the function. Describe the software capabilities that were designed to satisfy this function. State the findings as to the demonstrated capabilities from one or more tests.

3.1.2. Limits. Describe the range of data values tested, including both dynamic and static data. Identify the deficiencies, limitations, and constraints detected in the software during the testing with respect to this function.

Test Analysis Report

3.N. **Function (Identify).** Present the findings on the second and succeeding functions in a manner similar to that of paragraph 3.1.

4. ANALYSIS SUMMARY

4.1. **Capabilities.** Describe the capabilities of the software as demonstrated by the tests. Where tests were to demonstrate fulfillment of one or more specific performance requirements, prepare findings showing the comparison of the results with these requirements. Assess the effects any differences in the test envirment as compared to the operational environment may have had on this test demonstration of capabilities.

4.2. **Deficiencies.** Describe the deficiencies of the software as demonstrated by the tests. Describe the impact of each deficiency on the performance of the software. Describe the cumulative or overall impact on performance of all detected deficiencies.

4.3. **Recommendations and Estimates.** For each deficiency provide any estimates of time and effort required for its correction and any recommendations as to:

a. The urgency of each correction.
b. Parties responsible for corrections.
c. How the corrections should be made.

State the readiness for implementation of the software.

A.2 DOD-STD-2167

The material that follows is the Department of Defense standard DOD-STD-2167, "Military Standard Defense System Development."

Foreword

1. This standard contains requirements for the development of Mission-Critical Computer System software. It establishes a uniform software development process which is applicable throughout the system life cycle. The software development process defines development activities which result in: (1) the generation of different types and levels of software and documentation, (2) the application of development tools, approaches, and methods, and (3) project planning and control. It incorporates practices which have been demonstrated to be cost-effective from a life cycle perspective, based on information gathered by the Department of Defense (DOD) and industry.

2. This standard is intended to be dynamic and responsive to the rapidly evolving software technology field. As such, this standard should be selectively applied and tailored to fit the unique characteristics of each software acquisition program. To ensure that the requirements in this standard are appropriate and responsive to software acquisition needs, users of this standard are encouraged to provide feedback to the Preparing Activity. User experience in terms of benefits, pitfalls, and any other useful information encountered in applying this standard will be most helpful.

3. Data Item Descriptions (DIDs) applicable to this standard are listed in Section 6. When used in conjunction with this standard, these DIDs provide a set of concise and complete documents for recording and communicating information generated as a result of adherence to the requirements specified herein.

CONTENTS

5.2.3 Formal Reviews - Preliminary Design
5.2.4 Developmental Configuration - Preliminary Design
5.3 Detailed Design
5.3.1 Activities - Detailed Design
5.3.2 Products - Detailed Design
5.3.3 Formal Reviews - Detailed Design
5.3.4 Developmental Configuration - Detailed Design
5.4 Coding and Unit Testing
5.4.1 Activities - Coding and Unit Testing
5.4.2 Products - Coding and Unit Testing
5.4.3 Developmental Configuration - Coding and Unit Testing
5.5 CSC Integration and Testing
5.5.1 Activities - CSC Integration and Testing
5.5.2 Products - CSC Integration and Testing
5.5.3 Formal Reviews - CSC Integration and Testing
5.5.4 Developmental Configuration - CSC Integration and Testing
5.6 CSCI Testing
5.6.1 Activities - CSCI Testing
5.6.2 Products - CSCI Testing
5.6.3 Audits - CSCI Testing
5.6.4 Baselines - CSCI Testing
5.6.5 Software acceptance
5.6.6 Installation and checkout
5.7 Configuration Management (CM)
5.7.1 Activities - Configuration Management
5.7.1.1 Configuration identification
5.7.1.2 Configuration control
5.7.1.3 Configuration status accounting
5.7.2 Products - Configuration Management
5.7.3 Audits - Configuration Management
5.8 Software Quality Evaluation
5.8.1 Activities - Software Quality Evaluation
5.8.1.1 Planning
5.8.1.2 Internal reviews
5.8.1.2.1 Evaluation Criteria
5.8.1.2.2 Internal reviews - all phases
5.8.1.2.3 Internal review - Software Requirements Analysis
5.8.1.2.4 Internal review - Preliminary Design
5.8.1.2.5 Internal review - Detailed Design
5.8.1.2.6 Internal review - Coding and Unit Testing
5.8.1.2.7 Internal review - CSC Integration and Testing
5.8.1.2.8 Internal review - CSCI Testing
5.8.1.3 Formal reviews and audits
5.8.1.4 Acceptance inspection
5.8.1.5 Installation and checkout
5.8.1.6 Evaluation of subcontractor products

FIGURES

TABLES

APPENDIXES

A List of acronyms and abbreviations
B System life cycle
C Design and coding standards
D Guidelines for tailoring this standard

1. SCOPE

1.1 *Purpose.* This standard establishes requirements to be applied during the development and acquisition of Mission-Critical Computer System (MCCS) software, as defined in DOD Directive 5000.29. This standard may also be applied to non-MCCS software development and acquisition.

1.2 *Application.* Software development is usually an iterative process, in which an iteration of the software development cycle occurs one or more times during each of the system life cycle phases (Figure 1). Appendix B describes a typical system life cycle,

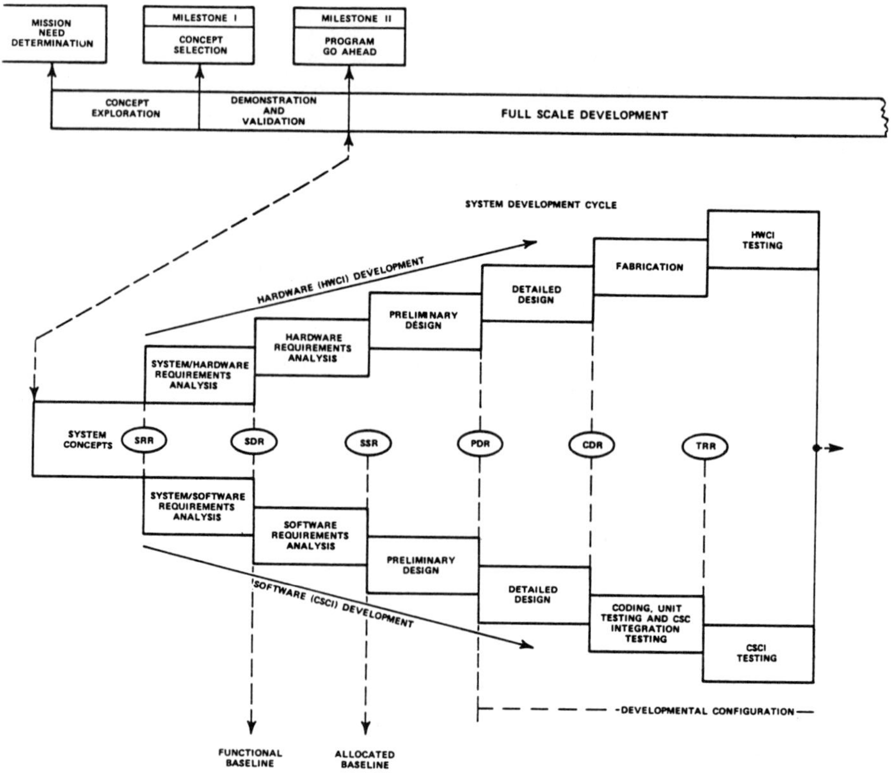

Figure 1. System development cycle within the system life cycle.

the activities that take place during each iteration of software development, and the documentation which typically exists at the beginning of an iteration in any given system life cycle phase. The requirements of this standard shall be applied to each iteration, as described below. The requirements of this standard shall also be applied to the development of software for firmware devices as described in 4.7.

1.2.1 *Application to Various Types of Software.* This standard applies to deliverable software designated as Computer Software Configuration Items (CSCIs). This standard, or portions thereof, such as configuration management, quality evaluation, and documentation also applies to:

a. Software developed and delivered as part of a system or a Hardware Configuration Item (HWCI) but not explicitly identified as a CSCI.
b. Non-deliverable software used in the development and testing of deliverable software and hardware (such as design and test tools).
c. Deliverable unmodified commercially available and reusable software.
d. Commercially available software, Government furnished software (GFS), and reusable software that is modified and delivered as part of the system.

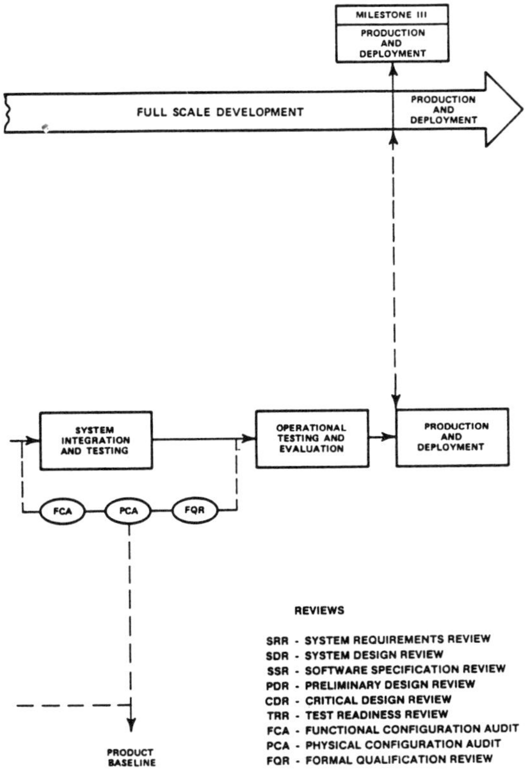

Figure 1. System development cycle within the system life cycle. (*continued*)

The specific requirements of this standard which apply to the above categories will be identified in the statement of work (SOW).

1.2.2 *Non-applicability of this Standard.* This standard, or portions thereof, may not apply to small applications which perform a fixed function that is not expected to change for the life of the system. Guidelines for applying specific portions of this standard to particular categories of software may be found in Appendix D. The SOW will specify the applicable requirements of this standard.

1.2.3 *Software Developed by Government Agencies.* Although this standard describes software development as performed by a contractor, the provisions of this standard also apply to Government agencies acting as software developers. In this case, the term "contractor" refers to the Government agency that is developing the software. Any contractor of that Government agency is classified as a subcontractor.

1.3 *Tailoring of this Standard.* Software shall be developed in accordance with this standard to the extent specified in the contract clauses, SOW, and the Contract Data Requirements List. Guidelines for applying this standard are provided in Appendix D. The contracting agency will tailor this standard to require only what is needed for each individual acquisition.

2. REFERENCED DOCUMENTS

2.1 *Government Documents.*

2.1.1 *Specifications, Standards, and Handbooks.* Unless otherwise specified, the following specifications, standards, and handbooks of the issue listed in that issue of the Department of Defense Index of Specifications and Standards (DODISS) specified in the solicitation form a part of this standard to the extent specified herein.

STANDARDS
MILITARY

- DOD-STD-480— Configuration Control - Engineering Changes, Deviations, and Waivers
- MIL-STD-481 — Configuration Control - Engineering Changes, Deviations, and Waivers (Short Form)
- MIL-STD-483 — Configuration Management Practices for Systems, Equipment, Munitions, and Computer Software
- MIL-STD-490 — Specification Practices
- MIL-STD-881 — Work Breakdown Structures for Defense Material Items
- MIL-STD-1521— Technical Reviews and Audits for Systems, Equipments, and Computer Software
- MIL-STD-1535— Supplier Quality Assurance Program Requirements

2.1.2 *Other Government Documents, Drawings, and Publications.* None.
(Copies of specifications, standards, handbooks, drawings, and publications required by contractors in connection with specific acquisition functions should be obtained from the contracting agency or as directed by the contracting officer.)

2.2 *Other Publications.* None.

2.3 *Order of Precedence.* In the event of a conflict between the text of this standard and the references cited herein, the text of this standard shall take precedence.

3. DEFINITIONS

3.1 *Allocated Baseline.* The initial approved allocated configuration identification as specified in DOD-STD-480.

3.2 *Authentication.* The procedure (essentially approval) used by the Government in verifying that specification content is acceptable. Authentication does not imply acceptance or responsibility by the Government for the specified item to perform successfully.

3.3 *Baseline.* A configuration identification document or a set of such documents (regardless of media) formally designated and fixed at a specific time during a configuration item's life cycle. Baselines, plus approved changes from those baselines, constitute the current configuration identification.

3.4 *Certification.* A process, which may be incremental, by which a contractor provides evidence to the contracting agency that a product meets contractual or otherwise specified requirements.

3.5 *Computer Data Definition.* A statement of the characteristics of basic elements of information operated upon by hardware in responding to computer instructions. These characteristics may include, but are not limited to, type, range, structure, and value.

3.6 *Computer Software (or Software).* A combination of associated computer instructions and computer data definitions required to enable the computer hardware to perform computational or control functions.

3.7 *Computer Software Component (CSC).* A functional or logically distinct part of a computer software configuration item. Computer software components may be top-level or lower-level.

3.8 *Computer Software Configuration Item (CSCI).* See Configuration Item.

3.9 *Computer Software Documentation.* Technical data or information, including computer listings and printouts, which documents the requirements, design, or details of computer software, explains the capabilities and limitations of the software, or provides operating instructions for using or supporting computer software during the software's operational life.

3.10 *Computer Software Quality (or Software Quality).* The degree to which the attributes of the software enable it to perform its specified end item use.

3.11 *Configuration Identification.* The current approved or conditionally approved technical documentation for a configuration item as set forth in specifications, drawings, and associated lists, and documents referenced therein.

3.12 *Configuration Item.* Hardware or software, or an aggregation of both, which is designated by the contracting agency for configuration management.

3.13 *Developmental Configuration.* The contractor's software and associated technical documentation that defines the evolving configuration of a CSCI during development. It is under the development contractor's configuration control and describes the software configuration of the design, coding, and testing effort. Any item in the Developmental Configuration may be stored on electronic media.

3.14 *Firmware.* The combination of a hardware device and computer instructions or computer data that reside as read-only software on the hardware device. The software cannot be readily modified under program control. The definition also applies to read-only digital data that may be used by electronic devices other than digital computers.

3.15 *Formal Test.* A test conducted in accordance with test plans and procedures approved by the contracting agency and witnessed by an authorized contracting agency representative, to show that the software satisfies a specified requirement.

3.16 *Functional Baseline.* The initial approved functional configuration identification as specified in DOD-STD-480.

3.17 *Hardware Configuration Item (HWCI).* See Configuration Item.

3.18 *Informal Test.* Any test which does not meet all the requirements of a formal test.

3.19 *Modular.* Pertaining to software that is organized into limited aggregates of data and contiguous code that perform identifiable functions.

3.20 *Product Baseline.* The initial approved product configuration identification as specified in DOD-STD-480.

3.21 *Software Development Library (SDL).* A controlled collection of software, documentation, and associated tools and procedures used to facilitate the orderly development and subsequent support of software. A software development library provides storage of and controlled access to software and documentation in both human-readable and machine-readable form. The library may also contain management data pertinent to the software development project.

3.22 *Top-down.* Pertaining to an approach that starts with the highest level of a hierarchy and proceeds through progressively lower levels. For example, top-down design, top-down coding, top-down testing.

3.23 *Unit.* The smallest logical entity specified in the detailed design which completely describes a single function in sufficient detail to allow implementing code to be produced and tested independently of other Units. Units are the actual physical entities implemented in code.

4. GENERAL REQUIREMENTS

4.1 *Software Development Cycle.* The contractor shall implement a software development cycle that includes the following six phases:

a. Software Requirements Analysis
b. Preliminary Design
c. Detailed Design
d. Coding and Unit Testing
e. Computer Software Component (CSC) Integration and Testing
f. CSCI Testing

4.1.1 Each iteration of the software development cycle, regardless of the system life cycle phase during which it occurs, is initiated by allocation of system requirements to that software or a subsequent revision to those requirements.

4.1.2 The relationship of the software development cycle phases with the products, reviews and audits, and baselines and Developmental Configurations required by Section 5 of this Standard are shown in Figure 2. Figure 2 reflects the sequential phases of a software development cycle, as well as the documentation which typically exists prior to initiating an iteration. During software development, more than one iteration of the software development cycle may be in progress at the same time. Each iteration represents a different version of the software. This process may be described as an "evolutionary acquisition" or "incremental build" approach. Within each iteration, the software development phases also typically overlap, rather than form a discrete termination-initiation sequence. For example, performing Unit code and test concurrently with CSC integration and test is useful in implementing incremental builds. The relationship of the software development cycle to the system life cycle, including system allocation of requirements to CSCIs, and system integration and testing of HWCIs and CSCIs, is described in Appendix B.

4.2 *Computer Software Organization.* Computer software developed in accordance with this standard shall be organized as one or more CSCIs or other types of software (see 1.2.1). Each CSCI is part of a system, segment, or prime item and shall consist of one or more Top Level Computer Software Components (TLCSCs). Each TLCSC shall consist of Lower-Level Computer Software Components (LLCSCs) or Units. LLCSCs may consist of other LLCSCs or Units. TLCSCs and LLCSCs are logical groupings. Units are the smallest logical entities, and the actual physical entities implemented in code. The static structure of CSCIs, TLCSCs, LLCSCs, and Units shall form a hierarchical structure as illustrated in Figure 3. The hierarchical structure shall uniquely identify all CSCIs, TLCSCs, LLCSCs, and Units.

4.2.1 The partitioning of the CSCI into TLCSCs, LLCSCs, and Units may be based on functional requirements, data flow requirements, or other design considerations. The hierarchical structure illustrated in Figure 3 demonstrates the static relationship of the TLCSCs, LLCSCs, and Units based on the partitioning considerations and does not represent either the control flow of the software during execution or the implemented code. Guidelines for selecting CSCIs are contained in MIL-STD-483, Appendix XVII. These guidelines may also be applied to selecting TLCSCs, LLCSCs, and Units.

4.3 *Software Quality.* The contractor shall plan and implement the software development project with the objective of building in quality. To achieve this quality, the contractor shall:

a. Establish and maintain a complete set of requirements for the software. These requirements shall serve as the standard against which software quality is evaluated. To establish the requirements, the contractor shall perform the tasks specified in 5.1. To maintain the requirements, the contractor shall perform the tasks specified in 5.7.

b. Establish and implement a complete process, including methodologies and tools, for developing the software and its documentation. The process shall be designed to build quality into the software and its documentation and to maintain the level of quality throughout the life cycle of the software. The development process shall include both contractor internal steps (specified in the Software Development Plan (SDP), Software Configuration Management Plan (SCMP), and Software Standards and Procedures Manual (SSPM)), and the formal steps specified in 5.1 through 5.7, and 5.9 (see 6.2).

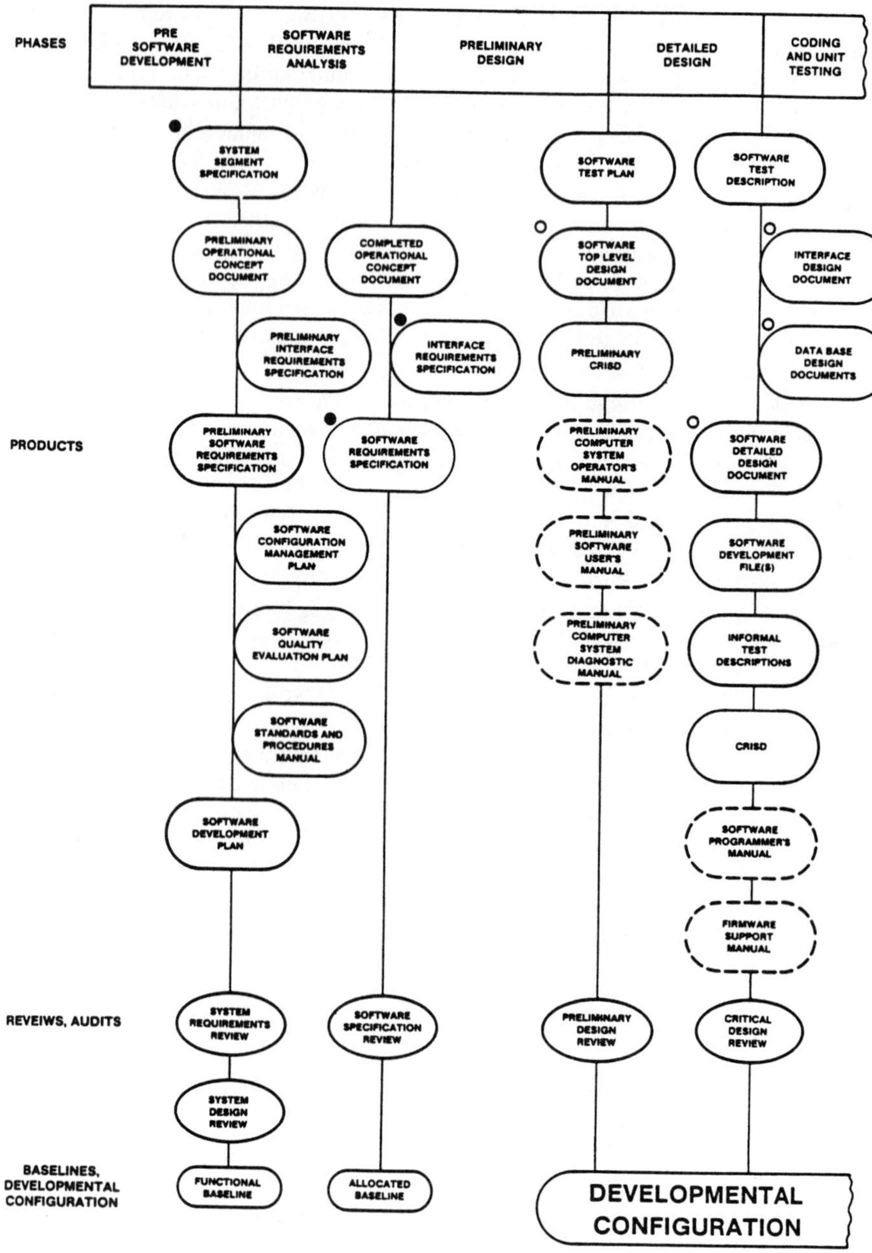

Figure 2. Software development cycle.

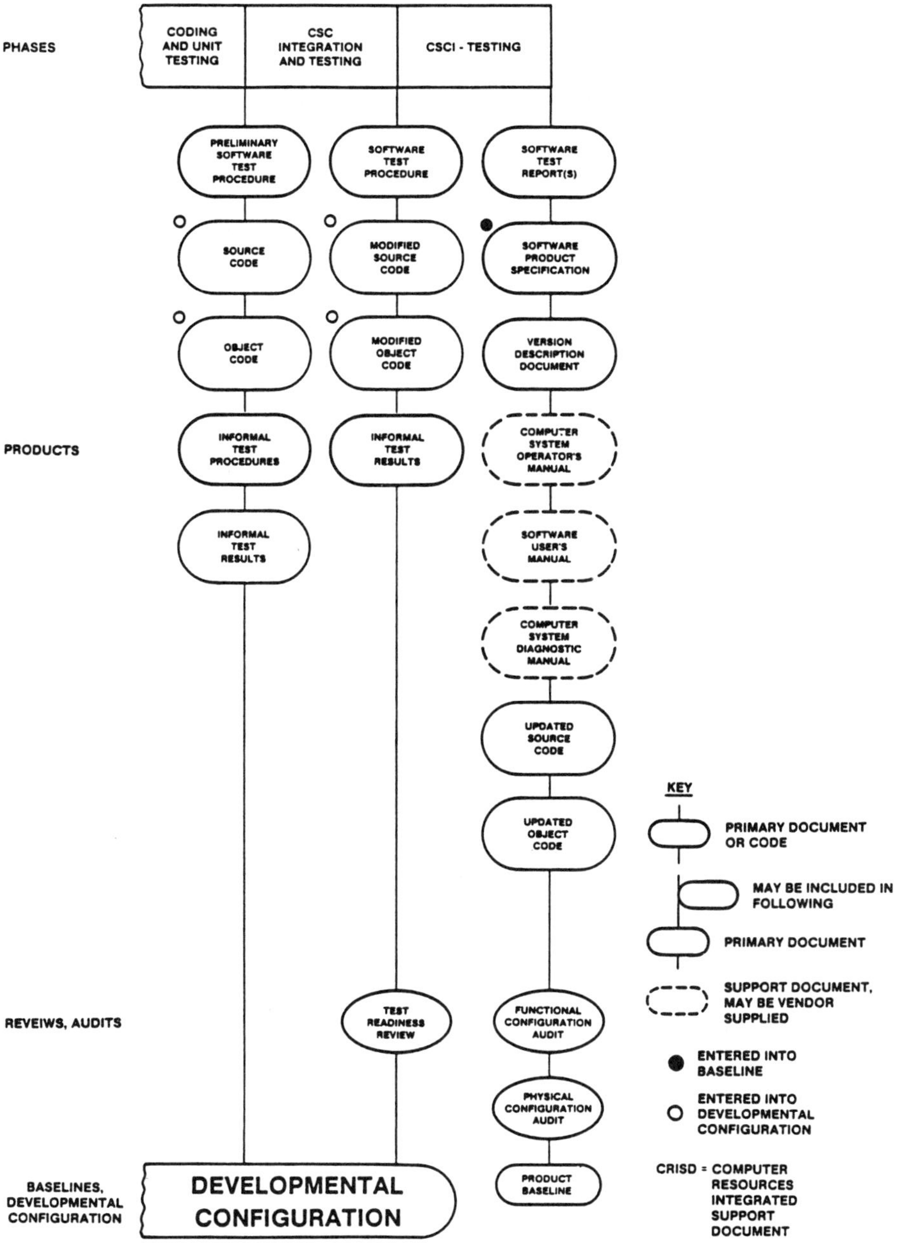

Figure 2. Software development cycle. (*continued*)

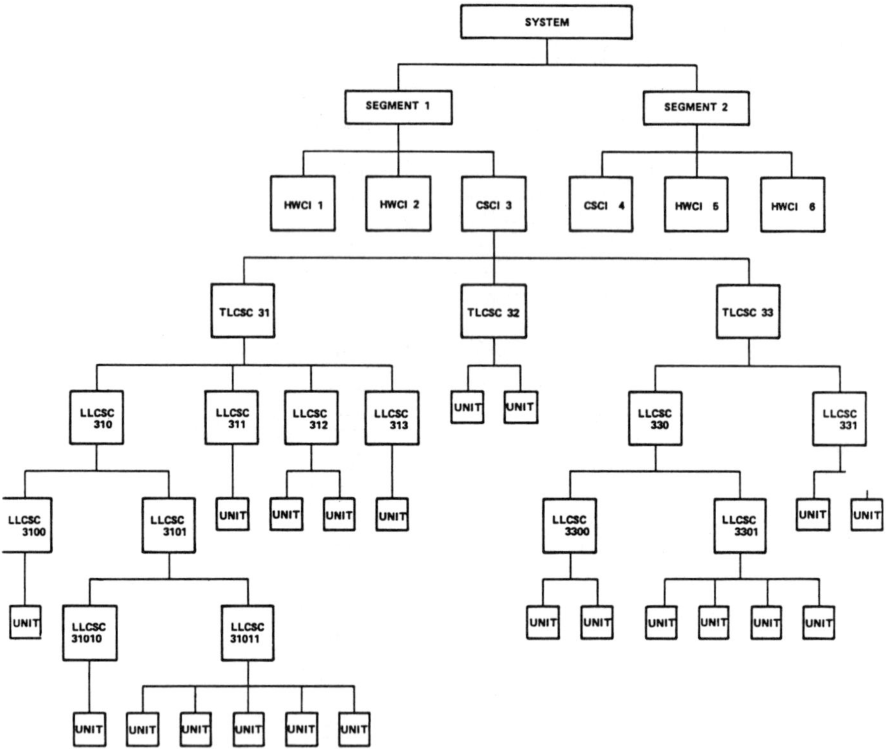

Figure 3. CSCI sample static structure.

c. Establish and maintain a process to evaluate the software, associated documentation, and the software development process. The objective of this process shall be to improve the quality of the software and its documentation, by providing feedback and ensuring that necessary corrections are made. The quality evaluation process shall include both contractor internal steps (specified in either the SDP or the Software Quality Evaluation Plan (SQEP)) and the formal steps specified in 5.8 (see 6.2).

4.4 *Use of Commercially Available, Reusable, and Government Furnished Software.* In order to facilitate cost-effective development and support of MCCS software, the contractor is encouraged to incorporate into the current software design commercially available software, GFS, and reusable software developed for other applications. However, the contractor shall perform the following activities prior to incorporating commercially available software, reusable software, GFS, or any combination of these, into the design: (1) describe in the SDP the data rights and documentation the contractor plans to provide the contracting agency regarding the commercially available and reusable software, (2) evaluate the commercially available, reusable, or Government furnished software to determine whether it performs as documented, (3) describe in the SDP the contractor's plans for certifying the commercially available or reusable software, and (4) obtain explicit contracting agency approval for use of commercially available software (see 5.8.1.7 and 6.2).

4.5 *Subcontractor Control.* The contractor shall ensure that all subcontractors developing software and documentation comply with subcontract requirements. The requirements of 4.4 shall apply to commercially available and reusable software procured from subcontractors. Additional guidance may be found in MIL-STD-1535.

4.6 *Non-deliverable Software, Firmware, and Hardware.* The contractor shall describe in the SDP the controls to be imposed on all non-deliverable software, firmware, and hardware used in the development and acquisition of deliverable software (see 6.2). As a minimum, the contractor shall describe the provisions for:

a. Modifications (as applicable)
b. Documentation
c. Configuration Management
d. Design & Coding Standards
e. Testing
f. Quality Evaluation
g. Certification

4.7 *Firmware.* The application of the requirements in this standard to firmware depends on whether the firmware is designated as a CSCI or as part of an HWCI. If the software to be implemented in firmware is designated as a CSCI, all the requirements in this standard apply, as tailored by the contract. If the software to be implemented in firmware is considered part of an HWCI, the contractor shall identify the applicable requirements in the SDP and apply these requirements subject to contracting agency approval (see 6.2).

4.8 *Development Methodologies.* The contractor shall use a top-down approach to design, code, integrate, and test all CSCIs, unless specific alternate methodologies have been proposed in either the SSPM or SDP (see Appendix D) and received contracting agency approval (see 6.2).

4.9 *Security.* The contractor shall implement applicable security measures during software design and development.

4.10 *Deliverable Data.* Deliverable data prepared in accordance with the requirements of sections 4 and 5 of this standard and identified on the DD Form 1423, Contract Data Requirements List, shall be prepared in accordance with the instructions in the applicable DIDs (see 6.2).

4.11 *Deviations and Waivers.* The contractor and, if applicable, subcontractors shall develop software in compliance with this standard, as required by the contract, unless a deviation or waiver has been approved by the contracting agency in accordance with DOD-STD-480 or MIL-STD-481.

5. DETAILED REQUIREMENTS

5.1 *Software Requirements Analysis.* The contractor shall define and analyze a complete set of functional, performance, interface, and qualification requirements for each CSCI. These requirements shall be derived from the system requirements as defined in the System/Segment Specification (SSS), prime item specification, critical item specification, or other sources specified in the contract. Additional requirements may be derived during the analysis and allocation of system-derived requirements. The contractor shall also prepare or update, as applicable (see Appendix B), an SDP, SSPM, SCMP, SQEP, and Operational Concept Document (OCD), and establish internal control over these documents.

5.1.1 *Activities - Software Requirements Analysis.* The contractor shall perform the following activities during Software Requirements Analysis.

5.1.1.1 If plans for developing the software have not previously been prepared and approved by the contracting agency (see Appendix B), the contractor shall prepare them. The contractor's plans for software development shall include:

a. Resources and organization, describing: (1) the contractor's facilities, (2) Government furnished equipment, software, and services required, and (3) organizational structure, personnel, and resources for software development, software configuration management, and software quality evaluation.

b. Development schedule and milestones, describing: (1) each individual activity of the project, (2) the activity network, (3) risk management procedures, and (4) identifiable high risk areas.

c. Software standards and procedures, describing: (1) tools, techniques, and methodologies to be used in the development, (2) if applicable, criteria for departing from a top-down approach (see 5.3.1.3, 5.3.1.4), (3) the software development library and associated access and control procedures, (4) the format and contents of software development files, associated procedures, and organizational responsibilities, (5) the format and contents of all informal test documentation, (6) design and coding standards, and (7) procedures and reports used to prepare for formal reviews.

d. Software configuration management, describing: (1) configuration identification procedures, (2) configuration control including software problem and change reports, and review boards, (3) configuration status accounting, (4) configuration audits, (5) preparation for configuration authentication procedures, and (6) configuration management major milestones.

e. Software quality evaluation, describing: (1) evaluation of development plans, standards, and procedures, (2) evaluation of the contractor's compliance with those plans, standards, and procedures, (3) evaluation of the products of software development, (4) implementation of a quality evaluation reporting system, and (5) implementation of a corrective action system.

f. Commercially available, reusable, and Government furnished software, describing: (1) rationale for its use, (2) plans for providing associated data rights and documentation for commercially available and reusable software, (3) plans for determining that the commercially available, reusable, and Government furnished software performs as documented, and (4) plans for certifying commercially available and reusable software.

g. Data rights and documentation for the software development library (SDL), describing the plans for providing associated data rights and documentation for the SDL.

h. Subcontractor control, describing: (1) the organization responsible for subcontractor control, and (2) the procedures to ensure that all subcontractor-developed software meets subcontract requirements.

i. Control provisions for non-deliverable software, firmware, and hardware, describing requirements for: (1) modifications (if applicable), (2) documentation, (3) configuration management, (4) design and coding standards, (5) testing, (6) quality evaluation, and (7) certification.

j. Control provisions for software that is part of a hardware item, describing procedures for: (1) requirements analysis and allocation, (2) design and coding, (3) hardware and software integration and test, (4) coordination of hardware and software design, (5) documentation, (6) software configuration management, and (7) software quality evaluation.

k. Interface management with associate contractors, describing the contractor's plan for coordinating development and data management efforts to ensure interface compatibility.

5.1.1.2 The contractor shall establish internal control over the SDP, SSPM, SCMP, and SQEP. The contractor shall monitor the development effort for consistency with the SDP, SSPM, SCMP, and SQEP (see 5.8.1.2.2). The contractor shall notify the contracting agency of proposed changes to these documents and make necessary revisions. All proposed changes shall be subject to disapproval by the contracting agency. In addition, the contractor shall notify the contracting agency at the next review, audit, or in the next status report (whichever comes first) of any actions or procedures occurring during Software Requirements Analysis that deviate from the SDP, SSPM, SCMP, or SQEP.

5.1.1.3 If provided by the Government, the contractor shall analyze the preliminary OCD (see Appendix B) for adequacy, understandability, validity, and completeness.

5.1.1.4 The contractor shall identify and describe the mission of the system and its operational and support environments. The contractor shall also describe the functions and characteristics of the computer system within the overall system (see 5.1.2.2).

5.1.1.5 The contractor shall analyze the SSS and, if provided, the preliminary Software Requirements Specifications (SRSs) and Interface Requirements Specifications (IRSs) for adequacy, testability, understandability, validity, and completeness. Circumstances under which the specifications are provided by the Government are described in Appendix B.

5.1.1.6 The contractor shall define a complete set of functional, performance, interface, and qualification requirements for each CSCI, incorporating the results of 5.1.1.5. Requirements specified by the contractor shall also include the following areas:

a. Programming constraints and standards
b. Design constraints and standards
c. Adaptation
d. Quality factors
e. Preparation for delivery

5.1.1.7 In the definition and analysis of software requirements, the contractor shall use structured requirements analysis tools, techniques, or a combination of both. The specific tools and techniques to be used shall be identified in either the SSPM or SDP (see Appendix D) and shall be subject to contracting agency approval. The contractor shall map the requirements defined in 5.1.1.6 to the applicable higher-level documents.

5.1.1.8 The contractor shall conduct internal in-process reviews during this phase (see 5.8.1.2.3) and shall make all necessary changes based on the results of the internal reviews prior to presenting the requirements document(s) to the contracting agency.

5.1.2 *Products - Software Requirements Analysis.* The contractor shall produce the following products during Software Requirements Analysis (see 6.2).

5.1.2.1 The contractor shall prepare or produce updated versions of (whichever is applicable, see Appendix B) the SDP, SSPM, SCMP, and SQEP.

5.1.2.2 The contractor shall produce an OCD for the system. In the event a preliminary OCD has been provided by the Government, the contractor shall update and complete the document.

5.1.2.3 The contractor shall produce records and summary reports of the internal reviews conducted (see 5.8.2.1 and 5.8.2.2).

5.1.2.4 The contractor shall produce an SRS and, if applicable, IRS(s) for each CSCI (see Appendix D). In the event preliminary SRSs and IRSs have been provided by the Government, the contractor shall produce updated and completed versions of these specifications (see Appendix B). Additional guidance on preparing specifications is provided in MIL-STD-490.

5.1.3 *Formal Reviews - Software Requirements Analysis.* The contractor shall present the newly prepared or updated OCD for the system and an SRS and IRS(s) for each CSCI at a Software Specification Review (SSR). The purpose of the SSR is to demonstrate to the contracting agency the adequacy of the OCD, SRS, and, if applicable, IRS(s). Specific details regarding the SSR process are contained in MIL-STD-1521.

5.1.4 *Baselines - Software Requirements Analysis.* Upon completion of the SSR, and when authenticated by the contracting agency, the SRS and IRS(s) will establish the Allocated Baseline for each CSCI. Specific details regarding the baseline process are contained in MIL-STD-483 and MIL-STD-490.

5.2 *Preliminary Design.* The contractor shall develop a top-level design of each CSCI which completely reflects the requirements specified in the SRS and IRS(s). The contractor may develop lower-level design for critical elements of the CSCI. The criteria for determining critical elements shall be described in either the SSPM or SDP (see Appendix D).

5.2.1 *Activities - Preliminary Design.* The contractor shall perform the following activities during Preliminary Design.

5.2.1.1 The contractor shall monitor the development effort for consistency with the SDP, SSPM, SCMP, and SQEP (see 5.8.1.2.2). The contractor shall notify the contracting agency of proposed changes to these documents, and make necessary revisions. All proposed changes shall be subject to disapproval by the contracting agency. In addition, the contractor shall notify the contracting agency at the next review, audit, or in the next status report (whichever comes first) of any actions or procedures occurring during Preliminary Design that deviate from the SDP, SSPM, SCMP, or SQEP.

5.2.1.2 The contractor shall establish the top-level design of each CSCI by allocating requirements from the SRS and, if applicable, IRS(s) to the TLCSCs of each CSCI. In defining each TLCSC the contractor shall identify:

a. The TLCSC's place in the CSCI's static structure
b. Functions allocated to the TLCSC
c. Memory size and processing time allocated (including reserve capacities) to the TLCSC
d. Functional control and data flow to and from the TLCSC
e. Known interrupt and special control features (such as non-standard subroutine returns) of the TLCSC
f. Global data shared with other TLCSCs
g. Applicable inputs, local data, interrupts, timing and sequencing, processing, and outputs of the TLCSC
h. Adaptation data needed by the TLCSC

5.2.1.3 The contractor may establish the lower-level design of critical elements of each CSCI, including external interfaces and data bases, by refining TLCSCs to LLCSCs and Units. The criteria for determining critical elements shall be described in either the SSPM or SDP (see Appendix D).

5.2.1.4 In establishing and defining the top-level and, as applicable, lower-level design of each CSCI, the contractor shall use a program design language or some other top-level design description tool or methodology. This tool or methodology shall be identified in either the SSPM or SDP (see Appendix D) and shall be subject to contracting agency approval.

5.2.1.5 In the development of the top-level design, the contractor shall incorporate applicable human factors engineering principles, including:

a. Human information processing capabilities and limitations
b. Anthropometric characteristics of the target population
c. Foreseeable human errors under both normal and extreme conditions
d. Implications for the total system environment (to include training, support, maintenance, and operational environment)

5.2.1.6 The contractor shall develop test plans for both informal and formal tests.

a. Informal tests shall test individual Units during Coding and Unit Testing and aggregates of Units during CSC Integration and Testing. For Unit testing, the contractor shall identify the overall test requirements, test responsibilities, and schedule information. For CSC integration testing, the contractor shall identify: (1) the overall test requirements, test responsibilities, and schedule information, and (2) different classes of CSC integration tests. Although informal test documentation does not require Government approval, it shall be made available for Government review.
b. Formal tests shall test the fully implemented CSCI during CSCI Testing, to show that the CSCI satisfies its specified requirements. Formal tests may also occur at the TLCSC, LLCSC, and Unit levels, when compliance with specified requirements cannot be shown at the CSCI level. Some CSCIs may require integration with other computer systems, HWCIs, or CSCIs before all formal testing can be completed. For formal testing, the contractor shall identify: (1)

the test requirements applicable to CSCI testing, (2) CSCI test organization, responsibilities, and schedule information, (3) different classes of formal tests, (4) data recording, reduction, and analysis requirements, and (5) the purpose of each formal test planned. The contractor shall plan for documenting formal test results as well. All individuals responsible for planning formal tests shall be sufficiently independent from the individuals responsible for development to permit objective testing.

c. The contractor shall identify all the resources (facilities, personnel, hardware, software) required for informal and formal testing.

5.2.1.7 The contractor shall define a preliminary version of the procedures and information for the operation of the computer system in which each CSCI executes (see 5.2.2.6). This definition shall include:

a. System preparation and set up
b. Operating procedures
c. Input/Output
d. Monitoring procedures
e. Off-line routines
f. Recovery and special procedures
g. Diagnostic features

5.2.1.8 The contractor shall define a preliminary version of the instructions for user personnel to execute each CSCI requiring user interaction (see 5.2.2.6). This definition shall include for each function the CSCI performs:

a. Name, number and purpose of the function
b. Initialization requirements
c. Execution options
d. User and system inputs
e. Termination and restart procedures
f. Expected outputs
g. Interrelationship with other functions
h. Error messages
i. Diagnostic features

5.2.1.9 The contractor shall define a preliminary version of the information necessary to identify a computer system malfunction and instructions to run the diagnostics (see 5.2.2.6). This definition shall include:

a. Identification of all support hardware, software, and procedures necessary to perform system diagnosis.
b. A description of each diagnostic tool available for the system.
c. A description of each diagnostic test available on the diagnostic tools, including: (1) the purpose of each test, (2) procedures for executing the test, (3) additional hardware, software, or firmware necessary for executing the test, and (4) all diagnostic messages.

5.2.1.10 The contractor shall define a preliminary version of the information required to perform life cycle support for the contractually deliverable software (see 5.2.2.6). This definition shall include identification of:

a. The support environment, describing required: (1) support software, (2) equipment, (3) facilities, and (4) personnel.
b. Support operations, describing: (1) general usage instructions (initiation, general operation, and monitoring operations of the support environment), (2) administration, (3) software modification, (4) software integration and testing, (5) system and software generation, (6) software quality evaluation, (7) corrective action system, (8) configuration management, (9) simulation, (10) emulation, (11) reproduction, and (12) operational distributions.
c. Training plans and provisions.
d. Predicted level of change to the deliverable software in the support environment.

5.2.1.11 The contractor shall conduct internal in-process reviews during this phase (See 5.8.1.2.4) and shall make all necessary changes based on the results of the internal reviews, prior to presenting the top-level design, test plans, and operation and support documents to the contracting agency.

5.2.2 *Products - Preliminary Design.* The contractor shall produce the following products during Preliminary Design (see 6.2).

5.2.2.1 The contractor shall produce updated versions of the SDP, SSPM, SCMP, and SQEP as necessary.

5.2.2.2 The contractor shall produce records and summary reports of the internal reviews conducted (see 5.8.2.1 and 5.8.2.2).

5.2.2.3 The contractor shall produce a Software Top-Level Design Document (STLDD) for each CSCI to describe the top-level design of the CSCI.

5.2.2.4 The contractor may produce preliminary versions of the Software Detailed Design Document (SDDD), Interface Design Document(s) (IDD(s)), and Data Base Design Document(s) (DBDD(s)) for critical lower-level elements of the CSCI.

5.2.2.5 The contractor shall produce a Software Test Plan (STP) for each CSCI to describe the plans for both informal and formal testing of the CSCI.

5.2.2.6 The contractor shall produce preliminary versions of the:

a. Computer System Operator's Manual (CSOM)
b. Software User's Manual (SUM) for one or more CSCIs
c. Computer System Diagnostic Manual (CSDM)
d. Computer Resources Integrated Support Document (CRISD)

5.2.3 *Formal Reviews - Preliminary Design.* The contractor shall present the STLDD and the STP for each CSCI, and preliminary versions of the CSOM, SUM(s), CSDM, and CRISD at a Preliminary Design Review (PDR). The purpose of the PDR is to review the top-level design, test plans, and preliminary operation and support documents with the contracting agency and to demonstrate to the contracting agency that: (1) the top-level design satisfies the software requirements allocated from the higher-level documents, (2) the test plans establish adequate test criteria for each CSCI and address all specified requirements, and (3) the preliminary versions of the CSOM, SUM(s), CSDM, and CRISD will, in final form, adequately address the operation and support of the computer system. In addition, the PDR may review preliminary versions of the SDDD, IDD(s), and DBDD(s) for critical lower-level elements, including external interfaces and data base(s), to demonstrate that the lower-level design for critical elements will satisfy the specified requirements. Specific details regarding the PDR process are contained in MIL-STD-1521.

5.2.4 *Developmental Configuration - Preliminary Design.* Upon successful completion of the PDR, the STLDD shall establish the contractor's Developmental Configuration for each CSCI.

5.3 *Detailed Design.* The contractor shall develop a modular, detailed design for each CSCI.

5.3.1 *Activities - Detailed Design.* The contractor shall perform the following activities during Detailed Design.

5.3.1.1 The contractor shall monitor the development effort for consistency with the SDP, SSPM, SCMP, and SQEP (see 5.8.1.2.2). The contractor shall notify the contracting agency of proposed changes to these documents and make necessary revisions. All proposed changes shall be subject to disapproval by the contracting agency. In addition, the contractor shall notify the contracting agency at the next review, audit, or in the next status report (whichever comes first) of any actions or procedures occurring during Detailed Design that deviate from the SDP, SSPM, SCMP, or SQEP.

5.3.1.2 The contractor shall establish the complete, modular, lower-level design for each CSCI, by refining TLCSCs into LLCSCs and Units. Each Unit shall perform a single function. In refining TLCSCs, the contractor shall identify:

a. All required details for implementing external interfaces, including item summary and item format for each interface
b. Global data definitions within each TLCSC
c. Inputs, local data definitions, process control requirements, processing, utilization of other elements, limitations, and outputs of all LLCSCs
d. Inputs, local data definitions, process control requirements, processing, special control features, protection, error handling, utilization of other elements, limitations, and outputs for all Units
e. Detailed data base design including data base management system overview, data base structure, data base file design, and data base references.

5.3.1.3 The contractor shall refine all TLCSCs using a top-down design approach, unless specific alternate methodologies have been proposed in either the SSPM or SDP (see Appendix D) and have received contracting agency approval.

5.3.1.4 The contractor may depart from a top-down approach to: (1) address critical lower-level elements or (2) incorporate commercially available, reusable, and Government furnished software. The contractor shall describe the criteria for determining critical lower-level elements in either the SSPM or SDP (see Appendix D). Examples of criteria for determining criticality are software performance, cost, and schedule.

5.3.1.5 In the development of the detailed design for each CSCI, the contractor shall employ a program design language. The language and other tools to be used shall be identified in either the SSPM or SDP (see Appendix D) and shall be subject to contracting agency approval.

5.3.1.6 The contractor shall ensure that the detailed design incorporates applicable human factors engineering principles (see 5.2.1.5).

5.3.1.7 The contractor shall monitor size and time estimates for the CSCI and adjust the estimates, if necessary. All modifications to controlled or baselined documentation shall be made in accordance with the configuration management requirements contained herein (see 5.7).

5.3.1.8 The contractor shall establish software development files (SDFs) for all Units. Each SDF may serve a single Unit or logically related group of Units. Unit requirements, design considerations and constraints, schedule, status information, and test documentation shall be incorporated into the corresponding SDF. All SDFs shall be in the format described in either the SSPM or SDP (see Appendix D). To reduce duplication, SDFs should not contain information provided in other documents. SDFs may be generated, maintained, and controlled by automated means.

5.3.1.9 The contractor shall document additional engineering information generated in the design process for each CSCI. The engineering information shall include rationale, results of analyses and trade-off studies, and any other information which aids in understanding the detailed design.

5.3.1.10 The contractor shall identify the test requirements, responsibilities, and schedule for the informal testing to be conducted for each Unit, and shall record them in the corresponding SDF.

5.3.1.11 The contractor shall describe test cases for each informal Unit test in terms of inputs, expected results, and evaluation criteria. The test cases for each Unit shall be described in the corresponding SDF.

5.3.1.12 The contractor shall identify the requirements, responsibilities, and schedule for each CSC integration test.

5.3.1.13 The contractor shall describe test cases for each informal CSC integration test in terms of inputs, expected results, and evaluation criteria.

5.3.1.14 The contractor shall describe test cases for each formal CSCI test identified in the STP. Test case descriptions shall include:

a. Initialization requirements
b. Input data
c. Expected intermediate test results
d. Expected output data
e. Criteria for evaluating results
f. Assumptions and constraints.

5.3.1.15 The contractor shall update with any additional known details all information and instructions pertaining to computer system operation, software operation by users, and computer system diagnostics (see 5.3.2.9).

5.3.1.16 The contractor shall complete the information that is required to perform life cycle support of the contractually deliverable software (see 5.3.2.10).

5.3.1.17 The contractor shall prepare information to facilitate programming or reprogramming software for the target computer (see 5.3.2.11). The information shall include:

a. Equipment configuration
b. Operational characteristics, capabilities, and limitations
c. Compilation and assembly information
d. Programming features
e. Program instructions
f. I/O control features
g. Examples of programming techniques
h. Special features
i. Error detection and diagnostic features

5.3.1.18 The contractor shall describe the information necessary to modify or replace the read-only memory (ROM), programmable read-only memory (PROM), and other such firmware components of the system (see 5.3.2.11). This description shall include:

a. Description of firmware components
b. Installation and repair procedures
c. Security implications
d. Operational and environment limitations
e. Hardware needed for programming firmware devices
f. Software needed for programming firmware devices
g. Procedures for programming firmware devices
h. Vendor information

5.3.1.19 The contractor shall conduct internal in-process reviews during this phase (see 5.8.1.2.5) and shall make all necessary changes based on the results of the internal review, prior to presenting the detailed design, formal test case documentation, and operation and support documentation to the contracting agency.

5.3.2 *Products - Detailed Design.* The contractor shall produce the following products during Detailed Design (see 6.2).

5.3.2.1 The contractor shall produce updated versions of the SDP, SSPM, SCMP, and SQEP as necessary.

5.3.2.2 The contractor shall produce records and summary reports of the internal reviews conducted (see 5.8.2.1 and 5.8.2.2).

5.3.2.3 The contractor shall produce an SDDD for each CSCI, to describe the detailed design. The contractor shall include in the SDDD, in Section 6 Notes, additional engineering information (rationale, results of analyses and trade-off studies, etc.) which aids in understanding the detailed design of the CSCI.

5.3.2.4 The contractor shall produce an IDD for each IRS to describe the details of external interfaces. The contractor shall include in the IDD(s), in Section 6 Notes, additional information (rationale, results of analyses and trade-off studies, etc.) which aids in understanding the details of external interfaces.

5.3.2.5 The contractor shall produce one or more DBDDs. Each DBDD shall describe the contents and structure of one or more data bases. (Data base interactions and control mechanisms are described in the top-level and detailed design documents). The contractor shall include in the DBDD(s), in Section 6 Notes, additional information (rationale, results of analyses and trade-off studies, etc.) which aids in understanding the details of the data base(s).

5.3.2.6 The contractor shall establish and maintain SDFs for all Units.

5.3.2.7 The contractor shall produce documents that identify each informal CSC integration test and describe the test cases, in the standard format described in either the SSPM or SDP (see Appendix D), for each informal test to be executed.

5.3.2.8 The contractor shall produce a Software Test Description (STD) for each CSCI, to define test cases for each formal test of the CSCI described in the STP.

5.3.2.9 The contractor shall produce updated versions of the CSOM, SUM(s), and CSDM.

5.3.2.10 The contractor shall produce a completed CRISD.

5.3.2.11 The contractor shall produce a Software Programmer's Manual (SPM) and a Firmware Support Manual (FSM).

5.3.3 *Formal Reviews - Detailed Design.* The contractor shall present the SDDD and the STD for each CSCI at a Critical Design Review (CDR). The contractor shall also present the IDD(s), DBDD(s), SPM, FSM, and updated CSOM, SUM, CSDM, and CRISD at this review. The purpose of the CDR is to review the detailed design, test description, and operation and support documents with the contracting agency, and to demonstrate to the contracting agency that: (1) the detailed design satisfies the requirements of the SRS and the IRS(s), (2) the SDDD, IDD(s), and DBDD(s) further refine the design details of the CSCI in a manner consistent with the STLDD, (3) the STD provides adequate test cases for the formal tests identified in the STP, (4) the updated versions of the CSOM, SUM(s), and CSDM will, in final form, adequately address the operation and support of the computer system, and (5) the SPM, FSM, and CRISD adequately address software programming support, firmware support, and integrated computer resources support. Specific details regarding the CDR process are contained in MIL-STD-1521.

5.3.4 *Developmental Configuration - Detailed Design.* Upon successful completion of the CDR, the contractor shall enter the SDDD, IDD(s), and the DBDD(s) for each CSCI into the Developmental Configuration for the CSCI.

5.4 *Coding and Unit Testing.* The contractor shall code and test each Unit making up the detailed design.

5.4.1 *Activities - Coding and Unit Testing.* The contractor shall perform the following activities during Coding and Unit Testing.

5.4.1.1 The contractor shall monitor the development effort for consistency with the SDP, SSPM, SCMP, and SQEP (see 5.8.1.2.2). The contractor shall notify the contracting agency of proposed changes to these documents, and make necessary revisions. All proposed changes shall be subject to disapproval by the contracting agency. In addition, the contractor shall notify the contracting agency at the next review, audit, or in the next status report (whichever comes first) of any actions or procedures occurring during Coding and Unit Testing that deviate from the SDP, SSPM, SCMP, or SQEP.

5.4.1.2 The contractor shall code and test Units in top-down sequence, unless alternate methodologies have been proposed in either the SSPM or SDP (see Appendix D) and have received contracting agency approval.

5.4.1.3 The contractor may depart from a top-down approach to: (1) code and test critical Units or (2) incorporate commercially available, reusable, or Government furnished software. The contractor shall describe the criteria for determining critical Units in either the SSPM or SDP (see Appendix D). Examples of criteria for determining criticality are software performance, cost, and schedule.

5.4.1.4 The contractor shall code all Units in accordance with coding standards. If the contractor has not proposed use of internal coding standards in either the SSPM or SDP (see Appendix D) and received contracting agency approval for the internal coding standards, then the coding standards of Appendix C shall apply.

5.4.1.5 The contractor shall produce deliverable code that can be regenerated and maintained using only Government-owned, contractually deliverable, or commercially available support software and hardware.

5.4.1.6 Prior to the testing of each Unit, the contractor shall prepare and record in the SDF test procedures for conducting each informal Unit test.

5.4.1.7 The contractor shall perform informal Unit tests according to the test plans for informal Unit testing contained in the STP and according to the Unit test cases and Unit test procedures contained in the SDF.

5.4.1.8 The contractor shall record in the SDF the test results of all informal Unit testing.

5.4.1.9 The contractor shall make necessary revisions to the design documentation and code, and shall update the SDFs of all Units that undergo design or coding changes based on Unit tests.

5.4.1.10 The contractor shall enter into the Developmental Configuration and release for integration each coded Unit that has been successfully tested and reviewed (see 5.8.1.2.6).

5.4.1.11 The contractor shall develop detailed test procedures for conducting each informal CSC integration test.

5.4.1.12 The contractor shall prepare preliminary versions of test procedures for conducting each formal CSCI test and for analyzing formal CSCI test results. Test procedures shall include:

a. Schedule
b. Pretest procedures, including equipment preparation and software preparation
c. Each step of the procedures
d. Applicable data reduction and data analysis procedures
e. Assumptions made and constraints imposed on formal test procedures

5.4.1.13 The contractor shall update with additional known details all information and instructions pertaining to computer system operation, software operation by users, computer system diagnostics, programming or reprogramming software for the target computer, and modifying or replacing firmware (see 5.4.2.7).

5.4.1.14 The contractor shall conduct internal in-process reviews during this phase (see 5.8.1.2.6) and shall make all necessary changes based on the results of the internal reviews.

5.4.2 *Products - Coding and Unit Testing.* The contractor shall produce the following products during Coding and Unit Testing (see 6.2).

5.4.2.1 The contractor shall produce updated versions of the SDP, SSPM, SCMP, and SQEP, as necessary.

5.4.2.2 The contractor shall produce records and summary reports of the internal reviews conducted (see 5.8.2.1 and 5.8.2.2).

5.4.2.3 The contractor shall produce the source and object code and, as necessary, updated design documentation for each Unit of each CSCI.

5.4.2.4 The contractor shall produce updated SDFs as necessary for all Units (e.g., modified Unit test procedures, retest results, etc.). All SDFs shall be in the standard format described in either the SSPM or SDP (see Appendix D).

5.4.2.5 The contractor shall produce detailed test procedures for conducting each informal CSC integration test. These procedures shall be in the format described in either the SSPM or SDP (see Appendix D).

5.4.2.6 The contractor shall produce a preliminary version of the Software Test Procedure (STPR) to describe the detailed procedures for conducting formal CSCI tests and for analyzing formal CSCI test results.

5.4.2.7 The contractor shall produce updated versions of the CSOM, SUM(s), CSDM, SPM, and FSM.

5.4.3 *Developmental Configuration - Coding and Unit Testing.* The contractor shall enter any updated design documentation, source and object code, and associated listings for each successfully tested and reviewed Unit into the Developmental Configuration for the CSCI (see 5.8.1.2.6).

5.5 *CSC Integration and Testing.* The contractor shall integrate Units of code entered in the Developmental Configuration and perform informal tests on aggregates of integrated Units. In order to test critical functions of each CSCI early, formal tests may be conducted during this phase. Formal tests conducted during this phase require: (1) the contractor to complete the applicable formal test procedures, (2) contracting agency approval of the applicable formal test procedures, and (3) the contractor to perform the tests in accordance with the approved test procedures.

5.5.1 *Activities - CSC Integration and Testing.* The contractor shall perform the following activities during CSC Integration and Testing.

5.5.1.1 The contractor shall monitor the development effort for consistency with the SDP, SSPM, SCMP, and SQEP (see 5.8.1.2.2). The contractor shall notify the contracting agency of proposed changes to these documents and make necessary revisions. All proposed changes shall be subject to disapproval by the contracting agency. In addition, the contractor shall notify the contracting agency at the next review, audit, or in the next status report (whichever comes first) of any actions or procedures occurring during CSC Integration and Testing that deviate from the SDP, SSPM, SCMP, or SQEP.

5.5.1.2 The contractor shall integrate and test aggregates of Units in a top-down sequence, unless alternate methodologies have been proposed in either the SSPM or SDP (see Appendix D) and have received contracting agency approval.

5.5.1.3 The contractor may depart from a top-down approach to: (1) integrate or test critical Units or (2) incorporate commercially available, reusable, and Government furnished software. The contractor shall describe the criteria for determining critical Units in either the SSPM or SDP (see Appendix D). Examples of criteria for determining criticality are software performance, cost, and schedule.

5.5.1.4 As Units are successively integrated with one another, the contractor shall compare memory and processing time values with allocations established during Preliminary and Detailed Design. The contractor shall also compare any system resources affected by the integrated Units with specified requirements (e.g., secondary storage, communication channel utilization, etc.). The contractor shall modify, as necessary, all controlled or baselined documentation based on the memory, processing time, and system resources comparisons. All modifications to controlled or baselined documentation shall be made in accordance with the configuration management requirements contained herein (see 5.7).

5.5.1.5 The contractor shall informally test aggregates of integrated Units according to the test plans contained in the STP and the test cases and test procedures developed in previous phases.

5.5.1.6 The contractor shall document the results of all integration testing in the standard format described in either the SSPM or SDP (see Appendix D).

5.5.1.7 The contractor shall make necessary revisions to the design documentation and code, perform all necessary retesting, and update the SDFs of all Units that undergo design or coding changes based on integration tests.

5.5.1.8 The contractor shall complete preparation of detailed procedures for conducting each formal CSCI test and for analyzing formal test results (see 5.4.1.12).

5.5.1.9 The contractor shall update with additional known details all information and instructions pertaining to computer system operation, software operation by users, computer system diagnostics, programming or reprogramming software for the target computer, and modifying or replacing firmware (see 5.5.2.7).

5.5.1.10 The contractor shall conduct internal in-process reviews during this phase (see 5.8.1.2.7) and shall make all necessary changes based on the results of the internal reviews, prior to presenting the informal test results, completed formal CSCI test procedures, and updated operation and support documentation to the contracting agency.

5.5.2 *Products - CSC Integration and Testing.* The contractor shall produce the following products during CSC Integration and Testing (see 6.2).

5.5.2.1 The contractor shall produce updated versions of the SDP, SSPM, SCMP, and SQEP, as necessary.

5.5.2.2 The contractor shall produce records and summary reports of the internal reviews conducted (see 5.8.2.1 and 5.8.2.2).

5.5.2.3 The contractor shall produce the source and object code for each complete CSCI by integrating its constituent parts.

5.5.2.4 The contractor shall produce the informal integration test results documented in the standard format described in either the SSPM or SDP (see Appendix D).

5.5.2.5 The contractor shall produce updated design documents and SDFs to reflect changes based on integration testing.

5.5.2.6 The contractor shall produce the completed STPR for each CSCI.

5.5.2.7 The contractor shall produce updated versions of the CSOM, SUM(s), CSDM, SPM, and FSM.

5.5.3 *Formal Reviews - CSC Integration and Testing.* The contractor shall present informal CSC integration test results and the STPR for each CSCI at a Test Readiness Review (TRR). The contractor shall also present the updated CSOM, SUM(s), and CSDM. The purpose of the TRR is to review the informal test results, formal test procedures, and operation and support documents with the contracting agency, and to demonstrate to the contracting agency that: (1) the STPR is complete, (2) the contractor is ready to begin formal testing, and (3) the updated versions of the CSOM, SUM(s), and CSDM will, in final form, adequately address the operation and support of the computer system. Specific details regarding the TRR process are contained in MIL-STD-1521.

5.5.4 *Developmental Configuration - CSC Integration and Testing.* The contractor shall enter any updated design documentation, source code, object code, and associated listings into the Developmental Configuration for each CSCI.

5.6 *CSCI Testing.* The contractor shall conduct formal tests on each CSCI to show that the CSCI satisfies its specified requirements. The contractor shall also record and analyze formal test results. Conducting and analyzing formal tests shall be performed by individuals sufficiently independent from the individuals responsible for development to permit objective testing.

5.6.1 *Activities - CSCI Testing.* The contractor shall perform the following activities during CSCI Testing.

5.6.1.1 The contractor shall monitor the development effort for consistency with the SDP, SSPM, SCMP, and SQEP (see 5.8.1.2.2). The contractor shall notify the contracting agency of proposed changes to these documents and make necessary revisions. All proposed changes shall be subject to disapproval by the contracting agency. In addition, the contractor shall notify the contracting agency at the next review, audit, or in the next status report (whichever comes first) of any actions or procedures occurring during CSCI Testing that deviate from the SDP, SSPM, SCMP, or SQEP.

5.6.1.2 Individuals sufficiently independent from the individuals responsible for development shall perform formal tests on each CSCI in accordance with the: (1) formal test plans described in the STP, (2) formal test cases described in the STD, and (3) formal test procedures contained in the STPR.

5.6.1.3 Individuals sufficiently independent from the individuals responsible for development shall report the results of all formal CSCI tests. The test reports shall include:

a. Summary and detail of the test results
b. Detailed test history
c. Evaluation of test results, and recommendations
d. Test procedure deviations

5.6.1.4 The contractor shall make necessary revisions to the design documentation and code, perform all necessary retesting, and update the SDFs of all Units that undergo design or coding changes based on formal tests.

5.6.1.5 The contractor shall identify the exact version of each deliverable CSCI and the interim changes occurring between versions. This identification shall include:

a. Inventory of materials to be released
b. Inventory of CSCI contents

c. Class I changes installed
d. Class II changes installed
e. Adaptation data
f. Interface compatibility
g. Bibliography of reference documents
h. Operational description
i. Installation instructions
j. Possible problems and known errors

5.6.1.6 The contractor shall complete all information and instructions pertaining to computer system operation, software operation by users, computer system diagnostics, programming or reprogramming software for the target computer, and modifying or replacing firmware (see 5.6.2.7).

5.6.1.7 The contractor shall conduct internal in-process reviews during this phase (see 5.8.1.2.8) and shall make all necessary changes based on the results of the internal reviews, prior to presenting the formal test results and completed operation and support documents to the contracting agency.

5.6.2 *Products - CSCI Testing.* The contractor shall produce the following products during CSCI Testing (see 6.2).

5.6.2.1 The contractor shall produce updated versions of the SDP, SSPM, SCMP, and SQEP, as necessary.

5.6.2.2 The contractor shall produce records and summary reports of the internal reviews conducted (see 5.8.2.1 and 5.8.2.2).

5.6.2.3 The contractor shall produce Software Test Reports (STRs) which document the results of formal CSCI tests, test data analysis, and any deviations or discrepancies discovered in the testing.

5.6.2.4 The contractor shall produce the updated source and object code for each CSCI and prepare them for delivery in accordance with the requirements of the SRS.

5.6.2.5 The contractor shall produce a Software Product Specification (SPS) for each CSCI, consisting of all the documents and listings comprising the Developmental Configuration for the CSCI. Some CSCIs may require integration with other computer systems, HWCIs, or CSCIs before all formal testing can be completed. In such cases the SPS cannot be completed until after such integration and testing. Additional guidance on preparing specifications is provided in MIL-STD-490.

5.6.2.6 The contractor shall produce a Version Description Document (VDD) for each CSCI.

5.6.2.7 The contractor shall produce completed versions of the CSOM, SUM(s), CSDM, SPM, and FSM.

5.6.3 *Audits - CSCI Testing.* The contractor shall present the STR(s) for each CSCI and the CSOM, SUM(s), and CSDM at a Functional Configuration Audit (FCA). The contractor shall present the SPS, VDD, and source and object code for each CSCI at a Physical Configuration Audit (PCA). The contractor shall also present the CSOM, SUM(s), CSDM, SPM, and FSM at the PCA. The purpose of the FCA is to demonstrate to the contracting agency that the CSCI was successfully tested and meets the requirements of the SRS and the IRS(s). The FCA also demonstrates to the contracting agency that the CSOM, SUM(s), and CSDM adequately address the operation and support of the computer system. The purpose of the PCA is to demonstrate to the contracting agency that the SPS is complete and reflects an up-to-date technical description of the CSCI. FCA and PCA for the CSCI may be postponed until the system level, if formal testing of the CSCI requires system level integration. Specific details regarding the FCA and PCA processes are contained in MIL-STD-1521.

5.6.4 *Baselines - CSCI Testing.* The configuration identification documents for the HWCIs and CSCIs that comprise a system form a single Product Baseline. Upon successful completion of the FCA and PCA for each CSCI and when authenticated by the contracting agency, the SPS for the CSCI will be entered into the Product Baseline. Upon SPS entry into the Product Baseline, the CSCI's Developmental Configuration shall cease to exist. Specific details regarding the baseline process are contained in MIL-STD-483 and MIL-STD-490.

5.6.5 *Software Acceptance.* Acceptance of the software by the contracting agency depends on the nature of the end items under contract. If only software is contracted for, then software acceptance follows PCA for each CSCI. If an integrated hardware and software system is contracted for, then software acceptance is part of system acceptance and follows system level PCA. Software acceptance shall be predicated on the following:

a. Satisfaction of criteria specified in the SOW and contract
b. Satisfactory completion of FCA and PCA
c. Number and severity of unresolved software and documentation errors
d. Documented evidence of correlation between the source code and object code
e. Consistency between the code and its associated SPS and VDD
f. Contractor recommendations for acceptance to the contracting agency or its designated representative
g. Certification of compliance with contractual requirements

Specific details regarding the software acceptance process are contained in MIL-STD-1521.

5.6.6 *Installation and Checkout.* If required by the SOW, the contractor shall install and checkout the deliverable software at Government-designated facilities. The contractor shall specify the installation and checkout procedures to be followed in the SDP.

5.7 *Configuration Management (CM).* The contractor shall implement the procedures described in either the SCMP, SDP, or system CM plan (see Appendix D) which provide technical and administrative direction and surveillance to: (1) identify and document the functional and physical characteristics of each CSCI, (2) control changes to those characteristics, and (3) record and report the processing of changes and the status of implementation. The contractor shall perform software configuration management within the framework of the system configuration management and shall ensure that integrated procedures address the total system requirements, including such items as hardware, related CSCIs, support and training elements and facilities, and Government furnished hardware or software, as applicable. The contractor shall perform configuration management on all non-deliverable software used in the development and on revisions to commercially-available computer resources, as described in either the

SCMP, SDP, or system CM plan (see Appendix D). The contractor is encouraged to use automated tools in performing configuration management (see 5.9.1.4). Additional guidance on configuration management practices and baselines may be found in MIL-STD-483 and MIL-STD-490.

5.7.1 *Activities - Configuration Management.* The contractor shall perform the following configuration management activities.

5.7.1.1 *Configuration Identification.* The contractor shall implement the procedures specified in either the SCMP, SDP, or system CM plan (see Appendix D) and approved by the contracting agency. These procedures shall identify the various TLCSCs, LLCSCs, and Units that make up the CSCI, and shall indicate the relationship between the CSCI elements and the documentation for the CSCI. Configuration identification by the contractor shall include the following activities.

5.7.1.1.1 The contractor shall identify the following documentation which establishes and defines:

a. The Functional and Allocated Baselines, which shall consist of system and CSCI requirements documents provided or approved by the contracting agency.
b. The Developmental Configuration, which consists of documentation defining the design and code (including revisions) for each CSCI and its constituent TLCSCs, LLCSCs, and Units. The Developmental Configuration also contains the complete and current software code (source and object) of all Units that have been successfully tested and reviewed. Documentation and code comprising the Developmental Configuration shall be designated for configuration control by the contractor until the documentation is entered into the Product Baseline and the source and object code are delivered. Documentation and code shall be provided to the contracting agency for information or provisional review in accordance with the contract data requirements.
c. The Product Baseline which will be established upon successful completion of FCA and PCA. The Product Baseline will include the approved Developmental Configuration documentation for each CSCI and shall be under contracting agency configuration control, unless otherwise stipulated in the contract.

5.7.1.1.2 The contractor shall identify all documentation and computer software media containing code, documentation, or both by titling, labeling, numbering, and cataloging procedures. The procedures shall accomplish the following:

a. Uniquely identify all the TLCSCs, LLCSCs, and Units of each CSCI, and the specific versions of each element to which a document applies.
b. Uniquely identify the serial, edition, change status, and other identification details of each document.
c. Identify the specific contents of each medium, including change status.

5.7.1.2 *Configuration Control.* The contractor shall implement the procedures specified in either the SCMP, SDP, or system CM plan (see Appendix D) and approved by the contracting agency, to control all changes to the Developmental Configuration, formally baselined documents, and code for each CSCI. Configuration control by the contractor shall include the following activities.

5.7.1.2.1 The contractor shall include under internal configuration control all items entered into the contractor's Developmental Configuration.

5.7.1.2.2 The contractor shall form a Software Configuration Control Board (SCCB) that shall have control over the Developmental Configuration. No changes shall be made to the Developmental Configuration without SCCB approval.

5.7.1.2.3 The contractor shall implement a corrective action system to report and track all problems and to implement necessary changes (see 5.8.1.10).

5.7.1.2.4 Proposed changes which impact the approved documentation comprising the Functional, Allocated, or Product Baselines shall be classified and processed in accordance with DOD-STD-480 or MIL-STD-481, as contractually specified, and shall be subject to contracting agency approval prior to implementation.

5.7.1.2.5 The contractor shall control the preparation and dissemination of changes to both the software and its documentation to reflect approved and implemented changes.

5.7.1.3 *Configuration Status Accounting.* The contractor shall implement the procedures specified in either the SCMP, SDP, or system CM plan (see Appendix D) and approved by the contracting agency, to generate periodic status reports on all products in the Developmental Configuration and in the Allocated and Product Baselines. Status reports shall: (1) provide traceability of changes to controlled products, (2) serve as a basis for communicating the status of configuration identifications and associated software, and (3) serve as a vehicle for ensuring that delivered documents describe and represent the associated software.

5.7.2 *Products - Configuration Management.* The contractor shall prepare the following products of configuration management (see 6.2).

5.7.2.1 The contractor shall prepare a software problem or change report to describe each problem discovered and the associated proposed change. All such reports shall be in the format specified in either the SCMP, SDP, or system CM plan (see Appendix D).

5.7.2.2 The contractor shall prepare an Engineering Change Proposal (ECP) in accordance with DOD-STD-480 or MIL-STD-481, as contractually specified, to propose each change to the Government that impacts the CSCI's cost, schedule, interfaces, or Government-controlled baselines.

5.7.2.3 The contractor shall prepare a Specification Change Notice (SCN) in accordance with MIL-STD-490 to describe changes to Government-controlled baselines. Preliminary SCNs shall accompany ECPs, as applicable. Additional guidance may be found in MIL-STD-483 and MIL-STD-490.

5.7.2.4 The contractor shall prepare a Version Description Document (VDD) to identify new and interim versions of each CSCI and associated software product specifications entered in the Product Baseline.

5.7.2.5 The contractor shall provide the contracting agency with CSCI configuration information from the status accounting system, in the form of reports, electronic data transmittal, or other media, as contractually required.

5.7.3 *Audits - Configuration Management.* The contracting agency will conduct, and the contractor shall support, an FCA and PCA of each CSCI in accordance with MIL-STD-1521.

5.8 *Software Quality Evaluation.* The contractor shall establish and implement internal procedures to: (1) evaluate the requirements established for the software, (2) evaluate the methodologies established and implemented for developing the software, (3) evaluate the products of the software development process, (4) provide feedback and recommendations based on these evaluations that can be used to effect improvements in the software quality, and (5) perform corrective action in terms of detecting, reporting, and tracking problems with controlled software and documentation. The methods of evaluation (e.g., sampling) shall be specified by the contractor in either the SQEP or the SDP.

5.8.1 *Activities - Software Quality Evaluation.* The contractor shall perform the following software quality evaluation activities.

5.8.1.1 *Planning.* The contractor shall perform the planning necessary to establish and implement the tasks specified in Section 5.8 herein.

5.8.1.2 *Internal Reviews.* The contractor shall conduct internal reviews of the methodologies proposed in the contractor's planning documents and of their implementation on the software development project. These reviews shall evaluate the compliance of proposed methodologies with this standard, their adequacy to produce software products that will meet established requirements, and compliance of the software development process with established methodologies. In addition, the contractor shall conduct internal in-process reviews of the software development products. The internal reviews in each software development phase shall be as follows.

5.8.1.2.1 *Evaluation Criteria.* In conducting reviews of software and documentation, the contractor shall use the following evaluation criteria in addition to those specified in 5.8.1.2.2 through 5.8.1.2.8:

a. Adherence to required format
b. Compliance with contractual requirements
c. Internal consistency
d. Understandability
e. Technical adequacy
f. Degree of completeness appropriate to the phase

5.8.1.2.2 *Internal Reviews - All Phases.* The contractor shall conduct the following internal reviews during all phases of the software development cycle:

a. Review the newly prepared or revised SDP, SSPM, SCMP, and SQEP for the criteria identified in 5.8.1.2.1, compliance with this standard, and consistency with one another.
b. Review the activities and the tools, procedures, and methodologies employed during the phase for consistency with the contractor's software development plans. Included in this review shall be evaluation of: (1) software configuration management, (2) software development library, (3) documentation control, (4) storage and handling of project media, (5) control of non-deliverables, (6) risk management, (7) corrective action, and (8) conformance to all approved standards and procedures.

5.8.1.2.3 *Internal Review - Software Requirements Analysis.* The contractor shall conduct internal reviews during Software Requirements Analysis. In addition to the reviews specified in 5.8.1.2.2, the contractor shall:

a. Review the OCD for: (1) the criteria in 5.8.1.2.1, (2) consistency with the SSS, and (3) ability to provide a high-level understanding of the system.
b. Review the evolving requirements and the SRS and IRS(s) for: (1) the criteria in 5.8.1.2.1, (2) traceability of the software requirements to the system/segment, prime item, or critical item specification requirements, (3) consistency of the interface requirements with specifications for interfacing elements, (4) consistency of the SRS and IRS(s) with one another, and (5) testability of the software functional, performance, and interface requirements.

5.8.1.2.4 *Internal Review - Preliminary Design.* The contractor shall conduct internal reviews during Preliminary Design. In addition to the reviews specified in 5.8.1.2.2, the contractor shall:

a. Review the evolving top-level design and STLDD for: (1) the criteria in 5.8.1.2.1, (2) traceability to software requirements, (3) use of appropriate design techniques, and (4) appropriate level of detail.
b. Review the STP for: (1) the criteria in 5.8.1.2.1, (2) adequate test coverage of all software requirements, (3) consistency with the software development plans, and (4) adequacy of test planning.
c. Review the preliminary versions of the CSOM, SUM(s), and CSDM for: (1) the criteria in 5.8.1.2.1, (2) consistency with software requirement specifications and design documents, (3) appropriateness of content for operators or users, and (4) consistency with one another.
d. Review the preliminary CRISD for: (1) the criteria in 5.8.1.2.1, (2) consistency with the Government's support concepts, and (3) adequacy of support planning.

5.8.1.2.5 *Internal Review - Detailed Design.* The contractor shall conduct internal reviews during Detailed Design. In addition to the reviews specified in 5.8.1.2.2, the contractor shall:

a. Review the evolving detailed design and the SDDD, IDD(s), and DBDD(s), as applicable for: (1) the criteria in 5.8.1.2.1, (2) traceability to software requirements specifications and top-level design documentation, (3) use of appropriate design techniques, and (4) consistency with one another.
b. Review the STD for: (1) the criteria in 5.8.1.2.1, (2) traceability to the STP, (3) adequate test coverage of the software requirements, and (4) consistency with design documentation.
c. Review a representative subset of the software development files for: (1) the criteria in 5.8.1.2.1, and (2) accuracy of schedule and status information. Review Unit test cases for: (1) the criteria in 5.8.1.2.1, (2) traceability to the STP, (3) adequate test coverage of Unit requirements, and (4) consistency with the design documentation.
d. Review the CSC integration test cases for: (1) the criteria in 5.8.1.2.1, (2) traceability to the STP, (3) adequate test coverage of the software requirements, and (4) consistency with design documentation.
e. Review the updated CSOM, SUM(s), and CSDM for: (1) the criteria in 5.8.1.2.1, (2) consistency with software requirement and design documents,

(3) appropriateness of content for operators or users, and (4) consistency with one another.

f. Review the completed CRISD for: (1) the criteria in 5.8.1.2.1, (2) consistency with the Government's support concepts, and (3) adequacy of support planning.

g. Review the SPM and FSM for: (1) the criteria in 5.8.1.2.1, (2) consistency with design documentation, and (3) appropriateness of content for support personnel.

5.8.1.2.6 *Internal Review - Coding and Unit Testing.* The contractor shall conduct internal reviews during Coding and Unit Testing. In addition to the reviews specified in 5.8.1.2.2, the contractor shall:

a. Review the evolving and completed source code of each software Unit for: (1) the criteria in 5.8.1.2.1, (2) compliance with coding standards, and (3) traceability to detailed design documentation.

b. Review a representative subset of the updated software development files for: (1) the criteria in 5.8.1.2.1, and (2) the accuracy of status and schedule information. Review the Unit test procedures and Unit test results for: (1) the criteria in 5.8.1.2.1, and (2) traceability to Unit test plans and Unit test cases. Based on Unit test results, evaluate whether each Unit is ready to be entered into the Developmental Configuration.

c. Review the updated STLDD, SDDD, IDD(s), and DBDD(s), as applicable, for: (1) the criteria in 5.8.1.2.1, (2) traceability to software requirements specifications, (3) use of appropriate design techniques, and (4) consistency with one another.

d. Review, as applicable, updated source code for: (1) the criteria in 5.8.1.2.1, (2) compliance with coding standards, and (3) consistency with the updated detailed design documentation.

e. Review the informal CSC integration test procedures for: (1) the criteria in 5.8.1.2.1, (2) traceability to CSC integration test plans and test cases, (3) adequate test coverage of software requirements, and (4) consistency with design documents.

f. Review the preliminary STPR for: (1) the criteria in 5.8.1.2.1, (2) traceability to the STP and STD, (3) adequate test coverage of the software requirements, and (4) consistency with the design documentation.

g. Review the updated CSOM, SUM(s), and CSDM for: (1) the criteria in 5.8.1.2.1, (2) consistency with software requirement and design documents, (3) appropriateness of content for operators or users, and (4) consistency with one another.

h. Review, as applicable, the updated SPM and FSM for: (1) the criteria in 5.8.1.2.1, (2) consistency with design documentation, and (3) appropriateness of content for support personnel.

5.8.1.2.7 *Internal Review - CSC Integration and Testing.* The contractor shall conduct internal reviews during CSC Integration and Testing. In addition to the reviews specified in 5.8.1.2.2, the contractor shall:

a. Review the informal test results of CSC integration testing for: (1) the criteria in 5.8.1.2.1, and (2) traceability to the CSC test cases and test procedures. Based on the informal integration test results, evaluate whether the integrated CSCI performs correctly and is ready to undergo formal testing.

b. Review the updated STLDD, SDDD, IDD(s), and DBDD(s), as applicable, for: (1) the criteria in 5.8.1.2.1, (2) traceability to software requirements specifications, (3) use of appropriate design techniques, and (4) consistency with one another.

c. Review updated source code for: (1) the criteria in 5.8.1.2.1, (2) compliance with coding standards, and (3) consistency with the updated design documentation.

d. Review a representative subset of the updated software development files, as applicable, for: (1) the criteria in 5.8.1.2.1, and (2) accuracy of status and schedule information.

e. Review the completed STPR for: (1) the criteria in 5.8.1.2.1, (2) traceability to the STP and STD, (3) adequate test coverage of the software requirements, and (4) consistency with the design documentation.

f. Review the updated CSOM, SUM(s), and CSDM for: (1) the criteria in 5.8.1.2.1, (2) consistency with software requirement and design documents, (3) appropriateness of content for operators or users, and (4) consistency with one another.

g. Review, as applicable, the updated SPM and FSM for: (1) the criteria in 5.8.1.2.1, (2) consistency with design documentation, and (3) appropriateness of content for support personnel.

5.8.1.2.8 *Internal Review - CSCI Testing.* The contractor shall conduct internal reviews during CSCI Testing. In addition to the reviews specified in 5.8.1.2.2, the contractor shall:

a. Monitor the CSCI testing to ensure that: (1) it is performed using the current controlled version of the code, (2) it is conducted in accordance with approved test plans, descriptions, and procedures, and (3) it includes all necessary retesting.

b. Review the STRs for: (1) the criteria in 5.8.1.2.1, and (2) traceability of the CSCI test results to the CSCI test plans, test cases, and test procedures. Based on the CSCI test results, evaluate whether the CSCI meets its specified requirements.

c. Review the updated STLDD, SDDD, IDD(s), and DBDD(s), as applicable, for: (1) the criteria in 5.8.1.2.1, (2) traceability to software requirements specifications, (3) use of appropriate design techniques, and (4) consistency with one another.

d. Review updated source code, as applicable, for: (1) the criteria in 5.8.1.2.1, (2) compliance with coding standards, and (3) consistency with the updated detailed design documentation.

e. Review a representative subset of updated software development files, as applicable, for: (1) the criteria in 5.8.1.2.1, and (2) accuracy of status and schedule information.

f. Review the SPS for: (1) the criteria in 5.8.1.2.1, and (2) incorporation of design documentation and software listings consistent with the "as-built" software.

g. Review the VDD for: (1) the criteria in 5.8.1.2.1, and (2) accuracy in reflecting the exact version of each CSCI.

h. Review the completed CSOM, SUM(s), and CSDM for: (1) the criteria in 5.8.1.2.1, (2) consistency with the SPS, (3) appropriateness of content for operators or users, and (4) consistency with one another.

i. Review, as applicable, the updated SPM and FSM for: (1) the criteria in 5.8.1.2.1, (2) consistency with design documentation, and (3) appropriateness of content for support personnel.

5.8.1.3 *Formal Reviews and Audits.* The contractor shall evaluate the planning and preparation performed for each formal review and audit in 5.1 through 5.6, to ensure that all required products will be available and ready for Government review.

5.8.1.4 *Acceptance Inspection.* The contractor shall support acceptance inspection by ensuring that all required products are available and ready for Government inspection, all required procedures have been performed, and evidence of these procedures is available for Government inspection.

5.8.1.5 *Installation and Checkout.* The contractor shall evaluate installation and checkout of the software, if required by the contract, to ensure that this activity has been carried out in compliance with procedures specified in the software development plans.

5.8.1.6 *Evaluation of Subcontractor Products.* Prior to accepting software or documentation developed by subcontractors, the contractor shall evaluate them for completeness, technical adequacy, and compliance with subcontract requirements.

5.8.1.7 *Commercially Available, Reusable, and Government Furnished Software.* The contractor shall evaluate the planning performed for the use of commercially available, reusable, and Government furnished software to ensure that all relevant factors have been considered. Upon acquisition, the contractor shall evaluate the software to determine whether it performs as documented, prior to incorporating it into the software being developed. The contractor shall certify that commercially available and reusable software performs as documented and that it is documented adequately.

5.8.1.8. *Preparation of Quality Records.* The contractor shall prepare and maintain records of each quality evaluation performed. These records shall identify the date of the evaluation, evaluation participants, items or activities reviewed, objectives of the evaluation, all detected problems, and any recommendations resulting from the evaluation.

5.8.1.9 *Quality Reporting.* The contractor shall prepare reports that provide to contractor management the results and recommendations from the quality evaluations specified herein. The quality evaluation reports shall identify the activities performed, all detected problems, necessary remedial action, identified trends in the problems reported, and recommended changes to improve software quality.

5.8.1.10 *Corrective Action System.* The contractor shall implement a corrective action system for all software and documentation that has been placed under contractor or Government control (e.g., development plans, test documentation, design documentation, etc.). The corrective action system shall include provisions for: (1) reporting detected problems, (2) analyzing these problems, (3) classifying problems by category and by priority, (4) identifying necessary corrective action, (5) identifying trends in the problems reported, (6) analyzing these trends to recommend changes that will improve software quality, (7) authorizing the implementation of corrective steps, (8) documenting the corrective actions taken, (9) performing reevaluation after corrections have been made, (10) tracking and closing out the problems reported, and (11) providing Government visibility into critical problems based on the categorization and priority schemes and problem/change reports.

5.8.1.11 *Quality Cost Data.* The contractor shall collect, analyze, and document data relative to the cost of detecting and correcting errors in all software and documentation that have been placed under contractor or Government control. The specific data to be collected and the analyses to be performed shall be proposed by the contractor in either the SQEP or SDP (see Appendix D) and shall be subject to contracting agency approval.

5.8.2 *Products - Software Quality Evaluation (see 6.2).*

5.8.2.1 *Quality Records.* The contractor shall prepare and maintain records of each quality evaluation performed.

5.8.2.2 *Quality Reports.* The contractor shall prepare and maintain reports that summarize the results and recommendations of the quality evaluations performed. These reports shall be available for Government review.

5.8.2.3 *Certification.* The contractor shall collect and make available for Government inspection evidence indicating the compliance with the requirements of the contract of each contract line item delivered under the contract.

5.8.3 *Independence.* Each activity specified in 5.8 herein shall be performed by individuals who have sufficient responsibility, authority, resources, and independence to accomplish objective evaluation of the products and activities being reviewed. The degree of independence varies with such factors as project complexity and criticality. The contractor shall specify the degree of independence in either the SQEP or SDP (see Appendix D).

5.9 *Software Project Planning and Control.* The contractor shall implement procedures for planning and controlling the software development project.

5.9.1 *Activities - Software Project Planning and Control.* The contractor shall perform the following planning and controlling activities.

5.9.1.1 *Sizing and Timing Assessments.* The contractor shall derive sizing and timing parameters appropriate for the CSCI, including minimum reserve capacities, and shall develop initial estimates during Software Requirements Analysis of these parameters' values and allowed margins. During the remainder of the development, the contractor shall monitor these parameters and reallocate as necessary to meet requirements specified in the SRS. As Units of code are completed, tested, and successively integrated with one another, the contractor shall measure these sizing and timing parameters, compare these measurements with estimates, and update overall CSCI sizing and timing records to reflect the results of these measurements. All modifications to controlled or baselined documentation shall be made in accordance with the configuration management requirements contained herein (see 5.7).

5.9.1.2 *Status and Cost Reporting.* The contractor shall maintain cost and schedule forecasts, analyses, and reports to at least the CSCI level. These reports shall indicate to the contracting agency predicted and planned progress versus actual progress. Cost reports shall include budgeted versus actual expenditures and shall conform to the Work Breakdown Structure (WBS) applicable to the development effort. Additional guidance for cost and status reporting may be found in MIL-STD-881.

5.9.1.3 *Test Documentation Control.* Once the contracting agency approves the STP, STD, and STPR the contractor shall establish internal control over these documents. The contractor shall notify the contracting agency at the next review, audit, or in the next status report (whichever comes first) of any proposed changes to these documents, and shall obtain contracting agency approval before making any of the proposed changes.

5.9.1.4 *Software Development Library (SDL).* The contractor shall establish and implement a software development library for controlling all software and associated documentation. Procedures and methodologies for establishing and implementing the SDL shall be specified in the SDP.

5.9.1.5 *Risk Management.* The contractor shall establish and implement the risk management procedures specified in the SDP for controlling risk. The procedures shall include:

a. Identifying the risk areas of the project and the constituent risk factors in each area.
b. Assessing the risk factors identified, including the probability of occurrence and the potential damage.
c. Assigning appropriate resources to reduce the risk factors.
d. Identifying and analyzing the alternatives available for reducing the risk factors.
e. Selecting the most promising alternative for each risk factor.
f. Planning implementation of the selected alternative for each risk factor.
g. Obtaining feedback to determine the success of the risk reducing action for each risk factor.

6. NOTES

6.1 *Intended Use.* This standard is intended for use during the development and acquisition of MCCS software, as defined in DOD Directive 5000.29. This standard may also be used for non-MCCS software development and acquisition.

6.2 *Data Requirements List and Cross Reference.* When this standard is used in an acquisition which incorporates a DD Form 1423, Contract Data Requirements List (CDRL), the data requirements identified below shall be developed as specified by an approved Data Item Description (DD Form 1664) and delivered in accordance with the approved CDRL incorporated into the contract. When the provisions of the DOD FAR Supplement 27.410-6 are invoked and the DD Form 1423 is not used, the data specified below shall be delivered by the contractor in accordance with the contract or purchase order requirements. Deliverable data required by this standard is cited in the following subparagraphs.

Paragraph No.	*Data Requirements Title*	*Applicable DID No.*
5.1, 5.1.1.5, 5.8.1.2.3, 20.4.1, 20.4.2, 20.4.5.2, 30.3.1, 30.3.1.1, 30.3.1.3, 40.6.2.2	System/Segment Specification	DI-CMAN-80008
4.3, 4.4, 4.6, 4.7, 4.8, 5.1, 5.1.1.1, 5.1.1.2, 5.1.1.7, 5.1.2.1, 5.2, 5.2.1.1, 5.2.1.3, 5.2.1.4, 5.2.2.1, 5.3.1.1, 5.3.1.3, 5.3.1.4, 5.3.1.5, 5.3.1.8, 5.3.2.1, 5.3.2.7, 5.4.1.1, 5.4.1.2, 5.4.1.3, 5.4.1.4, 5.4.2.1, 5.4.2.4, 5.4.2.5, 5.5.1.1, 5.5.1.2, 5.5.1.3, 5.5.1.6, 5.5.2.1, 5.5.2.4, 5.6.1.1, 5.6.2.1, 5.6.6, 5.7, 5.7.1.1, 5.7.1.2, 5.7.1.3, 5.7.2.1, 5.8.1.2.2, 5.8.1.11, 5.8.3, 5.9.1.4, 5.9.1.5, 20.4.3, 20.4.5.2, 30.1, 30.2, 30.3.1.1, 30.3.1.2, 40.5.1, 40.6.2.1	Software Development Plan	DI-MCCR-80030
4.3, 5.1, 5.1.1.1, 5.1.1.2, 5.1.2.1, 5.2.1.1, 5.2.2.1, 5.3.1.1, 5.3.2.1, 5.4.1.1, 5.4.2.1, 5.5.1.1, 5.5.2.1, 5.6.1.1, 5.6.2.1, 5.7, 5.7.1.1, 5.7.1.2, 5.7.1.3, 5.7.2.1, 5.8.1.2.2, 40.5.1, 40.6.2.1	Software Configuration Management Plan	DI-MCCR-80009
4.3, 5.1, 5.1.1.1, 5.1.1.2, 5.1.2.1,	Software Quality Evaluation Plan	DI-MCCR-80010

Paragraph No.	*Data Requirements Title*	*Applicable DID No.*
5.2.1.1, 5.2.1.4, 5.2.2.1, 5.3.1.1, 5.3.2.1, 5.4.1.1, 5.4.2.1, 5.5.1.1, 5.5.2.1, 5.6.1.1, 5.6.2.1, 5.8.1.2.2, 5.8.1.11, 5.8.3, 40.5.1, 40.6.2.1		
5.1.1.5, 5.1.1.6, 5.1.1.7, 5.1.2.4, 5.1.3, 5.1.4, 5.2, 5.2.1.2, 5.3.3, 5.6.3, 5.8.1.2.3, 5.9.1.1, 20.4.2, 20.4.3, 20.4.5.2, 40.6.2.2	Software Requirements Specification	DI-MCCR-80025
5.1.1.5, 5.1.1.6, 5.1.2.4, 5.1.3, 5.1.4, 5.2, 5.2.1.2, 5.3.2.4, 5.3.3, 5.6.3, 5.8.1.2.3, 20.4.2, 20.4.3, 20.4.5.2, 40.6.2.2	Interface Requirements Specification	DI-MCCR-80026
4.3, 4.8, 5.1, 5.1.1.1, 5.1.1.2, 5.1.1.7, 5.1.2.1, 5.2, 5.2.1.1, 5.2.1.3, 5.2.1.4, 5.2.2.1, 5.3.1.1, 5.3.1.3, 5.3.1.4, 5.3.1.5, 5.3.1.8, 5.3.2.1, 5.3.2.7, 5.4.1.1, 5.4.1.2, 5.4.1.3, 5.4.1.4, 5.4.2.1, 5.4.2.4, 5.4.2.5, 5.5.1.1, 5.5.1.2, 5.5.1.3, 5.5.1.6, 5.5.2.1, 5.5.2.4, 5.6.1.1, 5.6.2.1, 5.8.1.2.2, 20.4.3, 30.1, 30.2, 30.3.1.1, 40.5.1, 40.6.2.1	Software Standards and Procedures Manual	DI-MCCR-80011
5.2.1.2, 5.2.2.3, 5.2.3, 5.2.4, 5.3.3, 5.8.1.2.4,	Software Top Level Design Document	DI-MCCR-80012

Paragraph No.	*Data Requirements Title*	*Applicable DID No.*
5.8.1.2.6, 5.8.1.2.7, 5.8.1.2.8, 20.4.3, 40.6.2.2		
5.2.1.3, 5.2.2.4, 5.2.3, 5.3.1.2, 5.3.2.3, 5.3.3, 5.3.4, 5.8.1.2.5, 5.8.1.2.6, 5.8.1.2.7, 5.8.1.2.8, 20.4.3, 40.6.2.2	Software Detailed Design Document	DI-MCCR-80031
5.2.1.3, 5.2.2.4, 5.2.3, 5.3.1.2, 5.3.2.4, 5.3.3, 5.3.4, 5.8.1.2.5, 5.8.1.2.6, 5.8.1.2.7, 5.8.1.2.8, 20.4.3, 40.6.2.2	Interface Design Document	DI-MCCR-80027
5.2.1.3, 5.2.2.4, 5.2.3, 5.3.1.2, 5.3.2.5, 5.3.3, 5.3.4, 5.8.1.2.5, 5.8.1.2.6, 5.8.1.2.7, 5.8.1.2.8, 20.4.3, 40.6.2.2	Data Base Design Document	DI-MCCR-80028
5.6.2.5, 5.6.3, 5.6.4, 5.6.5, 5.8.1.2.8, 20.4.3, 40.6.2.2	Software Product Specification	DI-MCCR-80029
5.6.1.5, 5.6.2.6, 5.6.3, 5.6.5, 5.7.2.4, 5.8.1.2.8, 40.6.2.2	Version Description Document	DI-MCCR-80013
5.2.1.6, 5.2.2.5, 5.2.3, 5.3.1.14, 5.3.2.8, 5.3.3, 5.4.1.7, 5.5.1.5, 5.6.1.2, 5.8.1.2.4, 5.8.1.2.5, 5.8.1.2.6, 5.8.1.2.7, 5.9.1.3, 20.4.3, 40.6.2.3	Software Test Plan	DI-MCCR-80014
5.3.1.14, 5.3.2.8, 5.3.3, 5.6.1.2,	Software Test Description	DI-MCCR-80015

Paragraph No.	*Data Requirements Title*	*Applicable DID No.*
5.8.1.2.5, 5.8.1.2.6, 5.8.1.2.7, 5.9.1.3, 20.4.3, 40.6.2.3		
5.4.1.12, 5.4.2.6, 5.5.1.8, 5.5.2.6, 5.5.3, 5.6.1.2, 5.8.1.2.6, 5.8.1.2.7, 5.9.1.3, 40.6.2.3	Software Test Procedure	DI-MCCR-80016
5.6.1.3, 5.6.2.3, 5.6.3, 5.8.1.2.8, 40.6.2.3	Software Test Report	DI-MCCR-80017
5.2.1.7, 5.2.2.6, 5.2.3, 5.3.1.15, 5.3.2.9, 5.3.3, 5.4.1.13, 5.4.2.7, 5.5.1.9, 5.5.2.7, 5.5.3, 5.6.1.6, 5.6.2.7, 5.6.3, 5.8.1.2.4, 5.8.1.2.5, 5.8.1.2.6, 5.8.1.2.7, 5.8.1.2.8, 20.4.3, 40.6.2.4	Computer System Operator's Manual	DI-MCCR-80018
5.2.1.8, 5.2.2.6, 5.2.3, 5.3.1.15, 5.3.2.9, 5.3.3, 5.4.1.13, 5.4.2.7, 5.5.1.9, 5.5.2.7, 5.5.3, 5.6.1.6, 5.6.2.7, 5.6.3, 5.8.1.2.4, 5.8.1.2.5, 5.8.1.2.6, 5.8.1.2.7, 5.8.1.2.8, 20.4.3, 40.6.2.4	Software User's Manual	DI-MCCR-80019
5.2.1.9, 5.2.2.6, 5.2.3, 5.3.1.15, 5.3.2.9, 5.3.3, 5.4.1.13, 5.4.2.7, 5.5.1.9, 5.5.2.7, 5.5.3, 5.6.1.6, 5.6.2.7, 5.6.3, 5.8.1.2.4,	Computer System Diagnostic Manual	DI-MCCR-80020

Paragraph No.	*Data Requirements Title*	*Applicable DID No.*
5.8.1.2.5, 5.8.1.2.6, 5.8.1.2.7, 5.8.1.2.8, 20.4.3, 40.6.2.4		
5.3.1.17, 5.3.2.11, 5.3.3, 5.4.1.13, 5.4.2.7, 5.5.1.9, 5.5.2.7, 5.6.1.6, 5.6.2.7, 5.6.3, 5.8.1.2.5, 20.4.3, 40.6.2.4	Software Programmer's Manual	DI-MCCR-80021
5.3.1.18, 5.3.2.11, 5.3.3, 5.4.1.13, 5.4.2.7, 5.5.1.9, 5.5.2.7, 5.6.1.6, 5.6.2.7, 5.6.3, 5.8.1.2.5, 20.4.3, 40.6.2.4	Firmware Support Manual	DI-MCCR-80022
5.1, 5.1.1.3, 5.1.1.4, 5.1.2.2, 5.1.3, 5.8.1.2.3, 20.4.2, 20.4.3, 20.4.5.2, 40.6.2.4	Operational Concept Document	DI-MCCR-80023
5.2.1.10, 5.2.2.6, 5.2.3, 5.3.1.16, 5.3.2.10, 5.3.3, 5.8.1.2.4, 5.8.1.2.5, 20.4.3, 40.6.2.4	Computer Resources Integrated Support Document	DI-MCCR-80024
5.7, 5.7.1.2, 5.7.1.3, 5.7.2.1	Configuration Management Plan	DI-E-3108
5.7.2.2, 5.7.2.3, 40.6.2.2	Engineering Change Proposal	DI-E-3128
5.7.2.3, 40.6.2.2	Specification Change Notice	DI-E-3134

(Data item descriptions related to this standard, and identified in section 6 will be approved and listed as such in DoD 5000.19-L, Vol. II, AMSDL. Copies of data item descriptions required by the contractors in connection with specific acquisition functions should be obtained from the Naval Publications and Forms Center or as directed by the contracting officer.)

6.3 *Subject term (key word) listing.*

Acquisition
Code
Code and unit testing

Computer
Computer resources
Computer software
Computer software component
Computer software configuration item
Configuration item
Configuration management
CSC
CSC integration and testing
CSCI
CSCI testing
Data item descriptions
Detailed design
Firmware
Formal testing
Informal testing
LLCSC
Lower level computer software component
Mission-critical
Mission-critical computer resources
Mission-critical computer system
Preliminary design
Quality
Quality evaluation
Requirements analysis
Risk management
Software
Software acquisition
Software code
Software configuration item
Software configuration management
Software design
Software detailed design
Software development
Software integration
Software preliminary design
Software quality
Software quality evaluation
Software requirements
Software requirements analysis
Software standards
Software test
Tailoring
Tailoring of software requirements
Testing
TLCSC
Top-level computer software component
Unit

APPENDIX A

LIST OF ACRONYMS AND ABBREVIATIONS

10. *General.*

10.1 *Purpose.* This appendix provides a list of all acronyms and abbreviations used in this standard, with the associated meaning.

10.2 *Acronyms.*

CDR	Critical Design Review
CDRL	Contract Data Requirements List
CM	Configuration Management
CRISD	Computer Resources Integrated Support Document
CSC	Computer Software Component
CSCI	Computer Software Configuration Item
CSDM	Computer System Diagnostic Manual
CSOM	Computer System Operator's Manual
DBDD	Data Base Design Document
DID	Data Item Description
DOD	Department of Defense
DODISS	Department of Defense Index of Specifications and Standards
ECP	Engineering Change Proposal
FAR	Federal Acquisition Regulation
FCA	Functional Configuration Audit
FSM	Firmware Support Manual
GFE	Government Furnished Equipment
GFS	Government Furnished Software
HOL	Higher order language
HWCI	Hardware Configuration Item
IDD	Interface Design Document
IRS	Interface Requirements Specification
LLCSC	Lower-level computer software component
MCCS	Mission-Critical Computer System
NSCCA	Nuclear safety cross-check analysis
OCD	Operational Concept Document
PCA	Physical Configuration Audit
PDR	Preliminary Design Review
PROM	Programmable read-only memory
RFP	Request for proposal
ROM	Read-only memory
SCCB	Software Configuration Control Board
SCMP	Software Configuration Management Plan
SCN	Specification Change Notice
SDDD	Software Detailed Design Document
SDF	Software Development File
SDL	Software Development Library
SDP	Software Development Plan
SOW	Statement of Work
SPM	Software Programmer's Manual

SPS	Software Product Specification
SQEP	Software Quality Evaluation Plan
SRS	Software Requirements Specification
SSA	Software Support Agency
SSPM	Software Standards and Procedures Manual
SSR	Software Specification Review
SSS	System/Segment Specification
STD	Software Test Description
STLDD	Software Top Level Design Document
STP	Software Test Plan
STPR	Software Test Procedure
STR	Software Test Report
SUM	Software User's Manual
TLCSC	Top-level computer software component
TRR	Test Readiness Review
VDD	Version Description Document
WBS	Work Breakdown Structure

APPENDIX B

SYSTEM LIFE CYCLE

20. *General.*

20.1 *Purpose.* This appendix provides information on the system life cycle and the framework in which software development is conducted under the provisions of this standard.

20.2 *Scope.* This appendix briefly describes a typical system life cycle and its relationship to iterations of the software development cycle (see Figures 1 and 4). It also describes the documents that result from early system acquisition activities. The activities and phases described in this appendix include activities and phases for which the contractor is not responsible, as well as those for which the contractor is responsible.

20.3 *Applicability.* The information in this appendix is of a general, tutorial nature and is not a requirement of this standard.

20.4 *General Information.* The system life cycle consists of four phases: Concept Exploration, Demonstration and Validation, Full Scale Development, and Production and Deployment. The software development cycle consists of six phases: Software Requirements Analysis, Preliminary Design, Detailed Design, Coding and Unit Testing, CSC Integration and Testing, and CSCI Testing. The total software development cycle or a subset may be performed within each of the system life cycle phases. Successive iterations of software development usually build upon the products of previous iterations (see Figure 2).

20.4.1 *Concept Exploration.* The Concept Exploration Phase is the initial planning period when the technical, strategic, and economic bases are established through comprehensive studies, experimental development, and concept evaluation. This initial planning may be directed toward refining proposed solutions or developing alternative concepts to satisfy a required operational capability.

a. During this phase, proposed solutions are refined or alternative concepts are developed using feasibility assessments, estimates (cost and schedule, intelligence, logistics, etc.), trade-off studies, and analyses. The SSA and user should be involved in these activities.

b. For computer resources, the software development cycle should be tailored for use during this phase and may result in demonstration of critical algorithms, breadboards, etc.

c. The major document resulting from this phase is the initial SSS, which documents total system requirements. The SSS may differentiate between the requirements to be met by computer software and those applicable to hardware design. When applicable, definitions of interfaces between computer equipment functions, communication functions, and personnel functions are provided to enable the further definition and management of the computer software and computer equipment resources. Normally, this information is derived from system engineering studies. Deliverable products at the end of the Concept Exploration phase typically include preliminary SSS(s), preliminary Prime Item Development Specifications, software listings, and software test results, etc. The System Requirements Review is the technical review that should be accomplished.

20.4.2 *Demonstration and Validation.* The Demonstration and Validation Phase is the period when major system characteristics are refined through studies, system engineering, development of preliminary equipment and prototype computer software, and test and evaluation. The objectives are to validate the choice of alternatives and to provide the basis for determining whether or not to proceed into the next phase.

a. During this phase, system requirements, including requirements for computer resources, are further defined, and preferred development methodologies for computer software and data bases are selected. The results of validation activities are used to define the system characteristics (performance, cost, and schedule) and to provide confidence that risks have been resolved or minimized.

b. For computer resources, the software development cycle should be tailored for use during this phase, resulting in prototype software items.

c. The major documents resulting from this phase are the authenticated SSS(s), authenticated Prime Item Development Specifications, and preliminary IRS(s) and SRSs for each CSCI. The authenticated SSS(s) establish the system or segment Functional Baseline. Each authenticated Prime Item Development Specification contains the system requirements allocated to the equipment and software and establishes the Allocated Baseline for each prime item. Each preliminary SRS contains system or prime item requirements allocated to a CSCI. Each preliminary IRS defines the interfaces and qualification requirements for a CSCI within the system, segment, or prime item. The Allocated Baseline for each CSCI is established following Software Requirements Analysis within the software development cycle. A preliminary version of the Operational Concept Document (OCD) should also be prepared to identify and describe the mission of the system, operational and support environments of the system, and the functions and characteristics of the computer system

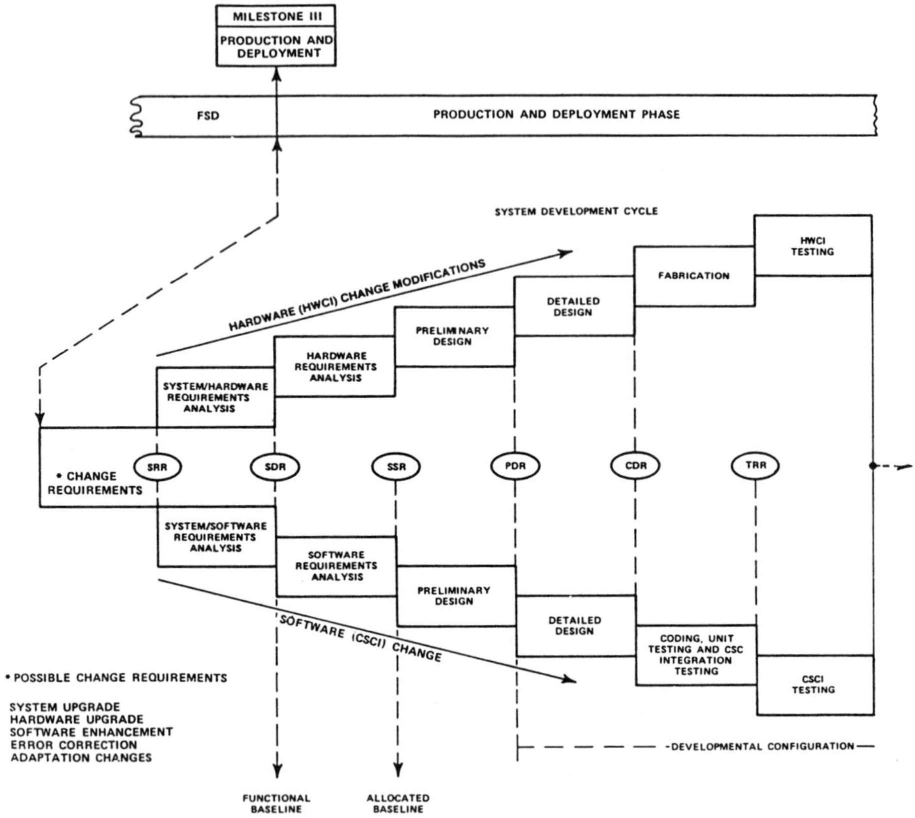

Figure 4. System support cycle within the system life cycle.

within the overall system. The System Design Review is the technical review that should be accomplished.

20.4.3 *Full Scale Development.* The Full Scale Development phase is the period when the system, equipment, computer software, facilities, personnel subsystems, training, and the principal equipment and software items necessary for support are designed, fabricated, tested, and evaluated. It includes one or more major iterations of the software development cycle. The intended outputs are a system which closely approximates the production item, the documentation necessary to enter the system's Production and Deployment phase, and the test results that demonstrate that the system to be produced will meet the stated requirements. During this phase the requirements for additional software items embedded in or associated with the equipment items may be identified. These requirements may encompass firmware, test equipment, environment simulation, mission support, development support, and many other kinds of software.

a. Software requirements analysis is performed in conjunction with system engineering activities related to equipment preliminary design. SRSs and IRSs

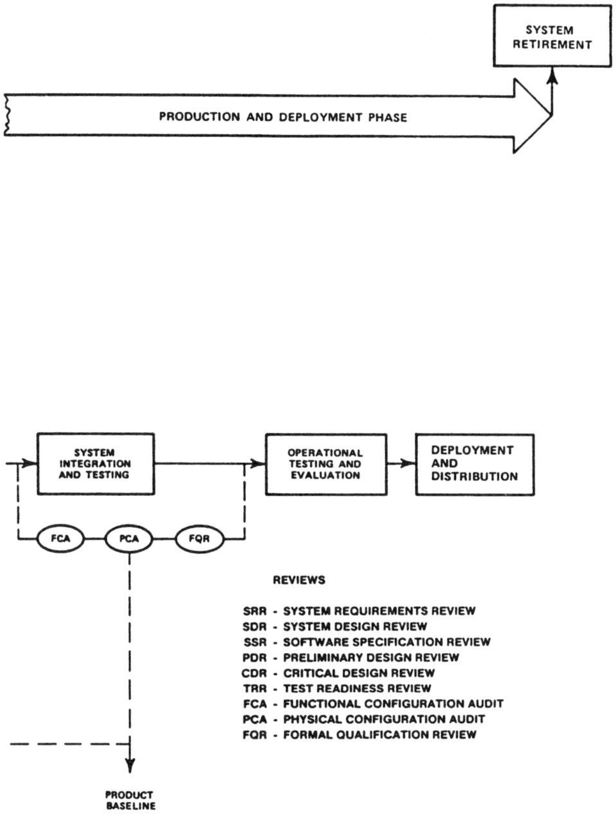

Figure 4. System support cycle within the system life cycle. (*continued*)

for each CSCI are completed and authenticated at the SSR, establishing the Allocated Baseline for each CSCI. Requirements for software that is part of an HWCI may be authenticated during HWCI design reviews. The OCD is completed and reviewed at the SSR as well.

b. A preliminary design effort is accomplished and results in a design approach. For computer software, preliminary design includes the definition of TLCSCs in terms of functions, external and internal interfaces, storage and timing allocation, operating sequences, and data base design. Detailed design of critical lower-level elements of the CSCI may be performed as well. A PDR is held to review the software top-level design document against the respective authenticated specifications for each equipment item and CSCI. The following documents are also presented at the PDR:

STP - to define the plans for informal and formal testing of the CSCI.
Preliminary CSOM - to define the procedures and information necessary to operate the computer system in which the CSCIs execute.

Preliminary SUM(s) - to define the instructions for users to execute each CSCI.
Preliminary CSDM - to define the information and procedures necessary to identify a malfunction and instructions to run the diagnostics.
Preliminary CRISD - to define the information that is required to perform life cycle support of the contractually deliverable software.

c. Formal engineering change control procedures are implemented to prepare, propose, review, approve, implement, and record engineering changes to each Allocated Baseline.

d. Informal engineering change control by the contractor starts with the establishment of each CSCI's Developmental Configuration. The Developmental Configuration is established at PDR by the STLDD as the repository for the approved design documents, software, and software listings. Following successful completion of FCA and PCA, the documents and listings of the Developmental Configuration are included in the SPS which establishes the Product Baseline. This baseline is used to control the software as it is integrated with other CSCIs and HWCIs.

e. Following an acceptable PDR for an item, detailed design of that item begins. During this activity, engineering documentation such as drawings, product specifications, test procedures, and descriptions are produced. For computer software, detailed design is accompanied by detailed design documentation of logical flows, functional sequences and relations, formats, constraints, data bases, and incorporation of reused design. The CDR should assure that the recommended design satisfies the requirements of the SRS and, if applicable, IRS(s). At the CDR, the detailed design documents (i.e. SDDD and, if applicable, DBDD(s) and IDD(s)) are reviewed. Equipment/personnel/computer software interfaces should be finalized at this time. A primary product of the CDR for software is the Government and contractor concurrence on the detailed design documents that will be released for coding and Unit testing. Additional documents prepared during detailed design and reviewed at CDR include:

STD - to describe the test cases for all formal testing of the CSCI.
CRISD - to define the information that is required to perform life cycle support of the contractually delivered software.
SPM - to define the information which facilitates programming or reprogramming software for the target computer.
FSM - to define the information necessary to modify or replace the firmware devices in the Mission-Critical Computer system.

f. Following CDR, software coding and testing, software integration and testing, software formal testing, system integration and testing, and initial operational test and evaluation are conducted. Software coding is performed in accordance with standards and procedures contained in the approved SDP (or SSPM, if applicable). Software testing is performed according to test plans submitted for review at PDR, test descriptions submitted for review at CDR, and test procedures submitted for review at TRR. These activities normally proceed in such a way that testing of selected functions begins early during development and proceeds by adding successive increments to the point where a complete CSCI is subjected to formal testing. Additional test equipment may be required to properly simulate an operational environment to test a CSCI. The scope and realism of software testing may be progressively expanded as additional increments are made available for this purpose. Adequacy of the performance of the software is checked to the maximum extent possible, sometimes through use of simulation, prior to software installation in a field site or operational computer. Nuclear safety cross-check analysis (NSCCA) is also performed on specified computer resource items during this phase. Satisfactory performance of the software for a large operational system may not be completely demonstrated and assessed until completion of system integration and operational test and evaluation of the equipment or of the system. Software that is relatively insensitive to the system's operational environments may be completely demonstrated earlier.

g. Functional and Physical Configuration Audits are performed on all items of hardware and software. FCA is conducted on the software at the completion of software formal testing. Based on the nature of the software, PCA may be conducted at the completion of software formal testing or after system integration and testing.

h. Functional and Physical Configuration Audits may be performed at the system level to authenticate the hardware product specification(s) and the software product specification(s) to establish the system Product Baseline. This baseline acts as an instrument for use in diagnosing troubles, adapting the computer resources to environmental and operational requirements of specific site locations, and proposing changes or enhancements.

i. Planning for transition of the computer resources to the user and the Software Support Agency (SSA) begins early in this phase. Necessary agreements should be prepared, coordinated, and approved prior to the end of this phase. The SSA and the user should be involved in this planning.

j. Provisions are made for follow-on support of the equipment and software configuration items and associated documentation. Failure to properly consider these provisions may result in support complications, obsolete documentation, and costly "modernization" programs. This is particularly true where the system is being developed in a phased manner, providing reduced capabilites for early system integration, operation, and evaluation.

20.4.4 *Production and Deployment.* The Production and Deployment Phase is the combination of two overlapping periods. The production period is from production approval until the last system item is delivered and accepted. The objective is to efficiently produce and deliver effective and supported systems to the user(s). The deployment period commences with delivery of the first operational system item and terminates when the last system items are removed from the operational inventory.

a. At system transition, the role of the contracting agency normally terminates except for identified residual tasks and phase-out responsibilities. The supporting and using agencies start providing the resources necessary to support the software throughout the Deployment phase.

b. Follow-on test and evaluation is performed on operational system items as they are deployed, to assess their operational effectiveness and suitability in a deployed configuration and environment.

c. After a system is in operational use, there are a variety of changes that may take place on the hardware items, software items, or both hardware and software items. Changes to software items may be necessary to remove latent errors, enhance operations, further system evolution, adapt to changes in mission requirements, or incorporate knowledge gained from operational use. Based upon complexity and other factors such as system interfaces, constraints, and priorities, control of the changes may vary from on-site management to complex checks and balances with mandatory security keys and access codes. The authority to change the software must be carefully and specifically delineated, particularly when security, safety, or special nuclear restrictions are involved. The same six phases of the software development cycle are utilized for each change during the Production and Deployment phase (see Figure 4).

20.4.5 *Software Development Cycle Application and Documentation.* The software development cycle may span more than one system life cycle phase, or may occur in any one phase. For example, mission simulation software may undergo one iteration of the software development cycle during the Concept Exploration, while mission application software may undergo many iterations of the software development cycle during the Demonstration and Validation, Full Scale Development, and Production and Deployment phases (see Figure 1).

20.4.5.1 The phases in the software development cycle may involve iterations back to previous phases. For example, design may reveal problems which lead to the revision of requirements and reinstitution of certain analyses; checkout may reveal errors in design, which in turn may lead to redesign or requirements revision; etc.

20.4.5.2 Prior to initiating software development during the Full Scale Development and the Production and Deployment phases, documented plans for software development (e.g., SDP); authenticated system, segment, or prime item specifications; and the OCD typically exist. In earlier life cycle phases, such plans may not yet exist. The software development plans include descriptions of all organizations and procedures to be used in the development effort. The system, segment, or prime item specification identifies the requirements of the system, segment, or prime item. In addition, these specifications identify the HWCIs and CSCIs making up the system, segment, or prime item. The OCD identifies and describes the mission of the system, the system operational and support environments, and the functions and characteristics of the computer system within the overall system. The six phases of the software development cycle are discussed below:

a. *Software Requirements Analysis.* The purpose of Software Requirements Analysis is to completely define and analyze the requirements for the software. These requirements include the functions the software is required to accomplish as part of the system, segment, or prime item. Additionally, the functional interfaces and the necessary design constraints are defined. During Full Scale Development, and Production and Deployment, this phase typically begins with the release of the SSS, Prime Item Specification(s), Critical Item Specification(s), or Preliminary SRS(s) and IRS(s), and terminates with the successful accomplishment of the SSR. During this phase, analyses and trade-off studies are performed, and requirements are made definitive. The results of this phase are documented and approved requirements for the software. At the initiation of Software Requirements Analysis, plans for developing the software are prepared or reviewed (as applicable).

b. *Preliminary Design.* The purpose of Preliminary Design is to develop a design approach which includes mathematical models, functional flows, and data flows. During this phase various design approaches are considered, analysis and trade-off studies are performed, and design approaches selected. Preliminary Design allocates software requirements to TLCSCs, describes the processing that takes place within each TLCSC, and establishes the interface relationship between TLCSCs. Design of critical lower-level elements of each CSCI may also be performed. The result of this phase is a documented and approved top-level design of the software. The top-level design is reviewed against the requirements prior to initiating the detailed design phase.

c. *Detailed Design.* The purpose of Detailed Design is to refine the design approach so that each TLCSC is decomposed into a complete structure of LLCSCs and Units. The detailed design approach is provided in detailed design documents and reviewed against the requirements and top-level design prior to initiating the coding phase.

d. *Coding and Unit Testing.* The purpose of Coding and Unit Testing is to code and test each Unit of code described in the detailed design documentation. Each Unit of code is reviewed for compliance with the corresponding detailed design description and applicable coding standards prior to establishing internal control of the Unit and releasing it for integration.

e. *CSC Integration and Testing.* The purpose of CSC Integration and Testing is to integrate and test aggregates of coded Units. Integration tests should be performed based on documented integration test plans, test descriptions, and test procedures. CSC Integration test results, and CSCI test plans, descriptions, and procedures for testing the fully implemented software are reviewed prior to the next phase of testing.

f. *CSCI Testing.* The purpose of CSCI testing is to test the fully implemented CSCI. Testing during this phase concentrates on showing that the software satisfies its specified requirements. Test results should be reviewed to determine whether the software satisfies its specified requirements.

APPENDIX C

DESIGN AND CODING STANDARDS

30. *General.*

30.1 *Purpose.* This appendix specifies default design and coding standards for the contractor. If the contractor has not proposed internal design and coding standards in either the SSPM or SDP (see Appendix D) and received approval, then the design and coding standards in this appendix shall be applied to all code written by the contractor.

30.2 *Applicability.* This appendix contains design and coding standards generally applicable to all programming languages. However, it does not provide complete design and coding standards for some higher order languages with advanced capabilities (e.g. Ada, PROLOG, etc.). In such cases, the contractor should propose additions to this appendix in either the SSPM or SDP (see Appendix D) and obtain contracting agency approval.

30.3 *Detailed Requirements.*

30.3.1 *Higher Order Language (HOL).* All code shall be written in the HOL specified in the SSS.

30.3.1.1 If one or more compilers are specified in the SSS, then all code shall be compiled by the specified compiler(s). Otherwise, all code shall be compiled by the compilers described in either the SDP or the SSPM (see Appendix D).

30.3.1.2 If the higher order language does not contain the control constructs of Section 30.3.2, the contractor shall use the precompiler specified in the SDP. If a precompiler which is acceptable to the contracting agency does not exist, then these control constructs shall be simulated (i.e. code in the language used shall follow the logic shown in figures 5 through 9 without explicitly using the names of the constructs in the code). If language simulation is used, the same form of the simulated constructs shall be uniformly applied throughout the code.

30.3.1.3 A waiver from the contracting agency shall be required in order for the contractor to write code in assembly language or in some HOL other than the HOL specified in the SSS.

30.3.2 *Control Constructs.* Code shall be written using only the five control constructs illustrated in Figures 5 through 9: SEQUENCE, IF-THEN-ELSE, DO-WHILE, DO-UNTIL, CASE. These control constructs refer to the control logic within a Unit while it is executing and do not preclude the calling or passing of processor control to other Units (e.g., subroutines, procedures, functions, exception handlers, interrupt service routines).

30.3.3 *Modularity.* The source code for each Unit shall not exceed, on the average, 100 executable, non-expandable statements or, at most, 200 executable, non-expandable statements. Additionally, Units shall exhibit the following characteristics:

a. Local variables within different Units shall not share the same storage locations.
b. Each Unit shall perform a single function.
c. Modification of a Unit's code during Unit execution shall be prohibited.
d. Each Unit shall be uniquely named.

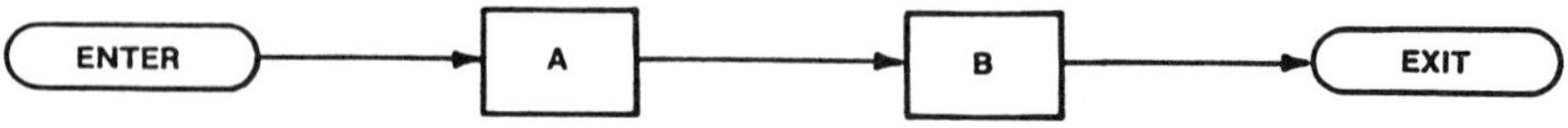

Figure 5. Sequence construct. Control flows from process A to the next in sequence, process B.

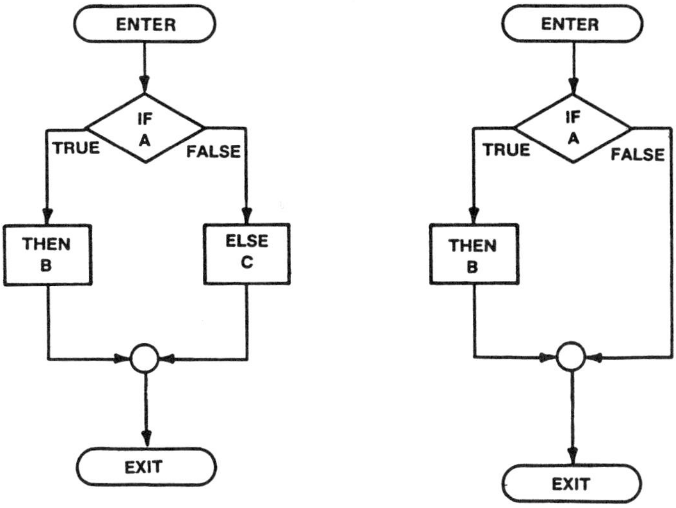

Figure 6. IF-THEN-ELSE construct. Left: Basic. Flow of control will return to common point after executing process B or C. A predicates the conditional execution. Right: Option. If option is to skip a process pending the condition of A.

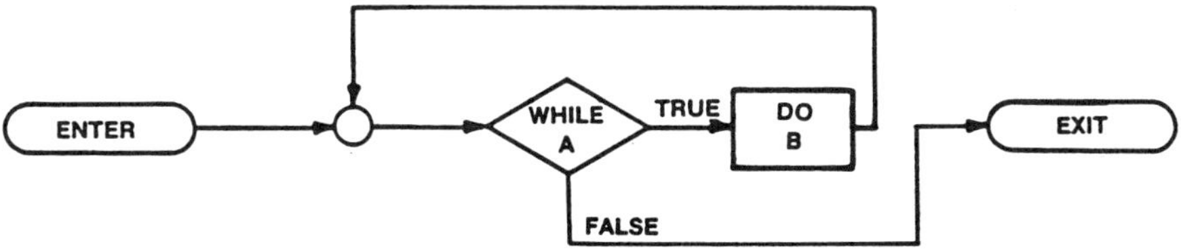

Figure 7. DO-WHILE construct. Condition A is evaluated. If found to be true, then control is passed to process B and condition A is (then) evaluated again. If condition A is false, control is passed out of the loop.

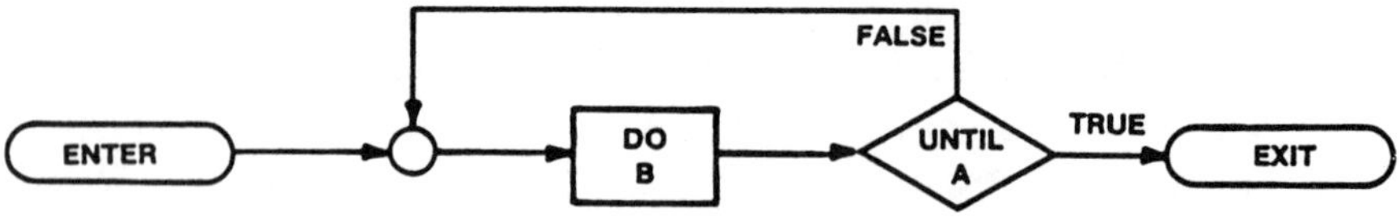

Figure 8. DO-UNTIL construct. Similar to DO WHILE, except that the test of condition A is performed after process B has executed. If condition A is true, control is passed out of the loop.

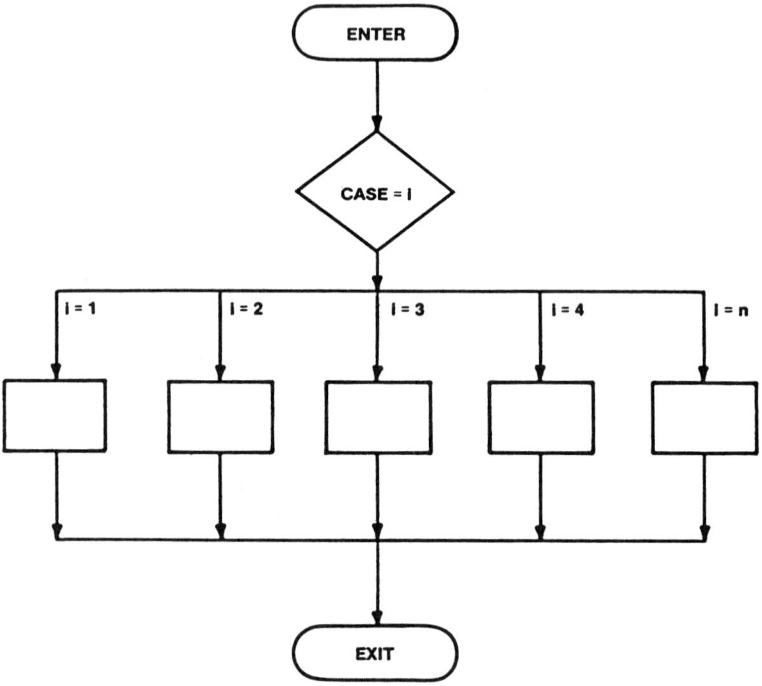

Figure 9. CASE construct. Control is passed to process based on the value of I.

e. All Units shall follow a standard format consisting of prologue, declarative statements, and executable statements or comments, in that order.
f. Except for error exits, each Unit shall have a single entry point and a single exit point.
g. Coding style conventions shall be consistent among all Units.

30.3.4 *Symbolic Parameters.* To the maximum extent practical, symbolic parameters shall be used, in lieu of specific numeric values, to represent constants, relative location within a table, and size of data structure.

30.3.5 *Naming.* Naming conventions shall be uniform throughout the CSCI and shall employ meaningful names which clearly identify the constant, variable, function performed, and any other objects used in the CSCI, to a reader of the source code. Language keywords shall not be used as identifiers.

30.3.6 *Mixed Mode Operations.* Mixed mode operations shall be avoided (e.g., arithmetic between real numbers and integer numbers). However, if it is necessary to use them, they shall be clearly identified and described using prominent comments within the source code.

30.3.7 *Paragraphing, Blocking, and Indenting.* Paragraphing, blocking by blank lines, and indenting shall be used to enhance the readability of the code.

30.3.8 *Complicated Expressions.* Compound negative Boolean expressions shall be prohibited. Nesting beyond five levels should be avoided.

30.3.9 *Compound Expressions.* The order of evaluation for compound expressions shall be clarified through the use of parentheses and spacing.

30.3.10 *Single Statement.* Each line of source code shall contain, at most, one executable statement.

30.3.11 *Comments.* Comments shall be set off from the executable source code in a uniform manner. Before each Unit's executable section, a prologue section shall describe the following details:

a. The Unit's purpose and how it works.
b. Functions, performance requirements, and external interfaces of the CSCI that the Unit helps implement.
c. Other Units (subroutines, procedures, functions) called and the calling sequence.
d. Inputs and outputs, including data files referenced during Unit entry or execution. For each referenced file, the name of the file, usage (input, output, or both), and brief summary of the purpose for referencing the file.
e. Use of global and local variables and, if applicable, registers and memory locations.
f. The identification of special tasks that are internally defined, and the size/structure of which are based on external requirements.
g. The programming department or section responsible for the Unit.
h. Date of creation of the Unit.
i. Date of latest revision, revision number, problem report number and title associated with revision.

30.3.12 *Error and diagnostic messages.* To the maximum extent practical, all error and diagnostic messages shall be presented in a uniform manner and shall be self-explanatory. They shall not require the operator to perform table look-ups or further processing of any kind to interpret the message.

APPENDIX D

GUIDELINES FOR TAILORING THIS STANDARD

40. *General.*

40.1 *Scope.* This appendix provides guidance for the cost-effective tailoring of the requirements of this standard for the development and acquisition of Mission-Critical Computer System software. This appendix serves as guidance for the agency responsible for the preparation of contract requirements and does not form a part of the contract. This appendix provides guidance for the tailoring of software requirements allocated from a System/Segment Specification (SSS). In cases where the software requirements are allocated from a Prime Item Development Specification (PIDS) or Critical Item Development Specification (CIDS), the guidance provided in the Tailoring Handbook* should be considered.

40.2 *Purpose.* The guidelines contained herein aid in implementing the Department of Defense Directive 4120.21, Specification and Standards Application, which requires all DOD components to apply selectively and to tailor military specifications and standards prior to their contractual imposition. This appendix provides guidelines for tailoring development requirements for Mission-Critical Computer System software. These guidelines help accommodate variations in:

a. The software development processes used during the system life cycle.
b. Software characteristics and intended end use.
c. Acquisition strategies and project management styles for software development.

40.3 *Objective.* The guidelines in this appendix address the following tailoring objectives:

a. Eliminating inapplicable and unnecessary requirements.
b. Eliminating redundancy and inconsistency with other contract specifications and standards.
c. Promote the use of commercial and reusable software.

40.4 *Tailoring Approach.* The above tailoring objectives are achieved by a four step-tailoring process:

a. Step 1 - Classify the required software by categories.
b. Step 2 - Select applicable contract data items.

*Planned for future release.

c. Step 3 - Tailor the activities, products, and reviews required during each software development phase.
d. Step 4 - Tailor the requirements for the selected data items.

40.5 *Tailoring Considerations.*

40.5.1 *Relationship to the Statement of Work (SOW) and the Contract Data Requirements List (CDRL).* A typical contract is defined by documents that include the following, or their equivalent:

a. A statement of work identifying tasks to be accomplished (SOW)
b. A schedule of contract line items, articles, services, or some combination to be delivered (schedule)
c. A list of data items, including format, content, and delivery requirements (CDRL)
d. A specification of the characteristics for the contract line items, articles, and services (Specification).

This software development standard is invoked as a work task by a citation in the SOW. Tailoring of this standard for each of the software categories is accomplished by including appropriate SOW statements which enumerate the changes. Selection of deliverable software documentation for each software category is invoked by citations in the CDRL. These citations cite the appropriate DID to invoke the format and content of the documentation. Tailoring of the DIDs for each software category is accomplished by deleting affected paragraphs in the DID which can be accomplished by entries in block 16 of the CDRL. Such changes could include incorporating the requirements of several DIDs into a single document and thereby eliminate the need for separate DIDs (e.g. incorporate the SCMP, SQEP, and SSPM into the SDP).

40.5.2 *Offeror Participation in Tailoring.* Cost-effective tailoring requires that this standard and its related DIDs be tailored to the project requirements and the unique characteristics of the software. The contracting agency is ultimately responsible for this effort. However, the offeror should be given an opportunity to recommend changes and to identify requirements considered appropriate. The contracting agency should request, in the instructions for proposal preparation, that the offeror recommend the tailoring details in the proposal. The tailoring process should be finalized prior to contract award.

40.6 *Tailoring Process*

40.6.1 *Step 1 - Classify the Required Software by Categories.* The software developed for Mission-Critical Computer Systems, and the software used in that development, can be divided into the five categories identified below.

40.6.1.1 *Category 1. Deliverable Software to be Developed and Designated as a CSCI.* Designating software as a CSCI typically imposes all of the development, documentation, test, review, and control requirements on the software. Some of the factors influencing the decision to designate software as a CSCI are:

a. Functional complexity
b. Size

c. Criticality
d. Interface complexity
e. Database complexity
f. Integration complexity
g. Complexity of security requirements
h. Certification requirements
i. Probability of change
j. Intended end-use
k. Support concept
l. Development location(s)
m. Schedule

40.6.1.2 *Category 2. Deliverable Software to be Developed and Designated as Part of a System or an HWCI.* Designating software as part of an HWCI typically imposes fewer requirements than Category 1. Such software may be embedded in firmware devices and may not be expected to undergo significant change. Within the framework of this standard, the contractor may propose the tailoring details applicable to such software, subject to contracting agency approval. Some of the factors influencing the decision to designate software as part of an HWCI are:

a. Size
b. Complexity
c. Probability of change
d. Intended end-use

40.6.1.3 *Category 3. Non-deliverable Software.* The controls imposed on non-deliverable software vary widely, depending on the use of the software. Within the framework of this standard, the contractor may propose control provisions for non-deliverable software, subject to contracting agency approval. Some of the factors to consider in establishing control provisions for non-deliverable software are:

a. Used in formal testing of deliverable products
b. Used in informal testing
c. Used to support manufacture of a deliverable item
d. Used for scientific simulation
e. Used as an analysis tool in hardware or software design
f. Probability of change
g. Duration of use within the software development cycle
h. Developed software vs. commercially available software

40.6.1.4 *Category 4. Unmodified Commercially Available and Reusable Software Used in a Deliverable CSCI or HWCI.* Within the framework of this standard, approval to use unmodified commercially available and reusable software in a deliverable CSCI or HWCI depends on the associated data rights, documentation, and certification evidence which the contractor proposes to provide the contracting agency. Some of the factors to consider in accepting the proposed data rights, documentation, and certification evidence are:

a. Support plans
b. Budget constraints
c. Proprietary information
d. Duration of project
e. Product evolution strategy

40.6.1.5 *Category 5. Previously Developed Software Undergoing Modifications (Such as Upgrades, Modified GFS, and Modified Commercially Available Software).* The requirements imposed on modifications to previously developed software vary widely. Some of the factors to consider in establishing the requirements are:

a. Existing documentation
b. Available support tools
c. Modification vs. enhancement
d. GFS vs. commercial software vs. developed software
e. Duration of project
f. Product evolution strategy

40.6.1.6 *Category Summary.* These categories reflect the software's past history (if any) and its intended end use. Each category requires a different approach to achieve cost effective management of its software through tailoring the application of this standard and its related DIDs. For this step, it is first necessary to identify each type of software associated with the development program (e.g., operational, diagnostic, and support software). Then, identify how each of these types might consist of software from one or more categories (e.g., operational software includes newly-developed, unmodified reuseable, and some modified GFS components). Then, summarize for each category the different types of software with components within the category. The nature of the software types within any given category will influence the tailoring process for that category.

40.6.2 *Step 2 - Select Contract Data Items.* The contract data items associated with this standard fall into four categories: Management, Engineering, Test, and Operational and Support. Each of the data items is typically associated with either a system, an individual CSCI, or group of CSCIs. Some of the data items are typically required, while others may be required depending upon project-unique characteristics (see Table I).

40.6.2.1 *Management Data Items.* The following data items are in the management category:

Software Development Plan (SDP)
Software Configuration Management Plan (SCMP)
Software Standards and Procedures Manual (SSPM)
Software Quality Evaluation Plan (SQEP)

The SDP, SCMP, SSPM, and SQEP typically define the contractor's approach to developing all the software in the system, or the software for a group of CSCIs. All

Table I. Typical data item selection range.

DID TITLE	TYPICALLY REQUIRED	MAY BE COVERED IN ANOTHER DATA ITEM	MAY BE VENDOR-SUPPLIED
SDP	X		
SCMP		X	
SSPM		X	
SQEP		X	
SSS	X		
SRS	X		
IRS		X	
STLDD	X		
SDDD	X		
IDD		X	
DBDD		X	
SPS	X		
VDD	X		
ECP	X		
SCN	X		
STP	X		
STD	X		
STPR	X		
STR	X		
OCD	X		
CSOM			X
SUM			X
CSDM			X
SPM			X
FSM			X
CRISD	X		

the development plans may be described in a single SDP, or broken out into two or more documents (see Figure 10). Some of the factors to consider in selecting the appropriate management documentation are:

a. Budget constraints
b. Multiple contractors or subcontractors
c. Proprietary information
d. Project size
e. Organizational complexity
f. Complexity of development process
g. Complexity of development environment
h. Applicable software categories

40.6.2.2 *Engineering Data Items.* The following data items are in the engineering category:

System/Segment Specification (SSS)
Software Requirements Specification (SRS)
Interface Requirements Specification (IRS)
Software Top Level Design Document (STLDD)

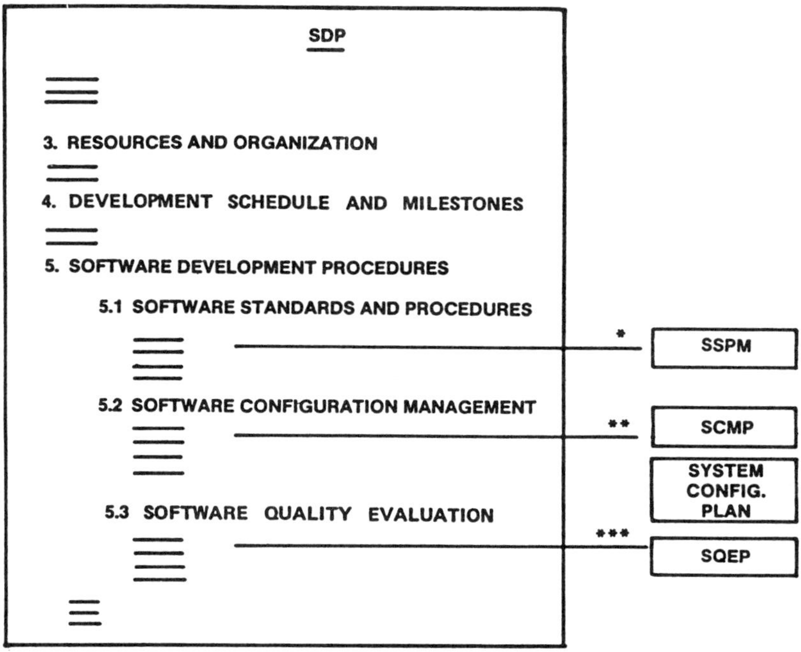

Figure 10. Relationship among management documents. Notes: * Software standards and procedures may be provided in a separate SSPM. ** Software configuration management procedures may be provided in a separate SCMP or system configuration management plan. *** Software quality evaluation procedures may be provided in a separate SQEP.

Software Detailed Design Document (SDDD)
Interface Design Document (IDD)
Data Base Design Document (DBDD)
Software Product Specification (SPS)
Version Description Document (VDD)
Engineering Change Proposal (ECP)
Specification Change Notice (SCN)

The SSS defines the requirements for the entire system, or segment of the system.

The SRS specifies the requirements for an individual CSCI. The interfaces for each CSCI may be specified in one or more IRSs (see Figure 11). Some of the factors to consider in selecting the appropriate requirements documentation are:

a. Number of interfaces

b. Number of development groups

c. Complexity of interfaces

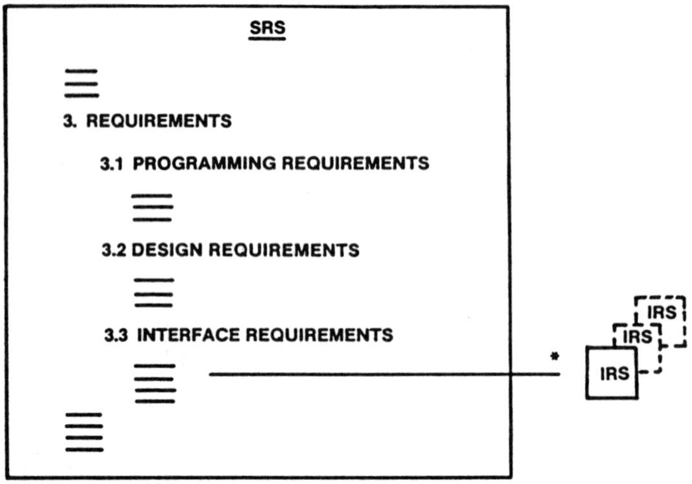

Figure 11. Relationship among requirements documents. Notes: * Interface requirements may be specified in one or more separate IRSs.

d. Number of contractors or subcontractors
e. Applicable software categories

The STLDD defines the top-level design and the SDDD defines the detailed design for an individual CSCI. The detailed design of the CSCI's data base(s) and external interfaces may be defined in the SDDD or one or more DBDDs and IDDs respectively (see Figure 12). Some of the factors to consider in selecting the appropriate design documentation are:

a. Interface requirements in separate IRS(s) (separate IDD for each IRS)
b. Number of data bases
c. Complexity of data base(s)
d. Probability of change to data base(s)

The SPS specifies the "as-built" description of an individual CSCI. The VDD identifies the exact version of an individual CSCI. ECPs and SCNs identify changes to formal baselines.

40.6.2.3 *Test Data Items.* The following data items are in the test category:

Software Test Plan (STP)
Software Test Description (STD)
Software Test Procedure (STPR)
Software Test Report (STR)

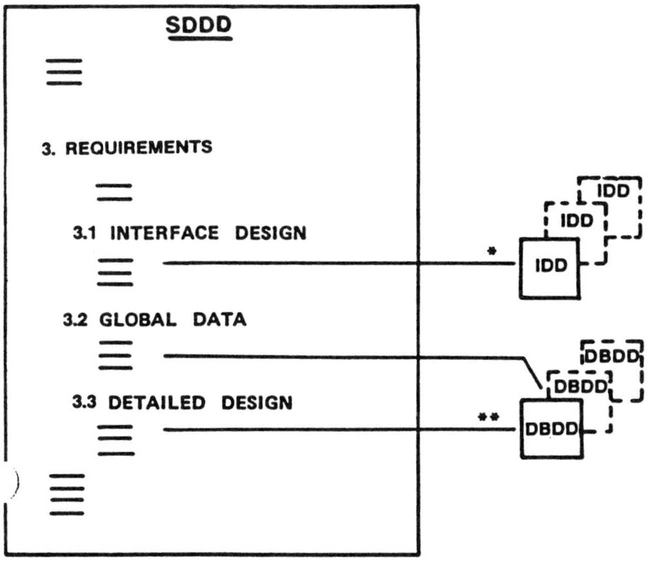

Figure 12. Relationship among design documents. Notes: * Detailed design of external interfaces may be provided in one or more separate IDDs. ** Detailed design of data base(s) may be provided in one or more separate DBDDs.

The test documents identify test information for an individual CSCI. The STP describes the contractor's plans for formal and informal testing. The STD identifies test cases for all formal tests of the CSCI. The STPR describes the step-by-step procedures for executing each formal test. STRs record the results of one or more formal tests.

40.6.2.4 *Operational and Support Data Items.* The following data items are in the operational and support category:

Operational Concept Document (OCD)
Computer System Operator's Manual (CSOM)
Software User's Manual (SUM)
Computer System Diagnostic Manual (CSDM)
Software Programmer's Manual (SPM)
Firmware Support Manual (FSM)
Computer Resources Integrated Support Document (CRISD)

The operational documents define the information required to operate the computer system(s) and associated software. The OCD identifies and describes the mission of the system and its operational and support environments. It also describes the functions and characteristics of the computer system within the overall system. The CSOM defines procedures for operating a computer system. The SUM defines procedures to execute one or more CSCIs. The entire SUM, or portions thereof, may be vendor-supplied, if commercially available software is used.

The support documents define the information required to support the computer system and associated software. The CSDM defines procedures to identify and isolate faults in a computer system. The SPM defines the programming aspects of a computer system. The FSM defines procedures to modify or replace firmware devices of a system. The CRISD defines the information required to support all the contractually deliverable software, or a portion thereof.

The CSDM, FSM, SPM, SUM, and CSOM, or portions thereof, may be vendor-supplied and may not be required from the development contractor.

40.6.2.5 *Additional Guidance.* Additional guidance on the selection of appropriate contract data items may be found in the Tailoring Handbook* related to this standard.

40.6.3 *Step 3 - Tailor the activities, products, and reviews.* This standard identifies applicable requirements for activities, products, reviews, and baselines/Developmental Configurations for each of the six software development phases identified in 4.1. The products of each phase consist of the contract deliverable data items as well as internal, non-deliverable items. Tailoring the requirements of each phase for each software category is accomplished by deletion of the affected paragraphs in this standard. Detailed tailoring guidance for each software development phase may be found in the Tailoring Handbook* related to this standard.

40.6.4 *Step 4 - Tailor the requirements of selected data items.* All of the requirements in the data items selected for the project may not be appropriate. Tailoring the data items is accomplished by deletion of the affected paragraphs in each selected data item for each software category. Detailed guidance for tailoring each data item may be found in the Tailoring Handbook* related to this standard.

Custodians:

Navy - NM
Army - AM
Air Force - 10,26

Preparing Activity:

Navy - NM

(Project MCCR-0005)

Review Activities:

Army - AD,AR,AY,CR,ER,MD,MI
Navy - EC,SH,AS,OM
Air Force - 10,26

*Planned for future release.

DOD-STD-2167 DATA ITEM DESCRIPTIONS (DIDs)

	DID No.	*Page No. (This Book)*
System/Segment Specification	DI-CMAN-80008 AMSC No. N3584	
Software Configuration Management Plan	DI-MCCR-80009 AMSC No. N3585	
Software Quality Evaluation Plan	DI-MCCR-80010 AMSC No. N3586	
Software Standards & Procedures Manual	DI-MCCR-80011 AMSC No. N3587	
*Software Top Level Design Document	DI-MCCR-80012 AMSC No. N3588	294
*Version Description Document	DI-MCCR-80013 AMSC No. N3589	306
*Software Test Plan	DI-MCCR-80014 AMSC No. N3590	310
*Software Test Description	DI-MCCR-80015 AMSC No. N3591	321
*Software Test Procedure	DI-MCCR-80016 AMSC No. N3592	326
*Software Test Report	DI-MCCR-80017 AMSC No. N3593	333
*Computer System Operator's Manual	DI-MCCR-80018 AMSC No. N3594	340
*Software User's Manual	DI-MCCR-80019 AMSC No. N3595	345
Computer Support Diagnostic Manual	DI-MCCR-80020 AMSC No. N3596	
Software Programmer's Manual	DI-MCCR-80021 AMSC No. N3597	
Firmware Support Manual	DI-MCCR-80022 AMSC No. N3598	
Operational Concept Document	DI-MCCR-80023 AMSC No. N3599	
Computer Resources Integ. Support Document	DI-MCCR-80024 AMSC No. N3600	
*Software Requirements Specification	DI-MCCR-80025 AMSC No. N3601	350
Interface Requirements Specification	DI-MCCR-80026 AMSC No. N3602	

*Included in this book (others may be obtained from the federal superintendent of public documents)

	DID No.	Page No. (This Book)
*Interface Design Document	DI-MCCR-80027 AMSC No. N3603	367
*Data Base Design Document	DI-MCCR-80028 AMSC No. N3604	373
*Software Product Specification	DI-MCCR-80029 AMSC No. N3605	380
*Software Development Plan	DI-MCCR-80030 AMSC No. N3606	385
*Software Detailed Design Document	DI-MCCR-80031 AMSC No. N3607	402

1. TITLE

SOFTWARE TOP LEVEL DESIGN DOCUMENT

2. IDENTIFICATION NUMBER

DI-MCCR-80012

3. DESCRIPTION/PURPOSE

3.1 The Software Top Level Design Document (STLDD) describes the structure and organization of a particular Computer Software Configuration Item (CSCI).

3.2 This document presents the allocation of the CSCI requirements specified in the Software Requirements Specification (SRS) and Interface Requirements Specifications (IRSs) to Top-Level Computer Software Components (TLCSCs) of the CSCI. Additionally, the STLDD defines the interface, data, and processing characteristics for each TLCSC in the CSCI design.

3.3 The STLDD describes the characteristics of each TLCSC to the Government. Upon completion of Physical Configuration Audit (PCA), the STLDD becomes a part of the Product Baseline for the CSCI.

3.4 The STLDD is used by the contractor as the basis for development of the TLCSCs and is the first document entered into the Developmental Configuration for the CSCI.

4. APPROVAL DATE (YYMMDD)

No entry.

*Included in this book (others may be obtained from the federal superintendent of public documents)

5. OFFICE OF PRIMARY RESPONSIBILITY (OPR)

NM

6a. DTIC REQUIRED

No entry.

6b. GIDEP REQUIRED

No entry.

7. APPLICATION/INTERRELATIONSHIP

7.1 This Data Item Description (DID) contains the format and content preparation instructions for that data generated under the work tasks described by 3.4.7.2 of MIL-STD-483, 3.1.3.3.5.1 of MIL-STD-490, and 5.2.1.2 and 5.2.2.3 of DOD-STD-2167.

7.2 The Government's Data Manager for this system must specify in the Statement of Work and Contract Data Requirements List whether this document is to be prepared and delivered on bound 8 1/2 by 11 inch bond paper or electronic media. If electronic media is selected, the precise format must be specified (e.g., magnetic tape, floppy disk, host system, etc.).

7.3 The STLDD is produced in the Preliminary Design phase of CSCI development. It documents the allocation of CSCI requirements from the SRS, DI-MCCR-80025, and IRSs, DI-MCCR-80026, to TLCSCs.

7.4 At PCA, the STLDD is included in the Software Product Specification (SPS), DI-MCCR-80029.

7.5 This DID supersedes DI-E-2138A and DI-E-25844A.

8. APPROVAL LIMITATION

No entry.

9a. APPLICABLE FORMS

No entry.

9b. AMSC NUMBER

No entry.

10. PREPARATION INSTRUCTIONS

10.1 *Source Document.* The applicable issue of the documents cited herein, including their approval date and dates of any applicable amendments and revisions, shall be as reflected in the contract.

10.2 *Content and Format Instructions.* This document shall be prepared on bound 8 1/2 by 11 inch bond paper (hardcopy) or a form of electronic media. The contract will specify the precise format. Each page prior to Section 1 shall be numbered in lower-case roman numeral beginning with page ii for the Table of Contents. Each page starting from Section 1 to the end of the document shall be consecutively numbered in arabic numerals. For hardcopy formats, this document may be printed on one or both sides of each page (single-sided/double-sided). For single-sided documents, all pages shall contain the document control number in the top right-hand corner. For double-sided documents, all even-numbered pages shall be on the left-hand side of the document and odd-numbered pages on the right-hand side. For double-sided documents, the control number shall be placed in the top right-hand corner for each odd-numbered page and the top left-hand corner for each even-numbered page. All paragraph and subparagraph headings listed below shall be included in the document. All paragraphs and subparagraphs starting with the phrase "This (sub)paragraph shall . . . " may be written as multiple (sub)paragraphs to enhance readability. The letter "X" serves as an identifier for a series of descriptions. For example, the paragraphs describing TLCSCs are designated as 3.6.X; if there is more than one TLCSC, the first paragraph is numbered 3.6.1 (Name) TLCSC, the second is 3.6.2 (Name) TLCSC, etc. (see 10.2.5.6.1). This document shall be as self-contained as possible. Reference to other documents should be minimal. This document shall consist of the following:

a. Cover Page
b. Table of Contents
c. Scope
d. Referenced Documents
e. Requirements
f. Notes
g. Appendixes

10.2.1 *Cover Page.* This page shall contain the document control number in the upper right hand corner. In the center of the page, these words shall appear in the following format:

SOFTWARE TOP LEVEL DESIGN DOCUMENT
FOR THE
[PROJECT NAME]

CONTRACT NO. [contract number]
CDRL SEQUENCE NO. [CDRL number]
[Date of document - day month year]

Prepared for:
[Contracting Agency Name, department code]

Prepared by:
[contractor name and address]

10.2.2 *Table of Contents.* This document shall contain a Table of Contents listing the title and page number of all titled paragraphs and subparagraphs. The Table of Contents shall then list the title and page number of all figures, tables, and appendixes, in that order.

10.2.3 *Scope.* This section shall be numbered 1. and divided into the following paragraphs.

10.2.3.1 *Identification.* This paragraph shall be numbered 1.1 and contain the approved identification number, title, and if applicable, abbreviation of the CSCI and the system to which this STLDD applies. This paragraph shall begin with the following sentence: "This Software Top Level Design Document describes the top-level design for the CSCI identified as (insert title, if applicable insert abbreviation in parenthesis, insert CSCI number) of the (insert title, if applicable insert abbreviation in parenthesis, insert system identification number) System."

10.2.3.2 *Purpose.* This paragraph shall be numbered 1.2, state the purpose of the system, and identify the TLCSCs of the CSCI to which this STLDD applies.

10.2.3.3 *Introduction.* This paragraph shall be numbered 1.3 and summarize the purpose and contents of this document.

10.2.4 *Referenced Documents.* This section shall be numbered 2. and list by document number and title all documents referenced in this document. This section shall also identify the source for all documents not available through normal Government stocking activities.

10.2.5 *Requirements.* This section shall be numbered 3. and divided into the following paragraphs.

10.2.5.1 *CSCI Architecture.* This paragraph shall be numbered 3.1 and describe the static structure used in the implementation of the CSCI. The TLCSCs defined by the top-level design shall be identified and their purpose briefly summarized. The relationships among these TLCSCs and critical Lower-Level Computer Software Components (LLCSCs) and Units, if known, shall be described. The CSCI top-level architecture may be provided by a CSCI top-level architecture diagram (see Figure 1).

10.2.5.2 *Functional Allocation.* This paragraph shall be numbered 3.2 and describe and discuss the considerations used in allocating CSCI functions and interfaces to TLCSCs. Text or tables shall be used to show that all the requirements identified in the requirements specification(s) have been allocated to TLCSCs. An example of a TLCSC requirements allocation table is provided in Table I.

10.2.5.3 *Memory and Processing Time Allocation.* This paragraph shall be numbered 3.3 and document the allocation of memory and processing time to TLCSCs. The allocation may be illustrated by a memory/processing time table. An example of a memory/processing time table is provided in Table II.

10.2.5.4 *Functional Control and Data Flow.* This paragraph shall be numbered 3.4

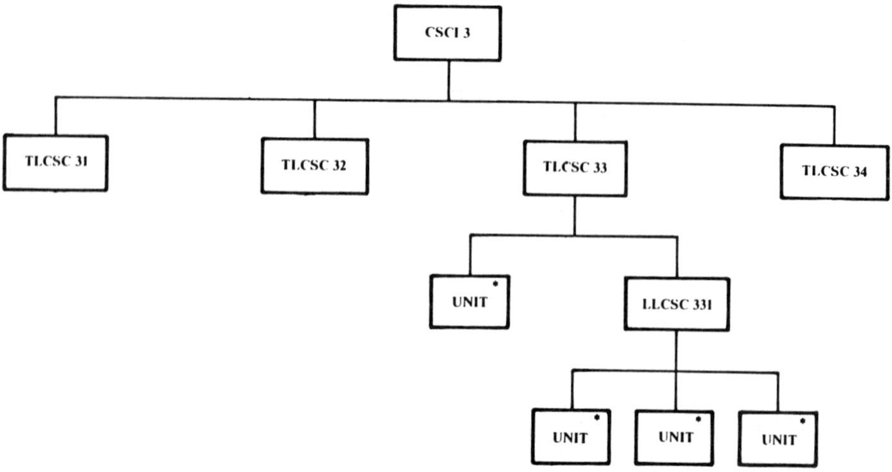

Figure 1. Sample CSCI architecture diagram. Notes: 1. TLCSC = Top-level CSC; 2. LLCSC = Lower-level CSC; 3. * = Critical units.

and describe the general top-level flow of both data and execution control within the CSCI. If the CSCI is designed to operate in more than one state (e.g., air ready, search, track), then each state shall be clearly distinguished. A state/TLCSC table may be provided to illustrate the states in which each TLCSC executes. An example of a state/TLCSC table is provided in Table III. A control flow diagram between TLCSCs may be used to illustrate top-level execution control. An example of a control flow diagram with an executive TLCSC is provided in Figure 2. A data flow diagram between top-level TLCSCs may be used to illustrate top-level data flow. An example of a data flow diagram is provided in Figure 3.

TABLE I. Sample allocation table.

STLDD Allocation			CSCI Requirement		
TLCSC Number	TLCSC Name	Paragraph Number	Requirement Name	Document Name	Paragraph Number
31	W (Interface 1)	3.6.1	Function 1 Function 2 Interface 1	SRS SRS SRS	3.4.1 3.4.2 3.3.3.2.1
32	X (Executive)	3.6.2	Function 3 Interface 5	SRS IRS for SC[1]	3.4.3 3.3.2
33	Y (Interface 2,3,4)	3.6.3	Function 4 Interface 2 Interface 3 Interface 4	SRS IRS for 1 IRS for 1 IRS for 1	3.4.4 3.3.1.1 3.3.1.2 3.3.1.3
34	Z (Interface 5)	3.6.4	Function 5 Interface 5	SRS IRS for SC	3.4.5 3.3.2

[1]SC = signal conditioner

TABLE II. Sample memory/processing time table.

TLCSC Name	TLCSC Number	Memory Budget (Words)	Allocated Processing Time
Mode control	25	1,700	128.0 ms
Coordinate conversion	69	900	156.0 ms
Radar control	26	3,000	96.0 ms
Weapon control	27	2,100	100.0 ms
Target engageability	11	1,700	10.0 ms
Executive	1	1,200	80.0 ms
Data base	100	2,000	N/A
Total		15,000	570 ms
Total available		16,384	740 ms
Reserve		1,384	170 ms
Reserve (%)		8.4	23.0

TABLE III. Sample state/TLCSC table.

System States \ TLCSCs Used In Each State	TLCSC 31	TLCSC 32	TLCSC 33	TLCSC 34	TLCSC 35
Air ready	X				X
Search	X	X	X		X
Track	X	X	X	X	X

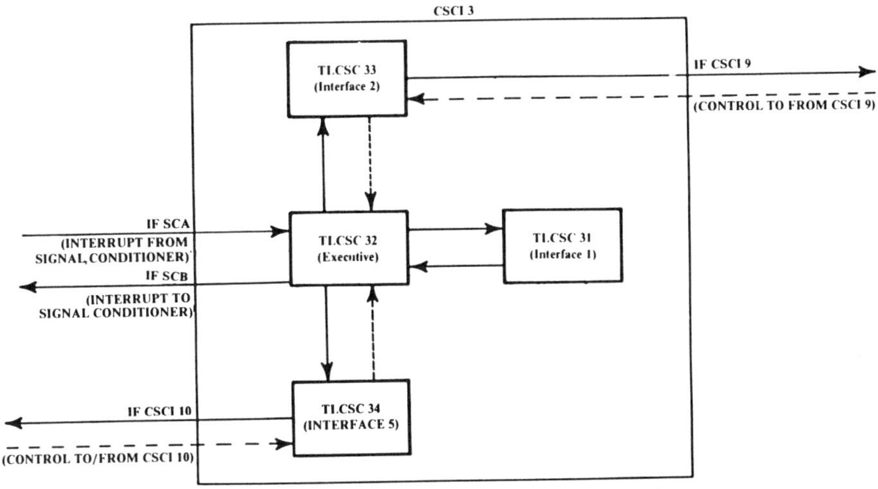

Figure 2. Sample control flow between TLCSCs. Notes: 1. → Control; 2. - - → Status; 3. IF = Interface; 4. SC = Signal conditioner.

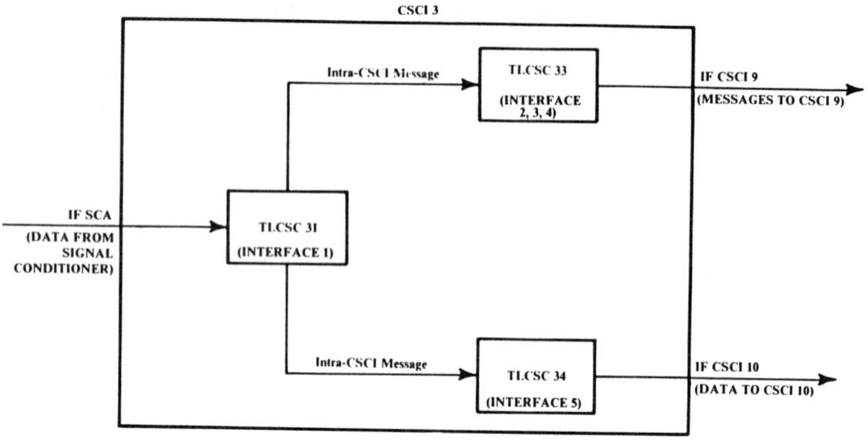

Figure 3. Sample data flow between TLCSCs.

10.2.5.5 *Global Data.* This paragraph shall be numbered 3.5 and identify, describe, and state the purpose of data that are common to more than one TLCSC in the top-level design. This paragraph shall include format of the global data, the TLCSCs which use the data, and all other characteristics of the global data needed to satisfy global data requirements. Examples are: limits or ranges of global data values, accuracy and precision. This information may be provided in a global data definition table. An example of a global data definition table is provided in Table IV. For convenience, information regarding global data may be provided as an appendix and referenced herein.

If files or a data base are part of the global data, this paragraph shall also provide the following details:

a. Purpose of each file or data base.
b. Structure of each file or data base in terms of records, fields, and items.
c. Access procedures (e.g., sequential, random access).

10.2.5.6 *Top-Level Design.* This paragraph shall be numbered 3.6 and divided into the following subparagraphs to identify and describe the requirements allocated to each TLCSC included in the top-level design. This information may be provided by automated tools or other techniques (e.g., program design language).

10.2.5.6.1 *(Name X) TLCSC.* This subparagraph shall be numbered 3.6.X (beginning with 3.6.1), identify TLCSC X, and describe in detail its purpose. If the system can exist in various states, this subparagraph shall list the states in which TLCSC X executes. In addition, this subparagraph may reference a TLCSC X functional block diagram to illustrate the source of inputs and destination of outputs of TLCSC X. The TLCSC X functional block diagram may also identify CSCI requirements allocated to TLCSC X (e.g., functions, external interfaces, etc.). An example of a TLCSC X functional block diagram is provided in Figure 4.

10.2.5.6.1.1 *Inputs.* This subparagraph shall be numbered 3.6.X.1 (beginning with 3.6.1.1) and identify and state the purpose of the input data required by TLCSC X.

TABLE IV. Sample global data definition table.

Identifier	Description	Data Type	Data Representation	Size	Units of Measure	Limit/ Range	Accuracy/ Precision	Applicable TLCSCs
Grange	Grid range	Real	Constant	1 word	Miles	N/A	N/A	TLCSC 31 TLCSC 32 TLCSC 33
Six 11	Emergency state	Boolean	Boolean	1 byte[1]	N/A	N/A	N/A	TLCSC 31 TLCSC 33
A list	Authorization list-data base user priority level	ASCII integer	File of 10 records	200 words 6 char[2] 1 word	N/A	50 records A-Z 0-4	N/A	TLCSC 31 TLCSC 32
Coords	Coordinates	Real	10 × 10 array	100 words[3]	N/A	N/A	6 dec. places ±.000005	TLCSC 32 TLCSC 33

[1]Byte = 8 Bits

[2]Char = 8 Bits

[3]Word = 16 Bits, 2 Bytes

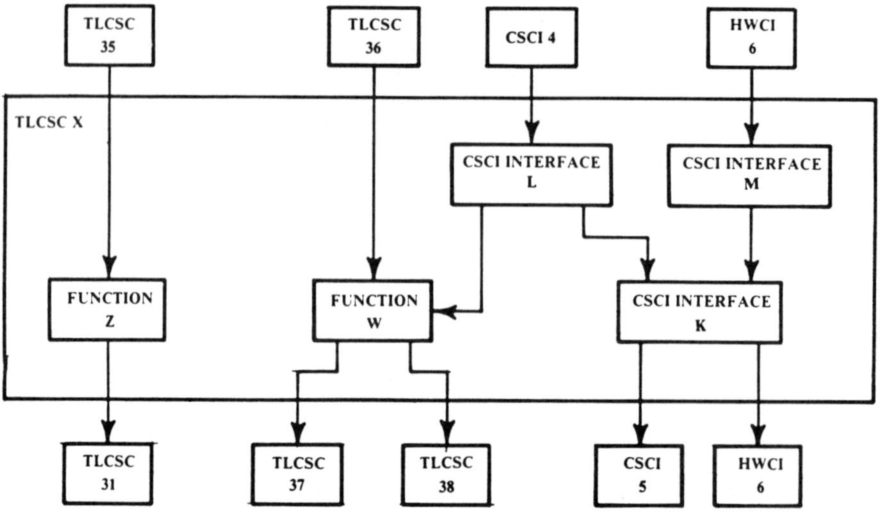

Figure 4. Sample TLCSC functional block diagram.

Input data may be transmitted as global data, direct I/O, passed parameters, or through shared memory. This subparagraph shall include the source(s), format(s), units of measure, and all other characteristics of the input data needed to satisfy the input requirements of TLCSC X. Examples are: limits or ranges of input values, accuracy and precision, frequency of input data arrival, and legality checks for erroneous information. This information may be provided in a TLCSC X input table. An example of a TLCSC X input table is provided in Table V.

10.2.5.6.1.2 *Local Data.* This subparagraph shall be numbered 3.6.X.2 (beginning with 3.6.1.2) and describe and state the purpose of the data that originate in TLCSC X and are not used by any other TLCSC. This subparagraph shall include the format and all other characteristics of the local data needed to satisfy the local data requirements of TLCSC X. Examples are: limits or ranges, values, accuracy and precision. This information may be provided in a TLCSC X local data definition table. An example of a TLCSC X local data definition table is provided in Table VI.

If files or a data base are part of the local data of TLCSC X, this subparagraph shall also provide the following details:

a. Purpose of each file or data base.

b. Structure of each file or data base in terms of records, fields, and items.

c. Access procedures (e.g., sequential, random access).

10.2.5.6.1.3 *Interrupts.* This subparagraph shall be numbered 3.6.X.3 (beginning with 3.6.1.3) and list the interrupts serviced by TLCSC X and for each interrupt identify the following:

a. Source of interrupt

b. Purpose of interrupt

TABLE V. Sample TLCSC X input table.

Identifier	Description	Data Type	Data Representation	Size	Units of Measure	Limit/ Range	Accuracy/ Precision	Frequency	Legal OK	Source(s)	Input Method
VMAG	Speed	Real	Fixed	2 words[3]	MPH	0–10,000	6 dec. places .000005	1 KH_z	N/A	TLCSC 33 TLCSC 34	Parameter
NUM	Number of objects	Integer	Positive	1 byte[1]	N/A	255	± 2	1 KH_z	Yes	TLCSC 33 TLCSC 34	Global
RPRI	Request priority	Integer	Mask	1 byte	N/A	0–4	N/A	Aperiodic	Yes	TLCSC 33 TLCSC 34	Direct I/O
ID	ID code	ASCII	String	6 char[2]	N/A	A-Z	N/A	Aperiodic	Yes	CSCI 3	Global

[1]Byte = 8 bits
[2]Char = 8 bits
[3]Word = 16 bits, 2 bytes

TABLE VI. Sample TLCSC X local data definition table.

Identifier	Description	Data Type	Data Representation	Size	Units of Measure	Limit/Range	Accuracy/ Precision
MYCOORD	Local coordinates	Array	10 × 10 matrix of fixed	100 words	Nautical mile	0–55	±.002
MYVMAG	Local speed	Real	Fixed	2 words	Knots	0–10,000	±.000005
KNOTS	Conversion factor	Real	Constant .869565	1 word	Nautical mile/ mile	N/A	±.000001
PICTURE	Pixel matrix	Array	100 × 100 matrix of binary	1000 words	N/A	0 = off 1 = on	N/A

TABLE VII. Sample TLCSC X output table.

Identifier	Description	Data Type	Data Representation	Size	Units	Limit/ Range	Accuracy/ Precision	Frequency	Destination	Output Method
VMAG	Speed	Real	Fixed	2 words	MPH	0–10,000	±.000005	1 KH_z	TLCSC 31 TLCSC 32	Parameter
NUM	Number of objects	Integer	Positive	1 byte	N/A	255	±	1 KH_z	TLCSC 31 TLCSC 32	Global
COORDS	Coordinates	Real	10 × 10 array	100 words	Mile	0–65	±.002	1 KH_z	TLCSC 32	Global
SIX 11	Emergency state	Boolean	Boolean	1 byte	N/A	N/A	N/A	1 KH_z	TLCSC 31	Global

c. Priority of interrupt
d. Required response and response time
e. Minimum, maximum, and probable frequency of interrupt

10.2.5.6.1.4 *Timing and Sequencing.* This subparagraph shall be numbered 3.6.X.4 (beginning with 3.6.1.4) and describe the control logic involved in invoking TLCSC X. The timing and sequencing conditions under which TLCSC X executes shall be described (e.g., TLCSC X executes 16 times a second and always follows TLCSC 31). If the sequencing is dynamically controlled during the CSCI's operations, the method for sequence control and the logic and input conditions of that method shall be described (e.g., timing variations, priority assignments, internal operations such as data transfer in and out of core, disc, drum or tape memory, sensing of discrete input signals, and timing relationships between interrupt operations with the CSCI).

10.2.5.6.1.5 *Processing.* This subparagraph shall be numbered 3.6.X.5 (beginning with 3.6.1.5) and describe the following processing characteristics of TLCSC X:

a. Algorithms. The algorithms incorporated in the execution of TLCSC X, in terms of the manipulation of the input and local data of TLCSC X and the operational functions performed.
b. *Special Control Features.* Special control features of TLCSC X which affect the design of the executive control logic, but are not part of the normal operational functions.
c. *Error Handling.* Error detection and recovery features of TLCSC X, including handling of erroneous input data and other conditions which affect the execution of TLCSC X (e.g., device faults).

These characteristics may be graphically illustrated (e.g., data flow diagram, control flow diagram, etc.), as applicable.

10.2.5.6.1.6 *Outputs.* This subparagraph shall be numbered 3.6.X.6 (beginning with 3.6.1.6) and identify and state the purpose of the output data of TLCSC X. Output data may be transmitted as global data, direct I/O, passed parameters, or through shared memory. This paragraph shall include the format(s), destination(s), units of measure, and all other characteristics of the output data needed to satisfy the output requirements of TLCSC X. Examples are: limits or ranges of output values, accuracy and precision, and frequency of output data. This information may be provided in a TLCSC X output table. An example of a TLCSC X output table is provided in Table VII.

10.2.5.7 *Adaptation Data.* This paragraph shall be numbered 3.7 and identify and describe all data and associated entry/initialization procedures required for adaptation of the CSCI to a particular site, mission, or state. In addition, for multi-site computer-based systems, a list of the actual data required to adapt the CSCI to the environment associated with each site shall be provided on a site-by-site basis. For convenience, this information may be contained in an appendix to this volume.

10.2.6 *Notes.* This section shall be numbered 6. and contain any general information that aids in understanding this document (e.g., background information, glossary, formula derivations). This section shall include an alphabetical listing of all acronyms, abbreviations, and their meanings as used in this document.

10.2.7 *Appendixes.* Appendixes may contain any supplemental information published separately for convenience in document maintenance (e.g., charts, classified data). Appendixes may be bound as separate documents for ease in handling. Appendixes shall be numbered sequentially in Roman numeral (I, II, etc.), and the paragraphs within each appendix shall all be numbered as multiples of 10 (e.g., Appendix I, paragraph 10.1, 10.2, Appendix II, paragraph 20.1, 20.2, etc.).

As applicable, each appendix shall be referenced in the main body of the document where the data would normally have been provided.

1. TITLE

VERSION DESCRIPTION DOCUMENT

2. IDENTIFICATION NUMBER

DI-MCCR-80013

3. DESCRIPTION/PURPOSE

3.1 The Version Description Document (VDD) identifies and describes a version of a Computer Software Configuration Item (CSCI) or interim changes (i.e., changes which occur between CSCI versions) to the previously released version.

3.2. The VDD records data pertinent to the status and usage of a CSCI version or interim change. It is used by the contractor to release CSCI versions or interim changes to the Government.

4. APPROVAL DATE (YYMMDD)

No entry.

5. OFFICE OF PRIMARY RESPONSIBILITY (OPR)

NM

6a. DTIC REQUIRED

No entry.

6b. GIDEP REQUIRED

No entry.

7. APPLICATION/INTERRELATIONSHIP

7.1. This Data Item Description (DID) contains the format and content preparation instructions for that data generated under the work tasks described by 80.5.4 of MIL-STD-483 and 5.6.1.5 and 5.6.2.6 of DOD-STD-2167.

7.2 The Government's Data Manager for this system must specify in the Statement of Work and Contract Data Requirements List whether this document is to be prepared and delivered on bound 8 1/2 by 11 inch bond paper or electronic media. If electronic media is selected, the precise format must be specified (e.g., magnetic tape, floppy disk, host system, etc.).

7.3 The VDD is a part of the integrated approach to Configuration Management as applied to a CSCI. As such, a VDD is prepared to accompany the release of: (1) each version of a CSCI, including the initial release, and (2) each interim change to a previously released version.

7.4 The VDD identifies, by reference to the applicable Engineering Change Proposal (ECP), DI-E-3128, and Specification Change Notice (SCN), DI-E-3134, all changes to the software since the last VDD was issued.

7.5 This DID supersedes DI-E-3121, DI-E-3122, and DI-E-3123.

8. APPROVAL LIMITATION

No entry.

9a. APPLICABLE FORMS

No entry.

9b. AMSC NUMBER

No entry.

10. PREPARATION INSTRUCTIONS

10.1 *Source Document.* The applicable issue of the document cited herein, including their approval date and dates of any applicable amendments and revisions, shall be as reflected in the contract.

10.2. *Content and Format Instructions.* This document shall be prepared on bound 8 1/2 by 11 inch bond paper (hardcopy) or a form of electronic media. The contract will specify the precise format. Each page prior to Section 1 shall be numbered in lowercase roman numeral beginning with page ii for the Table of Contents. Each page starting from Section 1 to the end of the document shall be consecutively numbered in arabic numerals. For hardcopy formats, this document may be printed on one or both sides of each page (single-sided/double-sided). For single-sided documents, all pages shall contain the document control number in the top right-hand corner. For double-sided documents, all even-numbered pages shall be on the left-hand side of the document and odd-numbered pages on the right-hand side. For double-sided documents, the control number shall be placed in the top right-hand corner for each odd-numbered page and the top left-hand corner for each even-numbered page. All paragraph headings listed below shall be included in the document. All paragraphs starting with the phrase "This paragraph shall . . . " may be written as multiple paragraphs to enhance readability. This document shall consist of the following:

a. Cover Page
b. Table of Contents
c. Scope
d. Referenced Documents
e. Version Description
f. Notes
g. Appendixes

10.2.1 *Cover Page.* This page shall contain the document control number in the upper right hand corner. In the center of the page, these words shall appear in the following format:

VERSION DESCRIPTION DOCUMENT
FOR THE
[PROJECT NAME]

CONTRACT NO. [contract number]
CDRL SEQUENCE NO. [CDRL number]
[Date of document - day month year]

Prepared for:
[Contracting Agency Name, department code]

Prepared by:
[contractor name and address]

10.2.2 *Table of Contents.* This document shall contain a Table of Contents listing the title and page number of all titled paragraphs and subparagraphs. The Table of Contents shall then list the title and page number of all figures, tables, and appendixes, in that order.

10.2.3 *Scope.* This section shall be numbered 1. and divided into the following paragraphs.

10.2.3.1 *Identification.* This paragraph shall be numbered 1.1 and contain the approved identification number, title, and if applicable, abbreviation of the CSCI and the system to which this VDD applies. For the release of a new CSCI version, this paragraph shall begin with the following sentence: "This Version Description Document describes version (insert new version number) for the CSCI identified as (insert title, if applicable insert abbreviation in parenthesis, insert CSCI number) of the (insert title, if applicable insert abbreviation in parenthesis, insert system identification number) System." For the release of an interim change, this paragraph shall begin with the following sentence: "This Version Description Document describes an interim change to (insert version number of the version to which the interim change is attached), incorporating ECP (insert ECP number) and SCN/change notice (insert SCN/change notice number) for the CSCI identified as (insert title, if applicable insert abbreviation in parenthesis, insert CSCI number) of the (insert title, if applicable insert abbreviation in parenthesis, insert system identification number) System."

10.2.3.2 *Purpose.* This paragraph shall be numbered 1.2, state the purpose of the system, and identify the functional capabilities added to the CSCI or problems corrected in the CSCI in this VDD.

10.2.3.3 *Introduction.* This paragraph shall be numbered 1.3 and summarize the purpose and contents of this document.

10.2.4 *Referenced Documents.* This section shall be numbered 2. and list by document number and title all documents referenced in this document. This section shall also identify the source for all documents not available through normal Government stocking activities.

10.2.5 *Version Description.* This section shall be numbered 3. and divided into the following paragraphs.

10.2.5.1 *Inventory of Materials Released.* This paragraph shall be numbered 3.1 and list all physical media (e.g., listings, tapes, cards, disks) and associated documentation which make up the new version or interim change package. This paragraph shall also identify all operation and support documents which are not a part of the released package, but which are required to operate, load, or regenerate the released CSCI.

10.2.5.2 *Inventory of CSCI Contents.* This paragraph shall be numbered 3.2 and identify all computer software which is being released (by reference to the appropriate specifications and manuals and by listings).

10.2.5.3 *Class I Changes Installed.* This paragraph shall be numbered 3.3 and contain a list of new Class I changes (as defined in MIL-STD-483) to the computer software incorporated since the previous version/change, with a cross reference to the affected CSCI specifications. This paragraph shall also indicate for each entry in this list the ECP number and date, and the related SCN/change package number and date.

Note: This information does not apply to an initial release.

10.2.5.4 *Class II Changes Installed.* This paragraph shall be numbered 3.4 and contain a list of new Class II changes (as defined in MIL-STD-483) to the computer software incorporated since the previous version/change, with a cross reference to the affected CSCI specifications. This paragraph shall also indicate for each entry in this list the ECP number and date, and the related SCN/change package number and date.

Note: This information does not apply to an initial release.

10.2.5.5 *Adaptation Data.* This paragraph shall be numbered 3.5. For the release of an initial CSCI version, this paragraph shall identify (by reference to appropriate specifications and listings) all unique-to-site data which are contained in the items being released. For CSCI versions subsequent to the initial version or for interim changes, this paragraph shall contain the necessary information to identify changes made to the adaptation data.

10.2.5.6 *Interface Compatibility.* This paragraph shall be numbered 3.6. For the release of a new CSCI version or for an interim change, this paragraph shall indicate other systems and configuration items affected by the changes incorporated in this release.

10.2.5.7 *Bibliography of Reference Documents.* This paragraph shall be numbered 3.7 and list all pertinent documents related to an initial CSCI version. For CSCI versions subsequent to the initial version or for interim changes, this paragraph shall identify changes to the listed documents.

10.2.5.8 *Operational Description.* This paragraph shall be numbered 3.8. For each ECP listed in 10.2.5.3 and 10.2.5.4 above, this paragraph shall contain a subparagraph describing the operational effect of the change as abstracted from the ECP.

10.2.5.9 *Installation Instructions.* This paragraph shall be numbered 3.9 and describe (either directly or by reference) the method to be used to install and checkout the delivered CSCI version or interim change.

10.2.5.10 *Possible Problems and Known Errors.* This paragraph shall be numbered 3.10 and identify aspects of the new version or interim change which should be further tested. Any possible problems or known errors shall be described and any steps being taken to resolve the problems or correct the errors shall be stated.

10.2.6 *Notes.* This section shall be numbered 6. and contain any general information that aids in understanding this document (e.g., background information, glossary). This section shall include an alphabetical listing of all acronyms, abbreviations, and their meanings as used in this document.

10.2.7 *Appendixes.* Appendixes may contain any supplemental information published separately for convenience in document maintenance (e.g., charts, classified data). Appendixes may be bound as separate documents for ease in handling. Appendixes shall be numbered sequentially in Roman numeral (I, II, etc.), and the paragraphs within each appendix shall all be numbered as multiples of 10 (e.g., Appendix I, paragraph 10.1, 10.2, Appendix II, paragraph 20.1, 20.2, etc.).

As applicable, each appendix shall be referenced in the main body of the document where the data would normally have been provided.

1. TITLE

SOFTWARE TEST PLAN

2. IDENTIFICATION NUMBER

DI-MCCR-80014

3. DESCRIPTION/PURPOSE

3.1 The Software Test Plan (STP) defines the total scope of testing for a particular Computer Software Configuration Item (CSCI). The STP establishes requirements, describes organizations and responsibilities, specifies resources required, and provides schedules for all CSCI testing. In addition, the STP identifies the individual tests that shall be performed during formal CSCI testing.

3.2 The STP enables the Government to assess the adequacy of planning for CSCI testing.

3.3 The STP is used by the contractor as the basis for the development of both formal and informal test programs.

4. APPROVAL DATE (YYMMDD)

No entry.

5. OFFICE OF PRIMARY RESPONSIBILITY (OPR)

NM

6a. DTIC REQUIRED

No entry.

6b. GIDEP REQUIRED

No entry.

7. APPLICATION/INTERRELATIONSHIP

7.1 This Data Item Description (DID) contains the format and content preparation instructions for that data generated under work tasks described by 5.2.1.6 and 5.2.2.5 of DOD-STD-2167.

7.2 The Government's Data Manager for this system must specify in the Statement of Work and Contract Data Requirements List whether this specification is to be prepared and delivered on bound 8 1/2 by 11 inch bond paper or electronic media. If electronic media is selected, the precise format must be specified (e.g., magnetic tape, floppy disk, host system, etc.).

7.3 The STP provides planning for the informal testing to be conducted on Computer Software Components (CSCs) and Units, to verify conformance with the design specified in the Software Top Level Design Document (STLDD), DI-MCCR-80012, Software Detailed Design Document (SDDD), DI-MCCR-80031, Interface Design Document (IDD), DI-MCCR-80027, and Data Base Design Document (DBDD), DI-MCCR-80028.

7.4 The STP provides planning for the formal testing to be used to validate the CSCI against the requirements of the Software Requirements Specification (SRS), DI-MCCR-80025, and the Interface Requirements Specifications (IRSs), DI-MCCR-80026.

7.5 This DID supersedes DI-T-2142A, DI-T-25851, DI-T-30715, and DI-T-3703A.

8. APPROVAL LIMITATION

No entry.

9a. APPLICABLE FORMS

No entry.

9b. AMSC NUMBER

No entry.

10. PREPARATION INSTRUCTIONS

10.1 *Source Document.* The applicable issue of the documents cited herein, including their approval date and dates of any applicable amendments and revisions, shall be as reflected in the contract.

10.2 *Content and Format Instructions.* This plan shall be prepared on bound 8 1/2 by 11 inch bond paper (hardcopy) or a form of electronic media. The contract will specify the precise format. Each page prior to Section 1 shall be numbered in lower-case roman numeral beginning with page ii for the Table of Contents. Each page starting from Section 1 to the end of the document shall be consecutively numbered in arabic numerals. For hardcopy formats, this document may be printed on one or both sides of each page (single-sided/double-sided). For single-sided documents, all pages shall contain the document control number in the top right-hand corner. For double-sided documents, all even-numbered pages shall be on the left-hand side of the document and odd-numbered pages on the right-hand side. For double-sided documents, the control number shall be placed in the top right-hand corner for each odd-numbered page and the top left-hand corner for each even-numbered page. All paragraph and subparagraph headings listed below shall be included in the plan. All paragraphs and subparagraphs starting with the phrase "This (sub)paragraph shall . . . " may be written as multiple (sub)paragraphs to enhance readability. The letter "X" serves as an identifier for a series of descriptions. For example, the subparagraphs describing formal tests are designated as 4.4.X; if there is more than one formal test, the first subparagraph is numbered 4.4.1 (Name) Formal Test, the second is 4.4.2 (Name) Formal Test, etc. (see 10.2.6.4.1). This plan shall be as self-contained as possible. Reference to other documents should be minimal. This plan shall consist of the following:

a. Cover Page
b. Table of Contents
c. Scope
d. Referenced Documents
e. Plans for Informal Testing
f. Plans for Formal Testing

g. Test Planning Assumptions and Constraints

h. Notes

i. Appendixes

10.2.1 *Cover Page.* This page shall contain the document control number in the upper right hand corner. In the center of the page, these words shall appear in the following format:

SOFTWARE TEST PLAN
FOR THE
[PROJECT NAME]

CONTRACT NO. [contract number]
CDRL SEQUENCE NO. [CDRL number]
[Date of document - day month year]

Prepared for:
[Contracting Agency Name, department code]

Prepared by:
[contractor name and address]

10.2.2 *Table of Contents.* This plan shall contain a Table of Contents listing the title and page number of all titled paragraphs and subparagraphs. The Table of Contents shall then list the title and page number of all figures, tables, and appendixes, in that order.

10.2.3 *Scope.* This section shall be numbered 1. and divided into the following paragraphs.

10.2.3.1 *Identification.* This paragraph shall be numbered 1.1 and contain the approved identification number, title, and if applicable, abbreviation of the CSCI and the system to which this STP applies. This paragraph shall begin with the following sentence: "This Software Test Plan establishes the plan for testing the CSCI identified as (insert title, if applicable insert abbreviation in parenthesis, insert CSCI number) of the (insert title, if applicable insert abbreviation in parenthesis, insert system identification number) System."

10.2.3.2 *Purpose.* This paragraph shall be numbered 1.2, state the purpose of the system, and identify the functions of the CSCI to which this STP applies.

10.2.3.3 *Introduction.* This paragraph shall be numbered 1.3 and summarize the purpose and contents of this document.

10.2.4 *Referenced Documents.* This section shall be numbered 2. and list by document number and title all documents referenced in this plan. This section shall also identify the source for all documents not available through normal Government stocking activities.

10.2.5 *Plans for Informal Testing.* This section shall be numbered 3. and divided into the following paragraphs and subparagraphs to describe the planning for the testing of each individual Unit after it has been coded, and for the integration and testing of aggregates of Units.

10.2.5.1 *Unit Test Planning.* This paragraph shall be numbered 3.1 and divided into the following subparagraphs. For all Units that shall be defined for the CSCI, the subparagraphs below shall describe the requirements, responsibilities, and schedules for their testing.

10.2.5.1.1 *Unit Test Requirements.* This subparagraph shall be numbered 3.1.1 and specify general requirements that shall apply to all Unit testing and unique requirements that shall apply to selected groups of Units implementing particular CSCI requirements.

For example:
"All Unit tests shall conform to the following general requirements:

a. Each Unit shall be tested using nominal, extreme, and erroneous input values.
b. Each Unit shall be tested for error detection and proper error recovery, including appropriate error messages.
c. Each option shall be tested for Units with data output options and formats.

All tests of Units implementing the weapon launch-control requirements shall conform to the following unique requirements:

a. All executable statements in each Unit shall be executed.
b. All options at each branch in each Unit shall be tested."

10.2.5.1.2 *Unit Test Responsibilities.* This subparagraph shall be numbered 3.1.2, identify the organizations responsible for the preparation, execution, reporting, review, audit, and control of Unit testing, and shall summarize their responsibilities in each of these areas. Reference may be made to other planning and control documents (e.g., Software Development Plan (SDP), Software Configuration Management Plan (SCMP), etc.), as appropriate.

For example:
"Organization X shall be responsible for:

a. Planning Unit tests.
b. Conducting Unit tests.
c. Reporting Unit tests.

Organization Y shall examine the Software Development Files (SDFs) for all Units and verify that:

a. All the requirements specified in 10.2.5.1.1 have been satisfied.
b. All the test results have been recorded in the SDFs.
c. All of the Units comply with the design and coding standards for the CSCI (as defined in the Software Standards and Procedures Manual (SSPM)).

Organization Z shall be responsible for:

a. Entering successfully tested Units into the Developmental Configuration.
b. Controlling changes to Units entered into the Developmental Configuration.
c. Establishment of procedures for the retention of Unit test results."

10.2.5.1.3 *Unit Test Schedule.* This subparagraph shall be numbered 3.1.3 and identify general Unit test schedules consistent with overall development plans. (Detailed schedules for testing individual Units shall not be included.)

10.2.5.2 *CSC Integration and Test Planning.* This paragraph shall be numbered 3.2 and divided into the following subparagraphs to describe plans for the integration of Units and the test of aggregates of integrated Units. The subparagraphs below shall focus on the overall design and structure of the CSCI and define:

a. CSC integration and test requirements
b. Responsibilities for CSC integration and test
c. Classes of CSC integration tests
d. CSC integration and test schedules

10.2.5.2.1 *CSC Integration and Test Requirements.* This subparagraph shall be numbered 3.2.1 and describe general requirements that apply to all CSC integration and testing and unique requirements that apply to selected integration tests.

For example:
"All integration tests shall conform to the following requirements:

a. Each aggregate of integrated Units shall be tested using nominal, extreme, and erroneous input values.
b. Each aggregate of integrated Units shall be tested for error detection and proper error recovery, including appropriate error messages.

Integration tests for the weapons launch control requirements shall conform to the following unique requirements:

a. Each aggregate of integrated Units shall be stressed with peak data loads.
b. Each aggregate of integrated Units shall be tested under all combinations of adaptation data."

10.2.5.2.2 *CSC Integration and Test Responsibilities.* This subparagraph shall be numbered 3.2.2, identify the organizations responsible for the preparation, execution, reporting, control, review, and audit of CSC integration and testing, and shall summarize their responsibilities in each of these areas. Reference may be made to other planning and control documents (e.g., Software Quality Evaluation Plan (SQEP), SDP, SCMP, etc.), as appropriate.

For example:
"Organization X shall:

a. Verify that a set of standard procedures have been established for the integration of Units.
b. Monitor CSC integration to verify that established integration procedures are followed.

Organization Y shall:

a. Perform the CSC integration tests.

b. Record results (in established format) and generate test reports (in established format).

c. Meet weekly with all the programming managers to discuss CSC integration test results and schedules.

Organization Z shall:

a. Maintain and control the hardware and software configuration during CSC integration tests as described in the SCMP.

b. Establish requirements for the retention of CSC versions and their test results.''

10.2.5.2.3 *CSC Integration Test Classes.* This subparagraph shall be numbered 3.2.3 and describe the various types or classes of tests that shall be executed during the CSC integration (e.g., Timing Tests, Erroneous Input Tests, Maximum Capacity Tests).

10.2.5.2.4 *CSC Integration and Test Schedules.* This subparagraph shall be numbered 3.2.4 and identify CSC Integration test schedules consistent with overall development plans.

10.2.5.3 *Resources Required for Informal Testing.* This paragraph shall be numbered 3.3 and divided into the following subparagraphs to identify and describe the facilities, personnel, hardware, and software required to conduct informal testing. The identification of each resource below shall include the activity and the test configuration during which the resource is required (Unit testing or CSC integration and testing).

10.2.5.3.1 *Facilities.* This subparagraph shall be numbered 3.3.1 and identify the facilities that shall be used for informal testing. If special facilities are required for certain classes of integration tests, the integration tests shall be identified. In addition, this subparagraph shall identify any classified processing or security issues and any planned transitions in facility location.

10.2.5.3.2 *Personnel.* This subparagraph shall be numbered 3.3.2 and identify, by title and number, the personnel necessary to conduct the test program described herein. A brief description of each position including skill level with regard to the particular CSCI application, facilities, hardware, and support software utilized, shall be provided. In addition, this subparagraph shall specify any requirements unique to particular positions (e.g., geographic location, security level, extended hours, etc.).

10.2.5.3.3 *Hardware.* This subparagraph shall be numbered 3.3.3 and identify the name and, if applicable, the computer hardware and interfacing equipment that shall be used for informal testing. If special computer hardware or interfacing equipment is required for certain classes of integration tests, the classes of integration tests shall be identified. In addition, this subparagraph shall identify any classified processing or security issues and any planned transitions in hardware.

10.2.5.3.4 *Interfacing/Support Software.* This subparagraph shall be numbered 3.3.4 and identify by name and, if applicable, number the interfacing and support software that shall be required for informal testing (e.g., operating systems, compilers, code auditors, dynamic path analyzers, test drivers, preprocessors, test data generators, postprocessors). In addition, this subparagraph shall identify any classified processing or security issues and any planned transitions associated with the software.

10.2.5.3.5 *Source.* This subparagraph shall be numbered 3.3.5, identify and describe the source of the required resources, and provide a plan for obtaining the resources.

The plan shall include estimates of resource utilization for all facilities, personnel, equipments, and support software and the time periods during which they are needed.

10.2.5.3.6 *Test Configuration.* This subparagraph shall be numbered 3.3.6 and describe or graphically portray the combinations of resources and their interrelationships required to conduct the informal testing described in 10.2.5.1 and 10.2.5.2.

10.2.6 *Plans for Formal Testing.* This section shall be numbered 4. and divided into the following paragraphs to describe the plans for formal CSCI testing. The description shall be oriented toward the validation of requirements specified in the SRS and IRSs. Formal testing is normally conducted on the fully integrated CSCI but may, with appropriate justification, also be conducted during CSC integration and unit testing.

10.2.6.1 *Formal Test Requirements.* This paragraph shall be numbered 4.1 and describe general requirements that apply to all formal tests of the CSCI and unique requirements that apply to selected formal tests.

For example:
"All formal tests shall include the following general test requirements:

a. CSCI size and execution time shall be measured.
b. The CSCI shall be tested using nominal, maximum, and erroneous input values.
c. The CSCI shall be tested for error detection and proper error recovery, including appropriate error messages.

Formal tests for radar tracking requirements shall include the following unique test requirements:

a. The CSCI shall be tested using simulated test data for all possible combinations of environmental conditions.
b. The CSCI shall be tested using input data taken from the environment ("live data")."

10.2.6.2 *Formal Test Responsibilities.* This paragraph shall be numbered 4.2 and identify the organizations responsible for the preparation, execution, reporting, review, audit, and control of formal tests; summarize their responsibilities in each of these areas; and describe their interrelationship to the organizations responsible for development. Reference shall be made, as applicable, to the appropriate planning documents (e.g., SCMP, SQEP, SDP).

For example:
"Organization X shall:

a. Using the test criteria in the Software Test Description, perform all the test procedures in the Software Test Procedure document.
b. Record all test results and prepare the Software Test Reports.

Organization Y shall monitor formal testing as described in the SQEP."

10.2.6.3 *Formal Test Classes.* This paragraph shall be numbered 4.3 and describe the various types or classes of formal tests that shall be executed (e.g., Timing Tests, Erroneous Input Tests, Maximum Capacity Tests).

10.2.6.4 *Formal Tests.* This paragraph shall be numbered 4.4 and divided into the following subparagraphs.

10.2.6.4.1 *Formal Test X.* This subparagraph shall be numbered 4.4.X (beginning with 4.4.1), identify Formal Test X by name and number, describe Formal Test X, and state its objectives. In addition, this subparagraph shall identify any special requirements necessary to perform Formal Test X (e.g., 48 hours of continuous facility time, Weapon Simulation, etc.).

10.2.6.5 *Formal Test Levels.* This paragraph shall be numbered 4.5 and describe the levels at which formal testing will be performed.

For example:

a. Unit level - to test critical algorithms.
b. CSC Integration and Test level - to test CSCI internal interfaces.
c. CSCI level - to validate baselined requirements of the CSCI.
d. System level - to validate CSCI external interfaces.

10.2.6.6 *Formal Test Summary.* This paragraph shall be numbered 4.6. For each formal test identified in 10.2.6.4, this paragraph shall identify the test level, test class, test method, and CSCI requirements validated by the test. Identification may be provided by referencing a formal test table. An example of a formal test table is provided in Table I.

Note: Test methods are allocated from the qualification methods specified in the SRS and IRSs: Demonstration, Test, Analysis, and Inspection.

10.2.6.7 *Formal Test Schedule(s).* This paragraph shall be numbered 4.7 and contain formal test schedule(s) consistent with overall development plans, including interdependencies among tests.

10.2.6.8 *Data Recording, Reduction, and Analysis.* This paragraph shall be numbered 4.8, identify data which must be recorded during the test, and describe how the data shall be recorded (by the CSCI, manually, or by instrumentation). This paragraph shall contain the format of the test log to be used to record all the chronological events relevant to formal testing. A sample test log is provided in Figure 1. Plans for data reduction and analysis shall also be described, as well as the format, content, and plans for the retention of raw data and data resulting from the reduction/analysis. The plans for data recording, reduction, and analysis shall be described in detail, such that the resulting information will clearly show whether the test objectives have been met.

10.2.6.9 *Formal Test Reports.* The results of all formal tests are documented in Software Test Reports (STRs). Each Software Test Report may contain the intermediate and final test results of one or more formal tests. This paragraph shall be numbered 4.9 and identify which groups of formal tests shall have their results documented in a single Software Test Report and which formal tests require a single Software Test Report for each formal test. In addition, this paragraph shall identify at what stages in the formal testing Software Test Reports are to be produced.

10.2.6.10 *Resources Required for Formal Testing.* This paragraph shall be numbered 4.10 and divided into the following subparagraphs to identify the facilities, personnel, hardware, and software required to conduct formal testing.

10.2.6.10.1 *Facilities.* This subparagraph shall be numbered 4.10.1 and identify the

TABLE I. Sample formal test table for CSCI X.

Test Name	Test Number	Test Level	Test Class	Test Method[1]	IRS/SRS Name	IRS/SRS Number	IRS/SRS Requirement Name	IRS/SRS Paragraph Number
Test A	1	Integrated CSCI 1	Erroneous input	T	SRS for CSCI 1	10741	Function A	3.4.2
Test B	2	HWCI 6 CSCI 1 integration	Erroneous input	T	IRS for interface HWCI 6	10841	Y interface	3.3.2
Test C	3	CSCI 3	Timing	T	IRS for CSCI 3	10842	Z interface	3.3.1
Test D	4	System level	Max capacity	A	SRS for CSCI 1	10741	Reliability requirement	3.6.3
Test E	5	System level	Erroneous input	I	SRS for CSCI 1	10741	System capacity data	3.5.3

[1]*Test Methods*

D - Demonstration
I - Inspection
A - Analysis
T - Test

CSCI Name ______
Test Name ______
Test Location ______
Person Completing Log ______
Witness(es) ______
Hardware Configuration ______
Software Configuration ______
Date ______

Time	Event
10:00 A.M.	Dick Z began pretest setup.
10:20 A.M.	Terminal A (serial no. XYZ) was defective and replaced with an identical terminal (serial no. YZX).
11:00 A.M.	Test data was generated by running the test data generation program (Revision B).
12:00 Noon	Break for lunch.
1:00 P.M.	Formal test X was begun with generated test data.
•	•
•	•
•	•

Figure 1. Sample test history.

facilities that shall be used for formal testing. In addition, this subparagraph shall identify any classified processing or security issues and any planned transitions in facility location.

10.2.6.10.2 *Personnel.* This subparagraph shall be numbered 4.10.2 and identify, by title and number, the personnel necessary to conduct the test program described herein. A brief description of each position including skill level with regard to the particular CSCI application, facilities, hardware, and support software utilized, shall be provided. In addition, this subparagraph shall specify any requirements unique to particular positions (e.g., geographic location, security level, extended hours, etc.).

10.2.6.10.3 *Hardware.* This subparagraph shall be numbered 4.10.3 and identify the name and, if applicable, the number of the computer hardware and interfacing equipment that shall be used for formal testing. In addition, this subparagraph shall identify any classified processing or security issues and any planned transitions in hardware.

10.2.6.10.4 *Interfacing/Support Software.* This subparagraph shall be numbered 4.10.4 and identify the name, and if applicable, the number of the interfacing and support software that shall be required for formal testing (e.g., operating systems, compilers, code auditors, dynamic path analyzers, environment simulators, preprocessors, test data generators, postprocessors). In addition, this subparagraph shall identify any classified processing or security issues and any planned transitions associated with the software.

10.2.6.10.5 *Source.* This subparagraph shall be numbered 4.10.5, identify and describe the source of the required resources, and provide a plan for obtaining the resources.

The plan shall include estimates of resource utilization for all facilities, personnel, equipments, and support software and the time periods for which they are needed.

10.2.6.10.6 *Test Configuration.* This subparagraph shall be numbered 4.10.6 and describe or graphically portray the combinations of resources and their interrelationships required to conduct the formal testing described in 10.7.

10.2.7 *Test Planning Assumptions and Constraints.* This section shall be numbered 5. and describe any assumptions that were made in test planning and any conditions that must be observed during testing to ensure valid results. Furthermore, this section shall describe any constraints imposed upon the test program by the Government (e.g., the use of software test analyzers or simulators provided to the contractor as Government furnished equipment, software, or information). In addition, this section shall identify any baselined CSCI requirements that are not tested and provide a rationale for not testing the requirements.

10.2.8 *Notes.* This section shall be numbered 6. and contain any general information that aids in understanding this document (e.g., background information, glossary). This section shall include an alphabetical listing of all acronyms, abbreviations, and their meanings as used in this document.

10.2.9 *Appendixes.* Appendixes may contain any supplemental information published separately for convenience in document maintenance (e.g., charts, classified data). Appendixes may be bound as separate documents for ease in handling. Appendixes shall be numbered sequentially in Roman numeral (I, II, etc.), and the paragraphs within each appendix shall all be numbered as multiples of 10 (e.g., Appendix I, paragraph 10.1, 10.2, Appendix II, paragraph 20.1, 20.2, etc.).

As applicable, each appendix shall be referenced in the main body of the document where the data would normally have been provided.

1. TITLE

SOFTWARE TEST DESCRIPTION

2. IDENTIFICATION NUMBER

DI-MCCR-80015

3. DESCRIPTION/PURPOSE

3.1 The Software Test Description (STD) identifies the input data, expected output data, and evaluation criteria that comprise the test cases for all of the formal tests of a Computer Software Configuration Item (CSCI).

3.2 The STD enables the Government to assess the adequacy of test case descriptions for formal CSCI testing.

3.3 The STP is used by the contractor as the basis for development of test procedures for formal CSCI testing.

4. APPROVAL DATE (YYMMDD)

No entry.

5. OFFICE OF PRIMARY RESPONSIBILITY (OPR)

NM

6a. DTIC REQUIRED

No entry.

6b. GIDEP REQUIRED

No entry.

7. APPLICATION/INTERRELATIONSHIP

7.1 This Data Item Description (DID) contains the format and content preparation instructions for that data generated under work tasks described by 5.3.1.14 and 5.3.2.8 of DOD-STD-2167.

7.2 The Government's Data Manager for this system must specify in the Statement of Work and Contract Data Requirements List whether this document is to be prepared and delivered on bound 8 1/2 by 11 inch bond paper or electronic media. If electronic media is selected, the precise format must be specified (e.g., magnetic tape, floppy disk, host system, etc.).

7.3 The STD documents the input data, expected output data, and evaluation criteria for each formal test identified in the Software Test Plan, DI-MCCR-80014.

7.4 This DID supersedes DI-T-2143A.

8. APPROVAL LIMITATION

No entry.

9a. APPLICABLE FORMS

No entry.

9b. AMSC NUMBER

No entry.

10. PREPARATION INSTRUCTIONS

10.1 *Source Document.* The applicable issue of the documents cited herein, including their approval date and dates of any applicable amendments and revisions shall be as reflected in the contract.

10.2 *Content and Format Instructions.* This document shall be prepared on bound 8 1/2 by 11 inch bond paper (hardcopy) or a form of electronic media. The contract will specify the precise format. Each page prior to Section 1 shall be numbered in lower-case roman numeral beginning with page ii for the Table of Contents. Each page starting from Section 1 to the end of the document shall be consecutively numbered in arabic numerals. For hardcopy formats, this document may be printed on one or both sides of each page (single-sided/double-sided). For single-sided documents, all pages shall contain the document control number in the top right-hand corner. For double-sided documents, all even-numbered pages shall be on the left-hand side of the document and odd-numbered pages on the right-hand side. For double-sided documents, the control number shall be placed in the top right-hand corner for each odd-numbered page and the top left-hand corner for each even-numbered page. All paragraph and subparagraph headings listed below shall be included in the document. All paragraphs and subparagraphs starting with the phrase "This (sub)paragraph shall . . . " may be written as multiple (sub)paragraphs to enhance readability. The letters "X" and "Y" serve as identifiers for a series of descriptions. "X" is used to identify a series of paragraphs describing formal tests. "Y" is used to identify a series of subparagraphs describing test cases for each formal test. For example, the paragraphs in Section 3 shall be structured as follows (see 10.2.5.1):

> 3.1 Title of the first formal test.
>
> 3.1.1 Title of the first test case of the first formal test.
>
> 3.1.2 Title of the second test case.
>
> 3.2 Title of the second formal test.

This paragraph format is used until all test cases for all formal tests are described.

This document shall be as self-contained as possible. Reference to other documents should be minimal. This document shall consist of the following:

a. Cover Page
b. Table of Contents
c. Scope
d. Referenced Documents
e. Formal Test Descriptions
f. Assumptions and Constraints
g. Notes
h. Appendixes

10.2.1 *Cover Page.* This page shall contain the document control number in the upper right hand corner. In the center of the page, these words shall appear in the following format:

SOFTWARE TEST DESCRIPTION
FOR THE
[PROJECT NAME]

CONTRACT NO. [contract number]
CDRL SEQUENCE NO. [CDRL number]
[Date of document - day month year]

Prepared for:
[Contracting Agency Name, department code]

Prepared by:
[contractor name and address]

10.2.2 *Table of Contents.* This document shall contain a Table of Contents listing the title and page number of all titled paragraphs and subparagraphs. The Table of Contents shall then list the title and page number of all figures, tables, and appendixes, in that order.

10.2.3 *Scope.* This section shall be numbered 1. and divided into the following paragraphs.

10.2.3.1 *Identification.* This paragraph shall be numbered 1.1 and contain the approved identification number, title, and if applicable, abbreviation of the CSCI and the system to which this STD applies. This paragraph shall begin with the following sentence: "This Software Test Description describes the input data, expected output data, and evaluation criteria for the formal testing of the CSCI identified as (insert title, if applicable insert abbreviation in parenthesis, insert CSCI number) of the (insert title, if applicable insert abbreviation in parenthesis, insert system identification number) System."

10.2.3.2 *Purpose.* This paragraph shall be numbered 1.2, state the purpose of the system, and identify the function(s) of the CSCI to which this STD applies.

10.2.3.3 *Introduction.* This paragraph shall be numbered 1.3 and summarize the purpose and contents of this document.

10.2.4 *Referenced Documents.* This section shall be numbered 2. and list by document number and title all documents referenced in this document. This section shall also identify the source for all documents not available through normal Government stocking activities.

10.2.5 *Formal Test Descriptions.* This section shall be numbered 3. and divided into the following paragraphs and subparagraphs to provide the requirements for initialization, input data, intermediate results, output data, and evaluation criteria for each formal test in the STP.

10.2.5.1 *Formal Test X.* This paragraph shall be numbered 3.X (beginning with 3.1), identify Formal Test X by name and number, and briefly describe its objectives. For each test case for Formal Test X, the following subparagraphs shall be provided.

10.2.5.1.1 *Test Case Y for Formal Test X.* This subparagraph shall be numbered 3.X.Y (beginning with 3.1.1) and divided into the following subparagraphs.

10.2.5.1.1.1 *Initialization.* This subparagraph shall be numbered 3.X.Y.1 (beginning with 3.1.1.1) and identify any prerequisite conditions that must be established or set prior to running Test Case Y for Formal Test X. When applicable, the following considerations shall be discussed:

a. Any flags, initial breakpoints, pointers, control parameters, or initial data identified in the Software Detailed Design Document to be set/reset prior to test commencement.
b. Any preset hardware conditions or electrical states necessary to run Test Case Y for Formal Test X.
c. The mechanism and initial conditions to be used in making any timing measurements.
d. Any conditioning of the simulated environment shall be described.
e. Any constraints or other special instructions peculiar to Formal Test X and not discussed in 10.2.6.

10.2.5.1.1.2 *Input Data.* This subparagraph shall be numbered 3.X.Y.2 (beginning with 3.1.1.2) and describe the input data necessary for Test Case Y of Formal Test X. For all input data, the following information shall be provided:

a. The name, purpose, range of values, and accuracy required of the input data.
b. The source of the input data and method to be used for selecting the input data.
c. Whether the input data is real or simulated.
d. The time or event sequence of the input data (e.g., in response to question Y, 4.375 will be input).

10.2.5.1.1.3 *Intermediate Test Results.* This subparagraph shall be numbered 3.X.Y.3 (beginning with 3.1.1.3) and identify any data or measurements to be taken during the running of Test Case Y for Formal Test X which, while not the result the test case was designed to produce, will be useful in evaluating those results (e.g., intermediate results in a complex algorithm). For each intermediate test result, the following shall be provided:

a. The purpose of recording the intermediate test result.
b. The conditions under which the intermediate test result is to be extracted (e.g., after a particular decision branch is chosen, every third time a routine is executed).

10.2.5.1.1.4 *Output Data.* This subparagraph shall be numbered 3.X.Y.4 (beginning with 3.1.1.4) and identify all predicted or expected test results for Formal Test X. Values shall be predicted for both intermediate and final test results if applicable.

10.2.5.1.1.5 *Criteria for Evaluating Results.* This subparagraph shall be numbered 3.X.Y.5 (beginning with 3.1.1.5) and identify the criteria for evaluating the intermediate and final results of Formal Test X. For each test result, the following information shall be provided, as applicable:

a. The accuracy requirements for the test result (e.g., ± .0005).
b. The CSCI or system capacity which establishes the upper bounds of the test result (e.g., timing stress test limit)
c. The duration of the test, in terms of time or number of events, in order to obtain the test result.

d. The conditions under which the test results are inconclusive and re-testing is to be performed.

e. The definition of any processing errors associated with the test result (e.g., "Input value is out of bounds").

f. Test results that signify success (e.g., acceptable error rates, acceptable confidence level).

g. Any additional criteria not mentioned above.

10.2.6 *Assumptions and Constraints.* This section shall be numbered 4. and identify any assumptions made and constraints to be imposed on the tests described in this document. If waivers or exceptions to specified limits and parameters are approved, they shall be addressed in the context of effects or impacts upon the tests involved. In addition, this section shall provide the rationale for any formal tests for which the input data or expected output data are not described in this document.

10.2.7 *Notes.* This section shall be numbered 6. and contain any general information that aids in understanding this document (e.g., background information, glossary). This section shall include an alphabetical listing of all acronyms, abbreviations, and their meanings as used in this document.

10.2.8 *Appendixes.* Appendixes may contain any supplemental information published separately for convenience in document maintenance (e.g., charts, classified data). Appendixes may be bound as separate documents for ease in handling. Appendixes shall be numbered sequentially in Roman numeral (I, II, etc.), and the paragraphs within each appendix shall all be numbered as multiples of 10 (e.g., Appendix I, paragraph 10.1, 10.2, Appendix II, paragraph 20.1, 20.2, etc.).

As applicable, each appendix shall be referenced in the main body of the document where the data would normally have been provided.

1. TITLE

SOFTWARE TEST PROCEDURE

2. IDENTIFICATION NUMBER

DI-MCCR-80016

3. DESCRIPTION/PURPOSE

3.1 The Software Test Procedure (STPR) describes detailed procedures for the performance of formal tests on a Computer Software Configuration Item (CSCI). In addition, the STPR describes detailed procedures for the reduction and analysis of CSCI formal test data.

3.2 The STPR assists the Government in evaluating and preparing CSCI testing. The Government observes the execution of the procedures described in this document.

3.3 The STPR is used by the contractor as the basis for the execution of formal CSCI tests.

4. APPROVAL DATE (YYMMDD)

850604

5. OFFICE OF PRIMARY RESPONSIBILITY (OPR)

EC

6a. DTIC REQUIRED

No entry.

6b. GIDEP REQUIRED

No entry.

7. APPLICATION/INTERRELATIONSHIP

7.1 This Data Item Description (DID) contains the format and content preparation instructions for that data generated under work tasks described by 5.4.1.12 and 5.4.2.6 of DOD-STD-2167.

7.2 The Government's Data Manager for this system must specify in the Statement of Work and Contract Data Requirements List whether this document is to be prepared and delivered on bound 8 1/2 by 11 inch bond paper or electronic media. If electronic media is selected, the precise format must be specified (e.g., magnetic tape, floppy disk, host system, etc.).

7.3 The STPR provides the step-by-step procedures for executing each formal test identified in the Software Test Plan (STP), DI-MCCR-80014, and described in the Software Test Description (STD), DI-MCCR-80015.

7.4 The STPR, in conjunction with the Software Test Report (STR), DI-MCCR-80017, documents the performance of the formal tests of the CSCI.

7.5 This DID supersedes DI-T-2144A, DI-T-25852, and DI-T-30716.

8. APPROVAL LIMITATION

No entry.

9a. APPLICABLE FORMS

No entry.

9b. AMSC NUMBER

N3592

10. PREPARATION INSTRUCTIONS

10.1 *Source Document.* The applicable issue of the documents cited herein, including their approval date and dates of any applicable amendments and revisions, shall be as reflected in the contract.

10.2 *Content and Format Instructions.* This document shall be prepared on bound 8 1/2 by 11 inch bond paper (hardcopy) or a form of electronic media. The contract will specify the precise format. Each page prior to Section 1 shall be numbered in lowercase roman numeral beginning with page ii for the Table of Contents. Each page starting from Section 1 to the end of the document shall be consecutively numbered in arabic numerals. For hardcopy formats, this document may be printed on one or both sides of each page (single-sided/double-sided). For single-sided documents, all pages shall contain the document control number in the top right-hand corner. For double-sided documents, all even-numbered pages shall be on the left-hand side of the document and odd-numbered pages on the right-hand side. For double-sided documents, the control number shall be placed in the top right-hand corner for each odd-numbered page and the top left-hand corner for each even-numbered page. All paragraph and subparagraph headings listed below shall be included in the document. All paragraphs and subparagraphs starting with the phrase "This (sub)paragraph shall . . . " may be written as multiple (sub)paragraphs to enhance readability. The letter "X" serves as an identifier for a series of descriptions. For example, the subparagraphs describing formal test procedures are designated as 3.3.X; if there is more than one test with procedures, the first subparagraph is numbered 3.3.1 Formal Test (Name) Test Procedures, the second is 3.3.2 Formal Test (Name) Test Procedures, etc. (see 10.2.5.3.1). This document shall be as self-contained as possible. Reference to other documents should be minimal. This document shall consist of the following:

a. Cover Page
b. Table of Contents
c. Scope
d. Referenced Documents
e. Test Schedule and Procedures
f. Assumptions and Constraints
g. Notes
h. Appendixes

10.2.1 *Cover Page.* This page shall contain the document control number in the upper right hand corner. In the center of the page, these words shall appear in the following format:

SOFTWARE TEST PROCEDURE
FOR THE
[PROJECT NAME]

CONTRACT NO. [contract number]
CDRL SEQUENCE NO. [CDRL number]
[Date of document - day month year]

Prepared for:
[Contracting Agency Name, department code]

Prepared by:
[contractor name and address]

10.2.2 *Table of Contents.* This document shall contain a Table of Contents listing the title and page number of all titled paragraphs and subparagraphs. The Table of Contents shall then list the title and page number of all figures, tables, and appendixes, in that order.

10.2.3 *Scope.* This section shall be numbered 1. and divided into the following paragraphs.

10.2.3.1 *Identification.* This paragraph shall be numbered 1.1 and contain the approved identification number, title, and if applicable, abbreviation of the CSCI and the system to which this STPR applies. This paragraph shall begin with the following sentence: "This Software Test Procedure describes the procedures for formal testing of the CSCI identified as (insert title, if applicable insert abbreviation in parenthesis, insert CSCI number) of the (insert title, if applicable insert abbreviation in parenthesis, insert system identification number) System."

10.2.3.2 *Purpose.* This paragraph shall be numbered 1.2, state the purpose of the system, and identify the functions of the CSCI to which this STPR applies.

10.2.3.3 *Introduction.* This paragraph shall be numbered 1.3 and summarize the purpose and contents of this document.

10.2.4 *Referenced Documents.* This section shall be numbered 2. and list by document number and title all documents referenced in this document. This section shall also identify the source for all documents not available through normal Government stocking activities.

10.2.5 *Test Schedule and Procedures.* This section shall be numbered 3. and divided into the following paragraphs and subparagraphs to provide the schedule and procedures for performing each formal test identified in the STP and STD.

10.2.5.1 *Schedule.* This paragraph shall be numbered 3.1 and provide the location and schedule for the following activities, if applicable:

a. Briefings
b. Pre-test activities (e.g., set-up, calibration, test data generation)
c. Formal tests
d. Debriefings
e. Data reduction and analysis

10.2.5.2 *Pre-test Procedures.* This paragraph shall be numbered 3.2 and divided into the following subparagraphs to provide the details for preparation and setup prior to formal testing.

10.2.5.2.1 *Equipment Preparation.* This subparagraph shall be numbered 3.2.1 and describe the procedures necessary to prepare the equipment for formal testing. When applicable, the following information shall be provided for each procedure:

a. When the procedure is to be followed (e.g., prior to all formal testing, prior to Formal Tests X and Y, etc.).

b. The specific equipment to be used. This equipment shall be identified by name and, if applicable, number.

c. Any switch settings and cabling necessary to connect the equipment. These shall be identified by name and location.

d. An optional block diagram to show equipment, interconnecting control, and data paths. An example of a block diagram is provided in Figure 1.

e. All of the individual steps necessary to apply power and place the equipment in a state of readiness.

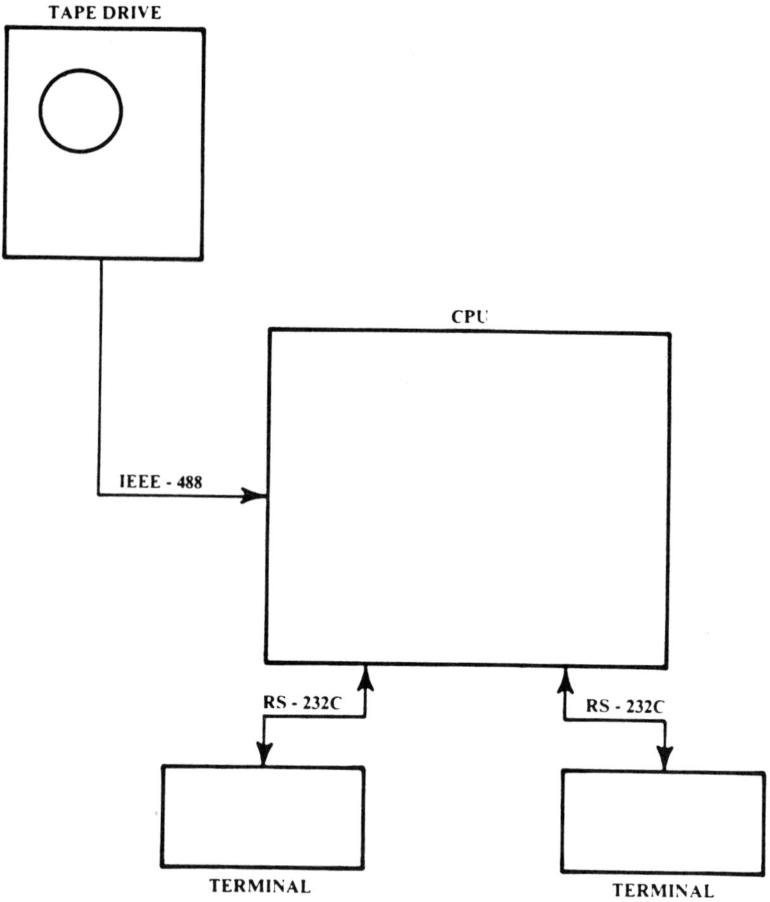

Figure 1. Sample block diagram.

When the procedures are lengthy or involved, reference may be made to the appropriate published operating manuals.

10.2.5.2.2 *Software Preparation.* This subparagraph shall be numbered 3.2.2 and provide the following information for the CSCI and support software required for formal testing:

a. The storage medium of the CSCI (e.g., magnetic tape, punch cards) and precise step-by-step instructions for loading the CSCI into the computer.
b. The storage medium of any support software (e.g., environment simulator, test drivers, data reduction programs) and precise step-by-step instructions for loading the support software. In addition, this paragraph shall identify when the support software shall be loaded (e.g., before the CSCI has been loaded, after Formal Test X has been executed, etc.).
c. The instructions for program initialization and setting of control parameters and initial data which are not unique to a particular formal test (for the CSCI or support software).

10.2.5.3 *Test Procedures.* This paragraph shall be numbered 3.3 and divided into the following subparagraphs to provide the test procedures for each formal test.

10.2.5.3.1 *Formal Test X Test Procedures.* This subparagraph shall be numbered 3.3.X (beginning with 3.3.1) and identify Formal Test X by name and number. In addition, this paragraph shall reference a Formal Test X test data sheet for each test case to define each step in the test procedure. Table I is an example of a test data sheet. For convenience in document maintenance, test data sheets may be included as an appendix.

The following rules shall apply to each test procedure:

a. If the test procedure covers several states or modes of operation, each state or mode of operation shall be described as a separate test case.
b. The test procedure shall be defined by a series of individual numbered steps, listed sequentially in the order in which the steps must be performed (see Table I, column 1).
c. The actions required by the test operator(s) and equipment required for each step shall be explicitly described (see Table I, column 2).
d. The expected result shall be identified for each step (see Table I, column 3).
e. If applicable, the evaluation criteria for each step shall be described (see Table I, column 5).
f. In the event of a program stop or indicated error, the correct actions to follow shall be described (see Table I, column 6).

10.2.5.4 *Data Reduction and Data Analysis Procedures.* This paragraph shall be numbered 3.4. For each Formal Test X requiring data reduction or data analysis, the procedure shall be described in a subparagraph below.

10.2.5.4.1 *Formal Test X Data Reduction/Data Analysis Procedure.* This paragraph shall be numbered 3.4.X (beginning with 3.4.1) and identify Formal Test X by name and number. In addition this paragraph shall identify and describe or reference, if lengthy, the procedures to be employed in reducing and analyzing Formal Text X data.

TABLE I. Sample formal test X data sheet.

Step	Operator/Equipment Action	Expected Results	Observed Results	Evaluation Criteria	Incorrect Result/Program Stop Action
1	Enter 'run' from terminal	'Enter number of targets' on terminal screen		Exact	If expected result does not occur cease all further testing.
2	Enter number 1 from terminal	'Enter X coordinate for target 1'		Exact	If expected result does not occur cease all further testing.
3	Enter 'A27.35' from terminal	'Erroneous X coordinate for target 1. Please reenter'		Exact	1. If result is 'enter Y coordinate for target 1' record error and proceed at step 5. 2. Cease all further testing if any other results. 3. If program stop occurs begin test again at step 1.
4	Enter number 27.35	'Enter Y coordinate for target 1'		Exact	If expected result does not occur cease all other testing.
5	Enter number 32.44	'Data base updated'		Exact	If expected result does not occur cease all other testing.
6	Enter 'range' from terminal	'Range = 42.43'		Within ±.01	If result fails to meet evaluation criteria enter in test log discrepency
	⋮	⋮	⋮	⋮	⋮

If support software is to be used to perform the data reduction or data analysis, procedures for initiating, executing, terminating, and restarting the software shall be included. (Reference may be made to a software manual in lieu of describing the support software procedures.)

10.2.6 *Assumptions and Constraints.* This section shall be numbered 4., identify any assumptions or constraints imposed on the test procedures, and define their impact on the formal tests. In addition, this section shall identify any formal tests for which test procedures are not described in this document and provide a rationale for the non-inclusion of these test procedures in this document (e.g., test requires classified data and is described in a separate document, or convenience of handling).

10.2.7 *Notes.* This section shall be numbered 6. and contain any general information that aids in understanding this document (e.g., background information, glossary). This section shall include an alphabetical listing of all acronyms, abbreviations, and their meanings as used in this document.

10.2.8 *Appendixes.* Appendixes may contain any supplemental information published separately for convenience in document maintenance (e.g., charts, classified data). Appendixes may be bound as separate documents for ease in handling. Appendixes shall be numbered sequentially in Roman numeral (I, II, etc.), and the paragraphs within each appendix shall all be numbered as multiples of 10 (e.g., Appendix I, paragraph 10.1, 10.2, Appendix II, Paragraph 20.1, 20.2 etc.).

As applicable, each appendix shall be referenced in the main body of the document where the data would normally have been provided.

1. TITLE

SOFTWARE TEST REPORT

2. IDENTIFICATION NUMBER

DI-MCCR-80017

3. DESCRIPTION/PURPOSE

3.1 The Software Test Report (STR) is a record of the formal testing performed for a particular Computer Software Configuration Item (CSCI). The STR consists of: (1) a summary of tests, (2) a test log which provides a history of the formal tests, (3) a test data sheet which provides formal test results, (4) a summary of the analysis and evaluation of test results, and (5) recommendations.

3.2 The STR provides the Government with a permanent record of the formal testing performed on a CSCI, to be used in the evaluation of changes to the CSCI.

3.3 The STR may be used by the contractor as a basis for re-test of a CSCI.

4. APPROVAL DATE (YYMMDD)

No entry.

5. OFFICE OF PRIMARY RESPONSIBILITY (OPR)

NM

6a. DTIC REQUIRED

No entry.

6b. GIDEP REQUIRED

No entry.

7. APPLICATION/INTERRELATIONSHIP

7.1 This Data Item Description (DID) contains the format and content preparation instructions for that data generated under work tasks described by 5.6.1.3 and 5.6.2.3 of DOD-STD-2167.

7.2 The Government's Data Manager for this system must specify in the Statement of Work and Contract Data Requirements List whether this document is to be prepared and delivered on bound 8 1/2 by 11 inch bond paper or electronic media. If electronic media is selected, the precise format must be specified (e.g., magnetic tape, floppy disk, host system, etc.).

7.3 The STR is used to record the actual results of one or more formal tests, as defined in the Software Test Plan (STP), DI-MCCR-80014, for a CSCI.

7.4 The STR includes the completed test data sheets provided in preliminary form in the Software Test Procedure (STPR), DI-MCCR-80016.

7.5 The STR is used to summarize any test discrepancies and to make reference to their documentation in software problem/change reports, as detailed in the Software Development Plan (SDP), DI-MCCR-80030, Software Configuration Management Plan (SCMP), DI-MCCR-80009, or System Configuration Management Plan.

7.6 This DID supersedes DI-T-2156A, DI-T-25852, and DI-T-3717A.

8. APPROVAL LIMITATION

No entry.

9a. APPLICABLE FORMS

No entry.

9b. AMSC NUMBER

No entry.

10. PREPARATION INSTRUCTIONS

10.1 *Source Document.* The applicable issue of the documents cited herein, including their approval date and dates of any applicable amendments and revisions, shall be as reflected in the contract.

10.2 *Content and Format Instructions.* This document shall be prepared on bound 8 1/2 by 11 inch bond paper (hardcopy) or a form of electronic media. The contract will specify the precise format. Each page prior to Section 1 shall be numbered in lowercase roman numeral beginning with page ii for the Table of Contents. Each page starting from Section 1 to the end of the document shall be consecutively numbered in arabic numerals. For hardcopy formats, this document may be printed on one or both sides of each page (single-sided/double-sided). For single-sided documents, all pages shall contain the document control number in the top right-hand corner. For double-sided documents, all even-numbered pages shall be on the left-hand side of the document and odd-numbered pages on the right-hand side. For double-sided documents, the control number shall be placed in the top right-hand corner for each odd-numbered page and the top left-hand corner for each even-numbered page. All paragraph and subparagraph headings listed below shall be included in the document. All paragraphs and subparagraphs starting with the phrase "This (sub)paragraph shall . . . " may be written as multiple (sub)paragraphs to enhance readability. The letter "X" serves as an identifier for a series of descriptions. For example, the subparagraphs describing formal test results are designated as 3.3.X; if there is more than one test with results, the first subparagraph is numbered 3.3.1 Formal Test (Name) Results, the second is 3.3.2 Formal Test (Name) Results, etc. (see 10.2.5.3.1). This document shall be as self-contained as possible. Reference to other documents should be minimal. This document shall consist of the following:

a. Cover Page
b. Table of Contents
c. Scope
d. Referenced Documents
e. Test Report
f. Deviations
g. Notes
h. Appendixes

10.2.1 *Cover Page.* This page shall contain the document control number in the upper right hand corner. In the center of the page, these words shall appear in the following format:

SOFTWARE TEST REPORT
FOR THE
[PROJECT NAME]

CONTRACT NO. [contract number]
CDRL SEQUENCE NO. [CDRL number]
[Date of document - day month year]

Prepared for:
[Contracting Agency Name, department code]

Prepared by:
[contractor name and address]

10.2.2 *Table of Contents.* This document shall contain a Table of Contents listing the title and page number of all titled paragraphs and subparagraphs. The Table of Contents shall then list the title and page number of all figures, tables, and appendixes, in that order.

10.2.3 *Scope.* This section shall be numbered 1. and divided into the following paragraphs.

10.2.3.1 *Identification.* This paragraph shall be numbered 1.1 and contain the approved identification number, title, and if applicable, abbreviation of the CSCI and the system to which this STR applies. In addition, this paragraph shall contain the name and number of all formal tests for which the results are recorded herein. This paragraph shall begin with the following sentence: "This Software Test Report contains the test history and test results of the formal test(s) identified as (insert formal test name, insert formal test number) for the CSCI identified as (insert title, if applicable insert abbreviation in parenthesis, insert CSCI number) of the (insert title, if applicable insert abbreviation in parenthesis, insert system identification number) System."

10.2.3.2 *Purpose.* This paragraph shall be numbered 1.2, state the purpose of the system, and identify the functions of the CSCI to which this STR applies.

10.2.3.3 *Introduction.* This paragraph shall be numbered 1.3 and summarize the purpose and contents of this document.

10.2.4 *Referenced Documents.* This section shall be numbered 2. and list by document number and title all documents referenced in this report. This section shall also identify the source for all documents not available through normal Government stocking activities.

10.2.5 *Test Report.* This section shall be numbered 3. and divided into the following paragraphs and subparagraphs.

10.2.5.1 *Summary of Tests.* This paragraph shall be numbered 3.1 and summarize the results of tests recorded by this document. The summary shall include the completion status of each test (i.e., success or failure). For failures, the step of the test procedure

TABLE I. Sample summary test results table.

Test	Success	Failure[1]	Software Problem Report Submitted	Remarks
Formal Test X	X			
Formal Test Y		Step 5	STR-011[2]	Not critical
Formal Test Z		Step 7 Step 29	STR-086	Needs immediate attention
•	•	•	•	•
•	•	•	•	•
•	•	•	•	•

[1]If a formal test produces a failure, the step(s) during which the failure occurred shall be recorded.

[2]STR = Software trouble report

which produced the failure and an identification of the problem report shall be submitted. This information may be provided by reference to a summary test results table. An example of a summary test results table is provided in Table I.

10.2.5.2 *Test History.* This paragraph shall be numbered 3.2 and present a summary of all events relevant to test preparation, test performance, and analysis and interpretation of formal test results recorded by this document. This paragraph shall reference a test log, which contains a chronological record of the actual conduct of a formal test, including the following information:

a. The date(s), time(s) and location(s) of the tests, as well as actual hardware and software configurations utilized for the tests. The description of the test configuration shall include, when available, part number, model number, serial number, manufacturer, revision level, and calibration date of all hardware; and version number and name for the software components utilized.
b. The occurrence date and time, the identity of the individual(s) who performed each test-related activity, and the identities of any witnesses.
c. Any problems encountered and the specific step(s) of the test procedures associated with the problem, including the number of times an individual step in a procedure had to be repeated in attempting to correct a problem and the outcome of each attempt.
d. Back-up points or test steps where tests were resumed for retesting.

An example of a test log is provided in Figure 1.

10.2.5.3 *Test Results.* This paragraph shall be numbered 3.3 and divided into the following subparagraphs to describe the results for each formal test.

10.2.5.3.1 *Formal Test X Results.* This subparagraph shall be numbered 3.3.X (beginning with 3.3.1) and present all the test results for Formal Test X. For each step of the test procedure, the actual result shall be recorded. The completed test data sheets from

CSCI Name ____________________
Test Name ____________________
Test Location ____________________
Person Completing Log ____________________
Witness(es) ____________________
Hardware Configuration ____________________
Software Configuration ____________________
Date ____________________

Time	Event
10:00 A.M.	Dick Z began pretest setup.
10:20 A.M.	Terminal A (serial no. XYZ) was defective and replaced with an identical terminal (serial no. YZX).
11:00 A.M.	Test data was generated by running the test data generation program (Revision B).
12:00 Noon	Break for lunch.
1:00 P.M.	Formal test X was begun with generated test data.
•	•
•	•
•	•

Figure 1. Sample test history.

the STPR shall be used (see Table II), included as an appendix, and referenced herein. Any anomalies, deviant results, changes in procedures, or discrepancies of any kind between execution of the formal test and the test plans, test description, and test procedures shall be described in this subparagraph. Amplifying information (e.g., memory dumps, record of registers, display diagrams) which may help to isolate and correct the cause of any discrepancies shall be included or referenced. In addition, the opinions of the test conductor as to the cause and means of correcting any discrepancies may be included.

10.2.5.4 *Test Result Evaluation and Recommendations.* This paragraph shall be numbered 3.4 and divided into the following subparagraphs.

10.2.5.4.1 *Test Result Evaluation.* This subparagraph shall be numbered 3.4.1 and provide an overall analysis of the capabilities of the CSCI demonstrated by the test results reported in this document. The analysis shall include any deficiencies, limitations, or constraints inherent in the CSCI which were detected by the testing performed. For each deficiency the analysis shall: (1) describe the impact on CSCI and system performance if the deficiency is not corrected, (2) describe the impact on the CSCI and system design to correct the deficiency, and (3) provide a recommended solution/approach. If software problem/change reports are utilized to provide deficiency information, they shall be included as an appendix and referenced herein.

10.2.5.4.2 *Recommendations.* This subparagraph shall be numbered 3.4.2 and recommend improvements that can be realized in the design, operation, or testing of the CSCI which were determined during the testing. Accompanying each recommendation

TABLE I. Sample formal test X test data sheet.

Step	Operator/Equipment Action	Expected Results	Observed Results	Evaluation Criteria	Incorrect Result/Program Stop Action
1	Enter 'run' from terminal	'Enter number of targets' on terminal screen		Exact	If expected result does not occur cease all further testing.
2	Enter number 1 from terminal	'Enter X coordinate for target 1'		Exact	If expected result does not occur cease all further testing.
3	Enter 'A27.35' from terminal	'Erroneous X coordinate for target 1. Please reenter'		Exact	1. If result is 'enter Y coordinate for target 1' record error and proceed at step 5. 2. Cease all further testing if any other results. 3. If program stop occurs begin test again at step 1.
4	Enter number 27.35	'Enter Y coordinate for target 1'		Exact	If expected result does not occur cease all other testing.
5	Enter number 32.44	'Data base updated'		Exact	If expected result does not occur cease all other testing.
6	Enter 'range' from terminal	'Range = 42.43'		Within $\pm .01$	If result fails to meet evaluation criteria enter in test log discrepency
	⋮	⋮	⋮	⋮	⋮

shall be a discussion of the added capability it provides and the impact on the CSCI and system design.

10.2.6 *Deviations.* This section shall be numbered 4. and discuss in detail any deviations from the procedures described in the corresponding STPR (e.g., substitution of required equipment, changes to support software, procedural steps not followed, and schedule deviations). For each deviation, the rationale for allowing it and its impact on the validity of the test shall be provided. The rationale shall include the opinions of those involved in the decision process (e.g., test conductor, quality evaluator, Government witness).

10.2.7 *Notes.* This section shall be numbered 6. and contain any general information that aids in understanding this document (e.g., background information, glossary). This section shall include an alphabetical listing of all acronyms, abbreviations, and their meanings as used in this document.

10.2.8 *Appendixes.* Appendixes may contain any supplemental information published separately for convenience in document maintenance (e.g., charts, classified data). Appendixes may be bound as separate documents for ease in handling. Appendixes shall be numbered sequentially in Roman numeral (I, II, etc.), and the paragraphs within each appendix shall all be numbered as multiples of 10 (e.g., Appendix I, paragraph 10.1, 10.2, Appendix II, paragraph 20.1, 20.2, etc.).

As applicable, each appendix shall be referenced in the main body of the document where the data would normally have been provided.

1. TITLE

COMPUTER SYSTEM OPERATOR'S MANUAL

2. IDENTIFICATION NUMBER

DI-MCCR-80018

3. DESCRIPTION/PURPOSE

3.1 The Computer System Operator's Manual (CSOM) provides information and detailed procedures for initiating, operating, and monitoring a specific computer system which is a part of the overall mission-critical system. The computer system, for which this CSOM applies, is the computer system in which one or more Computer Software Configuration Items (CSCIs) execute.

3.2 A CSOM is developed for each computer system in the overall mission-critical system in which one or more CSCIs execute.

4. APPROVAL DATE (YYMMDD)

No entry.

5. OFFICE OF PRIMARY RESPONSIBILITY (OPR)

NM

6a. DTIC REQUIRED

No entry.

6b. GIDEP REQUIRED

No entry.

7. APPLICATION/INTERRELATIONSHIP

7.1 This Data Item Description (DID) contains the format and content preparation instructions for that data generated under the work tasks described by 5.2.1.7 and 5.2.2.6 of DOD-STD-2167.

7.2 The Government's Data Manager for this system must specify in the Statement of Work and Contract Data Requirements List whether this manual is to be prepared and delivered on bound 8 1/2 by 11 inch bond paper or electronic media. If electronic media is selected, the precise format must be specified (e.g., magnetic tape, floppy disk, host system, etc.).

7.3 The CSOM will not apply if the information is provided in a commercially available document.

7.4 Paragraphs in 10.2.6 may reference a diagnostics manual for describing diagnostic features of the computer system (e.g., Computer System Diagnostic Manual (CSDM) DI-MCCR-80020).

7.5 This DID supersedes DI-M-2148A.

8. APPROVAL LIMITATION

No entry.

9a. APPLICABLE FORMS

No entry.

9b. AMSC NUMBER

No entry.

10. PREPARATION INSTRUCTIONS

10.1 *Source Document.* The applicable issue of the documents cited herein, including their approval date, and dates of any applicable amendments and revisions shall be as reflected in the contract.

10.2 *Content and Format Instructions.* This manual shall be prepared on bound 8 1/2 by 11 inch bond paper (hardcopy) or a form of electronic media. The contract will specify the precise format. Each page prior to Section 1 shall be numbered in lower-case roman numeral beginning with page ii for the Table of Contents. Each page starting from Section 1 to the end of the document shall be consecutively numbered in arabic numerals. For hardcopy formats, this document may be printed on one or both sides of each page (single-sided/double-sided). For single-sided documents, all pages shall contain the document control number in the top right-hand corner. For double-sided documents, all even-numbered pages shall be on the left-hand side of the document and odd-numbered pages on the right-hand side. For double-sided documents, the control number shall be placed in the top right-hand corner for each odd-numbered page and the top left-hand corner for each even-numbered page. All paragraph and subparagraph headings listed below shall be included in the manual. All paragraphs and subparagraphs starting with the phrase "This (sub)paragraph shall . . . " may be written as multiple (sub)paragraphs to enhance readability. The CSOM shall provide operating instructions in the form of self-contained checklists. Charts, tables, and diagrams may be used in lieu of written text. This manual shall be as self-contained as possible. Reference to other documents should be minimal. This manual shall consist of the following:

a. Cover Page
b. Table of Contents
c. Scope
d. Referenced Documents
e. Computer System Operation
f. Diagnostic Features
g. Notes
h. Appendixes

10.2.1 *Cover Page.* This page shall contain the document control number in the upper right hand corner. In the center of the page, these words shall appear in the following format:

COMPUTER SYSTEM OPERATOR'S MANUAL
FOR THE
[PROJECT NAME]

CONTRACT NO. [contract number]
CDRL SEQUENCE NO. [CDRL number]
[Date of document - day month year]

Prepared for:
[Contracting Agency Name, department code]

Prepared by:
[contractor name and address]

10.2.2 *Table of Contents.* This manual shall contain a Table of Contents listing the title and page number of all titled paragraphs and subparagraphs. The Table of Contents shall then list the title and page number of all figures, tables, and appendixes, in that order.

10.2.3 *Scope.* This section shall be numbered 1. and divided into the following paragraphs.

10.2.3.1 *Identification.* This paragraph shall be numbered 1.1 and contain the approved identification number, title, and if applicable, abbreviation of the system to which this CSOM applies. This paragraph shall begin with the following sentence: "This Computer System Operator's Manual provides the procedures for operating the computer system in the (insert system title, if applicable insert abbreviation in parenthesis, insert system identification number) System."

10.2.3.2 *Purpose.* This paragraph shall be numbered 1.2, state the purpose of the system, and identify the computer system function(s) and their operational environment to which this CSOM applies.

10.2.3.3 *Introduction.* This paragraph shall be numbered 1.3 and summarize the purpose and contents of this document.

10.2.4 *Referenced Documents.* This section shall be numbered 2. and list by document number and title all documents referenced in this manual. This section shall also identify the source for all documents not available through normal Government stocking activities.

10.2.5 *Computer System Operation.* This section shall be numbered 3. and divided into the following paragraphs and subparagraphs.

10.2.5.1 *Computer System Preparation and Set Up.* This paragraph shall be numbered 3.1 and divided into the following subparagraphs to describe the procedures for computer system preparation and setup prior to computer system operation.

10.2.5.1.1 *Power On and Off.* This subparagraph shall be numbered 3.1.1 and explain the step-by-step procedures required to power-on and power-off the equipment for operational and stand-by mode.

10.2.5.1.2 *Initiation.* This subparagraph shall be numbered 3.1.2 and contain the initiation procedures that are necessary to operate the computer system. As a minimum, this subparagraph shall describe the following:

a. The equipment setup and the procedures required for pre-operation.
b. The procedures necessary to bootstrap the computer system and to load programs.
c. The commands typically used during computer system initiation (e.g., system priority organization).
d. Any procedures necessary to initialize files, variables or other parameters.

10.2.5.2 *Operating Procedures.* This paragraph shall be numbered 3.2 and describe the steps for on-going operating procedures during computer system operation (e.g., establishing priority queues, mounting tapes, etc.). If more than one mode of operation is available, instructions for the selection of each mode shall be provided. This paragraph shall contain sufficient detail to identify all relevant options and to accomplish recovery from any step in error without starting over, if technically possible.

10.2.5.3 *Input and Output.* This paragraph shall be numbered 3.3, describe input and output media (e.g., magnetic tape, disk, cartridge, etc.), and explain the procedures required to read and write on these media. This paragraph shall briefly describe the operating system control language. This paragraph shall also list operator procedures for interactive messages and replies (e.g., describe password use, log on and log off procedures, and file protection requirements).

10.2.5.4 *Monitoring Procedures.* This paragraph shall be numbered 3.4 and describe the procedures for monitoring the software in operation. Applicable trouble and malfunction indications shall be included. Evaluation techniques for fault isolation shall be described to the maximum extent practical. This paragraph shall also include descriptions of conditions requiring computer system shutdown or aborting and the specific procedures for these actions. Procedures for on-line interventions, trap recovery, and operator communications shall also be included.

10.2.5.5 *Off-Line Routines.* This paragraph shall be numbered 3.5 and explain procedures required to operate all relevant off-line routines of the computer system.

10.2.5.6 *Recovery Procedures.* This paragraph shall be numbered 3.6 and explain procedures to follow for each trouble occurrence (e.g., give detailed instructions to obtain computer system dumps). This paragraph shall describe the steps to be taken by the operator to restart computer system operation after an abort or interruption of operation. Procedures for recording information concerning a malfunction shall also be included.

10.2.5.7 *Special Procedures.* This paragraph shall be numbered 3.7 and include any additional instructions required by the operator (e.g., computer system alarms, program or computer system security considerations, preparation of the computer system for a diagnostic run, switch over to a redundant computer system).

10.2.6 *Diagnostic Features.* This section shall be numbered 4. and divided into the following paragraphs.

10.2.6.1 *Error Detection and Diagnostic Features.* This paragraph shall be numbered 4.1 and briefly describe the on-line error detection and diagnostic features available to the computer system operator, including error messages. This paragraph shall include the purpose and value of each diagnostic feature.

10.2.6.2 *Computer System Diagnostic Features.* This paragraph shall be numbered 4.2 and list references to applicable publications (e.g., CSDM) and available software for performing diagnostics not available to the system operator.

10.2.7 *Notes.* This section shall be numbered 6. and contain any general information that aids in understanding this document (e.g., background information, glossary). This section shall include an alphabetical listing of all acronyms, abbreviations, and their meanings as used in this document.

10.2.8 *Appendixes.* Appendixes may contain any supplemental information published separately for convenience in document maintenance (e.g., charts, classified data). Appendixes may be bound as separate documents for ease in handling. Appendixes shall be numbered sequentially in Roman numeral (I, II, etc.), and the paragraphs within each appendix shall all be numbered as multiples of 10 (e.g., Appendix I, paragraph 10.1, 10.2, Appendix II, paragraph 20.1, 20.2, etc.).

As applicable, each appendix shall be referenced in the main body of the document where the data would normally have been provided.

1. TITLE

SOFTWARE USER'S MANUAL

2. IDENTIFICATION NUMBER

DI-MCCR-80019

3. DESCRIPTION/PURPOSE

3.1 The Software User's Manual (SUM) provides user personnel with instructions sufficient to execute the software of one or more related Computer Software Configuration Items (CSCIs).
3.2 The SUM provides the steps for executing the software, the expected output, and the corrective measures required when the expected output is not obtained.

4. APPROVAL DATE (YYMMDD)

No entry.

5. OFFICE OF PRIMARY RESPONSIBILITY (OPR)

NM

6a. DTIC REQUIRED

No entry.

6b. GIDEP REQUIRED

No entry.

7. APPLICATION/INTERRELATIONSHIP

7.1 This Data Item Description (DID) contains the format and content preparation instructions for that data generated under the work tasks described by 5.2.1.8 and 5.2.2.6 of DOD-STD-2167.

7.2 The Government's Data Manager for this system must specify in the Statement of Work and Contract Data Requirements List whether this manual is to be prepared and delivered on bound 8 1/2 by 11 inch bond paper or electronic media. If electronic media is selected, the precise format must be specified (e.g., magnetic tape, floppy disk, host system, etc.).

7.3 The SUM will not apply if the information is provided in a commercially available document.

7.4 Paragraphs in 10.2.5 may reference an operator's manual for operating instructions of the computer system (e.g., Computer System Operator's Manual (CSOM), DI-MCCR-80018).

7.5 Section 10.2.7 will be tailored out if a Computer System Diagnostic Manual (CSDM), DI-MCCR-80020, is to be required.

7.6 This DID supersedes DI-M-2145A, DI-M-25853, DI-M-3410, DI-M-30404, DI-M-30419, and DI-M-30421.

8. APPROVAL LIMITATION

No entry.

9a. APPLICABLE FORMS

No entry.

9b. AMSC NUMBER

No entry.

10. PREPARATION INSTRUCTIONS

10.1 *Source Document.* The applicable issue of the documents cited herein, including their approval date and the dates of any applicable amendments and revisions, shall be as reflected in the contract.

10.2 *Content and Format Instructions.* This manual shall be prepared on bound 8 1/2 by 11 inch bond paper (hardcopy) or a form of electronic media. The contract will specify the precise format. Each page prior to Section 1 shall be numbered in lowercase roman numeral beginning with page ii for the Table of Contents. Each page starting from Section 1 to the end of the document shall be consecutively numbered in arabic numerals. For hardcopy formats, this document may be printed on one or both sides of each page (single-sided/double-sided). For single-sided documents, all pages shall contain the document control number in the top right-hand corner. For double-sided documents, all even-numbered pages shall be on the left-hand side of the document and odd-numbered pages on the right-hand side. For double-sided documents, the control number shall be placed in the top right-hand corner for each odd-numbered page and the top left-hand corner for each even-numbered page. All paragraph and subparagraph headings listed below shall be included in the manual. All paragraphs and subparagraphs starting with the phrase "This (sub)paragraph shall . . . " may be written as multiple (sub)paragraphs to enhance readability. The letters "X" and "Y" serve as identifiers for a series of descriptions. "X" is used to identify a series of paragraphs describing a specific CSCI. "Y" is used to identify a series of subparagraphs describing functions of each CSCI "X". For example, the paragraphs in Section 3 shall be structured as follows (see 10.2.5):

3.1 Title of the first CSCI.

3.1.1 Title of the first function of CSCI 1.

3.1.2 Title of the second function of CSCI 1.

3.2 Title of the second CSCI

This paragraph format is used until all functions of each CSCI are described. This manual shall be as self-contained as possible. Reference to other documents should be minimal. This manual shall consist of the following:

a. Cover Page
b. Table of Contents
c. Scope
d. Referenced Documents
e. Instructions for Use
f. Errors
g. Diagnostic Features
h. Notes
i. Appendixes

10.2.1 *Cover Page.* This page shall contain the document control number in the upper right hand corner. In the center of the page, these words shall appear in the following format:

SOFTWARE USER'S MANUAL
FOR THE
[PROJECT NAME]

CONTRACT NO. [contract number]
CDRL SEQUENCE NO. [CDRL number]
[Date of document - day month year]

Prepared for:
[Contracting Agency Name, department code]

Prepared by:
[contractor name and address]

10.2.2 *Table of Contents.* This manual shall contain a Table of Contents listing the title and page number of all titled paragraphs and subparagraphs. The Table of Contents shall then list the title and page number of all figures, tables, and appendixes, in that order.

10.2.3 *Scope.* This section shall be numbered 1. and divided into the following paragraphs.

10.2.3.1 *Identification.* This paragraph shall be numbered 1.1 and contain the approved identification number(s), title(s), and if applicable, abbreviation(s) of the CSCI(s) and the system to which this SUM applies. This paragraph shall begin with the following sentence: "This Software User's Manual provides the procedures for executing the following CSCI(s) (insert title(s), if applicable insert abbreviation(s) in parenthesis, insert CSCI identification number(s)) for the (insert title, if applicable insert abbreviation in parenthesis, insert system identification number) System."

10.2.3.2 *Purpose.* This paragraph shall be numbered 1.2, state the purpose of the system, and identify the function(s) of the CSCI(s) to which the SUM applies.

10.2.3.3 *Introduction.* This paragraph shall be numbered 1.3 and summarize the purpose and contents of this document.

10.2.4 *Referenced Documents.* This section shall be numbered 2. and list by document number and title all documents referenced in this manual. This section shall also identify the source for all documents not available through normal Government stocking activities.

10.2.5 *Instructions for Use.* This section shall be numbered 3. and divided into the following paragraphs and subparagraphs for those CSCIs requiring user interaction.

10.2.5.1 *CSCI X.* This paragraph shall be numbered 3.X (beginning with 3.1) and divided into the following subparagraphs. This paragraph and the following subparagraphs shall be prepared for those functions specified in the Software Requirements Specification for CSCI X, requiring user interaction. The title of this paragraph shall be the title of CSCI X.

10.2.5.1.1 *Function Y.* This subparagraph shall be numbered 3.X.Y (beginning with 3.1.1) and prepared for each function performed by CSCI X requiring user interaction. Those functions which perform diagnostics shall be described in 10.2.7. This subparagraph shall identify function Y by name and number and shall describe the purpose it serves.

10.2.5.1.1.1 *Initialization.* This subparagraph shall be numbered 3.X.Y.1 (beginning with 3.1.1.1) and contain the initialization procedures for files, variables, or other parameters that are necessary in order to execute function Y.

10.2.5.1.1.2 *Execution Options.* This subparagraph shall be numbered 3.X.Y.2 (beginning with 3.1.1.2) and describe the execution options available to the user when executing function Y.

10.2.5.1.1.3 *User Inputs.* This subparagraph shall be numbered 3.X.Y.3 (beginning with 3.1.1.3) and completely describe the user inputs to function Y, including format, frequency, allowable range, and units of measure.

10.2.5.1.1.4 *System Inputs.* This subparagraph (if applicable) shall be numbered

3.X.Y.4 (beginning with 3.1.1.4) and describe the system inputs to function Y including format, frequency, allowable range, and units of measure (e.g., system inputs may be data from a remote sensor in the system).

10.2.5.1.1.5 *Execution.* This subparagraph shall be numbered 3.X.Y.5 (beginning with 3.1.1.5) and describe the step-by-step procedures for executing function Y (e.g., the format of the run command and the format of subsequent user inputs).

10.2.5.1.1.6 *Termination.* This subparagraph shall be numbered 3.X.Y.6 (beginning with 3.1.1.6) and describe the procedures for terminating function Y. Procedures for both normal and abnormal termination shall be described.

10.2.5.1.1.7 *Restart.* This subparagraph shall be numbered 3.X.Y.7 (beginning with 3.1.1.7) and describe the procedures for restarting function Y.

10.2.5.1.1.8 *Outputs.* This subparagraph shall be numbered 3.X.Y.8 (beginning with 3.1.1.8) and completely describe expected outputs of function Y, including format, frequency, allowable range, and units of measure. The procedures for evaluating the output to determine normal termination shall also be described.

10.2.5.1.1.9 *Interrelationship.* This subparagraph shall be numbered 3.X.Y.9 (beginning with 3.1.1.9) and describe the relationship of function Y to the other functions of the CSCI.

10.2.6 *Errors.* This section shall be numbered 4. and divided into the following paragraphs.

10.2.6.1 *Error Messages for (CSCI X title).* This paragraph shall be numbered 4.X (beginning with 4.1) and describe all error messages output by CSCI X and identify the applicable function(s) to which each error message applies. A description of each error and corrective action shall be included.

10.2.7 *Diagnostic Features.* This section shall be numbered 5. If a CSDM is not required, this section shall describe the diagnostic features of all CSCIs to which this SUM applies. If all the functions of the CSCI perform diagnostics, a paragraph structure similar to 10.2.5 shall be used to identify and describe each applicable CSCI and its associated functions. If some of the functions of the CSCI perform diagnostics, only those diagnostic functions shall be identified and described, using a paragraph structure similar to 10.2.5.

10.2.8 *Notes.* This section shall be numbered 6. and contain any general information that aids in understanding this document (e.g., background information, glossary). This section shall include an alphabetical listing of all acronyms, abbreviations, and their meanings used in this document.

10.2.9 *Appendixes.* Appendixes may contain any supplemental information published separately for convenience in document maintenance (e.g., charts, classified data). Appendixes may be bound as separate documents for ease in handling. Appendixes shall be numbered sequentially in Roman numeral (I, II, etc.), and the paragraphs within each appendix shall all be numbered as multiples of 10 (e.g., Appendix I, paragraph 10.1, 10.2, Appendix II, paragraph 20.1, 20.2, etc.).

As applicable, each appendix shall be referenced in the main body of the document where the data would normally have been provided.

1. TITLE

SOFTWARE REQUIREMENTS SPECIFICATION

2. IDENTIFICATION NUMBER

DI-MCCR-80025

3. DESCRIPTION/PURPOSE

3.1 The Software Requirements Specification (SRS) specifies in detail the complete requirements (functional, interface, performance, qualification, etc.) of a particular Computer Software Configuration Item (CSCI). The SRS includes requirements for programming design, adaptation, quality factors, and traceability of the CSCI.

3.2 The SRS specifies the requirements allocated to a CSCI and enables the Government to assess whether or not the completed CSCI complies with those requirements. Upon Government approval and authentication, the SRS becomes the Allocated Baseline for the CSCI.

3.3 The SRS is used by the contractor as the basis for development and formal testing of the CSCI.

4. APPROVAL DATE (YYMMDD)

850604

5. OFFICE OF PRIMARY RESPONSIBILITY (OPR)

EC

6a. DTIC REQUIRED

No entry.

6b. GIDEP REQUIRED

No entry.

7. APPLICATION/INTERRELATIONSHIP

7.1 This Data Item Description (DID) contains the format and content preparation instructions for that data generated under the work tasks described by 3.4.2 and 3.4.7.1

of MIL-STD-483, 3.1.3.2.5.1 of MIL-STD-490, and 5.1.1.6 and 5.1.2.4 of DOD-STD-2167.

7.2 The Government's Data Manager for this system must specify in the Statement of Work and Contract Data Requirements List whether this specification is to be prepared and delivered on bound 8 1/2 by 11 inch bond paper or electronic media. If electronic media is selected, the precise format must be specified (e.g., magnetic tape, floppy disk, host system, etc.).

7.3 The SRS is used to provide the detailed requirements for each CSCI specified in the System/Segment Specification (SSS), DI-CMAN-80008, Prime Item Development Specification (PIDS) or Critical Item Development Specification (CIDS), DI-E-3102A.

7.4 Paragraph 10.2.5.3 may reference one or more Interface Requirements Specifications (IRSs), DI-MCCR-80026, to identify all the external interfaces of the CSCI. Referenced IRSs become part of the Allocated Baseline for the CSCI.

7.5 This DID supersedes DI-E-2136B, DI-E-3119B, DI-E-25841A, DI-E-25843A, DI-E-30113 and DI-E-30130A.

8. APPROVAL LIMITATION

No entry.

9a. APPLICABLE FORMS

No entry.

9b. AMSC NUMBER

N3601

10. PREPARATION INSTRUCTIONS

10.1 *Source Document.* The applicable issue of the documents cited herein, including their approval date and dates of any applicable amendments and revisions, shall be as reflected in the contract.

10.2 *Content and Format Instructions.* This specification shall be prepared on bound 8 1/2 by 11 inch bond paper (hardcopy) or a form of electronic media. The contract will specify the precise format. Each page prior to Section 1 shall be numbered in lowercase roman numeral beginning with page ii for the Table of Contents. Each page starting from Section 1 to the end of the document shall be consecutively numbered in arabic numerals. For hardcopy formats, this document may be printed on one or both sides of each page (single-sided/double-sided). For single-sided documents, all pages shall contain the document control number in the top right-hand corner. For double-sided documents, all even-numbered pages shall be on the left-hand side of the document and odd-numbered pages on the right-hand side. For double-sided documents, the control number shall be placed in the top right-hand corner for each odd-numbered page and the top left-hand corner for each even-numbered page. All paragraph and subparagraph headings listed below shall be included in the specification. All paragraphs and subparagraphs starting with the phrase "This (sub)paragraph shall . . . " may be written as multiple (sub)paragraphs to enhance readability. The letters "X" and "Y" serve as identifiers for a series of descriptions. For example, the subparagraphs describing CSCI-to-CSCI interfaces are designated as 3.3.3.1.X; if there is more than one interface, the first paragraph is numbered 3.3.3.1.1 (Name) Interface, the second is 3.3.3.1.2 (Name) Interface, etc. (see 10.2.5.3.3.1.1). The subparagraphs describing HWCI-to-CSCI interfaces are designated as 3.3.3.2.Y; if there is more than one interface, the first paragraph is numbered 3.3.3.2.1 (Name) Interface, the second is 3.3.3.2.2 (Name) Interface, etc. (see 10.2.5.3.3.2.1). Similar paragraph structure is used in 10.2.5.4.1. This specification shall consist of the following:

a. Cover Page
b. Table of Contents
c. Scope
d. Applicable Documents
e. Requirements
f. Qualification Requirements
g. Preparation for Delivery
h. Notes
i. Appendixes

10.2.1 *Cover Page.* This page shall contain the document control number in the upper right hand corner. In the center of the page, these words shall appear in the following format:

SOFTWARE REQUIREMENTS SPECIFICATION
FOR THE
[PROJECT NAME]

CONTRACT NO. [contract number]
CDRL SEQUENCE NO. [CDRL number]
[Date of document - day month year]

Prepared for:
[Contracting Agency Name, department code]

Prepared by:
[contractor name and address]

10.2.2 *Table of Contents.* This specification shall contain a Table of Contents listing the title and page number of all titled paragraphs and subparagraphs. The Table of Contents shall then list the title and page number of all figures, tables, and appendixes, in that order.

10.2.3 *Scope.* This section shall be numbered 1. and divided into the following paragraphs.

10.2.3.1 *Identification.* This paragraph shall be numbered 1.1 and contain the approved identification number, title, and if applicable, abbreviation of the CSCI and the system to which this SRS applies. This paragraph shall begin with the following sentence: "This Software Requirements Specification establishes the requirements for the CSCI identified as (insert CSCI title, if applicable insert abbreviation in parenthesis, insert CSCI number) of the (insert title, if applicable insert abbreviation in parenthesis, insert system identification number) System."

10.2.3.2 *Purpose.* This paragraph shall be numbered 1.2, state the purpose of the system, identify the major functions the CSCI performs, and describe the role of the CSCI within the system or segment of which it is a part.

10.2.3.3 *Introduction.* This paragraph shall be numbered 1.3 and summarize the purpose and contents of this document.

10.2.4 *Applicable Documents.* This section shall be numbered 2. and divided into the following paragraphs.

10.2.4.1 *Government Documents.* This paragraph shall be numbered 2.1 and begin with the following paragraph: "The following documents of the exact issue shown form a part of this specification to the extent specified herein. In the event of conflict between the documents referenced herein and the contents of this specification, the contents of this specification shall be considered a superseding requirement."

Government documents shall be listed by document number and title in the following order:

SPECIFICATIONS:
- Federal
- Military
- Other Government Agency

STANDARDS:
- Federal
- Military
- Other Government Agency

DRAWINGS:

(Where detailed drawings referred to in a specification are listed on an assembly drawing, it is only necessary to list the assembly drawing.)

OTHER PUBLICATIONS:
- Manuals
- Regulations
- Handbooks
- Bulletins
- etc.

(Copies of specifications, standards, drawings, and publications required by suppliers in connection with specified procurement functions should be obtained from the contracting agency or as directed by the contracting officer.)

10.2.4.2 *Non-Government Documents.* This paragraph shall be numbered 2.1 and begin with the following paragraph: "The following documents of the exact issue shown form a part of this specification to the extent specified herein. In the event of conflict between the documents referenced herein and the contents of this specification, the contents of this specification shall be considered a superseding requirement."

Non-Government documents shall be listed by document number and title in the following order:

SPECIFICATIONS:
STANDARDS:
DRAWINGS:
OTHER PUBLICATIONS:

(List source for all documents not available through normal Government stocking activities.)

The following source paragraph shall be placed at the bottom of the list when applicable: "Technical society and technical association specifications and standards are generally available for reference from libraries. They are also distributed among technical groups and using Federal Agencies."

10.2.5 *Requirements.* This section shall be numbered 3. and divided into the following paragraphs and subparagraphs to specify all the requirements necessary to ensure proper development of the CSCI. Requirements to be included herein shall be allocated or derived from requirements established by the applicable SSS, PIDS, or CIDS.

10.2.5.1 *Programming Requirements.* This paragraph shall be numbered 3.1 and divided into the following subparagraphs to specify the programming requirements allocated to the CSCI.

10.2.5.1.1 *Programming Language(s).* This subparagraph shall be numbered 3.1.1 and specify the language(s) to be used to implement the CSCI.

10.2.5.1.2 *Compiler/Assembler.* This subparagraph shall be numbered 3.1.2 and specify the compiler and, if applicable, the assembler to be used to translate the CSCI implementation.

10.2.5.1.3 *Programming Standards.* This subparagraph shall be numbered 3.1.3 and specify directly or by reference the standards under which the CSCI shall be implemented.

10.2.5.2 *Design Requirements.* This paragraph shall be numbered 3.2 and divided into the following subparagraphs to specify the design requirements allocated to the CSCI.

10.2.5.2.1 *Sizing and Timing Requirements.* This subparagraph shall be numbered 3.2.1 and specify the amount and location of internal memory and processing time allocated to the CSCI, including spare capacity.

10.2.5.2.2 *Design Standards.* This subparagraph shall be numbered 3.2.2 and specify, directly or by reference, the design standards under which the CSCI shall be developed.

10.2.5.2.3 *Design Constraints.* This subparagraph shall be numbered 3.2.3 and specify other requirements which constrain the CSCI design (e.g., the use of a particular processing configuration).

10.2.5.3 *Interface Requirements.* This paragraph shall be numbered 3.3 and divided into the following subparagraphs to specify all interfaces to the CSCI. Interfaces shall be specified directly, or by reference to other specifications (e.g., IRSs) and standards (e.g., commercial and project). If data flows in both directions between the CSCIs, or between the CSCI and a Hardware Configuration Item (HWCI) or critical item (as defined in MIL-STD-490), each direction shall be specified.

10.2.5.3.1 *Interface Relationships.* This subparagraph shall be numbered 3.3.1 and describe the interface relationship of the CSCI to other HWCIs, CSCIs, and critical items of the system with which it interfaces. This description may be provided by an interface block diagram (see Figure 1).

10.2.5.3.2 *Interface Identification and Documentation.* This subparagraph shall be numbered 3.3.2 and specify the proper identification of each interfacing HWCI, CSCI, or critical item specified in 10.2.5.3.1 above, and associated documents containing interface information. This information may be specified in an interface identification table (see Table I).

10.2.5.3.3 *Detailed Interface Requirements.* This subparagraph shall be numbered 3.3.3 and divided into the following subparagraphs to specify the detailed interface requirements for those interfaces identified above which are not defined in separate specifications.

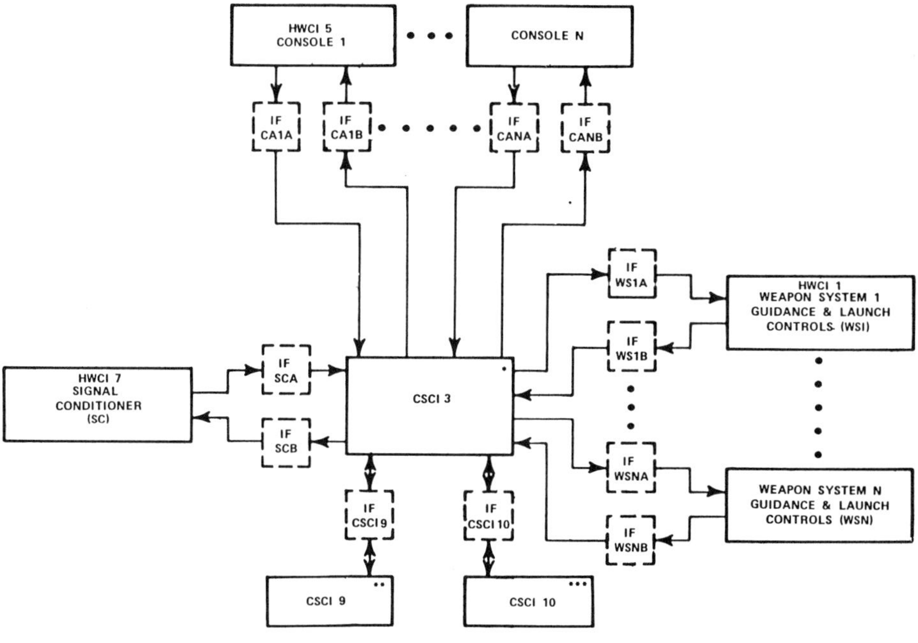

Figure 1. Sample interface block diagram. Notes: 1. IF = Interface; 2. Processor allocation: * = Processor 1; ** = Processor 2; *** = Processor 3.

TABLE I. Sample interface identification/documentation table for interface block diagram.

Interface Name	Interfacing Item: Title	Interfacing Item: CI Number	Interface Document Name	Interface Document No.
CA1A IF	Console A	5	B1 development spec - console A	5.2
CA1B IF	Console A	5	B1 development spec - console A	5.2
WS1A IF	Weapon system guidance & launch controls	1	B1 development spec - weapon system/ guidance & launch controls	1.2
WS1B IF	Weapon system guidance & launch controls	1	B1 development spec - weapon system/ guidance & launch controls	1.2
CSCI9 IF	A	9	IRS for A	9.2
CSCI10 IF	B	10	IRS for B	10.2

10.2.5.3.3.1 *CSCI-to-CSCI Interface Requirements.* This subparagraph shall be numbered 3.3.3.1 and divided into the following subparagraphs to specify each CSCI-to-CSCI interface.

10.2.5.3.3.1.1 *(Name X) Interface.* This subparagraph shall be numbered 3.3.3.1.X, (beginning with 3.3.3.1.1), specify the X interface by name and number, discuss its purpose, and provide a summary of the information communicated via the interface. This summary may be provided by an interface summary table (see Table II). In addition, this subparagraph shall specify:

a. Whether the interfacing CSCI executes concurrently or sequentially with the CSCI specified herein. If concurrently, the method of inter-CSCI synchronization shall be included.
b. Which CSCI transmits the data, which CSCI receives the data, and the communication protocol used.
c. The format and, when applicable, the units of measure, scaling, and conventions of the data communicated via the interface. This information may be provided in a CSCI-to-CSCI interface data transfer format table (see Table III).
d. Any shared memory between the CSCIs (if known) and the purpose for the shared memory.
e. The conditions for initiating each data transfer. If the transfer of data between CSCIs is cyclic, how often the cycle occurs.
f. The expected response to each data transfer, including the maximum time allowed for the receiving CSCI to acquire the data and the effects of not acquiring the data.

10.2.5.3.3.2 *CSCI-to-HWCI or Critical Item Requirements.* This subparagraph shall be numbered 3.3.3.2 and divided into the following subparagraphs to specify each CSCI to HWCI or critical item interface.

10.2.5.3.3.2.1 *(Name Y) Interface.* This subparagraph shall be numbered 3.3.3.2.Y, (beginning with 3.3.3.2.1), specify the Y interface by name and number, discuss its purpose, and provide a summary of the information communicated via the interface.

TABLE II. Sample interface summary table.

Interface Name	Information Description	Initiation Condition	Expected Response
IF SCA	SC[1]-to-CSCI 3	Buffer full	Clear
	Data ready	Received Sync	None
	Sync		
IF SCB	CSCI 3-to-SC	Mode change	Status
	Mode select	Start-up	Sync
	Sync	Cycle-1 H_Z	Status
	Status request		

[1]SC = signal conditioner

TABLE III. Sample CSCI-to-CSCI interface data transfer format table.

Data passed directly (e.g., messages, calling arguments)

Byte[1] Number	Data Type	Size	Units	Scaling	Conventions	Content
01-04	Real	2 words[2]	Feet	20-12[3]	MSB[4] = sign bit	X coordinate
05-08	Real	2 words	Feet	20-12	MSB = sign bit	Y coordinate
09-12	Real	2 words	Feet	20-12	MSB = sign bit	Z coordinate
13-16	Real	2 words	Feet/sec	14-18	N/A	Speed
17-20	ASCII	4 chars	N/A	N/A	See text	ID code

Total = 10 words, 20 bytes

Data passed by shared memory (e.g. data base file, global common area).

Byte Number	Data Type	Size	Unit	Scaling	Conventions	Content
01	Mask	Left-most 4 bits	N/A	N/A	0 = off	System state
01	Integer	Right-most 4 bits	N/A	N/A	15 = High	Priority of request
02	ACSII	1 char	N/A	N/A	N/A	Blank

Total = 1 word, 2 bytes

[1]Byte = 8 bits

[2]Word = 16 bits

[3]X-Y = X bits before the binary point
Y bits after the binary point

[4]MSB = Most significant bit

This summary may be provided by an interface summary table (see Table II). In addition, this subparagraph shall specify:

a. The direction of each signal (e.g., from HWCI to CSCI, or from CSCI to HWCI).
b. The format and, when applicable, the units of measure, scaling and conventions of each signal communicated via the interface. This information may be provided in a CSCI-to-HWCI interface message format table (see Table IV).
c. The memory buffer requirements for the CSCI and the memory locations used by the HWCI or critical item, if applicable.
d. The transfer protocol used for the interface (e.g., blocking, message switching, handshaking).
e. The conditions for initiating each signal and, if cyclic, how often the cycle occurs.
f. The priority level of the interface and of each signal, if applicable.
g. The expected response to each signal, including the maximum time allowed for responding to each signal and the effects of not responding to the signal within the allocated time interval (e.g., error control, alternate paths).

10.2.5.4 *Detailed Functional and Performance Requirements.* This paragraph shall be numbered 3.4 and list all system functional and performance requirements the CSCI must satisfy and, if applicable, the various states in which the system can exist (e.g., air ready, search, track). If the system can exist in various states, this paragraph shall correlate each identified function to the applicable states. This correlation may be provided in a system state/function table (see Table V). The subparagraphs below shall specify the requirements for each function.

10.2.5.4.1 *(Name X) Function.* This subparagraph shall be numbered 3.4.X (beginning with 3.4.1), specify function X by name, and describe the purpose it serves. If the system can exist in various states, this subparagraph shall specify the states in which this function operates. However, if this function operates differently in different states (e.g., receives different input, has different processing requirements, or produces different output), a separate function shall be specified for each unique set of input, processing, and output requirements.

The subparagraphs below shall specify the detailed requirements for input, processing, and output of function X. However, if function X is divided into subfunctions, a separate paragraph 3.4.X.Y shall describe each subfunction X.Y. (For example, paragraph 3.4.X.1 for subfunction X.1, paragraph 3.4.X.2 for subfunction X.2, etc.). If function X is divided into subfunctions, the subparagraphs below shall specify the input, processing, and output requirements for each subfunction, rather than for function X.

Note: The interface requirements between functions should not be confused with the interface requirements for the CSCI in 10.2.5.3. Figure 2 illustrates the difference between the CSCI interface requirements and function X inputs and outputs.

10.2.5.4.1.1 *Inputs.* This subparagraph shall be numbered 3.4.X.1 and identify and state the purpose of all inputs to function X. In addition, this subparagraph shall identify the source(s), frequency of arrival, legality checks, and units of measure for the

TABLE IV. Sample CSCI-to-HWCI interface message format table.

Launch Request Message						
Byte[1] Number	Data Type	Size	Units	Scaling	Conventions	Content
01-02	Integer	1 word[2]	N/A	N/A	Default = employee number	User ID number
03-08	ASCII	6 char	N/A	N/A	Default = last name	User password
09-12	ASCII	4 char	N/A	N/A	See text[4]	User request
13-16	Real	2 words	Feet	20-12[3]	MSB = sign bit	X coordinate
17-20	Real	2 words	Feet	20-12	MSB[5] = sign bit	Y coordinate
21-24	Real	2 words	Feet	20-12	MSB = sign bit	Z coordinate
25-28	Integer	2 words	Sec	N/A	N/A	Time

[1]Byte = 8 bits

[2]Word = 16 bits

[3]X-Y = X bits before the binary point
Y bits after the binary point

[4]Transfer rate = 1 m bits/sec

[5]MSB = most significant bit

TABLE V. Sample system state/function table.

System States \ CSCI Functions in Execution	Mode Determination	Radar Data Input	Track Filter	Director Control	Launcher Orders	Range Search	Angle Search	Normal Track	Passive Track	Weapon Control
Air ready	X	X	X							
Search	X	X	X	X		X	X	X	X	X
Track	X	X	X	X	X			X	X	X

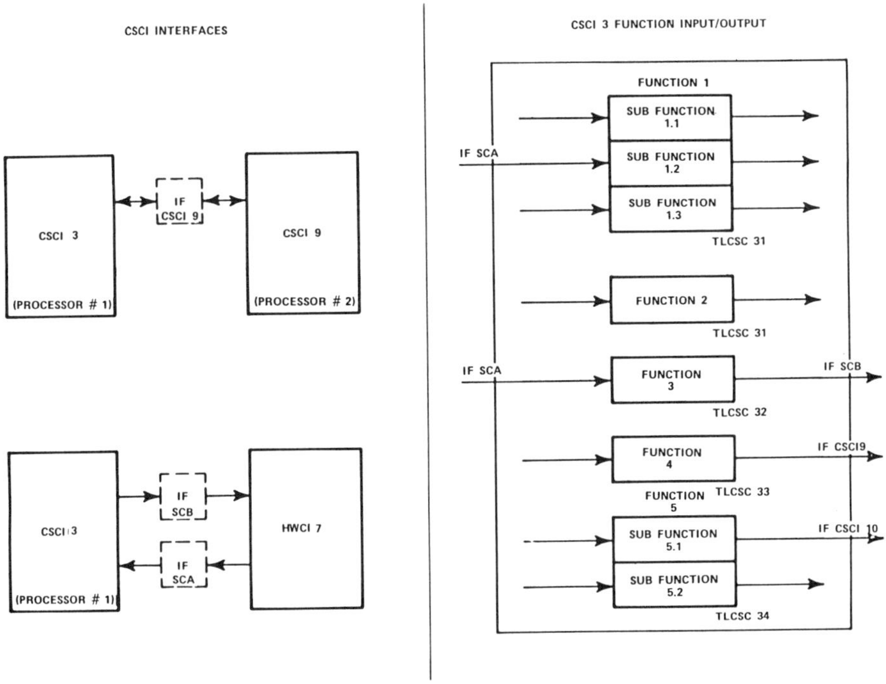

Figure 2. Sample CSCI external interfaces and function inputs/outputs. Notes: 1. IF = Interface; 2. SC = Signal conditioner.

TABLE VI. Sample function X input table.

Item	Description	Units of Measure	Frequency	Legality Check	Source(s)
1	Speed	MPH	1 kHz	N/A	Function 2 Function 4
2	Number of objects	N/A	1 kHz	Yes	Function 2 Function 4
3	Request priority	N/A	1 kHz	Yes	Function 2 Function 4
4	ID code	N/A	N/A	Yes	HWCI 5

inputs. The identification of source(s), frequency of arrival, legality checks, and units of measure for the inputs may be provided by a Function X input table (see Table VI).

Note: If function X is divided into subfunctions, this subparagraph shall be numbered 3.4.X.Y.1 Inputs and may reference a Subfunction X.Y input table (e.g., 3.4.X.1.1 Inputs, Subfunction X.1 input table).

10.2.5.4.1.2 *Processing.* Function X consists of one or more operations that are performed on its input. This subparagraph shall be numbered 3.4.X.2 and specify (by text, graphic portrayal, or a combination of both) the following processing requirements for function X:

a. The exact intent of the operation(s).
b. Parameters (including tolerances and accuracies) affected by the operation(s).
c. Sequence and timing of events.
d. Error detection and recovery (including erroneous input information).
e. Logical algorithms and mathematical equations to be employed by the function, if contractually constrained.
f. Any restrictions or limitations affecting the processing requirements of function X.
g. Allocation of CSCI performance requirements to function X.

If applicable, derivation of lengthy algorithms and mathematical equations shall be included in 10.2.8 (Section 6. Notes).

Note: If function X is divided into subfunctions, this subparagraph shall be numbered 3.4.X.Y.2 Processing and shall specify the processing requirements for subfunction X.Y (e.g., 3.4.X.1.2 Processing, Subfunction X.1).

10.2.5.4.1.3 *Outputs.* This subparagraph shall be numbered 3.4.X.3 and identify and state the purpose of the outputs to be generated by Function X. In addition, this subparagraph shall identify the destination(s), units of measure, and frequency of the outputs. The identification of the destination(s), units of measure, and frequency of the outputs may be provided in a Function X output table (see Table VII).

Note: If function X is divided into subfunctions, this subparagraph shall be numbered 3.4.X.Y.3 Outputs and shall reference a Subfunction X.Y output table (e.g., 3.4.X.1.3 Outputs, Subfunction X.1 output table).

TABLE VII. Sample function X output table.

Item	Description	Units of Measure	Frequency	Destination(s)
1	Speed	MPH	1 kHz	Function 1 Function 4
2	Number of objects	N/A	1 kHz	Function 1
3	Request priority	N/A	1 kHz	Function 1 Function 4
4	ID code	N/A	N/A	CSCI 9

10.2.5.5 *Adaptation Requirements.* Adaptation data is that data which can be centrally modified, as required, to change the scope of CSCI operational functions within prescribed limits. This paragraph shall be numbered 3.5 and divided into the following subparagraphs to specify the requirements with respect to system environment, system parameters, and system capacities.

10.2.5.5.1 *System Environment.* This subparagraph shall be numbered 3.5.1 and describe the environmental data from which each installation will select the required values for operational use. Examples of such data are: grid limits, radar ranges and areas of coverage, and prescribed safety limits. In addition, this subparagraph shall identify the functions and subfunctions of the CSCI in which these data are used. The identification of the functions and subfunctions of the CSCI in which these data are used may be provided in a system adaptation data usage table (see Table VIII).

10.2.5.5.2 *System Parameters.* This subparagraph shall be numbered 3.5.2 and describe constants required by one or more CSCIs that may change from time to time within a specified range according to operational needs. Examples of such data are: allowable trajectory deviations, navigation set model numbers, airplane tail number or performance characteristics, interaction/isolation of sorties, and missile performance characteristics. In addition, this subparagraph shall identify the functions and subfunctions of the CSCI in which these data are used. The identification of the functions and subfunctions of the CSCI in which these data are used may be provided in a system adaptation data usage table (see Table VIII).

TABLE VIII. Sample system adaptation data usage table.

	Environment Data Usage by CI			
Data Item	Subfunctions (of CSCI 3)	Functions (of CSCI 3)	Other CSCIs	Other HWCIs
Grid limit	1.1 1.3	3	9	1
Radar range		4	9 10	1 7
Safety limit	5.1 5.2	4	9	7

10.2.5.5.3 *System Capacities.* This subparagraph shall be numbered 3.5.3 and describe the features that are to be incorporated to permit the storage or work load capacities of the CSCI to be easily redefined according to operational needs and supported by appropriate changes in the computational devices. Examples of such parameters and their effect on performance are:

a. Storage, which affects the sizes of various on-line data base files
b. Execution time, which affects the number of simultaneous targets tracked
c. Interfaces, which affect the equipment's data transfer bandwidth

In addition, this subparagraph shall identify the functions and subfunctions affected by the system capacity parameters. The identification of the functions and subfunctions affected by the system capacity parameters may be provided in a system adaptation data usage table (see Table VIII).

10.2.5.6 *Quality Factors.* This paragraph shall be numbered 3.6 and divided into the following subparagraphs to specify the quality factor requirements applicable to the CSCI. If a particular method of quality factor compliance is required, it shall be specified with the requirements for that factor.

10.2.5.6.1 *Correctness Requirements.* This subparagraph shall be numbered 3.6.1 and specify the degree to which the implemented CSCI shall satisfy its requirements.

10.2.5.6.2 *Reliability Requirements.* This subparagraph shall be numbered 3.6.2 and specify the requirements for the implemented CSCI to consistently perform its intended function.

10.2.5.6.3 *Efficiency Requirements.* This subparagraph shall be numbered 3.6.3 and specify the efficiency with which the implemented CSCI shall use computer resources.

10.2.5.6.4 *Integrity Requirements.* This subparagraph shall be numbered 3.6.4 and specify the requirements for the implemented CSCI to control unauthorized access to operations and data.

10.2.5.6.5 *Usability Requirements.* This subparagraph shall be numbered 3.6.5 and specify the human engineering requirements of the implemented CSCI. The human engineering requirements shall consist of the maximum time and effort required to learn the human interface with the CSCI, prepare input, and interpret output of the CSCI.

10.2.5.6.6 *Maintainability Requirements.* This subparagraph shall be numbered 3.6.6 and specify the maximum effort required to locate and fix an error in the implemented CSCI.

10.2.5.6.7 *Testability Requirements.* This subparagraph shall be numbered 3.6.7 and specify the maximum effort required to ensure that the implemented CSCI performs its intended functions.

10.2.5.6.8 *Flexibility Requirements.* This subparagraph shall be numbered 3.6.8 and specify the maximum effort required for enhancement of the implemented CSCI.

10.2.5.6.9 *Portability Requirements.* This subparagraph shall be numbered 3.6.9 and specify the maximum effort required to transfer the implemented CSCI from one hardware or software system environment to another.

10.2.5.6.10 *Reusability Requirements.* This subparagraph shall be numbered 3.6.10 and specify requirements to use the implemented CSCI in other applications.

10.2.5.6.11 *Interoperability Requirements.* This subparagraph shall be numbered 3.6.11 and specify the requirements to facilitate interfacing the implemented CSCI with other systems.

10.2.5.6.12 *Additional Quality Factor Requirements.* This subparagraph shall be numbered 3.6.12 and specify any additional quality factor requirements not mentioned previously (e.g., availability), that apply to the implemented CSCI.

10.2.5.7 *CSCI Support.* This subparagraph shall be numbered 3.7 and specify the facilities, equipment, software, personnel, and training requirements affecting the development, operation, and support of the CSCI.

10.2.5.8 *Traceability.* This subparagraph shall be numbered 3.8 and contain a mapping of the requirements of 10.2.5 in this specification to corresponding requirements in the SSS, PIDS, or CIDS. This paragraph may reference a requirements traceability table (see Table IX).

10.2.6 *Qualification Requirements.* This section shall be numbered 4. and divided into the following paragraphs to specify the methods, techniques, tools, facilities, and acceptance tolerance limits necessary to establish that the CSCI satisfies the requirements of 10.2.5 and 10.2.7.

10.2.6.1 *General Qualification Requirements.* This paragraph shall be numbered 4.1 and specify the qualification methods to be used to ensure that each of the requirements of the CSCI have been satisfied.

Qualification methods used to show that the requirements of a CSCI have been satisfied typically include:

a. *Demonstration* - a qualification method that is carried out by operation of the CSCI (or some part of the CSCI) and that relies on observable functional operation not requiring the use of elaborate instrumentation or special test equipment.
b. *Test* - a qualification method that is carried out by operation of the CSCI (or some part of the CSCI) and that relies on the collection and subsequent examination of data.
c. *Analysis* - a qualification method that is carried out by the processing of accumulated data. An example of accumulated data is the compilation of data obtained from other qualification methods. Examples of the processing of accumulated data are interpretations or extrapolations made from the data.
d. *Inspection* - a qualification method that is carried out by visual examination.
e. *Additional Qualification Methods* - any additional qualification methods used to show that the CSCI requirements have been satisfied.

10.2.6.2 *Special Qualification Requirements.* This paragraph shall be numbered 4.2 and specify any special requirements associated with qualification of the requirements in 10.2.5 and 10.2.7. Special qualification requirements shall consist of special tools, techniques, (e.g., test formulas, algorithms), facilities, and acceptance limits.

10.2.7 *Preparation for Delivery.* This section shall be numbered 5. and specify the type and characteristics of the media of delivery for the CSCI (e.g., 8 track magnetic tape 1600 BPI, 150 megabyte disk). In addition, this section shall specify the labeling, packaging, handling, and classification marking requirements for the media,

TABLE IX. Sample requirement traceability table.

Software Requirement Specification			System/Segment Specification (SSS)				
Requirement Name	Requirement Number	Paragraph Number	SSS Name	SSS Number	SSS Paragraph Name	SSS Requirement Name	SSS Paragraph Number
Programming language	N/A	3.1.a	System A	10741	Programming requirements	Programming language	3.3.x.2.a
Compiler	N/A	3.1.b	System A	10741	Programming requirements	Compiler/assembler	3.3.x.2.b
Interface block diagram	N/A	3.3.1	System A	10741	Internal interface diagram	Internal interface diagram	3.1.7.2.1
Function X	Function No. 2	3.4.2	System A	10741	CSCI A	Functional requirement X	3.1.4.x

including name and number of the CSCI. Any unique delivery requirements shall also be specified in this section.

10.2.8 *Notes*. This section shall be numbered 6. and contain any general information that aids in understanding this specification (e.g., background information, glossary, formula derivations). This section shall include an alphabetical listing of all acronyms, abbreviations, and their meanings as used in this document.

10.2.9 *Appendixes*. Appendixes may contain any supplemental information published separately for convenience in document maintenance (e.g., charts, classified data). Appendixes may be bound as separate documents for ease in handling. Appendixes shall be numbered sequentially in Roman numeral (I, II, etc.), and the paragraphs within each appendix shall all be numbered as multiples of 10 (e.g., Appendix I, paragraph 10.1, 10.2, Appendix II, paragraph 20.1, 20.2, etc.).

As applicable, each appendix shall be referenced in the main body of the document where the data would normally have been provided.

1. TITLE

INTERFACE DESIGN DOCUMENT

2. IDENTIFICATION NUMBER

DI-MCCR-80027

3. DESCRIPTION/PURPOSE

3.1 The Interface Design Document (IDD) describes the detailed design of one or more interfaces between a Computer Software Configuration Item (CSCI) and other CSCIs, Hardware Configuration Items (HWCIs), or critical items.

3.2 The IDD and its companion Interface Requirements Specification (IRS) serve to communicate and control interface design decisions to the Government. Upon completion of Physical Configuration Audit, the IDD becomes a part of the Product Baseline for the CSCI(s).

3.3 The IDD is used by the contractor(s) during the detailed design of the CSCI(s) that implements the interface(s). It is entered into the Developmental Configuration for the CSCI.

4. APPROVAL DATE (YYMMDD)

850604

5. OFFICE OF PRIMARY RESPONSIBILITY (OPR)

EC

6a. DTIC REQUIRED

No entry.

6b. GIDEP REQUIRED

No entry.

7. APPLICATION/INTERRELATIONSHIP

7.1 This Data Item Description (DID) contains the format and content preparation instructions for that data generated under work tasks described by 3.4.7.2 of MIL-STD-483, 3.1.3.3.5.4 of MIL-STD-490, and 5.3.1.2 and 5.3.2.4 of DOD-STD-2167.

7.2 The Government's Data Manager for this system must specify in the Statement of Work and Contract Data Requirements List whether this document is to be prepared and delivered on bound 8 1/2 by 11 inch bond paper or electronic media. If electronic media is selected, the precise format must be specified (e.g., magnetic tape, floppy disk, host system, etc.).

7.3 The IDD is used to document the design of one or more interfaces with a CSCI specified by an IRS, DI-MCCR-80026. The IDD completes the description of the interface(s).

7.4 At PCA, the IDD is included in the Software Product Specification, DI-MCCR-80029. It describes the details of the information passed via the interface(s).

7.5 The CSCI elements which implement the interface designs detailed in this DID are described in the Software Top Level Design Document, DI-MCCR-80012, and the Software Detailed Design Document, DI-MCCR-80031.

7.6 The combination of this DID and the IRS supersede DI-E-2135A.

8. APPROVAL LIMITATION

No entry.

9a. APPLICABLE FORMS

No entry.

9b. AMSC NUMBER

N3603

10. PREPARATION INSTRUCTIONS

10.1 *Source Document.* The applicable issue of the documents cited herein, including their approval date and dates of any applicable amendments and revisions, shall be as reflected in the contract.

10.2 *Content and Format Instructions.* This document shall be prepared on bound 8 1/2 by 11 inch bond paper (hardcopy) or a form of electronic media. The contract will specify the precise format. Each page prior to Section 1 shall be numbered in lowercase roman numeral beginning with page ii for the Table of Contents. Each page starting from Section 1 to the end of the document shall be consecutively numbered in arabic numerals. For hardcopy formats, this document may be printed on one or both sides of each page (single-sided/double-sided). For single-sided documents, all pages shall contain the document control number in the top right-hand corner. For double-sided documents, all even-numbered pages shall be on the left-hand side of the document and odd-numbered pages on the right-hand side. For double-sided documents, the control number shall be placed in the top right-hand corner for each odd-numbered page and the top left-hand corner for each even-numbered page. All paragraph and subparagraph headings listed below shall be included in the document. All paragraphs and subparagraphs starting with the phrase "This (sub)paragraph shall . . . " may be written as multiple (sub)paragraphs to enhance readability. The letter "X" serves as an identifier for a series of descriptions. For example, the paragraphs describing interfaces are designated as 3.X; if there is more than one interface, the first paragraph is numbered 3.1 (Name) Interface, the second is 3.2 (Name) Interface, etc. (see 10.2.5.1). This document shall be as self-contained as possible. Reference to other documents should be minimal. This document shall consist of the following:

a. Cover Page
b. Table of Contents
c. Scope
d. Referenced Documents
e. Requirements
f. Notes
g. Appendixes

10.2.1 *Cover Page.* This page shall contain the document control number in the upper right hand corner. In the center of the page, these words shall appear in the following format:

INTERFACE DESIGN DOCUMENT
FOR THE
[PROJECT NAME]

CONTRACT NO. [contract number]
CDRL SEQUENCE NO. [CDRL number]
[Date of document - day month year]

Prepared for:
[Contracting Agency Name, department code]

Prepared by:
[contractor name and address]

10.2.2 *Table of Contents.* This document shall contain a Table of Contents listing the title and page number of all titled paragraphs and subparagraphs. The Table of Contents shall then list the title and page number of all figures, tables, and appendixes, in that order.

10.2.3 *Scope.* This section shall be numbered 1. and divided into the following paragraphs.

10.2.3.1 *Identification.* This paragraph shall be numbered 1.1 and contain the approved identification number, title, and if applicable, abbreviation of the interfaces, CSCI, and the system to which this IDD applies. This paragraph shall begin with the following sentence: "This Interface Design Document describes the detailed design of the interface(s) identified as (insert title) for the CSCI identified as (insert title, if applicable insert abbreviation in parenthesis, insert CSCI number) in the (insert title, if applicable insert abbreviation in parenthesis, insert system identification number) System."

10.2.3.2 *Purpose.* This paragraph shall be numbered 1.2, state the purpose of the interface(s), and identify the function(s) of the CSCI to which this IDD applies.

10.2.3.3 *Introduction.* This paragraph shall be numbered 1.3 and summarize the purpose and contents of this document.

10.2.4 *Referenced Documents.* This section shall be numbered 2. and list by document and title all documents referenced in this document. This section shall also identify the source for all documents not available through normal Government stocking activities.

10.2.5 *Requirements.* This section shall be numbered 3. and divided into the following paragraphs and subparagraphs to define the detailed design of one or more CSCI interfaces. All information passed across each interface shall be completely specified.

10.2.5.1 *(Name X) Interface.* This paragraph shall be numbered 3.X (beginning with 3.1) and divided into the following subparagraphs.

10.2.5.1.1 *Interface X Summary.* This subparagraph shall be numbered 3.X.1 (beginning with 3.1.1). The information passed across interface X shall be listed and its purpose described in this subparagraph. If interface X is bi-directional, each direction shall be separately listed. The initiation criteria for and response to each item of information passed shall be specified. A reference may be made to an interface summary table. An example of an interface summary table is provided in Table I.

10.2.5.1.2 *Interface X Item Summary.* This subparagraph shall be numbered 3.X.2 (beginning with 3.1.2) and describe, for each item listed in 3.X.1 above, the data, messages, or control information associated with that item. A reference may be made to an interface item summary table. An example of an interface item summary table is provided in Table II.

10.2.5.1.3 *Interface X Item Formats.* This subparagraph shall be numbered 3.X.3 (beginning with 3.1.3) and completely describe the format of each data, message, and control item passed via Interface X. The description of each field of each item shall include:

TABLE I. Sample interface summary table.

CSCI-to-HWCI		
Information	Initiation Criteria	Response
Launch	Operator input	Status word
Shutdown	Operator input or automatic for emergency state	Status word
Loop check	Periodic 1 H_Z rate	Loop check
Status request	Operator input or periodic at 10 H_Z rate	Status word
Presets	Operator input	N/A

a. A description of the information contained in the field.
b. The first and last bit positions of the field and word number(s), if applicable.
c. The name of the field, if variable, or the value of the field, if fixed.
d. The scaling, units of measure, and conventions associated with the field.

This subparagraph may reference an interface item format table to depict the required information. An example of an interface item format table is provided in Table III.

10.2.6 *Notes.* This section shall be numbered 6. and contain any general information that aids in understanding this document (e.g., background information, glossary, formula derivations). This section shall contain an alphabetical listing of all acronyms, abbreviations, and their meanings as used in this document.

10.2.7 *Appendixes.* Appendixes may contain any supplemental information published separately for convenience in document maintenance (e.g., charts, classified data). Appendixes may be bound as separate documents for ease in handling. Appendixes shall be numbered sequentially in Roman numeral (I, II, etc.), and the paragraphs within each appendix shall all be numbered as multiples of 10 (e.g., Appendix I, paragraph 10.1, 10.2, Appendix II, paragraph 20.1, 20.2, etc.).

TABLE II. Sample interface item summary table.

Information	Control	Data	Message
Launch request	—	ID code	Target X coord Y coord Z coord Timer
Launch	—	Launch code	—
Clock sync	Clock	—	—
Shutdown	Disable	Status code	—

TABLE III. Sample interface item format table.[3]

Byte[1] Number	Data Type	Size	Units	Scaling[5]	Conventions	Content
01-02	Integer	1 word[2]	N/A	N/A	Default = employee number	Used ID number
03-08	ASCII	6 char	N/A	N/A	Default = last name	User password
09-12	ASCII	4 char	N/A	N/A	See text	User request
13-16	Real	2 words	Feet	20-12	MSB[4] = sign bit	X coordinate
17-20	Real	2 words	Feet	20-12	MSB = sign bit	Y coordinate
21-24	Real	2 words	Feet	20-12	MSB = sign bit	Z coordinate
25-28	Integer	2 words	Sec	N/A	N/A	Time

[1]Byte = 8 bits

[2]Word = 16 bits

[3]Transfer rate = 1 m bits/sec

[4]MSB = most significant bit

[5]X-Y = X bits before the binary point
Y bits after the binary point

As applicable, each appendix shall be referenced in the main body of the document where the data would normally have been provided.

1. TITLE

DATA BASE DESIGN DOCUMENT

2. IDENTIFICATION NUMBER

DI-MCCR-80028

3. DESCRIPTION/PURPOSE

3.1 The Data Base Design Document (DBDD) describes the architecture and design of one or more data bases in the Computer Software Configuration Item (CSCI). The relationships among files in the data base are described, as well as the interactions between the data base files and the CSCI components and Units, including a Data Base Management System.

3.2 The DBDD serves to communicate and control data base design decisions to the Government. Upon completion of Physical Configuration Audit (PCA), the DBDD becomes a part of the Product Baseline for the CSCI.

3.3 The DBDD is used by the contractor during the detailed design and implementation of the CSCI. It is entered into the Developmental Configuration for the CSCI.

4. APPROVAL DATE (YYMMDD)

No entry.

5. OFFICE OF PRIMARY RESPONSIBILITY (OPR)

NM

6a. DTIC REQUIRED

No entry.

6b. GIDEP REQUIRED

No entry.

7. APPLICATION/INTERRELATIONSHIP

7.1 This Data Item Description (DID) contains the format and content preparation instructions for that data generated under work tasks described by 3.4.7.2 of MIL-STD-483, 3.1.3.3.5.3 of MIL-STD-490, and 5.3.1.2 and 5.3.2.5 of DOD-STD-2167.

7.2 The Government's Data Manager for this system must specify in the Statement of Work and Contract Data Requirements List whether this document is to be prepared and delivered on bound 8 1/2 by 11 inch bond paper or electronic media. If electronic media is selected, the precise format must be specified (e.g., magnetic tape, floppy disk, host system, etc.).

7.3 At PCA, the DBDD is included in the Software Product Specification (SPS), DI-MCCR-80029. It is used to describe in detail the contents and structure of both global and local data bases of the CSCI.

7.4 The Top-Level Computer Software Components (TLCSCs), Lower-Level Computer Software Components (LLCSCs), and Units of the CSCI which use the data base are described in the Software Top Level Design Document (STLDD), DI-MCCR-80012, and the Software Detailed Design Document (SDDD), DI-MCCR-80031.

7.5 If a CSCI contains more than one data base, a separate DBDD is normally prepared for each data base.

7.6 If a data base functions as an interface between CSCIs of a distributed system/segment, the DBDD may not apply. The controlling documentation in that application is either a Software Requirements Specification (SRS), DI-MCCR-80025, (when the data base is a CSCI), or an Interface Requirements Specification (IRS), DI-MCCR-80026, and Interface Design Document (IDD), DI-MCCR-80027, (otherwise).

7.7 This DID supersedes DI-S-2140A, DI-S-25850, DI-E-30144, and DI-E-30150.

8. APPROVAL LIMITATION

No entry.

9a. APPLICABLE FORMS

No entry.

9b. AMSC NUMBER

No entry.

10. PREPARATION INSTRUCTIONS

10.1 *Source Document.* The applicable issue of the documents cited herein, including their approval date and dates of any applicable amendments and revisions, shall be as reflected in the contract.

10.2 *Content and Format Instructions.* This document shall be prepared on bound 8 1/2 by 11 inch bond paper (hardcopy) or a form of electronic media. The contract will specify the precise format. Each page prior to Section 1 shall be numbered in lowercase roman numeral beginning with page ii for the Table of Contents. Each page starting from Section 1 to the end of the document shall be consecutively numbered in arabic numerals. For hardcopy formats, this document may be printed on one or both sides of each page (single-sided/double-sided). For single-sided documents, all pages shall contain the document control number in the top right-hand corner. For double-sided documents, all even-numbered pages shall be on the left-hand side of the document and odd-numbered pages on the right-hand side. For double-sided documents, the control number shall be placed in the top right-hand corner for each odd-numbered page and the top left-hand corner for each even-numbered page. All paragraph and subparagraph headings listed below shall be included in the document. All paragraphs and subparagraphs starting with the phrase "This (sub)paragraph shall . . . " may be written as multiple (sub)paragraphs to enhance readability. The letters "W", "X", "Y", and "Z" serve as identifiers for a series of descriptions. For example, the paragraphs describing files are designated as 3.2.2.X; if there is more than one file, the first paragraph is numbered 3.2.2.1 (Name) File, the second is 3.2.2.2 (Name) File, etc. (see 10.2.5.2.2.1). Similar identifiers are used in 10.2.5.3.1 in the paragraphs describing files, where "W", "X", "Y", and "Z" identify nested paragraph descriptions. For example, the paragraphs beginning with 3.3.W shall be structured as follows:

3.3.1 (Name) File 1.
3.3.1.1 (Name) Record 1 in File 1.
3.3.1.1.1 (Name) Field 1 in Record 1.
3.3.1.1.1.1 (Name) Item 1 in Field 1.
3.3.1.1.1.2 (Name) Item 2 in Field 1.
3.3.1.1.2 (Name) Field 2 in Record 1.
3.3.1.1.2.1 (Name) Item 1 in Field 2.
3.3.1.1.2.2 (Name) Item 2 in Field 2.
3.3.1.2 (Name) Record 2 in File 1.
3.3.2 (Name) File 2.

This structure shall be used until all files, records, fields, and items have been described.

This document shall be as self-contained as possible. Reference to other documents should be minimal. This document shall consist of the following:

a. Cover Page
b. Table of Contents
c. Scope
d. Referenced Documents
e. Requirements
f. Notes
g. Appendixes

10.2.1 *Cover Page.* This page shall contain the document control number in the upper right hand corner. In the center of the page, these words shall appear in the following format:

DATA BASE DESIGN DOCUMENT
FOR THE
[PROJECT NAME]

CONTRACT NO. [contract number]
CDRL SEQUENCE NO. [CDRL number]
[Date of document - day month year]

Prepared for:
[Contracting Agency Name, department code]

Prepared by:
[contractor name and address]

10.2.2 *Table of Contents.* This document shall contain a Table of Contents listing the title and page number of all titled paragraphs and subparagraphs. The Table of Contents shall then list the title and page number of all figures, tables, and appendixes, in that order.

10.2.3. *Scope.* This section shall be numbered 1. and divided into the following paragraphs.

10.2.3.1 *Identification.* This paragraph shall be numbered 1.1 and contain the approved identification number, title, and if applicable, abbreviation of the CSCI and the system to which this DBDD applies. In addition, this paragraph shall contain the identification of the data base by name and number. This paragraph shall begin with the following sentence: "This Data Base Design Document describes the detailed design of the data base identified as (insert data base title, insert data base number) for the CSCI identified as (insert title, if applicable insert abbreviation in parenthesis, insert CSCI number) of the (insert title, if applicable insert abbreviation in parenthesis, insert system identification number) System."

10.2.3.2 *Purpose.* This paragraph shall be numbered 1.2, state the purpose of the system, and identify the function(s) of the CSCI and its data base(s) for which this DBDD applies.

10.2.3.3 *Introduction.* This paragraph shall be numbered 1.3 and summarize the purpose and contents of this document.

10.2.4 *Referenced Documents.* This section shall be numbered 2. and list by document number and title all documents referenced in this document. This section shall also identify the source for all documents not available through normal Government stocking activities.

10.2.5 *Requirements.* This section shall be numbered 3. and divided into the following paragraphs and subparagraphs to describe in detail the structure and content of the data base(s) of the CSCI.

10.2.5.1 *Data Base Management System Overview.* This paragraph shall be numbered 3.1. If applicable, this paragraph shall briefly describe the Data Base Management

System which interacts with the data base described in this document. In addition this paragraph shall reference the appropriate software documentation for the following items:

a. Data Base Manager (DBM)
b. Data Base Definition Language (DBDL)
c. Data Base Query Language (DBQL)

10.2.5.2 *Data Base Structure.* This paragraph shall be numbered 3.2 and divided into the following subparagraphs. For the purpose of this document, the following terms are defined:

a. Item - a variable or a parameter.
b. Field - one or more contiguous items.
c. Record - a set of one or more consecutive fields on a related subject. A physical record is the entity for device storage and retrieval. A logical record is a user view of the physical record.
d. File - a physical collection of related records assembled as a unit.

10.2.5.2.1 *Data Base Structure Description.* This subparagraph shall be numbered 3.2.1 and describe the relationships among files and records. This description may be provided by referencing a data base structure diagram (see Figure 1).

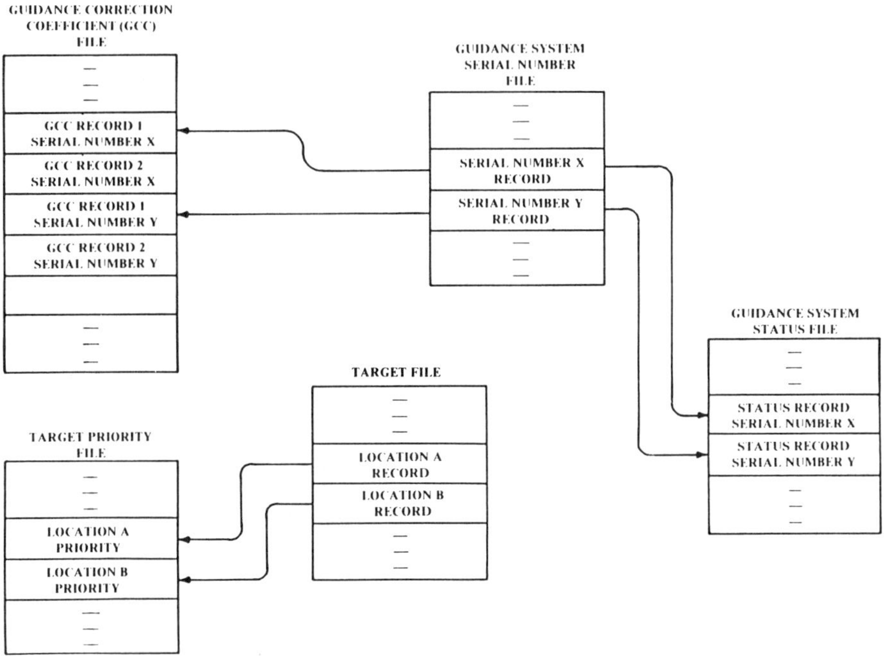

Figure 1. Sample data base structure diagram.

10.2.5.2.2 *Data Base File Interrelationships.* This subparagraph shall be numbered 3.2.2 and divided into the following subparagraphs.

10.2.5.2.2.1 *(Name X) File.* This subparagraph shall be numbered 3.2.2.X (beginning with 3.2.2.1) and describe:

a. How the file is related to the other files in the data base (e.g., the Guidance System Serial Number file contains pointers to associated entries in the Guidance System Status file and the GCC List file).
b. How the file interacts with the DBM, DBDL and DBQL (e.g., the Guidance System Serial Number file is used by the DBQL to associate a particular GCC list with its respective Guidance System Serial Number).

This subparagraph shall also relate (where possible) each design characteristic of the file (e.g., random access, fixed length record, sequenced by X, etc.) to a requirement in the SRS. This relation may be provided by a design characteristic/requirements traceability table (see Table I).

10.2.5.3 *Data Base File Design.* This paragraph shall be numbered 3.3 and divided into the following subparagraphs to describe the format of each file in the data base. The description shall be at a level of detail that will lead directly to the implementation of the data base and may be provided by a program design language.

10.2.5.3.1 *(Name W) File.* This subparagraph shall be numbered 3.3.W (beginning with 3.3.1) and describe the structure and size of file W (e.g., The Guidance System Serial Number file contains Guidance System Serial Number Records. The file will hold a maximum of 100 records).

10.2.5.3.1.1 *(Name X) Record.* This subparagraph shall be numbered 3.3.W.X (beginning with 3.3.1.1) and describe the structure and size of record X (e.g., A Guidance System Serial Number record contains a serial number field and two pointer fields: The GCC List Pointer and the Guidance System Status Pointer).

10.2.5.3.1.1.1 *(Name Y) Field.* This subparagraph shall be numbered 3.3.W.X.Y (beginning with 3.3.1.1.1) and describe the contents and size of field Y (e.g., The serial number field has a size of four ASCII characters and it contains numeric characters).

10.2.5.3.1.1.1.1 *(Name Z) Item.* This subparagraph shall be numbered 3.3.W.X.Y.Z (beginning with 3.3.1.1.1.1) and describe the representation, size, units of measure, and conventions for item Z. The most significant bit, least significant bit, and the bit

TABLE I. Design characteristic/requirements traceability table.

File Name	Characteristic	Requirement/Justification
GCC list file	Random access	To support requirement to quickly associate GCC lists with the appropriate guidance system serial number.
Guidance system serial number file	Sorted by increasing serial number	To support binary search on file to find correct serial number.
—	ASCII	To conform with requirement that system listing of serial number file be human readable.

representing unit of scaling shall be identified (e.g., The GCC List Pointer is a two ASCII character item containing the record number of the GCC List Record in the GCC List file).

10.2.5.4 *Data Base References.* This paragraph shall be numbered 3.4 and provide a cross reference of the architectural elements of the CSCI (e.g., TLCSCs, LLCSCs, Units) to the architectural elements of the data base (e.g., files, records, fields, items). For each data base element, the CSCI element directly referencing the data base element shall be listed and the type of reference (set, used, or both) provided. Data base references may be depicted by a set/used matrix. An example of a set/used matrix is provided in Table II. For convenience of generation and maintenance, this information may be produced by automated means and included as an appendix.

10.2.6 *6. Notes.* This section shall be numbered 6. and contain any general information that aids in understanding this document (e.g., background information, glossary, formula derivations). This section shall include an alphabetical listing of all acronyms, abbreviations, and their meanings as used in this document.

10.2.7. *Appendixes.* Appendixes may contain any supplemental information published separately for convenience in document maintenance (e.g., charts, classified data). Appendixes may be bound as separate documents for ease in handling. Appendixes shall be numbered sequentially in Roman numeral (I, II, etc.) and the paragraphs within each appendix shall all be numbered as multiples of 10 (e.g., Appendix I, paragraph 10.1, 10.2, Appendix II, paragraph 20.1, 20.2, etc.).

As applicable, each appendix shall be referenced in the main body of the document where the data would normally have been provided.

TABLE II. Sample set/used matrix.[1]

Data Base Element \ CSCI Element	TLCSC 31	LLCSC 310	LLCSC 3101	UNIT 31011	TLCSC 32	TLCSC 33	LLCSC 330	LLCSC 3300	UNIT 33001	UNIT 33002	TLCSC 34	TLCSC 35	LLCSC 351
OBJ													U
VELTBL		U											S
SIX 11	U	U					U	U	S				S
T				U									
NUM	U				U	S					S	B	
ID												U	
COORDS					U			B				S	
GRANGE			U		U								
A LIST		U		U	S								
GCC											U		

[1]S = set
U = used
B = both

1. TITLE

SOFTWARE PRODUCT SPECIFICATION

2. IDENTIFICATION NUMBER

DI-MCCR-80029

3. DESCRIPTION/PURPOSE

3.1 The Software Product Specification (SPS) consists of the design documents and software listings for a Computer Software Configuration Item (CSCI).

3.2 Upon Government approval and authentication at the Physical Configuration Audit (PCA), the SPS establishes the Product Baseline for the delivered CSCI.

3.3 Until establishment of the Product Baseline, the contents of the SPS are contained in the contractor's Developmental Configuration for the CSCI.

4. APPROVAL DATE (YYMMDD)

850604

5. OFFICE OF PRIMARY RESPONSIBILITY (OPR)

EC

6a. DTIC REQUIRED

No entry.

6b. GIDEP REQUIRED

No entry.

7. APPLICATION/INTERRELATIONSHIP

7.1 This Data Item Description (DID) contains the format and content preparation instructions for that data generated under the work tasks described by 3.4.7.3 of MIL-STD-483, 3.1.3.3.5 of MIL-STD-490, and 5.6.2.5 of DOD-STD-2167.

7.2 The Government's Data Manager for this system must specify in the Statement of Work and Contract Data Requirements List whether this specification is to be prepared and delivered on bound 8 1/2 by 11 inch bond paper or electronic media. If electronic media is selected, the precise format must be specified (e.g., magnetic tape, floppy disk, host system, etc.).

7.3 The SPS contains the: Software Top Level Design Document (STLDD), DI-MCCR-80012, Software Detailed Design Document (SDDD), DI-MCCR-80031, and any Interface Design Documents (IDDs), DI-MCCR-80027, and Data Base Design Documents (DBDDs), DI-MCCR-80028, applicable to the CSCI.

7.4 The release of the CSCI specified by the SPS is accomplished via the Version Description Document (VDD), DI-MCCR-80013.

7.5 This DID supersedes DI-S-2141A, DI-E-3120B, DI-A-30022, DI-E-30110A, DI-E-30111A, DI-E-30112A, DI-E-30145, DI-S-30568, DI-E-25841A, DI-E-25842A, and DI-E-25845A.

8. APPROVAL LIMITATION

No entry.

9a. APPLICABLE FORMS

No entry.

9b. AMSC NUMBER

N3605

10. PREPARATION INSTRUCTIONS

10.1 *Source Document.* The applicable issue of the documents cited herein, including their approval date and dates of any applicable amendments and revisions, shall be as reflected in the contract.

10.2 *Content and Format Instructions.* This specification shall be prepared on bound 8 1/2 by 11 inch bond paper (hardcopy) or a form of electronic media. The contract will specify the precise format. Each page prior to Section 1 shall be numbered in lower-case roman numeral beginning with page ii for the Table of Contents. Each page starting from Section 1 to the end of the document shall be consecutively numbered in arabic numerals. For hardcopy formats, this document may be printed on one or both sides of each page (single-sided/double-sided). For single-sided documents, all pages shall contain the document control number in the top right-hand corner. For double-sided documents, all even-numbered pages shall be on the left-hand side of the document and odd-numbered pages on the right-hand side. For double-sided documents, the control number shall be placed in the top right-hand corner for each odd-numbered page and the top left-hand corner for each even-numbered page. All paragraph headings listed below shall be included in the specification. All paragraphs starting with the phrase "This paragraph shall . . . " may be written as multiple paragraphs to enhance readability. The SPS is a collection of software design materials and listings. As a minimum, the SPS shall contain the STLDD and the SDDD. If one or more DBDDs have been created for the CSCI, the SPS shall contain the DBDDs. Likewise, if one or more IDDs have been created, the SPS shall contain the IDDs. CSCI listings shall be included. This specification shall consist of the following:

a. Cover Page
b. Table of Contents
c. Scope
d. Applicable Documents
e. Requirements
f. Notes
g. Appendixes

10.2.1 *Cover Page.* This page shall contain the document control number in the upper right hand corner. In the center of the page, these words shall appear in the following format:

SOFTWARE PRODUCT SPECIFICATION
FOR THE
[PROJECT NAME]

CONTRACT NO. [contract number]
CDRL SEQUENCE NO. [CDRL number]
[Date of document - day month year]

Prepared for:
[Contracting Agency Name, department code]

Prepared by:
[contractor name and address]

10.2.2 *Table of Contents.* This specification shall contain a Table of Contents listing the title and page number of all titled paragraphs and subparagraphs. The Table of Contents shall then list the title and page number of all figures, tables, and appendixes, in that order.

10.2.3 *Scope.* This section shall be numbered 1. and divided into the following paragraphs.

10.2.3.1 *Identification.* This paragraph shall be numbered 1.1 and contain the approved identification number, title, and if applicable, abbreviation of the CSCI and the system to which this SPS applies. This paragraph shall begin with the following sentence: "This Software Product Specification specifies the contents for the CSCI identified as (insert title, if applicable insert abbreviation in parenthesis, insert CSCI number) of the (insert title, if applicable insert abbreviation in parenthesis, insert system identification number) System."

10.2.3.2 *Purpose.* This paragraph shall be numbered 1.2, state the purpose of the system, identify the major functions the CSCI performs, and describe the role of the CSCI within the system or segment of which it is a part.

10.2.3.3 *Introduction.* This paragraph shall be numbered 1.3 and summarize the purpose and contents of the document.

10.2.4 *2. Applicable Documents.* This section shall be numbered 2. and divided into the following paragraphs.

10.2.4.1. *Government Documents.* This paragraph shall be numbered 2.1 and begin with the following paragraph: "The following documents of the exact issue shown form a part of this specification to the extent specified herein. In the event of conflict between the documents referenced herein and the contents of this specification, the contents of this specification shall be considered a superseding requirement."

Government documents shall be listed by document number and title in the following order:

SPECIFICATIONS:

- Federal
- Military
- Other Government Agency

STANDARDS:

- Federal
- Military
- Other Government Agency

DRAWINGS:

(Where detailed drawings referred to in a specification are listed on an assembly drawing, it is only necessary to list the assembly drawing.)

OTHER PUBLICATIONS:

- Manuals
- Regulations
- Handbooks
- Bulletins
- etc.

(Copies of specifications, standards, drawings, and publications required by suppliers in connection with specified procurement functions should be obtained from the contracting agency or as directed by the contracting officer.)

10.2.4.2 *Non-Government Documents.* This paragraph shall be numbered 2.2 and begin with the following paragraph: "The following documents of the exact issue shown form a part of this specification to the extent specified herein. In the event of conflict between the documents referenced herein and the contents of this specification, the contents of this specification shall be considered a superseding requirement."

Non-Government documents shall be listed by document number and title in the following order:

SPECIFICATIONS:
STANDARDS:
DRAWINGS:
OTHER PUBLICATIONS:

(List source for all documents not available through normal Government stocking activities.)

The following source paragraph shall be placed at the bottom of the list when applicable: "Technical society and technical association specifications and standards are generally available for reference from libraries. They are also distributed among technical groups and using Federal Agencies."

10.2.5 *Requirements.* This section shall be numbered 3. and divided into the following paragraphs to contain or reference the appendixes that contain all design documentation and listings applicable to the CSCI.

10.2.5.1 *Top-Level Design.* This paragraph shall be numbered 3.1 and contain or reference the appendix that contains the Software Top Level Design Document.

10.2.5.2 *Detailed Design.* This paragraph shall be numbered 3.2 and contain or reference the appendix that contains the Software Detailed Design Document.

10.2.5.3 *CSCI Listings.* This paragraph shall be numbered 3.3 and contain or reference the appendix that contains the source and object code listings of the CSCI, including a description of the physical media from which the listings are generated.

10.2.5.4 *Data Base Design.* This paragraph shall be numbered 3.4. If no Data Base Design Documents were prepared for the CSCI, then this paragraph shall state "NOT APPLICABLE". Otherwise, this paragraph shall contain or reference the appendix that contains the Data Base Design Document(s).

10.2.5.5 *Data Base Listings.* This paragraph shall be numbered 3.5 and contain or reference the appendix that contains the source and object code listings of the data base, including a description of the physical media from which the listings are generated.

10.2.5.6 *Interface Design.* This paragraph shall be numbered 3.6. If no Interface Design Documents were prepared for the CSCI, then this paragraph shall state "NOT APPLICABLE". Otherwise, this paragraph shall contain or reference the appendix that contains the Interface Design Document(s).

10.2.6 *Notes.* This section shall be numbered 6. and contain any general information that aids in understanding this specification (e.g., background information, glossary, formula derivations). This section shall include an alphabetical listing of all acronyms, abbreviations, and their meanings as used in this document.

10.2.7 *Appendixes.* Appendixes may contain any supplemental information published separately for convenience in document maintenance (e.g., charts, classified data). Appendixes may be bound as separate documents for ease in handling. To preclude renumbering of paragraphs, each appendix shall retain the numbering scheme of the original document, if applicable.

As applicable, each appendix shall be referenced in the main body of the document where the data would normally have been specified.

10.2.7.1 10. *Appendix I, Top-Level Design.* This appendix shall contain the STLDD if that document is not contained in 10.2.5.1.

10.2.7.2 *20. Appendix II, Detailed Design.* This appendix shall contain the SDDD if that document is not contained in 10.2.5.2.

10.2.7.3 *30. Appendix III, Source and Object Listings.* This appendix shall contain, in the paragraphs below, the source and object code listings of the CSCI, including a description of the listings media, if they are not contained in 10.2.5.3.

10.2.7.3.1 *Source Listings.* This paragraph shall contain listings of the source program (suitable for error-free translation by the applicable assembler or compiler).

10.2.7.3.2 *Object Listings.* This paragraph shall contain listings of the object program (generated from the source program and suitable for loading and executing on the specified processor).

10.2.7.3.3 *Program Media.* This paragraph shall describe the physical media from which listings are generated.

10.2.7.4 *40. Appendix IV, Data Base Design.* This appendix shall contain the DBDDs if they are not contained in 10.2.5.4.

10.2.7.5 *50. Appendix V, Data Base Listings.* This appendix shall contain, in the paragraphs below, the source and object listings of the data base(s), including a description of the listings media, if they are not contained in 10.2.5.5.

10.2.7.5.1 *Source Data Base.* This paragraph shall contain source listings of the data base(s) (suitable for error-free translation by the applicable assembler, compiler, or data base management system).

10.2.7.5.2 *Object Data Base.* This paragraph shall contain object listings of the data base(s) (generated from the source listings and suitable for loading and accessing on the specified processor).

10.2.7.5.3 *Data Base Media.* This paragraph shall describe the physical media from which the listings are generated.

10.2.7.6 *60. Appendix VI, Interface Design.* This appendix shall contain the IDDs if they are not contained in 10.2.5.6.

10.2.7.7 *Additional Appendixes.* Any additional appendixes shall commence with Appendix VII, section 70.

1. TITLE

SOFTWARE DEVELOPMENT PLAN

2. IDENTIFICATION NUMBER

DI-MCCR-80030

3. DESCRIPTION/PURPOSE

3.1 The Software Development Plan (SDP) describes the organization and procedures to be used by the contractor in performing software development.

3.2 The SDP is used to provide the Government insight into the organization(s) responsible for performing software development and the procedures to be followed by these organization(s).

3.3 The SDP is used by the Government to monitor the procedures, management, and contract work effort of the organizations performing software development.

4. APPROVAL DATE (YYMMDD)

850604

5. OFFICE OF PRIMARY RESPONSIBILITY (OPR)

EC

6a. DTIC REQUIRED

No entry.

6b. GIDEP REQUIRED

No entry.

7. APPLICATION/INTERRELATIONSHIP

7.1 This Data Item Description (DID) contains the format and content preparation instructions for that data generated under the work tasks described by 5.1.1.1 and 5.1.2.1 of DOD-STD-2167 and 3.1.1 of MIL-STD-483.

7.2 The Government's Data Manager for this system must specify in the Statement of Work and Contract Data Requirements List whether this plan is to be prepared and delivered on bound 8-1/2 by 11 inch bond paper or electronic media. If electronic media is selected, the precise format must be specified (e.g., magnetic tape, floppy disk, host system, etc.).

7.3 Paragraphs 10.2.7.1.1 through 10.2.7.1.7 will be tailored out if the software standards and procedures are to be provided in the corresponding Software Standards and Procedures Manual (SSPM), DI-MCCR-80011.

7.4 Paragraphs 10.2.5.3.1 through 10.2.5.3.3 and 10.2.7.2.1 through 10.2.7.2.7 will be tailored out if the configuration management information is to be provided in the corresponding Software Configuration Management Plan (SCMP), DI-MCCR-80009, or a System Configuration Management Plan DI-E-3108.

7.5 Paragraphs 10.2.5.4.1 through 10.2.5.4.3 and 10.2.7.3.1 through 10.2.7.3.2.2.4 will be tailored out if the software quality evaluation information is to be provided in the corresponding Software Quality Evaluation Plan (SQEP), DI-MCCR-80010.

7.6 This DID supersedes DI-A-2176A, DI-S-30567A, DI-A-25856, and DI-E-25868.

8. APPROVAL LIMITATION

No entry.

9a. APPLICABLE FORMS

No entry.

9b. AMSC NUMBER

N3606

10. PREPARATION INSTRUCTIONS

10.1 *Source Document.* The applicable issue of the documents cited herein, including their approval date and dates of any applicable amendments and revisions, shall be as reflected in the contract.

10.2 *Content and Format Instructions.* This plan shall be prepared on bound 8-1/2 by 11 inch bond paper (hardcopy) or a form of electronic media. The contract will specify the precise format. Each page prior to Section 1 shall be numbered in lower-case roman numerals beginning with page ii for the Table of Contents. Each page starting from Section 1 to the end of the document shall be consecutively numbered in arabic numerals. For hardcopy formats, this document may be printed on one or both sides of each page (single-sided/double-sided). For single-sided documents, all pages shall contain the document control number in the top right-hand corner. For double-sided documents, all even-numbered pages shall be on the left-hand side of the document and odd-numbered pages on the right-hand side. For double-sided documents, the control number shall be placed in the top right-hand corner of each odd-numbered page and the top left-hand corner of each even-numbered page. All paragraphs and subparagraph headings listed below shall be included in the plan. All paragraphs and subparagraphs starting with the phrase "This (sub)paragraph shall . . . ", may be written as multiple (sub)paragraphs to enhance readability. The letter "X" serves as an identifier for a series of descriptions. For example, the subparagraphs describing additional reports are numbered 5.2.2.2.X; the first report is described in 5.2.2.2.1 Report for Software Problems and Changes. Additional reports shall be described in subparagraphs starting with 5.2.2.2.2 Report (Name), 5.2.2.2.3 Report (Name), etc. (see 10.2.7.2.2.2.1, 10.2.7.2.2.2.2). A similar paragraph structure is used in 10.2.7.2.2.3.1 for subparagraphs describing review board procedures: 5.2.2.3.1 Review Board (Name) Procedures, 5.2.2.3.2 Review Board (Name) Procedures. This plan shall be as self-contained as possible. Reference to other documents should be minimal. This plan shall consist of the following:

a. Cover Page
b. Table of Contents

c. Scope
d. Referenced Documents
e. Resources and Organization
f. Development Schedule and Milestones
g. Software Development Procedures
h. Notes
i. Appendixes

10.2.1 *Cover Page.* This page shall contain the document control number in the upper right hand corner. In the center of the page, these words shall appear in the following format:

SOFTWARE DEVELOPMENT PLAN
FOR THE
[PROJECT NAME]

CONTRACT NO. [contract number]
CDRL SEQUENCE NO. [CDRL number]
[Date of document - day month year]

Prepared for:
[Contracting Agency Name, department code]

Prepared by:
[contractor name and address]

10.2.2 *Table of Contents.* This plan shall contain a Table of Contents listing the title and page number of all titled paragraphs and subparagraphs. The Table of Contents shall then list the title and page number of all figures, tables, and appendixes, in that order.

10.2.3 *Scope.* This section shall be numbered 1. and divided into the following paragraphs.

10.2.3.1 *Identification.* This paragraph shall be numbered 1.1 and contain the approved identification number, title, and if applicable, abbreviation of the system to which this SDP applies. If this SDP contains development plans for all the CSCI(s) developed for the system, then this paragraph shall begin with the following sentence: "This Software Development Plan establishes the plans for software development to be used during the development of all the CSCIs in the (insert title, if applicable insert abbreviation in parenthesis, insert system identification number) System." If this SDP contains development plans for only selected CSCI(s) of the system, then this paragraph shall begin with the following sentence: "This Software Development Plan establishes the plans for software development to be used during the development of the CSCI(s) identified as (insert title(s), if applicable insert abbreviation(s) in parenthesis, insert CSCI number(s)) in the (insert title, if applicable insert abbreviation in parenthesis, insert system identification number) System."

10.2.3.2 *Purpose.* This paragraph shall be numbered 1.2, state the purpose of the system, and identify the function(s) of the CSCI(s) to which this SDP applies.

10.2.3.3 *Introduction.* This paragraph shall be numbered 1.3 and summarize the purpose and contents of this document.

10.2.4 *Referenced Documents.* This section shall be numbered 2. and list by document number and title all documents referenced in this plan. This section shall also identify the source for all documents not available through normal Government stocking activities.

10.2.5 *Resources and Organization.* This section shall be numbered 3. and divided into the following paragraphs and subparagraphs to describe the required resources and the project organization of the contractor.

10.2.5.1 *Project Resources.* This paragraph shall be numbered 3.1 and divided into the following subparagraphs to summarize the resources necessary for the entire software development project.

10.2.5.1.1 *Contractor Facilities.* This subparagraph shall be numbered 3.1.1 and describe the contractor's facilities to be used for development and testing during the software development project. This subparagraph shall highlight project peculiar resources required (e.g., special purpose hardware and computer software). This subparagraph shall also describe the allocation of the contractor's facilities during each phase of the software development project.

10.2.5.1.2 *Government Furnished Equipment, Software, and Services.* This subparagraph shall be numbered 3.1.2 and summarize all Government furnished equipment, software, services, and facilities required for development and testing of the delivered software. A schedule detailing when these items will be needed shall also be included. This subparagraph shall highlight all required items not listed in the System/Segment Specification, Prime Item Development Specification, and Critical Item Development Specification.

10.2.5.1.3 *Personnel.* This subparagraph shall be numbered 3.1.3 and state the total number of personnel necessary to complete the software development project.

10.2.5.2 *Software Development.* This paragraph shall be numbered 3.2 and divided into the following subparagraphs to describe the organization(s) responsible for requirements analysis, design, coding, integration, and testing of the deliverable software. If more than one organization is involved, the precise structure, personnel, and resources of each organization and their interrelationships shall be highlighted.

10.2.5.2.1 *Organizational Structure - Software Development.* This subparagraph shall be numbered 3.2.1 and describe the organization(s) responsible for performing software requirements analysis, design, coding, integration, and testing. This subparagraph shall include the authority and responsibilities of each organization and its relationship to other organizational entities (e.g., the organization(s) responsible for performing configuration management). A chart may be used to illustrate the organizational structure of the organization(s) performing requirements analysis, design, coding, integration, and testing and their position within the project management system.

10.2.5.2.2 *Personnel - Software Development.* This subparagraph shall be numbered 3.2.2 and describe the number and skill levels of personnel that will perform software requirements analysis, design, coding, integration, and testing activities. The personnel shall be described by title and minimum qualifications for the position.

10.2.5.2.3 *Resources - Software Development.* This subparagraph shall be numbered 3.2.3 and identify and describe the specific resources necessary for performing software requirements analysis, design, coding, and integration. (Note: The resources for software configuration management and software quality evaluation are detailed in paragraphs 10.2.5.3.3 and 10.2.5.4.3 respectively.) The description of each resource shall reference the paragraph(s) in 10.2.7 describing requirements analysis, design, coding, and integration activities which require the resource.

10.2.5.3 *Software Configuration Management (CM).* This paragraph shall be numbered 3.3. If the plan for software CM is provided in another document (e.g., SCMP or System CM Plan), then this paragraph shall contain the following sentence: "The software configuration management plan is documented in the (enter approved title and identification number of the document)." In this case, the remaining subparagraphs in 10.2.5.3 shall not apply.

If the plan for software CM is not provided in another document, then the following content and format instructions for the subparagraphs of 10.2.5.3 shall apply.

10.2.5.3.1 *Organizational Structure - CM.* This subparagraph shall be numbered 3.3.1 and describe the organization(s) responsible for performing software CM. This subparagraph shall include the authority and responsibilities of each organization and its relationship to other organizational entities (e.g., the organization(s) responsible for performing software quality evaluation). A chart may be used to illustrate the organizational structure of the organization(s) performing software CM and their position within the project management system.

10.2.5.3.2 *Personnel - CM.* This subparagraph shall be numbered 3.3.2 and describe the number and skill levels of personnel that will perform the software CM. The personnel shall be described by title and minimum qualifications for the position.

10.2.5.3.3 *Resources - CM.* This subparagraph shall be numbered 3.3.3 and identify and describe the specific resources necessary for performing software CM. The description of each resource shall reference the paragraph(s) in 10.2.7 describing the CM activities which require the resource.

10.2.5.4 *Software Quality Evaluation.* This paragraph shall be numbered 3.4. If the plan for software quality evaluation is provided in another document (e.g., SQEP), then this paragraph shall contain the following sentence: "The software quality evaluation plan is documented in (enter approved title and identification number of the document)." In this case, the remaining subparagraphs in 10.2.5.4 shall not apply.

If the plan for software quality evaluation is not provided in another document, then the following content and format instructions for the subparagraphs of 10.2.5.4 shall apply.

10.2.5.4.1 *Organizational Structure - Software Quality Evaluation.* This subparagraph shall be numbered 3.4.1 and describe the organization(s) responsible for performing software quality evaluation. This subparagraph shall include the authority and responsibilities of each organization and its relationship to other organizational entities (e.g., the organization(s) responsible for performing CM). A chart may be used to illustrate the organizational structure of the organization(s) performing software quality evaluation and their position within the project management system.

10.2.5.4.2 *Personnel - Software Quality Evaluation.* This subparagraph shall be numbered 3.4.2 and describe the number and skill levels of personnel that will perform software quality evaluation. The personnel shall be described by title and minimum qualifications for the position.

10.2.5.4.3 *Resources - Software Quality Evaluation.* This subparagraph shall be numbered 3.4.3 and identify and describe the specific resources necessary for performing software quality evaluation. The description of each resource shall reference the paragraph(s) in 10.2.7 describing the software quality evaluation activities which require the resource.

10.2.5.5 *Other Software Development Functions.* For each other organization involved in the software development activity, a separate paragraph 3.X (beginning with 3.5) shall be prepared. The name of the function performed by the organization shall comprise the title of the paragraph.

10.2.5.5.1 *Organizational Structure - (Function X).* This subparagraph shall be numbered 3.X.1 (beginning with 3.5.1) and describe the organization(s) responsible for performing function X. This subparagraph shall include the authority and responsibilities of each organization and its relationship to other organizational entities (e.g., organizations responsible for performing CM and software quality evaluation). A chart may be used to illustrate the organizational structure of the organization(s) performing function X and their position within the project management system.

10.2.5.5.2 *Personnel - (Function X).* This subparagraph shall be numbered 3.X.2 (beginning with 3.5.2) and describe the number and skill levels of personnel that will perform function X. The personnel shall be described by title and minimum qualifications for the position.

10.2.5.5.3 *Resources - (Function X).* This subparagraph shall be numbered 3.X.3 (beginning with 3.5.3) and identify and describe the specific resources necessary for performing function X. The description of each resource shall reference the paragraph(s) in 10.2.7 describing function X activities which require the resource.

10.2.6 *Development Schedule and Milestones.* This section shall be numbered 4. and divided into the following paragraphs.

10.2.6.1 *Activities.* This paragraph shall be numbered 4.1 and briefly describe each individual software development activity of the project and its associated schedule, based on the contract master schedule (if applicable). For each activity the schedule shall indicate:

a. Activity initiation
b. Availability of draft and final copies of formal and informal documentation
c. Activity completion times.

The development schedule shall also indicate all significant events (e.g., reviews, audits, key meetings). The schedule may be described graphically.

10.2.6.2 *Activity Network.* This paragraph shall be numbered 4.2 and describe the sequential relationship among all individual activities of the project. This paragraph shall include identification of those activities which impose the greatest time restrictions on project completion and those activities with an excess of time for completion. The above information may be provided graphically (e.g., PERT Chart).

10.2.6.3 *Procedures for Risk Management.* This paragraph shall be numbered 4.3 and describe the contractor's procedures for risk management to be implemented during the development effort. As a minimum, this paragraph shall include procedures for:

a. Identifying the risk areas of the project and the constituent risk factors in each area (e.g., technical problems, requirements stability, acquisition strategy, inflation rate accuracy, socio-economic impacts).
b. Assessing the risk factors identified, including the probability of occurrence and the potential damage.
c. Assigning appropriate resources to reduce the risk factors.
d. Identifying and analyzing the alternatives available for reducing the risk factors.
e. Selecting the most promising alternative for each risk factor.
f. Planning implementation of the selected alternative for each risk factor.
g. Obtaining feedback to determine the success of the risk-reducing action for each risk factor.

10.2.6.4 *Identification of High Risk Areas.* This paragraph shall be numbered 4.4 and describe any known high risk areas in the development schedule or activity network and describe (if possible) the cost and schedule impacts. If alternatives to known high risk areas are available, these alternatives shall also be documented in this paragraph.

10.2.7 *Software Development Procedures.* This section shall be numbered 5. and divided into the following paragraphs and subparagraphs.

10.2.7.1 *Software Standards and Procedures.* This paragraph shall be numbered 5.1. If the software standards and procedures to be used on the project are provided in another document (e.g., SSPM), then this paragraph shall contain the following sentence: "The software standards and procedures to be used on this project are documented in the (enter approved title and identification number of the document)." In this case, the remaining subparagraphs in 10.2.7.1 shall not apply.

If the software standards and procedures are not provided in another document, then the following content and format instructions for the subparagraphs of 10.2.7.1 shall apply.

10.2.7.1.1 *Software Development Tools, Techniques, Methodologies.* This subparagraph shall be numbered 5.1.1 and identify and briefly describe the specific tools, techniques, and methodologies the contractor plans to use to perform:

a. Software Requirements Analysis (including structured requirements analysis tools, techniques, or a combination of both)
b. Preliminary Design
c. Detailed Design (including Program Design Language)
d. Coding and Unit Testing
e. CSC Integration and Testing
f. CSCI Testing

This subparagraph shall include identification and a brief description of all graphical representations, data dictionary representations, textual representations, and automated tools the contractor plans to use.

10.2.7.1.2 *Critical Lower-Level Computer Software Component (LLCSC) and Unit Selection Criteria.* If a top-down methodology is used in the development effort, it sometimes becomes necessary to depart from this approach to address critical lower-level elements. This subparagraph shall be numbered 5.1.2 and describe the criteria to be used by the contractor in determining which lower-level elements shall be deemed critical (e.g., lower-level elements that impact the software's performance, cost, schedule, or other contractual considerations).

10.2.7.1.3 *Software Development Library.* This subparagraph shall be numbered 5.1.3 and describe the software development library (SDL) to be used by the contractor for controlling the software and associated documentation. This subparagraph shall include a description of the contractor's procedures and methods for establishing and implementing the SDL and the contractor's access and control procedures for data stored in the SDL.

10.2.7.1.4 *Software Development Files.* This subparagraph shall be numbered 5.1.4 and define the contractor's plan, including the organization(s) responsible for the creation and maintenance of Software Development Files (SDFs). This subparagraph shall also define the format and contents of the SDFs and describe the procedures for maintaining SDFs.

10.2.7.1.5 *Documentation Formats for Informal Test.* This subparagraph shall be numbered 5.1.5 and describe the proposed documentation formats for all informal tests. As a minimum, this subparagraph shall include the formats for:

a. Unit test cases
b. Unit test procedures
c. Unit test results
d. CSC integration test cases
e. CSC integration test procedures
f. CSC integration test results

10.2.7.1.6 *Design and Coding Standards.* This subparagraph shall be numbered 5.1.6 and describe or reference the design and coding standards to be used in developing the software for the CSCIs. The rules and conventions to be used for: (1) assigning names to software design and data elements, (2) defining and describing interfaces, (3) commenting source code, and (4) chart or graphic standards shall be included. If this subparagraph references design and coding standards in a particular document (e.g., DOD-STD-2167, Appendix C), then any planned modifications to the referenced design and coding standards shall be explained.

10.2.7.1.7 *Formal Reviews.* This subparagraph shall be numbered 5.1.7 and describe the contractor's internal procedures for, and the formats of all reports used to prepare for and conduct, formal reviews.

10.2.7.2 *Software Configuration Management.* This paragraph shall be numbered 5.2. If the software configuration management activities are described in another document (e.g., SCMP, System CM Plan), then this paragraph shall contain the following sentence: "The software configuration management activities are documented in the (enter approved title and identification number of the document)." In this case, the remaining subparagraphs in 10.2.7.2 shall not apply.

If the software configuration management activities are not described in another document, then the following content and format instructions for the subparagraphs of 10.2.7.2 shall apply.

10.2.7.2.1 *Configuration Identification.* This subparagraph shall be numbered 5.2.1 and divided into the following subparagraphs.

10.2.7.2.1.1 *Developmental Configuration.* This subparagraph shall be numbered 5.2.1.1 and identify the contractor's internal Developmental Configuration(s) to be used in the development of the CSCI(s). For each Developmental Configuration identified, the method of establishing it shall be described and the contents shall be listed. For example, the engineering release of the first draft of the Software Top Level Design Document (STLDD), prior to submitting it at the Preliminary Design Review, shall establish the internal Developmental Configuration.

10.2.7.2.1.2 *CSCI and Related Documentation.* This subparagraph shall be numbered 5.2.1.2 and describe the methods to be used in identifying (e.g., naming, marking, numbering) Top-Level Computer Software Components (TLCSCs), LLCSCs, Units, and related documents (e.g., software design documents, specifications). This subparagraph shall also describe how revisions to TLCSCs, LLCSCs, Units, and related documents shall be identified.

10.2.7.2.2 *Configuration Control.* This subparagraph shall be numbered 5.2.2 and divided into the following subparagraphs to provide a detailed description of the procedures to be used in controlling changes to and maintaining the Developmental Configuration(s).

10.2.7.2.2.1 *Flow of Configuration Control.* This subparagraph shall be numbered 5.2.2.1 and describe the process by which problems and changes are submitted, reviewed, and subsequently approved or disapproved. This description may be accomplished graphically by a configuration control flow chart (see Figure 1).

10.2.7.2.2.2 *Reporting Documentation.* This paragraph shall be numbered 5.2.2.2 and divided into the following subparagraphs to describe the reporting documentation (e.g., Specification Change Notice, Engineering Change Proposal) to be used in controlling software problems and changes, starting with the report for software problems and changes.

10.2.7.2.2.2.1 *Report for Software Problems and Changes.* This subparagraph shall be numbered 5.2.2.2.1 and identify and describe the format used to document software problems and changes detected during software development. This report shall include:

a. System or Project Name - The name of the system or development project to which this report applies.
b. Originator - The name, telephone number, and designation of the organization submitting the report.
c. Problem Number - The assigned problem number (once a problem number has been assigned in accordance with established project configuration control procedures).
d. Problem Name - A brief phrase descriptive of the problem and descriptive of similar problems, if applicable.
e. Software Element or Document Affected - The specific software element(s), document(s) paragraph(s), or both to which the report applies, including ap-

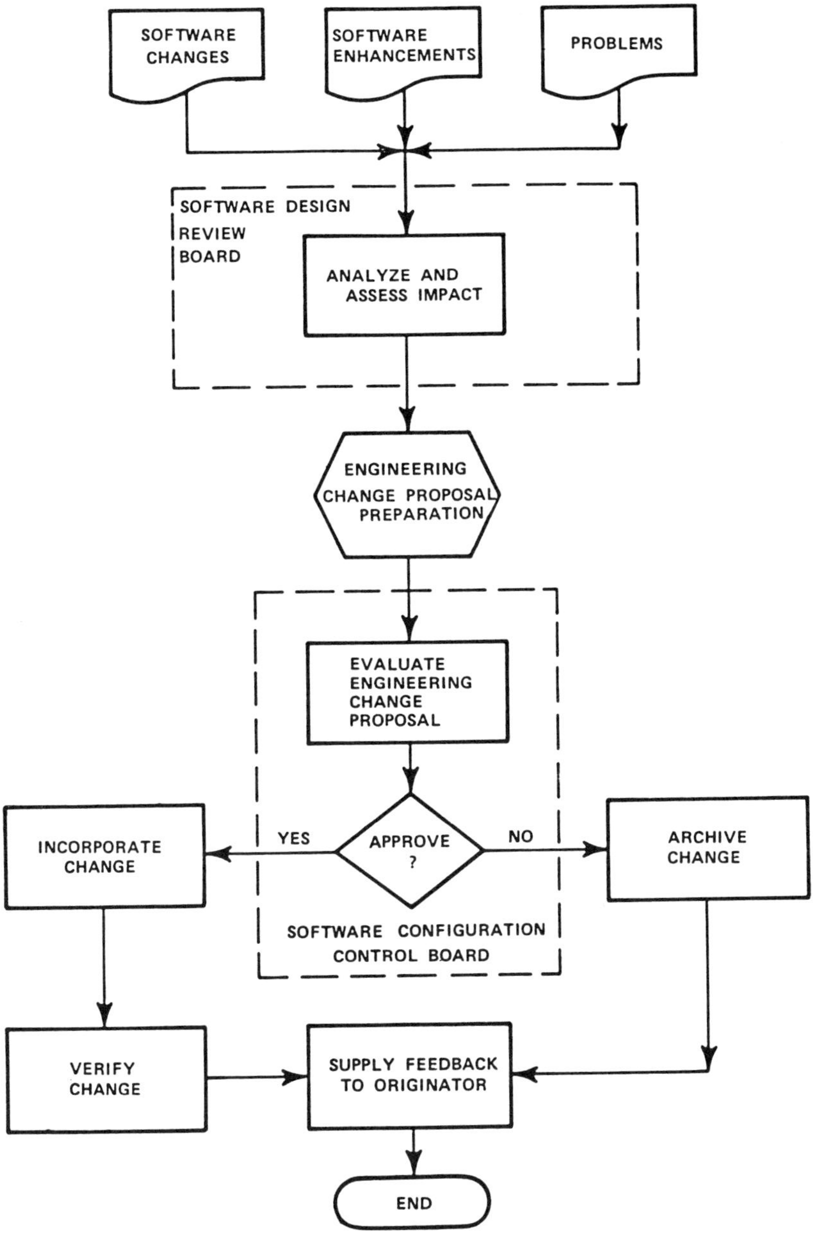

Figure 1. Sample configuration control flow chart.

propriate configuration identification and version number, if applicable. Include all established baselines or Developmental Configurations affected.

f. Origination Date - The date the report is first submitted.

g. Need Date or Priority - The date the fix is needed in order to maintain established schedules or priority in accordance with established standards.

h. Description of Problem - A description of the problem and the conditions, inputs, and equipment configuration under which the problem arises. A description of the activities leading up to the problem occurrence. Sufficient problem information to permit duplication and analysis. Include relationship to other reported problems and modifications.

i. Analyst - The name, telephone number, and organization of the individual assigned to analyze the problem.

j. Date Assigned - The date the analyst was assigned.

k. Date Complete - The date the analysis was completed.

l. Analysis Time - The time required to analyze the problem report.

m. Recommended Solution - After analysis of the problem, the recommended solution and alternative solutions, if available. The nature of the recommended solution by a short descriptive phrase. When applicable, supporting rationale and test results.

n. Impacts - The cost, schedule, and interface impacts if the solution is approved. Also, performance impacts if the solution is not approved. As applicable, include the impact on the other systems, configuration items, other contractors, system employment, integrated logistics support, system resources, training, etc.

o. Problem Status - The problem status designated by the configuration control procedures.

p. Approval of Solution - To be designated by the cognizant configuration control authority.

q. Follow-up Action - Actions following resolution of the problem.

r. Corrector - The name, telephone number, and organization of the individual correcting the problem.

s. Correction Date - The date the problem was corrected.

t. Version Number - The version in which the problem will be corrected.

u. Correction Time - The time required to correct the problem.

v. Implementation Solution - A brief description of the implemented solution to the problem.

10.2.7.2.2.2.2 *Report X (insert title).* This subparagraph shall be numbered 5.2.2.2.X (beginning with 5.2.2.2.2) and describe or reference the format, contents, and instructions for completing report X.

10.2.7.2.2.3 *Review Procedures.* This subparagraph shall be numbered 5.2.2.3 and divided into the following subparagraphs to describe the purpose of and the procedures to be employed by any review boards (e.g., Software Configuration Control Board) associated with the flow of configuration control.

10.2.7.2.2.3.1 *Review Board X (insert title) Procedures.* This subparagraph shall be numbered 5.2.2.3.X (beginning with 5.2.2.3.1) and describe the purpose of and the procedures to be followed by Review Board X. This subparagraph shall also describe how the procedures used by Review Board X, in conjunction with the configuration identification scheme, provide historical traceability.

10.2.7.2.2.4 *Storage, Handling, and Release of Project Media.* This subparagraph shall be numbered 5.2.2.4 and describe the methods to formally control the storage, handling, and release of software and documentation (including master copies) during the development process.

10.2.7.2.2.5 *Additional Control.* This subparagraph shall be numbered 5.2.2.5 and identify any additional configuration control activities not discussed above.

10.2.7.2.3 *Configuration Status Accounting.* This subparagraph shall be numbered 5.2.3 and define the configuration status accounting system. The content, format, and purpose of the status accounting records and reports shall be described.

10.2.7.2.4 *Configuration Audits.* This subparagraph shall be numbered 5.2.4 and describe the procedures for conducting configuration audits. The description of how the configuration status accounting reports and records will be used in conducting these audits shall be included.

10.2.7.2.5 *Preparation for Configuration Authentication.* This subparagraph shall be numbered 5.2.5 and describe the contractor's procedures to prepare for and respond to authentication of the applicable specifications. As a minimum, this subparagraph shall include the procedures for:

a. Submitting specifications to the contracting agency for review and authentication.
b. Ensuring the incorporation of approved changes.
c. Updating the configuration status accounting reports to reflect approved baseline(s).

10.2.7.2.6 *Configuration Management Major Milestones.* This subparagraph shall be numbered 5.2.6 and identify the major internal and Government CM-related milestones for the life cycle phase(s) of the contractual effort.

10.2.7.3 *Software Quality Evaluation.* This paragraph shall be numbered 5.3. If the software quality evaluation activities are described in another document (e.g. SQEP), then this paragraph shall contain the following sentence: "The software quality evaluation activities are documented in the (enter approved title and identification number of the document)." In this case, the remaining subparagraphs in 10.2.7.3 shall not apply.

If the software quality evaluation activities are not described in another document, then the following content and format instructions for the subparagraphs of 10.2.7.3 shall apply.

10.2.7.3.1 *Software Quality Evaluation Procedures, Methods, Tools and Facilities.* This subparagraph shall be numbered 5.3.1 and describe or reference the procedures, methods, tools, and facilities that will be used to evaluate the quality of the software and associated documentation and activities. Examples of methods that might be used are internal reviews, audits, walkthroughs, and inspections. Tool descriptions shall include the name, identification number, and version of each tool and its role in the evaluation process. Some or all of this information may be provided by reference to appropriate sections of the SSPM or other sections in the SDP.

10.2.7.3.2 *Quality Evaluation Activities.* This subparagraph shall be numbered 5.3.2 and divided into the following subparagraphs.

10.2.7.3.2.1 *Phase-Independent Activities.* This subparagraph shall be numbered 5.3.2.1 and divided into the following subparagraphs to describe the contractor's plans for software quality evaluation activities that will occur during all phases of the software development cycle. Each subparagraph shall identify the evaluation criteria to be used and the evaluation methods and tools to be employed.

10.2.7.3.2.1.1 *Evaluation of Development Plans, Standards, Procedures, Tools, and Facilities.* This subparagraph shall be numbered 5.3.2.1.1 and describe the contractor's plans for evaluating the SDP, SCMP, SSPM, and any updates to these documents to determine whether the selected methodologies, standards, procedures, tools, and facilities are in compliance with contractual requirements and are adequate to support the software development project.

10.2.7.3.2.1.2 *Evaluation of Configuration Management.* This subparagraph shall be numbered 5.3.2.1.2 and describe the contractor's plans for evaluating the configuration management methods applied to the software development project. Included shall be plans for evaluating configuration identification, configuration control, configuration status accounting and reporting, and preparation for configuration audits.

10.2.7.3.2.1.3 *Evaluation of Software Development Library.* This subparagraph shall be numbered 5.3.2.1.3 and describe the contractor's plans for evaluating the software development library. Included shall be plans for evaluating the content, procedures, and controls provided by the library.

10.2.7.3.2.1.4 *Evaluation of Documentation and Media Distribution.* This subparagraph shall be numbered 5.3.2.1.4 and describe the contractor's plans for evaluation of documentation and media distribution. Included shall be plans for evaluating the procedures and controls used for distribution of documentation and media.

10.2.7.3.2.1.5 *Evaluation of Storage and Handling.* This subparagraph shall be numbered 5.3.2.1.5 and describe the contractor's plans for evaluation of storage and handling of media and documentation. Included shall be plans for evaluating protection of materials, backup procedures, and compliance with security requirements.

10.2.7.3.2.1.6 *Evaluation of Non-Deliverables.* This subparagraph shall be numbered 5.3.2.1.6 and describe the contractor's plans for evaluating non-deliverables to be used on the project. Included shall be plans for evaluating compliance with applicable contractual requirements and adequacy of configuration management of non-deliverables.

10.2.7.3.2.1.7 *Evaluation of Risk Management.* This subparagraph shall be numbered 5.3.2.1.7 and describe the contractor's plans for evaluating the procedures employed and results achieved by risk management on the project.

10.2.7.3.2.1.8 *Subcontractor Products.* This subparagraph shall be numbered 5.3.2.1.8, identify the organization(s) responsible, and describe the contractor's plans and procedures for ensuring that software and associated documentation from subcontractors conform to contractual requirements. Included shall be plans for evaluating preaward surveys of prospective subcontractors, adequacy of requirements established for subcontractors, adequacy of subcontractor procedures as planned and as implemented, and adequacy of subcontractor products.

10.2.7.3.2.1.9 *Commercially Available, Reusable, and Government Furnished Software.* This subparagraph shall be numbered 5.3.2.1.9 and describe the contractor's plans for evaluating the planning performed for the use of commercially available, reusable, and Government furnished software. It shall also describe the contractor's plans for evaluating this software once acquired and for certifying commercially available and reusable software that meets specified criteria.

10.2.7.3.2.1.10 *Quality Evaluation Records.* This subparagraph shall be numbered 5.3.2.1.10 and describe the contractor's plans for preparing and maintaining records of each quality evaluation performed. It shall identify the formats to be used and the information to be recorded for each evaluation. It shall also describe plans for maintaining the records and for making them available for Government review.

10.2.7.3.2.1.11 *Corrective Action System.* This subparagraph shall be numbered 5.3.2.1.11 and describe the corrective action system to be implemented by the contractor. It shall include a description of the contractor's plans for: (1) reporting detected problems, (2) analyzing these problems, (3) classifying problems by category (such as requirements, design, code, or documentation) and by priority (such as high, medium, low), (4) identifying necessary corrective action, (5) identifying trends in the problems reported, (6) analyzing these trends to recommend changes that will improve software quality, (7) authorizing the implementation of corrective steps, (8) documenting the corrective actions taken, (9) performing re-evaluation after corrections have been made, (10) tracking and closing out the problems reported, and (11) providing Government visibility into critical problems based on the categorization and priority schemes and problem/change reports.

10.2.7.3.2.1.12 *Quality Evaluation Reports.* This subparagraph shall be numbered 5.3.2.1.12 and describe the types of reports that will be prepared to document the results of the software quality evaluation activities. It shall identify the formats to be used, the information to be included in each report, and the frequency and distribution of each report.

10.2.7.3.2.1.13 *Evaluation of Corrective Action System.* This subparagraph shall be numbered 5.3.2.1.13 and describe the contractor's plans for evaluating the corrective action system. Included shall be plans for evaluating each of the features identified in paragraph 5.3.2.1.11 of the contractor's SDP.

10.2.7.3.2.1.14 *Assessment of Software Quality Evaluation.* This subparagraph shall be numbered 5.3.2.1.14 and describe the contractor's plans for assessing the software quality evaluations performed.

10.2.7.3.2.1.15 *Certification.* This subparagraph shall be numbered 5.3.2.1.15 and describe the contractor's plans for providing evidence that deliverable products are in compliance with contract requirements. Included shall be a description of the evidence that will be presented in support of the certification.

10.2.7.3.2.1.16 *Interface with Software IV&V Contractor.* This subparagraph shall be numbered 5.3.2.1.16 and describe the contractor's plans for interfacing with the software independent verification and validation (IV&V) contractor, if applicable. Included shall be plans for providing the software IV&V contractor with materials to be evaluated, processing discrepancy reports submitted by the software IV&V contractor, participating in meetings with the software IV&V contractor, and coordinating on the status of discrepancies reported.

10.2.7.3.2.1.17 *Government Review at Contractor, Subcontractor, or Vendor Facility.* This subparagraph shall be numbered 5.3.2.1.17 and describe the contractor's plans for providing the contracting agency with facilities and access for reviews of products and activities at contractor, subcontractor, or vendor facilities.

10.2.7.3.2.1.18 *Quality Cost Data.* This subparagraph shall be numbered 5.3.2.1.18 and describe the contractor's plans for collecting, analyzing, and documenting data relative to the cost of detecting and correcting problems in software and associated documentation. It shall identify the specific cost data to be collected and the analysis to be performed on that data.

10.2.7.3.2.2 *Phase-dependent Activities.* This subparagraph shall be numbered 5.3.2.2. Each of the six phases of the software development life cycle shall have a separate subparagraph under 5.3.2.2 to describe phase-dependent activities. Subparagraph 5.3.2.2.1 shall cover Software Requirements Analysis, 5.3.2.2.2 shall cover Preliminary Design, and so on.

10.2.7.3.2.2.1 *Phase X Name.* This subparagraph shall be numbered 5.3.2.2.X (beginning with 5.3.2.2.1) and divided into the following subparagraphs.

10.2.7.3.2.2.1.1 *Activities Evaluation-Phase X Name.* This subparagraph shall be numbered 5.3.2.2.X.1 (beginning with 5.3.2.2.1.1) and describe the contractor's plans for conducting in-process internal reviews of the activities performed during Phase X to determine their compliance with approved plans, standards, and procedures. This description shall include evaluation of the planning and preparation for any formal reviews or audits to be conducted during Phase X. The description shall identify the specific activities to be evaluated and for each, the evaluation criteria to be used and the evaluation methods and tools to be employed.

10.2.7.3.2.2.1.2 *Products Evaluation-Phase X Name.* This subparagraph shall be numbered 5.3.2.2.X.2 (beginning with 5.3.2.2.1.2) and describe the contractor's plans for conducting in-process internal reviews of each of the products of Phase X. The description shall identify the specific products to be evaluated and for each, the evaluation criteria to be used and the evaluation methods and tools to be employed. Evaluation criteria shall include, at a minimum, adherence to required format, compliance with contractual requirements, traceability to and consistency with other software development products as appropriate, internal consistency, understandability, technical adequacy, and appropriate degree of completeness.

10.2.7.3.2.2.2 *Evaluations During System-Level Testing.* This subparagraph shall be numbered 5.3.2.2.7 and describe the contractor's plans for evaluation of software and documentation as a result of software changes occurring during System Integration and Testing, Development Test and Evaluation, and Operational Testing and Evaluation.

10.2.7.3.2.2.3 *Acceptance Inspection.* This subparagraph shall be numbered 5.3.2.2.8 and describe the contractor's plans for supporting Government acceptance inspection. Included shall be plans for ensuring that all required products will be available and ready for Government inspection, all required procedures have been performed, and evidence of these procedures will be available for Government inspection.

10.2.7.3.2.2.4 *Installation and Checkout.* This subparagraph shall be numbered 5.3.2.2.9 and describe the contractor's plans for evaluating installation and checkout of the software, if required by the contract, to ensure that this activity has been carried out in compliance with procedures specified in the software development plans.

10.2.7.4 *Additional Software Development Procedures.* This paragraph shall be numbered 5.4 and, if applicable, shall describe procedures to be used to perform the functions described in 10.2.5.5. Subparagraph 5.4.1 shall identify procedures for the first function described in 10.2.5.5, subparagraph 5.4.2 shall identify procedures for the second function described in 10.2.5.5 etc. This paragraph shall also describe any additional software development procedures not previously addressed (e.g., security procedures and controls, classification procedures).

10.2.7.5 *Commercially Available, Reusable, and Government Furnished Software.* This paragraph shall be numbered 5.5 and divided into the following subparagraphs.

10.2.7.5.1 *Identification, Data Rights, and Documentation.* This subparagraph shall be numbered 5.5.1 and briefly describe the commercially available, reusable, and Government furnished software the contractor plans to incorporate into the software product(s) and provide the rationale for its use. This subparagraph shall also include the plans for modifying the commercially available, reusable, and Government furnished software. In addition, this subparagraph shall include the plans for providing the contracting agency with associated data rights and documentation regarding any deliverable commercially available and reusable software. This subparagraph shall reference the appropriate CM section, in this document or another document, describing the contractor's procedures for controlling revisions to commercially available and reusable computer resources.

10.2.7.5.2 *Certification.* This subparagraph shall be numbered 5.5.2 and describe the contractor's plans for certifying commercially available and reusable software prior to its use in the software product.

10.2.7.6 *Data Rights and Documentation for Software Development Library.* This paragraph shall be numbered 5.6 and describe the contractor's plans for providing the contracting agency with associated data rights and documentation for the SDL.

10.2.7.7 *Non-deliverable Software, Firmware, and Hardware Controls.* This paragraph shall be numbered 5.7 and describe the controls the contractor plans to impose on any non-deliverable software, firmware, and hardware used in the development, testing, or acquisition of all deliverable software. These controls shall include requirements for commercially available, reusable, and newly developed hardware, firmware, and software. As a minimum, this paragraph shall include the requirements for:

a. Modifications (if applicable)
b. Documentation
c. Configuration management
d. Design and coding standards
e. Testing
f. Quality evaluation
g. Certification

10.2.7.8 *Software Developed for Hardware Configuration Items (HWCIs).* This paragraph shall be numbered 5.8 and describe the contractor's software development procedures for all software that is part of an HWCI (e.g., software in firmware devices). As a minimum, this paragraph shall include the procedures for:

a. Requirements analysis and allocation
b. Design and coding
c. Hardware and software integration and test
d. Coordination of hardware and software design

e. Documentation
f. Configuration management
g. Software quality evaluation

10.2.7.9 *Installation and Checkout.* This paragraph shall be numbered 5.9 and describe the contractor's procedures to install and checkout the deliverable software at the Government-designated facilities, if installation and checkout is a requirement of the contract.

10.2.7.10 *Interface Management.* This paragraph shall be numbered 5.10 and describe the contractor's plan for coordinating design and data management efforts to ensure compatibility at interfaces with associate contractors (i.e. where two or more contractors are participating in development or production of the system).

10.2.8 *Notes.* This section shall be numbered 6. and contain any general information that aids in understanding this document (e.g., background information, glossary). This section shall include an alphabetical listing of all acronyms, abbreviations, and their meanings as used in this document.

10.2.9 *Appendixes.* Appendixes may contain any supplemental information published separately for convenience in document maintenance (e.g., charts, classified data). Appendixes may be bound as separate documents for ease in handling. Appendixes shall be numbered sequentially in Roman numeral (I, II, etc.), and the paragraphs within each appendix shall all be numbered as multiples of 10 (e.g., Appendix I, paragraph 10.1, 10.2, Appendix II, paragraph 20.1, 20.2, etc.).

As applicable, each appendix shall be referenced in the main body of the document where the data would normally have been provided.

1. TITLE

SOFTWARE DETAILED DESIGN DOCUMENT

2. IDENTIFICATION NUMBER

DI-MCCR-80031

3. DESCRIPTION/PURPOSE

3.1 The Software Detailed Design Document (SDDD) describes in detail the structure and organization of a particular Computer Software Configuration Item (CSCI). This document describes the decomposition of the Top-Level Computer Software Components (TLCSCs) of the CSCI into Lower-Level Computer Software Components (LLCSCs) and Units. Additionally, the SDDD defines the interface, data, and processing characteristics for each LLCSC and Unit in the CSCI design.

3.2 The SDDD describes the characteristics of each LLCSC and Unit to the Government. Upon completion of Physical Configuration Audit (PCA), the SDDD becomes a part of the Product Baseline for the CSCI.

3.3 The SDDD is used by the contractor as the basis for development of the LLCSCs and Units. It is entered into the Developmental Configuration for the CSCI.

4. APPROVAL DATE (YYMMDD)

No entry.

5. OFFICE OF PRIMARY RESPONSIBILITY (OPR)

NM

6a. DTIC REQUIRED

No entry.

6b. GIDEP REQUIRED

No entry.

7. APPLICATION/INTERRELATIONSHIP

7.1 This Data Item Description (DID) contains the format and content preparation instructions for that data generated under work tasks described by 3.4.7.2 of MIL-STD-483, 3.1.3.3.5.2 of MIL-STD-490, and 5.3.1.2 and 5.3.2.3 of DOD-STD-2167.

7.2 The Government's Data Manager for this system must specify in the Statement of Work and Contract Data Requirements List whether this document is to be prepared and delivered on bound 8-1/2 by 11 inch bond paper or electronic media. If electronic media is selected, the precise format must be specified (e.g., magnetic tape, floppy disk, host system, etc.).

7.3 The SDDD is a product of the Detailed Design phase of CSCI development. It documents the completed design of the CSCI, based on the framework provided by the top-level design in the Software Top Level Design Document (STLDD), DI-MCCR-80012.

7.4 At PCA, the SDDD is included in the Software Product Specification (SPS), DI-MCCR-80029. It describes the detailed design and is the basis for coding the CSCI.

7.5 The design of one or more external interfaces of the CSCI implemented by the LLCSCs and Units of detailed design may be provided by one or more Interface Design Documents (IDDs), DI-MCCR-80027.

7.6 The structure and content of data base(s) used by the LLCSCs and Units of detailed design may be provided by one or more Data Base Design Documents (DBDDs), DI-MCCR-80028.

7.7 This DID supersedes DI-S-2139A and DI-S-25844A.

8. APPROVAL LIMITATION

No entry.

9a. APPLICABLE FORMS

No entry.

9b. AMSC NUMBER

No entry.

10. PREPARATION INSTRUCTIONS

10.1 *Source Document.* The applicable issue of documents cited herein, including their approval date and dates of any applicable amendments and revisions, shall be as reflected in the contract.

10.2 *Content and Format Instructions.* This document shall be prepared on bound 8-1/2 by 11 inch bond paper (hardcopy) or a form of electronic media. The contract will specify the precise format. Each page prior to Section 1 shall be numbered in lowercase roman numeral beginning with page ii for the Table of Contents. Each page starting from Section 1 to the end of the document shall be consecutively numbered in arabic numerals. For hardcopy formats, this document may be printed on one or both sides of each page (single-sided/double-sided). For single-sided documents, all pages shall contain the document control number in the top right-hand corner. For double-sided documents, all even-numbered pages shall be on the left-hand side of the document and odd-numbered pages on the right-hand side. For double-sided documents, the control number shall be placed in the top right-hand corner for each odd-numbered page and the top left-hand corner for each even-numbered page. All paragraph and subparagraph headings listed below shall be included in the document. All paragraphs and subparagraphs starting with the phrase "This (sub)paragraph shall . . . " may be written as multiple (sub)paragraphs to enhance readability. The letters "W", "X", and "Y" serve as identifiers for a series of descriptions. For example, the subparagraphs describing interfaces are designated as 3.1.X; if there is more than one interface, the first subparagraph is numbered 3.1.1 (Name) Interface, the second is 3.1.2 (Name) Interface, etc. (see 10.2.5.1.1). Each Interface X shall have subparagraphs containing a summary, an item summary, and an item format. A similar paragraph structure is used in 10.2.5.3.1, where "W", "X", and "Y" serve as identifiers for nested subparagraph descriptions. For example, the subparagraphs describing TLCSC decomposition are designated as 3.3.W, with subparagraphs for allocation and design. For each TLCSC decomposition, "W', there may be one or more LLCSCs, "X", (described in 3.3.W.2.X) or Units, "Y", (described in 3.3.W.3.Y), each with corresponding subparagraphs (see 10.2.5.3.1.2.1, 10.2.5.3.1.3.1). For example:

"3.3.1 TLCSC 1 Decomposition

3.3.1.1 TLCSC 1 Requirements Allocation

3.3.1.2 LLCSC Design
3.3.1.2.1 LLCSC 1 (of TLCSC 1)
3.3.1.2.1.1 LLCSC 1 Inputs
3.3.1.2.1.2 LLCSC 1 Local Data
3.3.1.2.1.3 LLCSC 1 Process Control
3.3.1.2.1.4 LLCSC 1 Processing
3.3.1.2.1.5 LLCSC 1 Utilization of other elements
3.3.1.2.1.6 LLCSC 1 Limitations
3.3.1.2.1.7 LLCSC 1 Outputs
3.3.1.3 Unit Level Design
3.3.1.3.1 Unit 1 (of TLCSC 1)
3.3.1.3.1.1 Unit 1 Inputs
3.3.1.3.1.2 Unit 1 Local Data
3.3.1.3.1.3 Unit 1 Process Control
3.3.1.3.1.4 Unit 1 Processing
3.3.1.3.1.5 Unit 1 Utilization of other elements
3.3.1.3.1.6 Unit 1 Limitations
3.3.1.3.1.7 Unit 1 Outputs
3.3.2 TLCSC 2 Decomposition''

This document shall be as self-contained as possible. Reference to other documents should be minimal. This document shall consist of the following:

a. Cover Page
b. Table of Contents
c. Scope
d. Referenced Documents
e. Requirements
f. Notes
g. Appendixes

10.2.1 *Cover Page.* This page shall contain the document control number in the upper right hand corner. In the center of the page, these words shall appear in the following format:

SOFTWARE DETAILED DESIGN DOCUMENT
FOR THE
[PROJECT NAME]

CONTRACT NO. [contract number]
CDRL SEQUENCE NO. [CDRL number]
[Date of document - day month year]

Prepared for:
[Contracting Agency Name, department code]

Prepared by:
[contractor name and address]

10.2.2 *Table of Contents.* This document shall contain a Table of Contents listing the title and page number of all titled paragraphs and subparagraphs. The Table of Contents shall then list the title and page number of all figures, tables, and appendixes, in that order.

10.2.3 *Scope.* This section shall be numbered 1. and divided into the following paragraphs.

10.2.3.1 *Identification.* This paragraph shall be numbered 1.1 and contain the approved identification number, title, and if applicable, abbreviation of the CSCI and the system to which this SDDD applies. This paragraph shall begin with the following sentence: "This Software Detailed Design Document describes the detailed design for the CSCI identified as (insert title, if applicable insert abbreviation in parenthesis, insert CSCI number) of the (insert title, if applicable insert abbreviation in parenthesis, insert system identification number) System."

10.2.3.2 *Purpose.* This paragraph shall be numbered 1.2, state the purpose of the system, and identify the LLCSCs and Units of the CSCI to which this SDDD applies.

10.2.3.3 *Introduction.* This paragraph shall be numbered 1.3 and summarize the purpose and contents of this document.

10.2.4 *Referenced Documents.* This section shall be numbered 2. and list by document and title all documents referenced in this document. This section shall also identify the source for all documents not available through normal Government Stocking activities.

10.2.5 *Requirements.* This section shall be numbered 3. and divided into the following paragraphs and subparagraphs to describe the detailed design of the CSCI. The decomposition of each TLCSC into LLCSCs and Units, as well as the algorithms employed by and the flow of data and execution control between LLCSCs and Units, shall be specified. The design shall be specified at a level of detail that will lead directly to production of the source code.

10.2.5.1 *Interface Design.* This paragraph shall be numbered 3.1 and divided into the following subparagraphs to identify and describe the detailed design information for all CSCI interfaces not described in an IDD.

10.2.5.1.1 *(Name X) Interface.* This subparagraph shall be numbered 3.1.X (beginning with 3.1.1) and divided into the following subparagraphs.

10.2.5.1.1.1 *Interface X Summary.* This subparagraph shall be numbered 3.1.X.1 (beginning with 3.1.1.1). The information passed across interface X shall be listed and its purpose described in this subparagraph. If interface X is bi-directional, each direction shall be separately listed. The initiation criteria for and response to each item of information passed shall be specified. A reference may be made to an interface summary table. An example of an interface summary table is provided in Table I.

10.2.5.1.1.2 *Interface X Item Summary.* This subparagraph shall be numbered 3.1.X.2 (beginning with 3.1.1.2) and describe, for each item listed in 3.1.X.1 above, the data, messages, or control information associated with that item. A reference may be made to an interface item summary table. An example of an interface item summary table is provided in Table II.

TABLE I. Sample interface summary table.

CSCI-to-HWCI		
Information	Initiation Criteria	Response
Launch	Operator input	Status word
Shutdown	Operator input or automatic for emergency state	Status word
Loop check	Periodic 1 H_Z rate	Loop check
Status request	Operator input or periodic at 10 H_Z rate	Status word
Presets	Operator input	N/A

10.2.5.1.1.3 *Interface X Item Format.* This subparagraph shall be numbered 3.1.X.3 (beginning with 3.1.1.3) and completely describe the format for each data, message, and control item passed via Interface X. The description of each field of each item shall include:

a. A description of the information contained in the field.
b. The first and last bit positions of the field and word number(s), if applicable.
c. The name of the field, if variable, or the value of the field, if fixed.
d. The scaling, units of measure, and conventions associated with the field.

This subparagraph may reference an interface item format table to depict the required information. An example of an interface item format table is provided in Table III.

10.2.5.2 *Global Data.* This paragraph shall be numbered 3.2, and identify, state the purpose of, and describe data common to more than one LLCSC or Unit in the detailed design and not provided in a separate DBDD. This paragraph shall include the format of the global data, the LLCSCs and Units which use the data, and all other characteristics of the global data needed to satisfy global data requirements. Examples are: limits or ranges of global data values, accuracy and precision. This information may be provided in a global data definition table. An example of a global data definition table is provided in Table IV.

TABLE II. Sample interface item summary table.

Information	Control	Data	Message
Launch request	—	ID Code	Target X coord Y coord Z coord Timer
Launch	—	Launch code	—
Clock sync	Clock	—	—
Shutdown	Disable	Status code	—

TABLE III. Sample interface item format table.[3]

Byte[1] Number	Data Type	Size	Units	Scaling[5]	Conventions	Content
01-02	Integer	1 word[2]	N/A	N/A	Default = employee number	User ID number
03-08	ASCII	6 char	N/A	N/A	Default = last name	User password
09-12	ASCII	4 char	N/A	N/A	See text	User request
13-16	Real	2 words	Feet	20-12	MSB = sign bit[4]	X coordinate
17-20	Real	2 words	Feet	20-12	MSB = sign bit	Y coordinate
21-24	Real	2 words	Feet	20-12	MSB = sign bit	Z coordinate
25-28	Integer	2 words	Sec	N/A	N/A	Time

[1]Byte = 8 bits

[2]Word = 16 bits

[3]Transfer rate = 1 m bits/sec

[4]MSB = most significant bit

[5]X-Y = X bits before the binary point
Y bits after the binary point

TABLE IV. Sample global data definition table.

Identifier	Description	Data Type	Data Representation	Size	Units of Measure	Limit/Range	Accuracy/Precision	Applicable TLCSCs
Grange	Grid range	Real	Constant	1 word	Miles	N/A	N/A	TLCSC 31 TLCSC 32 TLCSC 33
Six 11	Emergency state	Boolean	Boolean	1 byte[1]	N/A	N/A	N/A	TLCSC 31 TLCSC 33
A List	Authorization list—data base user priority level	ASCII integer	File of 10 records	200 words 6 char[2] 1 word	N/A	50 records A-Z 0-4	N/A	TLCSC 31 TLCSC 32
Coords	Coordinates	Real	10 × 10 array	100 words[3]	N/A	N/A	6 dec. places ± .000005	TLCSC 32 TLCSC 33

[1]Byte = 8 bits

[2]Char = 8 bits

[3]Word = 16 bits, 2 bytes

If files or a data base are part of the global data, this paragraph shall also provide the following details:

a. Purpose of each file or data base.
b. Structure of each file or data base in terms of contents and size.
c. Access procedures (e.g., sequential, random access).

For convenience of generation and maintenance, the information described in this subparagraph may be provided as an appendix and referenced herein.

10.2.5.3 *Detailed Design.* This paragraph shall be numbered 3.3 and divided into the following subparagraphs to describe the detailed design for each LLCSC and Unit. This information may be provided by automated tools or other techniques (e.g., program design language).

10.2.5.3.1 *TLCSC (Name W).* This subparagraph shall be numbered 3.3.W (beginning with 3.3.1) and identify by name and number TLCSC W. In addition, this subparagraph shall identify by name and number each CSCI interface which the TLCSC helps implement.

This subparagraph shall describe the decomposition of TLCSC W into LLCSCs and Units. This description may be provided by a TLCSC decomposition chart (or series of charts). Figure 1 is an example of a TLCSC decomposition chart. Each LLCSC shall

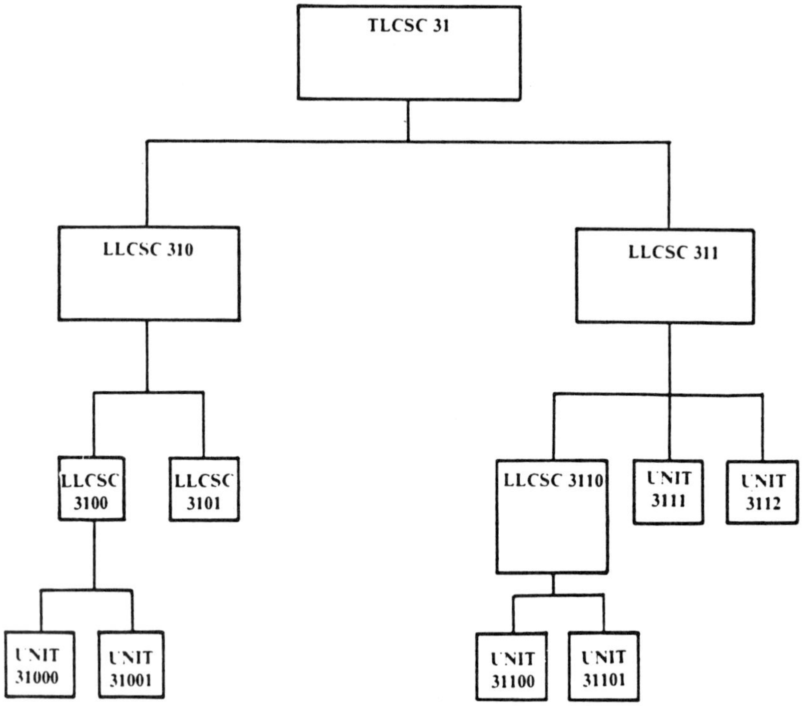

Figure 1. Sample TLCSC decomposition chart.

be described in 10.2.5.3.1.2 below by subparagraph 3.3.W.2.X and its subparagraphs. Each unit shall be described in 10.2.5.3.1.3 below by subparagraph 3.3.W.3.Y and its subparagraphs.

10.2.5.3.1.1 *TLCSC W Requirements Allocation.* This subparagraph shall be numbered 3.3.W.1 (beginning with 3.3.1.1) and describe the allocation of TLCSC W functional, performance, and interface requirements to the LLCSCs and Units described above. The allocation shall allow the traceability of the LLCSCs and Units to their originating requirements. The requirements allocation may be provided by a requirements allocation table. An example of a requirements allocation table is presented in Table V. In addition, this subparagraph shall allocate the memory and processing time constraints of TLCSC W to the LLCSCs and Units depicted in 10.2.5.3.1 above. The memory and processing time allocation may be provided by a memory processing time table. An example of a memory/processing time table is provided in Table VI.

10.2.5.3.1.2 *LLCSC Design.* This subparagraph shall be numbered 3.3.W.2 (beginning with 3.3.1.2) and divided into the following subparagraphs to specify the detailed design of each LLCSC included in TLCSC W.

10.2.5.3.1.2.1 *LLCSC X.* This subparagraph shall be numbered 3.3.W.2.X (beginning with 3.3.1.2.1) and identify LLCSC X by name, number, and level of decomposition and describe its purpose. If the system can exist in various states, this paragraph shall also list the states in which LLCSC X executes. The information on various states may be provided in a table.

The following information shall be provided for LLCSC X. A data or control flow diagram may be used to depict the information described.

10.2.5.3.1.2.1.1 *LLCSC X Inputs.* This subparagraph shall be numbered 3.3.W.2.X.1 (beginning with 3.3.1.2.1.1), and identify and state the purpose of the input data required by LLCSC X. Input data may be transmitted as global data, direct I/O, passed parameters, or through shared memory. This subparagraph shall include the source(s), format(s), units of measure, and all other characteristics of the input data needed to satisfy the input requirements of LLCSC X. Examples are: limits or ranges of input values, accuracy and precision, frequency of input arrival, and legality checks for erroneous information. This information may be provided in an LLCSC X input table. An example of an LLCSC X input table is provided in Table VII.

10.2.5.3.1.2.1.2 *LLCSC X Local Data.* This subparagraph shall be numbered 3.3.W.2.X.2 (beginning with 3.3.1.2.1.2). When not provided in a separate DBDD, this subparagraph shall identify and state the purpose of the data that originate in LLCSC X and are not used by other architectural elements of the CSCI. This subparagraph shall include the format and all other characteristics of the local data needed to satisfy the local data requirements of LLCSC X. Examples are: limits or ranges of local data values, accuracy and precision. This information may be provided in an LLCSC X local data definition table. An example of an LLCSC X local data definition table is provided in Table VIII.

If files or a data base are part of the local data of LLCSC X, this paragraph shall also provide the following details:

a. Purpose of each file or data base.
b. Structure of each file or data base in terms of contents and size.
c. Access procedures (e.g., sequential, random access).

TABLE V. Sample requirements allocation table.

SDDD			CSCI Requirement		
LLCSC/Unit Number	LLCSC/Unit Name	Paragraph Number	Requirement Name	Document Name	Paragraph Number
310	W1	3.3.1.2.1	Function 1	SRS	3.4.1
31001	W1V1	3.3.1.3.1	Interface 1	SRS	3.3.3.2
3101	W2	3.3.1.2.2	Function 2	SRS	3.4.2
3300	Y1	3.3.3.2.4	Function 4	SRS	3.4.4
33011	Y2	3.3.3.2.5	Interface 2	IRS for 1	3.3.1.1
33012	Y2U1	3.3.3.3.8	Interface 3	IRS for 1	3.3.1.2
33013	Y2U2	3.3.3.3.9	Interface 4	IRS for 1	3.3.1.3

TABLE VI. Sample memory/processing time table.

LLCSC/Unit Name	LLCSC/Unit Number	Memory Budget Words	Allocated Processing Time
Display processing	LLCSC 3101	20,000	20.0 ms
Refresh	Unit 31011	15,000	15.0 ms
Operator input	Unit 31012	3,000	5.0 ms
Subtotal		18,000	20.0 ms
Scheduler	LLCSC 331	10,000	100.0 ms
Total		28,000	120.0 ms
Total available		30,000	150.0 ms
Reserve		21,000	30.0 ms
Reserve %		6.7	20.0

10.2.5.3.1.2.1.3 *LLCSC X Process Control.* This subparagraph shall be numbered 3.3.W.2.X.3 (beginning with 3.3.1.2.1.3) and describe the generation of and response to process control requirements (e.g., signals and interrupts) by LLCSC X, including the following as applicable:

a. Source of signal/interrupt.
b. Purpose of signal/interrupt.
c. Priority of signal/interrupt.
d. Required response and response time.
e. Minimum, maximum, and probable frequency of signal/interrupt.

10.2.5.3.1.2.1.4 *LLCSC X Processing.* This subparagraph shall be numbered 3.3.W.2.X.4 (beginning with 3.3.1.2.1.4) and provide the following design characteristics for LLCSC X:

a. *Control.* The conditions under which LLCSC X receives control and passes control to interfacing CSCIs or architectural elements of CSCIs.
b. *Algorithms.* The algorithms incorporated in the execution of LLCSC X during normal operational functioning. The algorithms shall be described in terms of the manipulation of the input and local data and the generation of output.
c. *Special Control Features.* Special control features of LLCSC X which do not affect the main functions it performs (e.g., user control of printer, console display, system loop-test for on-line routine maintenance, program device checkouts).
d. *Error Handling.* The error detection and recovery features of LLCSC X. Error handling shall include handling of erroneous input data and other conditions which affect the execution of LLCSC X (e.g., device faults).
e. *Data Conversion.* Any data conversion operations performed by LLCSC X in order to implement the interface between LLCSC X and other CSCIs or architectural elements of CSCIs.
f. *Communication Interfaces.* The interface features in LLCSC X, such as syn-

TABLE VII. Sample LLCSC X input table.

Identifier	Description		Data Representation	Size[1]	Units of Measure	Limit/ Range	Accuracy/ Precision	Frequency	Legal OK	Source(s)	Input Method
VX	X-velocity	Real	Fixed	2 words	MPH	0-10,000	6 dec. places ± .000005	1 kh_Z	Yes	LLCSC 310 LLCSC 330	Parameter
VY	Y-velocity	Real	Fixed	2 words[2]	MPH	0-10,000	± .000005	1 kh_Z	Yes	LLCSC 310 LLCSC 330	Parameter
VZ	Z-velocity	Real	Fixed	2 words	MPH	0-10,000	± .000005	1 kh_Z	Yes	LLCSC 310 LLCSC 330	Parameter
OBJ	Object ID	ASCII	String	6 char	N/A	A-Z	N/A	Aperiodic	N/A	CSCI 3	Global

[1]Size
Char = 8 bits
Byte = 8 bits

[2]Word = 16 bits, 2 bytes

TABLE VIII. Sample LLCSCX local data definition table.

Identifier	Description	Data Type	Data Representation	Size	Units of Measure	Limit/Range	Accuracy/ Precision
MYVEL	Local velocity	Array	3 × 1 array of fixed	3 words	Knots	0-10,000	± .000005
MYVMAG	Local speed	Real	Fixed	2 words	Knots	0-10,000	± .000005
Knots	Conversion factor	Real	Constant .869565	1 word	Nautical mile/ mile	N/A	±.000010
OBJTBL	Object table	Array	100 × 2 array of (positive string)	400 words	N/A	100 objects	N/A

chronization and sequencing, that implement the required communication interfaces.

10.2.5.3.1.2.1.5 *LLCSC X Utilization of Other Elements.* This subparagraph shall be numbered 3.3.W.2.X.5 (beginning with 3.3.1.2.1.5) and describe any LLCSC X utilization of other elements in the CSCI or system (e.g., shared data, system hardware, external CSCIs, etc.).

10.2.5.3.1.2.1.6 *LLCSC X Limitations.* This subparagraph shall be numbered 3.3.W.2.X.6 (beginning with 3.3.1.2.1.6) and describe any special limitations or unusual features which restrict the performance of LLCSC X.

10.2.5.3.1.2.1.7 *LLCSC X Outputs.* This subparagraph shall be numbered 3.3.W.2.X.7 (beginning with 3.3.1.2.1.7), and identify and state the purpose of the output data generated by LLCSC X. Output data may be transmitted as global data, direct I/O, passed parameters, or through shared memory. This subparagraph shall include destination(s), format(s), units of measure, and all other characteristics of the output data needed to satisfy the output requirements of LLCSC X. Examples are: limits or ranges of output values, accuracy and precision, and frequency of output data. This information may be provided by an LLCSC X output table. An example of an LLCSC X output table is provided in Table IX.

10.2.5.3.1.3 *Unit Level Design.* This subparagraph shall be numbered 3.3.W.3 (beginning with 3.3.1.3) and divided into the following subparagraphs to specify the detailed design of each Unit of TLCSC W.

10.2.5.3.1.3.1 *Unit Y.* This subparagraph shall be numbered 3.3.W.3.Y (beginning with 3.3.1.3.1), identify Unit Y by name, number, and level of decomposition, and describe the function it performs. If Unit Y is to be coded in a programming language different from the specified CSCI language, the programming language shall be identified and the rationale for its use shall be provided. If Unit Y is a part of more than one TLCSC or LLCSC, it shall be described in detail only once, and remaining references to Unit Y shall be to the appropriate subparagraph numbers in this document. In addition, if Unit Y is used in many places and resides in a library, this subparagraph shall identify: (1) the library by name and number and (2) the Software Detailed Design Document, by configuration name and number, in which the library description can be found (if not found in this document).

The following information shall be provided for Unit Y.

10.2.5.3.1.3.1.1 *Unit Y Inputs.* This subparagraph shall be numbered 3.3.W.3.Y.1 (beginning with 3.3.1.3.1.1), and identify and state the purpose of the input data required by Unit Y. Input data may be transmitted as global data, direct I/O, passed parameters, or through shared memory. This subparagraph shall include source(s), format(s), units of measure, and all other characteristics of the data needed to satisfy the input requirements of Unit Y. Examples are: limits or ranges of input values, accuracy and precision, frequency of input data arrival, and legality checks for erroneous information. This information may be provided by a Unit Y input table. An example of a Unit Y input table is provided in Table X.

10.2.5.3.1.3.1.2 *Unit Y Local Data.* This subparagraph shall be numbered 3.3.W.3.Y.2 (beginning with 3.3.1.3.1.2). When not provided in a separate DBDD, this subparagraph shall identify and state the purpose of the data that originate in Unit Y and are

TABLE IX. Sample LLCSC X output table.

Identifier	Description	Data Type	Data Representation	Size	Units	Limit/ Range	Accuracy/ Precision	Frequency	Destination	Output Method
VELTBL	Table of object speeds	Array	100×1 array of fixed	200 words	MPH	0-10,000	$\pm$ .000005	1 kh_Z	LLCSC310 LLCSC321	Global
NUM-VEL	Number of object/ speeds	Integer	Positive	1 byte	N/A	255	$\pm$ 2	1 kh_Z	LLCSC310 LLCSC321	Parameter
SIX II	Emergency state	Boolean	Boolean	1 byte	N/A	N/A	N/A	1 kh_Z	TLCSC31 LLCSC310 LLCSC321	Global

TABLE X. Sample unit Y input table.

Indenti-fier	Description	Data Type	Data Represen-tation	Size[1]	Units of Measure	Limit/ Range	Accuracy/ Precision	Frequency	Legal OK	Source(s)	Input Method
VEL	Velocity	Array	3 × 1 array of fixed	6 words[2]	Knots	0-10,000	6 dec. places ± .000005	1 kh_Z	Yes	LLCSC X	Parameter (by value)
T	Time	Real	Float	1 word	Sec	0-59	± .001	1 kh_Z	Yes	CSCI5	Global

[1]Size
Char = 8 bits
Byte = 8 bits

[2]Word = 16 bits, 2 bytes

not used by other architectural elements of the CSCI. This subparagraph shall include the format and all other characteristics of the local data needed to satisfy the local data requirements of Unit Y. Examples are: limits or ranges of local data values, accuracy and precision. This information may be provided in a Unit Y local data definition table. An example of a Unit Y local data definition table is provided in Table XI.

If files or a data base are part of the local data of Unit Y, this paragraph shall also provide the following details:

a. Purpose of each file or data base.
b. Structure of each file or data base in terms of contents and size.
c. Access procedures (e.g., sequential, random access).

10.2.5.3.1.3.1.3 *Unit Y Process Control.* This subparagraph shall be numbered 3.3.W.3.Y.3 (beginning with 3.3.1.3.1.3) and describe the generation of and response to process control requirements (e.g., signals and interrupts), including the following, as applicable:

a. Source of signal/interrupt.
b. Purpose of signal/interrupt.
c. Priority of signal/interrupt.
d. Required response and response time.
e. Minimum, maximum, and probable frequency of signal/interrupt.

10.2.5.3.1.3.1.4 *Unit Y Processing.* This subparagraph shall be numbered 3.3.W.3.Y.4 (beginning with 3.3.1.3.1.4) and provide the following design characteristics for Unit Y:

a. *Control.* The conditions under which Unit Y receives control and passes control to interfacing CSCIs or architectural elements of CSCIs.
b. *Algorithms.* Describe Unit Y during normal operational functioning as a detailed algorithm. The algorithm shall include: (1) equations to be solved, (2) logic and data flow, (3) timing, sequencing, and resolution characteristics and requirements, (4) required numerical methods, (5) any special conditions for operations or contingencies to be handled by the unit, and (6) variable initialization. The description of the algorithm shall be in words, figures, equations, and charts, as appropriate, to convey the operation and design of the unit.
c. *Special Control Features.* Special control features of Unit Y which do not affect the main function it performs (e.g., user control of printer, alphanumeric or graphic display, user interactions, system loop-test for on-line routine maintenance, program device checkouts).
d. *Protection Features.* Any protection features implemented in Unit Y (e.g., Unit Y makes a local copy of global variable ID Code to protect against inconsistencies in data access).
e. *Error Handling.* The error detection and recovery features of Unit Y. Error handling shall include handling of erroneous input data and other conditions which affect the execution of Unit Y (e.g., device faults).

TABLE XI. Sample unit Y local data definition table.

Identifier	Description	Data Type	Data Representation	Size	Units of Measure	Limit/Range	Accuracy/ Precision
MY TIME	Local time	Array	3 × 1 array of real	3 words	(hrs, min, sec)	0-23 0-59 0-59	± .001
MY DATE	Date	Record	String, positive	3 char 1 byte	N/A	(Jan Dec) 1-31	N/A
SIXTY	Local constant	Real	Constant 60.0	1 word	Sec/min Min/hr	N/A	1.001

TABLE XII. Sample unit Y output table.

Identifier	Description	Data Type	Data Representation	Size	Units	Limit/ Range	Accuracy/ Precision	Frequency	Destination	Output Method
VMAG	Speed	Real	Fixed	2 words	MPH	0-10,000	± .000005	1 kh_Z	TLCSC 31	Parameter (by value)
TIME	Absolute time	Integer	Positive	2 words	Sec	1-1E9	± 1	1 kh_Z	TLCSC 31	Parameter (by value)

f. *Communication Interfaces.* The interface features of Unit Y, such as synchronization and sequencing, that implement the required communication interface.

10.2.5.3.1.3.1.5 *Unit Y Utilization of Other Elements.* This subparagraph shall be numbered 3.3.W.3.Y.5 (beginning with 3.3.1.3.1.5) and describe Unit Y's utilization of the following elements:

a. Other units (e.g., calls for library functions, and I/O services for access to data bases, mass storage devices, and real-time I/O channels).
b. Shared data stored in global or a common memory (e.g., input and output buffers, message buffers, constants, variables, data items, tables, and data bases).
c. System hardware through the issue of I/O commands, and desired response to hardware stimulus.
d. External CSCIs.
e. Any other elements not described above.

10.2.5.3.1.3.1.6 *Unit Y Limitations.* This subparagraph shall be numbered 3.3.W.3.Y.6 (beginning with 3.3.1.3.1.6) and describe any special limitations or unusual features which restrict the performance of Unit Y.

10.2.5.3.1.3.1.7 *Unit Y Outputs.* This subparagraph shall be numbered 3.3.W.3.Y.7 (beginning with 3.3.1.3.1.7), and identify and state the purpose of the output data generated by Unit Y. Output data may be transmitted as global data, direct I/O, passed parameters, or through shared memory. This subparagraph shall include the destination(s), format(s), units of measure, and all other characteristics of the output data needed to satisfy the output requirements of Unit Y. Examples are: limits or ranges of output values, accuracy and precision, and frequency of output data. This information may be provided in a Unit Y output table. An example of a Unit Y output table is provided in Table XII.

10.2.6 *Notes.* This section shall be numbered 6. and contain any general information that aids in understanding this document (e.g., background information, glossary, formula derivations). This section shall include an alphabetical listing of all acronyms, abbreviations, and their meanings as used in this document.

10.2.7 *Appendixes.* Appendixes shall contain any supplemental information published separately for convenience in document maintenance (e.g., charts, classified data). Appendixes may be bound as separate documents for ease in handling. Appendixes shall be numbered sequentially in Roman numeral (I, II, etc.), and the paragraphs within each appendix shall all be numbered as multiples of 10 (e.g., Appendix I, paragraph 10.1, 10.2, Appendix II, paragraph 20.1, 20.2, etc.).

As applicable, each appendix shall be referenced in the main body of the document where the data would normally have been provided.

A.3 DOD-STD-7935

The material that follows is the Department of Defense "Automated Data Systems (ADS) Documentation Standards," April 24, 1984, pages 3-2 through 3-126.

SECTION 2. DESCRIPTION OF DOCUMENT TYPES

2.1 Document Types. Figures 3-01 through 3-11 present the description of each of the technical documents as follows:

Figure 3-01. Functional Description (FD).
Figure 3-02. Data Requirements Document (RD).
Figure 3-03. System/Subsystem Specification (SS).
Figure 3-04. Program Specification (PS).
Figure 3-05. Data Base Specification (DS).
Figure 3-06. Users Manual (UM).
Figure 3-07. Computer Operation Manual (OM).
Figure 3-08. Program Maintenance Manual (MM).
Figure 3-09. Test Plan (PT).
Figure 3-10. Test Analysis Report (RT).
Figure 3-11. Implementation Procedures (IP).

2.2 Contents of Each Document Type. Included within each figure are a table of contents, a list of figures presented in that document type (if applicable), and the narrative description of the contents of that document type.

FIGURE 3-01. FUNCTIONAL DESCRIPTION
TABLE OF CONTENTS

FIGURE 3-01. Functional Description

SECTION 3. DETAILED CHARACTERISTICS
- 3.1 Specific Performance Requirements
  - 3.1.1 Accuracy and Validity
  - 3.1.2 Timing
- 3.2 Functional Area System Functions
- 3.3 Inputs-Outputs
- 3.4 Data Base Characteristics
- 3.5 Failure Contingencies
- 3.6 Security

SECTION 4. DESIGN DETAILS
- 4.1 System Description
- 4.2 System Functions
  - 4.2.1 Accuracy and Validity
  - 4.2.2 Timing
- 4.3 Flexibility
- 4.4 System Data
  - 4.4.1 Inputs
  - 4.4.2 Outputs
  - 4.4.3 Data Base

SECTION 5. ENVIRONMENT
- 5.1 Equipment Environment
- 5.2 Support Software Environment
- 5.3 Interfaces
- 5.4 Summary of Impacts
  - 5.4.1 ADP Organization Impacts
  - 5.4.2 ADP Operational Impacts
  - 5.4.3 ADP Development Impacts
- 5.5 Failure Contingencies
- 5.6 Security
- 5.7 Assumptions and Constraints

SECTION 6. COST FACTORS

SECTION 7. SYSTEM DEVELOPMENT PLAN

SECTION 1. GENERAL

1.1 Purpose of Functional Description. This paragraph shall describe the purpose of the FD (Functional Description) in the following words, modified when appropriate:

> This Functional Description for (Project Name) (Project Number) is written to provide:
>
> a. The system requirements to be satisfied which will serve as a basis for mutual understanding between the user and the developer.
>
> b. Information on performance requirements, preliminary design, and user impacts, including fixed and continuing costs.
>
> c. A basis for the development of system tests.

FIGURE 3-01. Functional Description

1.2 Project References. This paragraph shall provide a brief summary of the references applicable to the history and development of the project. The general nature of the computer programs (tactical, inventory control, war gaming, management information, etc.) to be developed shall be specified. The project sponsor, user, and operating center(s) that will run the completed computer programs shall be indicated.

At least the following documents,[1] when applicable, shall be specified by author or source, reference number, title, date, and security classification:

a. Project request, a copy of which must be included as an appendix.
b. Previously developed technical documentation relating to this project.
c. Significant correspondence relating to the project to include formal agreements to the requirements contained in the Functional Description.
d. Documentation concerning related projects.
e. Other manuals or documents that constrain or explain technical factors affecting project development.
f. Standards or reference documentation, such as:
   (1) Documentation standards and specifications.
   (2) Programming conventions.
   (3) DoD or Federal standards (data elements, programming languages, etc.).
   (4) Hardware manuals, support system documentation, etc., if necessary, for an understanding of the FD.

1.3 Terms and Abbreviations. This paragraph shall provide a listing or include in an appendix any terms, definitions, or acronyms unique to this document and subject to interpretation by the user of the document. This listing will not include item names or data codes.

SECTION 2. SYSTEM SUMMARY

This section shall provide a general description, written in non-ADP terminology, of the existing system and of the requirements for the proposed ADS.

2.1 Background. Included within this paragraph, as necessary, will be any information concerning the background of the uses and purposes of the system to orient the reader. Reference must be made to higher order and parallel systems when needed to enhance the general description. The relationships between the project and other capabilities being developed concurrently shall be described.

2.2 Objectives. Statements of the major performance requirements and goals of the proposed computer program system must be included. These statements should be concise, quantified if possible, and may include examples. When applicable, related events, such as exercises or impending military operations, may be discussed. Any anticipated operational changes that will affect the system and its use shall be identified and the provisions within the system for including them shall be explained.

[1]When applicable, specific reference should be made to the provisions of these documents in subsequent sections of the Functional Description.

FIGURE 3-01. Functional Description

2.3 Existing Methods and Procedures. This paragraph shall provide a brief description of the current methods and procedures being employed to satisfy the existing information requirements. A chart must be provided depicting the existing data flow through the functional system from data acquisition through its processing and eventual output. This chart may be complemented by an explanation or another chart showing the sequence in which the operational functions are performed by the user and pointing out the support of those decision making activities that is provided by the present system. Additionally, at least the following information should be included in this description:

a. Organizational/personnel responsibilities.
b. Equipment being utilized.
c. Inputs and outputs including volume and frequency.
d. Deficiencies, including limitations, such as time delays.

2.4 Proposed Methods and Procedures. A description of the proposed methods and procedures shall be presented in this and the following paragraphs. This description, written in non-ADP terminology, should explain how the proposed system will interact with the functional processes of which the automated system will be supportive. When products from other functional or automated systems will be utilized with, or will become part of the proposed system, they will be referenced in this description.

A chart depicting the proposed data flow should be provided to present an overall view of the planned capabilities. If the proposed system eliminates or degrades any capabilities in the existing system, these capabilities must also be described as well as the reasons for their elimination or degradation. Alternative methods and procedures that have been considered may be included. A chart showing the major functional processing steps and a chart showing the interacting organizations should be included within the following paragraphs wherever they best complement the narrative.

2.4.1 Summary of Improvements. This paragraph shall provide a qualitative and quantitative summary of the benefits to be obtained from the proposed system. A comparison of the deficiencies identified in paragraph 2.3 and the identification of any additional capabilities required, along with appropriate explanations, may be provided. Explicitly identified will be the required capabilities that will be satisfied by the proposed system. When improvements of the existing methods and procedures are a requirement, the extent of the anticipated improvements must be stated. The discussion may include:

a. Functional improvements (new capabilities).
b. Improvements of degree (upgrading existing capabilities).
c. Timeliness (improved response time).
d. The elimination or reduction of existing capabilities that are no longer needed.

2.4.2 Summary of Impacts. This and the following paragraphs shall describe the anticipated impacts and associated costs of the proposed system on the existing organizational and operational environments of the user. Impacts on the user during the development of the system shall be noted.

2.4.2.1 User Organization Impacts. Organizational impacts may include the modifications of responsibilities and the addition or elimination of responsibilities that will be necessary to use the proposed system. Any personnel eliminated will be identified and a discussion provided of the possibilities of retraining. Requirements for the number and skills of additional personnel will be identified. Included will be changes in authorized strength, location and position identifier, if known.

2.4.2.2 User Operational Impacts. The operational impacts on the organization during the use of the proposed system will be included. This discussion will consider the proposed interface between the user and the computer operating center; the impacts on the user to change from the current operational procedures; new data sources; quantity, type, and timeliness of data to be submitted for use in the system; data retention requirements; and modes of user operation based on peacetime, alert, and wartime conditions. Also included will be proposed methods for providing input data if these data are not already available.

2.4.2.3 User Development Impacts. Development impacts will include a discussion of all user effort that will be required prior to implementation of the system, such as training, manpower required to develop or modify the data base, etc. This paragraph will also include any user requirement for the parallel operation of the new and existing system along with the potential impact on the user during the testing phase of the proposed system. Any additional activities to be provided by the user to aid development also will be included in this paragraph.

2.5 Assumptions and Constraints. This paragraph shall describe any user assumptions and constraints that will affect development and operation of the system. Any limitations affecting the desired capability (including the prediction of expected types of errors) and explicit identification of any desired capabilities that will not be provided by the proposed system shall be discussed. Examples of assumptions include organizational actions, budget decisions, operational environment or deployment requirements. Examples of constraints include operation environment, budget limitations, system implementation deadlines or regulatory policy.

SECTION 3. DETAILED CHARACTERISTICS

This section shall provide a detailed description of the performance requirements of the proposed ADS written in non-ADP terminology.

3.1 Specific Performance Requirements. This paragraph shall describe the specific performance requirements to be satisfied by the ADS. This presentation shall be a delineation of requirements on which the system design is to be based.[2] The requirements will be stated in such a manner that system functions discussed in paragraph 3.2 and the system tests necessary for implementation can be related to them. A quantitative presentation of requirements will be included, such as the number of records that must be handled, maximum allowed time from query to receipt of requested information, and flexibility required to accommodate changing user requirements.

3.1.1 Accuracy and Validity. This paragraph shall provide a description of the accuracy requirements placed upon the system. The following items must be considered:

a. Accuracy requirements of mathematical calculations.

[2]Anticipated deviations from any of the standards specified by the documents listed in the above paragraph 1.2 must be specifically indicated.

b. Accuracy requirements of data.
c. Accuracy of transmitted data.

3.1.2 Timing. This paragraph shall provide a description of the timing requirements to be placed on the system. The following timing requirements must be considered:

a. Response time from receipt of input data to availability of ADS products.
b. Response time to queries and to updates of data files.
c. Sequential relationship of functions.
d. Priorities imposed by types of inputs and changes in modes of operation.
e. Any deviations from specified response times for peak load periods, as applicable.

3.2 Functional Area System Functions. This paragraph shall amplify and describe by individual function the major functional processing steps contained in paragraph 2.4. This description should relate the functions to the performance requirements in paragraph 3.1.

3.3 Inputs-Outputs. This paragraph shall describe each data element in the data inputs to and outputs from the ADS. For each data element may be listed information such as the following:

a. Data element name.
b. Synonymous name.
c. Definition.
d. Format.
e. Range of values.
f. Unit of measurement.
g. Data item names, abbreviations and codes.

When the information is published in a data element dictionary, reference to an entry in the dictionary will be made rather than including an extract from that dictionary. Any variations in either the inputs or outputs from the format or data item names that will be used on the data base of the ADS as discussed in paragraph 3.4 must be specifically identified.

When available, the various input data formats shall be shown and the input medium (disk, cards, magnetic tape, analog-originated signals from revolving radar, etc.) shall be specified. When available, the various output data formats including any quality control outputs shall be shown and the output medium shall be specified. When possible these outputs should be related to the system functions described in paragraph 3.2.

3.4 Data Base Characteristics. This paragrah shall provide a discussion concerning the data elements to be used in the data base. For each data element may be listed such information as:

a. Data element name.
b. Synonymous name.
c. Definition.

FIGURE 3-01. Functional Description

d. Format.

e. Range of values.

f. Unit of measurement.

g. Data item names, abbreviations, and codes.

When the information is published in a data element dictionary, reference to an entry in the dictionary will be made rather than including an extract from that dictionary. An estimate of the data storage requirements in terms of size and number of records will be provided. A description of the expected growth of the data and related components should be provided.

3.5 Failure Contingencies. This paragraph shall provide a discussion of the alternative courses of action that may be taken to satisfy the information requirements if the proposed ADS fails. There shall be included as appropriate:

a. *Back-up.* A discussion shall be provided of the back-up requirements for ensuring the continued achievement of system functions given in paragraph 3.2. "Back-up" as used means the redundancy available in the event the primary system element goes down.

b. *Fallback.* An explanation of the fallback techniques for ensuring the continued satisfaction of the specific requirements of the system shall be provided. "Fallback" as used indicates the use of another system or other means to accomplish the system requirements. For example, the fallback technique for an automated system might be manual manipulation and recording of data.

3.6 Security. This paragraph shall describe the degree of sensitivity of the data, data files, inputs and outputs of the system. Consideration must be given to classified, personal, proprietary and management data.

SECTION 4. DESIGN DETAILS

This section shall provide a description of how the proposed system will satisfy the functional requirements delineated in Sections 2 and 3.

4.1 System Description. This paragraph shall provide a general description of the proposed ADS. Related and interfacing systems and their documentation will be referenced as required to enhance this general description. Included within this description shall be a chart showing the relationship of the user organizations to the major components of the proposed ADS. This chart shall be based on the information included in paragraph 2.4.

4.2 System Functions. This paragraph shall describe the functions of the proposed ADS. There will be both quantitative and qualitative descriptions of how these functions will satisfy the requirements of paragraph 3.1. The functions must be described in such a manner that the system environment in Section 5 can be related to them.

4.2.1 Accuracy and Validity. This paragraph shall provide a description of the accuracy that will be achieved by the ADS. This description will be related to the requirements stated in paragraph 3.1.1. The following accuracy requirements must be considered:

a. Accuracy requirements of mathematical calculations.
b. Accuracy requirements of data.
c. Accuracy of transmitted data.

4.2.2 Timing. This paragraph shall provide a description of the timing considerations of the ADS. This description will be related to the requirements stated in paragraph 3.1.2. The following requirements must be considered:

a. Throughput time.
b. Response time to queries and to updates of data files.
c. Sequential relationship of system functions.
d. Priorities imposed by types of inputs and changes in modes of operation.
e. Timing requirements for the range of traffic load under varying operating conditions.

4.3 Flexibility. This paragraph shall provide a description of the capability to be incorporated for adapting the system to changing requirements such as anticipated operational changes, interaction with new or improved systems, and planned periodic changes. Components and procedures designed to be subject to change will be identified.

4.4 System Data. Included in this paragraph will be a description of the inputs, outputs, and data used. Each description will include the information below, if known.

4.4.1 Inputs.

a. Title and tag.
b. Format and acceptable range of values.
c. Number of items.
d. Means of entry and input initiation procedures, e.g., typewriter, card, tape, sensor, internal.
e. Expected volume and frequency, including special handling (such as queuing and priority handling) for peak load periods.
f. Priority, e.g., routine, emergency.
g. Sources, form at source, and disposition of source document.
h. Security considerations of input and individual items.
i. Requirements for timeliness.

4.4.2 Outputs.

a. Title and tag.
b. Format to include headings, line spacing, arrangement, totals, etc.
c. Number of items.
d. Preprinted form requirements.
e. Means of display, if known, e.g., CRT, printer, typewriter, projector, alarm type, internal.
f. Expected volume and frequency including special handling.
g. Priority, e.g., routine, emergency.

FIGURE 3-01. Functional Description

h. Timing requirements, e.g., response time.
i. Requirements for accuracy.
j. User recipients and use of displays, such as notification, trends or briefings.
k. Security considerations of output and individual items.

4.4.3 Data Base. Each data file, table, dictionary, or directory will be described as follows:

a. Title and tag.
b. Description of content.
c. Number of records or entries.
d. Storage media and size.
e. Security considerations.
f. Data retention.

SECTION 5. ENVIRONMENT

This section shall describe the current ADP environment and project the environment needed to satisfy those requirements delineated in Sections 2 and 3.

5.1 Equipment Environment. This paragraph shall provide a description of the equipment capabilities required for the operation of the proposed ADS. This paragraph will present broad descriptions of the equipment presently available and the characteristics of any new equipment necessary based on the information in Section 3. A guideline for equipment to be described follows:

a. Processor(s), including number of each online/offline, and size of internal storage.
b. Storage media, including number of disk units, tape units, etc.
c. Output devices, including number of each online/offline.
d. Input devices, including number of each online/offline.
e. Communications net, including line speeds.

5.2 Support Software Environment. This paragraph shall provide a description of the support software with which the computer programs to be developed must interact. Included will be both support software, input and equipment simulators, and test software, if needed. The correct nomenclature, level (version), and documentation references of each such software system, subsystem, and program shall be provided. In addition, the language (compiler, assembler, program, query, etc.), the operating system, and any Data Management System to be used will be identified.

5.3 Interfaces. This paragraph shall provide a description of the interfaces with other systems and subsystems. For each interface, the following should be specified:

a. Description of operational considerations of data transfer, such as security considerations.
b. General description of data transfer requirements to and from the subject system and characteristics of communications media/systems used for transfer.

FIGURE 3-01. Functional Description

c. Format, unit of measurement, range of values, data codes.
d. Type of anticipated interface, such as manual or automatic.
e. Anticipated interface procedures, including telecommunications considerations.

5.4 Summary of Impacts. This paragraph shall describe the anticipated organizational, operational and development impacts of the proposed ADS on the ADP organizations.

5.4.1 ADP Organization Impacts. Organizational impacts may include the modifications of positional responsibilities and the addition or elimination of responsibilities that will be required by the proposed system. Any personnel interactions eliminated will be identified and a discussion provided of the possibilities of retraining. ADP personnel responsibilities will be discussed. Requirements for the number and skills of additional personnel will be identified. Included will be changes in authorized strength, location and position identifier, if known.

5.4.2 ADP Operational Impacts. This paragraph shall discuss impacts on the operational procedures of the data processing center(s) to implement the ADS. Included will be operational impacts caused by a change in equipment configuration, if known.

5.4.3 ADP Development Impacts. This paragraph shall assess the personnel and ADP processing commitment necessary in the development and testing of the automated system. Additional requirements for program and data conversion will be addressed, if known, along with any additional development impacts resulting from the requirements in paragraph 2.4.2.3.

5.5 Failure Contingencies. This paragraph shall provide a discussion of possible failures of the hardware or software system, the consequences (in terms of system performance) of such failures, and the alternative courses of action that may be taken to satisfy the information requirements.

a. *Restart.* Include a discussion of the restart capabilities for ensuring effective and efficient recovery from a temporary problem within the hardware or software systems. The "restart" capability, as used, is a capability to resume operation from a point in the automated process prior to where the problem occurred, with appropriate restoration of data.

b. *Other.* The fallback and back-up contingencies described in paragraph 3.5 will be considered, as appropriate.

5.6 Security. This paragraph shall describe the degree of protection for the levels of availability, integrity and confidentiality that must be provided by the overall system and its components.

5.7 Assumptions and Constraints. This paragraph shall address any data automation assumptions and constraints that relate to development and operation of the automated system, as applicable.

SECTION 6. COST FACTORS

This section shall provide a summary of cost factors for the proposed system in accordance with DoD Instruction 7041.3, when applicable. While the proposed system responds directly to the project request, other factors may determine the need for this system, such as requirements of higher echelons of command, security considerations, telecommunications considerations, and the need to interface with other automated systems. General alternatives that may be discussed include those for system development and system design with consideration being given to equipment, software, supporting telecommunications requirements, organization, operation, etc. Reference may be made to such information contained in other documents.

SECTION 7. SYSTEM DEVELOPMENT PLAN

This section shall discuss the overall management approach to the development and implementation of the proposed computer system. Included may be a discussion of the documentation to be produced, time frames for the development of the system or the modules of the system, necessary liaison and participation by other organizations to ensure successful development, and any other factors that must be known prior to initiating development. Reference may be made to such information contained in other documents.

FIGURE 3-02. DATA REQUIREMENTS DOCUMENT
TABLE OF CONTENTS

SECTION 1. GENERAL

1.1 Purpose of the Data Requirements Document. This paragraph shall describe the purpose of the RD (Data Requirements Document) in the following words, modified when appropriate:

The objectives of this Data Requirements Document for (Project Name) (Project Number) are to list and define data elements which the system must handle and to communicate data collection requirements to the user.

1.2 Project References. This paragraph shall provide a brief summary of the references applicable to the history and development of the project. The general nature of the computer programs (tactical, inventory control, war gaming, management information, etc.) to be developed shall be specified. The project sponsor, user, and operating center(s) that will run the completed ADS shall be indicated. A general statement shall be included of the scope of user support necessary to furnish the required system data. Included shall be a brief statement of the project objectives and a description of the relationship of this project to other projects. At least the following documents, when applicable, shall be specified, by author or source, reference number, title, date, and security classification:

a. Project request.
b. Other technical documentation.
c. Functional Description.

1.3 Terms and Abbreviations. This paragraph shall provide a listing or include in an appendix any terms, definitions, or acronyms unique to this document and subject to interpretation by the user of the document. This listing will not include item names or data codes.

1.4 Modification of Data Requirements. This paragraph shall describe the procedures for implementing and documenting changes to the system data requirements, if applicable.

1.5 Security. This paragraph shall describe the degree of sensitivity of the data, data files, inputs and outputs of the system. Consideration must be given to classified, personal, proprietary and management data. It shall also reflect the authority for the degree of sensitivity and for the levels of availability, integrity and confidentiality. Examples of authority sources for the degree of sensitivity are classification authority for classified data, sensitivity measurement program and Federal Register reference for personal data, and sensitivity measurement algorithm for proprietary and other data. Examples of authority sources for the levels of availability, integrity and confidentiality are user, regulatory agency or federal statute.

SECTION 2. DATA DESCRIPTION

The data described in this section shall be separated into two categories, static data and dynamic data. Static data are defined as that data which are used mainly for reference during system operation and are usually generated or updated in widely separated time frames independent of normal system runs. Dynamic data include all data which are intended to be updated and which are input to a system during a normal run (including "real time" data such as targeting data) or are output by the system. Static data as described above are frequently referred to as parametric data and dynamic data as nonparametric data. Both, however, are composed of data elements. The data element names listed in paragraphs 2.1, 2.2, and 2.3 shall be the same as those contained in standard data element dictionaries, whenever applicable. Along with each data element name, either in the appropriate paragraph or summarized in some other place, shall be provided for each data element, as appropriate:

a. Synonymous name.
b. Definition.
c. Format.
d. Range of values.
e. Unit of measurement.
f. Data item names, abbreviations and codes.

When the information is published in a data element dictionary, reference to an entry in the dictionary will be made rather than including an extract from that dictionary.

2.1 Logical Organization of Static System Data. This paragraph shall list the titles of static data elements used by the system for either parametric control or reference purposes. The data elements will be arranged in any logical groupings, such as functions, subjects, or other categories which are most relevant to their usage.

2.2 Logical Organization of Dynamic Input Data. This paragraph shall provide a list of the titles of those dynamic input data elements which constitute the data that are intended to be updated by a normal system run or during online operation. The data elements will be arranged in logical groupings, such as functions, subjects, or other categories which are most relevant to their usage.

2.3 Logical Organization of Dynamic Output Data. This paragraph shall provide a list of the titles of those dynamic output data elements which constitute the data that are intended to be updated by a normal system run or during online operation. The data elements will be arranged in logical groupings, such as functions, subjects or other categories which are most relevant to their usage.

2.4 Internally Generated Data. This paragraph shall provide the internally generated data which are of interest to the user. The elements included in this paragraph need not be all inclusive, since they will be only of informational value to the user and will require no user action.

2.5 System Data Constraints. This paragraph shall contain only the known or anticipated system data constraints which have not been outlined in the FD. This information is to provide a general indication of the limits of the system with regard to future expansion or utilization; for example, a statement of the maximum size and the maximum number of files, records, and elements. Emphasis shall be placed on limits which could prove critical in future systems development.

SECTION 3. USER SUPPORT FOR DATA COLLECTION

All of the data elements required for the system will be listed in paragraphs 2.1, 2.2, and 2.3. This section will describe the data collection support necessary from the user to gather the data values for use by the particular system.

3.1 Data Collection Requirements and Scope. This paragraph shall describe the types of information required by the developer in order to establish the data values of each data element. It shall request, as a minimum, those types of information needed to describe the data element in accordance with the information required for the data element dictionary, such as the data element name, synonymous name, definition, format, range of values, unit of measurement, data item names, abbreviations and codes. When the information is published in a data element dictionary, reference to an entry in the dictionary will be made rather than including an extract from that dictionary.

a. *Input Source(s) of the Data Element.* This item names the source(s) from which the data element will be fed into the system. The source or origin of the data will be, for example, an operator, station, organizational unit, etc., or its component group—not the hardware device used for entering the data. An exception can be made in the case of automatic sensor devices, but in this case, the device should be linked to another data element set, such as a vehicle carrying the device, organization responsible for its use or maintenance, geographic location, etc.

b. *Input Device.* This item names the hardware device used for entering the data into the system. In those cases where only certain special stations are the legal entry points, those discrete devices shall be specified.

c. *Recipients.* This item specifies those users (other than the originator) who should be cognizant of the data. In specifying recipients, distinctions should be made among the following classes of data elements:

(1) Data elements input to the system, processed by it, and output from it essentially unchanged.
(2) Data elements generated by a program and output to the user.
(3) Data elements that are input to the system but that are not output by it. In this case, the program would substitute for the user as the recipient.

d. *Critical Value.* Many elements that have a range of values will have one value that is particularly significant to the user. This may be a breakpoint, a minimum stock level, a critical wind velocity, etc. When applicable, the critical value and its significance to the user should be included.

e. *Scales of Measurement.* For numeric scales, if the successive steps are not equal to "one" on the units of measurement, then the increment shall be specified. For example, a data element representing pressure in pounds per square inch (the unit of measurement) may be incremented by pound, half-pound, or 10-pound increments. For numeric scales, the "scale zero" should be specified if it is not implicit in the unit of measurement; e.g., pressure in pounds per square inch may be measured relative to absolute zero pressure or to atmospheric pressure. For numeric scales where average functions other than the arithmetic mean are appropriate, these other functions (e.g., geometric mean, root mean square, harmonic mean) should be indicated. For nonnumeric scales any relationships indicated by the legal values should be stated if not otherwise specified. For example, a code indicating lubricant type by values A, B, C, etc. should show whether the value is arbitrary (A = paraffin oils, B = graphite, etc.) or whether it indicates the ordering of the lubricants by some parameter (A = viscosity less than SAE 10, B = viscosity SAE 10 through SAE 40, etc.).

f. *Conversion Factors.* Measured quantities that must go through analog and digital conversion processes shall have the conversion factors specified.

g. *Output Form/Device.* Output data elements may be presented to the user symbolically, graphically, audibly, or may be used as input to some other automated system. If the user will receive a sensible presentation, the description should specify whether the user will receive the data element as part of a hard copy printout, a symbol in a CRT display, a line on a drawing, a colored light, an alarm bell, etc. If the output is passed along to some other automated system, the medium should be described, e.g., magnetic tape, punched cards, an electronic signal to a solenoid switch.

h. *Expansion Factors.* For systems that are expected to undergo future expansion, the expansion factor to be added to the maximum number of entries of this data element should be included. For instance, if the maximum number of input devices is now 12, but is expected to be 96 three years from now, the 700% expansion factor should be specified.

i. *Frequency of Update.* Data elements that are input to the system or that are expected to be modified by the system on a periodic basis should have the frequency of update specified. If the input arrives in a random or in an "as occurred" manner, both the average frequency and some measure of the variance must be specified.

3.2 Recommended Source of Input Data. This paragraph shall delineate the source(s) of input data. Recommendations as to who shall be responsible for providing specific data inputs shall be stated here. This shall include recommendations regarding the establishment of a user input reporting organization, if required. Those data inputs dependent on interfacing systems, unrelated agencies, or specific documents should be the source that is delineated.

3.3 Data Collection and Transfer Procedures. Specific instructions for data collection procedures shall be given in paragraph 3.3. These instructions shall include detailed formats where applicable. Communications media and timing of inputs and outputs shall be stated.

3.3.1 Input Formats. This paragraph shall describe all input formats (card layouts, tape layouts, etc.) to include master file formats used by the system.

3.3.2 Output Formats. This paragraph shall describe all output formats (printer layout, CRT display frame, tape layout, etc.) created by the system.

3.4 Data Base Impacts. This paragraph shall describe the impacts associated with collection and maintenance of the data base on equipment, software, organizational, operational, and developmental environments. These descriptions will amplify paragraph 2.4.2 of the Functional Description. Impacts on the system resulting from deficiencies in the data base shall also be given.

FIGURE 3-03. SYSTEM/SUBSYSTEM SPECIFICATION
TABLE OF CONTENTS

SECTION 2. SUMMARY OF REQUIREMENTS
- 2.1 System/Subsystem Description
- 2.2 System/Subsystem Functions
  - 2.2.1 Accuracy and Validity
  - 2.2.2 Timing
- 2.3 Flexibility

SECTION 3. ENVIRONMENT
- 3.1 Equipment Environment
- 3.2 Support Software Environment
- 3.3 Interfaces
- 3.4 Security
- 3.5 Controls

SECTION 4. DESIGN DETAILS
- 4.1 General Operating Procedures
- 4.2 System Logical Flow
- 4.3 System Data
  - 4.3.1 Inputs
  - 4.3.2 Outputs
  - 4.3.3 Data Base
- 4.4 Program Descriptions

SECTION 1. GENERAL

1.1 Purpose of the System/Subsystem Specification. This paragraph shall describe the purpose of the SS (System/Subsystem Specification) in the following words, modified when appropriate:

> The System/Subsystem Specification for (Project Name) (Project Number) is written to fulfill the following objectives:
>
> a. To provide a detailed definition of the system/subsystem functions.
>
> b. To communicate details of the on-going analysis between the user's operational personnel and the appropriate development personnel.
>
> c. To define in detail the interfaces with other systems and subsystems and the facilities to be utilized for accomplishing the interfaces.

1.2 Project References. This paragraph shall provide a brief summary of the references applicable to the history and development of the project. The general nature of the computer programs (tactical, inventory control, war gaming, management information, etc.) to be developed shall be specified. A brief description of the system shall include its purpose and uses. The project sponsor, user, and the operating center(s) that will run the completed computer programs shall be indicated. At least the following documents, when applicable, shall be specified by author or source, reference number, title, date, and security classification:

FIGURE 3-03. System/Subsystem Specification

a. Functional Description.
b. Related System/Subsystem Specifications.
c. Any other pertinent documentation or significant correspondence not specified in the Functional Description.

1.3 Terms and Abbreviations. This paragraph shall provide a listing or include in an appendix any terms, definitions, or acronyms unique to this document or subject to interpretation by the user of the document. This listing will not include item names or data codes.

SECTION 2. SUMMARY OF REQUIREMENTS

This section shall provide a summary of the system characteristics and requirements. This section shall be an expansion of the information published in the FD to reflect the determination of additional details. Any changes to the characteristics and requirements set forth in Sections 2 and 3 of the FD must be specifically identified.

2.1 System/Subsystem Description. This paragraph shall provide a general description of the system/subsystem to establish a frame of reference for the remainder of the document. Higher order and parallel systems/subsystems and their documentation will be referenced as required to enhance this general description. Included within this description shall be a chart showing the relationship of the user organizations to the major components of the system and a chart showing the interrelationships of the system components for the system/subsystem. These charts shall be based on or be updated versions of the charts included in paragraph 4.1 of the FD. The more detailed charts to be included in Section 4 shall be based on the charts included in this paragraph.

2.2 System/Subsystem Functions. This paragraph shall describe the system/subsystem functions. There will be both qualitative and quantitative descriptions of how the system/subsystem functions will satisfy the requirements. Although the descriptions of the system/subsystem functions may be refined and more detailed as a result of the on-going analysis and design, they must maintain a direct relationship to the system functions established in paragraph 4.2 of the FD, and be stated in such a manner that the system/subsystem environment in Section 3 can be related to them.

2.2.1 Accuracy and Validity. This paragraph shall provide a description of accuracy requirements imposed on the system/subsystem. The requirements will be related to paragraph 4.2.1 of the FD. The following accuracy requirements must be considered:

a. Accuracy requirements of mathematical calculations.
b. Accuracy requirements of data.
c. Accuracy of transmitted data.

2.2.2 Timing. This paragraph shall provide a description of the timing requirements placed on the system/subsystem, if they are applicable. The requirements will be related to paragraph 4.2.2 of the FD. The following timing requirements may be considered:

a. Throughput time.
b. Response time to queries and to updates of data files.
c. Sequential relationship of system/subsystem function.

FIGURE 3-03. System/Subsystem Specification

d. Priorities imposed by types of inputs and changes in modes of operation.
e. Timing requirements for the range of traffic load under varying operating conditions.
f. Sequencing and interleaving programs and systems (including the requirement for interrupting the operation of a program without loss of data).

2.3 Flexibility. This paragraph shall provide a description of the capability to be incorporated for adapting the system/subsystem to changing requirements, such as anticipated operational changes, interaction with new or improved systems, and planned periodic changes. Components and procedures designed to be subject to change will be identified.

SECTION 3. ENVIRONMENT

This section shall provide an expansion of the environment given in the FD to reflect the additional analysis and changes to the environment. Changes in the environment that do not affect the scope of the project as described in the FD and are the result of on-going analysis and design will be explicitly identified within the appropriate paragraphs of this section. These changes will be discussed in terms of the impacts on the currently available environmental components (equipment, software, etc.) as well as the impacts on estimates and functions which were based on the original planned environment.

3.1 Equipment Environment. This paragraph shall provide a description of the equipment required for the operation of the system/subsystem. Included will be descriptions of the equipment presently available as well as a more detailed discussion of the characteristics of any new equipment necessary. Equipment requirements will be related to the requirements stated in paragraph 5.1 of the FD. A guideline for equipment to be described follows:

a. Processor(s), including number of each online/offline and size of internal storage.
b. Storage media, including number of disk units, tape units, etc.
c. Input-output devices, including number of each online/offline.
d. Communications net, including line speeds.

3.2 Support Software Environment. This paragraph shall provide a description of the support software with which the computer programs to be developed must interact. Included will be both support software and test software, if needed. The correct nomenclature and documentation references of each such software system, subsystem, and program shall be provided. Included must be a reference to the languages (compiler, assembler, program, query, etc.), the operating system, and any Data Management System (DMS) to be used. This description must relate to and expand on the information provided in paragraph 5.2 of the FD. If operation of the computer programs to be developed is dependent upon forthcoming changes to support software, the nature, status, and anticipated availability date of such changes must be identified and discussed.

FIGURE 3-03. System/Subsystem Specification

3.3 Interfaces. This paragraph shall provide a description of the interfaces with other applications computer programs, including those of other operational capabilities and from other military organizations. The individual interfaces will be related to paragraph 5.3 of the FD. For each interface, the following shall be specified:

a. Type of interface, such as operator control of a terminal or program interfaces with other programs.
b. Description of operational implications of data transfer, including security considerations.
c. Data transfer requirements to and from the subject system/subsystem and characteristics of communications media/systems used for transfer.
d. Current formats of interchanged data for the sending and receiving systems including data item names, codes, or abbreviations that are to be interchanged.
e. Interface procedures, including telecommunications considerations.
f. Interface equipment.

If Subsystem Specifications are being written, interfaces with other subsystems which are to be developed will be described in the same manner.

3.4 Security. This paragraph shall be related to paragraph 5.6 of the FD and shall reflect the levels of availability, integrity and confidentiality of the system and its components. The relationship of the components to each other, how each affects the other, and their sequence of execution shall be discussed, when applicable.

3.5 Controls. This paragraph shall provide a presentation of overall system/subsystem controls. Included in this paragraph will be controls such as record counts, accumulated counts, batch controls, etc. If no specific controls are to be established at the subsystem level, this will be stated.

SECTION 4. DESIGN DETAILS

4.1 General Operating Procedures. Included in this paragraph will be a general description of the operating procedures such as load, start, stop, recovery, and restart.

4.2 System Logical Flow. This paragraph shall describe the logical flow of the system/subsystem. Logical flow of the system/subsystem will be presented primarily in the form of higher-level charts. A narrative presentation, when appropriate, will be used to supplement the chart. Charts will provide an integrated presentation of the system/subsystem dynamics, of entrances and exits, and of interfaces with other computer programs. Charts will effectively represent all modes of operations, priorities, cycles, and special handling. The charts will show general flow from input, through the system/subsystem, to the generation of output.

4.3 System Data. Included in this paragraph will be a description of the inputs, outputs, and data base.[1] For each record type and its data elements, information such as

[1]Optionally, inputs and outputs may be described with the individual programs to which they relate.

FIGURE 3-03. System/Subsystem Specification

the following will be provided. When the information is published in a data element dictionary, reference to an entry in the dictionary will be made rather than including an extract from that dictionary.

4.3.1 Inputs. Each input will be described as follows:

a. *Input Records.*

(1) Title and tag.
(2) Sources, medium of source, and disposition of source medium.
(3) Expected volume and frequency, including special handling (such as queuing and priority handling) for high density periods.
(4) Priority, e.g., routine, emergency.
(5) The degree of sensitivity.
(6) Requirements for timeliness.

b. *Input Data Elements.*

(1) Name and tag.
(2) Position in the input record type.
(3) Synonymous names.
(4) Definition.
(5) Unit of measurement.
(6) Format and acceptable range of values.
(7) The degree of sensitivity.
(8) Data item names, abbreviations and codes including a specification as to which is used in the input.

4.3.2 Outputs. Each output will be described as follows:

a. *Output Reports.*

(1) Title and tag.
(2) Format, to include headings, line spacing, arrangement, totals, etc. A report layout sheet may be included.
(3) Means of display, if known, e.g., CRT, printer, typewriter, projector.
(4) Expected volume and frequency including special handling.
(5) Priority, e.g., routine, emergency.
(6) Timing requirements, e.g., response time.
(7) User recipients and use of displays, such as notification, trends, or briefings.
(8) Preprinted form requirements.
(9) The degree of sensitivity.

b. *Output Data Elements.*

(1) Name and tag.
(2) Synonymous name.

(3) Definition.

(4) Unit of measurement.

(5) Format and acceptable range of values.

(6) The degree of sensitivity.

(7) Data item names, abbreviations, and codes including a specification as to which is used in the output.

4.3.3 Data Base. Each data base may be described as follows:

a. *Summary.*

(1) Title and tag.

(2) Narrative summary of content.

(3) Number of records or entries.

(4) Storage media and size.

(5) Degree of sensitivity.

(6) Retention schedule, including provisions for backup.

b. *Data Base Data Elements.*

(1) Name and tag.

(2) Position in the data base.

(3) Synonymous name.

(4) Definition.

(5) Unit of measurement.

(6) Format and acceptable range of values.

(7) The degree of sensitivity.

(8) Data item names, abbreviations and codes, including a specification as to which is used in the data base.

4.4 Program Descriptions. Paragraphs 4.4.1 through 4.4.n shall provide descriptions of the functions (related to paragraph 2.2) of the computer programs in the system/subsystem.

FIGURE 3-04. PROGRAM SPECIFICATION
TABLE OF CONTENTS

SECTION 1. GENERAL

1.1 Purpose of the Program Specification. This paragraph shall describe the purpose of the PS (Program Specification) in the following words or appropriate modifications thereto:

> The objective of this Program Specification[1] for (Project Name) (Project Number) is to describe the program design in sufficient detail to permit program production by the programmer/coder.

1.2 Project References. This paragraph shall provide a brief summary of the references applicable to the history and development of the project. The general nature of the computer programs (tactical, inventory control, war gaming, management information, etc.) to be developed shall be specified. A brief description of the system shall include its purpose and uses. The project sponsor, user, and operating center(s) that will run the completed computer programs shall be included. At least the following documents, when applicable, shall be specified by author or source, reference number, title, date, and security classification:

a. Functional Description.
b. Associated System/Subsystem Specifications.
c. Related Program Specifications.
d. Any other pertinent documentation or significant correspondence not specified in the Functional Description.

1.3 Terms and Abbreviations. This paragraph shall provide a listing or include in an appendix any terms, definitions, or acronyms unique to this document and subject to interpretation by the user of the document. This listing will not include item names or data codes.

[1]A Program Specification may be prepared for each program in the system or one Program Specification may be prepared for a group of related programs within the system.

FIGURE 3-04. Program Specification

SECTION 2. SUMMARY OF REQUIREMENTS

2.1 Program Description. This paragraph shall provide a general description of the program to establish a frame of reference for the remainder of the document. It shall include a summary of the system requirements. The documentation of higher order systems/subsystems and related programs will be referenced, as required, to enhance the general description of the program. If the program is common to more than one system or subsystem, appropriate references will be made to the applicable SS and FD documents.

2.2 Program Functions. This paragraph shall describe the functions of the program. If a program does not in itself satisfy system or subsystem requirements, this fact shall be noted in the presentation with a statement showing how the aggregate of programs completely satisfies the functions. Although the descriptions of the functions may be refined and more detailed as a result of the on-going analysis and design, they must be directly related to the subsystem or system functions and they must be stated in such a manner that program environment can be related to them.

2.2.1 Accuracy and Validity. This paragraph shall provide a description of accuracy requirements imposed on the program. The requirements will be related to paragraph 4.2.1 of the FD or to paragraph 2.2.1 of the SS. Changes in the accuracy requirements from the next higher order document will be explicitly identified. The following accuracy requirements must be considered:

a. Accuracy requirements of mathematical calculations.
b. Accuracy requirements of data.
c. Accuracy of transmitted data.

2.2.2 Timing. This paragraph shall provide a description of the timing requirements placed on the program, if they are applicable. The requirements will be related to paragraph 3.1.2 of the FD or to paragraph 2.2.2 of the SS. Changes in the timing requirements from the next higher order document will be explicitly identified. The following timing requirements must be considered:

a. Throughput time.
b. Response time to queries and to updates of data files.
c. Sequential relationship of program functions and data flows.
d. Priorities imposed by types of inputs and changes in modes of operation.
e. Timing requirements for the range of traffic load under varying operating conditions.
f. Sequencing and interleaving programs and systems (including the requirements for interrupting the operation of a program without loss of data).
g. I/O transfer time required for disk, drum, tape, etc.
h. Internal processing time.

2.3 Flexibility. This paragraph shall provide a description of the capability to be incorporated for adapting the program to changing requirements, such as anticipated operational changes, interaction with new or improved programs, and planned periodic changes. Components and procedures designed to be subject to change will be identified. This paragraph will be related to the portions of paragraph 2.3 of the SS that are applicable to the subject program.

SECTION 3. ENVIRONMENT

This section shall specify the current environment in which the system will operate indicating any changes made to the environment as reflected in the FD and SS.

3.1 Support Software Environment. This paragraph shall provide a description of the support software with which the computer programs to be developed must interact. Included will be both support software and test software, if needed. The correct nomenclature and documentation references of each such software system, subsystem, and program shall be provided. Included must be a reference to the languages (compiler, assembler, program, query, etc.) and to the operating system to be used. This description must relate to and expand on the information provided in paragraph 5.2 of the FD and paragraph 3.2 of the SS. If the operation of the computer programs to be developed is dependent upon forthcoming changes to support software, the nature, status, and anticipated availability date of such changes must be identified and discussed.

3.2 Interfaces. This paragraph shall provide a description of the interfaces with other applications computer programs, including those of other operational capabilities and from other organizations. The individual interfaces will be related to paragraph 5.3 of the FD and paragraph 3.3 of the SS. For each interface, the following shall be specified:

a. Type of interface, such as operator control of a terminal or program interfaces with other programs.
b. Description of operational implications of data transfer, including security considerations.
c. Data transfer requirements to and from the subject program (including data content, sequence, timing, format, volume, and processing), and characteristics of communications media/systems used for transfer.
d. Formats of data for both the sending and receiving systems including the data item names, codes or abbreviations that are to be interchanged.
e. Interface procedures, including telecommunications considerations.
f. Interface equipment.
g. Data conversion requirements.

3.3 Storage. This paragraph shall provide a description of storage requirements for the program. Included shall be internal storage requirements; use of internal storage and auxiliary storage such as tape, disk, drum; and the estimated quantity of storage required for each. Each type of program must give consideration to the following types of information for the various storage media:

a. Internal storage, number of words/auxiliary core bank or bytes/auxiliary core bank, number of banks.
b. Drum storage, number of words/field, number of fields/drum, number of drum assemblies.

c. Disk storage, number of words/zone or bytes/cylinder, number of zones/disk or cylinders/disk, number of disks/disk unit, number of disk units.

d. Tape storage, number of adapters, number of tape drives/adapter, number of tapes.

In addition, the machine storage will be further allocated into permanent and temporary areas.

3.4 Security. This paragraph shall reflect the type and degree of sensitivity of the data, and the degree of sensitivity of the algorithms. For all sensitive data, a statement shall be included as to whether the data are always sensitive, become sensitive upon the occurrence of specific events, or change their degree of sensitivity upon the occurrence of specific events. This paragraph shall also specify the operational environment that must exist within the ADP activity when any sensitive component of the system is being processed.

3.5 Controls. This paragraph shall provide a presentation of any program controls. Included in this paragraph will be controls such as record counts, accumulated counts, batch controls, etc. These controls will be related to that portion of paragraph 3.5 of the SS that relates to the program being described. If no specific controls are to be established at the program level, this will be so stated.

SECTION 4. DESIGN DETAILS

4.1 Program Operating Procedures. Any special program requirements necessary for the implementation of system operating procedures shall be delineated. Also discussed shall be the interaction of all programs with executive support programs.

4.2 Inputs. This paragraph shall provide a detailed description of all computer program inputs. For each input type and its data elements information such as the following may be provided. When the information is published in a data element dictionary, reference to an entry in the dictionary will be made rather than including an extract from that dictionary. Examples of prepared inputs and input preparation forms may be included. Optionally, inputs may be described with the program or subprogram.

a. *Input Records.*

(1) Title and tag.
(2) Source, medium, and disposition of source medium.
(3) Expected volume and frequency including special handling.
(4) Priority, e.g., routine emergency.
(5) The degree of sensitivity.
(6) Disposition other than processing, such as logging, hard copy reproduction of input, storage location, and custodian.
(7) Flexibility, such as capability of omitting and adding items.
(8) Requirements for timeliness, throughput time, etc.
(9) Special handling, such as specification of special control cards.

FIGURE 3-04. Program Specification

b. *Input Data Elements.*

(1) Name and tag.
(2) Position in the input record type.
(3) Synonymous name.
(4) Definition.
(5) Unit of measurement.
(6) Format and acceptable range of values.
(7) The degree of sensitivity.
(8) Data item names, abbreviations and codes, including a specification as to which is used in the input.

This paragraph shall include examples of prepared inputs and preparation forms, such as input creation sheets and communications message forms.

4.3 Outputs. This paragraph shall provide a detailed description of all computer program outputs. For each output type and its data elements information such as the following may be provided. When the information is published in a data element dictionary, reference to an entry in the dictionary will be made rather than including an extract from that dictionary.

a. *Output Reports.*

(1) Title and tag.
(2) Format, to include headings, line spacing, arrangement, totals, etc. A report layout sheet may be included.
(3) Means of display, if known, e.g., CRT, printer, typewriter, projector.
(4) Expected volume and frequency, including special handling.
(5) Priority, e.g., routine, emergency.
(6) Timing requirements, e.g., response time.
(7) User recipients and use of displays, such as notification, trends, or briefings.
(8) Preprinted form requirements.
(9) The degree of sensitivity.
(10) Data selection criteria will be presented to establish the basis for selecting information for display, e.g., selection for a maintenance report may be on the basis of information in a file of aircraft type and aircraft usage.
(11) Disposition, including logging, film and hard copy printout reproduction and storage, numbers of copies required for distribution, place of storage, office responsible for permanent copy, retention period, and special handling required because of bulk, security considerations, and timing.
(12) Description of plots or graphic displays will include the coordinates to be used, symbols to be used, type of graphic technique (i.e., points or continuous), number of curves per sheet, etc.

FIGURE 3-04. Program Specification

(13) Explanation of symbols.
(14) Conditional and status indicators (code and definition).
(15) Supporting background information, e.g., maps.

b. *Output Data Elements.*

(1) Name and tag.
(2) Synonymous name.
(3) Definition.
(4) Unit of measurement.
(5) Format and acceptable range of values.
(6) The degree of sensitivity.
(7) Data item names, abbreviations and codes, including a specification as to which is used in the output.

4.4 Data Environment. This paragraph shall provide a description of the data base. When the information is published in a data element dictionary, reference to an entry in the dictionary will be made rather than including an extract from that dictionary.

a. *Summary.*

(1) Title and tag.
(2) Narrative summary of content.
(3) Number of records or entries.
(4) Storage media and size.
(5) The degree of sensitivity.
(6) Relationship of each record to a common data base, if applicable.

b. *Data Base Data Elements.*

(1) Name and tag.
(2) Position in the data base.
(3) Synonymous name.
(4) Definition.
(5) Unit of measurement.
(6) Format and range of values.
(7) The degree of sensitivity.
(8) Data item names, abbreviations and codes including a specification as to which is used in the data base.

4.4.1 Storage Allocation. Storage allocation will be described for internal and auxiliary storage as follows:

a. Storage media.
b. Available storage on each medium.
c. Addresses of available storage.
d. Erasable working storage.

FIGURE 3-04. Program Specification

4.4.2 Data Retention. Data retention requirements will be described as follows:

a. Historic retention to include collection of data to be retained, format, storage medium, and time parameters.
b. Periodic report data, e.g., time retained after report generation and time retained to provide summary reports.
c. Summary report data, such as time retained after summary report.

4.4.3 Program Relationships. Interrelationships of a program with the data base(s) will be described to show those files and tables used in each program function.

4.5 Program Logic. This paragraph shall describe the logic of the program. Logical flow may be presented primarily in the form of charts. A narrative presentation, when appropriate, will be used to supplement the charts. All charts will be keyed to the higher-order charts in the SS, if applicable, or the FD.

The logical flow shall provide a detailed description of the processing performed by the program. There shall be included for each program function noted in paragraph 2.2 a description of the operation of the program. All processes will be described to include algorithmic or logic data manipulations and decision processes involved. Conditions being tested for purposes of branching will be explained in detail, as well as methods for identifying error conditions and the resulting actions of the program. The charts and narrative will be related to the information in paragraph 4.2 of the SS, if applicable.

FIGURE 3-05. DATA BASE SPECIFICATION
TABLE OF CONTENTS

FIGURE 3-05. Data Base Specification

LIST OF FIGURES

SECTION 1. GENERAL

1.1 Purpose of the Data Base Specification. This paragraph shall describe the purpose of the DS (Data Base Specification) in the following words, modified when appropriate:

> The objectives of this Data Base Specification for (Project Name) (Project Number) are to describe the storage allocation and data base organization and to provide the basic design data necessary for the construction of the system files, tables, dictionaries, and directories.

1.2 Project References. This paragraph shall include a brief description of the system providing its purpose and use. It shall identify the project sponsor, user, and the operating center(s) that will run the completed computer programs. A list of applicable documents shall be included. At least the following documents, when applicable, shall be specified by author or source, reference number, title, date, and security classification:

a. Functional Description.
b. Data Requirements Document.
c. System/Subsystem Specification.
d. Program Specifications.

1.3 Terms and Abbreviations. This paragraph shall provide a listing or include in an appendix any terms, definitions, or acronyms unique to this document and subject to interpretation by the user of the document. This listing will not include item names or data codes.

SECTION 2. DATA BASE IDENTIFICATION AND DESCRIPTION

This section shall provide all of the information necessary to identify and describe the data base being documented. It shall, in addition, contain various kinds of background information essential for proper utilization of the data base.

FIGURE 3-05. Data Base Specification

2.1 Data Base Identification. This paragraph shall give the code name, tag, or label by which each data base may be uniquely identified. Additional descriptive information shall also be given, whether or not it is implied in the identification code.

2.1.1 System Using the Data Base. The system of which this data base is a part shall be accurately and thoroughly identified. Included shall be the full system name; system code name; tag or label; and system model, modification, or version number. If more than one system uses this data base, each shall be identified.

2.1.2 Effective Dates. The first and last dates of the period during which this data base may be used with the above named system shall be given. The basis of the selection of the dates may vary. They may correspond to document publication dates, program testing periods, turnover periods, turnover or delivery dates, etc., depending upon the implementation plan being used for the system. This paragraph shall also indicate whether the data base is complete or incomplete, pre or post system delivery to the customer, experimental or permanent, and whether it supersedes or will be superseded by another data base. If it supersedes another data base, the availability date of the new data base must be specified.

2.1.3 Storage Requirements. This paragraph shall contain the estimated internal and peripheral storage assignments for all of the programs and data of a system. In addition, it will contain information relevant to certain constraints and conditions under which the programs must operate. Such constraints, based upon a design for the most efficient utilization of the storage media, can apply to both autonomously operated systems and systems that function within the environment of larger, machine operating systems.

2.1.4 Physical Description of Data Base Files. The physical characteristics of the master data base file(s) and duplicate working copies shall be given. This paragraph shall include the file media (disk, tape, or card deck), form of the file (symbolic or binary), and the respective codes used.

2.2 Labeling/Tagging Conventions. This paragraph shall discuss the system labeling/tagging conventions to the extent necessary for the programmer to use the conventions as a practical working tool. For example, specify the conventions used to identify new versions of the data base.

2.3 Organization of the Data Base. This paragraph shall provide system implementers with a single, central source of major design considerations for the handling of the data base. The purpose of this paragraph is to promote consistency of design concerning the organization and manipulation of the physical data base files. The following information shall be given for each kind of file media (tape, disk, etc.) containing the data base:

a. General file design and format.
b. Rationale of the design.

An example of the kind of information to be presented in this paragraph is shown in Figure 2-01 for a tape storage medium.

2.4 Special Instructions. This paragraph shall contain the instructions to be followed by all personnel who will contribute to the generation of the data base and who will use it for both testing and operational purposes. Such instructions may include:

FIGURE 3-05. Data Base Specification

2.3 Tapes.

2.3.1 Environmental Data Tape.

a. *File Design and Format.* The Environmental Data Tape will contain three tape files as shown below:

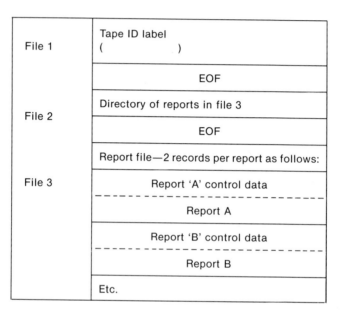

File 1	Tape ID label ( )
	EOF
File 2	Directory of reports in file 3
	EOF
	Report file—2 records per report as follows:
File 3	Report 'A' control data
	Report A
	Report 'B' control data
	Report B
	Etc.

b. *Design Rationale.* All system tapes will contain an identification label as the first tape file. All tape loading programs will check the labels against tape identification parameters input when the system is initialized.

The second tape file will contain the labels or tags of all reports in the third file in their sequential order, and a core/peripheral storage indicator. The loader program will use this to locate reports on the tape and to construct a report storage directory table in core.

The third tape file will contain two records per report. The first will contain detailed control data about the report; the second will contain the binary report itself. The tape loader will move the reports to their assigned peripheral storage areas, and place the contents of the control records into the permanent directory maintained in core.

Figure 2-01. Example of Textual Description of a Data Base

FIGURE 3-05. Data Base Specification

a. Criteria for entering data into the data base.
b. Rules and procedures to be followed when submitting data for entry into the data base.
c. Identification of a data control unit, if applicable.
d. Formats for data description sheets and cards.
e. Machine run instructions for generating, modifying, updating, or otherwise using the data base files. In very large systems, where the details of such instructions are extensive, this paragraph may reference sections of other programming documents (manuals or specifications) where this specific information can be found.

2.5 Support Programs Available for Handling the Data Base. In this paragraph, all of the support programs directly related to the data base shall be either referenced or, if required, discussed briefly. Descriptions shall include program name, functions, and major program operating considerations, such as operating time, hardware setup required, etc. The detailed program documentation shall also be cited. If the program is only referenced, the program name, document title, document number, and appropriate sections of the document shall be provided. Examples of such programs are:

a. Assemble Common Data Pool Programs (assemble symbolic data description information into binary system format and provide a common data pool for related system programs).
b. Data Base Analyzing Programs (reorganize, change, or compare data at the data-file and/or the record level).
c. Storage Allocation Programs (provide efficient facilities for modifying system control data and for maintaining sets of data at an organizational level).
d. Data Base Loading Programs (move or copy collections of data).
e. Information Processing and Data Management Systems (DMS, FIPS, NIPS).

Also to be included will be Electronic Accounting Machine (EAM) procedures created specifically to handle the data base.

2.6 Security. This paragraph shall contain an overview and discussion of the security considerations associated with the data of the overall system.

SECTION 3. DATA DEFINITIONS

This section shall include thorough, detailed definitions and descriptions of all of the data utilized by the system. The specific details of information required for each form of data may vary from system to system and will depend on the design characteristics of the operational or machine operating systems. The information specified below is intended to cover all kinds of systems and is not intended to be totally applicable to any system. In general, included is information about the physical data (as it is structured for direct use by the computer programs) and about the logical data represented by the physical data, i.e., the data as information regardless of how they are structured for use by the computer programs.

FIGURE 3-05. Data Base Specification

3.1 Data Files. For each data file information such as the following may be provided.

3.1.1 General Description of Data File.

a. Name and tag or label.
b. A brief statement of the purpose of the file and logical criteria used for its compilation.
c. The degree of sensitivity.
d. Conditions under which the file is modified or updated.
e. Restrictions and limitations on usage.

3.1.2 Physical Characteristics of Data Files.

a. File contents and format.
b. Primary and secondary storage media.
c. Form of the contents (symbolic, binary, mixed).
d. File control information used by programs, such as storage control items, directories, pointers, skip continue features, and end-of-file markers.
e. A representative of the file structure including tables, records, entries, items or other sub elements of the file.

3.1.3 Logical Characteristics of Data Files. Included in this paragraph shall be a description of each data element in the data base. For each data element may be listed information such as the following:

a. Data element name.
b. Synonymous name.
c. Definition.
d. Format.
e. Range of values.
f. Unit of measurement.
g. Data item names, abbreviations and codes.

When the information is published in a data element dictionary, reference to an entry in the dictionary will be made rather than including an extract from that dictionary. Any variations in either the inputs or outputs from the format or data items that will be used on the data base of the ADS must be specifically identified.

3.2 Tables. An adequate table definition shall contain the following information as applicable to the data base.

a. Table tag or label.
b. Full name or purpose of the table.
c. Data file containing the table.
d. Program subsystem that uses this table.
e. Logical divisions within table (internal table blocks or parts - not entries).
f. Basic table structure (fixed or variable length, fixed or variable entry structure).

FIGURE 3-05. Data Base Specification

(1) If fixed length table:

(a) Number of words/characters per entry.
(b) Number of entries in table.

(2) If variable length table:

(a) Maximum length (number of words/characters).
(b) Maximum number of entries (if entry structure is fixed).
(c) Number of kinds of entries.
(d) Key and control items of each kind of entry.
(e) Indication of presence or absence of table control information.
(f) Other directly related tables plus a statement of the relationship, for example:
"Table SRCHO, item LOOKUP contains the entry type code for the first entry in this table."
(g) Details of the structure of each entry type to include:
1 Contents and format of each entry type.
2 Tag or label of each item plus its entry position, for example, word/character number or bit position.
(h) Unique or significant characteristics, such as:
1 "To be loaded into hardware-protected registers only."
2 "Contents adapted to each installation" (for a multisite system).

3.3 Items. As used in this paragraph, the word "item" refers to a specific category of detailed information that has a defined position within a table, or is a discrete data entity (simple item), for direct and immediate manipulation by a program. Used in this sense, the definition of an item is machine and program oriented rather than operationally oriented. Item definitions shall include, as appropriate:

a. Tag or label.
b. Purpose of the item (a brief statement referenced to related data elements, when applicable).
c. The degree of sensitivity of the item and whether it maintains a specific degree of sensitivity or changes under certain conditions (e.g., removal or introduction of data files or specific data).
d. Table type in which it is found.
e. Position in table (word number and bit positions/level numbers/etc.).
f. Item use, e.g., table control item, entry structure key item, string control item, data item.
g. Item type, e.g., symbolic character, integer, fraction, mixed number (fixed or floating point), string, bead, status.
h. Item coding, depending upon the item type, for example:

(1) Symbolic - character code used.
(2) Integer - binary or binary coded decimal.

(3) Fraction - scaling factor.

(4) Mixed number, fixed point - point position.

(5) Status - the maximum number of conditions, form of status values (symbolic or numeric binary), a list of all acceptable status values or conditions.

i. Accessibility factor - coded to indicate machine instruction modifiers that can expedite retrieving and storing of the item, e.g., FW (full word), LHW or RHW (left or right-hand word), B (byte size), M (mask necessary), etc.

3.4 Records and Entries. Frequently, the basic unit of the data file is a record or an entry. These data units shall be defined to the same degree as tables (see paragraph 3.2). In addition to the file structure presented in the language being used, the following information for each data unit shall be given:

a. Full name and purpose.

b. An explanation of each item.

c. Maximum size.

d. Graphic representation as it is contained in the file, and examples of the output obtained from the file with significant output editing features, if applicable.

SECTION 4. INTEGRATED DATA BASE

If the system will use an integrated data base, that integrated data base shall be identified in this section. Included within this section shall be a discussion of any impacts on the integrated data base of the data that are to be used in this system as described in Section 2. Such impacts may include recommended changes in the organization of the data in the integrated data base that would enhance system efficiency, the addition to the integrated data base of new data elements needed for this system, etc. Recommendations concerning changes in existing support software of the integrated data base, such as data management systems, should also be included. If the system data base is designed based on the assumption that planned or recommended enhancements to either the integrated data base or its support software will be available at the time of system implementation, these assumptions will be stated.

FIGURE 3-06. USERS MANUAL
TABLE OF CONTENTS

SECTION 2. SYSTEM SUMMARY
2.1 System Application
2.2 System Operation
2.3 System Configuration
2.4 System Organization
2.5 Performance
2.6 Data Base
2.7 General Description of Inputs, Processing, Outputs

SECTION 3. STAFF FUNCTIONS RELATED TO TECHNICAL OPERATIONS
3.1 Initiation Procedures
3.2 Staff Input Requirements
3.2.1 Input Formats
3.2.2 Composition Rules
3.2.3 Input Vocabulary
3.2.4 Sample Inputs
3.3 Output Requirements
3.3.1 Output Formats
3.3.2 Sample Outputs
3.3.3 Output Vocabulary
3.4 Utilization of System Outputs
3.5 Recovery and Error Correction Procedures

SECTION 4. FILE QUERY PROCEDURES
4.1 System Query Capabilities
4.2 Data Base Format
4.3 Query Preparation
4.4 Control Instructions

SECTION 5. TERMINAL DATA DISPLAY AND RETRIEVAL PROCEDURES
5.1 Available Capabilities
5.2 Data Base Format
5.3 Access Procedures
5.4 Display and Retrieval Procedures
5.5 Recovery and Error Correction Procedures
5.6 Termination Procedures

SECTION 6. TERMINAL DATA UPDATE PROCEDURES
6.1 Frequency
6.2 Restrictions
6.3 Sources
6.4 Access Procedures
6.5 Update Procedures
6.6 Recovery and Error Correction Procedures
6.7 Termination Procedures

FIGURE 3-06. Users Manual

LIST OF FIGURES

SECTION 1. GENERAL

1.1 Purpose of the Users Manual. This paragraph shall describe the purpose of the UM (Users Manual) in the following words, modified when appropriate:

> The objective of the Users Manual for (Project Name) (Project Number) is to provide the user's non-ADP personnel with the information necessary to effectively use the system.

1.2 Project References. This paragraph shall provide a brief summary of the references applicable to the history and development of the project. The general nature of the computer programs (tactical, inventory control, war-gaming, management information, etc.) developed shall be specified. A brief description of the system shall include its purpose and uses. Also indicated shall be the project sponsor and user as well as the operating center(s) that will run the completed computer programs. At least the following documents, when applicable, shall be specified by author or source, reference number, title, date, and security classification.

a. Project request.
b. Previously published documentation on the project.
c. Documentation concerning related projects.
d. Standards or reference documentation, such as:
   (1) Documentation standards and specifications.
   (2) Programming conventions.
   (3) DoD or Federal standards (data elements, programming languages, etc.).

1.3 Terms and Abbreviations. This paragraph shall provide a list or include in an appendix any terms, definitions or acronyms unique to this document and subject to interpretation by the user of the document. This list will not include item names or data codes.

1.4 Security. This paragraph shall contain an overview and discussion of the security considerations associated with the data of the system.

SECTION 2. SYSTEM SUMMARY

2.1 System Application. The uses of the ADS in supporting the activities of the user's staff shall be generally stated and explained. The description shall include:

FIGURE 3-06. Users Manual

a. The purpose, reason, or rationale of the system.

b. Capabilities and operating improvements provided by the system.

c. Additional features, characteristics, and advantages considered appropriate in furnishing a clear, general description of the system and the benefits derived from it.

d. Functions performed by the system, such as preprocessing or postprocessing data input or output from a primary processor; maintenance of data files; display of submarine, surface or aircraft, etc.

2.2 System Operation. This paragraph will show the relationships of the functions performed by the system with the organizations or stations that are sources of input to the system and those that are recipients of output from it. Included shall be charts and a brief narrative description including *only* the who, what, where, and why concerning the inputs and outputs shown on the chart.

2.3 System Configuration. A brief narrative description of the equipment used by the system shall be given. It may include the type of computer and input and output devices.

2.4 System Organization. The objective of this paragraph shall be to present a general overview of the organization of the system. The presentation shall show, as appropriate, the logical parts of the system (such as subsystems and programs) and a brief description of their role in the operation of the system.

2.5 Performance. This paragraph shall present a brief description of the overall performance capabilities of the system, including how it meets the information requirements of the staff or how it supports associated activities. Performance measures and information of interest are represented by the following examples:

a. Input - types, volumes, rate of inputs accepted.

b. Output - types, volume, accuracy, rate of outputs that the system can produce.

c. Response time - include qualifications, where necessary, that affect response time in processing operational reports, such as listing a tape, compiling an object program, etc. Type and volume of input and equipment configuration are examples of items that may influence running time and, consequently, response time.

d. Limitations - for example, maximum size per unit of input, format constraints, restrictions on what data files may be queried and by what location, language constraints.

e. Error rate - capabilities for detecting various legal and logical errors and the means provided for error correction.

f. Processing time - show typical processing times.

g. Flexibility - note provisions allowing extension of the usage of the system.

h. Reliability - note system provisions that support, for example, alternatie processing or a switch-over capability.

2.6 Data Base. The data files that are referenced, supported, or kept current by the system shall be identified in functional terms. The brief description should include the type of data in the file and the usage made of it. If the system does not have a file query capability as described in Section 4, this paragraph will include a description of the data elements included in the data base. For each data element may be listed information such as the following:

a. Data element name.
b. Synonymous name.
c. Definition.
d. Format.
e. Range of values.
f. Unit of measurement.
g. Data item names, abbreviations and codes.

When the information is published in a data element dictionary, reference to an entry in the dictionary will be made rather than including an extract from that dictionary. Any variations in either the inputs or outputs from the format or data items that will be used on the data base of the ADS must be specifically identified.

2.7 General Description of Inputs, Processing, Outputs. This paragraph shall present a general narrative description of the inputs, the flow of data through the processing cycle, and the resultant outputs.

a. *Inputs.* In describing the inputs, consideration should be given to the following:

(1) Purpose of input - explain why the input is made to the program system and note conditions or events requiring its submission.
(2) Content of input - describe what the input contains in the way of operational, control, or reference data.
(3) Associated inputs - describe any other inputs required by the system in addition to the direct input.
(4) Origin of inputs - identify the source or preparer of the input.
(5) Data files - identify in general or functional terms the data files associated with the input.
(6) Security considerations.
(7) Other - include additional remarks of general information.

b. *Processing.* In this paragraph, the relationship of the input to the output should be described with a general description of the flow of data through the processing cycle.

c. *Outputs.* In describing the outputs, consideration should be given to the following:

(1) Output - list the outputs produced by the program system showing their relationship to the inputs.
(2) Purpose of output - explain the reason for the output and note conditions or events that require its generation by the system.
(3) Content of output - describe in general terms the information provided by the output.
(4) Associated outputs - reference other system outputs that complement the information in this output.

FIGURE 3-06. Users Manual

(5) Distribution of outputs - note the recipients in the organization who receive this output.
(6) Security considerations.
(7) Other - describe additional items of general information.

SECTION 3. STAFF FUNCTIONS RELATED TO TECHNICAL OPERATIONS

This section shall provide the details necessary to prepare staff inputs to the system. The logical arrangement of the information shall enable the staff and functional personnel to prepare required inputs. In addition, this section will explain in detail the characteristics and meaning of the information the program system produces as outputs. If an exclusively batch processing system or an exclusively online system is being described, the following paragraphs should provide the necessary procedures for the staff to utilize the system. If an online system with batch processing capabilities is being described, this paragraph may reference the manual that describes the terminal operations and the following paragraphs may detail the procedures to be followed for the batch processing runs, or both may be presented herein. Optionally, the following information may be presented with each capability.

3.1 Initiation Procedures. The procedures that must be followed to initiate system operation will be detailed in this paragraph. Included may be information such as sample job request forms, sample control card formats, or log-on procedures to be used for online terminal operations. If these procedures are standard or are detailed in another manual, that manual will be referenced.

3.2 Staff Input Requirements. The requirements to be observed in preparing entries to the program system shall be delineated in this paragraph for each different type or class of input. Typical considerations are the following:

a. Cause of input - note what operational conditions require the submission of the input (e.g., catastrophe, normal status report, need to enter parameters in a source program, need to update data, the desire to obtain particular data, the need to respond to a particular display).
b. Time of input - specify when the input must be prepared (e.g., periodically, randomly as a function of an operational situation).
c. Origin of input - identify the staff unit or station authorized to generate the input.
d. Medium of input - note the medium used to enter the input (e.g., keyboard, punched card, magnetic or paper tape).
e. Associated inputs - reference any related inputs that are required to be entered at the same time as this input.
f. Other - note any other applicable information, such as other recipients of the inputs; priority; security handling; variations on the basic input format using code or key indicators; limitations on what files may be interrogated by a particular type of input.

3.2.1 Input Formats. The layout form(s) used in the initial preparation of program system inputs shall be illustrated and the information which may be entered on the various sections and lines explained. The explanation of each entry provision shall be keyed to the sample form illustrated.

3.2.2 Composition Rules. This paragraph shall provide a description of the language and the grammatical rules and conventions that must be observed in order to prepare input that can be accepted by the program system. The rules of syntax, usage of punctuation, etc. will be explained. Items for consideration may include the following:

a. Input length - e.g., 100 characters maximum.
b. Line length - e.g., 30 characters maximum.
c. Format - e.g., all input items must be left-justified.
d. Labeling - i.e., usage of tags or identifier to denote major data sets to the system.
e. Sequencing - i.e., the order and placement of items in the input.
f. Punctuation - i.e., spacing and use of symbols (virgule, asterisk, character combinations, etc.) to denote start and end of input, of lines, of data groups, etc.
g. Combination - i.e., rules forbidding use of particular character or parameter sets in an input.

3.2.3 Input Vocabulary. This paragraph shall explain the legal character combinations or codes that must be used to identify or compose input items.[1] Included may be codes for submission or operational status, inventory items, statements or operations.

3.2.4 Sample Inputs. Each class or type of input acceptable by the system shall be illustrated. An introduction will be given as to what the sample represents. A complete explanation shall follow, describing the significance of the subsections of the sample input. Included in the explanation may be information on the following types of inputs:

a. Header - containing entries that denote the input class or type, date/time, origin, instruction codes to the system, etc.
b. Text - containing the subsections of the input representing data for operational files, request parameters for an information retrieval program, etc.
c. Trailer - containing control data denoting the end of input and any additional control data.
d. Omissions - indicating those classes or types of input that may be omitted at the option of the composer or because of particular circumstances concerning the input.
e. Repeats - indicating those subsections of the input that may be repeated up to a specified maximum number of entries, if required.

3.3 Output Requirements. The requirements relevant to each class or type of output shall be described. Representative information that may be included for each class of output is:

[1]An appendix may be provided containing an alphabetical listing of item codes that can be entered into an input to the system or that can appear on an output from the system, and an alphabetical listing of functional or generic categories, e.g., materiel control, weather, ship type. Each of these basic categories will contain an alphabetical listing of associated data items and their code representation. If extensive lists of codes have previously been promulgated in final form, those lists shall be referenced.

FIGURE 3-06. Users Manual

a. Purpose - the reasons why the output is generated e.g., the desire to obtain particular data, due to the existence of an "exception" situation, to identify different operating units at different ranges.

b. Time - whether the output is randomly or periodically produced. If produced periodically, the period must be specified.

c. Options - any modifications or variations of the basic output that are available.

d. Media - physical form of the output, such as printout, CRT, tape, cards.

e. Location - where the output is required to appear, such as in the computer area or remotely at a particular physical area or station.

f. Other - any additional requirements for this output, such as priority, security handling, associated outputs that complement the information in this output.

3.3.1 Output Formats. The layout in which each class or type of system output is presented shall be explained in detail. Explanations shall be keyed to particular parts of the format illustrated. Appropriate information that may be provided includes the following:

a. Header - the title, identification, time, number of output parts, and similar basic control data that may be contained in the header or control segment of the output shall be described.

b. Body - the information that may appear in the body or text of the output must be explained. Described shall be the significance of fixed data, such as columnar headings in tabular display types of output. The existence of subsets or sections in the output format (e.g., part A, part B) should be noted. In card/tape output, the position or column locations allocated to specific output information should be described.

c. Trailer - the control or reference information that may be appended to the body of information presented shall be discussed.

Additional characteristics concerning the make-up of outputs may include information such as the meanings of special symbols, etc.

3.3.2 Sample Outputs. Illustrations of the output obtainable from the system shall be given for each different class or type. The function or purpose of the output shall be explained. A detailed description including information such as the following may be provided:

a. Definition - the meaning and use of each information variable for the reader or user.

b. Source - item extracted from a specific input, from a data base file, calculated by system, etc.

c. Characteristics - concerning omissibility of the item under certain conditions of the output generation, range of values, unit of measure.

3.3.3 Output Vocabulary. Any codes or abbreviations that appear in the output in a form different from those used on the input described in paragraph 3.2.3 shall be described in this paragraph.

3.4 Utilization of System Outputs. An explanation shall be given of the use of the output by the operational area or activity which receives it. For example, a summary report of POL (petroleum, oil, and lubricant) stocks may be received by a materiel control activity and, depending on the information in the report, action might be required to initiate the purchase or transfer of stocks to a particular location; the appearance of a blinking symbol on a CRT may require keyboard entries by several stations; etc.

3.5 Recovery and Error Correction Procedures. A list of the error codes generated by the application program and the corrective actions to be taken by the user to correct the condition shall be included within this paragraph. Also included in this paragraph shall be the procedures to be followed by the user to ensure that any recovery and restart capabilities can be utilized.

SECTION 4. FILE QUERY PROCEDURES

This section shall be prepared for those ADSs with a file query retrieval capability. The instructions necessary for recognition, preparation, and processing of a query applicable to the data base shall be cited in detail. The descriptive techniques illustrated in paragraphs 4.1, 4.2, and 4.3 shall be utilized as applicable.

4.1 System Query Capabilities. This paragraph shall illustrate in tabular form the preprogrammed query capabilities provided by the system with a cross-reference to a query card format or query statement. An example is shown in Figure 4-01.

4.2 Data Base Format. This paragraph shall illustrate the data base format and content. An example is shown in Figure 4-02. If applicable, the format shall show both the data which are not subject to queries and the data which, even though not specifically requested, are extracted for some queries. For each data element may be listed information such as the following:

a. Data element name.
b. Synonymous name.
c. Definition.
d. Format.
e. Range of values.

QUERY	QUERY CARD FORMAT
Numbers of employees within an organization	A
Number of employees in a specific pay grade	B
Total gross pay for employees within an organization	C
State tax year-to-date for a specific state	D
FICA tax year-to-date for a specific employee	E
Total deductions for a specific employee	F
Net pay for a specific employee	G

Figure 4-01. Example of Preprogrammed Query Capability: Relationship of Queries to Card Formats

ITEM NAME	RECORD POSITIONS	KIND OF DATA
ORG-NAME	1-30	Alpha-numeric
ORG-ID	31-36	Alpha-numeric
SOC-SEC-NO	37-45	Alpha-numeric
NAME	46-65	Alpha-numeric
PAY-GRADE	66-69	Alpha-numeric
GROSS-PAY	70-75	Signed-numeric
GROSS-PAY-YTD	76–83	Signed-numeric
FED-TAX	84-89	Signed-numeric
FED-TAX-YTD	90-97	Signed-numeric
FICA	98-103	Signed-numeric
FICA-YTD	104-111	Signed-numeric
STATE-TAX	112-117	Signed-numeric
STATE-TAX-YTD	118-125	Signed-numeric
STATE-TAX-CODE	126-127	Alpha-numeric
ALLOTMENTS	128-133	Signed-numeric
NET-PAY	134-139	Signed-numeric

Figure 4-02. Example of Data Record Format: Format of Data Record 1

f. Unit of measurement.

g. Data item names, abbreviations and codes.

When the information is published in a data element dictionary, reference to an entry in the dictionary will be made rather than including an extract from that dictionary. Any variations in either the inputs or outputs from the format or data items that are used on the data base must be specifically identified.

4.3 Query Preparation. Instructions shall be provided for the preparation of any necessary query title, request, and parameter input. Figure 4-03 shows an example of this format. The details of query input preparation in the context of each specific data base and system retrieval capability shall be repeated as necessary in the form of positive instructions. In cases when the retrieval capability is part of a support program system and query input formats are not needed, the specific query statement required shall be listed. Figure 4-04 shows a specific query statement. The formats provided will be used by control personnel to transcribe queries into the technical phrasing of the retrieval system.

4.4 Control Instructions. Instructions shall be provided for the control of the sequencing of runs and of the program necessary to extract the response to the query request from the data base. These instructions shall include the requirements for, and the preparation of, control cards which may be required by the system or application programs. If extensive information concerning control card preparation is contained in support system documentation, this documentation may be referenced.

FORMAT OF QUERY CARD A (NUMBER OF EMPLOYEES WITHIN AN ORGANIZATION)			
Query Item Title	Begin in Char. Pos.	Content/Comments	
Query Designator	1	Q	Constant
File Number	2	01	Constant
Query Number	4	01	First Query
Security Classification	10	U	Unclassified
Query Card Format Code	12	A	
Organization	14		Insert ORG-ID as requested by query. Refer to data format for applicable code.

Figure 4-03. Example of Query Card Format: Format of Query Card A

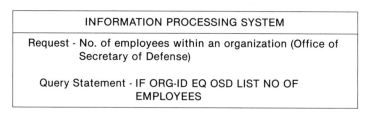

INFORMATION PROCESSING SYSTEM
Request - No. of employees within an organization (Office of Secretary of Defense)
Query Statement - IF ORG-ID EQ OSD LIST NO OF EMPLOYEES

Figure 4-04. Example of Query Statement

SECTION 5. TERMINAL DATA DISPLAY AND RETRIEVAL PROCEDURES

5.1 Available Capabilities. The data display and retrieval capabilities available through terminal operations will be stated and explained in general terms.

5.2 Data Base Content. This paragraph will discuss the content and, if applicable, the format of the data base used by the system with emphasis on the relationships among the data that can be displayed or retrieved.

5.3 Access Procedures. Presented in this paragraph will be the sequence of steps required to access the data base. Included will be such information as the name of the system or subsystem being called and other control information such as access restrictions.

5.4 Display and Retrieval Procedures. Paragraphs 5.4.1 through 5.4.n will describe the step-by-step procedures necessary to produce the various displays and retrievals that are available through the use of a terminal. For each procedure information such as the name of the operation, input formats, and sample responses may be included.

5.5 Recovery and Error Correction Procedures. Error codes and messages should be provided indicating their meanings and any corrective actions that should be taken.

5.6 Termination Procedures. This paragraph will present the sequence of steps necessary to terminate the display or retrieval operation.

FIGURE 3-06. Users Manual

SECTION 6. TERMINAL DATA UPDATE PROCEDURES

6.1 Frequency. This paragraph will describe the frequency of data updates from terminals. Information such as the events that caused the update may be included.

6.2 Restrictions. This paragraph shall describe any restrictions on updating the data base. Included may be such factors as:

a. The offices or personnel authorized to update.
b. Time periods when such updating is allowed.
c. Information for ensuring that only authorized updates are allowed.

6.3 Sources. Included in this paragraph will be a list of the sources used to obtain the data that will make up each update.

6.4 Access Procedures. Presented in this paragraph will be the sequence of steps required to access the data base. Included will be such information as the name of the system or subsystem being called and other control information such as access restrictions.

6.5 Update Procedures. Paragraph 6.5.1 through 6.5.n will provide information to enable an authorized user to update data in the system data base using a terminal. For each type of update procedure information such as the name of the operation, input formats, and sample responses may be included.

6.6 Recovery and Error Correction Procedures. Error codes and messages should be provided indicating their meanings and any corrective actions that should be taken. Any user initiated recovery procedures and validity checks should also be included in narrative form.

6.7 Termination Procedures. This paragraph shall present the step-by-step sequence of actions necessary to terminate the update.

FIGURE 3-07. COMPUTER OPERATION MANUAL
TABLE OF CONTENTS

FIGURE 3-07. Computer Operation Manual

3.3	Run Description (Identify)
3.3.1	Control Inputs
3.3.2	Management Information
3.3.3	Input-Output Files
3.3.4	Output Reports
3.3.5	Reproduced Output Reports
3.3.6	Restart/Recovery Procedures
3.4	Run Description (Identify)

SECTION 1. GENERAL

1.1 Purpose of the Computer Operation Manual. This paragraph shall describe the purpose of the OM (Computer Operation Manual) in the following words or appropriate modifications thereto:

> The objective of this Computer Operation Manual for (Project Name) (Project Number) is to provide computer control and computer operator personnel with a detailed operational description of the system and its associated environment with which they will be concerned during the performance of their duties.

1.2 Project References. At least the following documents, when applicable, shall be specified by author or source, reference number, title, date, and security classification:

a. Users Manual.

b. Program Maintenance Manual.

c. Other pertinent documentation on the project.

1.3 Terms and Abbreviations. This paragraph shall provide a listing or include in an appendix any terms, definitions, or acronyms unique to this document and subject to interpretation by the user of the document. This listing will not include item names or data codes.

SECTION 2. SYSTEM OVERVIEW

2.1 System Application. A brief description of the system including its purpose and uses shall be provided.

2.2 System Organization. This paragraph shall describe the operation of the system by use of a chart showing the data processing operations, including how the different operations are interrelated. If sets of runs are grouped by time periods or cycles, then each set of integrated operations required on a daily, weekly, etc. basis will be presented. If runs may be grouped logically by organizational level, the groups of runs that can be performed by each organizational level such as headquarters processing, field activity processing, etc., shall be presented.

2.3 Program Inventory. This paragraph shall provide an inventory of the various programs. This listing shall include the program full name, program ID, as well as security considerations of the programs and identification of those programs necessary to continue or resume operation of the ADS in case of an emergency.

FIGURE 3-07. Computer Operation Manual

2.4 File Inventory. This paragraph shall list all permanent files that are referenced, created, or updated by the system. This listing shall include information such as the file name, file ID, storage medium and required storage (number of tapes or disks) as well as security considerations. The listing shall also identify those files necessary to continue or resume operation of the ADS in case of an emergency.

2.5 Processing Overview. This paragraph will provide information which is applicable to the processing of the system. Separate paragraphs may be used as needed to cover system restrictions, waivers of operational standards, information oriented toward specific support areas (e.g., library, EAM support) or other processing requirements such as the following:

a. Interface with other systems.
b. Other pertinent system-related information.

2.6 Security. This paragraph shall contain an overview and discussion of the security considerations associated with the data of the system.

SECTION 3. DESCRIPTION OF RUNS

This section shall provide a description of the runs for operations and scheduling personnel to allow accurate and efficient scheduling of operations, assignment of equipment, the management of input and output data, and restart/recovery procedures. In online systems some information about system operational control will be related to the capabilities of the operating system and other information will need to be presented in a manner more directly useful to operators of online terminals. Much of the necessary information should be included in figures with additional information that is specifically oriented to the hardware and software set being used.

3.1 Run Inventory. This paragraph shall provide a list of the various runs (i.e., programs, jobs) that may be made by the system and include a brief summary of the purpose of the run. This list should relate to the runs that are included in the remainder of this section and should show the programs that are executed during the run.

3.2 Phasing. This paragraph shall provide a schedule of acceptable phasing of the program system into a logical series of operations. A system run may be phased to permit manual or semiautomatic checking of intermediate results, to provide the user with intermediate results for other purposes, or to permit a logical break if higher priority jobs are submitted. An example of the minimum division for most systems would be edit, file update, and report preparation.

3.3 Run Description (Identify). Paragraph 3.3 through 3.n will provide the detailed information needed to execute runs of the system. The information provided will be organized in a manner most useful to the operating centers and operations personnel that will perform the runs.

3.3.1 Control Inputs. This paragraph shall provide a listing of the runstream of job control statements needed to initiate the run.

3.3.2 Management Information. This paragraph shall present the information needed to manage the run including, for example, the following information:

a. Run identification.
b. Peripheral and resource requirements.

FIGURE 3-07. Computer Operation Manual

c. Security considerations.
d. Method of initiation, such as on request, as a result of another run, at a predetermined time, etc.
e. Estimated run time.
f. Required turnaround time.
g. Messages and responses.
h. Procedures for taking check points.
i. Waivers from operational standards.
j. Contacts for problems experienced with the run.

3.3.3 Input-Output Files. This paragraph shall list information about the files that serve as input to or that are created or updated by the run. Included for each file should be information such as the following:

a. File name.
b. Security and privacy.
c. Recording medium.
d. Retention schedule.
e. Disposition of file.

3.3.4 Output Reports. This paragraph shall list information about the reports that are produced during the run. Included for each report should be information such as the following:

a. Report identification.
b. Security and privacy.
c. Medium (i.e., hardcopy, tape).
d. Volume of report.
e. Number of copies.
f. Distribution of copies.

3.3.5 Reproduced Output Reports. This paragraph shall provide information about those computer-generated reports that are subsequently reproduced by other means. Included for each report shall be information such as the following:

a. Report identification.
b. Security and privacy.
c. Reproduction technique.
d. Paper size.
e. Binding method.
f. Number of copies.
g. Distribution of copies.

3.3.6 Restart/Recovery Procedures. This paragraph shall provide information to the operations center personnel concerning restart/recovery procedures that these personnel will follow in the event of a system failure.

3.4 Run Description (Identify). Paragraph 3.4 will present information about the second run in a manner similar to that used in paragraph 3.3.

FIGURE 3-07. Computer Operation Manual

FIGURE 3-08. PROGRAM MAINTENANCE MANUAL
TABLE OF CONTENTS

SECTION 1. GENERAL

1.1 Purpose of the Program Maintenance Manual. This paragraph shall describe the purpose of the MM (Program Maintenance Manual) in the following words or appropriate modifications thereto:

> The objective for writing this Program Maintenance manual for (Project Name) (Project Number) is to provide the maintenance programmer personnel with the information necessary to effectively maintain the system.

1.2 Project References. This paragraph shall provide a brief summary of the references applicable to the history and development of the project. The general nature of the system (tactical, inventory control, war-gaming, management information, etc.) developed shall be specified. A brief description of this system shall include its purpose and uses. Also indicated shall be the project sponsor and user as well as the operating center(s) that will run the completed computer programs. At least the following documents, when applicable, shall be specified by author or source, reference number, title, date, and security classification:

a. Users Manual.

b. Computer Operation Manual.

c. Other pertinent documentation on the project.

1.3 Terms and Abbreviations. This paragraph shall provide a list or include in an appendix any terms, definitions or acronyms unique to this document and subject to interpretation by the user of the document. This list will not include item names or data codes.

SECTION 2. SYSTEM DESCRIPTION

2.1 System Application. The purpose of the system and the functions it performs shall be explained. A particular application system, for example, might serve to control mission activities by accepting specific inputs (status reports, emergency conditions), extracting items of data, and deriving other items of data in order to produce both information about a specific mission and information for summary reports. These functions shall be related to paragraphs 3.1, Specific Performance Requirements, and 4.2, System Functions, of the FD.

2.2 Security. This paragraph shall contain an overview and discussion of the security considerations associated with the data of the system.

2.3 General Description. This paragraph will provide a comprehensive description of the system, subsystem, jobs, etc. in terms of their overall functions. This description will be accompanied by a chart showing the interrelationships of the major components of the system.

2.4 Program Description. The purpose of this paragraph is to supply details and characteristics of each program and subroutine that would be of value to a maintenance programmer in understanding the program and its relationship to other programs. (Special maintenance programs related to the specific system being documented will be discussed under paragraph 4.4, Special Maintenance Procedures.) This paragraph will initially contain a list of all programs to be discussed, followed by a narrative description of each program and its respective subroutines under separate paragraphs starting with 2.4.1 through 2.4.n. For each major item listed below include any applicable information on security considerations. Information to be included in the narrative description is represented by the following items:

a. Identification - program title or tag, including a designation of the version number of the program.

b. Functions - description of program functions and the method used in the program to accomplish the function.

c. Input - description of the input. Description used here must include all information pertinent to maintenance programming including:

(1) Data records used by the program during operation.

(2) Input data type and location(s) used by the program when its operation begins.

(3) Entry requirements concerning the initiation of the program.

d. Processing - description of the processing performed by the program, including:

   (1) Major operations - major operations of the program will be described. The description may reference chart(s) which may be included in an appendix. This chart will show the general logical flow of operations, such as read an input, access a data record, major decision, and print an output which would be represented by segments or subprograms within the program. Reference may be made to included charts that present each major operation in more detail.
   (2) Major branching conditions provided in the program.
   (3) Restrictions that have been designed into the system with respect to the operation of this program, or any limitations on the use of the program.
   (4) Exit requirements concerning termination of the operation of the program.
   (5) Communications or linkage to the next logical program (operational, control).
   (6) Output data type and location(s) produced by the program for use by related processing segments of the system.
   (7) Storage - Specify the amount and type of storage required to use the program and the broad parameters of the storage locations needed.

e. Output - description of the outputs produced by the program. While this description may reference output described in the Users Manual, any intermediate output, working files, etc., should be described for the benefit of the maintenance programmer.

f. Interfaces - description of the interfaces to and from this program.

g. Tables and Items - provide details and characteristics of the tables and items within each program. Items not part of a table must be listed separately. Items contained within a table may be referenced from the table descriptions. If the data description of the program provides sufficient information, the program listing may be referenced to provide some of the necessary information. At least the following will be included for each table:

   (1) Table tag, label or symbolic name.
   (2) Full name and purpose of the table.
   (3) Other programs that use this table.
   (4) Logical divisions within the table (internal table blocks or parts - not entries).
   (5) Basic table structure (fixed or variable length, fixed or variable entry structure).
   (6) Table layout (a graphic presentation should be used). Included in supporting description should be table control information, details of the structure of each type of entry, unique or significant characteristics of the use of the table, and information about the names and locations of items within the table.

FIGURE 3-08. Program Maintenance Manual

(7) Item - the term "item" refers to a specific category of detailed information that is coded for direct and immediate manipulation by a program. Used in this sense, the definition of an item is machine and program oriented rather than operationally oriented. Of primary importance is an explanation of the use of each item. At least the following will be included for each item:

(a) Item tag or label and full name.

(b) Purpose of the item.

(c) Item coding, depending upon the item type, such as integer, symbolic, status, etc.

h. Unique Run Features - description of any unique features of the running of this program that are not included in the OM.

SECTION 3. ENVIRONMENT

3.1 Equipment Environment. This paragraph shall discuss the equipment configuration and its general characteristics as they apply to the system.

3.2 Support Software. This paragraph shall list the various support software used by the system and identify the version or release number under which the system was developed.

3.3 Data Base. Information in this paragraph shall include a complete description of the nature and content of each data base used by the system including security considerations.

3.3.1 General Characteristics. Provide a general description of the characteristics of the data base, including:

a. Identification - name and mnemonic reference. List the programs utilizing the data base.

b. Data Permanency - note whether the data base contains static data that a program can reference, but may not change, or dynamic data that can be changed or updated during system operation. Indicate whether the change is periodic or random as a function of input data.

c. Storage - specify the storage media for the data base (e.g., tape, disk, internal storage) and the amount of storage required.

d. Restrictions - explain any limitations on the use of this data base by the program in the system.

3.3.2 Organization and Detailed Description. This paragraph will serve to define the internal structure of the data base. A layout will be shown and its composition, such as records and tables, will be explained. If available, computer-generated or other listings of this detailed information may be referenced or included, herein. The following items indicate the type of information desired:

a. Layout - show the structure of the data base including records and items.

b. Sections - note whether the physical record is a logical record or one of several that constitute a logical record. Identify the record parts, such as header or control segments and the body of the record.

c. Fields - identify each field in the record structure and, if necessary, explain its purpose. Include for each field the following items:
   (1) Tags/labels - indicate the tag or label assigned to reference each field.
   (2) Size - indicate the length and number of bits/characters that make up each data field.
   (3) Range - indicate the range of acceptable value for the field entry.
d. Expansion - note provisions, if any, for adding additional data fields to the record.

SECTION 4. PROGRAM MAINTENANCE PROCEDURES

This section shall provide information on the specific procedures necessary for the programmer to maintain the programs that make up the system.

4.1 Conventions. This paragraph will explain all rules, schemes, and conventions that have been used within the system. Information of this nature could include the following items:

a. Design of mnemonic identifiers and their application to the tagging or labeling of programs, subroutines, records, data fields, storage areas, etc.
b. Procedures and standards for charts, listings, serialization of cards, abbreviations used in statements and remarks, and symbols appearing in charts and listings.
c. The appropriate standards, fully identified, may be referenced in lieu of a detailed outline of conventions.
d. Standard data elements and related features.

4.2 Verification Procedures. This paragraph will include those requirements and procedures necessary to check the performance of a program section following its modification. Included may also be procedures for periodic verification of the program.

4.3 Error Conditions. A description of error conditions, not previously documented, may also be included. This description shall include an explanation of the source of the error and recommended methods to correct it.

4.4 Special Maintenance Procedures. This paragraph shall contain any special procedures required which have not been delineated elsewhere in this section. Specific information that may be appropriate for presentation would include:

a. Requirements, procedures, and verification which may be necessary to maintain the system input-output components, such as the data base.
b. Requirements, procedures, and verification methods necessary to perform a Library Maintenance System run.

4.5 Special Maintenance Programs. This paragraph shall contain an inventory and description of any special programs (such as file restoration, purging history files) used

FIGURE 3-08. Program Maintenance Manual

to maintain the system. These programs should be described in the same manner as those described in paragraphs 2.3 and 2.4 of the MM.

a. *Input-Output Requirements.* Included in this paragraph shall be the requirements concerning materials needed to support the necessary maintenance tasks. Materials may, for example, include card decks for loading a maintenance program and the inputs which represent the changes to be made. When a support system is being used, this paragraph should reference the appropriate manual.

b. *Procedures.* The procedures, presented in a step-by-step manner, shall detail the method of preparing the inputs, such as structuring and sequencing of inputs. The operations or steps to be followed in setting up, running, and terminating the maintenance task on the equipment shall be given.

4.6 Listings. This paragraph will contain or provide a reference to the location of the program listing. Comments appropriate to particular instructions shall be made if necessary to understand and follow the listing.

FIGURE 3-09. TEST PLAN
TABLE OF CONTENTS

LIST OF FIGURES

SECTION 1. GENERAL

1.1 Purpose of the Test Plan. This paragraph shall describe the purpose of the PT (Test Plan) in the following words, modified as appropriate:

The Test Plan for (Project Name) (Project Number) is written to fulfill the following objectives:

a. To provide guidance for the management and technical effort necessary throughout the test period.

b. To establish a comprehensive test plan and to communicate to the user(s) the nature and extent of the tests deemed necessary to provide a basis for evaluation of the system.

c. To coordinate with the user an orderly schedule of events, a specification of equipment and organizational requirements, the methodology

FIGURE 3-09. Test Plan

of testing, a list of materials to be delivered, and a schedule of user orientation.

d. To provide a written record of the actual test inputs to exercise system limits and critical capabilities, the instructions to permit execution of the test by the user staff and operator personnel, and the expected outputs.

1.2 Project References. This paragraph shall provide a brief summary of the references applicable to the history and development of the project. Documentation describing systems or procedures which supplement or provide for interaction with the subject system during the course of normal operation or at any point in the testing shall be specified. Included shall be a listing of at least all applicable documentation prepared for this project.

1.3 Terms and Abbreviations. This paragraph shall provide a listing or include in an appendix any terms, definitions, or acronyms unique to this document and subject to interpretation by the user of the document. This listing will not include item names or data codes.

SECTION 2. DEVELOPMENT TEST ACTIVITY

2.1 Statement of Pretest Activity. This paragraph shall provide a description of the testing completed as part of the system development activity. It may refer to an appendix in the form of a listing of the elements in the PS and SS against which the program operation has been explicitly checked.

2.2 Pretest Activity Results. This paragraph will provide an overall evaluation of the test results obtained from all tests conducted as part of the system development activity. It may refer to an appendix when multiple tests have been conducted. Included must be a statement of any known system deficiencies and their potential impact.

SECTION 3. TEST PLAN

3.1 System Description. A brief description or system chart showing inputs and outputs shall be included to provide a frame of reference for the description of the tests to be conducted.

3.2 Testing Schedule. This paragraph shall provide a listing or chart depicting the locations at which the testing will be scheduled and the time frames during which the testing will be conducted.

3.3 First Location (Identify) Testing. This paragraph shall identify the first location at which the testing will be conducted and the participating organizations. This paragraph will also list the test(s) to be performed at this location and will reference the appropriate section(s) that describe the test(s).

3.3.1 Milestone Chart. This paragraph shall provide a chart to depict the activities and events listed below. An example of this type of chart is shown in Figure 3-01. When preparing this chart, consideration will be given to all tests scheduled for this location. The chart will be in chronological order with supporting narrative as necessary and will show, for example:

Events \ Month and day	Mar 1	Mar 2	Mar 3	Mar 4	Mar 5	Mar 6	Mar 7	Mar 8	Mar 9	Mar 10	Mar 11
A						X	X	X	X	X	
B	X	X	X	X	X	X	X				
C					X	X	X				
D	X	X	X	X							
E			X	X	X				X		
F										X	X

Figure 3-01. Example of Milestone Chart: Milestone Chart for the Record Association System

a. Overall on-site test period by calendar date and portions of the period assigned to major portions of test.
b. Pretest on-site period required for system debugging, orientation, and familiarization.
c. Period assigned for the collection of data base values, input values, and other operational data required for system test.
d. Period assigned for user orientation and familiarization with system documentation.
e. Period assigned for user training, operator training, maintenance and control group training, and orientation briefing for non-ADP personnel.
f. Period assigned for preparation, review, and approval of the Test Analysis Report.

3.3.2 Equipment Requirements. This paragraph shall provide a chart or listing to depict the period of usage and quantity required of each item of equipment employed throughout the test period at each location where the system is to be installed. Any test data reduction equipment shall be included.

3.3.3 Software. This paragraph shall list software programs, including systems support and applications programs, and their form (tape, disk, etc.) used during and in support of the testing when they are not a part of the system being tested.

3.3.4 Personnel. This paragraph shall provide a chart or a listing of the number and period of use of personnel with indicated skill types required during the entire test period(s). It will indicate special requirements, such as multishift operation and assignment or the retention of key skills to ensure continuity and consistency in extensive test programs. This chart or listing should be related to the milestone chart.

3.3.5 Orientation Plan. This paragraph will describe the number of personnel providing training during the testing and the types of training to be undertaken. This information shall be related to the personnel requirements in paragraph 3.3.4. This plan shall include user instruction (classroom and computer), operator instruction, maintenance and control group instruction (if applicable), and the orientation briefing of noncomputer-oriented staff personnel. (If extensive training is anticipated, a separate manual may be developed and referenced here.)

3.3.6 Test Materials. This paragraph shall itemize the articles and apparatus associated with conducting test.

3.3.6.1 Deliverable Materials. This paragraph will itemize all materials that will be delivered as part of the system to include the quantity and full identification. Examples of these include:

a. Users, Computer Operation, and Program Maintenance Manuals.
b. Program card decks/listings/card image tapes/binary tapes/etc.
c. Data base card decks/listings/card image tapes/etc.
d. Sample listings of system output.

3.3.6.2 Site Supplied Materials. All items that are expected to be provided shall be listed in this paragraph. Examples of these include:

a. Data base and its form (card deck, tape, etc.), fully identified.
b. Other inputs and their form.

FIGURE 3-09. Test Plan

c. Test control programs or other special test programs and their form.
d. Test worksheets and other forms or instructions prepared to control and expedite the test activity. Their type, layout, and quantity must be fully explained.
e. Apparatus required during or in support of test, when it is not normally part of the equipment configuration or is not being delivered as part of the installation effort. Examples of this apparatus are extra peripherals (tape drives, printers, plotters), test message generators, test timing devices, test event records, etc. Such apparatus must be identified by name, type, and quantity required.

3.3.7 Security. Describe any security considerations associated with this test in addition to any privacy restrictions associated with the data being handled.

3.4 Second Location (Identify) Testing. This paragraph shall describe the testing to be conducted at the second location using the same information as outlined in paragraph 3.3.

SECTION 4. TEST SPECIFICATION AND EVALUATION

4.1 Test Specification.

4.1.1 Requirements. This paragraph shall list the individual requirements to be demonstrated by the test as derived from the Specific Performance Requirements given in paragraph 3.1 of the FD.

4.1.2 System Functions. This paragraph shall provide a detailed list of the system functions which will be exercised during the overall system testing. This list, derived from paragraph 4.2 of the FD, must be ordered in such a way that the functions are related to the requirements given in paragraph 4.1.1.

4.1.3 Test/Function Relationships. This paragraph shall provide a list of the tests which, taken as a whole, constitute the overall test activity. It will also provide, as applicable, Test/Function matrix chart summarizing the overall allocation of the system functions to the test. Figure 4-01 shows an example of this type of chart.

4.2 Test Methods and Constraints.

4.2.1 System Test Conditions. This paragraph shall indicate whether the system test is to be made using the normal system input and data base or whether a special set of inputs and data base is to be used.

4.2.2 Extent of System Test. This paragraph shall indicate the extent of the testing to be employed. Where total testing is not to be employed, the test requirements will be presented either as a percentage of some well defined total quantity or as a number of samples of discrete operating conditions or values. Also indicated will be the rationale for adopting limited testing.

4.2.3 Data Recording. This paragraph shall indicate data recording requirements, including those data types not normally recovered from system operation.

4.2.4 System Test Constraints. This paragraph shall indicate the anticipated limitations imposed on the test due to system or test conditions, such as limitations on timing, interfaces, equipment, personnel, and data base.

FIGURE 3-09. Test Plan

FUNCTION (paragraph)	Generate and maintain the data base (3.2.1)	Selectively retrieve data (3.2.2)						Produce special catalog (3.2.3)					
Program short name / Number/test	GNUP	DLPR	ASSC	PROJ	MDPR	FUAR	DAEL	DSPR	DATA	PRNT	DIRT	NAME	DPER
1. Add new record	X												
2. Add new SORU	X												
3. Add a card	X												
4. Change a card	X												
5. Delete a card	X												
6. Delete a record	X												
7. Delete a SORU		X											
8. Create index file			X										
Retrieve records with a requested:													
9. SORU				X									
10. Command designator					X								
11. Functional area						X							
12. Record ID code (RIC)							X						
13. Several RICs							X						
14. Index set and SORU								X					
15. Index set									X				
16. 2 different index sets									X				
17. 3 different index sets									X				
18. RIC and associated records									X				
19. Print full data base										X			
20. Extract record directory											X		
21. Extract record names/RICs												X	
22. Extract keywords, permuted													X

Figure 4-01. Example of Test/Function Relationship Chart: Test/Function Relationships for the Record Association System

4.3 Test Progression. In cases of progressive or cumulative test, an explanation shall be included concerning the manner in which progression is made from one test to another so that the cycle or activity for each test is completely accomplished.

4.4 Test Evaluation.

4.4.1 Test Data Criteria. This paragraph shall describe the rules by which test results will be evaluated; for example:

a. Tolerances - range over which a data value output by a system performance parameter can vary and still be considered acceptable.

b. Samples - the minimum number of combinations or alternatives of input conditions and output conditions that can be exercised to constitute an acceptable test of the parameters involved.
c. Counts - the maximum number of interrupts, halts, or other system breaks which may occur due to nontest conditions.

4.4.2 Test Data Reduction. This paragraph shall describe the technique to be used for manipulation of the raw test data into a form suitable for evaluation, if applicable. The available techniques could include:

a. Manual; i.e., manual collection and collation of system test outputs into test sequence order followed by visual inspection of the results.
b. Semiautomatic; i.e., automatic inspection of test results as obtained by data recording means using a test data reduction program followed by manual (visual) inspection of selected test results which do not lend themselves to complete reduction by automatic means.
c. Automatic; i.e., automatic inspection of test results specifically recorded for manipulation by the test data reduction program. Test results, as recorded, include all items of test significance. The test data reduction program contains an image of correct data output for an item-by-item comparison of data and provides a summary of an evaluated test as output.

SECTION 5. TEST (IDENTIFY) DESCRIPTION

This section shall describe major logical groups of tests to be performed. If appropriate, additional logical groups shall be described in subsequent sections following the same format as that used in this section.

5.1 Test Description. This paragraph shall provide a general description of the test to be performed.

5.2 Test Control.

5.2.1 System Test Means of Control. This paragraph shall indicate whether the test is to be controlled by:

a. Manual means; i.e., manual inspection of necessary inputs and manual control of test sequence.
b. Semiautomatic means; i.e., manual insertion of necessary inputs and automatic (test program) control of test sequence.
c. Automatic means; i.e., preparation and use of a special test program to provide necessary input, conduct tests, monitor and record test results.

5.2.2 Test Data. In each of the following paragraphs identify any security considerations.

5.2.2.1 Input Data. This paragraph will describe the manner in which input data are controlled in order to:

a. Test the system with a minimum number of data types and values.

FIGURE 3-09. Test Plan

b. Exercise the system with a range of bona fide data types and values which test for overload, saturation, and other "worst case" effects.
c. Exercise the system with bogus data types and values which test for rejection of irregular inputs.

5.2.2.2 Input Commands. This paragraph shall describe the manner in which input commands are used to control:

a. Initialization of test.
b. Halt or interrupt of test.
c. Repeat of unsuccessful or incomplete test.
d. Alternate modes of operation as required by test.
e. Termination of test.

5.2.2.3 Output Data. This paragraph shall describe the manner in which output data are analyzed in order to:

a. Detect occurrence (or ultimate nonoccurrence) of output data (as event).
b. Record or identify media and location of all output data for indication of test performance.
c. Evaluate output as a basis for continuation of test sequence.
d. Evaluate test output against required output to assess the performance of the test.

5.2.2.4 Output Notification. This paragraph shall describe the manner in which output notifications (messages output by the system concerning status or limitations on internal performance) are controlled in order to:

a. Indicate readiness for test (normal operation condition).
b. Provide indications of irregularities in input test data or test data base due to normal or erroneous test procedures.
c. Provide indications of irregularities in internal operations on test data due to normal or erroneous test procedures.
d. Provide indications on the control, status, and results of the test as available from auxiliary test supervisor program (if used).

5.3 Test Procedures. This paragraph shall contain the step-by-step procedures to accomplish each test of the system. Each step shall be assigned a test step number and this number, along with critical test data and test procedures information, shall be tabulated onto a test procedure form for test control and the recording of test results.

5.3.1 Test Setup. If not stated elsewhere or by standard operating procedures, this paragraph shall itemize the activities associated with setup of the computer facilities to conduct the test, including all routine machine activities from "power on" through "console setup" to "card/tape read-in." Included shall be the distribution of test documents, worksheets, and other forms.

5.3.2 Test Initialization. This paragraph shall itemize in test sequence order the activities associated with establishing the conditions of the first test starting with the equipment in the setup condition. Initialization may include such functions as:

a. Readout of control function locations and critical data from indicators and storage locations for reference purposes.
b. Queuing of data input values for first test.
c. Queuing of test support programs, if used.
d. Coordination of personnel actions associated with test.

5.3.3 Test Steps. This paragraph shall itemize the test(s) into test steps in test sequence order. It shall also include special operations, such as:

a. Visual inspection of test conditions.
b. Data dumps.
c. Instructions for data recording.
d. Modifications of data base.
e. Interim evaluation of test results.

5.3.4 Test Termination. This paragraph shall itemize in test sequence order the activities associated with termination of the test, such as:

a. Readout of critical data from indicators and location for reference purposes.
b. Termination of operation of time-sensitive test-support programs and test apparatus.
c. Collection of system and operator records of test results.

FIGURE 3-10. TEST ANALYSIS REPORT
TABLE OF CONTENTS

SECTION	1.	GENERAL
	1.1	Purpose of the Test Analysis Report
	1.2	Project References
	1.3	Terms and Abbreviations
	1.4	Security
SECTION	2.	TEST ANALYSIS
	2.1	Test (Identify)
	2.1.1	System Function (Identify)
	2.1.2	Function Performance
	2.1.3	Parameter Performance
	2.1.4	Data Performance
	2.2	Test (Identify)
SECTION	3.	SUMMARY AND CONCLUSIONS
	3.1	Demonstrated Capability
	3.2	System Deficiencies
	3.3	System Refinements

FIGURE 3-10. Test Analysis Report

SECTION 1. GENERAL

1.1 Purpose of the Test Analysis Report. This paragraph shall describe the purpose of the RT (Test Analysis Report) in the following words or appropriate modifications thereto:

The Test Analysis Report for (Project Name) (Project Number) is written to fulfill the following objectives:

a. To document the results of the implementation test.
b. To provide a basis for allocating responsibility for deficiency correction and follow-up.
c. To provide a basis for the preparation of the statement of project completion.
d. To establish user confidence in the operation of the system.

1.2 Project References. This paragraph shall provide a brief summary of the project objectives and identify the project sponsor and user. Also provided shall be a list of applicable documents by author or source, reference number, title, date, and security classification. This paragraph will include the following, when applicable:

a. Functional Description.
b. Users Manual.
c. Computer Operation Manual.
d. Program Maintenance Manual.
e. Test Plan.

1.3 Terms and Abbreviations. This paragraph shall provide a listing or include in an appendix any terms, definitions, or acronyms unique to this document and subject to interpretation by the user of the document. This listing will not include item names or data codes.

1.4 Security. This paragraph will describe any security considerations associated with the test analysis and the data being handled.

SECTION 2. TEST ANALYSIS

2.1 Test (Identify). Each test shall be separately identified in paragraphs 2.1 through 2.n and must be related to those presented in the Test Plan.

2.1.1 System Function (Identify). Each system function, corresponding to the functions presented in paragraph 4.1.2 of the PT, shall be separately described.

2.1.2 Function Performance. This paragraph shall describe the capability as it has been demonstrated in one or more system tests. It shall also assess the manner in which the environment may be different from the operational environment and the effect of this difference on the capability.

2.1.3 Parameter Performance. This paragraph shall compare the parameter performance of the test with the parameter performance described in the UM, OM, and PT, when applicable.

FIGURE 3-10. Test Analysis Report

2.1.4 Data Performance. This paragraph shall compare the I/O performance of the test with the I/O capabilities as described in the UM and the PT when applicable.

2.2 Test (Identify). This paragraph shall describe the second test in a manner similar to that used in paragraph 2.1.

SECTION 3. SUMMARY AND CONCLUSIONS

3.1 Demonstrated Capability. This paragraph shall provide a general statement of the capability of the system as demonstrated by the test, compared with the performance requirements contained in the system Functional Description. An individual discussion of conformance with specific requirements may be included on complex systems.

3.2 System Deficiencies. As required by the results of the testing, an individual statement will be provided for each deficiency in system operations, as measured against the Test Plan. Accompanying each deficiency will be a discussion of the impact:

a. On system performance if the deficiency is not corrected.
b. On the system design if the deficiency is corrected, along with the assignment of organizational responsibility for the correction.

3.3 System Refinements. An itemization of improvements which can be realized in system design or operation, as determined during the test period, will be given. Accompanying each improvement will be a discussion of the added capability it provides the system and the impact on the system design.

FIGURE 3-11. IMPLEMENTATION PROCEDURES
TABLE OF CONTENTS

FIGURE 3-11. Implementation Procedures

SECTION 1. GENERAL

1.1 Purpose of the Implementation Procedures. This paragraph shall describe the purpose of the IP (Implementation Procedures) in the following words, modified as appropriate:

> The objective of the Implementation Procedures for (Project Name) (Project Number) is to provide the necessary information to the functional users and data processing personnel to accomplish the installation of a previously tested ADS and to achieve operational status at additional sites.

1.2 Project References. This paragraph shall provide a brief summary of the references applicable to the history, development, operation, and maintenance of the system. As a minimum, the following shall be specified by source or author, reference number, title, date, and security classification.

a. Project request.

b. Users Manual.

c. Computer Operation Manual.

d. Other pertinent documentation on the project.

1.3 Terms and Abbreviations. This paragraph shall provide a list or include in an appendix any terms, definitions, or acronyms unique to this document and subject to interpretation by the user of this document. This list will not include item names or data codes.

SECTION 2. IMPLEMENTATION OVERVIEW

Section 2 shall provide a description of the implementation process, including support, user, and operations activities. It shall also identify who will accomplish the various segments of the implementation process, provide a schedule of events, and present additional information of common interest to both the functional user and data processing personnel.

FIGURE 3-11. Implementation Procedures

2.1 Description. This paragraph shall provide a general description of the implementation process to provide a frame of reference for the remainder of the document. A list of sites for ADS installation, the schedule dates, and the method of implementation shall be included.

2.2 Contact Point. This paragraph shall provide the organizational name, office symbol/code, and telephone number of a contact for questions relating to this implementation.

2.3 Support Materials. This paragraph shall list the type, source, and quantity of support materials required for the implementation. Included shall be items such as magnetic tapes, disk packs, punch cards, computer printer paper, and special forms.

2.4 Training. This paragraph shall describe the type and amount of special training required, if any.

2.5 Tasks. Each task required for the system installation shall be described or listed in general terms. Each task shall be identified with the organization that will accomplish this task, usually either the user, computer operations, or the developer. This task list or description shall include such items to be accomplished as:

a. Providing overall planning and coordination for the implementation and preparation of the Implementation Procedures.
b. Ensuring that all manuals applicable to the installation effort are available when needed.
c. Providing technical assistance.
d. Establishing criteria and supervising/conducting training activities associated with the implementation.
e. Scheduling processing required for the implementation.
f. Providing comprehensive support for the implementation.
g. Ensuring that all prerequisites have been fulfilled prior to the implementation date.
h. Providing personnel to the implementation team.
i. Arranging lodging, transportation, and office facilities for the implementation team.
j. Providing instructor and student personnel for training before and during the implementation effort.
k. Providing computer support.
l. Providing priority scheduling to ensure adequate turnaround.

2.6 Personnel Orientation. This paragraph shall identify those efforts such as briefings and seminars intended to orient personnel to the new system.

2.7 Personnel Requirements. This paragraph shall describe the number, time, and skill level of the personnel required during the implementation period, including the need for multishift operation, clerical support, etc.

2.8 Security. This paragraph shall contain an overview and discussion of the security considerations associated with the data of the system.

FIGURE 3-11. Implementation Procedures

SECTION 3. SITE INFORMATION - COMPUTER OPERATIONS

3.1 Site (Identify). The site or sites to be discussed in this paragraph shall be identified. Additional paragraphs (paragraphs 3.2 through 3.n) will be prepared as necessary to cover other sites. Multiple sites may be discussed within paragraph 3.1 when the information is generally consistent.

3.1.1 Schedule. This paragraph shall present a schedule of activities to be accomplished during implementation. It will depict the required tasks in chronological order with beginning and ending dates of each task with supporting narrative as necessary.

3.1.2 Software Inventory. This paragraph shall provide an inventory of the software required to support the implementation. The software will be identified by name, identification code or acronym, and security classification. It will be indicated if the software is expected to be on site or will be delivered for the implementation. Any software to be used only during the implementation process shall be identified.

3.1.3 Facilities. This paragraph shall detail the physical facilities and accommodations required during the implementation period. Some of the factors to be considered are:

a. Classroom/work space/training aids needed; hours per day, number of days, and shifts.
b. Hardware that must be operational and available.
c. The availability of transportation and lodging for the implementation team.

3.1.4 Implementation Team. When an implementation team is required, this paragraph shall describe its composition. Each team member's task should be defined.

3.1.5 Detailed Procedures. Paragraphs 3.1.5.1 through 3.1.5.n shall provide in step-by-step sequence the detailed procedures required to accomplish the implementation. Reference may be made to other documents, i.e., Computer Operation Manual. Examples of the areas to be considered are:

a. Control inputs.
b. Operating instructions.
c. Input-output files.
d. Output reports.
e. Special handling.
f. Diagnostic messages.
g. Recovery/restart procedures.

3.1.6 Data Update Procedures. This paragraph shall present the data update requirements that may occur during the implementation period. When the data update procedures are the same as the normal updating/processing procedures, reference may be made to the OM. Paragraph 3.1.6.1 through 3.1.6.n shall provide step-by-step procedures to update the converted data. Examples of the areas to be considered are:

a. Control inputs.
b. Operating instruction.
c. Input-output files.
d. Output reports.

FIGURE 3-11. Implementation Procedures

e. Special handling.
f. Diagnostic messages.
g. Restart/recovery procedures.

3.2 Site (Identify). This paragraph shall describe the computer operations at the second site using the same information as outlined in paragraph 3.1.

SECTION 4. SITE INFORMATION - USER

This section shall provide users with the information necessary to accomplish an orderly implementation. When more than one functional user is involved, a separate section (Sections 5 through N) may be written for each user and the section titles modified to reflect each user.

4.1 Site (Identify). The site or sites to be discussed in this paragraph shall be identified. Additional paragraphs (paragraphs 4.2 through 4.n) will be prepared as necessary to cover all sites. Multiple sites may be discussed within this paragraph when the information is generally consistent.

4.1.1 Schedule. This paragraph shall present a schedule of activities to be accomplished by the user during implementation. It will depict the required tasks in chronological order with beginning and ending dates of each task with supporting narrative as necessary.

4.1.2 Detailed Procedures. Paragraph 4.1.2.1 through 4.1.2.n shall provide in step-by-step sequence the detailed procedures required to accomplish the implementation. Reference may be made to other documents such as the UM. Examples of the areas to be considered are:

a. Initiation procedures.
b. Input formats.
c. Output formats.
d. Utilization of outputs.
e. Recovery and error correction procedures.

4.1.3 Data Update Procedures. This paragraph shall present the user's data update requirements that may occur during the implementation period. When update procedures are the same as normal processing, reference may be made to the UM and, if appropriate, to Section 3 of this document. Paragraphs 4.1.3.1 through 4.1.3.n shall provide step-by-step procedures for the update. Examples of areas to be considered are:

a. Initiation procedures.
b. Input formats.
c. Output formats.
d. Utilization of outputs.
e. Recovery and error correction procedures.

4.2 Site (Identify). This paragraph shall describe the user information at the second site using the same information as outlined in paragraph 4.1.

FIGURE 3-11. Implementation Procedures

APPENDIX B

Excerpts from the Prentice-Hall Author's Guide*

The following material dealing with legal and practical details of completing a manuscript may be useful to the author of software written communication. Although the material is intended specifically for the authors of Prentice-Hall books, much of it can be extended to more general forms of communication.

B.1 QUOTE, UNQUOTE

One problem you will probably run into in writing your book is to determine how much material, if any, you may quote from copyrighted publications without first obtaining written permission to do so. The new Copyright Law, which came into effect on January 1, 1978, attempts to deal with the problem to some extent by giving statutory recognition to the concept of "fair use" previously developed by the courts, which allowed some degree of quoting under certain circumstances.

The Copyright Law now specifically provides that " . . . the fair use of a copyrighted work . . . for purposes such as criticism, comment, news reporting, teaching (including multiple copies for classroom use), scholarship, or research, is not an infringement of copyright. . . . "

The Law also sets forth factors to be included in considering whether a use is

Prentice-Hall Author's Guide (Englewood Cliffs, NJ: Prentice-Hall, Inc., 1978), pp. 7–9, 17–20.

"fair." The factors specified are (1) the purpose and character of the use (is the use of a commercial nature or is it for nonprofit educational purposes?); (2) the nature of the copyrighted work; (3) the amount and the substantiality of the amount used in relation to the entirety of the copyrighted work; and (4) the effect of the use upon the potential market for or value of the copyrighted work.

If you are quoting from a *textbook*, our guidelines* permit use of up to 250 words without permission (except for charts and tables and material to be used in anthologies). *In all cases, be sure to credit the source.* All quotations of more than 250 words—and that means total number of words from one source, possibly in scattered quotes—require written permission. The quotation does not have to be exact to require permission; even if the material is paraphrased or adapted, get permission to use it in that form.

Our guidelines require written permission for quotations of fewer than 250 words under the following circumstances:

1. If the quotation is from a trade book (a book for the general public), obtain permission to use any quotation, whatever its length.
2. If the quotation exceeds 5 percent of the entire work from which it is taken—for example, if 135 words are taken from an essay of 2500 words.
3. If the quotation is poetry. No more than two lines should be used without permission, unless two lines constitute a stanza; then we require permission to quote even that amount.
4. If the quotation is to be used in an anthology or compilation, permission should be obtained for *every selection* in copyright, no matter how short.
5. If the quotation is from an unpublished work—for example, a thesis, lecture, or material prepared by a student as part of a course.
6. If the quotation is from a letter, published or unpublished. If the letter has been published under a copyright that has now expired, no permission is necessary. But if it is protected by a copyright still in force, written permission to quote from it is needed. For example, it is not safe to use a letter by Abraham Lincoln without investigation—it may have been published many years after it was written and may still be in copyright. If a letter has never been published, get the permission of the *writer* (not of the person to whom it was written) to quote from it. If the writer is dead, get the permission of whoever owns the right to publish the writer's literary legacy. If you solicit letters for publication, put your request in writing, making it clear that they are to be published.
7. If the quotation consists of music, either popular or classical, or of song lyrics that are still in copyright. Be careful of arrangements of old classical or folk music and lyrics. They are usually copyrighted.
8. If the quotation is a chart or table—or an adaptation thereof.
9. If the quotation is from a copyrighted dramatic composition, such as a play, motion picture film, or TV presentation.
10. If the quotation is used in an ornamental way (for example, as part of a chapter opening design).

*It should be understood that these are merely our *guidelines*. They should not be considered determinative of what does or does not constitute "fair use" in the legal sense, in every case.

B.2 BEWARE OF LIBEL

Another problem that sometimes plagues an author is where to draw the line between fair criticism of a person, group, or situation and libel or slurring. We hope the following section will help you make the distinction.

Libel, in "its most general sense [is] any publication that is injurious to the reputation of another" (*Black's Law Dictionary,* Revised Fourth Edition). As opposed to slander, it is defamation in "permanent form." It is usually printed, published, expressed in words, signs, symbols, or other permanent methods; it exposes the subject to "public hatred, shame, ridicule, or contempt," "disgraces him as a member of his community," "degrades him in his business, profession, or office."

Libel may be disguised or inadvertent. The portrayal of a character in a novel may be libelous even if the character is only partly modeled on a real person. The name used in the novel and the reprehensible actions of the character may be wholly fictitious, but if a real person is recognizable from the description in the book, the writer and the publisher may face a suit for libel.

Or a writer may describe a purely fictitious editor of a literary journal as being essentially self-promoting and malicious and may choose for the magazine a name that he or she believes to be nonexistent. If, unfortunately, a magazine with that name does exist and its actual editor believes that he or she has been defamed, he or she may threaten suit. The note often included in novels to the effect that all characters are fictitious and any resemblance to living persons is accidental is no defense to a claim for libel.

A word or a group of words may be considered libelous in one community at a particular time but not so under different circumstances. For example, to write that a United States citizen is a communist is libelous, but to so describe a Soviet citizen is not. Slang meanings, understood by large segments of the community but not yet found in any dictionary, may also be libelous. Some of the "vulgar" uses, although given in many recent dictionaries, might not alert a copy editor. Or a writer may use a word without realizing its full implications. Such a lack of knowledge or of actual intention to defame will not excuse libelous publication.

Certain libelous statements may be privileged and, therefore, not actionable. For example, a literary or drama critic may be critical in the extreme of a work being reviewed, provided he or she is honestly expressing personal opinion and is not motivated by actual malice. Criticism of a work, however, may not be used as a guise to attack its author personally. For example, a critique may say that a work is lacking in originality and is poorly expressed, but if it also says or implies that the author is a plagiarist, it invites a libel suit.

Truth has been a traditional defense to a claim of libel. In recent years the United States Supreme Court has also announced a new defense that attaches to libelous statements concerning "public officials" even if those statements are false. While the range of "public official" is quite broad, it has not yet been conclusively defined. The law now states that public officials may not prevail in a libel action even if a statement about them is defamatory and false unless they can show that it was published with actual knowledge of its falsity or with malice (i.e., in reckless disregard of whether it was true or false).

At one time the Supreme Court even went so far as to hold that this defense was available in cases where the object of the libel was not a "public official" but the statements concerned a matter of "public interest." That holding has since been modified so as to leave to each state the right to determine the extent to which libel of "private" persons in connection with a discussion of "public issues" may be excused. The laws of the various states differ in this respect, and you should exercise caution in writing about "private" persons even though they may be involved in matters of "public interest."

Biographers of living persons should be especially careful about the possibility of libel. Documented facts about the lives of public figures that are not of a purely personal nature are generally not actionable; usually the danger lies in statements about their friends and relatives who are not public figures. As to persons who are dead, the serious biographer or historian usually has nothing to fear. Danger exists only if malicious intention to injure the family or descendants of a deceased person and to expose them to defamation can be proved.

B.3 GUARD AGAINST PREJUDICE

Unintentional Slurs on Race or Religion

Of course no intelligent person would intentionally defame a whole group because the color of their skins, the country of their origin, or their religious beliefs were different from his or her own. But certain groups are understandably sensitive because their feelings have been so often—and quite intentionally—hurt by the bigoted. It is worth taking pains to avoid giving them offense. For example, one of our books on speech originally contained, quite innocently, as an exercise for developing an active tongue, the following quotation from a poem: "Oh the terrible, tyrannous, treacherous Turk!" Violent protests from Turkish quarters that the Turks had been slandered made it necessary to print and insert a substitute page.

Broad Accusations Against Professional Groups

Be careful, too, about making broad general accusations and blanket attacks on professional groups, associations, and businesses and industries as a whole. It is one thing to say that some lawyers are, unfortunately, ambulance chasers. It is quite another to imply, even indirectly, that all members of the legal profession are so disposed. The same considerations apply in discussing the medical profession or any other group.

Sexism

In your writing, be certain to treat men and women impersonally in regard to occupation, marital status, physical abilities, attitudes, interests, and so on. Depending on the requirements of your subject, avoid attributing particular characteristics to either sex; instead let your writing convey that one's abilities and achievements are not limited by gender. Your text should support the fact that both sexes play equally important roles in all facets of life and that activities on all levels are open to both women and men alike.

Men and women should be portrayed as people rather than as male or female. Be careful to avoid sexist language that excludes men or women from any activity or that implies that either sex is superior or dominant in a particular role. Where possible, in referring to people use words that have no sexual connotations; for example, human being, salesperson, supervisor, student, and the like. Try to avoid the use of *he* or *man* in the generic sense.

More specific guidelines for sexism are given in Appendix C.

APPENDIX C

Guidelines on Sexism

The following material is an elaboration, with examples, of the material found in Appendix B.3, focusing on sexism.*

Sexism in books includes sins of omission as well as of commission and bias in thought and concept as well as in language. Those who write and edit textbooks need to be particularly sensitive to both areas, for the portrayal of roles and life situations as exclusively masculine or exclusively feminine or the more subtle omission of women as participants in the action is just as much bias as is the general use of *he* or *man* to characterize all human beings. The purpose of establishing guidelines for nonsexist language is to help remove the conceptual and linguistic barriers that now artificially divide many aspects of life and work by gender. They are intended to sensitize both authors and editors to the many ways in which sexism may be expressed and to give them some tools with which to attack the problem.

These guidelines therefore contain "checklists" of things to look for in reading or in editing a manuscript as well as specific kinds of expressions to change or avoid. Eliminating sexism requires as much attention to thought and attitude as it does to pronouns and occupation titles. Much in the same way as one can observe the letter but not the spirit of the law, one can carefully use *he or she* or *they* and yet have a book that in fact ignores women as equal partners in the enterprise of transmitting or expanding human knowledge.

**Prentice-Hall College Division Guidelines on Sexism.*

Striking a balance is tricky; women in many cultures and in many eras have been treated as second-class citizens, and certainly the laws and rhetoric of recent years have yet to become part of everyday reality. But to recognize the contributions of women, past and present, is not only to correct the record; it is to make the facts available to those who will create and live out new social realities. And to treat people as human beings, as members of a common group, without identifying them by gender is to promote changes in attitude that can liberate both men and women and allow society to take advantage of each individual's full potential.

Bias in Concept and Coverage

Omission. Check the descriptive and illustrative material—the examples used to illustrate concepts, and the descriptions of processes, social structures, and typical situations: Are women simply ignored? Are they treated as exceptional cases or, on the other hand, as part of the landscape or the baggage? Are the subjects of studies all male? Is the work of women scholars cited? Certain subjects—history, the sciences, and business—are special candidates for careful scrutiny. The argument usually advanced—that there are no women involved or that women did not play certain roles in certain periods or cultures—does not justify ignoring women altogether or mentioning them only as auxiliaries or oddities.

Here and on the following pages are some examples of what to look for, accompanied by some possible unbiased alternatives.

Biased	*Unbiased*
The pioneers crossed the desert with their women, children, and possessions.	Pioneer families crossed the desert carrying all their possessions.
The slaves were allowed to marry and to have their wives and children with them.	Slave families were allowed to stay together. *or* Married slaves were allowed to live with their families.
Radium was discovered by a woman, Marie Curie.	Marie Curie discovered radium.
When setting up his experiment, the researcher must always check his sample for error.	When setting up an experiment, a researcher must always check for sampling error.
As knowledge of the physical world increased, men began to examine long-held ideas and traditions with a more critical eye.	As knowledge of the physical world increased, old ideas and traditions were examined with a more critical eye. *or* . . . people began to examine long-held ideas and traditions with a more critical eye.

Equal Treatment. Check the use of adjectives and modifiers: Do those used for women consistently create a negative impression or betray a patronizing attitude? Are women mentioned consistently as an afterthought? Does the inclusion of women seem like a conscious effort or a concession on the part of the author? an attempt to be trendy or up-to-date? Are women consistently described in physical or sexual terms that are never used when describing men? Is a woman's marital status always mentioned even though the context does not require it?

Biased	*Unbiased*
The poor women could no longer go on; the exhausted men . . .	The exhausted pioneers . . . or The exhausted men and women . . .
There were also some women painters in this period, most of them daughters or wives of painters.	The women painters of this period were . . . *or* worked primarily in . . . *or* Among the painters of this period, X, Y, and Z (both men and women) worked primarily in . . .
Though a woman, she ran the business efficiently.	She ran the business efficiently.
Mrs. Acton, a statuesque blonde, is Joe Granger's assistant.	Jan Acton is Joe Granger's assistant.
The little girls played with the boys.	The girls played with the boys; the children played; the little girls played with the little boys.
The line manager was angry; his secretary was upset.	The line manager and his secretary were both upset by the mistake.
All the strong young men of the village took part in the festival, as did the young girls.	All the young people of the village took part in the festival.

Stereotyping. Check the portrayal of roles, the description of jobs and skills, the treatment of life styles and life situations: Are people treated as human, or are all the portrayals done in male or female terms? Does the reader get the impression that only men do X and only women do Y? Are men portrayed one way and women another? Are all people in positions of authority or trust (the therapist, the politician, the scientist, the philosopher, the leader, the historian) male? In an education text, are all the teachers female and all the professors and administrators male? How is the family described and analyzed? Do "mommies" always stay at home? Does the author imply they should? What are the role models for children? How are recent changes in the family power structure treated? In a business text, are all the executives male and all the secretaries and assistants female? Can the reader instantly infer that all the participants in a meeting or conference are assumed to be male? Do examples of human behavior always reinforce the stereotyped idea that women and men are totally different kinds of creatures?

Biased	*Unbiased*
As a child, she was a tomboy; sports and not dolls were her main interest.	She was actively interested in sports as a child.
Most of the men in this plant are married heads of household.	In this plant, most of the married heads of household are men.
Current tax regulations allow a head of household to deduct for the support of a wife and children.	Current tax regulations allow a head of household to deduct for the support of a spouse and children.

Biased	*Unbiased*
The line manager is responsible for the productivity of his department; his foremen, for the day-to-day work of the girls on the line.	The line manager is responsible for the productivity of the department; the supervisors, for that of the workers on the line.
The secretary brought her boss his coffee.	The secretary brought the boss coffee.
The teacher must be sure her lesson plans are done well in advance of the day she plans to teach the material.	The teacher should prepare a lesson plan well in advance of the day the material will be taught *or* The teacher must be sure his or her lesson plans . . .

Completing this ''awareness checklist'' should give an editor (or an author) a good idea of whether or not a particular manuscript needs more than the adjustment of pronouns or changes in language to make it unbiased or nonsexist. At this point the editor or the copy editor can evaluate the scope of the problem and make recommendations for substantive work in addition to changes in language and expression. It is the overall presentation, not so much the occasional lapse in language, that can give a book a bias the author may not have intended.

Bias in Language and Expression

Pronouns. The use of *he, his, him* to denote any person or a person is the most common problem in editing language for bias, simply because English has no neutral pronoun in the singular. If there is no way to reword a passage or a sentence to avoid unnecessary pronouns or to change to the plural, the best current solution is to use *he or she, his or her.* Coined terms, such as *(s)he* or *she/he,* should be avoided; they are usually distracting to the reader and annoying to the author. In citing examples, individuals in the examples may sometimes be male, sometimes female. If this alternative is chosen, avoid stereotyping male and female roles (see page 4).

None of these suggestions—removing pronouns, changing to the plural, alternating examples, or substituting *he or she*—should be followed blindly as immutable rules. Context and clarity of expression are important considerations in a text and should not be sacrificed merely to ensure that every pronoun has been changed. The constant use of *her or she* leads to clumsy, repetitious phrases and sentence structure. A change to the plural may be wrong in a given context—for example, when the discussion is of one-to-one relationships such as that between parent and child. Alternating the *he* and *she* examples does not work well in many contexts. Both author and editor need to use a variety of approaches in sensitive, appropriate ways. It is advisable for the author to include a note in the preface to the book explaining what approach has been taken to avoid stereotyping and sexism.

Biased	*Unbiased*
A person's facial expression does not always reveal his true feelings.	Facial expression is not always an indicator of a person's true feelings.
Sometimes a doctor will see his patients only in a hospital.	Sometimes a doctor will see patients only in a hospital.

Biased	*Unbiased*
The clinician must take his measurements accurately and carefully.	The clinician must take accurate and careful measurements.
The typical child does his homework right after school.	Most children do their homework right after school.
A good lawyer will see that his clients are aware of their rights.	A good lawyer will see that his or her clients are aware of their rights.

Human, Not Man: Describing the World. One way to establish an unbiased tone that treats people as individuals who share universal human characteristics and traits is to avoid the use of the word *man* to mean all people and the use of *-man* words in general. If such words must be used, they should be accompanied by an explanation or be set in a context that clearly does not exclude women.

Biased	*Unbiased*
man, as in when man first walked upon the earth	human beings, humans, human race
mankind	human race, people, humankind, humanity
primitive man, early man	primitive people(s), primitive men and women
man-made	manufactured, made, synthetic, artificial
manpower	labor, workforce
the common man, the man in the street, the layman	the average citizen, the layperson, the nonspecialist
wise men	wise people, elders, leaders

Stereotyped Expressions	*Alternatives*
The committee decided he was the right man for the job.	The committee decided he was the right person for the job. *or* . . . was right for the job.
The teacher must always remember that her role in the learning process is a vital one.	Teachers must always remember that their role in the learning process is a vital one.
Research has shown that the smart shopper knows what she wants before she enters the store.	Research has shown that smart consumers know what they want before they enter the store.
One new specialty at which she may aim is that of nurse-practitioner.	One new specialty at which he [*or* he or she, the student] may aim is that of nurse-practitioner.
Mary is an extremely accurate typist; Alice is not.	Jack is an extremely accurate typist; Mary is not.

Stereotyped Expressions	*Alternatives*
Some chimpanzees in the experiment received no mothering.	Some chimpanzees in the experiment received no parental care [*or* nurturance].
Children need someone to mother them.	Children need a parent [*or* parental care, nurturing].
I'll have my girl call him.	I'll have my secretary [*or* assistant] call him.
girls' basketball team	women's basketball team
ladies' room	women's room
career girl	[give the occupation]

Parallel Treatment	*Alternatives*
The men in the office took the girls to lunch.	The men in the office took the women to lunch.
This is my secretary, Mrs. Smith and my aide, Jack Green.	This is my secretary, Alice Smith and my aide, Jack Green.
Dr. Jones and his wife Diane	Dr. and Mrs. Jones, Jack and Diane Jones
man and wife	husband and wife
co-ed	student
college men and girls	college men and women
the men and the ladies	the men and the women, the gentlemen and the ladies
at a meeting between President Nixon and Indira Gandhi [*or* Mrs. Gandhi[. . .	at a meeting between President Nixon and Prime Minister Gandhi [*or* Richard Nixon and Indira Gandhi, Mr. Nixon and Mrs. Gandhi]

Avoid using clichés such as the following:

the woman driver
the nagging mother-in-law
the little woman
the henpecked husband
gal Friday
boys' night out
dizzy blonde
catty women
female gossip
man-size job

Occupations and Titles. Naming a person's occupation has been an editorial problem, simply because so many job titles and occupations were themselves gender-linked terms. Many alternatives are now available, so that it is usually easy to use descriptive words that can apply to any person, whether male or female. Unnecessary gender identification can also be deleted.

Biased	*Unbiased*
actress	actor
authoress	author
businessman	businessperson, executive, manager
chairman	chair, chairperson
cleaning lady	household worker, cleaner
congressman	member of Congress, representative
foreman	supervisor
fireman	firefighter
houseboy	servant
housewife	homemaker, consumer
mailman	mail carrier, letter carrier
policeman, policewoman	police officer
salesman, saleswoman	sales representative, salesperson
stewardess	flight attendant
woman doctor	doctor
male nurse	nurse

APPENDIX D

Proofreader's Marks

This material is taken from the Prentice-Hall Author's Guide,* and explains the commonly used marks for correcting typeset material.

style of type

wf	Wrong font (size or style of type)
lc	lower Case letter
lc	Set in LOWER CASE
C	capital letter
Caps	SET IN capitals
c+lc	Set in lower case with INITIAL CAPITALS
sc	SET IN small capitals
c+sc	SET IN SMALL CAPITALS with initial capitals
rom.	Set in *roman* type
ital.	*Set in* italic *type*
ital. caps	*SET IN ITALIC* capitals
lf	Set in **lightface** type
bf	**Set in** boldface **type**
bf ital.	***Set in boldface*** italic
bf caps	Set in boldface **CAPITALS**
b	Superior letter b
2	Inferior figure 2

**Prentice-Hall Author's Guide* (Englewood Cliffs, NJ: Prentice-Hall, Inc., 1978), pp. 76–77. Adapted from "Roundup of Editors' and Proofreaders' Marks" by John Evans.

position

Move to right

Move to left

ctr Center

Lower (letters or words)

Raise (letters or words)

Straighten type (horizontally)

Align type (vertically)

tr Tranpsose

tr Transpose (order letters of or words)

spacing

ld in Insert lead (space) between lines

Sld Take out lead

Close up; take ou t space

Close up partly; leave some space

Eq # Equalize space between words

\# Insertspace (or more space)

Space out Morespacebetweenwords

insertion and deletion

the/) Caret (insert marginal addition

Delete (take it out)

Delete annd close up

e Correct latter or word marked

Stet Let it stand (all matter above dots)

paragraphing

¶ Begin a paragraph

No ¶ No paragraph.

Run in Run in or run on

flush No indention

punctuation

(Use caret in text to show point of insertion)

Insert period

Insert comma

Insert colon

;/ Insert semicolon

Insert quotation marks

Insert single quotes

Insert apostrophe

(set)? Insert question mark

! Insert exclamation point

=/ Insert hyphen

Insert one-em dash

(/) Insert parentheses

[/] Insert brackets

miscellaneous

Replace broken or imperfect type

Revers (upside down type)

(Sp) Spell out (twenty gr)

Au/(?) Query to author

Ed/(?) Query to editor

Mark off or break; start new line

Index

A

B

C

D

E

F

G

H

I

J

L

M

N

O

P

Q

R

S

T

U

V

W

Y